Peltzer · Voight
Handelsgesetzbuch
German Commercial Code

German Commercial Code

German-English Text
with an Introduction in English

by

Dr. Martin Peltzer
Rechtsanwalt und Notar
Frankfurt am Main

Elizabeth A. Voight
Attorney at Law
Munich

5th revised edition
2003

Verlag
Dr. Otto Schmidt
Köln

Handelsgesetzbuch

Deutsch-englische Textausgabe
mit einer englischen Einleitung

von

Dr. Martin Peltzer
Rechtsanwalt und Notar
Frankfurt am Main

Elizabeth A. Voight
Attorney at Law
München

5. erneuerte Auflage

2003

Verlag
Dr. Otto Schmidt
Köln

Bibliografische Information Der Deutschen Bibliothek
Die Deutsche Bibliothek verzeichnet diese Publikation in der Deutschen Nationalbibliografie; detaillierte bibliografische Daten sind im Internet über <http://dnb.ddb.de> abrufbar.

Verlag Dr. Otto Schmidt KG
Unter den Ulmen 96–98, 50968 Köln
Tel.: 02 21/9 37 38-01, Fax: 02 21/9 37 38-9 21
e-mail: info@otto-schmidt.de
www.otto-schmidt.de

ISBN 3-504-45509-8

© 2003 by Verlag Dr. Otto Schmidt KG

Das Werk einschließlich aller seiner Teile ist urheberrechtlich geschützt. Jede Verwertung, die nicht ausdrücklich vom Urheberrechtsgesetz zugelassen ist, bedarf der vorherigen Zustimmung des Verlages. Das gilt insbesondere für Vervielfältigungen, Bearbeitungen, Übersetzungen, Mikroverfilmungen und die Einspeicherung und Verarbeitung in elektronischen Systemen.

Das verwendete Papier ist aus chlorfrei gebleichten Rohstoffen hergestellt, holz- und säurefrei, alterungsbeständig und umweltfreundlich.

Umschlaggestaltung: Jan P. Lichtenford, Mettmann
Satz: reemers publishing services gmbh, Krefeld (www.reemers.de)
Druck und Verarbeitung: Bercker Graphischer Betrieb GmbH & Co. KG, Kevelaer
Printed in Germany

Foreword

The German Commercial Code (Handelsgesetzbuch) is the body of law governing the activities of merchants and thus a major part of business life in Germany. It defines the merchant and his legal relationship to his employees, agents, partners and customers. It also defines the common powers-of-attorney, contains the law governing commercial partnerships and prescribes standard bookkeeping practices. Finally, this Code regulates commercial transactions and the business of certain kinds of merchants, including forwarding agents, carriers and commission agents.

Since its inception, in the year 1900, the German Commercial Code has undergone many changes, not the least of which took place in 1998. On June 22, 1998 the German Federal Council (Bundestag) passed the Commercial Code Reform Act (Handelsrechtsformgesetz). This Act, among others, had a substantial impact on the Commercial Code and made the fourth edition necessary. The changes pertain particularly to the concept of the merchant, but to many other issues as well. They are discussed in greater detail in the Introduction. Since 1999 numerous further changes were brought about such that a fifth edition became necessary.

Not surprisingly, the Introduction is intended to be just that, an introduction to the German Commercial Code. It is intended as a comprehensive and helpful overview of the Code. That overview is based on a careful and relatively detailed summary of the legal text. Beyond that, it includes pointers to the most relevant or problematic Sections and Subsections of the Code, mentioning avoidable or inherent risks and liabilities as well as advantages that might be gained. This Introduction might be of particular use to those of our readers who are less familiar with the German Commercial Code and business practices in Germany. Thus, it comes as recommended reading for our international readers who wish to do business in Germany or hope to consult those who do.

This edition is, however, not only intended to broaden the readership of the German Commercial Code abroad, but aspires to serve as a guide and handy reference to German legal and business advisers who wish to advise their clients or draft documents and contracts concerning the Commercial Code in English. Finally, it may prove helpful to translators and interpreters who have in the last years expanded their presence in law firms and businesses in Germany and abroad.

We wish to thank those who have helped the authors make this resource available. This includes first and foremost the co-authors of the previous editions, who have laid the foundation on which we have built.

The authors would be pleased to receive any comments and suggestions for the sixth edition.

November 2002

Dr. Martin Peltzer

Elisabeth A. Voight

Inhaltsverzeichnis/Contents

Seite/Page

Foreword	V
Introduction	1
I. Necessity for a New Edition	1
1. Scope of Applicability of the Commercial Law	3
2. The Firm Name	6
3. The Commercial Register	7
4. Financial Records	9
II. Business Employees	10
1. Business Employees. Clerical Employees and Apprentices	10
2. The Employee's Power to Represent the Merchant	11
3. Hybrid Relationships	13
III. The Independent Business Agent	13
1. The Commercial Agent	14
2. The Commercial Broker	15
IV. The Commercial Partnership under the Commercial Code	16
1. The General Commercial Partnership	16
2. The Limited Partnership	20
3. The Silent Partnership	22
V. Accounting, Financial Statements and Audit of the Company and Amendments by the Transparency and Company Disclosure Act	23
VI. Commercial Transactions	25
1. Special Provisions for Commercial Transactions in General	25
2. Commercial Sales	27
3. Commission Transactions	30
4. Transportation Law	31

			Seite/Page
	Handelsgesetzbuch	**Commercial Code**	
	Erstes Buch. Handelsstand	Book One. Commercial Entities	
	Erster Abschnitt. Kaufleute	Part One. Merchants	
§ 1	[Istkaufmann]	Merchant by legal definition	35
§ 2	[Kannkaufmann]	Business operation by voluntary registration	35
§ 3	[Land- und Forstwirtschaft; Kannkaufmann]	Agriculture and forestry; merchant by voluntary registration	36
§ 4	*(aufgehoben)*	*(repealed)*	36
§ 5	[Kaufmann kraft Eintragung]	Merchant by registration	36
§ 6	[Handelsgesellschaften; Formkaufmann]	Commercial companies and partnerships; merchant by form of organization	36
§ 7	[Kaufmannseigenschaft und öffentliches Recht]	Merchant status and public law	37
	Zweiter Abschnitt. Handelsregister	Part Two. Commercial Register	
§ 8	[Führung des Registers]	Maintenance of the register	37
§ 8 a	[Ermächtigung der Landesregierungen; automatisierte Dateien]	Authorization of state governments; automated files	37
§ 9	[Einsicht des Handelsregisters; Abschriften; Bescheinigungen]	Inspection of the Commercial Register; copies; certificates	39
§ 9 a	[Zulässigkeit des automatisierten Verfahrens; Genehmigung; Datenschutz; Gebühren]	Admissibility of automated procedures; consent; data protection; fees	40
§ 10	[Bekanntmachung der Eintragungen]	Publication of registrations	41
§ 11	[Bezeichnung der Amtsblätter]	Designation of newspapers in which registration will be published	41
§ 12	[Anmeldungen; Zeichnung von Unterschriften; Nachweis der Rechtsnachfolge]	Filings to register; specimen signatures; proof of legal succession	42

Inhaltsverzeichnis/Contents

Seite/Page

§ 13	Zweigniederlassungen von Unternehmen mit Sitz im Inland	Branches of enterprises with domestic domicile	42
§ 13 a	Zweigniederlassungen von Aktiengesellschaften mit Sitz im Inland	Branches of stock corporations with domestic domicile	44
§ 13 b	Zweigniederlassungen von Gesellschaften mit beschränkter Haftung mit Sitz im Inland	Branches of limited liability companies with domestic domicile	44
§ 13 c	Bestehende Zweigniederlassungen von Unternehmen mit Sitz im Inland	Existing branches of enterprises with domestic domicile	45
§ 13 d	Sitz oder Hauptniederlassung im Ausland	Domicile or head office abroad	46
§ 13 e	Zweigniederlassungen von Kapitalgesellschaften mit Sitz im Ausland	Branches of corporations with foreign domicile	47
§ 13 f	Zweigniederlassungen von Aktiengesellschaften mit Sitz im Ausland	Branch offices of stock corporations with foreign domicile	49
§ 13 g	Zweigniederlassungen von Gesellschaften mit beschränkter Haftung mit Sitz im Ausland	Branches of limited liability companies with foreign domicile	50
§ 13 h	Verlegung des Sitzes einer Hauptniederlassung im Inland	Change of domicile of a domestic head office	52
§ 14	[Festsetzung von Zwangsgeld]	Setting of coercive fines	53
§ 15	[Publizität des Handelsregisters]	Publication in the Commercial Register	53
§ 16	[Entscheidung des Prozeßgerichts]	Judicial decision	54
	Dritter Abschnitt. Handelsfirma	**Part Three. Commercial Firm Name**	
§ 17	[Begriff]	Definition	55
§ 18	[Firma des Kaufmanns]	Firm name of the merchant	55
§ 19	[Bezeichnung der Firma bei Einzelkaufleuten, einer OHG oder KG]	Designation of the firm name for sole proprietors, a general commercial partnership or limited partnership	55

			Seite/Page
§ 20	(aufgehoben)	(repealed)	56
§ 21	[Fortführung bei Namensänderung]	Continuation in the event of a name change	56
§ 22	[Fortführung bei Erwerb des Handelsgeschäfts]	Continuation in the event of acquisition of the business	56
§ 23	[Veräußerungsverbot]	Prohibition on transfer	57
§ 24	[Fortführung bei Änderungen im Gesellschafterbestand]	Continuation in the event of changes within the partnership group	57
§ 25	[Haftung des Erwerbers bei Firmenfortführung]	Liability of the purchaser on continuation	57
§ 26	[Verjährung gegen den früheren Inhaber; Fristen]	Statute of limitations in respect of the former owner	58
§ 27	[Haftung des Erben bei Geschäftsfortführung]	Personal liability of the heirs on continuation	59
§ 28	[Eintritt in das Geschäft eines Einzelkaufmanns]	Joining a sole proprietorship	60
§ 29	[Anmeldung der Firma]	Registration of firm name	60
§ 30	[Unterscheidbarkeit]	Distinctiveness of the firm name	61
§ 31	[Änderung der Firma; Erlöschen]	Change of firm name; termination	61
§ 32	[Insolvenzverfahren]	Insolvency proceedings	62
§ 33	[Juristische Person]	Juridical person	63
§ 34	[Anmeldung und Eintragung von Änderungen]	Filing and registration of changes	63
§ 35	[Unterschriftszeichnung]	Specimen signatures	64
§ 36	(aufgehoben)	(repealed)	64
§ 37	[Unzulässiger Firmengebrauch]	Improper use of a firm name	64
§ 37 a	[Angaben auf Geschäftsbriefen]	Information on business letters	65
	Vierter Abschnitt. Handelsbücher	**Part Four. Commercial Records**	
§§ 38–47 b	(aufgehoben)	(repealed)	66

	Fünfter Abschnitt. Prokura und Handlungsvollmacht	**Part Five. General Agency (Prokura) and Commercial Power of Attorney**	
§ 48	[Erteilung der Prokura; Gesamtprokura]	Conferring the general agency (Prokura), joint Prokura	66
§ 49	[Umfang der Prokura]	Scope of the Prokura	66
§ 50	[Beschränkung des Umfanges]	Limiting the scope of the Prokura	66
§ 51	[Zeichnung des Prokuristen]	Signature of the Prokura holder	67
§ 52	[Widerruflichkeit; Unübertragbarkeit; Tod des Inhabers]	Revocability; non-transferability; death of the business owner	67
§ 53	[Anmeldung der Erteilung und des Erlöschens; Zeichnung des Prokuristen]	Notice of the conferral of the Prokura and termination thereof; Prokura holder's specimen signature	67
§ 54	[Handlungsvollmacht]	Commercial power of attorney	68
§ 55	[Abschlußvertreter]	Agent authorized to transact business	68
§ 56	[Angestellte in Laden oder Warenlager]	Sales clerks or warehouse employees	69
§ 57	[Zeichnung des Handlungsbevollmächtigten]	Signature of holder of commercial power of attorney	69
§ 58	[Unübertragbarkeit der Handlungsvollmacht]	Non-transferability of the commercial power of attorney	70
	Sechster Abschnitt. Handlungsgehilfen und Handlungslehrlinge	**Part Six. Clerical Employees and Apprentices**	
§ 59	[Handlungsgehilfe]	Clerical employees	70
§ 60	[Gesetzliches Wettbewerbsverbot]	Statutory prohibition of competition	70
§ 61	[Verletzung des Wettbewerbsverbots]	Violation of prohibition of competition	71
§ 62	[Fürsorgepflicht des Arbeitgebers]	Employer's duty to provide for the welfare of the employees	71
§ 63	*(aufgehoben)*	*(repealed)*	72
§ 64	[Gehaltszahlung]	Payment of salary	72
§ 65	[Provision]	Commission	72

			Seite/Page
§§ 66–72	*(aufgehoben)*	*(repealed)*	73
§ 73	[*Anspruch auf Zeugnis*]	*Right to a reference*	73
§ 74	[Vertragliches Wettbewerbsverbot; bezahlte Karenz]	Contractual prohibition of competition; paid abstention period	73
§ 74 a	[Unverbindliches oder nichtiges Verbot]	Non-binding or void prohibition of competition	74
§ 74 b	[Zahlung und Berechnung der Entschädigung]	Payment and calculation of compensation	74
§ 74 c	[Anrechnung anderweitigen Erwerbs]	Deduction of other earnings	75
§ 75	[Unwirksamwerden des Wettbewerbsverbots]	Invalidity of the prohibition of competition	76
§ 75 a	[Verzicht des Prinzipals auf Wettbewerbsverbot]	The principal's waiver of the prohibition of competition	77
§ 75 b	*(aufgehoben)*	*(repealed)*	77
§ 75 c	[Vertragsstrafe]	Contract penalty	77
§ 75 d	[Abweichende Vereinbarungen]	Deviating agreements	77
§ 75 e	*(aufgehoben)*	*(repealed)*	78
§ 75 f	[Sperrabrede unter Arbeitgebern]	Close-out agreements	78
§ 75 g	[Vermittlungsgehilfe]	Clerical employee capable of soliciting for the principal	78
§ 75 h	[Unkenntnis des Mangels der Vertretungsmacht]	Ignorance as to the absence of agency relationship	78
§§ 76–82	*(aufgehoben)*	*(repealed)*	79
§ 82 a	[Wettbewerbsverbot des Volontärs]	Prohibition of competition of unpaid trainees	79
§ 83	[Andere Arbeitnehmer]	Other employees	80
	Siebenter Abschnitt. Handelsvertreter	**Part Seven. Commercial Agents**	
§ 84	[Begriff des Handelsvertreters]	Definition of commercial agent	80
§ 85	[Vertragsurkunde]	Contract documents	81
§ 86	[Pflichten des Handelsvertreters]	Duties of the commercial agent	81
§ 86 a	[Pflichten des Unternehmers]	Principal's duties	81

			Seite/Page
§ 86 b	[Delkredereprovision]	*Del credere* commission	82
§ 87	[Provisionspflichtige Geschäfte]	Transactions for which commission is due	83
§ 87 a	[Fälligkeit der Provision]	Due date of the commission	84
§ 87 b	[Höhe der Provision]	Amount of the commission	85
§ 87 c	[Abrechnung über die Provision]	Accounting for the commission	85
§ 87 d	[Ersatz von Aufwendungen]	Reimbursement of expenses	86
§ 88	[Verjährung der Ansprüche]	Statute of limitations for claims	86
§ 88 a	[Zurückbehaltungsrecht]	Legal right of retention	87
§ 89	[Kündigung des Vertrages]	Termination of the agreement	87
§ 89 a	[Fristlose Kündigung]	Termination without observance of a notice period	88
§ 89 b	[Ausgleichsanspruch]	Compensation claim	88
§ 90	[Geschäfts- und Betriebsgeheimnisse]	Trade and business secrets	90
§ 90 a	[Wettbewerbsabrede]	Agreement prohibiting competition	90
§ 91	[Vollmachten des Handelsvertreters]	Authority of the commercial agent	91
§ 91 a	[Mangel der Vertretungsmacht]	Lack of authority	92
§ 92	[Versicherungs- und Bausparkassenvertreter]	Insurance and building and loan association agents	92
§ 92 a	[Mindestarbeitsbedingungen]	Minimum working conditions	93
§ 92 b	[Handelsvertreter im Nebenberuf]	Part-time commercial agent	94
§ 92 c	[Handelsvertreter außerhalb der EG; Schiffahrtsvertreter]	Commercial agent outside the EC; shipping agent	95
	Achter Abschnitt. Handelsmakler	**Part Eight. Commercial Broker**	
§ 93	[Begriff]	Definition	95
§ 94	[Schlußnote]	Memorandum of sale	96
§ 95	[Vorbehaltene Aufgabe]	Temporary reservation of disclosure of principal	97
§ 96	[Aufbewahrung von Proben]	Storage of samples	97

Inhaltsverzeichnis/Contents

			Seite/Page
§ 97	[Keine Inkassovollmacht]	No collection authority	98
§ 98	[Haftung gegenüber beiden Parteien]	Liability with respect to both parties	98
§ 99	[Lohnanspruch gegen beide Parteien]	Compensation right against both parties	98
§ 100	[Tagebuch]	Broker's transaction book	98
§ 101	[Auszüge aus dem Tagebuch]	Transaction book extracts	98
§ 102	[Vorlegung im Rechtsstreit]	Production during litigation	99
§ 103	[Ordnungswidrigkeiten]	Administrative violations	99
§ 104	[Krämermakler]	Petty broker	99
	Zweites Buch. Handelsgesellschaften und stille Gesellschaft	**Book Two. Commercial Partnerships and Silent Partnerships**	
	Erster Abschnitt. Offene Handelsgesellschaft	**Part One. General Commercial Partnership**	
	Erster Titel. Errichtung der Gesellschaft	*First Title. Establishment of the Partnership*	
§ 105	[Begriff der OHG; Anwendbarkeit des BGB]	Definition of general commercial partnership; applicability of the Civil Code	100
§ 106	[Anmeldung zum Handelsregister]	Application to the Commercial Register	100
§ 107	[Anzumeldende Änderungen]	Changes requiring application for registration	101
§ 108	[Anmeldung durch alle Gesellschafter; Aufbewahrung der Unterschriften]	Filing for registration by all partners; filing of signatures	101
	Zweiter Titel. Rechtsverhältnis der Gesellschafter untereinander	*Second Title. Legal Relationship of the Partners to One Another*	
§ 109	[Gesellschaftsvertrag]	Partnership agreement	101
§ 110	[Ersatz für Aufwendungen und Verluste]	Reimbursement for expenses and losses	102
§ 111	[Verzinsungspflicht]	Obligation to pay interest	102
§ 112	[Wettbewerbsverbot]	Prohibition of competition	102
§ 113	[Verletzung des Wettbewerbsverbots]	Violation of the prohibition of competition	103
§ 114	[Geschäftsführung]	Management of the business	104

Seite/Page

§ 115	[Geschäftsführung durch mehrere Gesellschafter]	Management of the business by more than one partner	104
§ 116	[Umfang der Geschäftsführungsbefugnis]	Scope of authority to manage the business	104
§ 117	[Entziehung der Geschäftsführungsbefugnis]	Withdrawal of authority to manage the business	105
§ 118	[Kontrollrecht der Gesellschafter]	Inspection right of partners	105
§ 119	[Beschlußfassung]	Passage of resolutions	105
§ 120	[Gewinn und Verlust]	Profits and losses	106
§ 121	[Verteilung von Gewinn und Verlust]	Distribution of profits and losses	106
§ 122	[Entnahmen]	Withdrawals	107
	Dritter Titel. Rechtsverhältnis der Gesellschafter zu Dritten	*Third Title. Legal Relationship of the Partners to Third Parties*	
§ 123	[Wirksamkeit im Verhältnis zu Dritten]	Effectiveness with respect to third parties	107
§ 124	[Rechtliche Selbständigkeit; Zwangsvollstreckung in Gesellschaftsvermögen]	Legal personality; execution on partnership assets	108
§ 125	[Vertretung der Gesellschaft]	Representation of the partnership	108
§ 125 a	[Angaben auf Geschäftsbriefen]	Information on business letters	109
§ 126	[Umfang der Vertretungsmacht]	Scope of the power to represent	110
§ 127	[Entziehung der Vertretungsmacht]	Withdrawal of the power to represent	110
§ 128	[Persönliche Haftung der Gesellschafter]	Personal liability of the partners	110
§ 129	[Einwendungen des Gesellschafters]	Defenses of the partner	111
§ 129 a	[Rückgewähr von Darlehen]	Repayment of loans	111
§ 130	[Haftung des eintretenden Gesellschafters]	Liability of a partner joining the partnership	112
§ 130 a	[Antragspflicht bei Zahlungsunfähigkeit oder Überschuldung]	Duty to file a petition in the event of inability to meet obligations or insolvency	112

			Seite/Page
§ 130 b	[Strafvorschriften]	Penal provisions	114
	Vierter Titel. Auflösung der Gesellschaft und Ausscheiden von Gesellschaftern	*Fourth Title. Dissolution of the Partnership and Withdrawal of Partners*	
§ 131	[Auflösungsgründe]	Reasons for dissolution	114
§ 132	[Kündigung eines Gesellschafters]	Notice of termination by one of the partners	115
§ 133	[Auflösung durch gerichtliche Entscheidung]	Dissolution by judicial decision	116
§ 134	[Gesellschaft auf Lebenszeit; fortgesetzte Gesellschaft]	Partnership for a term of life; continued partnership	116
§ 135	[Kündigung durch den Privatgläubiger]	Termination by the personal creditor of a partner	117
§§ 136–138	*(aufgehoben)*	*(repealed)*	117
§ 139	[Fortsetzung mit den Erben]	Continuation of the business with the heirs	117
§ 140	[Ausschließung eines Gesellschafters]	Exclusion of a partner	118
§§ 141, 142	*(aufgehoben)*	*(repealed)*	119
§ 143	[Anmeldung von Auflösung und Ausscheiden]	Registration of dissolution and withdrawal from the partnership	119
§ 144	[Fortsetzung nach Insolvenz der Gesellschaft]	Continuation of the partnership following insolvency	120
	Fünfter Titel. Liquidation der Gesellschaft	*Fifth Title. Liquidation of the Partnership*	
§ 145	[Notwendigkeit der Liquidation]	Necessity of liquidation	120
§ 146	[Bestellung der Liquidatoren]	Appointment of liquidators	121
§ 147	[Abberufung von Liquidatoren]	Removal of liquidators	121
§ 148	[Anmeldung der Liquidatoren]	Filing for registration of the liquidators	122
§ 149	[Rechte und Pflichten der Liquidatoren]	Rights and duties of liquidators	122
§ 150	[Mehrere Liquidatoren]	More than one liquidator	123
§ 151	[Unbeschränkbarkeit der Befugnisse]	Unlimited authority	123

			Seite/Page
§ 152	[Bindung an Weisungen]	Obligation to comply with directives	123
§ 153	[Unterschrift]	Signature	123
§ 154	[Bilanzen]	Balance sheets	124
§ 155	[Verteilung des Gesellschaftsvermögens]	Distribution of the partnership's assets	124
§ 156	[Rechtsverhältnisse der Gesellschafter]	Legal relationship of the partners	124
§ 157	[Anmeldung des Erlöschens; Geschäftsbücher]	Application for deletion of the firm name; business records	125
§ 158	[Andere Art der Auseinandersetzung]	Other types of dissolution	125
	Sechster Titel. Verjährung. Zeitliche Begrenzung der Haftung	*Sixth Title. Statute of Limitations. Time Limit on Liability*	
§ 159	[Ansprüche gegen einen Gesellschafter]	Claims against a partner	125
§ 160	[Haftung des ausscheidenden Gesellschafters; Fristen, Haftung als Kommanditist]	Liability of withdrawing partner; statutes of limitations; liability as limited partner	126
	Zweiter Abschnitt. Kommanditgesellschaft	**Part Two. Limited Partnership**	
§ 161	[Begriff der KG; Anwendbarkeit der OHG-Vorschriften]	Definition of the limited partnership; applicability of the general commercial partnership provisions	127
§ 162	[Anmeldung zum Handelsregister]	Filing for registration in the Commercial Register	128
§ 163	[Rechtsverhältnis der Gesellschafter untereinander]	Legal relationship of the partners to one another	128
§ 164	[Geschäftsführung]	Management of the business	128
§ 165	[Wettbewerbsverbot]	Prohibition of competition	129
§ 166	[Kontrollrecht]	Right of inspection	129
§ 167	[Gewinn und Verlust]	Profits and losses	129
§ 168	[Verteilung von Gewinn und Verlust]	Distribution of profits and losses	130
§ 169	[Gewinnauszahlung]	Payment of profits	130

XVII

			Seite/Page
§ 170	[Vertretung der KG]	Representing the limited partnership	130
§ 171	[Haftung des Kommanditisten]	Liability of the limited partner	131
§ 172	[Umfang der Haftung]	Scope of liability	131
§ 172 a	[Rückgewähr von Darlehen]	Repayment of loans	132
§ 173	[Haftung bei Eintritt als Kommanditist]	Liability upon joining as a limited partner	133
§ 174	[Herabsetzung der Einlage]	Reduction of capital contribution	133
§ 175	[Anmeldung der Änderung einer Einlage]	Filing for registration of change in capital contribution	133
§ 176	[Haftung vor Eintragung]	Liability prior to registration	133
§ 177	[Tod des Kommanditisten]	Death of a limited partner	134
§ 177 a	[Angaben auf Geschäftsbriefen; Antragspflicht bei Zahlungsunfähigkeit oder Überschuldung]	Information on business letters; duty to file a petition in the event of inability to meet obligations or insolvency	134
§§ 178–229	(aufgehoben)	(repealed)	135
	Dritter Abschnitt. Stille Gesellschaft	**Part Three. Silent Partnership**	
§ 230	[Begriff und Wesen der stillen Gesellschaft]	Definition and nature of the silent partnership	135
§ 231	[Gewinn und Verlust]	Profits and losses	135
§ 232	[Gewinn- und Verlustrechnung]	Calculation of profits and losses	135
§ 233	[Kontrollrecht des stillen Gesellschafters]	Inspection right of the silent partner	136
§ 234	[Kündigung der Gesellschaft; Tod des stillen Gesellschafters]	Termination of the partnership; death of the silent partner	136
§ 235	[Auseinandersetzung]	Settlement following dissolution	137
§ 236	[Insolvenz des Inhabers]	Insolvency of the business owner	137
§ 237	(aufgehoben)	(repealed)	137

Seite/Page

		Drittes Buch. Handelsbücher	**Book Three. Commercial Records**	
		Erster Abschnitt. Vorschriften für alle Kaufleute	**Part One. Regulations for all Merchants**	
		Erster Unterabschnitt. Buchführung. Inventar	**First Subpart. Bookkeeping. Inventory**	
	§ 238	Buchführungspflicht	Duty to keep books	138
	§ 239	Führung der Handelsbücher	Method of commercial bookkeeping	138
	§ 240	Inventar	Inventory	139
	§ 241	Inventurvereinfachungsverfahren	Procedures for simplifying the keeping of inventory	140
		Zweiter Unterabschnitt. Eröffnungsbilanz. Jahresabschluß	**Second Subpart. Opening Balance Sheet. Annual Financial Statements**	
		Erster Titel. Allgemeine Vorschriften	*First Title. General Regulations*	
	§ 242	Pflicht zur Aufstellung	Duty to prepare	142
	§ 243	Aufstellungsgrundsatz	Principle of preparation	142
	§ 244	Sprache. Währungseinheit	Language. Currency	142
	§ 245	Unterzeichnung	Signature	143
		Zweiter Titel. Ansatzvorschriften	*Second Title. Assessment Regulations*	
	§ 246	Vollständigkeit. Verrechnungsverbot	Completeness. Prohibition of offset	143
	§ 247	Inhalt der Bilanz	Contents of the balance sheet	143
	§ 248	Bilanzierungsverbote	Prohibitions in balancing accounts	144
	§ 249	Rückstellungen	Accruals	144
	§ 250	Rechnungsabgrenzungsposten	Accrued and deferred items	145
	§ 251	Haftungsverhältnisse	Contingencies and commitments	146
		Dritter Titel. Bewertungsvorschriften	*Third Title. Valuation Regulations*	
	§ 252	Allgemeine Bewertungsgrundsätze	General principles of valuation	146

XIX

Inhaltsverzeichnis/Contents

Seite/Page

§ 253	Wertansätze der Vermögensgegenstände und Schulden	Valuation of assets and liabilities	147
§ 254	Steuerrechtliche Abschreibungen	Depreciation under tax law	149
§ 255	Anschaffungs- und Herstellungskosten	Costs of acquisition and production	149
§ 256	Bewertungsvereinfachungsverfahren	Procedures for simplifying valuation	151

Dritter Unterabschnitt. Aufbewahrung und Vorlage

Third Subpart. Retention and Production

§ 257	Aufbewahrung von Unterlagen. Aufbewahrungsfristen	Retention of records; time periods of retention	151
§ 258	Vorlegung im Rechtsstreit	Production during litigation	153
§ 259	Auszug bei Vorlegung im Rechtsstreit	Excerpts from materials produced during litigation	153
§ 260	Vorlegung bei Auseinandersetzungen	Production of documents for distribution of assets	153
§ 261	Vorlegung von Unterlagen auf Bild- oder Datenträgern	Production of documents from film or data storage devices	153

Vierter Unterabschnitt. Landesrecht

Fourth Subpart. State Law

§ 262	*(aufgehoben)*	*(repealed)*	154
§ 263	Vorbehalt landesrechtlicher Vorschriften	Reservation of state law regulations	154

Zweiter Abschnitt. Ergänzende Vorschriften für Kapitalgesellschaften (Aktiengesellschaften, Kommanditgesellschaften auf Aktien und Gesellschaften mit beschränkter Haftung) sowie bestimmte Personenhandelsgesellschaften

Part Two. Additional Regulations for Corporations (Stock Corporations, Corporations Limited by Shares but having one or more General Partners and Limited Liability Companies) as well as certain Business Partnerships

Erster Unterabschnitt. Jahresabschluß der Kapitalgesellschaft und Lagebericht

First Subpart. Annual Financial Statements of the Corporation and Management Reports

Erster Titel. Allgemeine Vorschriften

First Title. General Regulations

§ 264	Pflicht zur Aufstellung	Duty to prepare	154

XX

			Seite/Page
§ 264 a	Anwendung auf bestimmte offene Handelsgesellschaften und Kommanditgesellschaften	Application to certain general commercial partnerships and limited partnerships	156
§ 264 b	Befreiung von der Pflicht zur Aufstellung eines Jahresabschlusses nach den für Kapitalgesellschaften geltenden Vorschriften	Exemption from the duty to prepare annual financial statements pursuant to the regulations applicable to corporations	157
§ 264 c	Besondere Bestimmungen für offene Handelsgesellschaften und Kommanditgesellschaften im Sinne des § 264 a	Special provisions for general commercial partnerships and limited partnerships within the meaning of § 264 a	158
§ 265	Allgemeine Grundsätze für die Gliederung	General principles of classification	160
	Zweiter Titel. Bilanz	*Second Title. The Balance Sheet*	
§ 266	Gliederung der Bilanz	Classification of the balance sheet	162
§ 267	Umschreibung der Größenklassen	Definition of class sizes	165
§ 268	Vorschriften zu einzelnen Posten der Bilanz. Bilanzvermerke	Regulations as to particular entries on the balance sheet; balance sheet notations	167
§ 269	Aufwendungen für die Ingangsetzung und Erweiterung des Geschäftsbetriebs	Expenses related to the formation and expansion of the business operation	169
§ 270	Bildung bestimmter Posten	Setting up certain entries	169
§ 271	Beteiligungen. Verbundene Unternehmen	Participations; related enterprises	170
§ 272	Eigenkapital	Shareholder's equity	171
§ 273	Sonderposten mit Rücklageanteil	Special entries in capital surplus	173
§ 274	Steuerabgrenzung	Tax deferrals	173
§ 274 a	Größenabhängige Erleichterungen	Size-related relief	174
	Dritter Titel. Gewinn- und Verlustrechnung	*Third Title. Profit and Loss Statement*	
§ 275	Gliederung	Presentation	175
§ 276	Größenabhängige Erleichterungen	Size-related relief	178

XXI

Inhaltsverzeichnis/Contents

			Seite/Page
§ 277	Vorschriften zu einzelnen Posten der Gewinn- und Verlustrechnung	Regulations for particular entries in the profit and loss statement	178
§ 278	Steuern	Taxes	179
	Vierter Titel. Bewertungsvorschriften	*Fourth Title. Regulations as to Valuation*	
§ 279	Nichtanwendung von Vorschriften. Abschreibungen	Inapplicability of regulations; depreciation	180
§ 280	Wertaufholungsgebot	Obligation to recover original value	180
§ 281	Berücksichtigung steuerrechtlicher Vorschriften	Consideration of tax regulations	181
§ 282	Abschreibung der Aufwendungen für die Ingangsetzung und Erweiterung des Geschäftsbetriebs	Amortization of expenses relating to the formation and expansion of the business operation	182
§ 283	Wertansatz des Eigenkapitals	Valuation of equity capital	182
	Fünfter Titel. Anhang	*Fifth Title. Notes*	
§ 284	Erläuterung der Bilanz und der Gewinn- und Verlustrechnung	Explanation of the balance sheet and the profit and loss statement	182
§ 285	Sonstige Pflichtangaben	Other mandatory disclosures	183
§ 286	Unterlassen von Angaben	Omission of disclosures	187
§ 287	Aufstellung des Anteilsbesitzes	List of share ownership	189
§ 288	Größenabhängige Erleichterungen	Size-related relief	189
	Sechster Titel. Lagebericht	*Sixth Title. Management Report*	
§ 289			189
	Zweiter Unterabschnitt. Konzernabschluß und Konzernlagebericht	**Second Subpart. The Consolidated Financial Statements and Consolidated Management Report**	
	Erster Titel. Anwendungsbereich	*First Title. Area of Application*	
§ 290	Pflicht zur Aufstellung	Duty to prepare	190

XXII

Inhaltsverzeichnis/Contents

Seite/Page

§ 291	Befreiende Wirkung von EU/EWR-Konzernabschlüssen	Exemptive effect of EU/EEA consolidated financial statements	192
§ 292	Rechtsverordnungsermächtigung für befreiende Konzernabschlüsse und Konzernlageberichte	Enabling rule for the exemptive consolidated financial statements and consolidated management reports	195
§ 292 a	Befreiung von der Aufstellungspflicht	Exemption from the duty to prepare consolidated financial statements and a consolidated management report	198
§ 293	Größenabhängige Befreiungen	Size-related exemptions	200
	Zweiter Titel. Konsolidierungskreis	*Second Title. Consolidated Group*	
§ 294	Einzubeziehende Unternehmen. Vorlage- und Auskunftspflichten	Enterprises to be included; duty to produce and inform	202
§ 295	Verbot der Einbeziehung	Prohibition of inclusion	203
§ 296	Verzicht auf die Einbeziehung	Waiver of the inclusion	204
	Dritter Titel. Inhalt und Form des Konzernabschlusses	*Third Title. Content and Form of the Consolidated Financial Statements*	
§ 297	Inhalt	Content	205
§ 298	Anzuwendende Vorschriften. Erleichterungen	Applicable regulations; relief	206
§ 299	Stichtag für die Aufstellung	Closing day for the preparation	207
	Vierter Titel. Vollkonsolidierung	*Fourth Title. Full Consolidation*	
§ 300	Konsolidierungsgrundsätze. Vollständigkeitsgebot	Principles of consolidation; requirement of completeness	208
§ 301	Kapitalkonsolidierung	Capital consolidation	209
§ 302	Kapitalkonsolidierung bei Interessenzusammenführung	Capital consolidation using the pooling-of-interest method	210
§ 303	Schuldenkonsolidierung	Debt consolidation	211
§ 304	Behandlung der Zwischenergebnisse	Treatment of interim results	212

XXIII

Inhaltsverzeichnis/Contents

Seite/Page

§ 305	Aufwands- und Ertragskonsolidierung	Consolidation of expenses and revenues	212
§ 306	Steuerabgrenzung	Tax deferral	213
§ 307	Anteile anderer Gesellschafter	Shares of other shareholders	213
	Fünfter Titel. Bewertungsvorschriften	*Fifth Title. Valuation Regulations*	
§ 308	Einheitliche Bewertung	Uniform valuation	214
§ 309	Behandlung des Unterschiedsbetrags	Treatment of difference in amounts	215
	Sechster Titel. Anteilmäßige Konsolidierung	*Sixth Title. Proportionate Consolidation*	
§ 310			216
	Siebenter Titel. Assoziierte Unternehmen	*Seventh Title. Associated Enterprises*	
§ 311	Definition. Befreiung	Definition; exemption	217
§ 312	Wertansatz der Beteiligung und Behandlung des Unterschiedsbetrags	Valuation of the participation and treatment of the difference in amounts	217
	Achter Titel. Konzernanhang	*Eighth Title. Consolidated Notes*	
§ 313	Erläuterung der Konzernbilanz und der Konzern-Gewinn- und Verlustrechnung. Angaben zum Beteiligungsbesitz	Discussion of the consolidated balance sheet and the consolidated profit and loss statement; reports on participations	220
§ 314	Sonstige Pflichtangaben	Other mandatory disclosures	223
	Neunter Titel. Konzernlagebericht	*Ninth Title. Consolidated Management Report*	
§ 315			226
	Dritter Unterabschnitt. Prüfung	**Third Subpart. Audit**	
§ 316	Pflicht zur Prüfung	Duty to audit	227
§ 317	Gegenstand und Umfang der Prüfung	Subject matter and extent of the audit	228
§ 318	Bestellung und Abberufung des Abschlußprüfers	Retaining and terminating the auditor	229
§ 319	Auswahl der Abschlußprüfer	Choice of the auditors	232

			Seite/Page
§ 320	Vorlagepflicht. Auskunftsrecht	Duty to produce; right to information	236
§ 321	Prüfungsbericht	Audit report	237
§ 322	Bestätigungsvermerk	Certification of the financial statements	239
§ 323	Verantwortlichkeit des Abschlußprüfers	The auditor's responsibilities	240
§ 324	Meinungsverschiedenheiten zwischen Kapitalgesellschaft und Abschlußprüfer	Differences of opinion between corporation and auditor	242
	Vierter Unterabschnitt. Offenlegung (Einreichung zu einem Register, Bekanntmachung im Bundesanzeiger). Veröffentlichung und Vervielfältigung. Prüfung durch das Registergericht.	**Fourth Subpart. Disclosure (Filing in the Register, Publication in the Federal Gazette). Publication and Reproduction. Examination by the Registry Court**	
§ 325	Offenlegung	Disclosure	243
§ 325 a	Zweigniederlassungen von Kapitalgesellschaften mit Sitz im Ausland	Branches of corporations with foreign domicile	246
§ 326	Größenabhängige Erleichterungen für kleine Kapitalgesellschaften bei der Offenlegung	Size-related relief for disclosures by small corporations	247
§ 327	Größenabhängige Erleichterungen für mittelgroße Kapitalgesellschaften bei der Offenlegung	Size-related relief for disclosures by medium-sized corporations	247
§ 328	Form und Inhalt der Unterlagen bei der Offenlegung, Veröffentlichung und Vervielfältigung	Form and content of records upon disclosure, publication and reproduction	249
§ 329	Prüfungspflicht des Registergerichts	Examination duty of the registry court of the Commercial Register	251
	Fünfter Unterabschnitt. Verordnungsermächtigung für Formblätter und andere Vorschriften	**Fifth Subpart. Enabling Rule for Printed Forms and Other Regulations**	
§ 330			251

				Seite/Page
	Sechster Unterabschnitt. Straf- und Bußgeldvorschriften. Zwangsgelder	**Sixth Subpart. Criminal Law and Civil Penalty Provisions. Coercive Fines**		
§ 331	Unrichtige Darstellung	False presentation		255
§ 332	Verletzung der Berichtspflicht	Violation of the duty to report		256
§ 333	Verletzung der Geheimhaltungspflicht	Violation of the duty of confidentiality		256
§ 334	Bußgeldvorschriften	Civil penalty provisions		257
§ 335	Festsetzung von Zwangsgeld	Setting of a coercive fine		260
§ 335a	Festsetzung von Ordnungsgeld	Setting of administrative fines		260
§ 335 b	Anwendung der Straf- und Bußgeldvorschriften sowie der Zwangs- und Ordnungsgeldvorschriften auf bestimmte offene Handelsgesellschaften und Kommanditgesellschaften	Application of criminal and civil penalty provisions and coercive and administrative fine provisions to certain general commercial partnerships and limited partnerships		261
	Dritter Abschnitt. Ergänzende Vorschriften für eingetragene Genossenschaften	**Part Three. Supplementary Provisions for Registered Cooperative Associations**		
§ 336	Pflicht zur Aufstellung von Jahresabschluß und Lagebericht	Duty to prepare annual financial statements and a management report		262
§ 337	Vorschriften zur Bilanz	Provisions as to the balance sheet		262
§ 338	Vorschriften zum Anhang	Provisions as to notes		263
§ 339	Offenlegung	Disclosure		264
	Vierter Abschnitt. Ergänzende Vorschriften für Unternehmen bestimmter Geschäftszweige	**Part Four. Supplementary Provisions for Enterprises of Certain Branches**		
	Erster Unterabschnitt. Ergänzende Vorschriften für Kreditinstitute und Finanzdienstleistungsinstitute	*First Subpart. Supplementary Provisions for Credit Institutions and Financial Service Institutions*		
	Erster Titel. Anwendungsbereich	*First Title. Area of Application*		
§ 340				266

Inhaltsverzeichnis/Contents

Seite/Page

	Zweiter Titel. Jahresabschluß. Lagebericht. Zwischenabschluß	*Second Title. Annual Financial Statements. Management Report. Interim Financial Statements*	
§ 340 a	Anzuwendende Vorschriften	Applicable provisions	268
§ 340 b	Pensionsgeschäfte	Cash sale coupled with a contract for subsequent repurchase	269
§ 340 c	Vorschriften zur Gewinn- und Verlustrechnung und zum Anhang	Provisions concerning the profit and loss statement and the notes	270
§ 340 d	Fristengliederung	Classification by due date	271
	Dritter Titel. Bewertungsvorschriften	*Third Title. Valuation Provisions*	
§ 340 e	Bewertung von Vermögensgegenständen	Valuation of assets	272
§ 340 f	Vorsorge für allgemeine Bankrisiken	Provision for general bank risks	273
§ 340 g	Sonderposten für allgemeine Bankrisiken	Special items for general bank risks	274
	Vierter Titel. Währungsumrechnung	*Fourth Title. Currency Conversion*	
§ 340 h			275
	Fünfter Titel. Konzernabschluß. Konzernlagebericht. Konzernzwischenabschluß	*Fifth Title. Consolidated Financial Statements. Consolidated Management Report. Interim Consolidated Financial Statements*	
§ 340 i	Pflicht zur Aufstellung	Duty to prepare	276
§ 340 j	Einzubeziehende Unternehmen	Includable enterprises	277
	Sechster Titel. Prüfung	*Sixth Title. Audit*	
§ 340 k			278
	Siebenter Titel. Offenlegung	*Seventh Title. Disclosure*	
§ 340 l			279
	Achter Titel. Straf- und Bußgeldvorschriften. Zwangsgelder	*Eighth Title. Criminal Law and Civil Penalty. Provisions, Coercive Fines*	
§ 340 m	Strafvorschriften	Criminal law provisions	281

			Seite/Page
§ 340 n	Bußgeldvorschriften	Civil penalty provisions	281
§ 340 o	Festsetzung von Zwangs- und Ordnungsgeld	Setting of a coercive and administrative fine	284
	Zweiter Unterabschnitt. Ergänzende Vorschriften für Versicherungsunternehmen und Pensionsfonds	**Second Subpart. Supplementary Rules for Insurance Companies and Pension Funds**	
	Erster Titel. Anwendungsbereich	*First Title. Area of Application*	
§ 341			285
	Zweiter Titel. Jahresabschluß, Lagebericht	*Second Title. Annual Financial Statements, Management Report*	
§ 341 a	Anzuwendende Vorschriften	Applicable provisions	287
	Dritter Titel. Bewertungsvorschriften	*Third Title. Valuation provisions*	
§ 341 b	Bewertung von Vermögensgegenständen	Valuation of assets	288
§ 341 c	Namensschuldverschreibungen, Hypothekendarlehen und andere Forderungen	Registered bonds, mortgage loans and other claims	290
§ 341 d	Anlagestock der fondsgebundenen Lebensversicherung	Investment holdings of life insurance bound to a fund	290
	Vierter Titel. Versicherungstechnische Rückstellungen	*Fourth Title. Actuarial Reserves*	
§ 341 e	Allgemeine Bilanzierungsgrundsätze	General balance sheet principles	291
§ 341 f	Deckungsrückstellung	Covering reserve	292
§ 341 g	Rückstellung für noch nicht abgewickelte Versicherungsfälle	Reserve for insurance cases not yet settled	293
§ 341 h	Schwankungsrückstellung und ähnliche Rückstellungen	Loss equalization reserve and similar reserves	294
	Fünfter Titel. Konzernabschluß, Konzernlagebericht	*Fifth Title. Consolidated Annual Financial Statements, Consolidated Management Report*	
§ 341 i	Aufstellung, Fristen	Preparation, deadlines	295
§ 341 j	Anzuwendende Vorschriften	Applicable provisions	296

				Seite/Page
§ 341 k	*Sechster Titel. Prüfung*	*Sixth Title. Audit*		297
§ 341 l	*Siebenter Titel. Offenlegung*	*Seventh Title. Disclosure*		297
	Achter Titel. Straf- und Bußgeldvorschriften. Zwangsgelder	*Eighth Title. Criminal Law and Civil Penalty Provisions. Coercive Fines*		
§ 341 m	Strafvorschriften	Criminal law provisions		298
§ 341 n	Bußgeldvorschriften	Civil penalty provisions		299
§ 341 o	Festsetzung von Zwangs- und Ordnungsgeld	Setting of coercive and administrative fines		302
§ 341 p	Anwendung der Straf- und Bußgeldvorschriften sowie der Zwangs- und Ordnungsgeldvorschriften auf Pensionsfonds	Application of the Criminal Law and Civil Penalty Provisions as well as the Coercive and Administrative Fine Provisions to Pension Funds		302
	Fünfter Abschnitt. Privates Rechnungslegungsgremium; Rechnungslegungsbeirat	**Part Five. Private Accounting Panel; Accounting Board**		
§ 342	Privates Rechnungslegungsgremium	Private accounting panel		303
§ 342 a	Rechnungslegungsbeirat	Accounting board		304
	Viertes Buch. Handelsgeschäfte	**Book Four. Commercial Transactions**		
	Erster Abschnitt. Allgemeine Vorschriften	**Part One. General Provisions**		
§ 343	[Begriff der Handelsgeschäfte]	Definition of commercial transactions		306
§ 344	[Vermutung für das Handelsgeschäft]	Presumption of a commercial transaction		306
§ 345	[Einseitige Handelsgeschäfte]	Unilateral commercial transactions		306
§ 346	[Handelsbräuche]	Commercial practices		306
§ 347	[Sorgfaltspflicht]	Duty of care		307
§ 348	[Vertragsstrafe]	Contract penalty		307

Inhaltsverzeichnis/Contents

Seite/Page

§ 349	[Keine Einrede der Vorausklage]	No defense by a guarantor that the creditor must first unsuccessfully try to execute his claim on the debtor	307
§ 350	[Formfreiheit]	Freedom from formal requirements	307
§ 351	*(aufgehoben)*	*(repealed)*	308
§ 352	[Gesetzlicher Zinssatz]	Statutory interest rate	308
§ 353	[Fälligkeitszinsen]	Interest from the date due	308
§ 354	[Provision; Lagergeld; Zinsen]	Commission; storage charges; interest	308
§ 354 a	[Wirksamkeit der Abtretung einer Geldforderung]	Effectiveness of transfer of monetary claim	309
§ 355	[Laufende Rechnung, Kontokorrent]	Revolving account, current account	309
§ 356	[Sicherheiten]	Security interests	310
§ 357	[Pfändung des Saldos]	Execution on the account balance	310
§ 358	[Zeit der Leistung]	Time of performance	311
§ 359	[Vereinbarte Zeit der Leistung; „acht Tage"]	Agreed time for performance; "eight days"	311
§ 360	[Gattungsschuld]	Obligation to deliver merchandise specified only by generic characteristics	311
§ 361	[Maß, Gewicht, Währung, Zeitrechnung und Entfernungen]	Measure, weight, currency, computation of time, distance	311
§ 362	[Schweigen des Kaufmanns auf Anträge]	Silence of merchant as to offers	312
§ 363	[Kaufmännische Orderpapiere]	Commercial negotiable instruments	312
§ 364	[Indossament]	Indorsement	313
§ 365	[Anwendung des Wechselrechts; Aufgebotsverfahren]	Applicability of the law governing bills of exchange; cancellation proceedings by public advertisement	313
§ 366	[Gutgläubiger Erwerb von beweglichen Sachen]	Good faith acquisition of tangible property	314
§ 367	[Gutgläubiger Erwerb gewisser Wertpapiere]	Good faith acquisition of certain securities	315

			Seite/Page
§ 368	[Pfandverkauf]	Sale of pledged items	315
§ 369	[Kaufmännisches Zurückbehaltungsrecht]	Merchant's right of retention	316
§ 370	*(aufgehoben)*	*(repealed)*	317
§ 371	[Befriedigungsrecht]	Right to satisfaction	317
§ 372	[Eigentumsfiktion und Rechtskraftwirkung bei Befriedigungsrecht]	Fictive ownership and effect of final judgment pertaining to the right to satisfaction	318
	Zweiter Abschnitt. Handelskauf	**Part Two. Commercial Sale of Goods**	
§ 373	[Annahmeverzug des Käufers]	Default in acceptance by the buyer	318
§ 374	[Vorschriften des BGB über Annahmeverzug]	Provisions of the Civil Code with respect to default in taking delivery	319
§ 375	[Bestimmungskauf]	Sale where the buyer specifies the item	320
§ 376	[Fixhandelskauf]	Sale to be performed at a fixed point in time	320
§ 377	[Untersuchungs- und Rügepflicht]	Duty to examine and object to defects	321
§ 378	*(aufgehoben)*	*(repealed)*	322
§ 379	[Einstweilige Aufbewahrung; Notverkauf]	Temporary storage; forced sale	322
§ 380	[Taragewicht]	Tare weight	322
§ 381	[Kauf von Wertpapieren; Werklieferungsvertrag]	Sale of securities	323
§ 382	*(aufgehoben)*	*(repealed)*	323
	Dritter Abschnitt. Kommissionsgeschäft	**Part Three. Transactions on a Commission Basis**	
§ 383	[Kommissionär; Kommissionsvertrag]	Commission agent; contract concluded by a commission agent	323
§ 384	[Pflichten des Kommissionärs]	Duties of the commission agent	324
§ 385	[Weisungen des Kommittenten]	Instructions of the principal	324
§ 386	[Preisgrenzen]	Buying and selling price limitations	325

XXXI

Inhaltsverzeichnis/Contents

Seite/Page

§ 387	[Vorteilhafter Abschluß]	More profitable conclusion of business	325
§ 388	[Beschädigtes oder mangelhaftes Kommissionsgut]	Damaged or defective goods on commission	326
§ 389	[Hinterlegung; Selbsthilfeverkauf]	Deposit; self-help sale	326
§ 390	[Haftung des Kommissionärs für das Gut]	The commission agent's liability for the goods	326
§ 391	[Untersuchungs- und Rügepflicht; Aufbewahrung; Notverkauf]	Duty to examine and object; storage; forced sale	327
§ 392	[Forderungen aus dem Kommissionsgeschäft]	Claims arising from transactions on a commission basis	327
§ 393	[Vorschuß; Kredit]	Advance; credit	328
§ 394	[Delkredere]	*Del credere* commission	328
§ 395	[Wechselindossament]	Bill of exchange indorsement	329
§ 396	[Provision des Kommissionärs; Ersatz von Aufwendungen]	Commission agent's commission; reimbursement for expenditures	329
§ 397	[Gesetzliches Pfandrecht]	Statutory lien	329
§ 398	[Befriedigung aus eigenem Kommissionsgut]	Satisfaction from one's own commission goods	330
§ 399	[Befriedigung aus Forderungen]	Satisfaction out of claims	330
§ 400	[Selbsteintritt des Kommissionärs]	Commission agent's substitution of himself for the third party he would otherwise deal with on the principal's behalf	330
§ 401	[Deckungsgeschäft]	Covering transactions	331
§ 402	[Unabdingbarkeit]	Unalterable rights	332
§ 403	[Provision bei Selbsteintritt]	Commission for entry of the commission agent simultaneously as third party	332
§ 404	[Gesetzliches Pfandrecht]	Statutory lien	332
§ 405	[Ausführungsanzeige und Selbsteintritt; Widerruf der Kommission]	Notice of performance and substitution of commission agent for the third party he would otherwise deal with on the principal's behalf; revocation of the commission	333

			Seite/Page
§ 406	[Ähnliche Geschäfte]	Similar transactions	333
	Vierter Abschnitt. Frachtgeschäft	**Part Four. Carrier Business**	
	Erster Unterabschnitt. Allgemeine Vorschriften	**First Subpart. General Provisions**	
§ 407	Frachtvertrag	Freight agreement	334
§ 408	Frachtbrief	Waybill	335
§ 409	Beweiskraft des Frachtbriefs	Evidentiary value of the waybill	336
§ 410	Gefährliches Gut	Dangerous goods	337
§ 411	Verpackung. Kennzeichnung	Packaging; labelling	337
§ 412	Verladen und Entladen	Loading and unloading	338
§ 413	Begleitpapiere	Documents accompanying the goods	339
§ 414	Verschuldensunabhängige Haftung des Absenders in besonderen Fällen	Strict liability of the shipper in special cases	339
§ 415	Kündigung durch den Absender	Termination by the shipper	340
§ 416	Anspruch auf Teilbeförderung	Claim to partial shipment	341
§ 417	Rechte des Frachtführers bei Nichteinhaltung der Ladezeit	Rights of the carrier in case of non-observance of the loading time	342
§ 418	Nachträgliche Weisungen	Subsequent instructions	343
§ 419	Beförderungs- und Ablieferungshindernisse	Hindrances to shipment and delivery	344
§ 420	Zahlung. Frachtberechnung	Payment; computation of freight charges	346
§ 421	Rechte des Empfängers. Zahlungspflicht	Rights of the consignee; payment obligation	346
§ 422	Nachnahme	Cash due on delivery	347
§ 423	Lieferfrist	Term for delivery	348
§ 424	Verlustvermutung	Presumption of loss	348
§ 425	Haftung für Güter- und Verspätungsschäden. Schadensteilung	Liability for damages to goods and for delay; partition of damages	349
§ 426	Haftungsausschluß	Exclusion of liability	349

Inhaltsverzeichnis/Contents

Seite/Page

§ 427	Besondere Haftungsausschlußgründe	Special grounds for exclusion of liability	350
§ 428	Haftung für andere	Liability for others	351
§ 429	Wertersatz	Compensation for lost value	351
§ 430	Schadensfeststellungskosten	Costs of determining the damage	352
§ 431	Haftungshöchstbetrag	Maximum liability	352
§ 432	Ersatz sonstiger Kosten	Reimbursement of other costs	353
§ 433	Haftungshöchstbetrag bei sonstigen Vermögensschäden	Maximum amount of liability in case of other pecuniary loss	354
§ 434	Außervertragliche Ansprüche	Non-contractual claims	354
§ 435	Wegfall der Haftungsbefreiungen und -begrenzungen	Loss of exemptions from and limitations of liability	355
§ 436	Haftung der Leute	Liability of employees	355
§ 437	Ausführender Frachtführer	Acting carrier	355
§ 438	Schadensanzeige	Notification of damage	356
§ 439	Verjährung	Statute of limitations	357
§ 440	Gerichtsstand	Place of jurisdiction	358
§ 441	Pfandrecht	Lien	358
§ 442	Nachfolgender Frachtführer	Subsequent carrier	359
§ 443	Rang mehrerer Pfandrechte	Priority among multiple liens	359
§ 444	Ladeschein	Bill of lading	360
§ 445	Ablieferung gegen Rückgabe des Ladescheins	Delivery against return of the bill of lading	361
§ 446	Legitimation durch Ladeschein	Identification by means of the bill of lading	361
§ 447	Ablieferung und Weisungsbefolgung ohne Ladeschein	Delivery and compliance with instructions without inland bill of lading	361
§ 448	Traditionspapier	Negotiable document of title	361
§ 449	Abweichende Vereinbarungen	Deviating agreements	362
§ 450	Anwendung von Seefrachtrecht	Application of maritime shipping law	363

Inhaltsverzeichnis/Contents

Seite/Page

		Zweiter Unterabschnitt. Beförderung von Umzugsgut	Second Subpart. Shipment of Personal and Household Goods in Course of Relocation	
§ 451		Umzugsvertrag	Relocation agreement	363
§ 451 a		Pflichten des Frachtführers	Duties of the carrier	363
§ 451 b		Frachtbrief. Gefährliches Gut. Begleitpapiere. Mitteilungs- und Auskunftspflichten	Waybill. Dangerous goods. Accompanying documents; duties to notify and inform	364
§ 451 c		Haftung des Absenders in besonderen Fällen	Liability of the shipper in special cases	364
§ 451 d		Besondere Haftungsausschlußgründe	Special reasons for exemption from liability	365
§ 451 e		Haftungshöchstbetrag	Maximum amount of liability	366
§ 451 f		Schadensanzeige	Notification of damage	366
§ 451 g		Wegfall der Haftungsbefreiungen und -begrenzungen	Loss of the exemptions from and limitations of liability	366
§ 451 h		Abweichende Vereinbarungen	Deviating agreements	367
		Dritter Unterabschnitt. Beförderung mit verschiedenartigen Beförderungsmitteln	Third Subpart. Shipment by Different Means of Transportation	
§ 452		Frachtvertrag über eine Beförderung mit verschiedenartigen Beförderungsmitteln	Freight agreement pertaining to a shipment by different means of transportation	368
§ 452 a		Bekannter Schadensort	Identified place where damage occurred	369
§ 452 b		Schadensanzeige. Verjährung	Notification of damage. Statute of limitations	369
§ 452 c		Umzugsvertrag über eine Beförderung mit verschiedenartigen Beförderungsmitteln	Relocation agreement pertaining to shipment by different means of transportation	370
§ 452 d		Abweichende Vereinbarungen	Deviating agreements	370
		Fünfter Abschnitt. Speditionsgeschäft	Part Five. The Forwarding Business	
§ 453		Speditionsvertrag	Forwarding agreement	371
§ 454		Besorgung der Versendung	Handling the shipment	371
§ 455		Behandlung des Gutes. Begleitpapiere. Mitteilungs- und Auskunftspflichten	Handling of the goods; accompanying documents; duties to notify and inform	372

XXXV

Inhaltsverzeichnis/Contents

			Seite/Page
§ 456	Fälligkeit der Vergütung	Due date of the remuneration	373
§ 457	Forderungen des Versenders	Claims of the shipper	373
§ 458	Selbsteintritt	The forwarding agent's right to substitute himself for the third party he would otherwise deal with on the principal's behalf	374
§ 459	Spedition zu festen Kosten	Forwarding at fixed costs	374
§ 460	Sammelladung	Mixed Consignment	374
§ 461	Haftung des Spediteurs	Liability of the forwarding agent	375
§ 462	Haftung für andere	Liability for others	375
§ 463	Verjährung	Statute of limitations	376
§ 464	Pfandrecht	Lien	376
§ 465	Nachfolgender Spediteur	Subsequent forwarding agent	376
§ 466	Abweichende Vereinbarungen	Deviating agreements	376
	Sechster Abschnitt. Lagergeschäft	**Part Six. Warehousing**	
§ 467	Lagervertrag	Warehousing contract	378
§ 468	Behandlung des Gutes. Begleitpapiere. Mitteilungs- und Auskunftspflichten	Handling of the goods; accompanying documents; duties to notify and inform	378
§ 469	Sammellagerung	Mixed deposit storage	379
§ 470	Empfang des Gutes	Acceptance of the goods	380
§ 471	Erhaltung des Gutes	Maintenance of the goods	380
§ 472	Versicherung. Einlagerung bei einem Dritten	Insurance. Warehousing at a third Party	381
§ 473	Dauer der Lagerung	Duration of the warehousing	381
§ 474	Aufwendungsersatz	Reimbursement of expenditures	382
§ 475	Haftung für Verlust oder Beschädigung	Liability for loss or damage	382
§ 475 a	Verjährung	Statute of limitations	382
§ 475 b	Pfandrecht	Lien	383
§ 475 c	Lagerschein	Warehouse receipt	383
§ 475 d	Wirkung des Lagerscheins	Effect of the warehouse receipt	384

			Seite/Page
§ 475 e	Auslieferung gegen Rückgabe des Lagerscheins	Delivery against return of the warehouse receipt	385
§ 475 f	Legitimation durch Lagerschein	Proof of identity by means of the warehouse receipt	386
§ 475 g	Traditionsfunktion des Orderlagerscheins	Function of negotiable warehouse receipt	386
§ 475 h	Abweichende Vereinbarungen	Deviating agreements	386
	Fünftes Buch. Seehandel	**Book Five. Maritime Trade**	
§§ 476 bis 905	*(nicht abgedruckt)*	*(not printed)*	386

Stichwortverzeichnis 387

Index 397

Introduction

I. Necessity for a New Edition

The fourth and last edition of this book appeared in 2000. Since 1996, and especially in 1998, the German Commercial Code (*Handelsgesetzbuch*) had been significantly changed and amended, such that the 4th revised edition became necessary.

The Act to Reform the Commercial Code (*Handelsrechtsreformgesetz* of June 22, 1998, BGBl.[1] 1998/I/1474) brought about material changes to the scope of applicability of the Commercial Code and the provisions pertaining to the firm name, the commercial register (*Handelsregister*) and partnerships.

The Act to Reform the Transportation Law (*Transportrechtsreformgesetz* of June 25, 1998, BGBl. 1998/I/1588) was a completely new codification of the rules pertaining to all transports by road, rail and internal waterways, broadly following the example of the Convention on the Contract for the International Carriage of Goods by Road (CMR, compare BGBl. 1961/II/1119 and 1962/II/12) and doing away with a multitude of old and widely scattered provisions, ordinances and laws. This reform act, although it had not drawn a lot of public attention, was one of the most thorough and radical legal changes of the last years. It has been incorporated in the Commercial Code since the trades involved, namely freight carrying, forwarding and warehousing, are trades which fall under the revised Commercial Code – as does each and every commercial activity except the exercise of a profession – and had already been incorporated in rudimentary form and, as mentioned above, scattered manner in the old version of the Commercial Code.

In addition, the Commercial Code had been amended by the so-called "KonTraG" (*Gesetz zur Kontrolle und Transparenz im Unternehmensbereich* of April 27, 1998, BGBl. 1998/I/786), the main thrust of which was to amend the Stock Corporation Act. This law required, *inter alia*, every stock corporation to introduce a warning system by which dangers to the corporation will be detected in timely manner; this danger-detecting system – in the case of stock corporations the shares of which are publicly quoted – has to be audited. The KonTraG, further, strengthened the role of the auditor generally, causing the long-form audit reports to be more meaningful and more easily intelligible and the auditor to work together more closely with the supervisory board. Most of these ideas have been incorporated in the Stock Corporation Act[2], but some of them are also contained in

---

1 Bundesgesetzblatt – Federal Gazette
2 See Peltzer/Hickinbotham, bilingual edition of the new Stock Corporation Act, Otto-Schmidt-Verlag, 1999.

the Commercial Code since the auditing of the accounts of a commercial enterprise – together with the accounting – is dealt with in the Commercial Code (§§ 316 et seq.).

These changes, having been brought about as of April 1st or July 1st, 1998 or in some cases only as of January 1st, 1999, are arguably the most important changes to the Commercial Code in its one-hundred-year history (it came into force on January 1, 1900). One would expect that, after such a major revision, the law would remain unchanged for some time. We live, however, in a rapidly changing world, and this cannot be without consequences for the main law dealing with the world of business. It is therefore not surprising that close to 100 paragraphs were changed since the 4th edition appeared. The changes – some of which minor – were brought about by the following acts

- Act concerning Guidelines to Partnerships in which the General Partner itself is a Corporate Entity (*Kapitalgesellschaften- und Co-Richtlinie-Gesetz*), BGBl. 2000/I/154 ff.
- Act for Acceleration of Payments Due (*Gesetz zur Beschleunigung fälliger Zahlungen*), BGBl. 2000/I/330 ff.
- Act on Long Distance Sales Contracts and Other Questions of Consumer Law as well as for Conversion of Regulations to Euro (*Gesetz über Fernabsatzverträge und andere Fragen des Verbraucherrechts sowie zur Umstellung von Vorschriften auf Euro*), BGBl. 2000/I/897 ff.
- A law pertaining to maritime matters, BGBl. 2000/I/938
- Act for Amendment of Regulations on the Activities of Certified Accountants – Certified Accountants Rules Amendment Act (*Gesetz zur Änderung von Vorschriften über die Tätigkeit der Wirtschaftsprüfer – Wirtschaftsprüferordnungs-Änderungsgesetz*), BGBl. 2000/I/1769 ff.
- Fourth Euro Introduction Act (*4. Euro-Einführungsgesetz*), BGBl. 2000/I/1983 ff.
- Act for Registered Shares and for Simplification of the Exercise of Voting Rights – Registered Share Act (*Gesetz zur Namensaktie und zur Erleichterung der Stimmrechtsausübung – Namensaktiengesetz*), BGBl. 2001/I/123 ff.
- Act for Amendment of Recovery Law in International and National Maritime Transportation (*Gesetz zur Neuregelung des Bergungsrechts in der See- und Binnenschifffahrt*), BGBl. 2001/I/898 ff.
- Act on Private and Company Pensions (*Altersvermögensgesetz*), BGBl. 2001/I/1310 ff.
- Act on Conforming the Formal Requirements to the Modern Legal Transactions (*Gesetz zur Anpassung der Formvorschriften an den modernen Rechtsverkehr*), BGBl. 2001/I/1542 ff.
- Seventh Order on Amendment of Jurisdiction (*7. Zuständigkeitsanpassungsverordnung*), BGBl. 2001/I/2785 ff.

- Act on Reform of the Law of Obligations (*Gesetz zur Modernisierung des Schuldrechts*), BGBl. 2001/I/3138 ff.
- Euro Accounting Act (*Euro-Bilanzgesetz*), BGBl. 2001/I/3414 ff.
- Act on Electronic Register and Judicial Costs for Telecommunications (*Gesetz über elektronische Register und Justizkosten für Telekommunikation*), BGBl. 2001/I/3422 ff.
- Act for Amendment of Regulations regarding the Valuation of Capital Investments of Insurance Companies and Repeal of the Bank Rate Transition Act – Insurance Capital Investments-Valuation Act (*Gesetz zur Änderung von Vorschriften über die Bewertung der Kapitalanlagen von Versicherungsunternehmen und zur Aufhebung des Diskontsatz-Überleitungs-Gesetzes – Versicherungskapitalanlagen-Bewertungsgesetz – VersKapAG*), BGBl. 2002/I/1219 ff.)
- Act for Further Development of the Federal Republic of Germany as a Financial Center – Fourth Capital Market Subsidy Act (*Gesetz zur weiteren Fortentwicklung des Finanzplatzes Deutschland – Viertes Finanzmarktförderungsgesetz*), BGBl. 2002/I/2010 ff.)
- Second Act on Amendment of Legal Regulations on Damages (*Zweites Gesetz zur Änderung schadensersatzrechtlicher Vorschriften*), BGBl. 2002/I/2674 ff.
- Act for Further Reform of Stock Corporation and Accounting Law, for Transparency and Company Disclosure – Transparency and Company Disclosure Act (*Gesetz zur weiteren Reform des Aktien- und Bilanzrechts, zu Transparenz und Publizität – Transparenz- und Publizitätsgesetz*), BGBl. 2002/I/2681 ff.
- Third Act for Amendment of the Trade, Commerce and Industry Regulation Act and other Trade regulations (*Drittes Gesetz zur Änderung der Gewerbeordnung und sonstiger gewerberechtlicher Vorschriften*), BGBl. 2002/I/3412 ff.

1. Scope of Applicability of the Commercial Law

§ 1 of the new Commercial Code starts with the definition of a merchant: Anyone who conducts a commercial enterprise is a merchant.

The radical expansion of what qualifies as a commercial enterprise, thus, constitutes a major amendment to the law and broadens the scope of its applicability considerably.

a) Under the old system (§ 1 Subsection 2), a commercial enterprise (and thereby a merchant *per se*) was only an undertaking active in one of a certain number of commercial activities listed in the law itself and corresponding largely to what a legislator some hundred years ago considered to be the main commercial activities, like e. g. trading in wares and securities, insurance business, banking, transportation, publishing and printing. Accordingly, many service industries which in the meantime had become

increasingly important (cinemas, theatres, schools, hotels, advertising, etc.) did not fall under this list, the same as e. g. the entire construction business.

Anyone who operated a business contained in the list was automatically a merchant, regardless of whether or not he had his enterprise registered in the commercial register. Anyone falling under the list was supposed to apply for registration in the commercial register, provided the type and volume of his enterprise required a commercially organized business operation. Accordingly, the registration would only be declaratory.

By contrast, anyone not falling within the business categories mentioned in § 1 Subsection 2 of the Commercial Code, but whose business required a commercially organized business operation, was supposed to apply for registration in the commercial register. This registration did have a constitutive effect, i. e. only upon registration would the business in question become that of a merchant (so-called *"Sollkaufleute"*).

It follows from this how the Commercial Code is made applicable and how it is determined to whom the law applies: It applies to all merchants and, therefore, the question of who is a merchant is of utmost importance.

b) The revised Commercial Code has a very different approach; the list contained in § 1 Subsection 2 has been completely eliminated. Now anyone conducting a business is a merchant regardless of his field of commercial activity, be it production, trade or services (it should be noted that, in German, the word for Commercial Code is *"Handelsgesetzbuch"*, *"Gesetzbuch"* meaning code and *"Handel"* meaning trading as opposed to production or services. Obviously, were it not for an old tradition, the code in German should now be named *"Unternehmensgesetzbuch"* (Enterprise Code) or the like).

There are, however, two exceptions to the applicability of the Commercial Code.

One is the professions, like lawyers, notaries, doctors, etc. The German notion is that exercising a profession is not commercial (*"gewerblich"*). This has a very practical advantage, namely, that no trade tax is levied. German law firms are, therefore, mostly civil law associations.

The other exception is taken over from the old system. Where a business is so small that no commercially organized business operation is required, the person or persons conducting the business are not merchants. In this case, however, the persons can apply for registration in the commercial register, and upon registration a single person becomes a registered merchant or two or more persons become a partnership (by constitutive act, §§ 2 and 105 Commercial Code).

Accordingly, the system in a nutshell operates as follows: Anyone conducting a business is a merchant, be he registered or not. The revised Commercial Code applies to him. The merchant has a duty to register and can be compelled to file for registration by coercive fine (§ 14 Commercial Code).

Members of the professions do not carry on a commercial business, and, therefore, the Commercial Code does not apply to them.

The very small business is exempted from the application of the Commercial Code, but it can file for registration and thereby become a merchant (§ 2 Commercial Code).

Whether the exemption of the small-sized business does or does not apply may be difficult to determine in individual cases (the one-person service office is surely exempt, but is the carpenter with three helpers exempt?).

According to the wording of the law (§ 1 Subsection 2 Commercial Code), there is a presumption ("unless") that the exemption does not apply. Once the firm name has been entered in the commercial register, the small businessman may change his mind and file for deletion (§ 2 sentence 3 Commercial Code – "return ticket").

Agriculture and forestry are also exempted, but can likewise file for registration in the commercial register where a commercially organized business operation is required (§ 3 Subsection 2 Commercial Code). In this case, however, no return ticket is issued. The registration is permanent.

The question obviously remains why a small businessman, or members of a civil law association administering its own assets, would file for registration, only to become subject to a much more stringent and sometimes dangerous legal system (e. g. oral guarantees being valid and enforceable – § 350 Commercial Code, duty to immediately examine objects bought and object to defects – § 377 Commercial Code, silence deemed to be acceptance of an offer – § 362 Commercial Code).

The answer is that the application of the Commercial Code may also bring with it considerable advantages, such as the clearly defined and undisputable limitation of liability for the limited partner of a limited partnership (§§ 161, 171 and 172 Commercial Code), which cannot be brought about in a civil law association or at least only with a lot of ado.

The question of applicability of the Commercial Code necessarily leads to the next question: Whether the Commercial Code supplants or is supplementary to the provisions of the Civil Code, or vice versa – both codes date back to January 1st, 1900.

The side-by-side relationship of the two codes is complicated. The Civil Code consists of five books:

I. General
II. 1. Contracts General
II. 2. Contracts Special (giving a set of rules for a number of contracts (but there is freedom to conclude other contracts and stipulate other rules with a very strong consumer protection in the meantime))
III. *In rem* Contracts
IV. Family Law
V. Succession Law

Introduction

It should be noted that the German Parliament promulgated an Act on October 11 2001 (*Schuldrechtmodernisierungsgesetz*, BGBl. 2001/I/3138) by which many institutions which had not been touched by the legislation for over 100 years were significantly amended. The changes apply especially to purchase/sale contracts and to prescription. This Act also brought about changes in the Commercial Code itself. In applying the Commercial Code, one has to be awave, accordingly, that complementary provisions of the Civil Code may also have changed.

Most rules of books I, II, III, IV and V Civil Code will also apply for merchants. There is not too much potential for conflict between books IV and V Civil Code and the Commercial Code; however, both codes must be carefully checked in drafting contracts. What happens upon the death of a partner of a partnership? What does the Civil Code say and what does the Commercial Code say? What happens upon the divorce of an entrepreneur? Has nothing been agreed upon between the spouses such that the entrepreneur will have to pay half of the appreciation of his assets during the marriage to his estranged wife?

The rules of books I and II. 1. Civil Code will mostly apply also to merchants. As for book II. 2. Civil Code (Special Contracts), many contracts are not dealt with in the Commercial Code, and the rules of the Civil Code will apply (e. g. lease). In other cases (e. g. sale and purchase, guarantee), both codes have rules, and here the special rules of the Commercial Code will supplant or supplement – as the case may be – (compare chapter 15 below) the rules of the Civil Code. In other cases still only the Commercial Code contains rules (e. g. freight carrier, forwarding agent). The rules of the Civil Code about the civil law association (§§ 705 et seq.) supplement the rules in the Commercial Code about the general and the limited partnership.

2. The Firm Name

The German word *"Firma"* has a double meaning in German. In legal language it only stands for the firm name, but in colloquial German it is used, as in English, to mean the enterprise as such.

In the context of the Commercial Code, it is obviously only used as a firm name. This topic has also been radically changed – and improved (!) – by the amendments to the law brought about in 1998.

Under the old system, a set of complicated rules had to be adhered to, depending on whether the merchant was a corporation, a partnership or a sole proprietor. A sole proprietor had to use his surname and at least one forename (§ 18 of the old version of the Commercial Code) as his firm name. The firm name of a partnership had to consist of the surname of at least one general partner. The firm name of a corporation was supposed to derive from its activity (*"Sachfirma"*, § 4 of the old Stock Corporation Act).

All this has been abolished.

The firm name according to the revised Commercial Code only has to meet three criteria, namely:
- designation, distinction and identification (§ 18 Subsection 1);
- interdiction to confuse the public (§ 18 Subsection 2); and
- designation of the legal form, including the fact that, if this is the case, the general partner is not a physical person, but rather a legal entity with the limited liability which follows from this (§ 18 Subsection 3).

Within these parameters the merchant is, irrespective of legal form, free to choose the firm name. He can, provided the three criteria are met, choose his own name, a fancy word or a name derived from the activity of the enterprise.

Adhering to the three parameters mentioned above means that no firm name may be chosen which could be confused with a firm name already in use at the same place and that no firm name may be chosen which would confuse the public about the activity of the firm or its type and volume, e. g. "German" or "National" for a small firm with only regional and restricted activity.

The legal form must always be part of the firm name. For a sole proprietor, "registered merchant" or an appropriate abbreviation should be chosen. For a general or limited partnership, the proper designation must be used and – as mentioned above – if there is no physical person as general partner, an appropriate designation pointing out this fact. The most popular form is a limited partnership with a limited liability company (*Gesellschaft mit beschränkter Haftung*, GmbH) as a general partner; the common abbreviation is "... GmbH & Co. KG", but the designation "beschränkt haftende KG" (limited partnership with limited liability) would also suffice.

Corporations must always have the pertinent form of organization as part of their firm name. Accordingly, the stock corporation must add "... *Aktiengesellschaft*" or "... AG" or "... AktGes." (§ 4 Stock Corporation Act), and the limited liability company must add "... Gesellschaft mit beschränkter Haftung", "... GmbH" or the like (§ 4 Limited Liability Companies Act).

The gist of the amendment is that the merchant after the reform has a far wider range of possibilities to choose from for his firm name than before.

The firm name is the name under which the merchant transacts business and executes agreements. A merchant may sue and be sued under his firm name (§ 17 Commercial Code).

3. The Commercial Register

The commercial register contains specific information which is of great legal significance for commercial transactions. It is maintained by the District Court in the area in which the firm to be registered has its head office (§ 8 Commercial Code, § 125 FGG[1]). It has been discussed at length

---
[1] Law concerning Administrative Acts of the Judiciary.

Introduction

whether this competence should be transferred to the chambers of commerce, but – at least for the time being – this idea has been abandoned. The commercial register is open to public inspection (§ 9 Commercial Code). A very recent change of the law has, however, determined (by amending §§ 9 and 9a), that the information obtained may only be used for the information of the enquirer in question (and not for commercial purposes) (*Gesetz über elektronische Register und Justizkosten*, BGBl. 2001/I/3422). Pursuant to § 29 Commercial Code, every merchant must file for registration of his firm name and the location of his business with the court for the district in which the business is domiciled; the establishment of a branch of the business is also to be registered with the court (§ 13 Commercial Code). The granting of a Prokura (general commercial power of representation) is to be registered in the commercial register by the owner of the business (§ 53 Commercial Code).

In addition, the formation of a general commercial partnership or of a limited partnership is to be registered with the commercial register, as is the organization of a limited liability company (§§ 7 et seq. of the Limited Liability Companies Act) or a stock corporation (§ 36 of the Stock Corporation Act). The commercial register is divided into a so-called "Department A" for sole proprietorships and partnerships, and a "Department B" for corporations.

All filings for registration are to be submitted in officially certified form (§ 12 Commercial Code). The merchant no longer has to sign with the firm name (in case of a sole proprietorship or a partnership), but – according to the revised code – signs with his own name and adds the firm name.

Registration in the commercial register is generally competent evidence of an existing legal fact, but it normally does not have the effect of constituting or establishing rights. Thus, for example, the effectiveness of a Prokura is not dependent upon its registration in the commercial register.

In certain cases, however, the registration does have the effect of constituting or establishing rights, for example, registration pursuant to §§ 2 and 3 Commercial Code (very small businesses and agriculture and forestry), registration of a stock corporation or a limited liability company. In these cases, the entities named come into existence only upon registration with the commercial register.

A third party may rely in good faith on the contents of the commercial register and may, thus, assume that items which have not been registered do not exist. Moreover, the merchant who permits an incorrect registration in the commercial register must allow third parties acting in good faith to deal with him as if the registration were correct (cf. § 15 Subsections 1 and 3 Commercial Code). The same applies to the merchant who negligently fails to correct an erroneous registration.

Where, on the other hand, a fact has been registered and published, the fact may be asserted against a third party (§ 15 Subsection 2 Commercial Code).

It should be noted that on all business letters of the merchant to a specific addressee, the firm name, the form of legal organization, the domicile of the enterprise, the competent commercial register and the number under which the merchant is registered must be disclosed.

Where a business is taken over by a third party, the business may be continued under the existing firm name if the name of the successor company indicates the successor relationship (§ 22 Commercial Code). Furthermore, each firm name must be clearly distinguished from all other firm names already being used in the same area (§ 30 Commercial Code).

Protection of the firm name from improper use by a third party is provided for in § 37 Commercial Code.

Pursuant to §§ 31 through 35 Commercial Code, specific alterations and statements which concern the firm name are to be registered in the commercial register.

A person acquiring a business is liable, if the firm name is continued, for the debts of the former owner, unless this is expressly excluded and such exclusion is published and registered in the commercial register (§ 25 Commercial Code). Similar rules apply where a commercial business is continued by the heirs of the owner (§ 27 Commercial Code). Moreover, if someone joins an existing sole proprietorship and a registerable partnership results, the new partner is liable pursuant to § 28 Commercial Code if the partnership has continued operation of the business of the sole proprietorship and liability has not been excluded by publication and registration in the commercial register.

4. Financial Records

The few provisions pertaining to financial record keeping formerly contained in §§ 38 et seq. of the Commercial Code have been replaced by a comprehensive body of rules (§§ 238 et seq.). For this purpose, a special part (or in this case the third book) was inserted in the Commercial Code. This made it necessary to transfer the provisions pertaining to the silent partnership from §§ 335 et seq. to §§ 230 et seq. The former third and fourth books were renumbered as the fourth and fifth books.

The third book was made part of the Commercial Code by the Financial Statements Act (Bilanzrichtliniengesetz) of December 19, 1985. The Bilanzrichtliniengesetz transforms into German law the 4th, 7th and 8th EU Directives concerning this topic, and the full name of the Bilanzrichtliniengesetz is accordingly "Act to Implement the 4th, 7th and 8th Directives of the Council of the European Union for Co-ordination of Company Law."

The third book commences in §§ 238 et seq. Commercial Code by imposing certain duties on all merchants. They must, for example, keep accounts and establish certain reports and records at the end of the fiscal year.

The second chapter (§§ 264 et seq.) contains additional provisions for corporations (stock corporations, partnerships limited by shares and limited

liability companies). In this chapter, the provisions pertaining to consolidation of the financial statements of groups of companies are especially important.

The third chapter (§§ 336 et seq.) deals with co-operatives, and §§ 340 et seq. pertain to financial institutions.

A merchant who violates the duties imposed by this book is liable to be fined or subject to criminal prosecution.

II. Business Employees

1. Business Employees. Clerical Employees and Apprentices

A clerical employee is one who is employed in a business for the performance of services in return for compensation. The provisions of the Commercial Code with respect to clerical employees (§§ 59 et seq. Commercial Code) govern the relationship between the clerical employee and the principal arising from the employment contract. As a consequence of the extraordinarily broad definition of the term "clerical employee", these provisions are of great practical significance. Clerical employees may be bookkeepers, purchasing agents, dispatchers, management personnel, branch managers, typists or apprentices, as long as they are employed for the performance of commercial services (cf. § 83 Commercial Code).

In addition to the employment duties of the clerical employee and his right to compensation (§ 59 Commercial Code), the Commercial Code also regulates his duty of loyalty to the principal, his employer (§ 60 Commercial Code). Additional provisions concern the time at which salary is due (§ 64 Commercial Code), commission rights (§ 65 Commercial Code) and the right to an employment reference (§ 73 Commercial Code).

A basic provision with respect to the clerical employee is the prohibition on competition with the employer. § 60 Commercial Code provides that a clerical employee may not, without the principal's consent, conduct a separate commercial business or undertake transactions in the business field of the principal for his own account or that of another person. Where the clerical employee violates this duty, he is liable for damages (§ 61 Commercial Code).

Competition may also be prohibited for a period of up to two years subsequent to termination of the employment relationship between the employer and the clerical employee. This obligation, however, must be in writing and is binding only if the principal is obligated to pay compensation for the period of the restraint. Such compensation must equal, for each year of the restraint, at least one-half of the most recent annual contractual compensation received by the clerical employee (§ 74 Commercial Code). On the other hand, however, the clerical employee must allow deduction from such compensation of any income he earns (or maliciously fails to

earn) through other employment during the period for which compensation is to be paid (§ 74 c Commercial Code). The prohibition is only binding if it serves to protect a legitimate business interest of the principal (§ 74 a Commercial Code). For managing directors of a corporation clauses restricting competition after termination of employment may even be agred upon without compensation; provided, however, they last no longer than two years.

Where a clerical employee terminates his employment for an important reason ("*aus wichtigem Grund*"), the prohibition of competition becomes invalid if the clerical employee declares in writing within one month following the termination of employment that he does not consider himself bound by the agreement. The same invalidity results if the employer terminates the employment relationship, unless an important reason (having to do with the person or the conduct of the clerical employee) exists. In the first case, accordingly, the employee may elect between termination of the prohibition of competition (no compensation) and continuation thereof (with compensation); in the latter case, the employer has the analogous right.

The provisions of §§ 74 through 75 c Commercial Code cannot be altered to the disadvantage of the clerical employee. It should be kept in mind that the Commercial Code regulates only part of the relationship between the employer and the employee. A very important additional body of rules governing this relationship is found in German labour law, which is only partly codified and in which case law plays an important role. It is also important to determine whether the employee is a "commercial" or a "technical" employee (of § 83). In the latter case, in addition to labour law, the Trade Ordinance (Gewerbeordnung), and not the Commercial Code, would apply. Messengers or drivers in a sales organization would represent "borderline cases" in this regard.

2. The Employee's Power to Represent the Merchant

While the internal relationship between the employer and the employees is treated under the heading "Clerical Employees and Apprentices", the Section entitled "Prokura and Business Proxy" deals with the ability of the clerical employee to represent the principal in the external relationship of the employer with respect to third parties. It follows, therefore, that a Prokura holder, or a holder of a business proxy, is almost always at the same time a clerical employee.

In addition to the forms of agency which the Civil Code regulates in §§ 164 et seq., the Commercial Code recognises three specific kinds of agency powers. The commercial forms of agency are distinguishable from the forms of agency regulated in the Civil Code in that third parties may rely in good faith on the legally-defined scope of the agency power.

Introduction

a) Prokura

A Prokura holder is a legal agent of the company, partnership or merchant. The granting of the Prokura is registered in the commercial register (§ 53 Commercial Code); the registration is only of declaratory nature. The specimen signature of the Prokura holder (together with the firm name) must be filed with the court (§ 53 Subsection 2 Commercial Code) so that the genuineness of the signature can be examined by third parties at any time.

The scope of the power of attorney conferred with the Prokura is described in §§ 49 and 50 Commercial Code.

This power includes all judicial and non-judicial transactions relating to the operation of a commercial business. Only private affairs of the principal and transactions which do not serve the business operations, such as termination and sale of the entire business, are not within the scope of the Prokura.

The Prokura holder is only authorized to sell and encumber real estate in connection with the operation of a commercial business if this power has been specifically conferred, according to § 49 Subsection 2 Commercial Code. It is generally assumed, however, that the holder of the Prokura can mortgage real property in order to provide security for payment of the purchase price, even without this special authorization.

A limitation of the Prokura is invalid with respect to third parties. The Prokura can, however, be limited internally, i. e. between the Prokura holder and the principal. A third party cannot rely on the unlimited agency power if he knowingly acted to the disadvantage of the person represented or if the Prokura holder acted intentionally to the disadvantage of his principal and the third party knew or should have known this.

The Prokura can be conferred with either sole or joint power of representation. In the latter case, the Prokura holder can only represent the enterprise together with another Prokura holder or a managing director. In the vast majority of cases in Germany, Prokura is conferred only with joint power of representation.

The Prokura may also be restricted to a particular branch office of an enterprise, provided the firm name of the branch is different from the firm name generally. Large banks usually restrict the Prokura to the business of a branch. They are entitled to do so since for the bank branch, the name of the bank is always followed by the word "Branch" and the name of the location.

b) Business Proxy

Like the Prokura, the business proxy is a power of attorney, the scope and content of which have been codified (§§ 54 et seq. Commercial Code). The business proxy is narrower than the Prokura and does not cover unusual or uncommon transactions, endorsement or acceptance of bills of exchange, assumption of loans, conduct of litigation or the sale and mortgage of real property, unless the holder of the business proxy has been given specific authorization for these transactions.

Moreover, additional limitations are possible (§ 54 Subsection 3 Commercial Code), but these can only be validly asserted against a third party where it knew or should have known of them.

c) The Agency Power of Sales Clerks or Warehouse Employees

Here, agency power is not expressly conferred, but exists by operation of law (§ 56 Commercial Code). Anyone employed in a store or warehouse open to the public is deemed to be authorized to sell and receive (but not buy) merchandise customary for such store or warehouse. § 56 Commercial Code is an example of apparent authority on which a third party may rely in good faith. A borderline case to be found in every textbook (based on a decision of the Federal Supreme Court) is the customer who pays the sales clerk for merchandise despite clearly visible signs within the store indicating that payment should only be made to the cashiers.

3. Hybrid Relationships

A phenomenon much discussed recently is hybrid forms of principal–dependent relationships where the dependent person is deemed to be neither an employee nor an independent agent (*Scheinselbständige*). Previously, all the circumstances had to be considered to establish whether the working person was an employee or an independent agent. Now a presumption has been established in the Mandatory Social Insurance Law according to which a person is presumed to be a dependent employee (with the consequence that social security contributions are to be levied, half from the employer and half from the employee – § 7 Subsection 4 Sozialgesetzbuch IV) where:

– the person does not employ employees subject to the mandatory old age insurance system (other than members of the family);
– the person works as a rule only for one principal;
– the person is subject to instructions of the principal and is integrated into his organization; and
– the person does not act as an entrepreneur in the market.

The presumption does not apply to commercial agents where they can freely dispose of their time and are free to organize their own activities.

All this, for the time being, only applies to the rules of the mandatory social insurance system, but it may well be that labour courts will follow suit and also apply this to the labour relationship between employer and employee.

III. The Independent Business Agent

In addition to clerical employees, the Commercial Code recognises other types of independent agents of the merchant, such as the commercial agent (*Handelsvertreter* – § 84 Commercial Code) and the commercial broker

(*Handelsmakler* – §§ 93 et seq. Commercial Code). Unlike clerical employees, commercial agents and commercial brokers are not employees of the principal, but independent merchants. The function of the commercial broker is to solicit transactions in a commercial sense.

1. The Commercial Agent

A commercial agent is an individual who, as an independent person engaged in business, is permanently authorized to solicit or enter into business transactions for another merchant in such merchant's name.

A person is independent if he is essentially free to arrange his own activity and specify his hours of work (§ 84 Subsection 1 sentence 2 Commercial Code).

Generally, a commercial agent may work for several companies, provided this does not impair his ability to fulfil his duty to protect the interests of each merchant.

The statutory duties of the commercial agent, especially the duty to safeguard the interests and commercial secrets of the merchant, are found in §§ 86 and 90 Commercial Code. The commercial agent is further obligated to work actively on behalf of the merchant.

The principal duty of the merchant is to support the commercial agent and place at his disposal the materials necessary for the performance of his duties, such as samples, drawings, price lists, advertising materials and the terms and conditions of business (§ 86 a Commercial Code).

The commercial agent has a right to a commission for all transactions concluded during the contractual relationship which are attributable to his efforts or are concluded with third parties whom he acquired as customers in transactions of the same kind (§ 87 Commercial Code). The amount of commission is normally expressly agreed by the parties; otherwise, the customary rate is deemed agreed (§ 87 b Commercial Code). The due date of and accounting for commissions is determined by §§ 87 a and 87 c Commercial Code. Pursuant to § 92 a Commercial Code, the Federal Ministries of Justice, Economics and Labour may issue regulations mandating certain minimum working conditions for specific commercial agents.

Where the commercial agent is assigned to a specific district or a particular group of customers, he also has the right to a commission for transactions concluded without his assistance with persons in his district or among his group of customers during the term of his contractual relationship (§ 87 Subsection 2 Commercial Code). This is based on the idea that these transactions are usually connected in some way with the activity of the agent.

The commercial agent is only liable to fulfil the contractual obligations of the customers procured (upon their default) where this is expressly agreed. This *"del credere"* liability (§ 86 b Commercial Code) is in reality much like a guaranty. With respect to a merchant who resides in Germany, *del credere* liability will be valid for a specific transaction only when it is in writing and specific additional compensation *(del credere* commission) is agreed to.

These prerequisites for validity do not apply if the merchant or his customer has his business establishment abroad (§ 86 b Subsection 3 Commercial Code).

§ 89 Commercial Code contains provisions regarding termination of the contractual relationship with the commercial agent. The relationship with the commercial agent may be terminated at any time for an important reason without observance of a notice period (§ 89 a Commercial Code).

Insofar as it is intended that the commercial agent be limited in his activity following the expiration of the contractual relationship, the agreement must be in writing. The maximum duration of such a prohibition of competition is two years. The merchant must pay the commercial agent reasonable compensation for the term of the prohibition (§ 90 a Subsection 1 Commercial Code). If the relationship is terminated for an important reason, either by the merchant or by the agent, the special rules of § 90 a Subsections 2 and 3 Commercial Code apply.

Pursuant to § 89 b Commercial Code, the commercial agent may demand reasonable compensation from the merchant after expiration of the commercial agency agreement if the merchant obtains substantial advantages, following the expiration of the commercial agency agreement, from the prior activity of the commercial agent and if the commercial agent, by reason of the expiration of the contractual relationship, loses rights to commission. The amount of such compensation must be appropriate in light of all the circumstances.

The maximum claim is one year's commission based on the average of the last five years, or on the average of a shorter period if the relationship did not last five years. Any claim of the agent for such compensation must be brought within one year after termination.

§ 89 b Commercial Code is arguably the most important provision in the Code relating to the commercial agent, and certainly one that frequently leads to disputes.

The provisions designed to protect the agent are mandatory, and any agreement to the contrary is invalid unless § 92 c Commercial Code applies.

2. The Commercial Broker

A commercial broker (*Handelsmakler*) is one who commercially undertakes the solicitation of agreements with respect to commercial matters for other persons in exchange for a commission, without being authorized to do so on a regular basis by contractual relationship (§ 93 Commercial Code). Like the commercial agent, the commercial broker must also be independent. The commercial broker's activity distinguishes itself from that of the commercial agent in that the commercial broker is not active for a merchant on a regular, but only on a case-to-case, basis.

Further, an essential characteristic of the commercial broker's activity is that he is continuously active. Where his work is only occasional, the Civil Code provisions with respect to brokers apply (§§ 652 et seq. Civil Code).

In contrast to the commercial agent, the commercial broker may be the agent of both parties to a transaction if the relationship with the customer permits this. Accordingly, in the absence of agreement or custom, one-half of his commission is to be paid by each party (§ 99 Commercial Code). Further, the commercial broker is also liable to both parties for damages arising by reason of his fault (§ 98 Commercial Code).

Immediately following the conclusion of a transaction, the commercial broker must supply each of the parties with a memorandum of sale which contains the essential terms of the transaction and is signed by him (§§ 94 et seq. Commercial Code). The agreement between the parties, however, does not arise by reason of this memorandum of sale, which merely indicates that the broker drew up the agreement in such a manner. However, where the memorandum of sale is accepted by both parties without protest, it is deemed to be equivalent to a commercial confirmation memorandum, i. e. the agreement comes into being just as it is set forth in the memorandum of sale (cf. the discussion of commercial confirmations in Section V.I.b below).

Additional provisions regulate the broker's duty to store samples (§ 96 Commercial Code), the prohibition with regard to the commercial broker's accepting payments or any other contractual stipulated consideration (§ 97 Commercial Code) and the duty of maintaining a transaction book (§ 100 Commercial Code).

IV. The Commercial Partnership under the Commercial Code

Commercial Code §§ 105 et seq. on the general commercial partnership (*offene Handelsgesellschaft*) and §§ 161 et seq. on limited partnerships (*Kommanditgesellschaft*) contain essential provisions governing commercial partnerships. There are, however, only a very few rules, and much is left to the discretion of the parties.

1. The General Commercial Partnership

a) Definition and Legal Nature

Pursuant to § 105 Subsection 1 Commercial Code the general commercial partnership (*offene Handelsgesellschaft* – OHG) is a partnership for the purpose of operating a commercial business under a firm name where all of the partners have unlimited liability with regard to the partnership's creditors.

As indicated by the reference in § 105 Subsection 2 Commercial Code to the Civil Code's provision on partnership (§§ 705 et seq. Civil Code), the general commercial partnership is a subcategory of the BGB partnership, or civil law association. The latter is described as an agreement between persons to contribute to a common purpose to be pursued jointly by the partners, without the association constituting a legal entity (both the BGB partnership and the general commercial partnership would be classified as a "general partnership" under American law).

In contrast to the incorporated entities such as the stock corporation (*Aktiengesellschaft* – AG) or the limited liability company (*Gesellschaft mit beschränkter Haftung* – GmbH), the general commercial partnership is not a legal entity. It is, however, similar to a legal entity (which, in turn, distinguishes it from the civil law partnership).

This results particularly from the provisions of § 124 Commercial Code whereby the general commercial partnership may, under its firm name, acquire rights and enter into obligations, acquire ownership and other rights *in rem* in real property and sue and be sued in court.

The status of the general commercial partnership as a partnership (as contrasted with an incorporated entity) has vital significance for tax law. The general commercial partnership is not subject to corporate tax; rather, the individual partners must pay personal income tax on their portion of the commercial partnership's profits. The general commercial partnership is, however, subject to trade tax, a tax levied by the municipalities and varying widely from one locality to the other.

b) Formation of the General Commercial Partnership

There are three stages to the formation of a general commercial partnership: the conclusion of the partnership agreement, registration of the partnership and the commencement of business by the partners.

In the internal relationship between the partners, the conclusion of the partnership agreement is conclusive for the formation of the partnership. The rights and duties of the partners among themselves result from this agreement.

Externally, i. e. with respect to third parties, the formation of a general commercial partnership requires registration in the commercial register (§§ 106, 123 Commercial Code). All of the partners are legally obligated to file for registration (§ 108 Commercial Code).

§ 123 Subsection 2 Commercial Code provides that the partnership is established upon the commencement of business if the partnership commences business before registration. However, this applies only if the business activity constitutes the operation of a commercial business within the meaning of § 1 Subsection 1 Commercial Code. If § 1 Subsection 2 Commercial Code (very small business) applies, or if merely its own assets are administered, the partnership is subject to the Civil Code provisions and becomes a merchant only upon registration in the commercial register (§ 105 Subsection 2 Commercial Code).

Where the partnership agreement is void or voidable, this has no effect on the legal relationship with third parties if the partnership has been registered or has conducted commercial transactions. Following execution of the partnership agreement, the commercial partnership is deemed to be in existence with respect to the partners' relations to one another in spite of defects in conclusion of the agreement; the agreement may only be dissolved by judicial decree pursuant to § 133 Commercial Code.

c) Legal Relationship of the Partners to One Another

The partners of a general commercial partnership can be natural persons, legal entities or partnerships without legal personality, insofar as they appear as an independent unit in legal dealings and can assume liability independently. Thus, a general commercial partnership may itself be a partner in another general commercial partnership.

The legal relationship of the partners to one another is determined by the partnership agreement (§ 109 Commercial Code). Absent contrary provisions in the partnership agreement, the relationship of the partners to one another is regulated by §§ 110 through 122 Commercial Code.

The Commercial Code provides that each individual partner is authorized to manage the business (§ 114 Subsection 1 Commercial Code). Where the partnership agreement grants only one or several partners the right to manage the business, the remaining partners are automatically excluded from the management.

Where all or several partners are authorized to manage the business, each one is authorized to manage the business alone. However, in this case, all of the other partners authorized to manage the business have a veto right (§ 115 Commercial Code). § 117 Commercial Code regulates the right of the other partners to apply to a court in order to have the authority to manage the business withdrawn from one of the partners for an important reason. An important reason, in the sense of § 117 Commercial Code, is an especially gross violation of duties and/or incompetence to maintain proper management.

In general, the authority to manage the business extends to all acts relating to the normal operation of the partnership's commercial undertaking (§ 116 Subsection 1 Commercial Code). For activities beyond this scope, a resolution by all of the partners is required. For the appointment of a Prokura holder, the consent of all of the partners authorized to manage the business is necessary, pursuant to § 116 Subsection 3 Commercial Code.

Additional provisions apply to the internal relationship of the partners to one another where the partnership agreement does not otherwise provide, e. g., the right to reimbursement of expenses and losses – § 110 Commercial Code, the passage of resolutions at the partnership meeting – § 119 Commercial Code, the computation and distribution of profits and losses – §§ 120 and 121 Commercial Code and the right of each partner to withdraw limited amounts from the partnership's account – § 122 Commercial Code.

d) The Legal Relationship of the Partners to Third Parties

Each partner is authorized to represent the partnership in all matters concerning which he has not been expressly excluded from such representation (§ 125 Commercial Code). The Code also contains special provisions for joint representation (§ 125 Subsections 2 through 4 Commercial Code).

The scope of authority extends to all judicial and non-judicial proceedings and transactions, including transfer and encumbrance of real property and

conferral or revocation of a Prokura. In this connection, § 126 Subsection 2 Commercial Code is of prime importance, providing that limitation of the scope of authority is invalid vis-à-vis third parties. As noted above, the authority of a partner may be withdrawn by judicial determination upon application by the remaining partners pursuant to § 127 Commercial Code.

An essential characteristic of the general commercial partnership is the unlimited personal liability of the partners for partnership obligations to third parties (§ 128 Commercial Code). In order to ensure that this liability is not undermined, § 129 Commercial Code provides that a partner may raise a defense against a third-party claim only to the extent that he has a personal defense or the defense could be asserted by the partnership itself.

A person who enters an existing general commercial partnership as a partner is liable in the same manner as the prior partners for the obligations of the partnership arising before his entry. This provision is mandatory and may not be restricted contractually (§ 130 Commercial Code).

For similar reasons of creditor protection, § 130 a Commercial Code regulates the duty of the general managers of a general commercial partnership (or the liquidators, where none of the general partners is a physical person) to initiate insolvency proceedings upon the partnership's overindebtedness or inability to meet its obligations.

e) Dissolution of Partnership and Withdrawal of the Partners

The events or conditions leading to a dissolution of a general commercial partnership are enumerated in § 131 Commercial Code. The statutory reform of 1998 has radically changed this provision. Under the old system, death and bankruptcy of a partner would lead to the dissolution of the partnership, unless the partnership agreement provided differently. This was almost always the case, such that, in practice, rule and exception were reversed. The idea of the unrevised code to safeguard the continuity of the persons forming the partnership has been replaced by the idea to safeguard the partnership as such.

According to § 131 Subsection 3 in the revised form, death, insolvency proceedings and termination by a partner himself or by his personal creditors will only lead to the partner withdrawing from the partnership, but the partnership, as such, will not be affected. In case of the death of a partner, this only applies to general partners. In case of the death of a limited partner, the partnership is continued with his heirs (§ 177 Commercial Code). Both cases are subject to any different rules contained in the partnership agreement.

The partnership is dissolved by the events listed in § 131 Subsections 1 and 2 Commercial Code.

One may doubt the wisdom of § 131 Subsection 3, number 1 Commercial Code, to have the general partner withdraw from the company upon his death and have his heirs, accordingly, inherit a claim for the full value of his participation against the partnership. It would have been better to have

the partnership continue with the heirs of the deceased as limited partners. In any case, this question must be dealt with in drafting the partnership agreement. The claim of the heirs should be structured such that the financial stability of the partnership is not jeopardised, unless one would prefer a solution along the lines of § 177 Commercial Code.

f) Liquidation of the General Commercial Partnership

Unless the partners have agreed otherwise, or insolvency proceedings have been commenced with respect to the assets of the partnership (§ 145 Commercial Code), liquidation and distribution of the partnership assets to the individual partners occurs following dissolution.

The identity of the partnership is not affected by liquidation. The general commercial partnership merely alters its purpose, i. e. the partnership which was established for the operation of a commercial business becomes a liquidating company.

Liquidation is effected by the liquidators. The partners are the liquidators, unless the partnership agreement provides otherwise (§ 146 Commercial Code). Beginning with the commencement of liquidation, the general commercial partnership is no longer represented by the general managers, but by the liquidators. Limitation of the liquidators' authority is invalid with respect to third parties (§ 151 Commercial Code).

The liquidators' duties are to wind up the on-going business, collect claims, convert assets to cash and pay off the creditors (§ 149 Commercial Code). The partnership assets remaining after satisfaction of liabilities are then distributed to the partners according to their respective shares in the capital of the partnership (§ 155 Commercial Code). The liquidators must also prepare a balance sheet at the beginning and at the conclusion of liquidation proceedings (§ 154 Commercial Code).

All of the partners are to file for registration of the liquidators in the commercial register (§ 148 Commercial Code). From this point on the general commercial partnership is to be identified as a firm "in liquidation" ("i. L.") (§ 153 Commercial Code). Further, following the conclusion of liquidation, the entry concerning the firm name in the commercial register must be deleted. The books and records of the partnership are given into the charge of one of the partners or a third party (§ 157 Commercial Code). It goes without saying that liquidation without insolvency is, in practice, a rare incident.

2. The Limited Partnership

The limited partnership (*Kommanditgesellschaft* – KG) is distinct from the general commercial partnership in that not all of the partners have unlimited liability for partnership obligations. The liability of the limited partners with respect to partnership creditors is limited to the amount of their respective specific capital contributions (limited partnership contributions) (§ 161 Subsection 1 Commercial Code).

The general commercial partnership provisions of the Commercial Code are generally applicable to the limited partnership (§§ 161 Subsection 2, 163 Commercial Code). §§ 164 through 177 a Commercial Code have priority, however, in the event of conflict.

A limited partner is supposed to maintain a purely financial participation in the business. A limited partner is, thus, excluded from management (§ 164 Commercial Code), is not subject to a prohibition of competition (§ 165 Commercial Code) and is not authorized to represent the partnership (§ 170 Commercial Code); further, his death does not automatically result in dissolution of the partnership (§ 177 Commercial Code).

Since a limited partner is liable to partnership creditors only up to the amount of his contribution payable, the partnership's filing with the Commercial Register must specify the amount of the limited partner's capital contribution (§ 162 Subsection 1 Commercial Code). Where the limited partnership commences business before registration, limited partners are personally liable for liabilities of the partnership incurred before registration (§ 176 Commercial Code). If the capital contribution of a limited partner is paid back, e. g. by distribution of profits in a loss situation, the personal liability of the limited partner is reinstated up to the amount of the repayment of the capital contribution.

Pursuant to §§ 174 and 175 Commercial Code, any reduction of a limited partner's capital contribution must be registered in the Commercial Register in order to be legally effective.

A person who enters an existing commercial partnership as a limited partner is liable for obligations of the partnership which arose before his entry only up to the amount of his capital contribution (§ 173 Commercial Code), provided that his name is entered in the Commercial Register along with the amount of his capital contribution. The same applies if a share in a commercial partnership is transferred. The transferee must ensure that his name is entered immediately or, in order to avoid a risk of liability, the effectiveness of the transfer should be expressly conditioned upon registration in the Commercial Register.

Like general partners not authorized to manage the business, limited partners have the right to inspect the affairs of the partnership (§ 166 Commercial Code). The difference, however, is that the right of the general partner excluded from management is much more comprehensive (§ 118 Commercial Code), an arrangement which is plausible since the general partner is at risk with his entire assets.

Like general partners, limited partners have a share in the total net worth of the limited partnership. The share of profits and losses is computed pursuant to §§ 167 through 169 Commercial Code.

As in the general commercial partnership, the partners in a limited partnership need not be natural persons. Legal entities may participate in a limited partnership, both as general partners and as limited partners. Thus, the general partner of many limited partnerships is a corporation, such as a GmbH.

Introduction

This kind of limited partnership is identified as a "GmbH & Co." The management and representation of this entity is normally conducted by the body authorized to represent the corporation, i. e. the managing director of the GmbH, who does not necessarily need to be a partner in the limited partnership.

The GmbH & Co. KG, i. e. a partnership with a corporation (nearly always a GmbH) as a general partner, is a popular form of legal organization. It is very flexible inasmuch as the statutes concerning the limited partnership and the limited liability company are flexible. It combines the tax advantages of a partnership with the limited liability of a corporation.

The GmbH & Co. KG also has advantages from the point of view of labour participation in management, since – unlike a GmbH, where a supervisory board with labour participation must be established if the number of employees exceeds 500 – no supervisory board with labour participation is necessary unless the number of employees exceeds 2000. When labour participation becomes necessary, § 4 of the Co-determination Act (*Mitbestimmungsgesetz*) applies, and a supervisory board of 12 (or 16 or 20), with an equal number of shareholders' and labour representatives, must be established.

The GmbH & Co. KG is – liability-wise – very close to a GmbH, and certain rules which protect the creditors of a GmbH must, accordingly, also apply to a GmbH & Co. KG. Shareholders' loans are, in many instances, deemed to be capital (§ 172 a Commercial Code), and in case of insolvency or overindebtedness, the managing directors of the GmbH, as the general partner, must initiate insolvency proceedings without undue delay (§§ 177 a and 130 a Commercial Code).

3. The Silent Partnership

The silent partnership (*stille Gesellschaft*) is a partnership in which one partner: (a) participates in the commercial enterprise of another by paying in a capital contribution to the assets of the business owner and (b) shares in the profits arising from the operation of the business (cf. § 230 Commercial Code).

Unlike the OHG or the KG, the silent partner's capital contribution does not result in partnership business assets; rather, such contribution becomes the property of the active participant.

Although the silent partner normally participates in the losses of the partnership as well as in its profits, liability for losses can be excluded (§ 231 Subsection 2 Commercial Code).

Management is conducted exclusively by the active participant. The silent partner merely has the right, pursuant to § 233 Commercial Code, to request a copy of the annual financial statements and examine their accuracy by inspecting the books and records.

With respect to third parties, the active participant is the sole owner of the commercial enterprise. He carries on the business in his own name and is alone authorized to conclude transactions within the operation of the business.

Additional provisions concern termination of the partnership by a partner (§ 234 Commercial Code), apportionment of the partnership assets (§ 235 Commercial Code) and insolvency of the active participant (§ 236 Commercial Code).

The most important advantage of silent partner status is the absence of personal liability. This advantage, however, must be viewed in light of the less advantageous provisions of § 235 Commercial Code, whereby the silent partner, in the event of dissolution, is merely entitled to a claim for the repayment of the credit balance of his capital account (in other words, he does not participate in any increase in hidden reserves).

Some partnership agreements seek to avoid this disadvantage such that the silent partner receives a contractual claim against the active partner, including a right to hidden reserves upon dissolution of the partnership. Distribution of the assets would then be handled as if the assets of the business belonged to both partners jointly. The silent partner would then participate in any increase in the value of the partnership's assets not reflected on the books (*atypische stille Gesellschaft*).

V. Accounting, Financial Statements and Audit of the Company and Amendments by the Transparency and Company Disclosure Act

§§ 238–342 a of the German Commercial Code deal with accounting and the financial statements of merchants and companies as well as affiliated groups and finally the audit of these financial statements. Up to now these regulations have not been included in the Introduction since they are relatively explicit and moreover financial statements under the Commercial Code for large enterprises have been superseded more and more by consolidated financial statements under IAS or US GAAP (§ 292 a Commercial Code).

The Transparency and Company Disclosure Act of July 19, 2002 (BGBl. 2002/I/2681 ff.), which was amended in particular by §§ 285, 286, 291, 297, 299 and 321 Commercial Code, has a special influence on the accounting, the financial statements and the audit. This Act and the Fourth Capital Market Subsidy Act of June 26, 2002 (BGBl. 2002/I/2009 ff.) are the reactions of the legislators, *inter alia*, to the grievances that occurred on the *Neue Markt* and that cheated the numerous investors out of their savings as well as company failures (Holzmann, Babcock), exorbitant management compensation packages concurrent with plunging stock prices (Deutsche Bank, Telekom) and fraudulent false bookings that were not detected by any auditor (Flowtech).

The reforms which both Acts contain find their expression for the most part outside the Commercial Code and at most peripheral parts of legal amendments find their way into our Code.

A good example of this is the introduction of a corporate governance code in German jurisprudence. A committee of thirteen corporate practitioners,

Introduction

scholars and trade unionists were appointed by the Federal Minister of Justice to a Corporate Governance Commission and developed a German Corporate Governance Code ("the Code") in a few months at the turn of the year 2001/2002 which in turn could be based on the preliminary work of other commissions. The "recommendations" of this Code do not have to be followed; however, if they are not followed, then this must be explained ("comply or explain"). The Code contains, in addition to the recommendations, repetitions of the Act – which has to be complied with in any event – and "suggestions" with respect to which there is neither a duty to comply nor a duty to explain.

The obligation for the managing board (*Vorstand*) and supervisory board (*Aufsichtsrat*) of quoted companies to make an appropriate statement is contained in new § 161 of the Stock Corporation Act (*Aktiengesetz*). This procedure is reflected in the Commercial Code only to the extent that it now has to be stated in the notes (new § 285 No. 16 Commercial Code) that the statement under § 161 Stock Corporation Act has been made and has been made available to the shareholders. The parent company has to make the statement in the notes to the consolidated financial statements, also for its quoted subsidiaries (new § 314 Subsection 1 No. 8 Commercial Code). The statement must also be filed with the Commercial Register (supplemented § 325 Subsection 1 sentence 1). Finally, the auditor of the annual financial statements also has to audit and report whether the statement has been made.

The Transparency and Company Disclosure Act further cautiously reforms the law relating to consolidated financial statements, whereby it should, however, be pointed out that in the meantime a directive has been issued at the EU level which provides that in the future for fiscal years beginning after January 1, 2005 consolidated financial statements may only be prepared under IAS so that the provisions of the Commercial Code regarding accounting standards for affiliated groups will become obsolete in a relatively short period of time.

According to § 285 No. 9a from now on all "stock based compensation" of members of the managing board or managing directors has to be specified in the notes. Only the situation at the time of the grant of the right is to serve as the basis for the report. Further developments or a non-exercise, etc. do not have to be reported. This amendment will not accomplish much. What is missing are legal regulations which bring about a parallelism of interests of agent and principal regarding the development of the stock price.

Of significance is further the revision of § 321 Subsection 2 which deals with the contents of the audit report. In Germany – just like in America – the auditors were blamed many times not to have detected the balance sheet scandals or even to have turned two blind eyes to the cover-up of false bookings. § 321 Subsection 2 is supposed to lead to more exact, problem oriented audit and reporting. However, one can question whether the writing on the wall of Arthur Anderson will not exert a much greater pressure on the auditors than the – not particularly clear – implementation of § 321 Subsection 2.

VI. Commercial Transactions

The fourth book of the Commercial Code contains special provisions which apply to transactions with and between merchants.

1. Special Provisions for Commercial Transactions in General

§§ 343 through 372 of the Commercial Code set forth provisions which apply to all commercial transactions. Commercial transactions are all transactions relating to the operation of a merchant's business (§ 343 Subsection 1 Commercial Code).

A commercial transaction is "unilateral" or "bilateral," depending on whether one or both of the parties thereto are merchants. The commercial transaction provisions generally apply to both parties, even if the transaction is unilateral (§ 345 Commercial Code).

An essential prerequisite for a commercial transaction within the meaning of § 343 Subsection 1 Commercial Code is that the transaction relates to the operation of a merchant's business. Normally, however, a presumption exists, pursuant to § 344 Subsection 1 Commercial Code, that all transactions undertaken by a merchant are "commercial transactions."

Specific provisions deviating from the terms of the Civil Code apply only to merchants (e. g. § 349 Commercial Code with respect to the prohibition of the defense of the guarantor that the creditor must first try unsuccessfully to execute his claim directly against the debtor, § 350 Commercial Code with respect to the form requirements of the Civil Code as to guaranties [§ 766 Civil Code], admission of liability by the debtor [§ 780 Civil Code] and acknowledgement of debt [§ 781 Civil Code]). According to the Civil Code, these latter declarations must be in writing in order to be valid; under the Commercial Code, no form is required if they are commercial transactions on the part of the obligor or guarantor.

A number of general provisions are of importance for all commercial transactions, e. g. § 347 Commercial Code, concerning the merchant's duty of care, creates a heightened standard of liability compared with the provisions of § 276 Civil Code. §§ 352 and 355 Commercial Code allow the charging of a five percent (5 %) rate of interest on obligations, which is higher than the four percent (4 %) rate allowed by the Civil Code. Notwithstanding this 5 % standard rate, a higher rate may be charged if the party asserting the claim can prove that it itself had to pay higher interest charges to finance the claim asserted.

§ 354 Commercial Code allows the merchant to assert claims with respect to commission, storage charges and interest thereon even without express agreement. §§ 358 and 359 Commercial Code specify the time for performance. § 360 Commercial Code defines the obligation to deliver merchandise specified only by generic characteristics.

§§ 363 through 365 Commercial Code describe the negotiation of commercial negotiable instruments.

Introduction

§§ 366 and 367 Commercial Code broaden the possibilities for good faith acquisition of chattel in commercial business dealings by the merchant. Normally, good faith must pertain to the title to property (§§ 932 et seq. Civil Code), whereas the good faith of the merchant according to § 366 Commercial Code must only pertain to the authority of the other person to dispose rightfully of the chattel. § 366 Subsection 3 Commercial Code has been expanded by the reform of the law. By contrast, in transactions with bearer securities, the requirements for the merchant are more stringent than for the non-merchant set forth in § 935 Subsection 2 of the Civil Code. The merchant does not act in good faith if the bearer security has been published as lost in the Official Gazette.

§ 361 Commercial Code provides that, with respect to measure, weight, currency and computation of time and distance in written contracts, the usage at the place of performance is deemed to have been agreed upon, absent any specific agreement.

a) § 346 Commercial Code dealing with "commercial practices" is especially significant. A commercial practice results from regular, standard, voluntary and actual usage between or among merchants. A commercial practice is normally to be adhered to in dealings between merchants; in transactions with non-merchants, however, it must be expressly agreed to.

The International Chamber of Commerce's International Commercial Terms (INCOTERMS) determine what is commercial practice, particularly in the area of sales.

In commercial contracts, the clause "freibleibend" (subject to change without notice) is of particular significance. Such an agreement is to be interpreted to the effect that the "offeror" does not actually make a binding offer, but rather that the "offeree" is requested to make an offer himself, or that the buyer reserves the right to withdraw the offer.

b) Another important commercial practice pertains to commercial confirmations. A commercial confirmation is a memorandum from one party to another in which the sender confirms his understanding concerning the formation and content of an oral agreement. An agreement is formed pursuant to the terms of the confirmation if the party receiving the memorandum does not contest the confirmation in a timely manner, provided the following conditions exist: Both parties must be merchants or be sophisticated in business affairs and, in a clear departure from the rules relating to order confirmation, it must be clearly evident from the confirmation that the confirming party views the agreement as finalised, such that the commercial confirmation serves as evidence for the contents of the transaction, rather than as a means of bringing about the transaction. Finally, the party confirming may not knowingly confirm something false, and the contents of the confirmation memorandum may not deviate to such an extent from the earlier agreement that the consent of the other party cannot be expected.

c) § 362 Commercial Code provides a statutory exception to the principle that silence with regard to an offer generally does not signify acceptance. In normal life, one does not need to respond to offers, but for a merchant, such an obligation does exist towards someone with whom he maintains a business relationship or to whom he has made commercial offers. In such a case, the merchant is obligated to answer; otherwise, his silence is deemed to be acceptance.

d) Of great practical significance are the current account provisions, §§ 355 et seq. Commercial Code. A current account relationship within the meaning of § 355 Commercial Code exists if two parties, at least one of whom is a merchant, arrange the legal relationship between them in such a way that mutual claims and payments are placed on account and balanced out, i. e. adjusted by means of offset. Because only one of the two parties must be a merchant, a major application for these provisions is the relationship of a bank customer to his bank. The claims lose their independent nature by becoming part of the current account relationship. As long as the current account exists, the individual claims cannot be asserted, transferred or pledged individually, nor can they be attached or taken in pledge; they are in essence "paralysed". Only the surplus balance is attachable (cf. § 357 Commercial Code).

The individual entries in the current account are balanced by means of an overall computation. Setting off the debit and credit sides of the current account against one another establishes the open balance remaining. Where the balance established in such a way is acknowledged (which can be done not only in writing, but also by silent acquiescence), such acknowledgement is deemed to be equivalent to an abstract debt acknowledgement within the meaning of §§ 781, 782 Civil Code. Moreover, the continuation of the current account relationship, where the balance is incorporated therein, is deemed to be an acknowledgement in the foregoing sense.

e) Pursuant to §§ 369, 370 Commercial Code, a merchant who holds a matured claim for money against another merchant has a right of retention with respect to the debtor's chattels or securities. The commercial right of retention, which is far more extensive than the right of retention provided for by § 273 Civil Code, authorizes, where it is based on a bilateral commercial transaction, not only the right to retention of the debtor's property prior to performance of the outstanding payment, but, in addition, satisfaction out of these items pursuant to § 371 Subsections 2 through 4 Commercial Code.

The creditor who has exercised his right to satisfaction out of an item in good faith, receives special protection as a result of § 372 Commercial Code, if the debtor has in the meantime transferred title to the property to a third party.

2. Commercial Sales

A commercial sale is a sale which is a commercial transaction, i. e. one made within the scope of a merchant's business (§ 343 Subsection 1 Com-

Introduction

mercial Code), the subject matter of which is either goods or securities (§ 381 Commercial Code). Commercial sales thus pertain only to chattels and securities and not to real estate, patents, claims or other assets.

Sales with respect to such latter property may also be concluded by a merchant within the scope of his business and, thereby, constitute commercial transactions, but they are not subject to the specific provisions of §§ 373 et seq. Commercial Code concerning commercial sales.

The provisions pertaining to the commercial sale can only be understood in the context of the provisions of the Civil Code concerning sale and purchase (§§ 433 et seq. Civil Code). They basically amend these provisions in favor of the seller and aim to bring about swift resolution if anything goes wrong with the sale/purchase transaction.

One must distinguish between unilateral and bilateral commercial sales. The provisions of §§ 373 through 376 Commercial Code relating to the seller's depositing of goods at the buyer's expense, allocation of risk for goods in a public warehouse, the self-help sale, the sale subject to the specific directives of the buyer and the commercial sale to be performed at a fixed point in time are all applicable if either the buyer or the seller is a merchant and carries out the sale within the operation of his business (§ 345 Commercial Code). On the other hand, the provisions of §§ 377 through 379 Commercial Code, which regulate the duty to examine goods delivered and object to defects and the duty to store temporarily and protect goods, apply only to bilateral commercial sales which are commercial transactions for both parties and in which both the buyer and the seller are merchants.

The provisions with respect to the commercial sale also apply to the delivery of chattel still to be made or produced.

a) Provisions Applicable to the Unilateral Commercial Sale

If the buyer defaults on his obligation to take delivery of the goods, the seller has the right to deposit the goods in a public warehouse or in some other secure place (§ 373 Subsection 1 Commercial Code). This right is more extensive than that granted by corresponding provisions in the Civil Code.

In the event of such default, the seller simultaneously has the right to conduct a self-help sale of all goods and securities pursuant to § 373 Subsections 2 through 5 Commercial Code. Because the self-help sale is deemed to be for the defaulting buyer's account, the completion of the self-help sale is considered to be fulfillment of the sales agreement by the seller. The self-help sale extinguishes the buyer's right to demand delivery.

Whether the buyer is in default in taking delivery is determined by §§ 280 et seq. Civil Code. The seller's rights pursuant to the Civil Code will not be affected by the special provisions of the Commercial Code (§ 374 Commercial Code).

The claim against the buyer for payment of the purchase price is not extinguished by utilisation of the self-help sale by the seller, despite the fact that the latter has received the proceeds. Moreover, pursuant to § 670 Civil Code, the seller may demand damages from the buyer for expenses and a commission pursuant to § 354 Subsection 1 Commercial Code. On the other hand, the buyer has a right to receive the proceeds realised from the self-help sale.

A special sub-category of commercial sales is a transaction in which the buyer is to specify the form, size, etc. of the goods. In these cases, the buyer is obligated to make the specification, and if he fails to do so, the seller is entitled to make the specifications in his stead (§ 375 Commercial Code); the seller may also demand damages according to §§ 280 and 281 of the Civil Code or withdraw from the contract according to § 323 of the Civil Code. A further type is the sale to be performed at a fixed point in time (cf. § 376 Commercial Code). This is a sales transaction in which performance by one of the parties must be made at an exact time or within a specific period, and the buyer has the rights specified in § 376 Commercial Code in the event these deadlines are not met.

b) Provisions Applicable to the Bilateral Commercial Sale

The Civil Code does not obligate a normal buyer, in the event of defective delivery, to inspect the items for defects and to give notice of the defects or discrepancy in amount immediately. Under the Civil Code, warranty claims may be asserted under normal circumstances within two years following delivery (§ 438 Subsection 1 No. 3 Civil Code). § 377 of the Commercial Code, however, standardises the duty of the buyer to examine the goods and object to defects in a bilateral commercial sale. Where the buyer fails to object in timely manner (as discussed below), the goods are deemed to be approved. The seller may, thus, be immediately certain that the transaction has been completed according to the buyer's order.

The duty to lodge an objection does not exist if the seller has maliciously concealed the defect (§ 377 Subsection 5 Commercial Code).

Where patent defects exist (defects which are apparent upon ordinary inspection), objection must be lodged immediately, i. e. without undue delay (definition in § 121 Civil Code). When defects are latent (not apparent upon ordinary examination), notice must be given immediately after such defects become apparent (§ 377 Subsection 3 Commercial Code). With respect to mass shipments, examination of samples is necessary and sufficient to fulfil the buyer's duty to inspect.

Where the buyer gives timely notice of the defect, his Civil Code warranty claims are unaffected.

§ 379 Commercial Code establishes the buyer's duty to provide for temporary storage of goods which he has refused to accept and his obligation to sell the goods if they are perishable and time is of the essence.

3. Commission Transactions

§ 383 Subsection 2 has been added by the Act to Reform the Commercial Code of 1998 and gives an interesting example of the fact that the Commercial Code can, in exceptional cases, also apply to a non-merchant. A "commission transaction" within the meaning of § 383 Commercial Code is any transaction concluded by a merchant in his own name for the account of a third party within the operation of his business. A commission agent (Kommissionär) is one who commercially undertakes to buy and sell goods or securities in his own name for the account of another (principal) (§ 383 Commercial Code).

Of great practical significance today are bank commission transactions, especially securities transactions, because the sales of these securities for the customers are made in the bank's name, but for the account of the customer.

In addition, under the provisions of § 406 Commercial Code, the provisions relating to the commission sale are also applicable to transactions similar to commission sales.

Three distinct contractual relationships are to be distinguished in commission transactions:

(i) the agreement between the commission agent and the principal;
(ii) the primary transaction (the transaction based on (i) above – normally, the agreement concluded by the commission agent with the third party); and
(iii) the winding-up transaction with which the commission agent turns over the proceeds for the goods to the principal and the principal pays the commission.

The primary transaction (ii) establishes a contractual relationship only between the commission agent and the third party, not between the principal and the third party. Claims arising from the primary transaction can, therefore, be asserted by the principal against the debtor only after the claim has been assigned to him (§ 392 Commercial Code). Economically, all advantages and disadvantages from the principal transaction accrue to the principal. This is particularly apparent in § 386 Commercial Code, under which a transaction by the commission agent is deemed to have been consented to by the principal if he does not reject it immediately, and in § 387 Commercial Code, under which the principal receives the benefit of any terms of the transaction which are more advantageous than those originally stipulated by the principal.

Upon completion of the transaction, the commission agent has the right to a commission (§ 396 Commercial Code). In order to secure this right, he has a statutory lien on the commission goods and claims based on the principal transaction (§§ 397 to 399 Commercial Code).

The commission agent is obligated to conclude the transaction with the care of a prudent merchant and to protect the interests of the principal

(§ 384 Subsection 1 Commercial Code). Where the goods sent to the agent are damaged or defective, he must perform the duties set forth in § 388 Commercial Code. Pursuant to § 390 Commercial Code, the commission agent is liable for loss or damage to goods in his custody. On the other hand, the principal may not withhold instructions or fail to perform his obligations arising from the commercial transaction. Where the principal is negligent, for example, by failing to accept goods although he is obligated to do so, the agent may deposit the goods in storage in compliance with § 373 Commercial Code (§ 389 Commercial Code) or, under certain circumstances, sell the goods (§§ 379, 391 Commercial Code) if continued custody of the goods can no longer be reasonably expected.

Generally, the commission agent must follow the principal's directions precisely. He is, otherwise, liable for subsequent damages, and the principal need not ratify the transaction (§ 385 Commercial Code). Following completion of the transaction, the commission agent must render an account to the principal and forward the amounts due to the principal in accordance therewith (§ 384 Subsection 2 Commercial Code).

The commission agent is liable, irrespective of fault, if he pays an advance or grants credit to the third party with whom he concludes the primary transaction without the approval of the principal (§ 393 Commercial Code). He may also be obligated by commercial custom to fulfil the third party's obligations (*del credere* liability, cf. § 394 Commercial Code).

Finally, §§ 400 through 405 Commercial Code set forth the conditions under which the commission agent may enter into a transaction simultaneously as the third party he would otherwise deal with on the principal's behalf, i. e., when he may deliver the goods as seller or purchase the goods which he is instructed to sell. This is of great practical significance for banks dealing in securities.

4. Transportation Law

As mentioned above, the transportation law has been totally re-codified by the so-called "*Transportrechtsreformgesetz*" of June 25, 1998 (BGBl. 1998/I/1588) and has been incorporated in the Commercial Code.

The new transportation law applies to freight carrying, forwarding and warehousing. All contracts in this field which are subject to German law now have a clear legal basis in §§ 407 et seq. of the Commercial Code. The only exception is maritime transports, which are dealt with in the fifth book of the Commercial Code (the field of application is, however, so restricted that in most editions of the Commercial Code – as in this one – the fifth book is simply left out).

The great merit of the re-codification of transportation law is that all German transports, regardless of whether by road, rail, air or internal waterways – also if several means of transportation are chosen, even some with maritime transport routes in between – now have one – and only one – legal

Introduction

basis and that a lot of provisions, laws and ordinances regulating transportation, therefore, have become obsolete.

Among the rules which have been done away with or have become partly or totally obsolete are the *"Binnenschiffahrtsgesetz"*, the *"Eisenbahnverkehrsordnung"*, the *"Kraftverkehrsordnung"* and the *"Allgemeine Deutsche Spediteurbedingungen"*. Many of these rules had been developed in times when a government-controlled economy prevailed, and they have since proved totally unfit in a free market economy.

Since even experts had difficulty in finding their way through the jungle of scattered legal rules, the Federal Ministry of Justice appointed in 1992 a commission of experts to submit a first draft of a bill. This draft was submitted in 1996 to the Federal Ministry of Justice and served as the basis for the bill of the government. In this bill, a phenomenon of ever greater importance was dealt with for the first time, namely the freight agreement where the carrier chooses different means of transportation (*Multimodaler Transport* – §§ 452 through 452 d Commercial Code).

The bill was submitted to parliament in May 1997 and was promulgated as law a year later.

The sequence of the different trades, freight carrying, forwarding and warehousing, was changed, and freight carrying was placed at the beginning, because it now contains many rules which also apply by reference to forwarding and warehousing.

a) Freight Carrying

Freight carrying is dealt with in §§ 407 through 452 d Commercial Code, and this is a body of rules for the German freight business which is complete; no rules exist other than those contained in the Commercial Code.

One restriction of the applicability must, however, be emphasised, although it is not expressly laid down in the Code as being self-evident: International transports where the freight carrier crosses a frontier are frequently regulated by international conventions such as the CMR in the case of transportation by road, the CIM by rail and the Warsaw Convention by air. The rules dealing with the freight carrier business are divided into general rules (§§ 407 through 450 Commercial Code), rules pertaining to the relocation of personal and household goods (§§ 451 through 451 h Commercial Code) and shipment by different means of transportation (§§ 452 through 452 d Commercial Code).

The contractual duties of the parties have been described in detail in the general provisions of the revised code. Thereby, a number of institutions from specialised fields have been introduced in the general freight agreement, such as the right of the freight carrier to demand lump-sum indemnification (one-third of the freight charges agreed upon – *"Fautfracht"*) in case the shipper terminates the freight contract unilaterally (§ 415 Subsection 2 Commercial Code).

The freight agreement requires no form. The freight carrier may demand that a waybill be issued (§ 408 Commercial Code), but a freight contract is perfectly valid without such a waybill. If the waybill is issued, it serves to prove or establish a presumption of certain facts (§ 409 Commercial Code).

Instead of a waybill (§ 408 Commercial Code), an inland bill of lading (§ 444 Commercial Code) can be issued which is very similar to the bill of lading used in maritime transports. So far, an inland bill of lading has not been used frequently, but this may change since its legal consequences were previously only insufficiently regulated. The important – and now clearly defined – functions of the inland bill of lading are dealt with, *inter alia*, in §§ 447 and 448 Commercial Code. The freight carrier shall not deliver the goods or follow instructions pertaining to returning or delivering the goods without having the inland bill of lading handed over to him, and handing over the inland bill of lading causes title to the goods to pass over to the recipient.

A shipper has to package the goods (§ 411 Commercial Code) and is liable to the freight carrier for all damages resulting from insufficient packaging etc. (§ 414 Commercial Code) up to the limit of 8.33 accounting units (for the time being approximately 10 Euro) per kilogram (§ 414 Subsection 2 Commercial Code). The shipper need not have been at fault in order to become liable, unless he is a consumer (§ 414 Subsections 3 and 4 Commercial Code).

Special legal remedies are provided if the goods are not put at the disposal of the freight carrier in a timely manner. The freight carrier is entitled to reasonable compensation if he has to wait for the goods (§ 412 Subsection 2 Commercial Code). The freight carrier can then fix a term within which the goods have to be loaded or, where the shipper is not obligated to load, within which the goods shall be put at the disposal of the freight carrier, and if this is unsuccessful, the freight carrier can unilaterally terminate the freight contract and assert the claims according to § 415 Subsection 2 Commercial Code.

Where only part of the goods are ready for shipping, the shipper can demand partial shipment; in this case the freight carrier remains entitled to the full freight charges, but he is required to set off such freight charges which he earns or maliciously omits to earn by utilising the free space left vacant by the part of the goods which were left behind (§ 416 Commercial Code).

The main obligations of the consignee follow from § 421 Commercial Code.

The claim of the shipper and/or the consignee against the freight carrier in case of damage to the goods or loss of the goods is of great importance. The carrier is responsible for the goods in his custody, and he is liable unless loss and damage could not be avoided despite "exercise of the utmost care" (§§ 425, 426 Commercial Code); it goes without saying that this is very close to strict liability. § 427 Commercial Code lists a number of exemptions from the liability of the carrier, mostly due to a contributing causality brought about by the shipper or consignee or due to certain properties of the goods.

Introduction

The scope of the payments for damages is determined by the value of the goods at the place of acceptance by the carrier. This may seem arbitrary, but this is what CMR provides, and, to a great extent, the new set of rules is modelled on the CMR (§§ 429 through 432 Commercial Code).

If the goods have been sold immediately before shipment, the price agreed upon is deemed to be the value of the goods (§ 429 Subsection 3 sentence 2 Commercial Code). The maximum liability is 8.33 accounting units per kilogram (other than in the realm of consumer protection, most of the provisions of the freight agreement are at the free disposal of the parties). No limitation of liability exists, however, where the carrier acted wilfully or recklessly and with knowledge that damage would probably arise (§ 435 Commercial Code).

The lien of the carrier is dealt with in §§ 441 et seq. Commercial Code.

b) Forwarding

Forwarding is dealt with in §§ 453 et seq. Commercial Code. Like in the chapter on the freight-carrying business, the law dwells on the duties of the parties. One of the difficulties here is that the duties of the forwarding agent in the era of "logistics" are much more varied than follows from the definition of the forwarding agency agreement in § 453 Commercial Code.

The shipper has duties which are similar to his duties towards the freight carrier, and the liability is also similar (§ 455 Commercial Code). The liability of the forwarding agent is laid down in § 461 Commercial Code and follows the example of the liability of the freight carrier.

c) Warehousing

The main amendment to the chapter on warehousing is that the so-called Regulation for Negotiable Bills of Lading (*Verordnung über Orderlagerscheine*) has been abolished and, accordingly, the warehouseman can issue negotiable bills of lading without being officially empowered to do so.

d) Conclusion

Altogether, a new, comprehensive and modern legal system for the transportation trades has been created, and the German legislature has shown that, at least in specialised fields, it can produce reasonable laws and simplify and clarify confused legal subjects. One can only hope that similar achievements will one day be brought about by legislation in other areas of the economy, especially in the realm of taxation.

Handelsgesetzbuch

Erstes Buch. Handelsstand

Erster Abschnitt. Kaufleute

§ 1 [Istkaufmann]

(1) Kaufmann im Sinne dieses Gesetzbuchs ist, wer ein Handelsgewerbe betreibt.

(2) Handelsgewerbe ist jeder Gewerbebetrieb, es sei denn, daß das Unternehmen nach Art oder Umfang einen in kaufmännischer Weise eingerichteten Geschäftsbetrieb nicht erfordert.

§ 2 [Kannkaufmann]

Ein gewerbliches Unternehmen, dessen Gewerbebetrieb nicht schon nach § 1 Abs. 2 Handelsgewerbe ist, gilt als Handelsgewerbe im Sinne dieses Gesetzbuchs, wenn die Firma des Unternehmens in das Handelsregister eingetragen ist. Der Unternehmer ist berechtigt, aber nicht verpflichtet, die Eintragung nach den für die Eintragung kaufmännischer Firmen geltenden Vorschriften herbeizuführen. Ist die Eintragung erfolgt, so findet eine Löschung der Firma auch auf Antrag des Unternehmers statt, sofern nicht die Voraussetzung des § 1 Abs. 2 eingetreten ist.

Commercial Code

Book One. Commercial Entities

Part One. Merchants

§ 1 Merchant by legal definition

(1) A Merchant within the meaning of this Code is one who conducts a business.

(2) A business is every commercial operation unless the enterprise by type and volume does not require a commercially organized business operation.

§ 2 Business operation by voluntary registration

A business enterprise whose operation is not already defined as a business pursuant to § 1 Subsection 2 is deemed to be a business within the meaning of this Code if the firm name of the enterprise has been registered in the Commercial Register. The entrepreneur is entitled, but not obligated, to register pursuant to the provisions applicable to the registration of commercial companies. If the firm name has been registered, the firm name shall also be deleted from the Commercial Register upon application of the entrepreneur unless the requirement of § 1 Subsection 2 has been fulfilled in the meantime.

§ 3 [Land- und Forstwirtschaft; Kannkaufmann]

(1) Auf den Betrieb der Land- und Forstwirtschaft finden die Vorschriften des § 1 keine Anwendung.

(2) Für ein land- oder forstwirtschaftliches Unternehmen, das nach Art und Umfang einen in kaufmännischer Weise eingerichteten Geschäftsbetrieb erfordert, gilt § 2 mit der Maßgabe, daß nach Eintragung in das Handelsregister eine Löschung der Firma nur nach den allgemeinen Vorschriften stattfindet, welche für die Löschung kaufmännischer Firmen gelten.

(3) Ist mit dem Betrieb der Land- oder Forstwirtschaft ein Unternehmen verbunden, das nur ein Nebengewerbe des land- oder forstwirtschaftlichen Unternehmens darstellt, so finden auf das im Nebengewerbe betriebene Unternehmen die Vorschriften der Absätze 1 und 2 entsprechende Anwendung.

§ 4 *(aufgehoben)*

§ 5 [Kaufmann kraft Eintragung]

Ist eine Firma im Handelsregister eingetragen, so kann gegenüber demjenigen, welcher sich auf die Eintragung beruft, nicht geltend gemacht werden, daß das unter der Firma betriebene Gewerbe kein Handelsgewerbe sei.

§ 6 [Handelsgesellschaften; Formkaufmann]

(1) Die in betreff der Kaufleute gegebenen Vorschriften finden auch auf die Handelsgesellschaften Anwendung.

§ 3 Agriculture and forestry; merchant by voluntary registration

(1) The provisions of § 1 do not apply to an agricultural or forestry operation.

(2) § 2 applies to agricultural or forestry enterprises which by type and volume require a commercially organized business operation, with the proviso that after registration in the Commercial Register, deletion of the firm name can be only effected pursuant to the provisions generally applicable to the deletion of commercial firm names.

(3) If such an agricultural or forestry operation has a related enterprise representing only a business ancillary to the agricultural or forestry operation, the provisions of Subsections 1 and 2 will apply analogously to that enterprise.

§ 4 *(repealed)*

§ 5 Merchant by registration

Where a firm name is registered in the Commercial Register, it may not be asserted against those who claim reliance on the registration that the operation carried out under the firm name is not a commercial business.

§ 6 Commercial companies and partnerships; merchant by form of organization

(1) The provisions applicable to merchants also apply to commercial companies and partnerships.

(2) Die Rechte und Pflichten eines Vereins, dem das Gesetz ohne Rücksicht auf den Gegenstand des Unternehmens die Eigenschaft eines Kaufmanns beilegt, bleiben unberührt, auch wenn die Voraussetzungen des § 1 Abs. 2 nicht vorliegen.

§ 7 [Kaufmannseigenschaft und öffentliches Recht]

Durch die Vorschriften des öffentlichen Rechtes, nach welchen die Befugnis zum Gewerbebetrieb ausgeschlossen oder von gewissen Voraussetzungen abhängig gemacht ist, wird die Anwendung der die Kaufleute betreffenden Vorschriften dieses Gesetzbuchs nicht berührt.

Zweiter Abschnitt. Handelsregister

§ 8 [Führung des Registers]

Das Handelsregister wird von den Gerichten geführt.

§ 8 a [Ermächtigung der Landesregierungen; automatisierte Dateien]

(1) Die Landesregierungen können durch Rechtsverordnung bestimmen, daß und in welchem Umfang das Handelsregister einschließlich der zu seiner Führung erforderlichen Verzeichnisse in maschineller Form als automatisierte Datei geführt wird. Hierbei muß gewährleistet sein, daß

1. die Grundsätze einer ordnungsgemäßen Datenverarbeitung eingehalten, insbesondere Vorkehrungen gegen einen Datenverlust getroffen sowie die erforderlichen Kopien der Datenbestände mindestens tages-

(2) The rights and duties of an association to which the law attributes merchant status irrespective of the purpose of the enterprise, are not affected even if the requirements of § 1 Subsection 2 are not fulfilled.

§ 7 Merchant status and public law

The provisions of this Code applying to merchants will not be affected by public law provisions pursuant to which the right to carry on a business operation can be denied or conditioned on certain prerequisites.

Part Two. Commercial Register

§ 8 Maintenance of the register

The Commercial Register shall be maintained by the courts.

§ 8 a Authorization of state governments; automated files

(1) The state (Land) governments can determine by administrative rule that and to what extent the Commercial Register, including the indices necessary for its maintenance, shall be operated in electronic form as an automated file. It must be ensured that

1. the principles of orderly data processing are observed, especially that measures are taken against a losses of data, that necessary copies of data portfolios are updated at least daily and that the original

aktuell gehalten und die originären Datenbestände sowie deren Kopien sicher aufbewahrt werden,

2. die vorzunehmenden Eintragungen alsbald in einen Datenspeicher aufgenommen und auf Dauer inhaltlich unverändert in lesbarer Form wiedergegeben werden können,

3. die nach der Anlage zu § 126 Abs. 1 Satz 2 Nr. 3 der Grundbuchordnung erforderlichen Maßnahmen getroffen werden.

Die Landesregierungen können ferner durch Rechtsverordnung bestimmen, dass die Einreichung von Jahres- und Konzernabschlüssen, von Lageberichten sowie sonstiger einzureichender Schriftstücke in einer maschinell lesbaren und zugleich für die maschinelle Bearbeitung durch das Registergericht geeigneten Form zu erfolgen hat; die Bestimmung kann auch für einzelne Handelsregister getroffen werden. Die Landesregierungen können durch Rechtsverordnung die Ermächtigung nach nach den Sätzen 1 oder 3 auf die Landesjustizverwaltungen übertragen.

(2) Eine Eintragung wird wirksam, sobald sie in den für die Handelsregistereintragungen bestimmten Datenspeicher aufgenommen ist und auf Dauer inhaltlich unverändert in lesbarer Form wiedergegeben werden kann.

(3) Die zum Handelsregister eingereichten Schriftstücke können zur Ersetzung der Urschrift auch als Wiedergabe auf einem Bildträger oder auf anderen Datenträgern aufbewahrt werden, wenn sichergestellt ist, daß die Wiedergaben oder die Daten innerhalb angemessener Zeit lesbar gemacht werden können. Bei der Herstellung der Bild- oder Datenträger ist ein

data portfolios and their copies are stored safely,

2. the entries to be registered can be promptly stored in an electronic data processor and can be permanently reproduced in legible form unchanged in content,

3. the measures necessary pursuant to the Appendix to § 126 Subsection 1 sentence 2 No. 3 of the Land Title Register Ordinance are taken.

The state (Land) governments can additionally determine by administrative rule that the submission of annual financial statements, management reports and other documents requiring submission must be made in electronic form suitable for electronic processing by the registry court; this determination can also be made for individual commercial registries. The state (Land) governments can delegate the authority pursuant to sentences 1 or 3 by administrative rule to the state (Land) Departments of Justice.

(2) An entry is effective as soon as it is stored in the electronic data processor assigned to the Commercial Register registrations and can be permanently reproduced in legible form with no change in content.

(3) Documents submitted to the Commercial Register can be kept as reproductions on film or in other data storage devices in place of the original documents if it is ensured that the reproductions or the data can be rendered legible within a reasonable time. In producing film or data storage devices, written documentation shall be produced as to their contents being

schriftlicher Nachweis über ihre inhaltliche Übereinstimmung mit der Urschrift anzufertigen.

(4) Das Gericht kann gestatten, daß die zum Handelsregister einzureichenden Jahresabschlüsse und Konzernabschlüsse und die dazugehörigen Unterlagen sowie sonstige einzureichende Schriftstücke in der in Absatz 3 Satz 1 bezeichneten Form eingereicht werden.

(5) Die näheren Anordnungen über die maschinelle Führung des Handelsregisters, die Aufbewahrung von Schriftstücken nach Absatz 3 und die Einreichung von Abschlüssen und Schriftstücken nach Absatz 1 Satz 3 und Absatz 4 sowie deren Aufbewahrung trifft die Landesjustizverwaltung, soweit nicht durch Rechtsverordnung nach § 125 Abs. 3 des Gesetzes über die Angelegenheiten der freiwilligen Gerichtsbarkeit Vorschriften erlassen werden.

§ 9 [Einsicht des Handelsregisters; Abschriften; Bescheinigungen]

(1) Die Einsicht des Handelsregisters sowie der zum Handelsregister eingereichten Schriftstücke ist jedem zu Informationszwecken gestattet.

(2) Von den Eintragungen und den zum Handelsregister eingereichten Schriftstücken kann eine Abschrift gefordert werden. Werden die Schriftstücke nach § 8 a Abs. 3 aufbewahrt, so kann eine Abschrift nur von der Wiedergabe gefordert werden. Die Abschrift ist von der Geschäftsstelle zu beglaubigen, sofern nicht auf die Beglaubigung verzichtet wird. Wird das Handelsregister in maschineller Form als automati-

true copies of the original document.

(4) The court can allow the annual financial statements and consolidated financial statements to be submitted to the Commercial Register and the documents pertaining thereto and other documents to be submitted be submitted in the form described in Subsection 3 sentence 1.

(5) The state (Land) Department of Justice shall issue more detailed rules as to the electronic operation of the Commercial Register, the keeping of documents pursuant to Subsection 3 and the submission of financial statements and documents pursuant to Subsection 1 sentence 3 and Subsection 4 as well as their storage to the extent that provisions are not issued by administrative rule pursuant to § 125 Subsection 3 of the Law concerning on Administrative Acts of the Judiciary.

§ 9 Inspection of the Commercial Register; copies; certificates

(1) Any person may inspect the Commercial Register and the documents filed therewith for information purposes.

(2) Copies can be requested of the registrations and the documents filed in the Commercial Register. If the documents are stored according to § 8 a Subsection 3, a copy can only be demanded of the form in which it has been stored. The copy is to be certified by the registry office unless such certification is waived. If the Commercial Register is maintained in electronic form as an automated file, then the

sierte Datei geführt, so tritt an die Stelle der Abschrift der Ausdruck und an die Stelle der beglaubigten Abschrift der amtliche Ausdruck.

(3) Der Nachweis, wer der Inhaber einer in das Handelsregister eingetragenen Firma eines Einzelkaufmanns ist, kann Behörden gegenüber durch ein Zeugnis des Gerichts über die Eintragung geführt werden. Das gleiche gilt von dem Nachweis der Befugnis zur Vertretung eines Einzelkaufmanns oder einer Handelsgesellschaft.

(4) Das Gericht hat auf Verlangen eine Bescheinigung darüber zu erteilen, daß bezüglich des Gegenstandes einer Eintragung weitere Eintragungen nicht vorhanden sind oder daß eine bestimmte Eintragung nicht erfolgt ist.

§ 9 a [Zulässigkeit des automatisierten Verfahrens; Genehmigung; Datenschutz; Gebühren]

(1) Die Einrichtung eines automatisierten Verfahrens, das die Übermittlung der Daten aus dem maschinell geführten Handelsregister durch Abruf ermöglicht, ist zulässig, wenn der Abruf von Daten auf die Eintragungen in das Handelsregister sowie die zum Handelsregister eingereichten aktuellen Gesellschafterlisten und jeweils gültigen Satzungen beschränkt ist und insoweit die nach § 9 Abs. 1 zulässige Einsicht nicht überschreitet.

(2) Der Nutzer ist darauf hinzuweisen, dass er die übermittelten Daten nur zu Informationszwecken verwenden darf. Die zuständige Stelle hat (z.B. durch Stichproben) zu prüfen, ob sich Anhaltspunkte dafür ergeben, dass die nach Satz 1 zulässige Einsicht überschritten oder übermittelte Daten missbraucht werden.

printout replaces the copy and the official printout replaces the certified copy.

(3) Proof of ownership of the registered firm name of a sole proprietorship can be made to the authorities by means of a certificate from the court concerning the registration. The same applies to proof of authority to represent a sole proprietorship or partnership.

(4) On demand, the court shall provide a certificate stating that additional entries do not exist with respect to the subject of registration or that a specific entry has not been made.

§ 9 a Admissibility of automated procedures; consent; data protection; fees

(1) The establishment of an automated procedure which renders possible the transmission of data from the electronically operated Commercial Register by automated retrieval is permitted if the automated retrieval of data is limited to the entries in the Commercial Register as well as the current shareholders list and the currently valid Articles of Association filed with the Commercial Register and to the extent that inspection permitted pursuant to § 9 Subsection 1 is not exceeded.

(2) It shall be pointed out to the user that he may only use the transmitted data for information purposes. The responsible office shall review (e. g., by spot checks) wether there are reasons to believe that the inspection permitted under sentence 1 is exceeded or transmitted data is misused.

Handelsregister §§ 9a–11

(3) Die zuständige Stelle kann einen Nutzer, der die Funktionsfähigkeit der Abrufeinrichtung gefährdet, die nach Absatz 2 Satz 1 zulässige Einsicht überschreitet oder übermittelte Daten missbraucht, von der Teilnahme am automatisierten Abrufverfahren ausschließen; dasselbe gilt bei drohender Überschreitung oder drohendem Missbrauch.

(4) Zuständige Stelle ist die Landesjustizverwaltung. Örtlich zuständig ist die Behörde, in deren Bezirk das betreffende Gericht liegt. Die Zuständigkeit kann durch Rechtsverordnung der Landesregierung abweichend geregelt werden. Sie kann diese Ermächtigung durch Rechtsverordnung auf die Landesjustizverwaltung übertragen.

§ 10 [Bekanntmachung der Eintragungen]

(1) Das Gericht hat die Eintragungen in das Handelsregister durch den Bundesanzeiger und durch mindestens ein anderes Blatt bekanntzumachen. Soweit nicht das Gesetz ein anderes vorschreibt, werden die Eintragungen ihrem ganzen Inhalte nach veröffentlicht.

(2) Mit dem Ablaufe des Tages, an welchem das letzte der die Bekanntmachung enthaltenden Blätter erschienen ist, gilt die Bekanntmachung als erfolgt.

§ 11 [Bezeichnung der Amtsblätter]

(1) Das Gericht hat jährlich im Dezember die Blätter zu bezeichnen, in denen während des nächsten Jahres

(3) The responsible office can exclude from participation in the automated retrieval system any user who jeopardizes the operation of the retrieval system, who exceeds the inspection permitted under Subsection 2 sentence 1 or misuses transmitted data; the same applies in the event of threatened excess or threatened misuse.

(4) The responsible office shall be the State Office for Judicial Administration. The agency in whose district the relevant court is located shall have local jurisdiction. The jurisdiction may be regulated otherwise by executive order of the State Government. It may delegate this authority by executive order to the State Office for Judicial Administration.

§ 10 Publication of registrations

(1) The court shall publish registrations in the Commercial Register by means of the Federal Gazette and in at least one other newspaper. The entire contents of the registrations shall be published unless the law prescribes otherwise.

(2) Publication is effective as of the end of the day on which the last paper appeared in which the publication is included.

§ 11 Designation of newspapers in which registration will be published

(1) Once a year in December the court shall designate the newspapers in which, during the following year, the

41

die in § 10 vorgesehenen Veröffentlichungen erfolgen sollen.

(2) Wird das Handelsregister bei einem Gerichte von mehreren Richtern geführt und einigen sich diese über die Bezeichnung der Blätter nicht, so wird die Bestimmung von dem im Rechtszug vorgeordneten Landgerichte getroffen; ist bei diesem Landgericht eine Kammer für Handelssachen gebildet, so tritt diese an die Stelle der Zivilkammer.

§ 12 [Anmeldungen; Zeichnung von Unterschriften; Nachweis der Rechtsnachfolge]

(1) Die Anmeldungen zur Eintragung in das Handelsregister sowie die zur Aufbewahrung bei dem Gerichte bestimmten Zeichnungen von Unterschriften sind in öffentlich beglaubigter Form einzureichen.

(2) Die gleiche Form ist für eine Vollmacht zur Anmeldung erforderlich. Rechtsnachfolger eines Beteiligten haben die Rechtsnachfolge soweit tunlich durch öffentliche Urkunden nachzuweisen.

§ 13 Zweigniederlassungen von Unternehmen mit Sitz im Inland

(1) Die Errichtung einer Zweigniederlassung ist von einem Einzelkaufmann oder einer juristischen Person beim Gericht der Hauptniederlassung, von einer Handelsgesellschaft beim Gericht des Sitzes der Gesellschaft zur Eintragung in das Handelsregister des Gerichts der Zweigniederlassung anzumelden. Das Gericht der Hauptniederlassung oder des Sitzes hat die Anmeldung unverzüglich mit einer

publications provided for in § 10 shall be made.

(2) Where the Commercial Register is maintained within one court by more than one judge and agreement cannot be reached over designation of the newspapers, the determination will be made by the District Court (Ed.: District Court superior to the local Court (Amtsgericht) within the German court system). Where a commercial division exists within the District Court, it will replace the civil division.

§ 12 Filings to register; specimen signatures; proof of legal succession

(1) Filings to register in the Commercial Register as well as the specimen signatures to be kept on file with the court are to be submitted in a publicly certified form.

(2) The same form is required for a power of attorney for purposes of registration. The legal successor of a party should prove succession to the extent feasible by means of official documents.

§ 13 Branches of enterprises with domestic domicile

(1) A sole proprietor or a juridical person shall file to register the establishment of a branch at the court of the head office, and a partnership shall apply for registration of the establishment of a branch at the court of the domicile of the partnership. The court at the main branch or at the domicile shall pass to the court of the branch office without delay the filing with a certified copy of its registrations, to

beglaubigten Abschrift seiner Eintragungen, soweit sie nicht ausschließlich die Verhältnisse anderer Niederlassungen betreffen, an das Gericht der Zweigniederlassung weiterzugeben.

(2) Die gesetzlich vorgeschriebenen Unterschriften sind zur Aufbewahrung beim Gericht der Zweigniederlassung zu zeichnen; für die Unterschriften der Prokuristen gilt dies nur, soweit die Prokura nicht ausschließlich auf den Betrieb einer anderen Niederlassung beschränkt ist.

(3) Das Gericht der Zweigniederlassung hat zu prüfen, ob die Zweigniederlassung errichtet und § 30 beachtet ist. Ist dies der Fall, so hat es die Zweigniederlassung einzutragen und dabei die ihm mitgeteilten Tatsachen nicht zu prüfen, soweit sie im Handelsregister der Hauptniederlassung oder des Sitzes eingetragen sind. Die Eintragung hat auch den Ort der Zweigniederlassung zu enthalten; ist der Firma für die Zweigniederlassung ein Zusatz beigefügt, so ist auch dieser einzutragen.

(4) Die Eintragung der Zweigniederlassung ist von Amts wegen dem Gericht der Hauptniederlassung oder des Sitzes mitzuteilen und in dessen Register zu vermerken; ist der Firma für die Zweigniederlassung ein Zusatz beigefügt, so ist auch dieser zu vermerken. Der Vermerk wird nicht veröffentlicht.

(5) Die Vorschriften über die Errichtung einer Zweigniederlassung gelten sinngemäß für ihre Aufhebung.

(6) Die Bekanntmachung von Eintragungen im Handelsregister des Gerichts der Zweigniederlassung beschränkt sich auf

1. die Errichtung und Aufhebung der Zweigniederlassung,
2. die Firma,

the extent that they do not concern exclusively the relations of other branches.

(2) The statutorily required specimen signatures shall be submitted for filing to the court of the branch: this applies to the signatures of the holders of a general agency (Prokura) only to the extent that their power to represent is not limited exclusively to the operation of another branch.

(3) The court at the branch must review whether the branch has been established and § 30 has been observed. If this is the case, then the court must register the branch and shall not review facts of which it is informed to the extent that they are registered in the Commercial Register of the head office or of the domicile. The registration shall also contain the place of the branch; if an addendum is added to the company name for the branch, then this must also be registered.

(4) The registration of the branch shall be reported by the court on its own motion to the court of the head office or of the domicile and is to be noted in its register; if an addendum has been added to the company name for the branch, then this must also be noted. The note shall not be published.

(5) The provisions concerning establishment of a branch apply analogously for its dissolution.

(6) The publication of entries in the Commercial Register of the court of the branch is restricted to

1. the establishment and dissolution of the branch,
2. the corporate name,

3. den Zusatz, wenn der Firma für die Zweigniederlassung ein Zusatz beigefügt ist,
4. den Ort der Zweigniederlassung,
5. den Ort der Hauptniederlassung oder den Sitz und
6. die Tatsachen, die nur die Verhältnisse der Zweigniederlassung betreffen.

§ 13 a Zweigniederlassungen von Aktiengesellschaften mit Sitz im Inland

(1) Für Zweigniederlassungen von Aktiengesellschaften gelten ergänzend die folgenden Vorschriften.

(2) Die Errichtung einer Zweigniederlassung ist durch den Vorstand anzumelden. Der Anmeldung ist eine öffentlich beglaubigte Abschrift der Satzung beizufügen.

(3) Die Eintragung hat auch die Angaben nach § 39 des Aktiengesetzes zu enthalten.

(4) Die Vorschriften über die Zweigniederlassungen von Aktiengesellschaften gelten sinngemäß für die Zweigniederlassungen von Kommanditgesellschaften auf Aktien, soweit sich aus den Vorschriften der §§ 278 bis 290 des Aktiengesetzes oder aus dem Fehlen eines Vorstands nichts anderes ergibt.

§ 13 b Zweigniederlassungen von Gesellschaften mit beschränkter Haftung mit Sitz im Inland

(1) Für Zweigniederlassungen von Gesellschaften mit beschränkter Haftung gelten ergänzend die folgenden Vorschriften.

3. the addendum, if an addendum is added to the company name for the branch,
4. the place of the branch,
5. the place of the head office or domicile and
6. facts pertaining only to the circumstances of the branch.

§ 13 a Branches of stock corporations with domestic domicile

(1) The following supplemental provisions apply to branches of stock corporations.

(2) The managing board shall file to register the establishment of a new branch. A publicly certified copy of the articles of association shall be attached to such filing.

(3) The entry shall also contain the information required by § 39 of the Stock Corporation Act.

(4) The provisions concerning branches of stock corporations shall apply analogously for branches of partnerships limited by shares, to the extent not provided otherwise by §§ 278 through 290 of the Stock Corporation Act or by the lack of a managing board.

§ 13 b Branches of limited liability companies with domestic domicile

(1) The following supplemental provisions apply to branches of limited liability companies.

(2) Die Errichtung einer Zweigniederlassung ist durch die Geschäftsführer anzumelden. Der Anmeldung ist eine öffentlich beglaubigte Abschrift des Gesellschaftsvertrages und der Liste der Gesellschafter beizufügen.

(3) Die Eintragung hat auch die in § 10 Abs. 1 und 2 des Gesetzes betreffend die Gesellschaften mit beschränkter Haftung bezeichneten Angaben zu enthalten.

§ 13 c Bestehende Zweigniederlassungen von Unternehmen mit Sitz im Inland

(1) Ist eine Zweigniederlassung in das Handelsregister eingetragen, so sind alle Anmeldungen, die die Hauptniederlassung oder die Niederlassung am Sitz der Gesellschaft oder die eingetragenen Zweigniederlassungen betreffen, beim Gericht der Hauptniederlassung oder des Sitzes zu bewirken; es sind so viel Stücke einzureichen, wie Niederlassungen bestehen.

(2) Das Gericht der Hauptniederlassung oder des Sitzes hat seine Eintragung unverzüglich mit einem Stück der Anmeldung von Amts wegen den Gerichten der Zweigniederlassungen mitzuteilen. Die Gerichte der Zweigniederlassungen haben die Eintragungen ohne Nachprüfung in ihr Handelsregister zu übernehmen. Eintragungen im Register der Zweigniederlassungen werden von den Gerichten der Zweigniederlassungen nur bekannt gemacht, soweit sie die in § 13 Abs. 6 angeführten Tatsachen betreffen. Im Bundesanzeiger wird die Eintragung im Handelsregister der Zweigniederlassung nicht bekanntgemacht. Sind für mehrere Zweigniederlassungen von demselben Gericht übereinstimmende Eintragungen bekanntzumachen, ist in der Be-

(2) The managing directors shall file to register the establishment of a branch. A publicly certified copy of the articles of association and of the list of shareholders shall be attached to such filing.

(3) The application shall also contain the information designated in § 10 Subsections 1 and 2, of the Limited Liability Companies Act.

§ 13 c Existing branches of enterprises with domestic domicile

(1) If a branch has been entered in the Commercial Register, all filings for registration affecting the head office, the branch located at the domicile of the company or the registered branche, shall be made at the court for the head office or the domicile; one counterpart shall be submitted for each existing branch.

(2) The court of the head office or the domicile shall without delay communicate on its own motion to the courts for the branches its entry, with a counterpart of the filing for registration. The courts for the branches shall make the entries in their Commercial Registers without further examination. Entries into the registry of the branches shall be published by the courts of the branches to the extent the entries include the facts stated in § 13 Subsection 6. The entry in the Commercial Register of the branch shall not be published in the Federal Gazette. If identical entries have to be communicated by the same court for several branches, the entry shall be reproduced only once in the communication and it shall be specified for

§§ 13c, d — Handelsstand

kanntmachung die Eintragung nur einmal wiederzugeben und anzugeben, für welche einzelnen Zweigniederlassungen sie vorgenommen worden ist.

(3) Betrifft die Anmeldung ausschließlich die Verhältnisse einzelner Zweigniederlassungen, so sind außer dem für das Gericht der Hauptniederlassung oder des Sitzes bestimmten Stück nur so viel Stücke einzureichen, wie Zweigniederlassungen betroffen sind. Das Gericht der Hauptniederlassung oder des Sitzes teilt seine Eintragung nur den Gerichten der Zweigniederlassungen mit, deren Verhältnisse sie betrifft. Die Eintragung im Register der Hauptniederlassung oder des Sitzes wird in diesem Fall nur im Bundesanzeiger bekanntgemacht.

(4) Absätze 1 bis 3 gelten sinngemäß für die Einreichung von Schriftstücken und die Zeichnung von Unterschriften.

§ 13 d Sitz oder Hauptniederlassung im Ausland

(1) Befindet sich die Hauptniederlassung eines Einzelkaufmanns oder einer juristischen Person oder der Sitz einer Handelsgesellschaft im Ausland, so haben alle eine inländische Zweigniederlassung betreffenden Anmeldungen, Zeichnungen, Einreichungen und Eintragungen bei dem Gericht zu erfolgen, in dessen Bezirk die Zweigniederlassung besteht.

(2) Die Eintragung der Errichtung der Zweigniederlassung hat auch den Ort der Zweigniederlassung zu enthalten; ist der Firma der Zweigniederlassung ein Zusatz beigefügt, so ist auch dieser einzutragen.

which individual branches the entry has been made.

(3) If the filing for registration solely affects individual branches, then, in addition to the counterpart for the court of the head office or domicile, only so many counterparts shall be submitted as there are branches affected. The court of the head office or domicile shall communicate its entry only to the courts of those branches which are affected thereby. In such event, the entry in the Commercial Register of the head office or domicile shall be published only in the Federal Gazette.

(4) Subsections 1 through 3 apply analogously to the submission of documents and the submission of specimen signatures.

§ 13 d Domicile or head office abroad

(1) In the event the head office of a sole proprietorship, a juridical person or the domicile of a commercial company is located in a foreign country, all filings for registration, specimen signatures, submissions and entries with respect to a domestic branch shall be made with the court in whose jurisdiction the branch exists.

(2) The entry concerning establishment of the branch office shall also indicate the town or city where the same is located; if an addendum is added to the company name for the branch, then this fact must also be registered.

(3) Im übrigen gelten für die Anmeldungen, Zeichnungen, Einreichungen, Eintragungen und Bekanntmachungen, die die Zweigniederlassung eines Einzelkaufmanns, einer Handelsgesellschaft oder einer juristischen Person mit Ausnahme von Aktiengesellschaften, Kommanditgesellschaften auf Aktien und Gesellschaften mit beschränkter Haftung betreffen, die Vorschriften für Hauptniederlassungen oder Niederlassungen am Sitz der Gesellschaft sinngemäß, soweit nicht das ausländische Recht Abweichungen nötig macht.

§ 13 e Zweigniederlassungen von Kapitalgesellschaften mit Sitz im Ausland

(1) Für Zweigniederlassungen von Aktiengesellschaften und Gesellschaften mit beschränkter Haftung mit Sitz im Ausland gelten ergänzend zu § 13 d die folgenden Vorschriften.

(2) Die Errichtung einer Zweigniederlassung einer Aktiengesellschaft ist durch den Vorstand, die Errichtung einer Zweigniederlassung einer Gesellschaft mit beschränkter Haftung ist durch die Geschäftsführer zur Eintragung in das Handelsregister anzumelden. Bei der Anmeldung ist das Bestehen der Gesellschaft als solcher und, wenn der Gegenstand des Unternehmens oder die Zulassung zum Gewerbebetrieb im Inland der staatlichen Genehmigung bedarf, auch diese nachzuweisen. Die Anmeldung hat auch die Anschrift und den Gegenstand der Zweigniederlassung zu enthalten. In der Anmeldung sind ferner anzugeben

1. das Register, bei dem die Gesellschaft geführt wird, und die Nummer des Registereintrags, sofern das Recht des Staates, in dem die

(3) Otherwise, the provisions concerning head offices or branches at the domicile of the company apply analogously to filings for registration, specimen signatures, submissions, entries and publications which affect the branches of a sole proprietorship, a commercial company or a juridical person (with the exception of stock corporations, partnerships limited by shares and limited liability companies) to the extent that foreign law does not necessitate deviations therefrom.

§ 13 e Branches of corporations with foreign domicile

(1) In addition to § 13 d, the following provisions apply to branches of stock corporations and limited liability companies with foreign domicile.

(2) In the case of a stock corporation, the managing board shall file for registration of the establishment of a branch office in the Commercial Register; in the case of a limited liability company, the managing directors shall file. With the filing, proof shall be provided of the existence of the company as such, and if the purpose of the company or permission to conduct business in this country requires government approval, proof of such approval shall be submitted. The filing shall also contain the mailing address and an indication of the purpose of the branch. The filing for registration shall further contain

1. the name of the Commercial Register in which the company is entered and the number of its entry, to the extent that the law of the

Gesellschaft ihren Sitz hat, eine Registereintragung vorsieht;

2. die Rechtsform der Gesellschaft;
3. die Personen, die befugt sind, als ständige Vertreter für die Tätigkeit der Zweigniederlassung die Gesellschaft gerichtlich und außergerichtlich zu vertreten, unter Angabe ihrer Befugnisse;
4. wenn die Gesellschaft nicht dem Recht eines Mitgliedstaates der Europäischen Gemeinschaft oder eines anderen Vertragsstaates des Abkommens über den Europäischen Wirtschaftsraum unterliegt, das Recht des Staates, dem die Gesellschaft unterliegt.

(3) Die in Absatz 2 Satz 4 Nr. 3 genannten Personen haben jede Änderung dieser Personen oder der Vertretungsbefugnis einer dieser Personen zur Eintragung in das Handelsregister anzumelden.

(4) Die in Absatz 2 Satz 4 Nr. 3 genannten Personen oder, wenn solche nicht angemeldet sind, die gesetzlichen Vertreter der Gesellschaft haben die Eröffnung oder die Ablehnung der Eröffnung eines Insolvenzverfahrens oder ähnlichen Verfahrens über das Vermögen der Gesellschaft zur Eintragung in das Handelsregister anzumelden.

(5) Errichtet eine Gesellschaft mehrere Zweigniederlassungen im Inland, so brauchen die Satzung oder der Gesellschaftsvertrag sowie deren Änderungen nach Wahl der Gesellschaft nur zum Handelsregister einer dieser Zweigniederlassungen eingereicht zu werden. In diesem Fall haben die nach Absatz 2 Satz 1 Anmeldepflichtigen zur Eintragung in den Handelsregistern der übrigen Zweigniederlassun-

country in which the company has its domicile foresees such registration;

2. the legal form of the company;
3. the names of the persons who are empowered to represent the company in judicial and non-judicial matters as permanent representatives for the activities of the branch, including an indication of their powers;
4. if the company is not subject to the law of a member state of the European Union or of another contracting party to the European Economic Area Agreement, the law of the country to which the company is subject.

(3) The persons named in Subsection 2 sentence 4 No. 3 shall file for registration in the Commercial Register every change in the identity of such persons or in the representation powers of one of these persons.

(4) The persons named in Subsection 2 sentence 4 No. 3, or if none are entered, the legal representatives of the company, shall file for registration in the Commercial Register of the commencement or denial of commencement of insolvency or similar proceeding concerning the assets of the company.

(5) In the event a company establishes more than one branch within this country, the articles of association or similar constitutive agreements and any amendments thereto may, at the option of the company, be submitted to the Commercial Register of only one of such branches. In such event, the persons obligated pursuant to Subsection 2 sentence 1 to file for registration in the Commercial Registers of

gen anzumelden, welches Register die Gesellschaft gewählt hat und unter welcher Nummer die Zweigniederlassung eingetragen ist.

§ 13 f Zweigniederlassungen von Aktiengesellschaften mit Sitz im Ausland

(1) Für Zweigniederlassungen von Aktiengesellschaften mit Sitz im Ausland gelten ergänzend die folgenden Vorschriften.

(2) Der Anmeldung ist die Satzung in öffentlich beglaubigter Abschrift und, sofern die Satzung nicht in deutscher Sprache erstellt ist, eine beglaubigte Übersetzung in deutscher Sprache beizufügen. Die Vorschriften des § 37 Abs. 3, 5 und 6 des Aktiengesetzes finden Anwendung. Soweit nicht das ausländische Recht eine Abweichung nötig macht, sind in die Anmeldung die in § 23 Abs. 3 und 4, §§ 24, 25 Satz 2 des Aktiengesetzes vorgesehenen Bestimmungen, Bestimmungen der Satzung über die Zusammensetzung des Vorstandes und, wenn die Anmeldung in den ersten zwei Jahren nach der Eintragung der Gesellschaft in das Handelsregister ihres Sitzes erfolgt, auch die Angaben nach § 40 Abs. 1 Nr. 1, 2 und 3 des Aktiengesetzes aufzunehmen. Der Anmeldung ist die für den Sitz der Gesellschaft ergangene gerichtliche Bekanntmachung beizufügen.

(3) Die Eintragung der Errichtung der Zweigniederlassung hat auch die Angaben nach § 39 des Aktiengesetzes sowie die in § 13 e Abs. 2 Satz 4 vorgeschriebenen Angaben zu enthalten.

(4) In die Bekanntmachung der Eintragung sind außer deren Inhalt auch die

the other branches shall file to register which Commercial Register the company has chosen and under which number the branch has been entered.

§ 13 f Branch offices of stock corporations with foreign domicile

(1) The following supplemental provisions apply to branches of stock corporation with foreign domicile.

(2) A publicly certified copy of the articles of association and, to the extent that such articles are not in the German language, a certified translation into German shall be attached to the filing for registration. The provisions of § 37 Subsections 3, 5 and 6 of the Stock Corporation Act shall apply. To the extent that foreign law does not necessitate a departure, herefrom, the provisions set forth in § 23 Subsections 3 and 4, §§ 24, 25 sentence 2, of the Stock Corporation Act, provisions in the articles of association concerning the composition of the managing board and, if the entry is made within the first two years following registration of the company in the Commercial Register of its domicile, also the information pursuant to § 40 Subsection 1 Nos. 1, 2 and 3 of the Stock Corporation Act shall be included in the filing. The judicial publication for the domicile of the company shall be attached to the filing.

(3) The entry concerning the establishment of a branch shall also contain the information required by § 39 of the Stock Corporation Act as well as the information required in § 13 e Subsection 2 sentence 4.

(4) The publication of the entry shall contain, in addition to its contents,

Angaben nach § 40 Abs. 1 Nr. 1, 2 und 3 des Aktiengesetzes aufzunehmen, soweit sie nach den vorstehenden Vorschriften in die Anmeldung aufzunehmen sind.

(5) Änderungen der Satzung der ausländischen Gesellschaft sind durch den Vorstand zur Eintragung in das Handelsregister anzumelden. Für die Anmeldung gelten die Vorschriften des § 181 Abs. 1 und 2 des Aktiengesetzes sinngemäß, soweit nicht das ausländische Recht Abweichungen nötig macht.

(6) Im übrigen gelten die Vorschriften der § 81 Abs. 1, 2 und 4, § 263 Satz 1, § 266 Abs. 1, 2 und 5, § 273 Abs. 1 Satz 1 des Aktiengesetzes sinngemäß, soweit nicht das ausländische Recht Abweichungen nötig macht.

(7) Für die Aufhebung einer Zweigniederlassung gelten die Vorschriften über ihre Errichtung sinngemäß.

(8) Die Vorschriften über Zweigniederlassungen von Aktiengesellschaften mit Sitz im Ausland gelten sinngemäß für Zweigniederlassungen von Kommanditgesellschaften auf Aktien mit Sitz im Ausland, soweit sich aus den Vorschriften der §§ 278 bis 290 des Aktiengesetzes oder aus dem Fehlen eines Vorstands nichts anderes ergibt.

§ 13 g Zweigniederlassungen von Gesellschaften mit beschränkter Haftung mit Sitz im Ausland

(1) Für die Zweigniederlassungen von Gesellschaften mit beschränkter Haftung mit Sitz im Ausland gelten ergänzend die folgenden Vorschriften.

the information pursuant to § 40 Subsection 1 Nos. 1, 2 and 3 of the Stock Corporation Act to the extent that such items are to be included in the filing for registration pursuant to the above provisions.

(5) The managing board shall file to register amendments to the articles of association of the foreign company in the Commercial Register. To the extent that foreign law does not necessitate deviations therefrom, the provisions of § 181 Subsections 1 and 2 of the Stock Corporation Act shall apply analogously to the filing.

(6) Otherwise, the provisions of § 81 Subsections 1, 2 and 4, § 263 sentence 1, § 266 Subsections 1, 2 and 5, and § 273 Subsection 1 sentence 1, of the Stock Corporation Act apply analogously to the extent that foreign law does not necessitate deviations therefrom.

(7) The provisions concerning establishment of a branch apply analogously to its dissolution.

(8) The provisions concerning branches of stock corporations with foreign domicile apply analogously to branches of partnerships limited by shares with foreign domicile, to the extent not provided otherwise by §§ 278 through 290 of the Stock Corporation Act or by reason of the lack of an managing board.

§ 13 g Branches of limited liability companies with foreign domicile

(1) The following supplemental provisions apply to branches of limited liability companies with foreign domicile.

(2) Der Anmeldung ist der Gesellschaftsvertrag in öffentlich beglaubigter Abschrift und, sofern der Gesellschaftsvertrag nicht in deutscher Sprache erstellt ist, eine beglaubigte Übersetzung in deutscher Sprache beizufügen. Die Vorschriften des § 8 Abs. 1 Nr. 2, Abs. 4 und 5 des Gesetzes betreffend die Gesellschaften mit beschränkter Haftung sind anzuwenden. Wird die Errichtung der Zweigniederlassung in den ersten zwei Jahren nach der Eintragung der Gesellschaft in das Handelsregister ihres Sitzes angemeldet, so sind in die Anmeldung auch die nach § 5 Abs. 4 des Gesetzes betreffend die Gesellschaften mit beschränkter Haftung getroffenen Festsetzungen aufzunehmen, soweit nicht das ausländische Recht Abweichungen nötig macht.

(3) Die Eintragung der Errichtung der Zweigniederlassung hat auch die Angaben nach § 10 Abs. 1 und 2 des Gesetzes betreffend die Gesellschaften mit beschränkter Haftung sowie die in § 13 e Abs. 2 Satz 4 vorgeschriebenen Angaben zu enthalten.

(4) In die Bekanntmachung der Eintragung sind außer deren Inhalt auch die in § 10 Abs. 3 des Gesetzes betreffend die Gesellschaften mit beschränkter Haftung bezeichneten Bestimmungen aufzunehmen, die dort nach § 5 Abs. 4 Satz 1 getroffenen Festsetzungen jedoch nur dann, wenn die Eintragung innerhalb der ersten zwei Jahre nach der Eintragung in das Handelsregister des Sitzes der Gesellschaft erfolgt.

(5) Änderungen des Gesellschaftsvertrages der ausländischen Gesellschaft sind durch die Geschäftsführer zur Eintragung in das Handelsregister anzumelden. Für die Anmeldung gelten die Vorschriften des § 54 Abs. 1 und 2 des Gesetzes betreffend die Gesell-

(2) A publicly certified copy of the articles of association and, to the extent that such articles are not in the German language, a certified translation into German shall be attached to the filing for registration. The provisions of § 8 Subsection 1 No. 2, Subsections 4 and 5 of the Limited Liability Companies Act shall apply. If filing for registration of establishment of a branch is made within the first two years after registration of the company in the Commercial Register of its domicile, the determinations made pursuant to § 5 Subsection 4 of the Limited Liability Companies Act shall be included in the filing, to the extent that foreign law does not necessitate deviations therefrom.

(3) The entry concerning the establishment of a branch shall also contain the information required by § 10 Subsections 1 and 2 of the Limited Liability Companies Act, as well as the information required in § 13 e Subsection 2 sentence 4.

(4) The publication of the entry shall contain, in addition to its contents, the provisions described in § 10 Subsection 3 of the Limited Liability Companies Act; the determinations made pursuant to § 5 Subsection 4 sentence 1 thereof, however, shall only be included if the entry is made within the first two years following registration of the company in the Commercial Register of its domicile.

(5) The general managers shall file to register all amendments to the articles of association of the foreign company in the Commercial Register. To the extent that foreign law does not necessitate deviations therefrom, the provisions of § 54 Subsections 1

schaften mit beschränkter Haftung sinngemäß, soweit nicht das ausländische Recht Abweichungen nötig macht.

(6) Im übrigen gelten die Vorschriften der § 39 Abs. 1, 2 und 4, § 65 Abs. 1 Satz 1, § 67 Abs. 1, 2 und 5, § 74 Abs. 1 Satz 1 des Gesetzes betreffend die Gesellschaften mit beschränkter Haftung sinngemäß, soweit nicht das ausländische Recht Abweichungen nötig macht.

(7) Für die Aufhebung einer Zweigniederlassung gelten die Vorschriften über deren Errichtung sinngemäß.

§ 13 h Verlegung des Sitzes einer Hauptniederlassung im Inland

(1) Wird die Hauptniederlassung eines Einzelkaufmanns oder einer juristischen Person oder der Sitz einer Handelsgesellschaft im Inland verlegt, so ist die Verlegung beim Gericht der bisherigen Hauptniederlassung oder des bisherigen Sitzes anzumelden.

(2) Wird die Hauptniederlassung oder der Sitz aus dem Bezirk des Gerichts der bisherigen Hauptniederlassung oder des bisherigen Sitzes verlegt, so hat dieses unverzüglich von Amts wegen die Verlegung dem Gericht der neuen Hauptniederlassung oder des neuen Sitzes mitzuteilen. Der Mitteilung sind die Eintragungen für die bisherige Hauptniederlassung oder den bisherigen Sitz sowie die bei dem bisher zuständigen Gericht aufbewahrten Urkunden beizufügen. Das Gericht der neuen Hauptniederlassung oder des neuen Sitzes hat zu prüfen, ob die Hauptniederlassung oder der Sitz ordnungsgemäß verlegt und § 30 beachtet ist. Ist dies der Fall, so hat es die Verlegung einzutragen und dabei die ihm

and 2 of the Limited Liability Companies Act shall apply analogously to the filing.

(6) Otherwise, the provisions of § 39 Subsections 1, 2 and 4, § 65 Subsection 1 sentence 1, § 67 Subsections 1, 2 and 5 and § 74 Subsection 1 sentence 1 of the Limited Liability Companies Act apply analogously, to the extent that foreign law does not necessitate deviations therefrom.

(7) The provisions concerning establishment of a branch apply analogously to its dissolution.

§ 13 h Change of domicile of a domestic head office

(1) Where the head office of a sole proprietorship or a juridical person, or the domicile of a commercial company or partnership, is relocated domestically, notification of relocation is to be filed for registration with the court of the previous head office or domicile.

(2) Where the head office or domicile is relocated outside the court district of the previous head office or domicile, this relocation must be communicated immediately by that court to the court of the new head office. The notification must be accompanied by the registrations for the previous head office or domicile, as well as the records filed with the court having jurisdiction hitherto. The court of the new head office or domicile shall determine whether the relocation is valid and § 30 has been complied with. If this is the case, it shall register the relocation and entries of which it has been notified in its Commercial Register without further investigation. Notice of the registration shall be

mitgeteilten Eintragungen ohne weitere Nachprüfung in sein Handelsregister zu übernehmen. Die Eintragung ist dem Gericht der bisherigen Hauptniederlassung oder des bisherigen Sitzes mitzuteilen. Dieses hat die erforderlichen Eintragungen von Amts wegen vorzunehmen.

(3) Wird die Hauptniederlassung oder der Sitz an einen anderen Ort innerhalb des Bezirks des Gerichts der bisherigen Hauptniederlassung oder des bisherigen Sitzes verlegt, so hat das Gericht zu prüfen, ob die Hauptniederlassung oder der Sitz ordnungsgemäß verlegt und § 30 beachtet ist. Ist dies der Fall, so hat es die Verlegung einzutragen.

§ 14 [Festsetzung von Zwangsgeld]

Wer seiner Pflicht zur Anmeldung, zur Zeichnung der Unterschrift oder zur Einreichung von Schriftstücken zum Handelsregister nicht nachkommt, ist hierzu von dem Registergericht durch Festsetzung von Zwangsgeld anzuhalten. Das einzelne Zwangsgeld darf den Betrag von fünftausend Euro nicht übersteigen.

§ 15 [Publizität des Handelsregisters]

(1) Solange eine in das Handelsregister einzutragende Tatsache nicht eingetragen und bekanntgemacht ist, kann sie von demjenigen, in dessen Angelegenheiten sie einzutragen war, einem Dritten nicht entgegengesetzt werden, es sei denn, daß sie diesem bekannt war.

(2) Ist die Tatsache eingetragen und bekanntgemacht worden, so muß ein Dritter sie gegen sich gelten lassen.

given to the court of the previous head office or domicile. This court must make the necessary entries on its own motion.

(3) Where the head office or domicile is relocated to another location within the court district of the previous head office or domicile, the court shall determine whether the relocation is valid and whether § 30 has been complied with. If this is the case, the relocation shall be registered.

§ 14 Setting of coercive fines

Any person who fails to comply with his duty to file for registration, provide specimen signatures or the file documents with the Commercial Register, shall be induced to do so by the registry court by means of a coercive fine. An individual fine may not exceed the amount of five thousand Euro.

§ 15 Publication in the Commercial Register

(1) As long as a fact requiring registration in the Commercial Register is not registered and published, knowledge thereof cannot be asserted against a third party by the one to whom the entry pertains, unless the third party knew of such fact.

(2) Where the fact is registered and published, it may be asserted against a third party. This does not apply to le-

Dies gilt nicht bei Rechtshandlungen, die innerhalb von fünfzehn Tagen nach der Bekanntmachung vorgenommen werden, sofern der Dritte beweist, daß er die Tatsache weder kannte noch kennen mußte.

(3) Ist eine einzutragende Tatsache unrichtig bekanntgemacht, so kann sich ein Dritter demjenigen gegenüber, in dessen Angelegenheiten die Tatsache einzutragen war, auf die bekanntgemachte Tatsache berufen, es sei denn, daß er die Unrichtigkeit kannte.

(4) Für den Geschäftsverkehr mit einer in das Handelsregister eingetragenen Zweigniederlassung ist im Sinne dieser Vorschriften die Eintragung und Bekanntmachung durch das Gericht der Zweigniederlassung entscheidend. Für Zweigniederlassungen von Unternehmen mit Sitz im Inland gilt dies nur für die in § 13 Abs. 6 angeführten Tatsachen.

§ 16 [Entscheidung des Prozeßgerichts]

(1) Ist durch eine rechtskräftige oder vollstreckbare Entscheidung des Prozeßgerichts die Verpflichtung zur Mitwirkung bei einer Anmeldung zum Handelsregister oder ein Rechtsverhältnis, bezüglich dessen eine Eintragung zu erfolgen hat, gegen einen von mehreren bei der Vornahme der Anmeldung Beteiligten festgestellt, so genügt zur Eintragung die Anmeldung der übrigen Beteiligten. Wird die Entscheidung, auf Grund deren die Eintragung erfolgt ist, aufgehoben, so ist dies auf Antrag eines der Beteiligten in das Handelsregister einzutragen.

(2) Ist durch eine rechtskräftige oder vollstreckbare Entscheidung des Pro-

gal transactions effected within fifteen days following publication, where the third party proves he neither knew nor should have known of the fact.

(3) Where the fact was published incorrectly, a third party may claim reliance on the fact as published against the one to whom the entry pertained, unless the third party knew the publication to be incorrect.

(4) With respect to business transacted with a branch registered in the Commercial Register within the meaning of these provisions, filing for registration and publication of such entry by the court of the branch is determinative. With respect to branches of enterprises with a domestic domicile, this applies only to the facts cited in § 13 Subsection 6.

§ 16 Judicial decision

(1) If by a final or enforceable trial court decision the obligation to cooperate in the filing for registration in the Commercial Register, or a legal transaction with reference to which a registration must be effected, is determined as against one of several persons participating in the registration, the filing of the remaining participants is sufficient for registration. If the decision pursuant to which such registration was undertaken is reversed, this fact is to be entered in the Commercial Register upon application by one of the parties concerned.

(2) If registration is prohibited by a final or enforceable trial court decision,

zeßgerichts die Vornahme einer Eintragung für unzulässig erklärt, so darf die Eintragung nicht gegen den Widerspruch desjenigen erfolgen, welcher die Entscheidung erwirkt hat.

Dritter Abschnitt. Handelsfirma

§ 17 [Begriff]

(1) Die Firma eines Kaufmanns ist der Name, unter dem er seine Geschäfte betreibt und die Unterschrift abgibt.

(2) Ein Kaufmann kann unter seiner Firma klagen und verklagt werden.

§ 18 [Firma des Kaufmanns]

(1) Die Firma muß zur Kennzeichnung des Kaufmanns geeignet sein und Unterscheidungskraft besitzen.

(2) Die Firma darf keine Angaben enthalten, die geeignet sind, über geschäftliche Verhältnisse, die für die angesprochenen Verkehrskreise wesentlich sind, irrezuführen. Im Verfahren vor dem Registergericht wird die Eignung zur Irreführung nur berücksichtigt, wenn sie ersichtlich ist.

§ 19 [Bezeichnung der Firma bei Einzelkaufleuten, einer OHG oder KG]

(1) Die Firma muß, auch wenn sie nach den §§ 21, 22, 24 oder nach anderen gesetzlichen Vorschriften fortgeführt wird, enthalten:

1. bei Einzelkaufleuten die Bezeichnung „eingetragener Kaufmann", „eingetragene Kauffrau" oder eine

registration cannot be effected contrary to the objections of the one who obtained the decision.

Part Three. Commercial Firm Name

§ 17 Definition

(1) The firm name (Firma) of a merchant is the name under which he transacts his business and executes his signature.

(2) A merchant may sue and be sued under his firm name.

§ 18 Firm name of the merchant

(1) The firm name shall be suitable to identify the merchant and shall be distinctive.

(2) The firm name may not contain data which is apt to mislead concerning business circumstances which are material for the pertinent business circles. In the proceeding before the registry court the aptness to mislead will only be taken into consideration if it is apparent.

§ 19 Designation of the firm name for sole proprietors, a general commercial partnership or limited partnership

(1) The firm name shall, even if it is continued pursuant to §§ 21, 22, 24 or other legal provisions, contain:

1. In case of sole proprietors, the designation "registered businessman", "registered businesswoman" or a

allgemein verständliche Abkürzung dieser Bezeichnung, insbesondere „e.K.", „e.Kfm." oder „e.Kfr.";

2. bei einer offenen Handelsgesellschaft die Bezeichnung „offene Handelsgesellschaft" oder eine allgemein verständliche Abkürzung dieser Bezeichnung;

3. bei einer Kommanditgesellschaft die Bezeichnung „Kommanditgesellschaft" oder eine allgemein verständliche Abkürzung dieser Bezeichnung.

(2) Wenn in einer offenen Handelsgesellschaft oder Kommanditgesellschaft keine natürliche Person persönlich haftet, muß die Firma, auch wenn sie nach den §§ 21, 22, 24 oder nach anderen gesetzlichen Vorschriften fortgeführt wird, eine Bezeichnung enthalten, welche die Haftungsbeschränkung kennzeichnet.

§ 20 *(aufgehoben)*

§ 21 [Fortführung bei Namensänderung]

Wird ohne eine Änderung der Person der in der Firma enthaltene Name des Geschäftsinhabers oder eines Gesellschafters geändert, so kann die bisherige Firma fortgeführt werden.

§ 22 [Fortführung bei Erwerb des Handelsgeschäfts]

(1) Wer ein bestehendes Handelsgeschäft unter Lebenden oder von Todes wegen erwirbt, darf für das Geschäft die bisherige Firma, auch wenn sie den Namen des bisherigen Geschäftsinhabers enthält, mit oder ohne Beifü-

readily comprehensible abbreviation of this designation, especially "e.K.", "e.Kfm." or "e.Kfr.";

2. in case of a general commercial partnership, the designation "general partnership" or a readily comprehensible abbreviation of this designation;

3. in case of a limited partnership, the designation "limited partnership" or a readily comprehensible abbreviation of this designation.

(2) If no natural person is personally liable in a commercial general partnership or limited partnership, the firm name shall contain a designation indicating the limitation of liability even if the firm name is continued pursuant to §§ 21, 22, 24 or other legal provisions.

§ 20 *(repealed)*

§ 21 Continuation in the event of a name change

Where the name of the business owner or partner whose name is included in the firm name is changed without there being a change in the identity of the person involved, the present firm name may be continued.

§ 22 Continuation in the event of acquisition of the business

(1) One who acquires an existing business "inter vivos" or by inheritance may continue the present firm name (even if it includes the name of the previous business owner) with or without an addition indicating the

gung eines das Nachfolgeverhältnis andeutenden Zusatzes fortführen, wenn der bisherige Geschäftsinhaber oder dessen Erben in die Fortführung der Firma ausdrücklich willigen.

(2) Wird ein Handelsgeschäft auf Grund eines Nießbrauchs, eines Pachtvertrags oder eines ähnlichen Verhältnisses übernommen, so finden diese Vorschriften entsprechende Anwendung.

§ 23 [Veräußerungsverbot]

Die Firma kann nicht ohne das Handelsgeschäft, für welches sie geführt wird, veräußert werden.

§ 24 [Fortführung bei Änderungen im Gesellschafterbestand]

(1) Wird jemand in ein bestehendes Handelsgeschäft als Gesellschafter aufgenommen oder tritt ein neuer Gesellschafter in eine Handelsgesellschaft ein oder scheidet aus einer solchen ein Gesellschafter aus, so kann ungeachtet dieser Veränderung die bisherige Firma fortgeführt werden, auch wenn sie den Namen des bisherigen Geschäftsinhabers oder Namen von Gesellschaftern enthält.

(2) Bei dem Ausscheiden eines Gesellschafters, dessen Name in der Firma enthalten ist, bedarf es zur Fortführung der Firma der ausdrücklichen Einwilligung des Gesellschafters oder seiner Erben.

§ 25 [Haftung des Erwerbers bei Firmenfortführung]

(1) Wer ein unter Lebenden erworbenes Handelsgeschäft unter der bisheri-

successor relationship if the previous business owner or his heirs expressly consent to the continuation of the firm name.

(2) Where a business is assumed on the basis of beneficial use, lease contract or a similar relationship, these provisions apply analogously.

§ 23 Prohibition on transfer

The firm name cannot be transferred separately from the business for which it was used.

§ 24 Continuation in the event of changes within the partnership group

(1) If a person is admitted as a partner in an existing business, a new partner joins a business or a partner retires or withdraws from such business, the present firm name may be continued in spite of this change even if it includes the name of the previous business owner or names of partners.

(2) Where a partner whose name is included within the firm name withdraws, the continued use of the firm name requires the express consent of the partner or his heirs.

§ 25 Liability of the purchaser on continuation

(1) One who carries on a business acquired "inter vivos" under the previ-

gen Firma mit oder ohne Beifügung eines das Nachfolgeverhältnis andeutenden Zusatzes fortführt, haftet für alle im Betriebe des Geschäfts begründeten Verbindlichkeiten des früheren Inhabers. Die in dem Betriebe begründeten Forderungen gelten den Schuldnern gegenüber als auf den Erwerber übergegangen, falls der bisherige Inhaber oder seine Erben in die Fortführung der Firma gewilligt haben.

(2) Eine abweichende Vereinbarung ist einem Dritten gegenüber nur wirksam, wenn sie in das Handelsregister eingetragen und bekanntgemacht oder von dem Erwerber oder dem Veräußerer dem Dritten mitgeteilt worden ist.

(3) Wird die Firma nicht fortgeführt, so haftet der Erwerber eines Handelsgeschäfts für die früheren Geschäftsverbindlichkeiten nur, wenn ein besonderer Verpflichtungsgrund vorliegt, insbesondere wenn die Übernahme der Verbindlichkeiten in handelsüblicher Weise von dem Erwerber bekanntgemacht worden ist.

§ 26 [Verjährung gegen den früheren Inhaber; Fristen]

(1) Ist der Erwerber des Handelsgeschäfts auf Grund der Fortführung der Firma oder auf Grund der in § 25 Abs. 3 bezeichneten Kundmachung für die früheren Geschäftsverbindlichkeiten haftbar, so haftet der frühere Geschäftsinhaber für diese Verbindlichkeiten nur, wenn sie vor Ablauf von fünf Jahren fällig und daraus Ansprüche gegen ihn in einer in § 197 Abs. 1 Nr. 3 bis 5 des Bürgerlichen Gesetzbuchs bezeichneten Art festgestellt sind oder eine gerichtliche oder behördliche Vollstreckungshandlung vorgenommen oder beantragt wird;

ous firm name, with or without an addition revealing the successor relationship, assumes liability for all obligations of the previous owner arising out of his conduct of the business. Where the former owner or his heirs have expressly agreed to continued use of the firm name, claims are deemed, with respect to the debtors thereon, to have been transferred to the purchaser.

(2) Any agreement to the contrary is only effective against third parties if it is registered in the Commercial Register and published, or the third party has been informed thereof by either the purchaser or the seller of the business.

(3) Where use of the firm name is not continued, the purchaser or a business is liable for prior business obligations only if a specific basis for liability exists, in particular if assumption of liability by the purchaser is published by the purchaser in a commercially customary manner.

§ 26 Statute of limitations in respect of the former owner

(1) If the purchaser of the business is liable for earlier business obligations because of continuation of the firm name or because of the declaration specified in § 25 Subsection 3, then the former business owner is liable for such obligations only if they are due before five years have elapsed and claims against him arising therefrom have been determined in a manner specified in § 197 Subsection 1 No. 3 to 5 of the Civil Code or legal or official enforcement action has been undertaken or applied for; in the event of public law obligations, the issuance of

bei öffentlich-rechtlichen Verbindlichkeiten genügt der Erlass eines Verwaltungsakts. Die Frist beginnt im Falle des § 25 Abs. 1 mit dem Ende des Tages, an dem der neue Inhaber der Firma in das Handelsregister des Gerichts der Hauptniederlassung eingetragen wird, im Falle des § 25 Abs. 3 mit dem Ende des Tages, an dem die Übernahme kundgemacht wird. Die für die Verjährung geltenden §§ 204, 206, 210, 211 und 212 Abs. 2 und 3 des Bürgerlichen Gesetzbuches sind entsprechend anzuwenden.

(2) Einer Feststellung in einer in § 197 Abs. 1 Nr. 3 bis 5 des Bürgerlichen Gesetzbuchs bezeichneten Art bedarf es nicht, soweit der frühere Geschäftsinhaber den Anspruch schriftlich anerkannt hat.

§ 27 [Haftung des Erben bei Geschäftsfortführung]

(1) Wird ein zu einem Nachlasse gehörendes Handelsgeschäft von dem Erben fortgeführt, so finden auf die Haftung des Erben für die früheren Geschäftsverbindlichkeiten die Vorschriften des § 25 entsprechende Anwendung.

(2) Die unbeschränkte Haftung nach § 25 Abs. 1 tritt nicht ein, wenn die Fortführung des Geschäfts vor dem Ablaufe von drei Monaten nach dem Zeitpunkt, in welchem der Erbe von dem Anfalle der Erbschaft Kenntnis erlangt hat, eingestellt wird. Auf den Lauf der Frist finden die für die Verjährung geltenden Vorschriften des § 210 des Bürgerlichen Gesetzbuchs entsprechende Anwendung. Ist bei dem Ablaufe der drei Monate das Recht zur Ausschlagung der Erbschaft noch nicht verloren, so endigt die Frist nicht vor dem Ablaufe der Ausschlagungsfrist.

an administrative decision is sufficient. The statute of limitations begins to run in the case of § 25 Subsection 1 with the end of the day on which the new owner of the firm name is registered in the Commercial Register of the court of the main office and in the case of § 25 Subsection 3 it begins with the end of the day on which the takeover is announced. §§ 204, 206, 210, 211 and 212 Subsection 2 and 3 of the Civil Code regarding the statute of limitations apply analogously.

(2) To the extent that the former business owner has recognized the claim in writing, there is no need for determination in a manner specified in § 197 Subsection 1 No. 3 to 5 of the Civil Code.

§ 27 Personal liability of the heirs on continuation

(1) Where a business which is part of an estate is carried on by the heirs, the provisions of § 25 apply analogously as to the liability of the heirs for prior business obligations.

(2) Unlimited liability pursuant to § 25 Subsection 1 does not arise where conduct of the business has been terminated within three months following the date on which the heir acquired knowledge of the inheritance. The provisions of § 210 of the Civil Code concerning the statute of limitations apply analogously to the running of the period. Where the right to reject the inheritance has not expired at the end of the three months, the period does not cease prior to the expiration of the rejection period.

§§ 28, 29 — Handelsstand

§ 28 [Eintritt in das Geschäft eines Einzelkaufmanns]

(1) Tritt jemand als persönlich haftender Gesellschafter oder als Kommanditist in das Geschäft eines Einzelkaufmanns ein, so haftet die Gesellschaft, auch wenn sie die frühere Firma nicht fortführt, für alle im Betriebe des Geschäfts entstandenen Verbindlichkeiten des früheren Geschäftsinhabers. Die in dem Betriebe begründeten Forderungen gelten den Schuldnern gegenüber als auf die Gesellschaft übergegangen.

(2) Eine abweichende Vereinbarung ist einem Dritten gegenüber nur wirksam, wenn sie in das Handelsregister eingetragen und bekanntgemacht oder von einem Gesellschafter dem Dritten mitgeteilt worden ist.

(3) Wird der frühere Geschäftsinhaber Kommanditist und haftet die Gesellschaft für die im Betrieb seines Geschäfts entstandenen Verbindlichkeiten, so ist für die Begrenzung seiner Haftung § 26 entsprechend mit der Maßgabe anzuwenden, daß die in § 26 Abs. 1 bestimmte Frist mit dem Ende des Tages beginnt, an dem die Gesellschaft in das Handelsregister eingetragen wird. Dies gilt auch, wenn er in der Gesellschaft oder einem ihr als Gesellschafter angehörenden Unternehmen geschäftsführend tätig wird. Seine Haftung als Kommanditist bleibt unberührt.

§ 29 [Anmeldung der Firma]

Jeder Kaufmann ist verpflichtet, seine Firma und den Ort seiner Handelsniederlassung bei dem Gericht, in dessen Bezirke sich die Niederlassung befindet, zur Eintragung in das Handelsregister anzumelden; er hat seine Na-

§ 28 Joining a sole proprietorship

(1) Where one joins a sole proprietorship as a general or limited partner, the partnership is liable for all obligations of the former owner arising out of the operation of the business, even where the partnership does not continue to use the former firm name. With respect to debtors, claims resulting from the business of the sole proprietor are deemed to have been transferred to the partnership.

(2) Any agreement to the contrary is only effective against third parties if it is registered in the Commercial Register and published, or the third party has been informed thereof by a partner.

(3) If the former business owner becomes a limited partner and the partnership is liable for obligations arising in the operation of his business, then § 26 shall apply analogously to limit his liability, to the extent that the time period set in § 26 Subsection 1 begins with the end of the day on which the partnership has been registered in the Commercial Register. This applies also if he becomes active in the management of the partnership or of an enterprise belonging to the partnership as shareholder. His liability as limited partner remains unaffected.

§ 29 Registration of firm name

Every merchant is obligated to file to register his firm name and the location of the business in the Commercial Register of the court of the district in which the business is domiciled; he must provide his specimen signature

Handelsfirma §§ 29–31

mensunterschrift unter Angabe der Firma zur Aufbewahrung bei dem Gericht zu zeichnen.

giving the firm name for filing with the court.

§ 30 [Unterscheidbarkeit]

(1) Jede neue Firma muß sich von allen an demselben Ort oder in derselben Gemeinde bereits bestehenden und in das Handelsregister oder in das Genossenschaftsregister eingetragenen Firmen deutlich unterscheiden.

(2) Hat ein Kaufmann mit einem bereits eingetragenen Kaufmanne die gleichen Vornamen und den gleichen Familiennamen und will auch er sich dieser Namen als seiner Firma bedienen, so muß er der Firma einen Zusatz beifügen, durch den sie sich von der bereits eingetragenen Firma deutlich unterscheidet.

(3) Besteht an dem Orte oder in der Gemeinde, wo eine Zweigniederlassung errichtet wird, bereits eine gleiche eingetragene Firma, so muß der Firma für die Zweigniederlassung ein der Vorschrift des Absatzes 2 entsprechender Zusatz beigefügt werden.

(4) Durch die Landesregierungen kann bestimmt werden, daß benachbarte Orte oder Gemeinden als ein Ort oder als eine Gemeinde im Sinne dieser Vorschriften anzusehen sind.

§ 30 Distinctiveness of the firm name

(1) Every new firm name must be clearly distinct from all other firm names already existing and registered in the Commercial Register or the Cooperatives Register in the same location or the same community.

(2) Where a merchant has the same first name and family name as a previously registered merchant and also wishes to utilise this name as his firm name, he must include an addition to the firm name by which it can be distinguished clearly from the firm name already registered.

(3) If the same firm name is already registered in the location or community where a branch is to be established, the firm name of the branch must include an addition pursuant to Subsection 2 above.

(4) State governments may decree that adjacent locations or communities are to be considered as one location within the meaning of these provisions.

§ 31 [Änderung der Firma; Erlöschen]

(1) Eine Änderung der Firma oder ihrer Inhaber sowie die Verlegung der Niederlassung an einen anderen Ort ist nach den Vorschriften des § 29 zur Eintragung in das Handelsregister anzumelden.

(2) Das gleiche gilt, wenn die Firma erlischt. Kann die Anmeldung des Erlö-

§ 31 Change of firm name; termination

(1) Filing for registration in the Commercial Register pursuant to the provisions of § 29 is to be made for a change in the name of the firm or its owner as well as the relocation of the business.

(2) The same applies if the name is terminated. If the filing for registration of

61

schens einer eingetragenen Firma durch die hierzu Verpflichteten nicht auf dem in § 14 bezeichneten Wege herbeigeführt werden, so hat das Gericht das Erlöschen von Amts wegen einzutragen.

§ 32 [Insolvenzverfahren]

(1) Wird über das Vermögen eines Kaufmanns das Insolvenzverfahren eröffnet, so ist dies von Amts wegen in das Handelsregister einzutragen. Das gleiche gilt für

1. die Aufhebung des Eröffnungsbeschlusses,

2. die Bestellung eines vorläufigen Insolvenzverwalters, wenn zusätzlich dem Schuldner ein allgemeines Verfügungsverbot auferlegt oder angeordnet wird, daß Verfügungen des Schuldners nur mit Zustimmung des vorläufigen Insolvenzverwalters wirksam sind, und die Aufhebung einer derartigen Sicherungsmaßnahme,

3. die Anordnung der Eigenverwaltung durch den Schuldner und deren Aufhebung sowie die Anordnung der Zustimmungsbedürftigkeit bestimmter Rechtsgeschäfte des Schuldners,

4. die Einstellung und Aufhebung des Verfahrens und

5. die Überwachung der Erfüllung eines Insolvenzplans und die Aufhebung der Überwachung.

(2) Die Eintragungen werden nicht bekanntgemacht. Die Vorschriften des § 15 sind nicht anzuwenden.

termination of a registered firm name cannot be effected by the person obligated thereto in the manner described by § 14, the court must register the termination on its own motion.

§ 32 Insolvency proceedings

(1) Where insolvency proceedings have been commenced with respect to the assets of a merchant, this must be registered by a court on its own motion in the Commercial Register. The same applies for

1. the cancellation of the court order by which insolvency proceedings have been commenced,

2. the appointment of an interim insolvency administrator if additionally a general restraint on disposition of his assets is imposed on the debtor or it is ordered that dispositions of the debtor are effective only with the consent of the interim insolvency administrator, and the cancellation of such a security measure,

3. the court order of self-administration by the debtor and its cancellation as well as the court order that certain legal transactions of the debtor require consent,

4. the termination or cancellation of the proceedings and

5. the supervision of the fulfilment of an insolvency plan and the cancellation of the supervision.

(2) The registrations will not be published. The provisions of § 15 do not apply.

Handelsfirma §§ 33, 34

§ 33 [Juristische Person]

(1) Eine juristische Person, deren Eintragung in das Handelsregister mit Rücksicht auf den Gegenstand oder auf die Art und den Umfang ihres Gewerbebetriebes zu erfolgen hat, ist von sämtlichen Mitgliedern des Vorstandes zur Eintragung anzumelden.

(2) Der Anmeldung sind die Satzung der juristischen Person und die Urkunden über die Bestellung des Vorstandes in Urschrift oder in öffentlich beglaubigter Abschrift beizufügen; ferner ist anzugeben, welche Vertretungsmacht die Vorstandsmitglieder haben. Bei der Eintragung sind die Firma und der Sitz der juristischen Person, der Gegenstand des Unternehmens, die Mitglieder des Vorstandes und ihre Vertretungsmacht anzugeben. Besondere Bestimmungen der Satzung über die Zeitdauer des Unternehmens sind gleichfalls einzutragen.

(3) Die Errichtung einer Zweigniederlassung ist durch den Vorstand unter Beifügung einer öffentlich beglaubigten Abschrift der Satzung anzumelden.

(4) Für juristische Personen im Sinne von Absatz 1 gilt die Bestimmung des § 37 a entsprechend.

§ 34 [Anmeldung und Eintragung von Änderungen]

(1) Jede Änderung der nach § 33 Abs. 2 Satz 2 und 3 einzutragenden Tatsachen oder der Satzung, die Auflösung der juristischen Person, falls sie nicht die Folge der Eröffnung des Insolvenzverfahrens ist, sowie die Personen der Liquidatoren, ihre Vertretungsmacht,

§ 33 Juridical person

(1) All of the members of the managing board must file for registration of a juridical person if registration in the Commercial Register must be made because of the type and volume of its business.

(2) The articles of association of the juridical person and the originals, or publicly certified copies, of documents concerning the appointment of the managing board are to be attached to the filing for registration; in addition, it shall be specified what authority the members of the managing board have to represent the juridical person. The name and domicile of the juridical person, as well as its business purpose, the members of the managing board an their authority to represent the juridical person are to be submitted at the time of registration. Specific provisions in the articles of association concerning the duration of the company shall likewise be registered.

(3) The establishment of a branch shall be registered by the managing board by a filing containing a publicly certified copy of the articles of association.

(4) For juridical persons within the meaning of Subsection 1, the provision of § 37 a shall apply analogously.

§ 34 Filing and registration of changes

(1) Any change in the facts to be registered pursuant to § 33 Subsection 2 sentences 2 and 3, or to the articles of association or the dissolution of the legal entity, unless it is the result of the commencement of the insolvency proceeding, as well as the identity of

jeder Wechsel der Liquidatoren und jede Änderung ihrer Vertretungsmacht sind zur Eintragung in das Handelsregister anzumelden.

(2) Bei der Eintragung einer Änderung der Satzung genügt, soweit nicht die Änderung die in § 33 Abs. 2 Satz 2 und 3 bezeichneten Angaben betrifft, die Bezugnahme auf die bei dem Gericht eingereichten Urkunden über die Änderung.

(3) Die Anmeldung hat durch den Vorstand oder, sofern die Eintragung erst nach der Anmeldung der ersten Liquidatoren geschehen soll, durch die Liquidatoren zu erfolgen.

(4) Die Eintragung gerichtlich bestellter Vorstandsmitglieder oder Liquidatoren geschieht von Amts wegen.

(5) Im Falle des Insolvenzverfahrens finden die Vorschriften des § 32 Anwendung.

§ 35 [Unterschriftszeichnung]

Die Mitglieder des Vorstandes und die Liquidatoren einer juristischen Person haben ihre Unterschrift zur Aufbewahrung bei dem Gerichte zu zeichnen.

§ 36 *(aufgehoben)*

§ 37 [Unzulässiger Firmengebrauch]

(1) Wer eine nach den Vorschriften dieses Abschnitts ihm nicht zustehende Firma gebraucht, ist von dem

liquidators, their authority to represent the juridical entity, every change of the liquidators and every amendment of their authority to represent the juridical entity shall be filed for registration in the Commercial Register.

(2) For registration of a change in the articles of incorporation it is sufficient, unless the changes outlined in § 33 Subsection 2 sentences 2 and 3 above are concerned, to refer to those documents relating to the changes filed with the court.

(3) The managing board or, if registration is to occur after the registration of the first liquidators, the liquidators, must file for registration of the change.

(4) Registration of court-appointed members of the managing board or liquidators shall be made by the court on its own motion without further filing.

(5) In case of the insolvency proceeding, the provisions of § 32 apply.

§ 35 Specimen signatures

The members of the managing board of a juridical person and the liquidators of such a juridical person must provide their specimen signatures for filing with the court.

§ 36 *(repealed)*

§ 37 Improper use of a firm name

(1) One who uses a firm name to which he is not entitled, pursuant to the provisions of this Part, is to be in-

Registergerichte zur Unterlassung des Gebrauchs der Firma durch Festsetzung von Ordnungsgeld anzuhalten.

(2) Wer in seinen Rechten dadurch verletzt wird, daß ein anderer eine Firma unbefugt gebraucht, kann von diesem die Unterlassung des Gebrauchs der Firma verlangen. Ein nach sonstigen Vorschriften begründeter Anspruch auf Schadensersatz bleibt unberührt.

§ 37 a [Angaben auf Geschäftsbriefen]

(1) Auf allen Geschäftsbriefen des Kaufmanns, die an einen bestimmten Empfänger gerichtet werden, müssen seine Firma, die Bezeichnung nach § 19 Abs. 1 Nr. 1, der Ort seiner Handelsniederlassung, das Registergericht und die Nummer, unter der die Firma in das Handelsregister eingetragen ist, angegeben werden.

(2) Der Angaben nach Absatz 1 bedarf es nicht bei Mitteilungen oder Berichten, die im Rahmen einer bestehenden Geschäftsverbindung ergehen und für die üblicherweise Vordrucke verwendet werden, in denen lediglich die im Einzelfall erforderlichen besonderen Angaben eingefügt zu werden brauchen.

(3) Bestellscheine gelten als Geschäftsbriefe im Sinne des Absatzes 1. Absatz 2 ist auf sie nicht anzuwenden.

(4) Wer seiner Pflicht nach Absatz 1 nicht nachkommt, ist hierzu von dem Registergericht durch Festsetzung von Zwangsgeld anzuhalten. § 14 Satz 2 gilt entsprechend.

duced to desist from using such firm name by imposition of a coercive fine by the registry court.

(2) Any person whose rights have been violated by improper use of his firm name by another can demand that such other person desist from using the firm name. A right to damages pursuant to other provisions remains unaffected.

§ 37 a Information on business letters

(1) All business letters of the merchant directed to a specific addressee shall contain his firm name, the designation pursuant to § 19 Subsection 1 No. 1, the domicile of his business, the registry court and the number under which the firm name is registered in the Commercial Register.

(2) The data pursuant to Subsection 1 need not be included on notifications or reports issued in connection with an existing business relationship and for which it is customary to use printed forms on which only the special details necessary for the individual case have to be inserted.

(3) Order forms are deemed to be business letters within the meaning of Subsection 1. Subsection 2 shall not apply to them.

(4) Whoever does not comply with his duty under Subsection 1 shall be induced to do so by the registry court by imposition of an administrative fine. § 14 sentence 2 shall apply analogously.

Vierter Abschnitt. Handelsbücher

§§ 38–47 b *(aufgehoben)*

Fünfter Abschnitt. Prokura und Handlungsvollmacht

§ 48 [Erteilung der Prokura; Gesamtprokura]

(1) Die Prokura kann nur von dem Inhaber des Handelsgeschäfts oder seinem gesetzlichen Vertreter und nur mittels ausdrücklicher Erklärung erteilt werden.

(2) Die Erteilung kann an mehrere Personen gemeinschaftlich erfolgen (Gesamtprokura).

§ 49 [Umfang der Prokura]

(1) Die Prokura ermächtigt zu allen Arten von gerichtlichen und außergerichtlichen Geschäften und Rechtshandlungen, die der Betrieb eines Handelsgewerbes mit sich bringt.

(2) Zur Veräußerung und Belastung von Grundstücken ist der Prokurist nur ermächtigt, wenn ihm diese Befugnis besonders erteilt ist.

§ 50 [Beschränkung des Umfanges]

(1) Eine Beschränkung des Umfanges der Prokura ist Dritten gegenüber unwirksam.

(2) Dies gilt insbesondere von der Beschränkung, daß die Prokura nur für gewisse Geschäfte oder gewisse Arten von Geschäften oder nur unter gewissen Umständen oder für eine gewisse Zeit oder an einzelnen Orten ausgeübt werden soll.

Part Four. Commercial Records

§§ 38–47 b *(repealed)*

Part Five. General Agency (Prokura) and Commercial Power of Attorney

§ 48 Conferring the general agency (Prokura), joint Prokura

(1) The Prokura can be conferred only by the owner of the business or his legal representative and only by means of an express declaration.

(2) The Prokura can be conferred jointly on several persons (joint Prokura).

§ 49 Scope of the Prokura

(1) The Prokura constitutes authority to enter into every kind of judicial and non-judicial business and legal transaction related to the operation of a commercial business.

(2) The holder of the Prokura is authorized to transfer and encumber real property only where this power has been specifically conferred.

§ 50 Limiting the scope of the Prokura

(1) A limitation on the scope of the Prokura is ineffective as to third parties.

(2) This applies especially to a limitation whereby the Prokura may only be exercised for certain transactions or kinds of transactions, only under certain circumstances, for a limited period of time or at certain specific locations.

(3) Eine Beschränkung der Prokura auf den Betrieb einer von mehreren Niederlassungen des Geschäftsinhabers ist Dritten gegenüber nur wirksam, wenn die Niederlassungen unter verschiedenen Firmen betrieben werden. Eine Verschiedenheit der Firmen im Sinne dieser Vorschrift wird auch dadurch begründet, daß für eine Zweigniederlassung der Firma ein Zusatz beigefügt wird, der sie als Firma der Zweigniederlassung bezeichnet.

(3) A limitation of the Prokura to the operation of one of several branches operated by the business owner is only effective as to third parties if the branches operate under different firm names. A firm name is different within the meaning of this provision where an addition is attached to the firm name which designates it as the firm name of the branch.

§ 51 [Zeichnung des Prokuristen]

Der Prokurist hat in der Weise zu zeichnen, daß er der Firma seinen Namen mit einem die Prokura andeutenden Zusatze beifügt.

§ 51 Signature of the Prokura holder

The holder of the Prokura must sign in such a manner as to add to the firm name his own signature with an addition indicating his Prokura.

§ 52 [Widerruflichkeit; Unübertragbarkeit; Tod des Inhabers]

(1) Die Prokura ist ohne Rücksicht auf das der Erteilung zugrunde liegende Rechtsverhältnis jederzeit widerruflich, unbeschadet des Anspruchs auf die vertragsmäßige Vergütung.

(2) Die Prokura ist nicht übertragbar.

(3) Die Prokura erlischt nicht durch den Tod des Inhabers des Handelsgeschäfts.

§ 52 Revocability; non-transferability; death of the business owner

(1) The Prokura is revocable at any time regardless of the legal relationship underlying the conferral thereof, without prejudice to the right to contractual compensation.

(2) The Prokura is not transferrable.

(3) The Prokura is not terminated upon the death of the commercial business owner.

§ 53 [Anmeldung der Erteilung und des Erlöschens; Zeichnung des Prokuristen]

(1) Die Erteilung der Prokura ist von dem Inhaber des Handelsgeschäfts zur Eintragung in das Handelsregister anzumelden. Ist die Prokura als Gesamtprokura erteilt, so muß auch dies zur Eintragung angemeldet werden.

§ 53 Notice of the conferral of the Prokura and termination thereof; Prokura holder's specimen signature

(1) The owner of the commercial business must file for registration of the conferral of the Prokura in the Commercial Register. Where the Prokura has been conferred as a joint Prokura, this must also be indicated in the registration.

(2) Der Prokurist hat seine Namensunterschrift unter Angabe der Firma und eines die Prokura andeutenden Zusatzes zur Aufbewahrung bei dem Gericht zu zeichnen.

(3) Das Erlöschen der Prokura ist in gleicher Weise wie die Erteilung zur Eintragung anzumelden.

§ 54 [Handlungsvollmacht]

(1) Ist jemand ohne Erteilung der Prokura zum Betrieb eines Handelsgewerbes oder zur Vornahme einer bestimmten zu einem Handelsgewerbe gehörigen Art von Geschäften oder zur Vornahme einzelner zu einem Handelsgewerbe gehöriger Geschäfte ermächtigt, so erstreckt sich die Vollmacht (Handlungsvollmacht) auf alle Geschäfte und Rechtshandlungen, die der Betrieb eines derartigen Handelsgewerbes oder die Vornahme derartiger Geschäfte gewöhnlich mit sich bringt.

(2) Zur Veräußerung oder Belastung von Grundstücken, zur Eingehung von Wechselverbindlichkeiten, zur Aufnahme von Darlehen und zur Prozeßführung ist der Handlungsbevollmächtigte nur ermächtigt, wenn ihm eine solche Befugnis besonders erteilt ist.

(3) Sonstige Beschränkungen der Handlungsvollmacht braucht ein Dritter nur dann gegen sich gelten zu lassen, wenn er sie kannte oder kennen mußte.

§ 55 [Abschlußvertreter]

(1) Die Vorschriften des § 54 finden auch Anwendung auf Handlungsbevollmächtigte, die Handelsvertreter

(2) The Prokura holder must provide his specimen signature giving the firm name with an addition indicating his Prokura for filing with the court.

(3) Termination of the Prokura is to be registered in the same manner as conferral thereof.

§ 54 Commercial power of attorney

(1) Where any person is authorized, without conferral of a Prokura, to operate a commercial business, to undertake a certain kind of transaction relating to a business or to undertake individual transactions relating to a business, this power of attorney (commercial power of attorney) extends to all business and legal transactions which normally relate to the conduct of such business or the undertaking of such transactions.

(2) The holder of a commercial power of attorney is only authorized to transfer or encumber real property, to endorse or accept bills of exchange, to assume loans and conduct litigation if such authority has been specifically conferred on him.

(3) Other limitations of the commercial power of attorney are effective as against a third party only where the third party knew or should have known thereof.

§ 55 Agent authorized to transact business

(1) The provisions of § 54 are also applicable to holders of a commercial power of attorney who are commer-

sind oder die als Handlungsgehilfen damit betraut sind, außerhalb des Betriebes des Prinzipals Geschäfte in dessen Namen abzuschließen.

(2) Die ihnen erteilte Vollmacht zum Abschluß von Geschäften bevollmächtigt sie nicht, abgeschlossene Verträge zu ändern, insbesondere Zahlungsfristen zu gewähren.

(3) Zur Annahme von Zahlungen sind sie nur berechtigt, wenn sie dazu bevollmächtigt sind.

(4) Sie gelten als ermächtigt, die Anzeige von Mängeln einer Ware, die Erklärung, daß eine Ware zur Verfügung gestellt werde, sowie ähnliche Erklärungen, durch die ein Dritter seine Rechte aus mangelhafter Leistung geltend macht oder sie vorbehält, entgegenzunehmen; sie können die dem Unternehmer (Prinzipal) zustehenden Rechte auf Sicherung des Beweises geltend machen.

cial agents or are entrusted as clerical employees with the transaction of business in the principal's name outside the premises of the principal's business.

(2) The power conferred on such persons to transact business does not authorize them to amend existing agreements, especially to extend periods for payment.

(3) Such persons are only authorized to accept payments if they have been specifically granted such power.

(4) Such persons are deemed to be authorized to accept notice of defective goods, statements that goods have been rejected as well as similar statements by which a third party asserts or reserves its rights arising from defective contractual performance; they can assert rights of the business owner (principal) to preserve the evidence.

§ 56 [Angestellte in Laden oder Warenlager]

Wer in einem Laden oder in einem offenen Warenlager angestellt ist, gilt als ermächtigt zu Verkäufen und Empfangnahmen, die in einem derartigen Laden oder Warenlager gewöhnlich geschehen.

§ 56 Sales clerks or warehouse employees

Any person who is employed in a store or warehouse open to the public is deemed to be authorized to sell and receive anything which is customary for such a business or warehouse.

§ 57 [Zeichnung des Handlungsbevollmächtigten]

Der Handlungsbevollmächtigte hat sich bei der Zeichnung jedes eine Prokura andeutenden Zusatzes zu enthalten; er hat mit einem das Vollmachtsverhältnis ausdrückenden Zusatze zu zeichnen.

§ 57 Signature of holder of commercial power of attorney

The holder of a commercial power of attorney must refrain from using with his signature an addition indicating a Prokura. He must sign with an addition which indicates the power of attorney.

§ 58 [Unübertragbarkeit der Handlungsvollmacht]

Der Handlungsbevollmächtigte kann ohne Zustimmung des Inhabers des Handelsgeschäfts seine Handlungsvollmacht auf einen anderen nicht übertragen.

Sechster Abschnitt. Handlungsgehilfen und Handlungslehrlinge

§ 59 [Handlungsgehilfe]

Wer in einem Handelsgewerbe zur Leistung kaufmännischer Dienste gegen Entgelt angestellt ist (Handlungsgehilfe), hat, soweit nicht besondere Vereinbarungen über die Art und den Umfang seiner Dienstleistungen oder über die ihm zukommende Vergütung getroffen sind, die dem Ortsgebrauch entsprechenden Dienste zu leisten sowie die dem Ortsgebrauch entsprechende Vergütung zu beanspruchen. In Ermangelung eines Ortsgebrauchs gelten die den Umständen nach angemessenen Leistungen als vereinbart.

§ 60 [Gesetzliches Wettbewerbsverbot]

(1) Der Handlungsgehilfe darf ohne Einwilligung des Prinzipals weder ein Handelsgewerbe betreiben noch in dem Handelszweige des Prinzipals für eigene oder fremde Rechnung Geschäfte machen.

(2) Die Einwilligung zum Betrieb eines Handelsgewerbes gilt als erteilt, wenn dem Prinzipal bei der Anstellung des Gehilfen bekannt ist, daß er das Gewerbe betreibt, und der Prinzipal die Aufgabe des Betriebs nicht ausdrücklich vereinbart.

§ 58 Non-transferability of the commercial power of attorney

The holder of a commercial power of attorney may not transfer his commercial power of attorney to another without the business owner's consent.

Part Six. Clerical Employees and Apprentices

§ 59 Clerical employees

One who is employed in a business for the performance of business services in return for compensation (clerical employee) shall, unless special agreements have been made with respect to the type and scope of his duties or the compensation due, perform such services as are in accordance with local custom and have a right to compensation in accordance with local custom. In the absence of local custom, the parties will be deemed to have agreed to services reasonable under the circumstances.

§ 60 Statutory prohibition of competition

(1) Without the principal's consent, the clerical employee may neither carry on a business venture on his own nor undertake transactions in the field of the principal's trade, for his own account or that of another person.

(2) The principal shall be deemed to have consented to the operation of the business venture if the principal had knowledge of such business at the time of hiring the clerical employee and did not expressly agree to the cessation thereof.

§ 61 [Verletzung des Wettbewerbsverbots]

(1) Verletzt der Handlungsgehilfe die ihm nach § 60 obliegende Verpflichtung, so kann der Prinzipal Schadensersatz fordern; er kann statt dessen verlangen, daß der Handlungsgehilfe die für eigene Rechnung gemachten Geschäfte als für Rechnung des Prinzipals eingegangen gelten lasse und die aus Geschäften für fremde Rechnung bezogene Vergütung herausgebe oder seinen Anspruch auf die Vergütung abtrete.

(2) Die Ansprüche verjähren in drei Monaten von dem Zeitpunkt an, in welchem der Prinzipal Kenntnis von dem Abschlusse des Geschäfts erlangt; sie verjähren ohne Rücksicht auf diese Kenntnis in fünf Jahren von dem Abschlusse des Geschäfts an.

§ 62 [Fürsorgepflicht des Arbeitgebers][1]

(1) Der Prinzipal ist verpflichtet, die Geschäftsräume und die für den Geschäftsbetrieb bestimmten Vorrichtungen und Gerätschaften so einzurichten und zu unterhalten, auch den Geschäftsbetrieb und die Arbeitszeit so zu regeln, daß der Handlungsgehilfe gegen eine Gefährdung seiner Gesundheit, soweit die Natur des Betriebs es gestattet, geschützt und die Aufrechterhaltung der guten Sitten und des Anstandes gesichert ist.

(2) Ist der Handlungsgehilfe in die häusliche Gemeinschaft aufgenommen, so hat der Prinzipal in Ansehung des Wohn- und Schlafraums, der Ver-

---

§ 61 Violation of prohibition of competition

(1) Where the clerical employee violates his duty pursuant to § 60, the principal may assert a claim for damages; alternatively, he may demand that transactions made for the clerical employee's own account be deemed to be made for the principal's account and that the employee either turn over compensation received from transactions for the account of third parties or assign his rights to such compensation.

(2) The statute of limitation for claims is three months from the time the principal acquires knowledge of the conclusion of the transaction. Regardless of knowledge, the period of limitation is five years from the date of the transaction.

§ 62 Employer's duty to provide for the welfare of the employees[1]

(1) The principal is obligated to equip and maintain the business premises and the specific devices and equipment used in the business, and to regulate the business operation and daily working hours, so that the clerical employee is protected against any danger to his health, insofar as the nature of the operation permits, and so that the maintenance of good morals and decency is assured.

(2) Where the clerical employee is accommodated in the principal's household, the principal shall, with respect to living and sleeping quarters and

---

1 § 62 Abs. 2 bis 4 ist für das Gebiet der ehemaligen DDR nicht anzuwenden (Einigungsvertrag vom 31. 8. 1990, BGBl. II S. 889, 959, 1020).

1 § 62 Subsection 2 through 4 is not applicable in the territory of the former G.D.R. (Unification Treaty of August 31, 1990, BGBl. II p. 889, 959, 1020).

pflegung sowie der Arbeits- und Erholungszeit diejenigen Einrichtungen und Anordnungen zu treffen, welche mit Rücksicht auf die Gesundheit, die Sittlichkeit und die Religion des Handlungsgehilfen erforderlich sind.

(3) Erfüllt der Prinzipal die ihm in Ansehung des Lebens und der Gesundheit des Handlungsgehilfen obliegenden Verpflichtungen nicht, so finden auf seine Verpflichtung zum Schadensersatze die für unerlaubte Handlungen geltenden Vorschriften der §§ 842 bis 846 des Bürgerlichen Gesetzbuchs entsprechende Anwendung.

(4) Die dem Prinzipal hiernach obliegenden Verpflichtungen können nicht im voraus durch Vertrag aufgehoben oder beschränkt werden.

§ 63 *(aufgehoben)*

§ 64 [Gehaltszahlung]¹

Die Zahlung des dem Handlungsgehilfen zukommenden Gehalts hat am Schlusse jedes Monats zu erfolgen. Eine Vereinbarung, nach der die Zahlung des Gehalts später erfolgen soll, ist nichtig.

§ 65 [Provision]

Ist bedungen, daß der Handlungsgehilfe für Geschäfte, die von ihm geschlossen oder vermittelt werden, Provision erhalten solle, so sind die für die Handelsvertreter geltenden Vorschriften des § 87 Abs. 1 und 3 sowie der §§ 87 a bis 87 c anzuwenden.

---

1 § 64 ist für das Gebiet der ehemaligen DDR nicht anzuwenden (Einigungsvertrag vom 31. 8. 1990, BGBl. II S. 889, 959, 1020).

board, as well as working and leisure time, maintain arrangements and regulations which are necessary with regard to the health, morals and religious beliefs of the clerical employee.

(3) Where the principal does not fulfil his obligations with regard to the life and health of the clerical employee, the tort provisions of §§ 842 through 846 of the Civil Code apply analogously with regard to his liability for damages.

(4) The obligations of the principal hereunder cannot be contractually waived or limited in advance.

§ 63 *(repealed)*

§ 64 Payment of salary¹

Payment of the salary due the clerical employee shall be made at the end of every month. Any agreement pursuant to which payment of salary is to be made later is void.

§ 65 Commission

Where it is provided that the clerical employee shall receive commissions for transactions concluded or arranged by him, the provisions of § 87 Subsections 1 and 3 as well as §§ 87 a through 87 c, applicable to commercial agents, shall apply.

---

1 § 64 is not applicable in the territory of the former G.D.R. (Unification Treaty of August 31, 1990, BGBl. II p. 889, 959, 1020).

§§ 66–72 *(aufgehoben)*

§§ 66–72 *(repealed)*

§ 73 [Anspruch auf Zeugnis]¹

Bei der Beendigung des Dienstverhältnisses kann der Handlungsgehilfe ein schriftliches Zeugnis über die Art und Dauer der Beschäftigung fordern. Das Zeugnis ist auf Verlangen des Handlungsgehilfen auch auf die Führung und die Leistungen auszudehnen. Die Erteilung des Zeugnisses in elektronischer Form ist ausgeschlossen.

§ 73 Right to a reference¹

Upon termination of the employment relationship, the clerical employee may demand a written reference pertaining to the type and duration of employment. The employment reference shall, at the employee's request, extend to matters of conduct and services. The provision of the reference in electronic form is excluded.

§ 74 [Vertragliches Wettbewerbsverbot; bezahlte Karenz]

(1) Eine Vereinbarung zwischen dem Prinzipal und dem Handlungsgehilfen, die den Gehilfen für die Zeit nach Beendigung des Dienstverhältnisses in seiner gewerblichen Tätigkeit beschränkt (Wettbewerbsverbot), bedarf der Schriftform und der Aushändigung einer vom Prinzipal unterzeichneten, die vereinbarten Bestimmungen enthaltenden Urkunde an den Gehilfen.

(2) Das Wettbewerbsverbot ist nur verbindlich, wenn sich der Prinzipal verpflichtet, für die Dauer des Verbots eine Entschädigung zu zahlen, die für jedes Jahr des Verbots mindestens die Hälfte der von dem Handlungsgehilfen zuletzt bezogenen vertragsmäßigen Leistungen erreicht.

§ 74 Contractual prohibition of competition; paid abstention period

(1) An agreement between the principal and the clerical employee which limits the clerical employee in his business activity (prohibition of competition) for the period following termination of the employment relationship must be in writing, and a copy of the document signed by the principal and containing the agreed conditions must be provided to the clerical employee.

(2) The prohibition of competition is only binding where the principal is obligated, for the term of the prohibition, to pay annual compensation equal to at least one-half of the most recent contractual remuneration received by the clerical employee.

---

1 § 73 ist aufgehoben mit Wirkung ab 1.1.2003 durch Gesetz vom 24.8.2002, BGBl. I S. 3412.

1 § 73 is repealed effective January 1, 2003 by Act dated August 24, 2002, Federal Gazette I, page 3412.

§ 74 a [Unverbindliches oder nichtiges Verbot]

(1) Das Wettbewerbsverbot ist insoweit unverbindlich, als es nicht zum Schutze eines berechtigten geschäftlichen Interesses des Prinzipals dient. Es ist ferner unverbindlich, soweit es unter Berücksichtigung der gewährten Entschädigung nach Ort, Zeit oder Gegenstand eine unbillige Erschwerung des Fortkommens des Gehilfen enthält. Das Verbot kann nicht auf einen Zeitraum von mehr als zwei Jahren von der Beendigung des Dienstverhältnisses an erstreckt werden.

(2) Das Verbot ist nichtig, wenn der Gehilfe zur Zeit des Abschlusses minderjährig ist oder wenn sich der Prinzipal die Erfüllung auf Ehrenwort oder unter ähnlichen Versicherungen versprechen läßt. Nichtig ist auch die Vereinbarung, durch die ein Dritter an Stelle des Gehilfen die Verpflichtung übernimmt, daß sich der Gehilfe nach der Beendigung des Dienstverhältnisses in seiner gewerblichen Tätigkeit beschränken werde.

(3) Unberührt bleiben die Vorschriften des § 138 des Bürgerlichen Gesetzbuchs über die Nichtigkeit von Rechtsgeschäften, die gegen die guten Sitten verstoßen.

§ 74 b [Zahlung und Berechnung der Entschädigung]

(1) Die nach § 74 Abs. 2 dem Handlungsgehilfen zu gewährende Entschädigung ist am Schlusse jedes Monats zu zahlen.

(2) Soweit die dem Gehilfen zustehenden vertragsmäßigen Leistungen in einer Provision oder in anderen wechselnden Bezügen bestehen, sind sie bei der Berechnung der Entschädigung

§ 74 a Non-binding or void prohibition of competition

(1) The prohibition of competition is non-binding insofar as it does not serve to protect a legitimate business interest of the principal. Furthermore, it is non-binding insofar as, with respect to the compensation allowed, the place, time or subject matter, it constitutes an unreasonable interference with the clerical employee's career. The prohibition cannot extend beyond a period of two years following the end of the employment relationship.

(2) The prohibition is void, if the clerical employee is a minor at the time the contract was concluded or if the principal causes the clerical employee to give his word of honour or a similar assurance. The agreement by which a third party, in lieu of the clerical employee, assumes the obligation to ensure that the clerical employee will restrict his professional activity following the end of the employment relationship, is also void.

(3) The provisions of § 138 of the Civil Code with regard to the nullity of legal acts contrary to public policy remain unaffected.

§ 74 b Payment and calculation of compensation

(1) Compensation guaranteed to the clerical employee pursuant to § 74 Subsection 2 is to be paid at the end of every month.

(2) Insofar as the contractual remuneration due the clerical employee is based upon a commission or other variable payment, the average of such remuneration received over the last

nach dem Durchschnitt der letzten drei Jahre in Ansatz zu bringen. Hat die für die Bezüge bei der Beendigung des Dienstverhältnisses maßgebende Vertragsbestimmung noch nicht drei Jahre bestanden, so erfolgt der Ansatz nach dem Durchschnitt des Zeitraums, für den die Bestimmung in Kraft war.

(3) Soweit Bezüge zum Ersatze besonderer Auslagen dienen sollen, die infolge der Dienstleistung entstehen, bleiben sie außer Ansatz.

§ 74 c [Anrechnung anderweitigen Erwerbs]

(1) Der Handlungsgehilfe muß sich auf die fällige Entschädigung anrechnen lassen, was er während des Zeitraums, für den die Entschädigung gezahlt wird, durch anderweite Verwertung seiner Arbeitskraft erwirbt oder zu erwerben böswillig unterläßt, soweit die Entschädigung unter Hinzurechnung dieses Betrags den Betrag der zuletzt von ihm bezogenen vertragsmäßigen Leistungen um mehr als ein Zehntel übersteigen würde. Ist der Gehilfe durch das Wettbewerbsverbot gezwungen worden, seinen Wohnsitz zu verlegen, so tritt an die Stelle des Betrags von einem Zehntel der Betrag von einem Viertel. Für die Dauer der Verbüßung einer Freiheitsstrafe kann der Gehilfe eine Entschädigung nicht verlangen.

(2) Der Gehilfe ist verpflichtet, dem Prinzipal auf Erfordern über die Höhe seines Erwerbes Auskunft zu erteilen.

three years is to be used to calculate the compensation due the employee. Where the applicable provision of the contract with respect to such amounts has not been in force three years at the end of the employment relationship, the estimate of the compensation amount is to be made by averaging the contractual remuneration paid during the period for which the provision was in force.

(3) Insofar as certain amounts were intended to compensate for specific expenses arising in connection with the employment performance, they are not to be included in the estimate.

§ 74 c Deduction of other earnings

(1) The clerical employee must allow all amounts that he earns through employment elsewhere (or maliciously fails to earn) during the period for which compensation is to be paid to be deducted from the compensation due, insofar as the compensation plus this amount would exceed by more than ten percent the contractual remuneration last received by him. Where the clerical employee has been compelled by the prohibition of competition to change his residence, the foregoing amount of ten percent shall be replaced by twenty-five percent. The clerical employee may not claim compensation for any period in which he is imprisoned.

(2) The clerical employee is obligated, on demand, to give information to the principal concerning the amount of his earnings.

§ 75 [Unwirksamwerden des Wettbewerbsverbots]

(1) Löst der Gehilfe das Dienstverhältnis gemäß den Vorschriften der §§ 70 und 71[1] wegen vertragswidrigen Verhaltens des Prinzipals auf, so wird das Wettbewerbsverbot unwirksam, wenn der Gehilfe vor Ablauf eines Monats nach der Kündigung schriftlich erklärt, daß er sich an die Vereinbarung nicht gebunden erachte.

(2) In gleicher Weise wird das Wettbewerbsverbot unwirksam, wenn der Prinzipal das Dienstverhältnis kündigt, es sei denn, daß für die Kündigung ein erheblicher Anlaß in der Person des Gehilfen vorliegt oder daß sich der Prinzipal bei der Kündigung bereit erklärt, während der Dauer der Beschränkung dem Gehilfen die vollen zuletzt von ihm bezogenen vertragsmäßigen Leistungen zu gewähren. Im letzteren Falle finden die Vorschriften des § 74 b entsprechende Anwendung.

(3) ²Löst der Prinzipal das Dienstverhältnis gemäß den Vorschriften der §§ 70 und 72 wegen vertragswidrigen Verhaltens des Gehilfen auf, so hat der Gehilfe keinen Anspruch auf die Entschädigung.

§ 75 Invalidity of the prohibition of competition

(1) Where the clerical employee terminates the employment relationship pursuant to the provisions of §§ 70 and 71[1] because of breach of contract by the principal, the prohibition of competition will be invalid if the employee declares in writing within one month following the termination of employment that he does not consider himself bound by the agreement.

(2) The prohibition of competition will similarly be invalid if the principal terminates the employment relationship, unless a significant cause relating to the person of the clerical employee exists for the termination or the principal declares, upon giving notice, that he will pay to the clerical employee the full contractual remuneration last earned by him for the term of the prohibition of competition. In the latter case the provisions of § 74 b apply analogously.

(3) ²Where the principal dissolves the employment relationship pursuant to the provisions of §§ 70 and 72 due to breach of contract by the clerical employee, the clerical employee shall have no right to compensation.

---

1 Die §§ 70 und 71 sind seit 1969 aufgehoben; die außerordentliche Kündigung ist jetzt in § 626 BGB geregelt.

2 § 75 Abs. 3 ist nichtig; das Bundesarbeitsgericht hat die Vorschrift mit Urteil vom 23. 7. 1977 (BAGE 22, 215) für verfassungswidrig erklärt. Für das Gebiet der ehemaligen DDR ist § 75 Abs. 3 daher auch nicht anzuwenden (Einigungsvertrag vom 31. 8. 1990, BGBl. II S. 889, 959, 1020).

1 § 70 and 71 have been repealed since 1969; the extraordinary notice of termination is now regulated in § 626 Civil Code.

2 § 75 Subsection 3 is void; the Federal Labor Court declared the provision to be unconstitutional by decision dated July 23, 1977 (BAGE 22,215). § 75 Subsection 3 is, therefore, also not applicable in the territory of the former German Democratic Republic (DDR) (Unification Treaty (Einigungsvertrag) dated August 31, 1990 BGBl. II, page 889, 959, 1020).

§ 75 a [Verzicht des Prinzipals auf Wettbewerbsverbot]

Der Prinzipal kann vor der Beendigung des Dienstverhältnisses durch schriftliche Erklärung auf das Wettbewerbsverbot mit der Wirkung verzichten, daß er mit dem Ablauf eines Jahres seit der Erklärung von der Verpflichtung zur Zahlung der Entschädigung frei wird.

§ 75 b *(aufgehoben)*

§ 75 c [Vertragsstrafe]

(1) Hat der Handlungsgehilfe für den Fall, daß er die in der Vereinbarung übernommene Verpflichtung nicht erfüllt, eine Strafe versprochen, so kann der Prinzipal Ansprüche nur nach Maßgabe der Vorschriften des § 340 des Bürgerlichen Gesetzbuchs geltend machen. Die Vorschriften des Bürgerlichen Gesetzbuchs über die Herabsetzung einer unverhältnismäßig hohen Vertragsstrafe bleiben unberührt.

(2) Ist die Verbindlichkeit der Vereinbarung nicht davon abhängig, daß sich der Prinzipal zur Zahlung einer Entschädigung an den Gehilfen verpflichtet, so kann der Prinzipal, wenn sich der Gehilfe einer Vertragsstrafe der in Absatz 1 bezeichneten Art unterworfen hat, nur die verwirkte Strafe verlangen; der Anspruch auf Erfüllung oder auf Ersatz eines weiteren Schadens ist ausgeschlossen.

§ 75 d [Abweichende Vereinbarungen]

Auf eine Vereinbarung, durch die von den Vorschriften der §§ 74 bis 75 c zum Nachteil des Handlungsgehilfen

§ 75 a The principal's waiver of the prohibition of competition

The principal may effectively waive, by means of a written statement, the prohibition of competition prior to expiration of the employment relationship. In such a case, the principal will, beginning one year after the date of the declaration, be free of the obligation to pay compensation.

§ 75 b *(repealed)*

§ 75 c Contract penalty

(1) Where the clerical employee is subject to a penalty in the event of non-fulfilment of his contractual obligation, the principal can assert claims only pursuant to the provisions of § 340 of the Civil Code. The provisions of the Civil Code with regard to reduction of a disproportionate contractual penalty remain unaffected.

(2) Where the contractual obligation does not depend on the principal's obligation to pay compensation to the clerical employee, the principal can, if the clerical employee is subject to a contractual penalty of the kind outlined in Subsection 1, only assert the penalty forfeited by the employee; the right to specific performance or compensation for additional damages is prohibited.

§ 75 d Deviating agreements

The principal cannot, to the prejudice of the clerical employee, assert rights resulting from an agreement which

§§ 75d–h   Handelsstand

abgewichen wird, kann sich der Prinzipal nicht berufen. Das gilt auch von Vereinbarungen, die bezwecken, die gesetzlichen Vorschriften über das Mindestmaß der Entschädigung durch Verrechnungen oder auf sonstige Weise zu umgehen.

deviates from the provisions of §§ 74 through 75 c. This also applies to agreements intended, by means of set-off or other methods, to circumvent legal provisions concerning the minimum compensation.

§ 75 e *(aufgehoben)*

§ 75 e *(repealed)*

§ 75 f [Sperrabrede unter Arbeitgebern]

§ 75 f Close-out agreements

Im Falle einer Vereinbarung, durch die sich ein Prinzipal einem anderen Prinzipal gegenüber verpflichtet, einen Handlungsgehilfen, der bei diesem im Dienst ist oder gewesen ist, nicht oder nur unter bestimmten Voraussetzungen anzustellen, steht beiden Teilen der Rücktritt frei. Aus der Vereinbarung findet weder Klage noch Einrede statt.

In the event of an agreement by which a principal obligates himself to another principal not to employ a clerical employee who has been employed by the latter, or to employ him only under specific conditions, both parties are free to rescind the agreement. Neither a cause of action nor a defense is created by the agreement.

§ 75 g [Vermittlungsgehilfe]

§ 75 g Clerical employee capable of soliciting for the principal

§ 55 Abs. 4 gilt auch für einen Handlungsgehilfen, der damit betraut ist, außerhalb des Betriebes des Prinzipals für diesen Geschäfte zu vermitteln. Eine Beschränkung dieser Rechte braucht ein Dritter gegen sich nur gelten zu lassen, wenn er sie kannte oder kennen mußte.

§ 55 Subsection 4 also applies to a clerical employee entrusted to solicit business for the principal as an agent outside the premises of the principal's place of business. Limitations of this authority are deemed to be valid against a third party only where the third party knew or should have known thereof.

§ 75 h [Unkenntnis des Mangels der Vertretungsmacht]

§ 75 h Ignorance as to the absence of agency relationship

(1) Hat ein Handlungsgehilfe, der nur mit der Vermittlung von Geschäften außerhalb des Betriebes des Prinzipals betraut ist, ein Geschäft im Namen

(1) Where a clerical employee only authorized to solicit business outside the premises of the principal's place of business has concluded a transaction

des Prinzipals abgeschlossen, und war dem Dritten der Mangel der Vertretungsmacht nicht bekannt, so gilt das Geschäft als von dem Prinzipal genehmigt, wenn dieser dem Dritten gegenüber nicht unverzüglich das Geschäft ablehnt, nachdem er von dem Handlungsgehilfen oder dem Dritten über Abschluß und wesentlichen Inhalt benachrichtigt worden ist.

(2) Das gleiche gilt, wenn ein Handlungsgehilfe, der mit dem Abschluß von Geschäften betraut ist, ein Geschäft im Namen des Prinzipals abgeschlossen hat, zu dessen Abschluß er nicht bevollmächtigt ist.

§§ 76–82 *(aufgehoben)*

§ 82 a [Wettbewerbsverbot des Volontärs]¹

Auf Wettbewerbsverbote gegenüber Personen, die, ohne als Lehrlinge angenommen zu sein, zum Zwecke ihrer Ausbildung unentgeltlich mit kaufmännischen Diensten beschäftigt werden (Volontäre), finden die für Handlungsgehilfen geltenden Vorschriften insoweit Anwendung, als sie nicht auf das dem Gehilfen zustehende Entgelt Bezug nehmen.

in the principal's name, and the third party did not know of this lack of authority, the ransaction will be regarded as ratified by the principal if he fails to repudiate it without undue delay after he has been informed by the clerical employee or the third party of the conclusion of the agreement and its material terms.

(2) The same applies where a clerical employee authorized to enter into business transactions has concluded in the principal's name a transaction which he is not authorized to conclude.

§§ 76–82 *(repealed)*

§ 82 a Prohibition of competition of unpaid trainees[1]

With regard to prohibition of competition with respect to persons employed gratuitously – without being employed as apprentices – for the purpose of their vocational training (unpaid trainees), the provisions pertaining to clerical employees apply insofar as they do not relate to remuneration due the clerical employee.

---

1 § 82 a ist gegenstandslos, vgl. §§ 5, 19 Berufsbildungsgesetz. Für das Gebiet der ehemaligen DDR ist § 82 a daher auch nicht anzuwenden (Einigungsvertrag vom 31. 8. 1990, BGBl. II S. 889, 959, 1020).

1 § 82 a is obsolete, compare §§ 5, 19 Vocational Education Act (*Berufsbildungsgesetz*). § 82 a is, therefore, also not applicable to the territory of the former German Democratic Republic (DDR) (Unification Treaty (*Einigungsvertrag*) dated August 31, 1990, BGBl. II, page 889, 959, 1020).

§ 83 [Andere Arbeitnehmer][1]

Hinsichtlich der Personen, welche in dem Betrieb eines Handelsgewerbes andere als kaufmännische Dienste leisten, bewendet es bei den für das Arbeitsverhältnis dieser Personen geltenden Vorschriften.

Siebenter Abschnitt. Handelsvertreter

§ 84 [Begriff des Handelsvertreters]

(1) Handelsvertreter ist, wer als selbständiger Gewerbetreibender ständig damit betraut ist, für einen anderen Unternehmer (Unternehmer) Geschäfte zu vermitteln oder in dessen Namen abzuschließen. Selbständig ist, wer im wesentlichen frei seine Tätigkeit gestalten und seine Arbeitszeit bestimmen kann.

(2) Wer, ohne selbständig im Sinne des Absatzes 1 zu sein, ständig damit betraut ist, für einen Unternehmer Geschäfte zu vermitteln oder in dessen Namen abzuschließen, gilt als Angestellter.

(3) Der Unternehmer kann auch ein Handelsvertreter sein.

(4) Die Vorschriften dieses Abschnittes finden auch Anwendung, wenn das Unternehmen des Handelsvertreters nach Art oder Umfang einen in kaufmännischer Weise eingerichteten Geschäftsbetrieb nicht erfordert.

§ 83 Other employees[1]

With regard to persons who in the operation of a commercial enterprise perform services other than commercial services, the rules applicable to the employment relationships of such persons apply.

Part Seven. Commercial Agents

§ 84 Definition of commercial agent

(1) A commercial agent is one who, as an independent person engaged in business, is regularly authorized to solicit business for another entrepreneur (the "principal") or to enter into transactions in his name. A person is independent if he is essentially free to structure his activity and determine his hours of work.

(2) Any person who, without being independent within the meaning of Subsection 1, is regularly authorized to solicit business for a principal or to enter into transactions in his name, is deemed to be an employee.

(3) The principal can also be a commercial agent.

(4) The provisions of this part also apply if the business of the commercial agent by type and volume does not require a commercially organized business operation.

---

[1] § 83 ist für das Gebiet der ehemaligen DDR nicht anzuwenden (Einigungsvertrag vom 31. 8. 1990, BGBl. II S. 889, 959, 1020).

[1] § 83 is not applicable in the territory of the former G.D.R. (Unification Treaty of August 31, 1990, BGBl. II p. 889, 959, 1020).

§ 85 [Vertragsurkunde]

Jeder Teil kann verlangen, daß der Inhalt des Vertrages sowie spätere Vereinbarungen zu dem Vertrag in eine vom anderen Teil unterzeichnete Urkunde aufgenommen werden. Dieser Anspruch kann nicht ausgeschlossen werden.

§ 86 [Pflichten des Handelsvertreters]

(1) Der Handelsvertreter hat sich um die Vermittlung oder den Abschluß von Geschäften zu bemühen; er hat hierbei das Interesse des Unternehmers wahrzunehmen.

(2) Er hat dem Unternehmer die erforderlichen Nachrichten zu geben, namentlich ihm von jeder Geschäftsvermittlung und von jedem Geschäftsabschluß unverzüglich Mitteilung zu machen.

(3) Er hat seine Pflichten mit der Sorgfalt eines ordentlichen Kaufmanns wahrzunehmen.

(4) Von den Absätzen 1 und 2 abweichende Vereinbarungen sind unwirksam.

§ 86 a [Pflichten des Unternehmers]

(1) Der Unternehmer hat dem Handelsvertreter die zur Ausübung seiner Tätigkeit erforderlichen Unterlagen, wie Muster, Zeichnungen, Preislisten, Werbedrucksachen, Geschäftsbedingungen, zur Verfügung zu stellen.

(2) Der Unternehmer hat dem Handelsvertreter die erforderlichen Nachrichten zu geben. Er hat ihm unverzüglich die Annahme oder Ablehnung eines vom Handelsvertreter vermittelten oder ohne Vertretungsmacht

§ 85 Contract documents

Either party can demand that the terms of the contract, as well as any subsequent amendment thereof, be set out in a document signed by the other party. This right may not be excluded.

§ 86 Duties of the commercial agent

(1) The commercial agent is obligated to make efforts toward the solicitation or conclusion of business transactions. In connection herewith he must act in the interest of the principal.

(2) He shall give the principal all necessary information, i. e. inform him immediately of every solicitation and conclusion of every transaction.

(3) He must fulfil his duties with the care of a prudent merchant.

(4) Any agreement contrary to Subsections 1 and 2 hereof is void.

§ 86 a Principal's duties

(1) The principal shall provide the commercial agent with all materials which are necessary for the performance of his duties, such as samples, drawings, price lists, advertising material and terms and conditions of business.

(2) The principal shall keep the commercial agent generally informed. In particular, he shall inform him promptly of the acceptance or rejection of a transaction solicited by the agent or a transaction concluded by

abgeschlossenen Geschäfts und die Nichtausführung eines von ihm vermittelten oder abgeschlossenen Geschäfts mitzuteilen. Er hat ihn unverzüglich zu unterrichten, wenn er Geschäfte voraussichtlich nur in erheblich geringerem Umfange abschließen kann oder will, als der Handelsvertreter unter gewöhnlichen Umständen erwarten konnte.

(3) Von den Absätzen 1 und 2 abweichende Vereinbarungen sind unwirksam.

§ 86 b [Delkredereprovision]

(1) Verpflichtet sich ein Handelsvertreter, für die Erfüllung der Verbindlichkeit aus einem Geschäft einzustehen, so kann er eine besondere Vergütung (Delkredereprovision) beanspruchen; der Anspruch kann im voraus nicht ausgeschlossen werden. Die Verpflichtung kann nur für ein bestimmtes Geschäft oder für solche Geschäfte mit bestimmten Dritten übernommen werden, die der Handelsvertreter vermittelt oder abschließt. Die Übernahme bedarf der Schriftform.

(2) Der Anspruch auf die Delkredereprovision entsteht mit dem Abschluß des Geschäfts.

(3) Absatz 1 gilt nicht, wenn der Unternehmer oder der Dritte seine Niederlassung oder beim Fehlen einer solchen seinen Wohnsitz im Ausland hat. Er gilt ferner nicht für Geschäfte, zu deren Abschluß und Ausführung der Handelsvertreter unbeschränkt bevollmächtigt ist.

the agent without authority, and of the non-completion of a transaction solicited or concluded by him. He shall inform him promptly if he (the principal) desires, or will likely be able to, conclude transactions only on a significantly reduced scale in comparison to that which the agent could expect under normal circumstances.

(3) Any agreement contrary to Subsections 1 and 2 hereof is void.

§ 86 b *Del credere* commission

(1) Where the commercial agent guarantees the fulfilment of the obligation arising from the transaction, he may demand special compensation (*del credere* commission). This right may not be excluded in advance. The guaranty may only be undertaken for a specific transaction or for transactions with specific third parties which the commercial agent solicits or concludes. This undertaking must be in writing.

(2) The right to a *del credere* commission arises upon conclusion of the transaction.

(3) Subsection 1 does not apply if the principal or third party has his office or, failing such, his residence abroad. Furthermore, it does not apply to transactions for the conclusion and performance of which the commercial agent has unlimited authority.

Handelsvertreter § 87

§ 87 [Provisionspflichtige Geschäfte]

(1) Der Handelsvertreter hat Anspruch auf Provision für alle während des Vertragsverhältnisses abgeschlossenen Geschäfte, die auf seine Tätigkeit zurückzuführen sind oder mit Dritten abgeschlossen werden, die er als Kunden für Geschäfte der gleichen Art geworben hat. Ein Anspruch auf Provision besteht für ihn nicht, wenn und soweit die Provision nach Absatz 3 dem ausgeschiedenen Handelsvertreter zusteht.

(2) Ist dem Handelsvertreter ein bestimmter Bezirk oder ein bestimmter Kundenkreis zugewiesen, so hat er Anspruch auf Provision auch für die Geschäfte, die ohne seine Mitwirkung mit Personen seines Bezirkes oder seines Kundenkreises während des Vertragsverhältnisses abgeschlossen sind. Dies gilt nicht, wenn und soweit die Provision nach Absatz 3 dem ausgeschiedenen Handelsvertreter zusteht.

(3) Für ein Geschäft, das erst nach Beendigung des Vertragsverhältnisses abgeschlossen ist, hat der Handelsvertreter Anspruch auf Provision nur, wenn

1. er das Geschäft vermittelt hat oder es eingeleitet und so vorbereitet hat, daß der Abschluß überwiegend auf seine Tätigkeit zurückzuführen ist, und das Geschäft innerhalb einer angemessenen Frist nach Beendigung des Vertragsverhältnisses abgeschlossen worden ist oder

2. vor Beendigung des Vertragsverhältnisses das Angebot des Dritten zum Abschluß eines Geschäfts, für das der Handelsvertreter nach Absatz 1 Satz 1 oder Absatz 2 Satz 1 Anspruch auf Provision hat, dem Handelsvertreter oder dem Unternehmer zugegangen ist.

§ 87 Transactions for which commission is due

(1) The commercial agent has a right to commissions for all transactions concluded during the term of his contractual relationship which are to be attributed to his activity or which have been concluded with third parties whom he had acquired as customers for similar business. He has no right to a commission if this is owed to the prior commercial agent pursuant to Subsection 3.

(2) Where the commercial agent has been assigned to a specific district or a particular group of customers, he also has a right to commission for transactions concluded without his assistance with persons in his district or among his group of customers during the term of his contractual relationship. This does not apply if the commission is owed to the prior commercial agent pursuant to Subsection 3.

(3) For transactions concluded after the termination of the contractual agency relationship, the agent shall have a right to commission only if:

1. he solicited, initiated or prepared it in such a way that conclusion thereof was predominantly due to his activity, and the transaction was concluded within a reasonable time after termination of the agency contract, or

2. prior to the termination of the agency contract, the offer of a third party to conclude a transaction for which the agent has a claim for commission under Subsection 1 sentence 1 or Subsection 2 sentence 1 hereof has been received by the agent or the principal.

Der Anspruch auf Provision nach Satz 1 steht dem nachfolgenden Handelsvertreter anteilig zu, wenn wegen besonderer Umstände eine Teilung der Provision der Billigkeit entspricht.

(4) Neben dem Anspruch auf Provision für abgeschlossene Geschäfte hat der Handelsvertreter Anspruch auf Inkassoprovision für die von ihm auftragsgemäß eingezogenen Beträge.

§ 87 a [Fälligkeit der Provision]

(1) Der Handelsvertreter hat Anspruch auf Provision, sobald und soweit der Unternehmer das Geschäft ausgeführt hat. Eine abweichende Vereinbarung kann getroffen werden, jedoch hat der Handelsvertreter mit der Ausführung des Geschäfts durch den Unternehmer Anspruch auf einen angemessenen Vorschuß, der spätestens am letzten Tag des folgenden Monats fällig ist. Unabhängig von einer Vereinbarung hat jedoch der Handelsvertreter Anspruch auf Provision, sobald und soweit der Dritte das Geschäft ausgeführt hat.

(2) Steht fest, daß der Dritte nicht leistet, so entfällt der Anspruch auf Provision; bereits empfangene Beträge sind zurückzugewähren.

(3) Der Handelsvertreter hat auch dann einen Anspruch auf Provision, wenn feststeht, daß der Unternehmer das Geschäft ganz oder teilweise nicht oder nicht so ausführt, wie es abgeschlossen worden ist. Der Anspruch entfällt im Falle der Nichtausführung, wenn und soweit diese auf Umständen beruht, die vom Unternehmer nicht zu vertreten sind.

(4) Der Anspruch auf Provision wird am letzten Tag des Monats fällig, in dem nach § 87 c Abs. 1 über den Anspruch abzurechnen ist.

The subsequent agent shall have a claim to a share of the commission when, due to special circumstances, fairness requires that the commission be split.

(4) In addition to the right to commission for transactions concluded, the commercial agent has a right to a collection commission for amounts collected by him pursuant to instructions.

§ 87 a Due date of the commission

(1) The commercial agent has a right to commission as soon as, and insofar as, the principal has completed the transaction. An agreement to the contrary may be made, but the commercial agent, upon completion of the transaction by the principal, has in any event a right to a reasonable advance due no later than the last day of the following month. Independent of any agreement, however, the commercial agent has a right to commission as soon as, and insofar as, the third party has completed the transaction.

(2) Where it has been determined that the third party will not perform, there is no right to commission. Amounts already received are to be returned.

(3) The commercial agent also has a right to commission when it is determined that the principal will not perform the transaction, will perform only partially, or will not perform in the manner agreed upon. No right to commission shall exist in the event of non-performance due to reasons beyond the control of the principal.

(4) The commission is due on the last day of the month in which the claim is accounted for pursuant to § 87 c Subsection 1.

(5) Von Absatz 2 erster Halbsatz, Absätzen 3 und 4 abweichende, für den Handelsvertreter nachteilige Vereinbarungen sind unwirksam.

§ 87 b [Höhe der Provision]

(1) Ist die Höhe der Provision nicht bestimmt, so ist der übliche Satz als vereinbart anzusehen.

(2) Die Provision ist von dem Entgelt zu berechnen, das der Dritte oder der Unternehmer zu leisten hat. Nachlässe bei Barzahlung sind nicht abzuziehen; dasselbe gilt für Nebenkosten, namentlich für Fracht, Verpackung, Zoll, Steuern, es sei denn, daß die Nebenkosten dem Dritten besonders in Rechnung gestellt sind. Die Umsatzsteuer, die lediglich auf Grund der steuerrechtlichen Vorschriften in der Rechnung gesondert ausgewiesen ist, gilt nicht als besonders in Rechnung gestellt.

(3) Bei Gebrauchsüberlassungs- und Nutzungsverträgen von bestimmter Dauer ist die Provision vom Entgelt für die Vertragsdauer zu berechnen. Bei unbestimmter Dauer ist die Provision vom Entgelt bis zu dem Zeitpunkt zu berechnen, zu dem erstmals von dem Dritten gekündigt werden kann; der Handelsvertreter hat Anspruch auf weitere entsprechend berechnete Provisionen, wenn der Vertrag fortbesteht.

§ 87 c [Abrechnung über die Provision]

(1) Der Unternehmer hat über die Provision, auf die der Handelsvertreter Anspruch hat, monatlich abzurechnen; der Abrechnungszeitraum kann auf höchstens drei Monate erstreckt

(5) Agreements contrary to Subsection 2, first half-sentence or Subsections 3 and 4, to the disadvantage of the commercial agent, are void.

§ 87 b Amount of the commission

(1) Where the amount of commission is not specified, the customary rate is deemed to be agreed upon.

(2) Commission is to be calculated on the basis of the amount that the third party or the principal is obligated to pay. Discounts for cash payment are not to be made; the same applies to miscellaneous costs, such as freight, packaging, customs duties and taxes, unless the miscellaneous costs have been itemised separately in the invoice sent to the third party. Value-added tax which is itemised separately solely by reason of the tax law is deemed not to be separately itemised.

(3) With respect to rental and use agreements of specific duration, commission is to be calculated on the consideration received for the term of the contract. With respect to agreements of indefinite duration, commission is to be calculated on the consideration received up until the time when the third party can terminate the agreement; the commercial agent has a right to additional commission calculated accordingly if the contract continues in force.

§ 87 c Accounting for the commission

(1) The principal shall account monthly for the commission to which the commercial agent is entitled. The accounting period can be extended to a maximum of three months. The ac-

werden. Die Abrechnung hat unverzüglich, spätestens bis zum Ende des nächsten Monats, zu erfolgen.

(2) Der Handelsvertreter kann bei der Abrechnung einen Buchauszug über alle Geschäfte verlangen, für die ihm nach § 87 Provision gebührt.

(3) Der Handelsvertreter kann außerdem Mitteilung über alle Umstände verlangen, die für den Provisionsanspruch, seine Fälligkeit und seine Berechnung wesentlich sind.

(4) Wird der Buchauszug verweigert oder bestehen begründete Zweifel an der Richtigkeit oder Vollständigkeit der Abrechnung oder des Buchauszuges, so kann der Handelsvertreter verlangen, daß nach Wahl des Unternehmers entweder ihm oder einem von ihm zu bestimmenden Wirtschaftsprüfer oder vereidigten Buchsachverständigen Einsicht in die Geschäftsbücher oder die sonstigen Urkunden soweit gewährt wird, wie dies zur Feststellung der Richtigkeit oder Vollständigkeit der Abrechnung oder des Buchauszuges erforderlich ist.

(5) Diese Rechte des Handelsvertreters können nicht ausgeschlossen oder beschränkt werden.

counting shall be made without delay, in any case not later than by the end of the succeeding month.

(2) At the time of accounting, the commercial agent may demand an excerpt from the books concerning all transactions for which he has a claim to commission pursuant to § 87.

(3) In addition, the commercial agent may demand information regarding all matters which are material to a determination of the right to commission, its due date and amount.

(4) Where the excerpt from the books is withheld, or reasonable doubt exists as to the accuracy or completeness of the account or the excerpt, the commercial agent may demand that, at the principal's option, either he or an auditor or certified accountant designated by him shall be permitted to inspect the business books and other documents to the extent that necessary to establish the accuracy or completeness of the accounting or excerpt.

(5) These rights of the commercial agent cannot be excluded or limited.

§ 87 d [Ersatz von Aufwendungen]

Der Handelsvertreter kann den Ersatz seiner im regelmäßigen Geschäftsbetrieb entstandenen Aufwendungen nur verlangen, wenn dies handelsüblich ist.

§ 87 d Reimbursement of expenses

The commercial agent may only demand reimbursement of his regular business expenses if this is customary within the trade.

§ 88 [Verjährung der Ansprüche]

Die Ansprüche aus dem Vertragsverhältnis verjähren in vier Jahren, beginnend mit dem Schluß des Jahres, in dem sie fällig geworden sind.

§ 88 Statute of limitations for claims

Claims arising from the contractual relationship are barred after four years, beginning with the end of the year in which they became due.

§ 88 a [Zurückbehaltungsrecht]

(1) Der Handelsvertreter kann nicht im voraus auf gesetzliche Zurückbehaltungsrechte verzichten.

(2) Nach Beendigung des Vertragsverhältnisses hat der Handelsvertreter ein nach allgemeinen Vorschriften bestehendes Zurückbehaltungsrecht an ihm zur Verfügung gestellten Unterlagen (§ 86 a Abs. 1) nur wegen seiner fälligen Ansprüche auf Provision und Ersatz von Aufwendungen.

§ 89 [Kündigung des Vertrages]

(1) Ist das Vertragsverhältnis auf unbestimmte Zeit eingegangen, so kann es im ersten Jahr der Vertragsdauer mit einer Frist von einem Monat, im zweiten Jahr mit einer Frist von zwei Monaten und im dritten bis fünften Jahr mit einer Frist von drei Monaten gekündigt werden. Nach einer Vertragsdauer von fünf Jahren kann das Vertragsverhältnis mit einer Frist von sechs Monaten gekündigt werden. Die Kündigung ist nur für den Schluß eines Kalendermonats zulässig, sofern keine abweichende Vereinbarung getroffen ist.

(2) Die Kündigungsfristen nach Absatz 1 Satz 1 und 2 können durch Vereinbarung verlängert werden; die Frist darf für den Unternehmer nicht kürzer sein als für den Handelsvertreter. Bei Vereinbarung einer kürzeren Frist für den Unternehmer gilt die für den Handelsvertreter vereinbarte Frist.

(3) Ein für eine bestimmte Zeit eingegangenes Vertragsverhältnis, das nach Ablauf der vereinbarten Laufzeit von beiden Teilen fortgesetzt wird, gilt als auf unbestimmte Zeit verlängert. Für die Bestimmung der Kündigungsfri-

§ 88 a Legal right of retention

(1) The commercial agent cannot waive his legal rights of retention in advance.

(2) After expiration of the contractual relationship the commercial agent has the right, pursuant to general statutory law, to retain materials placed at his disposal (§ 86 a Subsection 1) only by reason of unpaid commissions or reimbursement of expenses due to him.

§ 89 Termination of the agreement

(1) If the contractual relationship is of indefinite duration, it may be terminated with prior notice of one month during the first year, two months during the second year and three months in the third through the fifth years. After a duration of five years, the contractual relationship may be terminated with prior notice of six months. Absent any agreement to the contrary, termination is effective only as of the end of a calendar month.

(2) The notice periods under Subsection 1 sentences 1 and 2, may be extended by contract; the period may not be shorter for the principal than for the agent. If a shorter period for the principal is agreed upon, the period for the agent shall apply instead.

(3) A contractual relationship of definite duration which, upon expiration, is extended by both parties, shall be deemed to be extended indefinitely. For calculation of the termination notice periods under Subsection 1 sen-

sten nach Absatz 1 Satz 1 und 2 ist die Gesamtdauer des Vertragsverhältnisses maßgeblich.

§ 89 a [Fristlose Kündigung]

(1) Das Vertragsverhältnis kann von jedem Teil aus wichtigem Grunde ohne Einhaltung einer Kündigungsfrist gekündigt werden. Dieses Recht kann nicht ausgeschlossen oder beschränkt werden.

(2) Wird die Kündigung durch ein Verhalten veranlaßt, das der andere Teil zu vertreten hat, so ist dieser zum Ersatz des durch die Aufhebung des Vertragsverhältnisses entstehenden Schadens verpflichtet.

§ 89 b [Ausgleichsanspruch]

(1) Der Handelsvertreter kann von dem Unternehmer nach Beendigung des Vertragsverhältnisses einen angemessenen Ausgleich verlangen, wenn und soweit

1. der Unternehmer aus der Geschäftsverbindung mit neuen Kunden, die der Handelsvertreter geworben hat, auch nach Beendigung des Vertragsverhältnisses erhebliche Vorteile hat,
2. der Handelsvertreter infolge der Beendigung des Vertragsverhältnisses Ansprüche auf Provision verliert, die er bei Fortsetzung desselben aus bereits abgeschlossenen oder künftig zustande kommenden Geschäften mit den von ihm geworbenen Kunden hätte, und
3. die Zahlung eines Ausgleichs unter Berücksichtigung aller Umstände der Billigkeit entspricht.

tences 1 and 2, the total duration of the relationship shall be decisive.

§ 89 a Termination without observance of a notice period

(1) The contractual relationship can be terminated without observance of a notice period by either party for an important reason. This right cannot be excluded or limited.

(2) Where termination results from conduct of the other party, that party is obligated to compensate for damages arising from the termination of the contractual relationship.

§ 89 b Compensation claim

(1) The commercial agent may, after expiration of the contractual relationship, demand from the principal reasonable compensation if and insofar as

1. the principal retains substantial advantages, after termination of the contractual relationship, from business relations with new customers solicited by the commercial agent,
2. the commercial agent, by reason of termination of the contractual relationship, loses rights to commissions relating to concluded business or business to be concluded in the future with those customers he had solicited, and which rights he would have had if the contractual relationship had been continued, and
3. the payment of compensation is equitable after consideration of all the circumstances.

| Handelsvertreter | § 89b |

Der Werbung eines neuen Kunden steht es gleich, wenn der Handelsvertreter die Geschäftsverbindung mit einem Kunden so wesentlich erweitert hat, daß dies wirtschaftlich der Werbung eines neuen Kunden entspricht.

(2) Der Ausgleich beträgt höchstens eine nach dem Durchschnitt der letzten fünf Jahre der Tätigkeit des Handelsvertreters berechnete Jahresprovision oder sonstige Jahresvergütung; bei kürzerer Dauer des Vertragsverhältnisses ist der Durchschnitt während der Dauer der Tätigkeit maßgebend.

(3) Der Anspruch besteht nicht, wenn

1. der Handelsvertreter das Vertragsverhältnis gekündigt hat, es sei denn, daß ein Verhalten des Unternehmers hierzu begründeten Anlaß gegeben hat oder dem Handelsvertreter eine Fortsetzung seiner Tätigkeit wegen seines Alters oder wegen Krankheit nicht zugemutet werden kann, oder

2. der Unternehmer das Vertragsverhältnis gekündigt hat und für die Kündigung ein wichtiger Grund wegen schuldhaften Verhaltens des Handelsvertreters vorlag oder

3. auf Grund einer Vereinbarung zwischen dem Unternehmer und dem Handelsvertreter ein Dritter anstelle des Handelsvertreters in das Vertragsverhältnis eintritt; die Vereinbarung kann nicht vor Beendigung des Vertragsverhältnisses getroffen werden.

(4) Der Anspruch kann im voraus nicht ausgeschlossen werden. Er ist innerhalb eines Jahres nach Beendigung des Vertragsverhältnisses geltend zu machen.

"Solicitation of new customers" shall also include the expansion of business relations with an existing customer which corresponds economically to the acquisition of a new customer.

(2) Compensation may amount to no more than the average of the annual commission or other annual remuneration over the last five years of the activity of the commercial agent; in the event that the contractual relationship has been shorter than five years, the average during the period of activity applies.

(3) No claim for compensation shall exist where:

1. the commercial agent has terminated the contractual relationship, unless the actions of the principal constituted sufficient grounds therefor, or the commercial agent cannot be expected to continue his activities by reason of his age or health, or

2. the principal has terminated the contractual relationship for an important reason relating to culpable conduct of the commercial agent, or

3. by reason of an agreement between the principal and the commercial agent, a third party assumes the rights and obligations of the commercial agent; such an agreement cannot be made prior to the termination of the contractual relationship.

(4) The compensation claim may not be excluded in advance. It must be asserted within one year after termination of the contractual relationship.

(5) Die Absätze 1, 3 und 4 gelten für Versicherungsvertreter mit der Maßgabe, daß an die Stelle der Geschäftsverbindung mit neuen Kunden, die der Handelsvertreter geworben hat, die Vermittlung neuer Versicherungsverträge durch den Versicherungsvertreter tritt und der Vermittlung eines Versicherungsvertrages es gleichsteht, wenn der Versicherungsvertreter einen bestehenden Versicherungsvertrag so wesentlich erweitert hat, daß dies wirtschaftlich der Vermittlung eines neuen Versicherungsvertrages entspricht. Der Ausgleich des Versicherungsvertreters beträgt abweichend von Absatz 2 höchstens drei Jahresprovisionen oder Jahresvergütungen. Die Vorschriften der Sätze 1 und 2 gelten sinngemäß für Bausparkassenvertreter.

(5) Subsections 1, 3 and 4 hereof shall apply to insurance agents in such a manner that the concept of business relationships with new customers solicited by the commercial agent shall be replaced by the concept of conclusion of new insurance contracts by the insurance agent, and expansion by the insurance agent of an existing insurance contract which corresponds economically to the conclusion of a new insurance contract shall be deemed to be the conclusion of a new insurance contract. In derogation of Subsection 2 hereof, the compensation claim of an insurance agent shall equal, at a maximum, three years worth of commissions or remuneration. Sentences 1 and 2 hereof shall apply analogously to agents of building and savings associations.

§ 90 [Geschäfts- und Betriebsgeheimnisse]

Der Handelsvertreter darf Geschäfts- und Betriebsgeheimnisse, die ihm anvertraut oder als solche durch seine Tätigkeit für den Unternehmer bekanntgeworden sind, auch nach Beendigung des Vertragsverhältnisses nicht verwerten oder anderen mitteilen, soweit dies nach den gesamten Umständen der Berufsauffassung eines ordentlichen Kaufmannes widersprechen würde.

§ 90 Trade and business secrets

The commerical agent may not, even after termination of the contractual relationship, utilise or divulge to others trade or business secrets which have been entrusted to him or which he has learned by reason of his activity for the principal insofar as this would under all the circumstances be contrary to the professional standards of a prudent merchant.

§ 90 a [Wettbewerbsabrede]

(1) Eine Vereinbarung, die den Handelsvertreter nach Beendigung des Vertragsverhältnisses in seiner gewerblichen Tätigkeit beschränkt (Wettbewerbsabrede), bedarf der Schriftform und der Aushändigung einer vom Un-

§ 90 a Agreement prohibiting competition

(1) An agreement by which a commercial agent is restricted in his commercial activity following termination of the contractual relationship (agreement prohibiting competition), must be in writing, and the document con-

ternehmer unterzeichneten, die vereinbarten Bestimmungen enthaltenden Urkunde an den Handelsvertreter. Die Abrede kann nur für längstens zwei Jahre von der Beendigung des Vertragsverhältnisses an getroffen werden; sie darf sich nur auf den dem Handelsvertreter zugewiesenen Bezirk oder Kundenkreis und nur auf die Gegenstände erstrecken, hinsichtlich deren sich der Handelsvertreter um die Vermittlung oder den Abschluß von Geschäften für den Unternehmer zu bemühen hat. Der Unternehmer ist verpflichtet, dem Handelsvertreter für die Dauer der Wettbewerbsbeschränkung eine angemessene Entschädigung zu zahlen.

(2) Der Unternehmer kann bis zum Ende des Vertragsverhältnisses schriftlich auf die Wettbewerbsbeschränkung mit der Wirkung verzichten, daß er mit dem Ablauf von sechs Monaten seit der Erklärung von der Verpflichtung zur Zahlung der Entschädigung frei wird.

(3) Kündigt ein Teil das Vertragsverhältnis aus wichtigem Grund wegen schuldhaften Verhaltens des anderen Teils, kann er sich durch schriftliche Erklärung binnen einem Monat nach der Kündigung von der Wettbewerbsabrede lossagen.

(4) Abweichende für den Handelsvertreter nachteilige Vereinbarungen können nicht getroffen werden.

§ 91 [Vollmachten des Handelsvertreters]

(1) § 55 gilt auch für einen Handelsvertreter, der zum Abschluß von Geschäften von einem Unternehmer bevollmächtigt ist, der nicht Kaufmann ist.

taining the conditions agreed to must be signed by the principal and delivered to the commercial agent. The agreement may run for no longer than two years following the termination of the contractual relationship. The agreement may cover only the geographical area or group of customers assigned to the commercial agent and may only refer to the type of business in which the commercial agent was responsible for soliciting transactions. The principal is obligated to pay reasonable compensation to the commercial agent for the duration of the prohibition of competition.

(2) The principal may waive the prohibition of competition in writing up to the end of the contractual relationship with the effect that he will be free from the obligation to pay compensation as of the end of six months after the date of such declaration.

(3) Where one party terminates the contractual relationship for an important reason because of culpable conduct of other party, he may, by a declaration in writing made within one month after such termination, declare that he is not bound by the prohibition of competition.

(4) Agreements deviating from these provisions to the disadvantage of the commercial agent cannot be made.

§ 91 Authority of the commercial agent

(1) § 55 also applies to a commercial agent who is authorized to conclude transactions for a principal who is not a merchant.

(2) Ein Handelsvertreter gilt, auch wenn ihm keine Vollmacht zum Abschluß von Geschäften erteilt ist, als ermächtigt, die Anzeige von Mängeln einer Ware, die Erklärung, daß eine Ware zur Verfügung gestellt werde, sowie ähnliche Erklärungen, durch die ein Dritter seine Rechte aus mangelhafter Leistung geltend macht oder sich vorbehält, entgegenzunehmen; er kann die dem Unternehmer zustehenden Rechte auf Sicherung des Beweises geltend machen. Eine Beschränkung dieser Rechte braucht ein Dritter gegen sich nur gelten zu lassen, wenn er sie kannte oder kennen mußte.

§ 91 a [Mangel der Vertretungsmacht]

(1) Hat ein Handelsvertreter, der nur mit der Vermittlung von Geschäften betraut ist, ein Geschäft im Namen des Unternehmers abgeschlossen, und war dem Dritten der Mangel an Vertretungsmacht nicht bekannt, so gilt das Geschäft als von dem Unternehmer genehmigt, wenn dieser nicht unverzüglich, nachdem er von dem Handelsvertreter oder dem Dritten über Abschluß und wesentlichen Inhalt benachrichtigt worden ist, dem Dritten gegenüber das Geschäft ablehnt.

(2) Das gleiche gilt, wenn ein Handelsvertreter, der mit dem Abschluß von Geschäften betraut ist, ein Geschäft im Namen des Unternehmers abgeschlossen hat, zu dessen Abschluß er nicht bevollmächtigt ist.

§ 92 [Versicherungs- und Bausparkassenvertreter]

(1) Versicherungsvertreter ist, wer als Handelsvertreter damit betraut ist, Versicherungsverträge zu vermitteln oder abzuschließen.

(2) Even if he is not authorized to conclude transactions, a commercial agent is deemed to have authority to accept notice of defective goods, statements that goods have been rejected, as well as similar statements by which a third party asserts or reserves rights arising from defective contractual performance; he may assert the principal's rights to preserve evidence. Limitation of this authority is deemed to be valid against a third party only where the third party knew or should have known thereof.

§ 91 a Lack of authority

(1) Where a commercial agent only authorized to solicit business has concluded a transaction in the principal's name, and the third party did not know of this lack of authority, the transaction will be regarded as ratified by the principal if he fails to repudiate it without undue delay upon being informed by the commercial agent or third party of the conclusion of the agreement and its material terms.

(2) The same applies where a commercial agent authorized to enter into business transactions has concluded in the principal's name a transaction which he is not authorized to conclude.

§ 92 Insurance and building and loan association agents

(1) An insurance agent is one who, as a commercial agent, is authorized to solicit or conclude insurance contracts.

(2) Für das Vertragsverhältnis zwischen dem Versicherungsvertreter und dem Versicherer gelten die Vorschriften für das Vertragsverhältnis zwischen dem Handelsvertreter und dem Unternehmer vorbehaltlich der Absätze 3 und 4.

(3) In Abweichung von § 87 Abs. 1 Satz 1 hat ein Versicherungsvertreter Anspruch auf Provision nur für Geschäfte, die auf seine Tätigkeit zurückzuführen sind. § 87 Abs. 2 gilt nicht für Versicherungsvertreter.

(4) Der Versicherungsvertreter hat Anspruch auf Provision (§ 87 a Abs. 1), sobald der Versicherungsnehmer die Prämie gezahlt hat, aus der sich die Provision nach dem Vertragsverhältnis berechnet.

(5) Die Vorschriften der Absätze 1 bis 4 gelten sinngemäß für Bausparkassenvertreter.

§ 92 a [Mindestarbeitsbedingungen]

(1) Für das Vertragsverhältnis eines Handelsvertreters, der vertraglich nicht für weitere Unternehmer tätig werden darf oder dem dies nach Art und Umfang der von ihm verlangten Tätigkeit nicht möglich ist, kann das Bundesministerium der Justiz im Einvernehmen mit den Bundesministerien für Wirtschaft und Technologie und für Arbeit und Sozialordnung nach Anhörung von Verbänden der Handelsvertreter und der Unternehmer durch Rechtsverordnung, die nicht der Zustimmung des Bundesrates bedarf, die untere Grenze der vertraglichen Leistungen des Unternehmers festsetzen, um die notwendigen sozialen und wirtschaftlichen Bedürfnisse dieser Handelsvertreter oder einer bestimmten Gruppe von ihnen si-

(2) The provisions applicable to the contractual relationship between the commercial agent and the principal apply, subject to Subsections 3 and 4 hereof, to the contractual relationship between the insurance agent and the insurer.

(3) As an exception to § 87 Subsection 1 sentence 1, an insurance agent has a right to commission only for transactions which are a result of his activity. Section 87 Subsection 2 does not apply to insurance agents.

(4) The insurance agent has a right to commission (§ 87 a Subsection 1) as soon as the insured has paid the premium on which the commission, according to the contractual relationship, is calculated.

(5) The provisions of Subsections 1 through 4 apply analogously to building and loan association agents.

§ 92 a Minimum working conditions

(1) For the contractual relationship of a commercial agent who is not permitted to represent other principals, or for whom this is impossible because of the type and volume of business activity demanded of him, the Federal Ministry of Justice may, in conjunction with the Federal Ministries for Economics and Technology and for Labor and Social Welfare, after a hearing with the commercial agent's and principal's representative associations, establish regulations which determine the minimum contractual duties of the principal in order to ensure that the requisite social and economic needs of these commercial agents or a particular group of commercial agents are provided for. Such regulations shall not require the con-

cherzustellen. Die festgesetzten Leistungen können vertraglich nicht ausgeschlossen oder beschränkt werden.

(2) Absatz 1 gilt auch für das Vertragsverhältnis eines Versicherungsvertreters, der auf Grund eines Vertrages oder mehrerer Verträge damit betraut ist, Geschäfte für mehrere Versicherer zu vermitteln oder abzuschließen, die zu einem Versicherungskonzern oder zu einer zwischen ihnen bestehenden Organisationsgemeinschaft gehören, sofern die Beendigung des Vertragsverhältnisses mit einem dieser Versicherer im Zweifel auch die Beendigung des Vertragsverhältnisses mit den anderen Versicherern zur Folge haben würde. In diesem Falle kann durch Rechtsverordnung, die nicht der Zustimmung des Bundesrates bedarf, außerdem bestimmt werden, ob die festgesetzten Leistungen von allen Versicherern als Gesamtschuldnern oder anteilig oder nur von einem der Versicherer geschuldet werden und wie der Ausgleich unter ihnen zu erfolgen hat.

§ 92 b [Handelsvertreter im Nebenberuf]

(1) Auf einen Handelsvertreter im Nebenberuf sind §§ 89 und 89 b nicht anzuwenden. Ist das Vertragsverhältnis auf unbestimmte Zeit eingegangen, so kann es mit einer Frist von einem Monat für den Schluß eines Kalendermonats gekündigt werden; wird eine andere Kündigungsfrist vereinbart, so muß sie für beide Teile gleich sein. Der Anspruch auf einen angemessenen Vorschuß nach § 87 a Abs. 1 Satz 2 kann ausgeschlossen werden.

(2) Auf Absatz 1 kann sich nur der Unternehmer berufen, der den Handelsvertreter ausdrücklich als Handels-

sent of the Federal upper house of Parliament (Bundesrat). The duties thus determined may not be excluded or limited by any contract.

(2) Subsection 1 also applies to the contractual relationship of an insurance agent who, by reason of one or more contracts, has been authorized to solicit or conclude business transactions for numerous insurers who belong to an insurance concern or an organization common to all of them, to the extent that termination of the contractual relationship with one of these insurers may have the effect of terminating the contractual relationship with the other insurers. In this case it can be determined, by means of regulation which shall not require the consent of the Federal upper house of Parliament, whether the duties established are to be performed by all insurers jointly and severally or by only one insurer and how the compensation is to be apportioned among them.

§ 92 b Part-time commercial agent

(1) §§ 89 and 89 b are not applicable to a part-time commercial agent. Where the contractual relationship is for an indefinite period, it can be terminated as of the end of a calendar month on prior notice of one month. Where a different notice period is agreed to, it must be the same for both parties. The right to a reasonable advance pursuant to § 87 a Subsection 1 sentence 2 can be excluded by agreement.

(2) Subsection 1 can only be asserted by a principal who has authorized the commercial agent to solicit or con-

vertreter im Nebenberuf mit der Vermittlung oder dem Abschluß von Geschäften betraut hat.

(3) Ob ein Handelsvertreter nur als Handelsvertreter im Nebenberuf tätig ist, bestimmt sich nach der Verkehrsauffassung.

(4) Die Vorschriften der Absätze 1 bis 3 gelten sinngemäß für Versicherungsvertreter und für Bausparkassenvertreter.

§ 92 c [Handelsvertreter außerhalb der EG; Schiffahrtsvertreter]

(1) Hat der Handelsvertreter seine Tätigkeit für den Unternehmer nach dem Vertrag nicht innerhalb des Gebietes der Europäischen Gemeinschaft oder der anderen Vertragsstaaten des Abkommens über den Europäischen Wirtschaftsraum auszuüben, so kann hinsichtlich aller Vorschriften dieses Abschnittes etwas anderes vereinbart werden.

(2) Das gleiche gilt, wenn der Handelsvertreter mit der Vermittlung oder dem Abschluß von Geschäften betraut wird, die die Befrachtung, Abfertigung oder Ausrüstung von Schiffen oder die Buchung von Passagen auf Schiffen zum Gegenstand haben.

Achter Abschnitt. Handelsmakler

§ 93 [Begriff]

(1) Wer gewerbsmäßig für andere Personen, ohne von ihnen auf Grund eines Vertragsverhältnisses ständig damit betraut zu sein, die Vermittlung von Verträgen über Anschaffung oder Veräußerung von Waren oder Wertpapieren, über Versicherungen, Güter-

clude business transactions expressly as a part-time commercial agent.

(3) Whether or not a commercial agent is active only as a part-time agent is determined by the custom of the trade.

(4) The provisions of Subsections 1 through 3 apply analogously to insurance agents and building and loan association agents.

§ 92 c Commercial agent outside the EC; shipping agent

(1) Where the commercial agent is not contractually obligated to carry out his activities for the principal within the territory of the European Community or the other contracting states of the European Economic Area Agreement, all provisions of this part may be altered by agreement.

(2) The same applies if the commercial agent is authorized to solicit or conclude business transactions in the area of shipping charters, dispatch or equipping of vessels, or the booking of passages on ships.

Part Eight. Commercial Broker

§ 93 Definition

(1) Someone who undertakes commercially the solicitation of contracts concerning the purchase and sale of goods or securities, insurance, shipping and forwarding of goods, marine charter or other commercial matters for other persons, without being au-

beförderungen, Schiffsmiete oder sonstige Gegenstände des Handelsverkehrs übernimmt, hat die Rechte und Pflichten eines Handelsmaklers.

(2) Auf die Vermittlung anderer als der bezeichneten Geschäfte, insbesondere auf die Vermittlung von Geschäften über unbewegliche Sachen, finden, auch wenn die Vermittlung durch einen Handelsmakler erfolgt, die Vorschriften dieses Abschnitts keine Anwendung.

(3) Die Vorschriften dieses Abschnittes finden auch Anwendung, wenn das Unternehmen des Handelsmaklers nach Art oder Umfang einen in kaufmännischer Weise eingerichteten Geschäftsbetrieb nicht erfordert.

§ 94 [Schlußnote]

(1) Der Handelsmakler hat, sofern nicht die Parteien ihm dies erlassen oder der Ortsgebrauch mit Rücksicht auf die Gattung der Ware davon entbindet, unverzüglich nach dem Abschlusse des Geschäfts jeder Partei eine von ihm unterzeichnete Schlußnote zuzustellen, welche die Parteien, den Gegenstand und die Bedingungen des Geschäfts, insbesondere bei Verkäufen von Waren oder Wertpapieren deren Gattung und Menge sowie den Preis und die Zeit der Lieferung, enthält.

(2) Bei Geschäften, die nicht sofort erfüllt werden sollen, ist die Schlußnote den Parteien zu ihrer Unterschrift zuzustellen und jeder Partei die von der anderen unterschriebene Schlußnote zu übersenden.

(3) Verweigert eine Partei die Annahme oder Unterschrift der Schlußnote, so hat der Handelsmakler davon der anderen Partei unverzüglich Anzeige zu machen.

thorized to do so on a regular basis by contractual relationship, has the rights and duties of a commercial broker.

(2) The provisions of this part have no application to the solicitation of business other than the kind set forth above, especially the solicitation of business relating to intangible assets, even if the solicitation is effected through a commercial broker.

(3) The provisions of this Part also apply if the business of the commercial broker by type and volume does not require a commercially organized business operation.

§ 94 Memorandum of sale

(1) The commercial broker must, unless released therefrom by the parties or by local custom with regard to the nature of the goods involved, supply each party, without undue delay following the conclusion of the transaction, with a memorandum of sale signed by him and setting forth the names of the parties, the subject and terms of the transaction, especially in the case of a sale of goods or securities, their type and quantity, as well as the price and date of delivery.

(2) With transactions which are not to be performed immediately, the memorandum of sale is to be forwarded to the parties for signature and each party is to be sent the memorandum of sale signed by the other party.

(3) Where one party refuses to accept or sign the memorandum, the commercial broker must notify the other party without undue delay.

§ 95 [Vorbehaltene Aufgabe]

(1) Nimmt eine Partei eine Schlußnote an, in der sich der Handelsmakler die Bezeichnung der anderen Partei vorbehalten hat, so ist sie an das Geschäft mit der Partei, welche ihr nachträglich bezeichnet wird, gebunden, es sei denn, daß gegen diese begründete Einwendungen zu erheben sind.

(2) Die Bezeichnung der anderen Partei hat innerhalb der ortsüblichen Frist, in Ermangelung einer solchen innerhalb einer den Umständen nach angemessenen Frist zu erfolgen.

(3) Unterbleibt die Bezeichnung oder sind gegen die bezeichnete Person oder Firma begründete Einwendungen zu erheben, so ist die Partei befugt, den Handelsmakler auf die Erfüllung des Geschäfts in Anspruch zu nehmen. Der Anspruch ist ausgeschlossen, wenn sich die Partei auf die Aufforderung des Handelsmaklers nicht unverzüglich darüber erklärt, ob sie Erfüllung verlange.

§ 96 [Aufbewahrung von Proben]

Der Handelsmakler hat, sofern nicht die Parteien ihm dies erlassen oder der Ortsgebrauch mit Rücksicht auf die Gattung der Ware davon entbindet, von jeder durch seine Vermittlung nach Probe verkauften Ware die Probe, falls sie ihm übergeben ist, so lange aufzubewahren, bis die Ware ohne Einwendung gegen ihre Beschaffenheit angenommen oder das Geschäft in anderer Weise erledigt wird. Er hat die Probe durch ein Zeichen kenntlich zu machen.

§ 95 Temporary reservation of disclosure of principal

(1) Where one party accepts a memorandum of sale in which the commercial broker has not disclosed the identity of the other party, the party accepting is bound to the transaction with the other party, the identity of whom is to be disclosed later, unless justifiable objections are raised against the other party.

(2) The identification of the other party must be made within the locally customary period and, in the absence thereof, within a period reasonable under the circumstances.

(3) Where identification is not made or justifiable objections can be raised against the person or company identified, the party is entitled to demand that the commercial broker perform the contract. The right does not exist if the party does not, on request by the commercial broker, declare without undue delay whether it demands performance.

§ 96 Storage of samples

The commercial broker must, unless released therefrom by the parties or by local custom with respect to the nature of the goods, retain a sample of each piece of merchandise sold by sample by his solicitation, provided the sample has been given to him, until the merchandise is accepted without objection as to quality or the transaction has been concluded otherwise. He must identify the sample by marking.

§ 97 [Keine Inkassovollmacht]

Der Handelsmakler gilt nicht als ermächtigt, eine Zahlung oder eine andere im Vertrage bedungene Leistung in Empfang zu nehmen.

§ 98 [Haftung gegenüber beiden Parteien]

Der Handelsmakler haftet jeder der beiden Parteien für den durch sein Verschulden entstehenden Schaden.

§ 99 [Lohnanspruch gegen beide Parteien]

Ist unter den Parteien nichts darüber vereinbart, wer den Maklerlohn bezahlen soll, so ist er in Ermangelung eines abweichenden Ortsgebrauchs von jeder Partei zur Hälfte zu entrichten.

§ 100 [Tagebuch]

(1) Der Handelsmakler ist verpflichtet, ein Tagebuch zu führen und in dieses alle abgeschlossenen Geschäfte täglich einzutragen. Die Eintragungen sind nach der Zeitfolge zu bewirken; sie haben die in § 94 Abs. 1 bezeichneten Angaben zu enthalten. Das Eingetragene ist von dem Handelsmakler täglich zu unterzeichnen oder gemäß § 126a Abs. 1 des Bürgerlichen Gesetzbuchs elektronisch zu signieren.

(2) Die Vorschriften der §§ 239 und 257 über die Einrichtung und Aufbewahrung der Handelsbücher finden auf das Tagebuch des Handelsmaklers Anwendung.

§ 101 [Auszüge aus dem Tagebuch]

Der Handelsmakler ist verpflichtet, den Parteien jederzeit auf Verlangen Auszüge aus dem Tagebuche zu ge-

§ 97 No collection authority

The commercial broker is not deemed to be authorized to accept payment or any other contractually stipulated consideration.

§ 98 Liability with respect to both parties

The commercial broker is liable to each of the two parties for damages arising through his fault.

§ 99 Compensation right against both parties

Where it is not agreed upon between the parties as to who should pay the broker's fee, in the absence of a contrary local custom, one-half is to be paid by each party.

§ 100 Broker's transaction book

(1) The commercial broker is obligated to maintain a transaction book and to enter into such book all transactions concluded each day. Entries are to be made chronologically; they must include the information set forth in § 94 Subsection 1. The entry shall, on a daily basis, be signed by the commercial broker or be electronically signed in accordance with §126 a Subsection 1 of the Civil Code.

(2) The provisions of §§ 239 and 257 concerning the establishment and storage of commercial records apply to the commercial broker's transaction book.

§ 101 Transaction book extracts

The commercial broker is obligated to give excerpts from the transaction book signed by him and containing

Handelsmakler §§ 101–104

ben, die von ihm unterzeichnet sind und alles enthalten, was von ihm in Ansehung des vermittelten Geschäfts eingetragen ist.

everything entered by him with regard to the transaction negotiated to the parties at any time on request.

§ 102 [Vorlegung im Rechtsstreit]

Im Laufe eines Rechtsstreits kann das Gericht auch ohne Antrag einer Partei die Vorlegung des Tagebuchs anordnen, um es mit der Schlußnote, den Auszügen oder anderen Beweismitteln zu vergleichen.

§ 102 Production during litigation

In the course of litigation, the court can, on its own motion, order the production of the transaction book in order to compare it with the memorandum of sale, the excerpts or other evidence.

§ 103 [Ordnungswidrigkeiten]

(1) Ordnungswidrig handelt, wer als Handelsmakler

1. vorsätzlich oder fahrlässig ein Tagebuch über die abgeschlossenen Geschäfte zu führen unterläßt oder das Tagebuch in einer Weise führt, die dem § 100 Abs. 1 widerspricht oder

2. ein solches Tagebuch vor Ablauf der gesetzlichen Aufbewahrungsfrist vernichtet.

(2) Die Ordnungswidrigkeit kann mit einer Geldbuße bis zu fünftausend Euro geahndet werden.

§ 103 Administrative violations

(1) It shall be an administrative violation for a commercial broker to

1. intentionally or negligently, fail either to maintain a transaction book with regard to the transactions concluded or to maintain the transaction book in a manner inconsistent with § 100 Subsection 1 or

2. destroy such a transaction book before expiration of the retention period required by law.

(2) The administrative violation can be punished with a fine of up to five thousand Euro.

§ 104 [Krämermakler]

Auf Personen, welche die Vermittlung von Warengeschäften im Kleinverkehre besorgen, finden die Vorschriften über Schlußnoten und Tagebücher keine Anwendung. Auf Personen, welche die Vermittlung von Versicherungs- oder Bausparverträgen übernehmen, sind die Vorschriften über Tagebücher nicht anzuwenden.

§ 104 Petty broker

The provisions concerning memoranda of sale and transaction books do not apply to persons who provide for the solicitation of merchandise transactions of small value. The provisions concerning transaction books do not apply to persons who solicit insurance or building and savings contracts.

Zweites Buch. Handelsgesellschaften und stille Gesellschaft

Erster Abschnitt. Offene Handelsgesellschaft

Erster Titel. Errichtung der Gesellschaft

§ 105 [Begriff der OHG; Anwendbarkeit des BGB]

(1) Eine Gesellschaft, deren Zweck auf den Betrieb eines Handelsgewerbes unter gemeinschaftlicher Firma gerichtet ist, ist eine offene Handelsgesellschaft, wenn bei keinem der Gesellschafter die Haftung gegenüber den Gesellschaftsgläubigern beschränkt ist.

(2) Eine Gesellschaft, deren Gewerbebetrieb nicht schon nach § 1 Abs. 2 Handelsgewerbe ist oder die nur eigenes Vermögen verwaltet, ist offene Handelsgesellschaft, wenn die Firma des Unternehmens in das Handelsregister eingetragen ist. § 2 Satz 2 und 3 gilt entsprechend.

(3) Auf die offene Handelsgesellschaft finden, soweit nicht in diesem Abschnitt ein anderes vorgeschrieben ist, die Vorschriften des Bürgerlichen Gesetzbuchs über die Gesellschaft Anwendung.

§ 106 [Anmeldung zum Handelsregister]

(1) Die Gesellschaft ist bei dem Gericht, in dessen Bezirke sie ihren Sitz hat, zur Eintragung in das Handelsregister anzumelden.

Book Two. Commercial Partnerships and Silent Partnerships

Part One. General Commercial Partnership

First Title. Establishment of the Partnership

§ 105 Definition of general commercial partnership; applicability of the Civil Code

(1) A partnership formed for the purpose of operating a commercial enterprise under a common firm name is a general commercial partnership where no partner's liability is limited with regard to the partnership's creditors.

(2) A company whose operation is not already defined as a business pursuant to § 1 Subsection 2, or which only manages its own assets, is a general commercial partnership if the firm name of the enterprise has been registered in the Commercial Register. § 2 sentences 2 and 3 apply analogously.

(3) Unless this Part provides otherwise, the provisions of the Civil Code regarding the partnership apply to the general commercial partnership.

§ 106 Application to the Commercial Register

(1) The partnership shall file for registration in the Commercial Register of the court in whose district it is domiciled.

(2) Die Anmeldung hat zu enthalten:

1. den Namen, Vornamen, Geburtsdatum und Wohnort jedes Gesellschafters;
2. die Firma der Gesellschaft und den Ort, wo sie ihren Sitz hat;
3. den Zeitpunkt, mit welchem die Gesellschaft begonnen hat;
4. die Vertretungsmacht der Gesellschafter.

§ 107 [Anzumeldende Änderungen]

Wird die Firma einer Gesellschaft geändert oder der Sitz der Gesellschaft an einen anderen Ort verlegt, tritt ein neuer Gesellschafter in die Gesellschaft ein oder ändert sich die Vertretungsmacht eines Gesellschafters, so ist dies ebenfalls zur Eintragung in das Handelsregister anzumelden.

§ 108 [Anmeldung durch alle Gesellschafter; Aufbewahrung der Unterschriften]

(1) Die Anmeldungen sind von sämtlichen Gesellschaftern zu bewirken.

(2) Die Gesellschafter, welche die Gesellschaft vertreten sollen, haben ihre Namensunterschrift unter Angabe der Firma zur Aufbewahrung bei dem Gericht zu zeichnen.

Zweiter Titel. Rechtsverhältnis der Gesellschafter untereinander

§ 109 [Gesellschaftsvertrag]

Das Rechtsverhältnis der Gesellschafter untereinander richtet sich zunächst nach dem Gesellschaftsver-

(2) The filing must contain:

1. the family name, the first name, date of birth and residence of every partner;
2. the firm name of the partnership and its place of domicile;
3. the date on which the partnership commenced;
4. the authority of the partners to represent the partnership.

§ 107 Changes requiring application for registration

Where the firm name of a partnership is altered, the domicile of the partnership is changed to another location, a new partner enters the partnership or the authority of a partner to represent the partnership is changed, this fact must likewise be filed for registration in the Commercial Register.

§ 108 Filing for registration by all partners; filing of signatures

(1) Filing for registration is to be made by all the partners.

(2) The partners who are to represent the partnership must provide their specimen signatures giving the firm name for filing with the court.

Second Title. Legal Relationship of the Partners to One Another

§ 109 Partnership agreement

The legal relationship of the partners to one another is determined principally by the partnership agreement;

trage; die Vorschriften der §§ 110 bis 122 finden nur insoweit Anwendung, als nicht durch den Gesellschaftsvertrag ein anderes bestimmt ist.

§ 110 [Ersatz für Aufwendungen und Verluste]

(1) Macht der Gesellschafter in den Gesellschaftsangelegenheiten Aufwendungen, die er den Umständen nach für erforderlich halten darf, oder erleidet er unmittelbar durch seine Geschäftsführung oder aus Gefahren, die mit ihr untrennbar verbunden sind, Verluste, so ist ihm die Gesellschaft zum Ersatze verpflichtet.

(2) Aufgewendetes Geld hat die Gesellschaft von der Zeit der Aufwendung an zu verzinsen.

§ 111 [Verzinsungspflicht]

(1) Ein Gesellschafter, der seine Geldeinlage nicht zur rechten Zeit einzahlt oder eingenommenes Gesellschaftsgeld nicht zur rechten Zeit an die Gesellschaftskasse abliefert oder unbefugt Geld aus der Gesellschaftskasse für sich entnimmt, hat Zinsen von dem Tage an zu entrichten, an welchem die Zahlung oder die Ablieferung hätte geschehen sollen oder die Herausnahme des Geldes erfolgt ist.

(2) Die Geltendmachung eines weiteren Schadens ist nicht ausgeschlossen.

§ 112 [Wettbewerbsverbot]

(1) Ein Gesellschafter darf ohne Einwilligung der anderen Gesellschafter weder in dem Handelszweige der Gesellschaft Geschäfte machen noch an

the provisions of §§ 110 through 122 apply only to the extent that the partnership agreement does not provide otherwise.

§ 110 Reimbursement for expenses and losses

(1) If, in the course of partnership matters, a partner incurs expenses which he reasonably deems necessary under the circumstances, or if he sustains losses directly through his business management or from risks inseparable from such business management, the partnership is obligated to reimburse him.

(2) The partnership must pay interest on money paid for expenses, from the date of payment.

§ 111 Obligation to pay interest

(1) A partner who fails to pay in his partnership contribution on time, who fails to deliver to the partnership funds in his possession belonging to the partnership or who withdraws money from a partnership account for his own use without authorization, must pay interest from the day on which the payment or delivery should have occurred or the withdrawal was made.

(2) The assertion of a further claim for damages is not barred.

§ 112 Prohibition of competition

(1) A partner may not, without the consent of the other partners, conduct business in the partnerhip's branch of business or participate as a general

einer anderen gleichartigen Handelsgesellschaft als persönlich haftender Gesellschafter teilnehmen.

(2) Die Einwilligung zur Teilnahme an einer anderen Gesellschaft gilt als erteilt, wenn den übrigen Gesellschaftern bei Eingehung der Gesellschaft bekannt ist, daß der Gesellschafter an einer anderen Gesellschaft als persönlich haftender Gesellschafter teilnimmt, und gleichwohl die Aufgabe dieser Beteiligung nicht ausdrücklich bedungen wird.

§ 113 [Verletzung des Wettbewerbsverbots]

(1) Verletzt ein Gesellschafter die ihm nach § 112 obliegende Verpflichtung, so kann die Gesellschaft Schadensersatz fordern; sie kann statt dessen von dem Gesellschafter verlangen, daß er die für eigene Rechnung gemachten Geschäfte als für Rechnung der Gesellschaft eingegangen gelten lasse und die aus Geschäften für fremde Rechnung bezogene Vergütung herausgebe oder seinen Anspruch auf die Vergütung abtrete.

(2) Über die Geltendmachung dieser Ansprüche beschließen die übrigen Gesellschafter.

(3) Die Ansprüche verjähren in drei Monaten von dem Zeitpunkt an, in welchem die übrigen Gesellschafter von dem Abschlusse des Geschäfts oder von der Teilnahme des Gesellschafters an der anderen Gesellschaft Kenntnis erlangen; sie verjähren ohne Rücksicht auf diese Kenntnis in fünf Jahren von ihrer Entstehung an.

(4) Das Recht der Gesellschafter, die Auflösung der Gesellschaft zu verlangen, wird durch diese Vorschriften nicht berührt.

partner in another similar commercial partnership.

(2) Consent to participation in another partnership is deemed to be given if the other partners know on entering the partnership that the partner is participating as a general partner in another partnership and renunciation of such participation is not expressly demanded.

§ 113 Violation of the prohibition of competition

(1) Where a partner violates his obligation pursuant to § 112, the partnership may assert a claim for damages; alternatively, it can demand of the partner that the business he conducted for his own account be deemed as made for the account of the partnership and that the partner either turn over compensation received from transactions for the account of third parties or assign his rights to such compensation.

(2) The remaining partners shall determine whether to assert these rights.

(3) The statute of limitations for these claims is three months from the time the remaining partners acquire knowledge of the conclusion of the transaction or of the participation of the partner in another partnership. Regardless of knowledge, the statute of limitations is five years from the date of the transaction.

(4) The right of the partners to demand the dissolution of the partnership is not affected by these provisions.

§ 114 [Geschäftsführung]

(1) Zur Führung der Geschäfte der Gesellschaft sind alle Gesellschafter berechtigt und verpflichtet.

(2) Ist im Gesellschaftsvertrage die Geschäftsführung einem Gesellschafter oder mehreren Gesellschaftern übertragen, so sind die übrigen Gesellschafter von der Geschäftsführung ausgeschlossen.

§ 115 [Geschäftsführung durch mehrere Gesellschafter]

(1) Steht die Geschäftsführung allen oder mehreren Gesellschaftern zu, so ist jeder von ihnen allein zu handeln berechtigt; widerspricht jedoch ein anderer geschäftsführender Gesellschafter der Vornahme einer Handlung, so muß diese unterbleiben.

(2) Ist im Gesellschaftsvertrage bestimmt, daß die Gesellschafter, denen die Geschäftsführung zusteht, nur zusammen handeln können, so bedarf es für jedes Geschäft der Zustimmung aller geschäftsführenden Gesellschafter, es sei denn, daß Gefahr im Verzug ist.

§ 116 [Umfang der Geschäftsführungsbefugnis]

(1) Die Befugnis zur Geschäftsführung erstreckt sich auf alle Handlungen, die der gewöhnliche Betrieb des Handelsgewerbes der Gesellschaft mit sich bringt.

(2) Zur Vornahme von Handlungen, die darüber hinausgehen, ist ein Beschluß sämtlicher Gesellschafter erforderlich.

(3) Zur Bestellung eines Prokuristen bedarf es der Zustimmung aller geschäftsführenden Gesellschafter, es sei denn, daß Gefahr im Verzug ist.

§ 114 Management of the business

(1) All partners are authorized and obligated to manage the business of the partnership.

(2) Where the management of the business has been assigned to one or more of the partners in the partnership agreement, the remaining partners are excluded from the management of the business.

§ 115 Management of the business by more than one partner

(1) Where all or several of the partners are entitled to manage the business, each one of them is authorized to transact business acting alone; where, however, another partner who is authorized to transact business objects to a transaction, it may not be undertaken.

(2) Where the partnership agreement provides that the managing partners may transact business only jointly, every business transaction requires the consent of all managing partners unless there is risk in delay.

§ 116 Scope of authority to manage the business

(1) The authority to manage the business extends to all acts associated with the normal operation of the business of the partnership.

(2) Transactions which are beyond such scope require a resolution of all the partners.

(3) The appointment of a Prokurist requires the consent of all managing partners unless there is risk in delay. Revocation of the Prokura can be ef-

Der Widerruf der Prokura kann von jedem der zur Erteilung oder zur Mitwirkung bei der Erteilung befugten Gesellschafter erfolgen.

§ 117 [Entziehung der Geschäftsführungsbefugnis]

Die Befugnis zur Geschäftsführung kann einem Gesellschafter auf Antrag der übrigen Gesellschafter durch gerichtliche Entscheidung entzogen werden, wenn ein wichtiger Grund vorliegt; ein solcher Grund ist insbesondere grobe Pflichtverletzung oder Unfähigkeit zur ordnungsmäßigen Geschäftsführung.

§ 118 [Kontrollrecht der Gesellschafter]

(1) Ein Gesellschafter kann, auch wenn er von der Geschäftsführung ausgeschlossen ist, sich von den Angelegenheiten der Gesellschaft persönlich unterrichten, die Handelsbücher und die Papiere der Gesellschaft einsehen und sich aus ihnen eine Bilanz und einen Jahresabschluß anfertigen.

(2) Eine dieses Recht ausschließende oder beschränkende Vereinbarung steht der Geltendmachung des Rechtes nicht entgegen, wenn Grund zu der Annahme unredlicher Geschäftsführung besteht.

§ 119 [Beschlußfassung]

(1) Für die von den Gesellschaftern zu fassenden Beschlüsse bedarf es der Zustimmung aller zur Mitwirkung bei der Beschlußfassung berufenen Gesellschafter.

(2) Hat nach dem Gesellschaftsvertrage die Mehrheit der Stimmen zu

fected by any of the partners authorized to confer or participate in the conferral of the Prokura.

§ 117 Withdrawal of authority to manage the business

The authority to manage the business can be withdrawn from one of the partners for an important reason by means of a judicial determination on application by the remaining partners. In particular, an important reason includes gross violation of duty or the inability to manage the business in a proper manner.

§ 118 Inspection right of partners

(1) A partner, even if he has been excluded from the management of the business, may inform himself concerning the partnership's affairs, examine the books and records of the partnership and prepare therefrom a balance sheet and annual financial statements.

(2) Any agreement excluding or limiting this right will not prevent assertion thereof if there is reason to believe that the business is being managed in a dishonest manner.

§ 119 Passage of resolutions

(1) The passage of resolutions by the partners requires consent of all partners entitled to participate in the resolution.

(2) If, pursuant to the partnership agreement, a majority vote is required

entscheiden, so ist die Mehrheit im Zweifel nach der Zahl der Gesellschafter zu berechnen.

§ 120 [Gewinn und Verlust]

(1) Am Schlusse jedes Geschäftsjahrs wird auf Grund der Bilanz der Gewinn oder der Verlust des Jahres ermittelt und für jeden Gesellschafter sein Anteil daran berechnet.

(2) Der einem Gesellschafter zukommende Gewinn wird dem Kapitalanteile des Gesellschafters zugeschrieben; der auf einen Gesellschafter entfallende Verlust sowie das während des Geschäftsjahrs auf den Kapitalanteil entnommene Geld wird davon abgeschrieben.

§ 121 [Verteilung von Gewinn und Verlust]

(1) Von dem Jahresgewinne gebührt jedem Gesellschafter zunächst ein Anteil in Höhe von vier vom Hundert seines Kapitalanteils. Reicht der Jahresgewinn hierzu nicht aus, so bestimmen sich die Anteile nach einem entsprechend niedrigeren Satze.

(2) Bei der Berechnung des nach Absatz 1 einem Gesellschafter zukommenden Gewinnanteils werden Leistungen, die der Gesellschafter im Laufe des Geschäftsjahrs als Einlage gemacht hat, nach dem Verhältnisse der seit der Leistung abgelaufenen Zeit berücksichtigt. Hat der Gesellschafter im Laufe des Geschäftsjahrs Geld auf seinen Kapitalanteil entnommen, so werden die entnommenen Beträge nach dem Verhältnisse der bis zur Entnahme abgelaufenen Zeit berücksichtigt.

to pass a resolution, the majority shall be calculated, in case of doubt, according to the number of partners.

§ 120 Profits and losses

(1) At the close of every fiscal year, the profits and losses for the year will be computed based on the annual balance sheet and every partner's share thereof will be determined.

(2) The profits due to a partner will be credited to the partner's share in capital; the losses attributable to a partner, as well as money withdrawn from the share capital during the fiscal year, will be deducted therefrom.

§ 121 Distribution of profits and losses

(1) Every partner is entitled to an initial share in the annual profits in the amount of four percent of his share in capital. Where the annual profits are not sufficient for this, the profit share shall be computed at a correspondingly lower rate.

(2) In computing profit shares to which a partner is entitled pursuant to Subsection 1, payments which the partner made in the course of the fiscal year as contributions to capital will be taken into consideration in proportion to the time elapsed since payment. Where the partner, during the course of the fiscal year, has withdrawn money from his share in capital, the sums withdrawn will be taken into consideration in proportion to the time elapsed prior to the withdrawal.

(3) Derjenige Teil des Jahresgewinns, welcher die nach den Absätzen 1 und 2 zu berechnenden Gewinnanteile übersteigt, sowie der Verlust eines Geschäftsjahrs wird unter die Gesellschafter nach Köpfen verteilt.

§ 122 [Entnahmen]

(1) Jeder Gesellschafter ist berechtigt, aus der Gesellschaftskasse Geld bis zum Betrage von vier vom Hundert seines für das letzte Geschäftsjahr festgestellten Kapitalanteils zu seinen Lasten zu erheben und, soweit es nicht zum offenbaren Schaden der Gesellschaft gereicht, auch die Auszahlung seines den bezeichneten Betrag übersteigenden Anteils am Gewinne des letzten Jahres zu verlangen.

(2) Im übrigen ist ein Gesellschafter nicht befugt, ohne Einwilligung der anderen Gesellschafter seinen Kapitalanteil zu vermindern.

Dritter Titel. Rechtsverhältnis der Gesellschafter zu Dritten

§ 123 [Wirksamkeit im Verhältnis zu Dritten]

(1) Die Wirksamkeit der offenen Handelsgesellschaft tritt im Verhältnisse zu Dritten mit dem Zeitpunkt ein, in welchem die Gesellschaft in das Handelsregister eingetragen wird.

(2) Beginnt die Gesellschaft ihre Geschäfte schon vor der Eintragung, so tritt die Wirksamkeit mit dem Zeitpunkte des Geschäftsbeginns ein, soweit nicht aus § 2 oder § 105 Abs. 2 sich ein anderes ergibt.

(3) Eine Vereinbarung, daß die Gesellschaft erst mit einem späteren Zeitpunkt ihren Anfang nehmen soll, ist Dritten gegenüber unwirksam.

(3) That portion of the annual profits which exceeds the profit shares calculated pursuant to Subsections 1 and 2, as well as the losses from a fiscal year, will be distributed among the partners equally.

§ 122 Withdrawals

(1) Every partner is entitled to withdraw funds from the partnership account up to an amount equal to four per cent of his share in capital as ascertained for the last fiscal year and, insofar as it does not clearly cause injury to the partnership, also to demand payment of his share of the profits of the preceding fiscal year which exceeds the aforementioned amount.

(2) A partner is not otherwise authorized, without consent of the other partners, to reduce his share capital.

Third Title. Legal Relationship of the Partners to Third Parties

§ 123 Effectiveness with respect to third parties

(1) The effectiveness of the general commercial partnership with respect to third parties begins with the time the partnership has been registered in the Commercial Register.

(2) Where the partnership begins business before registration, effectiveness begins with the time when business commences, unless § 2 or § 105 Subsection 2 provides otherwise.

(3) Any agreement by which the partnership is to begin existence at a later date is ineffective with respect to third parties.

§ 124 [Rechtliche Selbständigkeit; Zwangsvollstreckung in Gesellschaftsvermögen]

(1) Die offene Handelsgesellschaft kann unter ihrer Firma Rechte erwerben und Verbindlichkeiten eingehen, Eigentum und andere dingliche Rechte an Grundstücken erwerben, vor Gericht klagen und verklagt werden.

(2) Zur Zwangsvollstreckung in das Gesellschaftsvermögen ist ein gegen die Gesellschaft gerichteter vollstreckbarer Schuldtitel erforderlich.

§ 125 [Vertretung der Gesellschaft]

(1) Zur Vertretung der Gesellschaft ist jeder Gesellschafter ermächtigt, wenn er nicht durch den Gesellschaftsvertrag von der Vertretung ausgeschlossen ist.

(2) Im Gesellschaftsvertrage kann bestimmt werden, daß alle oder mehrere Gesellschafter nur in Gemeinschaft zur Vertretung der Gesellschaft ermächtigt sein sollen (Gesamtvertretung). Die zur Gesamtvertretung berechtigten Gesellschafter können einzelne von ihnen zur Vornahme bestimmter Geschäfte oder bestimmter Arten von Geschäften ermächtigen. Ist der Gesellschaft gegenüber eine Willenserklärung abzugeben, so genügt die Abgabe gegenüber einem der zur Mitwirkung bei der Vertretung befugten Gesellschafter.

(3) Im Gesellschaftsvertrage kann bestimmt werden, daß die Gesellschafter, wenn nicht mehrere zusammen handeln, nur in Gemeinschaft mit einem Prokuristen zur Vertretung der Gesellschaft ermächtigt sein sollen. Die Vorschriften des Absatzes 2 Satz 2 und 3 finden in diesem Falle entsprechende Anwendung.

§ 124 Legal personality; execution on partnership assets

(1) The general commercial partnership can acquire rights and enter into obligations, acquire ownership and other rights in real property and sue and be sued in its own name.

(2) For execution on the assets of the partnership, a legally executable judgment of debt against the partnership is required.

§ 125 Representation of the partnership

(1) Each of the partners is authorized to represent the partnership if he has not been excluded from such representation by the terms of the partnership agreement.

(2) The partnership agreement may provide that all or more than one of the partners should be authorized to represent the partnership only jointly (joint representation). The partners authorized to represent jointly may among themselves authorize individual partners to undertake specific transactions or specific kinds of transactions. Where a statement of intent is to be made to the partnership, it is sufficient that it be made to one of the partners authorized to participate in representing the partnership.

(3) The partnership agreement may provide that, where the partners do not act jointly, they are authorized to represent the partnership only jointly with a Prokurist. The provisions of Subsection 2 sentences 2 and 3 apply analogously to this case.

(4) *(aufgehoben)* | (4) *(repealed)*

§ 125 a [Angaben auf Geschäftsbriefen]

(1) Auf allen Geschäftsbriefen der Gesellschaft, die an einen bestimmten Empfänger gerichtet werden, müssen die Rechtsform und der Sitz der Gesellschaft, das Registergericht und die Nummer, unter der die Gesellschaft in das Handelsregister eingetragen ist, angegeben werden. Bei einer Gesellschaft, bei der kein Gesellschafter eine natürliche Person ist, sind auf den Geschäftsbriefen der Gesellschaft ferner die Firmen der Gesellschafter anzugeben sowie für die Gesellschafter die nach § 35 a des Gesetzes betreffend die Gesellschaften mit beschränkter Haftung oder § 80 des Aktiengesetzes für Geschäftsbriefe vorgeschriebenen Angaben zu machen. Die Angaben nach Satz 2 sind nicht erforderlich, wenn zu den Gesellschaftern der Gesellschaft eine offene Handelsgesellschaft oder Kommanditgesellschaft gehört, bei der ein persönlich haftender Gesellschafter eine natürliche Person ist.

(2) Für Vordrucke und Bestellscheine ist § 37 a Abs. 2 und 3, für Zwangsgelder gegen die zur Vertretung der Gesellschaft ermächtigten Gesellschafter oder deren organschaftliche Vertreter und die Liquidatoren ist § 37 a Abs. 4 entsprechend anzuwenden.

§ 125 a Information on business letters

(1) All business letters of the company directed to a specific addressee shall contain the legal form and domicile of the partnership, the registry court and the number under which the partnership is registered in the Commercial Register. In a partnership where no partner is a natural person, the business of the partnership must also contain the firm names of the partners as well the information with respect to the partners which must appear on business pursuant to § 35 a of the Limited Liability Companies Act or § 80 of the Stock Corporation Act. The information pursuant to sentence 2 is not required if one of the partners is a commercial general partnership or a limited partnership in which a general partner is a natural person.

(2) § 37 a Subsections 2 and 3 of the Limited Liability Companies Act shall apply analogously for printed forms and order forms; likewise § 37 a Subsection 4 of the Limited Liability Companies Act shall apply analogously for coercive fines against the partners authorized to represent the partnership or the corporate representatives and the liquidators.

§ 126 [Umfang der Vertretungsmacht]

(1) Die Vertretungsmacht der Gesellschafter erstreckt sich auf alle gerichtlichen und außergerichtlichen Geschäfte und Rechtshandlungen einschließlich der Veräußerung und Belastung von Grundstücken sowie der Erteilung und des Widerrufs einer Prokura.

(2) Eine Beschränkung des Umfanges der Vertretungsmacht ist Dritten gegenüber unwirksam; dies gilt insbesondere von der Beschränkung, daß sich die Vertretung nur auf gewisse Geschäfte oder Arten von Geschäften erstrecken oder daß sie nur unter gewissen Umständen oder für eine gewisse Zeit oder an einzelnen Orten stattfinden soll.

(3) In betreff der Beschränkung auf den Betrieb einer von mehreren Niederlassungen der Gesellschaft finden die Vorschriften des § 50 Abs. 3 entsprechende Anwendung.

§ 127 [Entziehung der Vertretungsmacht]

Die Vertretungsmacht kann einem Gesellschafter auf Antrag der übrigen Gesellschafter durch gerichtliche Entscheidung entzogen werden, wenn ein wichtiger Grund vorliegt; ein solcher Grund ist insbesondere grobe Pflichtverletzung oder Unfähigkeit zur ordnungsgemäßen Vertretung der Gesellschaft.

§ 128 [Persönliche Haftung der Gesellschafter]

Die Gesellschafter haften für die Verbindlichkeiten der Gesellschaft den Gläubigern als Gesamtschuldner per-

§ 126 Scope of the power to represent

(1) The partners' power of representation extends to all court and non-court proceedings and transactions, including the alienation and encumbrance of real property and the conferral and revocation of a Prokura.

(2) A limitation of the scope of the power of representation is ineffective as to third parties; this applies especially to limitations which restrict the representation to only certain transactions or kinds of transactions or by which the power is only to be exercised under certain circumstances, for a specific period of time or at a certain location.

(3) The provisions of § 50 Subsection 3 apply analogously to the limitation of the power to operation of one of several branches of the partnership.

§ 127 Withdrawal of the power to represent

The power of representation can be withdrawn from one partner for an important reason by judicial determination on application by the other partners. In particular, an important reason includes the gross violation of duty or the inability to manage the business in a proper manner.

§ 128 Personal liability of the partners

The partners are jointly and severally liable to creditors for the obligations of the partnership. Any agreement to

sönlich. Eine entgegenstehende Vereinbarung ist Dritten gegenüber unwirksam.

§ 129 [Einwendungen des Gesellschafters]

(1) Wird ein Gesellschafter wegen einer Verbindlichkeit der Gesellschaft in Anspruch genommen, so kann er Einwendungen, die nicht in seiner Person begründet sind, nur insoweit geltend machen, als sie von der Gesellschaft erhoben werden können.

(2) Der Gesellschafter kann die Befriedigung des Gläubigers verweigern, solange der Gesellschaft das Recht zusteht, das ihrer Verbindlichkeit zugrunde liegende Rechtsgeschäft anzufechten.

(3) Die gleiche Befugnis hat der Gesellschafter, solange sich der Gläubiger durch Aufrechnung gegen eine fällige Forderung der Gesellschaft befriedigen kann.

(4) Aus einem gegen die Gesellschaft gerichteten vollstreckbaren Schuldtitel findet die Zwangsvollstreckung gegen die Gesellschafter nicht statt.

§ 129 a [Rückgewähr von Darlehen]

Bei einer offenen Handelsgesellschaft, bei der kein Gesellschafter eine natürliche Person ist, gelten die §§ 32 a und 32 b des Gesetzes betreffend die Gesellschaften mit beschränkter Haftung sinngemäß mit der Maßgabe, daß an die Stelle der Gesellschafter der Gesellschaft mit beschränkter Haftung die Gesellschafter oder Mitglieder der Gesellschafter der offenen Handelsgesellschaft treten. Dies gilt

the contrary is invalid with respect to third parties.

§ 129 Defenses of the partner

(1) If a claim based on an obligation of the partnership is asserted against a partner, the partner may assert defenses which are not personal defenses only insofar as they could be raised by the partnership.

(2) The partner can refuse payment to the creditor as long as the partnership has the right to challenge the legal transaction underlying the obligation.

(3) The partner has the same right for so long as the creditor can satisfy the obligation by means of set-off against a claim due to the partnership.

(4) Execution against the partners cannot be accomplished by a legally executable judgment of debt directed against the partnership.

§ 129 a Repayment of loans

With respect to a general partnership in which none of the partners is a natural person, §§ 32 a and 32 b of the Limited Liability Companies Act apply analogously, with the proviso that the partners or members of the partners of the general partnership shall take the place of the shareholders of the limited liability company. This does not apply where one of the partners of the general partnership is an-

nicht, wenn zu den Gesellschaftern der offenen Handelsgesellschaft eine andere offene Handelsgesellschaft oder Kommanditgesellschaft gehört, bei der ein persönlich haftender Gesellschafter eine natürliche Person ist.

§ 130 [Haftung des eintretenden Gesellschafters]

(1) Wer in eine bestehende Gesellschaft eintritt, haftet gleich den anderen Gesellschaftern nach Maßgabe der §§ 128 und 129 für die vor seinem Eintritte begründeten Verbindlichkeiten der Gesellschaft, ohne Unterschied, ob die Firma eine Änderung erleidet oder nicht.

(2) Eine entgegenstehende Vereinbarung ist Dritten gegenüber unwirksam.

§ 130 a [Antragspflicht bei Zahlungsunfähigkeit oder Überschuldung]

(1) Wird eine Gesellschaft, bei der kein Gesellschafter eine natürliche Person ist, zahlungsunfähig oder ergibt sich die Überschuldung der Gesellschaft, so ist die Eröffnung des Insolvenzverfahrens zu beantragen; dies gilt nicht, wenn zu den Gesellschaftern der offenen Handelsgesellschaft eine andere offene Handelsgesellschaft oder Kommanditgesellschaft gehört, bei der ein persönlich haftender Gesellschafter eine natürliche Person ist. Antragspflichtig sind die organschaftlichen Vertreter der zur Vertretung der Gesellschaft ermächtigten Gesellschafter und die Liquidatoren. Der Antrag ist ohne schuldhaftes Zögern, spätestens aber drei Wochen nach Eintritt der Zahlungsunfähigkeit oder der Überschuldung der Gesellschaft zu stellen.

other general partnership or limited partnership, of which one of the general partners is a natural person.

§ 130 Liability of a partner joining the partnership

(1) One who joins an existing partnership is liable in the same manner as the other partners in accordance with §§ 128 and 129 for the obligations of the partnership incurred before his joining, irrespective of whether the firm name is changed.

(2) Any agreement to the contrary is ineffective with respect to third parties.

§ 130 a Duty to file a petition in the event of inability to meet obligations or insolvency

(1) Where a partnership in which none of the partners is a natural person is unable to meet its debts, or the assets of the partnership no longer cover the debts, a petition for commencement of insolvency proceedings shall be filed; this does not apply if one of the partners is a general commercial partnership or a limited partnership in which a general partner is a natural person. The legal representatives of the partners authorized to represent the partnership and the liquidators are obligated to file the petition. The petition shall be filed without culpable delay, and not later than three weeks following the commencement of the partnership's insolvency or inability to meet its debts.

(2) Nachdem die Zahlungsunfähigkeit der Gesellschaft eingetreten ist oder sich ihre Überschuldung ergeben hat, dürfen die organschaftlichen Vertreter der zur Vertretung der Gesellschaft ermächtigten Gesellschafter und die Liquidatoren für die Gesellschaft keine Zahlungen leisten. Dies gilt nicht von Zahlungen, die auch nach diesem Zeitpunkt mit der Sorgfalt eines ordentlichen und gewissenhaften Geschäftsleiters vereinbar sind.

(3) Wird entgegen Absatz 1 die Eröffnung des Insolvenzverfahrens nicht oder nicht rechtzeitig beantragt oder werden entgegen Absatz 2 Zahlungen geleistet, nachdem die Zahlungsunfähigkeit der Gesellschaft eingetreten ist oder sich ihre Überschuldung ergeben hat, so sind die organschaftlichen Vertreter der zur Vertretung der Gesellschaft ermächtigten Gesellschafter und die Liquidatoren der Gesellschaft gegenüber zum Ersatz des daraus entstehenden Schadens als Gesamtschuldner verpflichtet. Ist dabei streitig, ob sie die Sorgfalt eines ordentlichen und gewissenhaften Geschäftsleiters angewandt haben, so trifft sie die Beweislast. Die Ersatzpflicht kann durch Vereinbarung mit den Gesellschaftern weder eingeschränkt noch ausgeschlossen werden. Soweit der Ersatz zur Befriedigung der Gläubiger der Gesellschaft erforderlich ist, wird die Ersatzpflicht weder durch einen Verzicht oder Vergleich der Gesellschaft noch dadurch aufgehoben, daß die Handlung auf einem Beschluß der Gesellschafter beruht. Satz 4 gilt nicht, wenn der Ersatzpflichtige zahlungsunfähig ist und sich zur Abwendung des Insolvenzverfahrens mit seinen Gläubigern vergleicht oder wenn die Ersatzpflicht in

(2) Upon commencement of the partnership's inability to meet its debts or its insolvency, the legal representatives of the partners authorized to represent the partnership and the liquidators may not make any payments on behalf of the partnership. This does not apply to payments which, even after such point in time, are consistent with the care of a prudent business manager.

(3) Where, contrary to Subsection 1, the petition for commencement of insolvency proceedings has not been filed, where it has not been filed in a timely manner or where payments are made, contrary to Subsection 2, following the commencement of the partnership's inability to meet its debts or insolvency, the legal representatives of the partners authorized to represent the partnership and the liquidators of the partnership are jointly liable to the partnership for resultant damages. Where it is contested as to whether they have acted in accordance with the care of a prudent business manager, they shall bear the burden of proof. The duty to pay damages may be neither limited nor excluded by agreement with the partners. Insofar as payment of damages is necessary to satisfy the partnership's creditors, the duty to pay damages will be affected neither by renunciation or settlement by the partnership, nor by the fact that the action was based on a resolution of the partners. Sentence 4 does not apply where the party obligated to pay damages is insolvent and enters into a composition with its creditors in order to avert the insolvency proceedings or where the obligation to pay damages is laid

einem Insolvenzplan geregelt wird. Die Ansprüche aus diesen Vorschriften verjähren in fünf Jahren.

(4) Diese Vorschriften gelten sinngemäß, wenn die in den Absätzen 1 bis 3 genannten organschaftlichen Vertreter ihrerseits Gesellschaften sind, bei denen kein Gesellschafter eine natürliche Person ist, oder sich die Verbindung von Gesellschaften in dieser Art fortsetzt.

§ 130 b [Strafvorschriften]

(1) Mit Freiheitsstrafe bis zu drei Jahren oder mit Geldstrafe wird bestraft, wer es entgegen § 130 a Abs. 1 oder 4 unterläßt, als organschaftlicher Vertreter oder Liquidator bei Zahlungsunfähigkeit oder Überschuldung der Gesellschaft die Eröffnung des Insolvenzverfahrens zu beantragen.

(2) Handelt der Täter fahrlässig, so ist die Strafe Freiheitsstrafe bis zu einem Jahr oder Geldstrafe.

Vierter Titel. Auflösung der Gesellschaft und Ausscheiden von Gesellschaftern

§ 131 [Auflösungsgründe]

(1) Die offene Handelsgesellschaft wird aufgelöst:
1. durch den Ablauf der Zeit, für welche sie eingegangen ist;
2. durch Beschluß der Gesellschafter;
3. durch die Eröffnung des Insolvenzverfahrens über das Vermögen der Gesellschaft;
4. durch gerichtliche Entscheidung.

down in an insolvency plan. The statute of limitation for claims arising from these provisions is five years.

(4) These provisions apply analogously if the corporate representatives referred to in Subsections 1 through 3 are partnerships in which no natural persons are partners or the chain of partnerships is continued in this manner.

§ 130 b Penal provisions

(1) One who as legal representative or liquidator fails to file a petition to commence insolvency proceedings, contrary to § 130 a Subsections 1 or 4, where the partnership is insolvent or unable to pay its debts, will be punished with up to three years' imprisonment or by fine.

(2) Where such person has acted negligently, the penalty shall be up to one year's imprisonment or a fine.

Fourth Title. Dissolution of the Partnership and Withdrawal of Partners

§ 131 Reasons for dissolution

(1) The general commercial partnership will be dissolved
1. by expiration of the period for which it was entered into;
2. by resolution of the partners;
3. by commencement of the insolvency proceeding with respect to the assets of the partnership;
4. by judical decision.

(2) Eine offene Handelsgesellschaft, bei der kein persönlich haftender Gesellschafter eine natürliche Person ist, wird ferner aufgelöst:
1. mit der Rechtskraft des Beschlusses, durch den die Eröffnung des Insolvenzverfahrens mangels Masse abgelehnt worden ist;
2. durch die Löschung wegen Vermögenslosigkeit nach § 141 a des Gesetzes über die Angelegenheiten der freiwilligen Gerichtsbarkeit.

Dies gilt nicht, wenn zu den persönlich haftenden Gesellschaftern eine andere offene Handelsgesellschaft oder Kommanditgesellschaft gehört, bei der ein persönlich haftender Gesellschafter eine natürliche Person ist.

(3) Folgende Gründe führen mangels abweichender vertraglicher Bestimmung zum Ausscheiden eines Gesellschafters:
1. Tod des Gesellschafters,
2. Eröffnung des Insolvenzverfahrens über das Vermögen des Gesellschafters,
3. Kündigung des Gesellschafters,
4. Kündigung durch den Privatgläubiger des Gesellschafters,
5. Eintritt von weiteren im Gesellschaftsvertrag vorgesehenen Fällen,
6. Beschluß der Gesellschafter.

Der Gesellschafter scheidet mit dem Eintritt des ihn betreffenden Ereignisses aus, im Falle der Kündigung aber nicht vor Ablauf der Kündigungsfrist.

§ 132 [Kündigung eines Gesellschafters]

Die Kündigung eines Gesellschafters kann, wenn die Gesellschaft für unbestimmte Zeit eingegangen ist, nur für

(2) A general commercial partnership in which none of the general partners is a natural person shall also be dissolved:
1. Upon the finality of the court order by which the commencement of the insolvency proceeding is rejected because of lack of assets;
2. by deletion in the Commercial Register because of lack of assets pursuant to § 141a of the Law Concerning Administrative Acts of the Judiciary.

This does not apply if one of the general partners is another commercial general partnership or a limited partnership in which a general partner is a natural person.

(3) The following reasons lead to the withdrawal of a partner, unless contractual provisions provide otherwise:
1. The death of a partner,
2. commencement of the insolvency proceeding pertaining to the assets of a partner,
3. termination of a partner,
4. termination by the personal creditor of the partner,
5. occurrence of other events provided for in the partnership agreement,
6. resolution of the partners.

The partner withdraws upon the occurrence of the relevant event in case of termination, however, not before the expiration of the notice period.

§ 132 Notice of termination by one of the partners

Notice of termination by a partner can only be effective as of the close of a fiscal year if the partnership is of indefi-

den Schluß eines Geschäftsjahrs erfolgen; sie muß mindestens sechs Monate vor diesem Zeitpunkte stattfinden.

§ 133 [Auflösung durch gerichtliche Entscheidung]

(1) Auf Antrag eines Gesellschafters kann die Auflösung der Gesellschaft vor dem Ablaufe der für ihre Dauer bestimmten Zeit oder bei einer für unbestimmte Zeit eingegangenen Gesellschaft ohne Kündigung durch gerichtliche Entscheidung ausgesprochen werden, wenn ein wichtiger Grund vorliegt.

(2) Ein solcher Grund ist insbesondere vorhanden, wenn ein anderer Gesellschafter eine ihm nach dem Gesellschaftsvertrag obliegende wesentliche Verpflichtung vorsätzlich oder aus grober Fahrlässigkeit verletzt oder wenn die Erfüllung einer solchen Verpflichtung unmöglich wird.

(3) Eine Vereinbarung, durch welche das Recht des Gesellschafters, die Auflösung der Gesellschaft zu verlangen, ausgeschlossen oder diesen Vorschriften zuwider beschränkt wird, ist nichtig.

§ 134 [Gesellschaft auf Lebenszeit; fortgesetzte Gesellschaft]

Eine Gesellschaft, die für die Lebenszeit eines Gesellschafters eingegangen ist oder nach dem Ablaufe der für ihre Dauer bestimmten Zeit stillschweigend fortgesetzt wird, steht im Sinne der Vorschriften der §§ 132 und 133 einer für unbestimmte Zeit eingegangenen Gesellschaft gleich.

nite duration; it must be given at least six months before such time.

§ 133 Dissolution by judicial decision

(1) Upon motion by one of the partners, the dissolution of the partnership can be declared by judicial decision before expiration of the period specified for its duration, or if the partnership is to continue for an indefinite period, without notice if an important reason exists.

(2) Such an important reason is particularly present if another partner intentionally or by reason of gross negligence violates a material obligation set forth in the partnership agreement, or if the fulfilment of such an obligation becomes impossible.

(3) An agreement by which the partner's right to demand dissolution of the partnership is excluded or limited contrary to these provisions, is void.

§ 134 Partnership for a term of life; continued partnership

A partnership which has been entered into for the term of the life of one of the partners or which is tacitly continued after expiration of the specific period of its duration, constitutes a partnership of indefinite duration within the meaning of the provisions of §§ 132 and 133.

§ 135 [Kündigung durch den Privatgläubiger]

Hat ein Privatgläubiger eines Gesellschafters, nachdem innerhalb der letzten sechs Monate eine Zwangsvollstreckung in das bewegliche Vermögen des Gesellschafters ohne Erfolg versucht ist, auf Grund eines nicht bloß vorläufig vollstreckbaren Schuldtitels die Pfändung und Überweisung des Anspruchs auf dasjenige erwirkt, was dem Gesellschafter bei der Auseinandersetzung zukommt, so kann er die Gesellschaft ohne Rücksicht darauf, ob sie für bestimmte oder unbestimmte Zeit eingegangen ist, sechs Monate vor dem Ende des Geschäftsjahrs für diesen Zeitpunkt kündigen.

§§ 136–138 *(aufgehoben)*

§ 139 [Fortsetzung mit den Erben]

(1) Ist im Gesellschaftsvertrage bestimmt, daß im Falle des Todes eines Gesellschafters die Gesellschaft mit dessen Erben fortgesetzt werden soll, so kann jeder Erbe sein Verbleiben in der Gesellschaft davon abhängig machen, daß ihm unter Belassung des bisherigen Gewinnanteils die Stellung eines Kommanditisten eingeräumt und der auf ihn fallende Teil der Einlage des Erblassers als seine Kommanditeinlage anerkannt wird.

(2) Nehmen die übrigen Gesellschafter einen dahingehenden Antrag des Erben nicht an, so ist dieser befugt, ohne Einhaltung einer Kündigungsfrist sein Ausscheiden aus der Gesellschaft zu erklären.

§ 135 Termination by the personal creditor of a partner

Where a personal creditor of a partner, after having sought execution on the tangible assets of the partner without success within the last six months, effects, on the basis of other than a merely preliminary enforceable judgment of debt, a seizure and transfer of what is due the partner in the case of dissolution, he may give notice to terminate the partnership as of the end of the fiscal year, without regard as to whether the partnership has been entered into for a definite or indefinite period of time, by giving notice at least six months prior to the end of such fiscal year.

§§ 136–138 *(repealed)*

§ 139 Continuation of the business with the heirs

(1) Where a partnership agreement provides that, on the death of one of the partners, the partnership shall be carried on with the heirs of such partner, each heir can make his continued participation in the partnership conditional upon his being given the position of a limited partner, with retention of the then-existing profit share, and upon the recognition of the portion of the decedent's partnership contribution attributable to him as his limited partnership contribution.

(2) Where the remaining partners do not accept such request by the heir, he may declare his immediate withdrawal from the partnership without compliance with a notice period.

(3) Die bezeichneten Rechte können von dem Erben nur innerhalb einer Frist von drei Monaten nach dem Zeitpunkt, in welchem er von dem Anfalle der Erbschaft Kenntnis erlangt hat, geltend gemacht werden. Auf den Lauf der Frist finden die für die Verjährung geltenden Vorschriften des § 210 des Bürgerlichen Gesetzbuchs entsprechende Anwendung. Ist bei dem Ablaufe der drei Monate das Recht zur Ausschlagung der Erbschaft noch nicht verloren, so endigt die Frist nicht vor dem Ablaufe der Ausschlagungsfrist.

(4) Scheidet innerhalb der Frist des Absatzes 3 der Erbe aus der Gesellschaft aus oder wird innerhalb der Frist die Gesellschaft aufgelöst oder dem Erben die Stellung eines Kommanditisten eingeräumt, so haftet er für die bis dahin entstandenen Gesellschaftsschulden nur nach Maßgabe der die Haftung des Erben für die Nachlaßverbindlichkeiten betreffenden Vorschriften des bürgerlichen Rechtes.

(5) Der Gesellschaftsvertrag kann die Anwendung der Vorschriften der Absätze 1 bis 4 nicht ausschließen; es kann jedoch für den Fall, daß der Erbe sein Verbleiben in der Gesellschaft von der Einräumung der Stellung eines Kommanditisten abhängig macht, sein Gewinnanteil anders als der des Erblassers bestimmt werden.

§ 140 [Ausschließung eines Gesellschafters]

(1) Tritt in der Person eines Gesellschafters ein Umstand ein, der nach § 133 für die übrigen Gesellschafter das Recht begründet, die Auflösung der Gesellschaft zu verlangen, so kann vom Gericht anstatt der Auflösung die Ausschließung dieses Gesellschaf-

(3) The foregoing rights can only be asserted by the heir within a period of three months following the time he acquired knowledge of the vesting of the inheritance. The provisions of § 210 of the Civil Code concerning the statute of limitations apply analogously to the running of the period. Where the right to reject the inheritance has not expired at the end of the three months, the period does not end prior to expiration of the rejection period.

(4) Where, within the period in Subsection 3, the heir withdraws from the partnership, the partnership is dissolved or the heir is given the position of a limited partner, he is liable for the then-existing partnership liabilities only in accordance with the civil law provisions concerning liability of the heirs for obligations of the estate.

(5) The partnership agreement cannot exclude application of the provisions of Subsections 1 through 4; however, in the event that the heir has made his remaining in the partnership conditional upon being granted the position of a limited partner, his profit share may be determined differently from that of the decedent.

§ 140 Exclusion of a partner

(1) Where a circumstance relating to the person of a partner occurs which, pursuant to § 133, gives the remaining partners the right to demand dissolution of the partnership, the court can order the exclusion of such partner from the partnership instead of disso-

ters aus der Gesellschaft ausgesprochen werden, sofern die übrigen Gesellschafter dies beantragen. Der Ausschließungsklage steht nicht entgegen, daß nach der Ausschließung nur ein Gesellschafter verbleibt.

(2) Für die Auseinandersetzung zwischen der Gesellschaft und dem ausgeschlossenen Gesellschafter ist die Vermögenslage der Gesellschaft in dem Zeitpunkte maßgebend, in welchem die Klage auf Ausschließung erhoben ist.

§§ 141, 142 *(aufgehoben)*

§ 143 [Anmeldung von Auflösung und Ausscheiden]

(1) Die Auflösung der Gesellschaft ist von sämtlichen Gesellschaftern zur Eintragung in das Handelsregister anzumelden. Dies gilt nicht in den Fällen der Eröffnung oder der Ablehnung der Eröffnung des Insolvenzverfahrens über das Vermögen der Gesellschaft (§ 131 Abs. 1 Nr. 3 und Abs. 2 Nr. 1). In diesen Fällen hat das Gericht die Auflösung und ihren Grund von Amts wegen einzutragen. Im Falle der Löschung der Gesellschaft (§ 131 Abs. 2 Nr. 2) entfällt die Eintragung der Auflösung.

(2) Absatz 1 Satz 1 gilt entsprechend für das Ausscheiden eines Gesellschafters aus der Gesellschaft.

(3) Ist anzunehmen, daß der Tod eines Gesellschafters die Auflösung oder das Ausscheiden zur Folge gehabt hat, so kann, auch ohne daß die Erben bei der Anmeldung mitwirken, die Eintragung erfolgen, soweit einer solchen Mitwirkung besondere Hindernisse entgegenstehen.

lution, provided the remaining partners have made a motion to this effect. A court action to exclude a partner is not rendered impossible by the fact that only one partner will remain after the exclusion.

(2) The financial condition of the partnership at the time the motion for exclusion was made is determinative in the settlement between the partnership and the excluded partner.

§§ 141, 142 *(repealed)*

§ 143 Registration of dissolution and withdrawal from the partnership

(1) All of the partners shall file to register the dissolution of the partnership in the Commercial Register. This does not apply where insolvency proceedings pertaining to the assets of the partnership are commenced or the commencement is rejected (§ 131 Subsection 1 No. 3 and Subsection 2 No. 1). The court shall in these cases register in the Commercial Register on its own motion the dissolution and its reason. No registration of the dissolution is necessary where the company is deleted from the Commercial Register (§ 131 Subsection 2 No. 2).

(2) Subsection 1 sentence 1 applies analogously to the withdrawal of a partner from the partnership.

(3) Where it can be assumed that the death of a partner has caused the dissolution or withdrawal, registration can also occur without the heirs' participation in the filing insofar as special obstacles prevent such participation.

§ 144 [Fortsetzung nach Insolvenz der Gesellschaft]

(1) Ist die Gesellschaft durch die Eröffnung des Insolvenzverfahrens über ihr Vermögen aufgelöst, das Verfahren aber auf Antrag des Schuldners eingestellt oder nach der Bestätigung eines Insolvenzplans, der den Fortbestand der Gesellschaft vorsieht, aufgehoben, so können die Gesellschafter die Fortsetzung der Gesellschaft beschließen.

(2) Die Fortsetzung ist von sämtlichen Gesellschaftern zur Eintragung in das Handelsregister anzumelden.

Fünfter Titel. Liquidation der Gesellschaft

§ 145 [Notwendigkeit der Liquidation]

(1) Nach der Auflösung der Gesellschaft findet die Liquidation statt, sofern nicht eine andere Art der Auseinandersetzung von den Gesellschaftern vereinbart oder über das Vermögen der Gesellschaft das Insolvenzverfahren eröffnet ist.

(2) Ist die Gesellschaft durch Kündigung des Gläubigers eines Gesellschafters oder durch die Eröffnung des Insolvenzverfahrens über das Vermögen eines Gesellschafters aufgelöst, so kann die Liquidation nur mit Zustimmung des Gläubigers oder des Insolvenzverwalters unterbleiben; ist im Insolvenzverfahren Eigenverwaltung angeordnet, so tritt an die Stelle der Zustimmung des Insolvenzverwalters die Zustimmung des Schuldners.

§ 144 Continuation of the partnership following insolvency

(1) Where the partnership is dissolved by the commencement of insolvency proceedings with respect to its assets, but insolvency proceedings have been discontinued on application of the debtor or cancelled upon ratification of an insolvency plan which provides for the continuation of the partnership, the partners may by resolution continue the partnership.

(2) Filing for registration in the Commercial Register of continuation shall be made by all of the partners.

Fifth Title. Liquidation of the Partnership

§ 145 Necessity of liquidation

(1) Liquidation shall take place after dissolution of the partnership unless some other manner of settlement has been agreed to by the partners or insolvency proceedings are commenced with respect to the assets of the partnership.

(2) Where the partnership has been dissolved by notice of a creditor of one of the partners or by the commencement of insolvency proceedings with respect to the assets of one of the partners, liquidation can be avoided only with the consent of the creditor or the insolvency administrator; where it has been decreed in the insolvency proceedings that the partners may administer their own assets, the consent of the debtor takes the place of the consent of the insolvency administrator.

(3) Ist die Gesellschaft durch Löschung wegen Vermögenslosigkeit aufgelöst, so findet eine Liquidation nur statt, wenn sich nach der Löschung herausstellt, daß Vermögen vorhanden ist, das der Verteilung unterliegt.

§ 146 [Bestellung der Liquidatoren]

(1) Die Liquidation erfolgt, sofern sie nicht durch Beschluß der Gesellschafter oder durch den Gesellschaftsvertrag einzelnen Gesellschaftern oder anderen Personen übertragen ist, durch sämtliche Gesellschafter als Liquidatoren. Mehrere Erben eines Gesellschafters haben einen gemeinsamen Vertreter zu bestellen.

(2) Auf Antrag eines Beteiligten kann aus wichtigen Gründen die Ernennung von Liquidatoren durch das Gericht erfolgen, in dessen Bezirke die Gesellschaft ihren Sitz hat; das Gericht kann in einem solchen Falle Personen zu Liquidatoren ernennen, die nicht zu den Gesellschaftern gehören. Als Beteiligter gilt außer den Gesellschaftern im Falle des § 135 auch der Gläubiger, durch den die Kündigung erfolgt ist. Im Falle des § 145 Abs. 3 sind die Liquidatoren auf Antrag eines Beteiligten durch das Gericht zu ernennen.

(3) Ist über das Vermögen eines Gesellschafters das Insolvenzverfahren eröffnet und ist ein Insolvenzverwalter bestellt, so tritt dieser an die Stelle des Gesellschafters.

§ 147 [Abberufung von Liquidatoren]

Die Abberufung von Liquidatoren geschieht durch einstimmigen Beschluß der nach § 146 Abs. 2 und 3 Beteilig-

(3) Where the partnership is dissolved by deletion from the Commercial Register because of lack of assets, liquidation shall take place only where after the deletion from the Commercial Register it is determined that assets exist which are subject to distribution.

§ 146 Appointment of liquidators

(1) Liquidation shall be effected by all of the partners as liquidators, unless responsibility therefor is transferred by resolution of the partners or the partnership agreement to individual partners or other persons. If there is more than one heir of a partner, they must appoint a common representative.

(2) Liquidators may, for important reasons, be appointed by the court for the district in which the partnership has its domicile on application of a participant; in such event, the court may nominate as liquidators persons who are not partners. In the event of § 135, a participant shall include, in addition to the partners, the creditor who has given notice of termination. Where § 145 Subsection 3 applies, the liquidators shall be appointed by the court upon motion of one of the participants.

(3) Where insolvency proceedings are commenced with respect to the assets of a partner and an insolvency administrator is appointed, the insolvency administrator takes the place of the partner.

§ 147 Removal of liquidators

Removal of liquidators is effected by unanimous resolution of the participants pursuant to § 146 Subsections 2

ten; sie kann auf Antrag eines Beteiligten aus wichtigen Gründen auch durch das Gericht erfolgen.

§ 148 [Anmeldung der Liquidatoren]

(1) Die Liquidatoren und ihre Vertretungsmacht sind von sämtlichen Gesellschaftern zur Eintragung in das Handelsregister anzumelden. Das gleiche gilt von jeder Änderung in den Personen der Liquidatoren oder in ihrer Vertretungsmacht. Im Falle des Todes eines Gesellschafters kann, wenn anzunehmen ist, daß die Anmeldung den Tatsachen entspricht, die Eintragung erfolgen, auch ohne daß die Erben bei der Anmeldung mitwirken, soweit einer solchen Mitwirkung besondere Hindernisse entgegenstehen.

(2) Die Eintragung gerichtlich bestellter Liquidatoren sowie die Eintragung der gerichtlichen Abberufung von Liquidatoren geschieht von Amts wegen.

(3) Die Liquidatoren haben ihre Namensunterschriften unter Angabe der Firma zur Aufbewahrung bei dem Gericht zu zeichnen.

§ 149 [Rechte und Pflichten der Liquidatoren]

Die Liquidatoren haben die laufenden Geschäfte zu beendigen, die Forderungen einzuziehen, das übrige Vermögen in Geld umzusetzen und die Gläubiger zu befriedigen; zur Beendigung schwebender Geschäfte können sie auch neue Geschäfte eingehen. Die Liquidatoren vertreten innerhalb ihres Geschäftskreises die Gesellschaft gerichtlich und außergerichtlich.

and 3; removal may be made by the court on motion of one of the participants for important reasons.

§ 148 Filing for registration of the liquidators

(1) All of the partners shall file to register the liquidators and their authority to represent the partnership in the Commercial Register. The same applies to every change of liquidators or alteration of their power of representation. In the event of the death of a partner, registration may also be made without the heirs' participation insofar as special obstacles prevent such participation, if it can be assumed that the filing is consistent with the facts.

(2) Registration of court-appointed liquidators as well as registration of a liquidator's removal by the court occurs on the court's own motion.

(3) The liquidators must provide their specimen signatures giving the firm name for filing with the court.

§ 149 Rights and duties of liquidators

The liquidators shall wind up on-going business, collect claims, liquidate the remaining assets and pay off the creditors; for the purpose of terminating pending business, they may conclude new transactions. Within the scope of their operations, the liquidators represent the partnership in judicial and non-judicial proceedings.

§ 150 [Mehrere Liquidatoren]

(1) Sind mehrere Liquidatoren vorhanden, so können sie die zur Liquidation gehörenden Handlungen nur in Gemeinschaft vornehmen, sofern nicht bestimmt ist, daß sie einzeln handeln können.

(2) Durch die Vorschrift des Absatzes 1 wird nicht ausgeschlossen, daß die Liquidatoren einzelne von ihnen zur Vornahme bestimmter Geschäfte oder bestimmter Arten von Geschäften ermächtigen. Ist der Gesellschaft gegenüber eine Willenserklärung abzugeben, so findet die Vorschrift des § 125 Abs. 2 Satz 3 entsprechende Anwendung.

§ 151 [Unbeschränkbarkeit der Befugnisse]

Eine Beschränkung des Umfanges der Befugnisse der Liquidatoren ist Dritten gegenüber unwirksam.

§ 152 [Bindung an Weisungen]

Gegenüber den nach § 146 Abs. 2 und 3 Beteiligten haben die Liquidatoren, auch wenn sie vom Gerichte bestellt sind, den Anordnungen Folge zu leisten, welche die Beteiligten in betreff der Geschäftsführung einstimmig beschließen.

§ 153 [Unterschrift]

Die Liquidatoren haben ihre Unterschrift in der Weise abzugeben, daß sie der bisherigen, als Liquidationsfirma zu bezeichnenden Firma ihren Namen beifügen.

§ 150 More than one liquidator

(1) Where there are several liquidators, they may undertake transactions related to the liquidation only jointly unless it has been agreed that they may act individually.

(2) Subsection 1 shall not prevent the liquidators from authorizing individual liquidators to undertake specific transactions or specific kinds of transactions. The provision of § 125 Subsection 2 sentence 3 applies analogously where a declaration of intent is to be made to the partnership.

§ 151 Unlimited authority

A limitation of the scope of the liquidators' authority is ineffective with respect to third parties.

§ 152 Obligation to comply with directives

Vis-à-vis the participants pursuant to § 146 Subsections 2 and 3, the liquidators, even if they are appointed by the court, must comply with directives which such participants have resolved unanimously in regard to the management of the business.

§ 153 Signature

The liquidators shall sign such that they append their own names to the prior firm name, which must be designated as the firm "in liquidation".

§ 154 [Bilanzen]

Die Liquidatoren haben bei dem Beginne sowie bei der Beendigung der Liquidation eine Bilanz aufzustellen.

§ 155 [Verteilung des Gesellschaftsvermögens]

(1) Das nach Berichtigung der Schulden verbleibende Vermögen der Gesellschaft ist von den Liquidatoren nach dem Verhältnisse der Kapitalanteile, wie sie sich auf Grund der Schlußbilanz ergeben, unter die Gesellschafter zu verteilen.

(2) Das während der Liquidation entbehrliche Geld wird vorläufig verteilt. Zur Deckung noch nicht fälliger oder streitiger Verbindlichkeiten sowie zur Sicherung der den Gesellschaftern bei der Schlußverteilung zukommenden Beträge ist das Erforderliche zurückzubehalten. Die Vorschriften des § 122 Abs. 1 finden während der Liquidation keine Anwendung.

(3) Entsteht über die Verteilung des Gesellschaftsvermögens Streit unter den Gesellschaftern, so haben die Liquidatoren die Verteilung bis zur Entscheidung des Streites auszusetzen.

§ 156 [Rechtsverhältnisse der Gesellschafter]

Bis zur Beendigung der Liquidation kommen in bezug auf das Rechtsverhältnis der bisherigen Gesellschafter untereinander sowie der Gesellschaft zu Dritten die Vorschriften des zweiten und dritten Titels zur Anwendung, soweit sich nicht aus dem gegenwärtigen Titel oder aus dem Zwecke der Liquidation ein anderes ergibt.

§ 154 Balance sheets

The liquidators shall prepare a balance sheet at the beginning as well as at the conclusion of the liquidation proceedings.

§ 155 Distribution of the partnership's assets

(1) The assets of the partnership remaining after settlement of debts are to be distributed by the liquidators among the partners in proportion to their capital shares as indicated by the closing balance sheet.

(2) Funds not needed for the liquidation proceeding will be temporarily distributed. The amounts needed to cover obligations not yet due or disputed and to ensure the amounts due to the partners in the final distribution are to be retained. The provisions of § 122 Subsection 1 do not apply during the liquidation.

(3) Where a dispute arises among the partners concerning the distribution of partnership assets, the liquidators shall suspend the distribution until the dispute has been resolved.

§ 156 Legal relationship of the partners

Until conclusion of the liquidation proceedings the provisions of the Second and Third Titles apply to the legal relationship of the partners to one another and that of the partnership to third parties, unless otherwise provided by this Title or by the purpose of the liquidation.

§ 157 [Anmeldung des Erlöschens; Geschäftsbücher]

(1) Nach der Beendigung der Liquidation ist das Erlöschen der Firma von den Liquidatoren zur Eintragung in das Handelsregister anzumelden.

(2) Die Bücher und Papiere der aufgelösten Gesellschaft werden einem der Gesellschafter oder einem Dritten in Verwahrung gegeben. Der Gesellschafter oder der Dritte wird in Ermangelung einer Verständigung durch das Gericht bestimmt, in dessen Bezirke die Gesellschaft ihren Sitz hat.

(3) Die Gesellschafter und deren Erben behalten das Recht auf Einsicht und Benutzung der Bücher und Papiere.

§ 158 [Andere Art der Auseinandersetzung]

Vereinbaren die Gesellschafter statt der Liquidation eine andere Art der Auseinandersetzung, so finden, solange noch ungeteiltes Gesellschaftsvermögen vorhanden ist, im Verhältnisse zu Dritten die für die Liquidation geltenden Vorschriften entsprechende Anwendung.

Sechster Titel. Verjährung. Zeitliche Begrenzung der Haftung

§ 159 [Ansprüche gegen einen Gesellschafter]

(1) Die Ansprüche gegen einen Gesellschafter aus Verbindlichkeiten der Gesellschaft verjähren in fünf Jahren nach der Auflösung der Gesellschaft, sofern nicht der Anspruch gegen die Gesellschaft einer kürzeren Verjährung unterliegt.

§ 157 Application for deletion of the firm name; business records

(1) Following the conclusion of liquidation proceedings, the liquidators shall file for the deletion of the firm name from the Commercial Register.

(2) The books and documents of the dissolved partnership will be given into the charge of one of the partners or a third party. In absence of agreement, the partner or third party will be determined by the court for the district in which the partnership has its domicile.

(3) The partners and their heirs retain the right to inspect and use the books and documents.

§ 158 Other types of dissolution

Where the partners agree to dissolution other than by liquidation, the provisions concerning liquidation apply analogously in relation to third parties as long as undistributed partnership assets exist.

Sixth Title. Statute of Limitations. Time Limit on Liability

§ 159 Claims against a partner

(1) Claims against a partner arising from liabilities of the partnership are time-barred five years after dissolution of the partnership, unless the claim against the partnership is subject to a shorter statute of limitations.

(2) Die Verjährung beginnt mit dem Ende des Tages, an welchem die Auflösung der Gesellschaft in das Handelsregister des für den Sitz der Gesellschaft zuständigen Gerichts eingetragen wird.

(3) Wird der Anspruch des Gläubigers gegen die Gesellschaft erst nach der Eintragung fällig, so beginnt die Verjährung mit dem Zeitpunkte der Fälligkeit.

(4) Der Neubeginn der Verjährung und ihre Hemmung nach § 204 des Bürgerlichen Gesetzbuchs gegenüber der aufgelösten Gesellschaft wirken auch gegenüber den Gesellschaftern, die der Gesellschaft zur Zeit der Auflösung angehört haben.

§ 160 [Haftung des ausscheidenden Gesellschafters; Fristen, Haftung als Kommanditist]

(1) Scheidet ein Gesellschafter aus der Gesellschaft aus, so haftet er für ihre bis dahin begründeten Verbindlichkeiten, wenn sie vor Ablauf von fünf Jahren nach dem Ausscheiden fällig und daraus Ansprüche gegen ihn in einer in § 197 Abs. 1 Nr. 3 bis 5 des Bürgerlichen Gesetzbuchs bezeichneten Art festgestellt sind oder eine gerichtliche oder behördliche Vollstreckungshandlung vorgenommen oder beantragt wird; bei öffentlich-rechtlichen Verbindlichkeiten genügt der Erlass eines Verwaltungsakts. Die Frist beginnt mit dem Ende des Tages, an dem das Ausscheiden in das Handelsregister des für den Sitz der Gesellschaft zuständigen Gerichts eingetragen wird. Die für die Verjährung geltenden §§ 204, 206, 210, 211 und 212 Abs. 2 und 3 des Bürgerlichen Gesetzbuches sind entsprechend anzuwenden.

(2) The statute begins to run with the end of the day on which the dissolution of the partnership is registered in the Commerial Register of the court having jurisdiction over the domicile of the partnership.

(3) Where the creditor's claim against the partnership becomes due only after the registration, the statute begins to run on the due date.

(4) The new beginning of the statute and its tolling under § 204 of the Civil Code regarding the dissolved partnership shall also be effective vis-à-vis the partners who belonged to the partnership at the time of its dissolution.

§ 160 Liability of withdrawing partner; statutes of limitations; liability as limited partner

(1) If a partner withdraws from the partnership, then he is liable for obligations incurred up to that point if they become due before the end of five years after his withdrawal and claims resulting therefrom against him determined in a manner specified in § 197 Subsection 1 No. 3 to 5 of the Civil Code or legal or official enforcement action has been undertaken or applied for; for public law obligations, the issuance of an administrative decision is sufficient. The statute of limitations begins to run with the end of the day on which the withdrawal is entered in the Commercial Register of the court having jurisdiction over the domicile of the partnership. §§ 204, 206, 210, 211 and 212 Subsection 2 and 3 of the Civil Code regarding statutes of limitations shall apply analogously.

(2) Einer Feststellung in einer in § 197 Abs. 1 Nr. 3 bis 5 des Bürgerlichen Gesetzbuchs bezeichneten Art bedarf es nicht, soweit der Gesellschafter den Anspruch schriftlich anerkannt hat.

(3) Wird ein Gesellschafter Kommanditist, so sind für die Begrenzung seiner Haftung für die im Zeitpunkt der Eintragung der Änderung in das Handelsregister begründeten Verbindlichkeiten die Absätze 1 und 2 entsprechend anzuwenden. Dies gilt auch, wenn er in der Gesellschaft oder einem ihr als Gesellschafter angehörenden Unternehmen geschäftsführend tätig wird. Seine Haftung als Kommanditist bleibt unberührt.

(2) To the extent that the partner has recognized the claim in writing, a determination in a manner specified in § 197 Subsection 1 No. 3 to 5 of the Civil Code is not necessary.

(3) If a partner becomes a limited partner, then Subsections 1 and 2 apply analogously to limit his liability for the obligations already existing at the time of the entry of the change in the Commercial Register. This applies also if he becomes active in management of the partnership or of an enterprise belonging to the partnership as shareholder. His liability as limited partner remains unaffected.

Zweiter Abschnitt. Kommanditgesellschaft

§ 161 [Begriff der KG; Anwendbarkeit der OHG-Vorschriften]

(1) Eine Gesellschaft, deren Zweck auf den Betrieb eines Handelsgewerbes unter gemeinschaftlicher Firma gerichtet ist, ist eine Kommanditgesellschaft, wenn bei einem oder bei einigen von den Gesellschaftern die Haftung gegenüber den Gesellschaftsgläubigern auf den Betrag einer bestimmten Vermögenseinlage beschränkt ist (Kommanditisten), während bei dem anderen Teile der Gesellschafter eine Beschränkung der Haftung nicht stattfindet (persönlich haftende Gesellschafter).

(2) Soweit nicht in diesem Abschnitt ein anderes vorgeschrieben ist, finden auf die Kommanditgesellschaft die für die offene Handelsgesellschaft geltenden Vorschriften Anwendung.

Part Two. Limited Partnership

§ 161 Definition of the limited partnership; applicability of the general commercial partnership provisions

(1) A partnership formed for the purpose of operating a commercial enterprise under a common firm name is a limited partnership where the liability of one or more of the partners is limited with respect to the partnership's creditors to the amount of a specific capital contribution (limited partners) and there is no limitation of liability for the other partners (general partners).

(2) Unless this Part otherwise provides, the provisions applicable to the general partnership apply to the limited partnership.

§ 162 [Anmeldung zum Handelsregister]

(1) Die Anmeldung der Gesellschaft hat außer den in § 106 Abs. 2 vorgesehenen Angaben die Bezeichnung der Kommanditisten und den Betrag der Einlage eines jeden von ihnen zu enthalten. Ist eine Gesellschaft bürgerlichen Rechts Kommanditist, so sind auch deren Gesellschafter entsprechend § 106 Abs. 2 und spätere Änderungen in der Zusammensetzung der Gesellschafter zur Eintragung anzumelden.

(2) Bei der Bekanntmachung der Eintragung der Gesellschaft sind keine Angaben zu den Kommanditisten zu machen; die Vorschriften des § 15 sind insoweit nicht anzuwenden.

(3) Diese Vorschriften finden im Falle des Eintritts eines Kommanditisten in eine bestehende Handelsgesellschaft und im Falle des Ausscheidens eines Kommanditisten aus einer Kommanditgesellschaft entsprechende Anwendung.

§ 163 [Rechtsverhältnis der Gesellschafter untereinander]

Für das Verhältnis der Gesellschafter untereinander gelten in Ermangelung abweichender Bestimmungen des Gesellschaftsvertrags die besonderen Vorschriften der §§ 164 bis 169.

§ 164 [Geschäftsführung]

Die Kommanditisten sind von der Führung der Geschäfte der Gesellschaft ausgeschlossen; sie können einer Handlung der persönlich haftenden Gesellschafter nicht widersprechen, es sei denn, daß die Handlung

§ 162 Filing for registration in the Commercial Register

(1) The filing for registration by the partnership shall contain, in addition to the information specified in § 106 Subsection 2, the names of the limited partners and the amount of the capital contribution of each of them. If a civil law association (*Gesellschaft bürgerlichen Rechts*) is limited partner, then its partners in accordance with § 106 Subsection 2 and subsequent changes in the composition of its partners shall also be filed for registration.

(2) In the publication of the entry of the partnership, no disclosure regarding the limited partners shall be made; to this extent the provisions of § 15 are not applicable.

(3) These provisions apply analogously in the event of a limited partner joining an existing commercial partnership and in the event of withdrawal of a limited partner from a limited partnership.

§ 163 Legal relationship of the partners to one another

Unless the partnership agreement provides otherwise, the specific provisions of §§ 164 through 169 apply to the relationship of the partners among one another.

§ 164 Management of the business

The limited partners are excluded from the management of the business; they cannot object to an action taken by the general partners unless the action goes beyond the ordinary course of business of the partnership. The

über den gewöhnlichen Betrieb des Handelsgewerbes der Gesellschaft hinausgeht. Die Vorschriften des § 116 Abs. 3 bleiben unberührt.

§ 165 [Wettbewerbsverbot]

Die §§ 112 und 113 finden auf die Kommanditisten keine Anwendung.

§ 166 [Kontrollrecht]

(1) Der Kommanditist ist berechtigt, die abschriftliche Mitteilung des Jahresabschlusses zu verlangen und dessen Richtigkeit unter Einsicht der Bücher und Papiere zu prüfen.

(2) Die in § 118 dem von der Geschäftsführung ausgeschlossenen Gesellschafter eingeräumten weiteren Rechte stehen dem Kommanditisten nicht zu.

(3) Auf Antrag eines Kommanditisten kann das Gericht, wenn wichtige Gründe vorliegen, die Mitteilung einer Bilanz und eines Jahresabschlusses oder sonstiger Aufklärungen sowie die Vorlegung der Bücher und Papiere jederzeit anordnen.

§ 167 [Gewinn und Verlust]

(1) Die Vorschriften des § 120 über die Berechnung des Gewinns oder Verlustes gelten auch für den Kommanditisten.

(2) Jedoch wird der einem Kommanditisten zukommende Gewinn seinem Kapitalanteil nur so lange zugeschrieben, als dieser den Betrag der bedungenen Einlage nicht erreicht.

provisions of § 116 Subsection 3 remain unaffected.

§ 165 Prohibition of competition

§§ 112 and 113 do not apply to limited partners.

§ 166 Right of inspection

(1) The limited partner is entitled to request a copy of the annual financial statements and to determine their accuracy by inspection of the books and records.

(2) The limited partner does not have the additional rights granted by § 118 to partners excluded from the management of the business.

(3) The court may at any time, upon application by a limited partner and recognition of important reasons therefor, order the communication of a balance sheet, annual financial statements or other clarification, as well as the production of the books and records.

§ 167 Profits and losses

(1) The provisions of § 120 concerning the calculation of profits and losses also apply to limited partners.

(2) However, the profits due to a limited partner will only be added to his capital contribution so long as this has not reached the amount of the required contribution to capital.

(3) An dem Verluste nimmt der Kommanditist nur bis zum Betrage seines Kapitalanteils und seiner noch rückständigen Einlage teil.

§ 168 [Verteilung von Gewinn und Verlust]

(1) Die Anteile der Gesellschafter am Gewinne bestimmen sich, soweit der Gewinn den Betrag von vier vom Hundert der Kapitalanteile nicht übersteigt, nach den Vorschriften des § 121 Abs. 1 und 2.

(2) In Ansehung des Gewinns, welcher diesen Betrag übersteigt, sowie in Ansehung des Verlustes gilt, soweit nicht ein anderes vereinbart ist, ein den Umständen nach angemessenes Verhältnis der Anteile als bedungen.

§ 169 [Gewinnauszahlung]

(1) § 122 findet auf den Kommanditisten keine Anwendung. Dieser hat nur Anspruch auf Auszahlung des ihm zukommenden Gewinns; er kann auch die Auszahlung des Gewinns nicht fordern, solange sein Kapitalanteil durch Verlust unter den auf die bedungene Einlage geleisteten Betrag herabgemindert ist oder durch die Auszahlung unter diesen Betrag herabgemindert werden würde.

(2) Der Kommanditist ist nicht verpflichtet, den bezogenen Gewinn wegen späterer Verluste zurückzuzahlen.

§ 170 [Vertretung der KG]

Der Kommanditist ist zur Vertretung der Gesellschaft nicht ermächtigt.

(3) The limited partner only participates in losses up to the amount of his capital contribution and unpaid contribution.

§ 168 Distribution of profits and losses

(1) The partners' shares in the profits are computed pursuant to the provisions of § 121 Subsections 1 and 2, to the extent that profits do not exceed four percent of the capital contributions.

(2) With regard to profits in excess of this amount, and to losses, a distribution which is reasonable under the circumstances is deemed to have been agreed upon absent any other agreement.

§ 169 Payment of profits

(1) § 122 has no application to a limited partner. He has a right only to payment of profits due to him; he cannot demand payment of profits so long as his capital contribution has been reduced by losses to less than the amount required to be paid in as contribution or would be so reduced as a result of such payment.

(2) The limited partner is not obligated to repay profits received in the event of subsequent losses.

§ 170 Representing the limited partnership

The limited partner is not authorized to represent the partnership.

§ 171 [Haftung des Kommanditisten]

(1) Der Kommanditist haftet den Gläubigern der Gesellschaft bis zur Höhe seiner Einlage unmittelbar; die Haftung ist ausgeschlossen, soweit die Einlage geleistet ist.

(2) Ist über das Vermögen der Gesellschaft das Insolvenzverfahren eröffnet, so wird während der Dauer des Verfahrens das den Gesellschaftsgläubigern nach Absatz 1 zustehende Recht durch den Insolvenzverwalter oder den Sachwalter ausgeübt.

§ 172 [Umfang der Haftung]

(1) Im Verhältnisse zu den Gläubigern der Gesellschaft wird nach der Eintragung in das Handelsregister die Einlage eines Kommanditisten durch den in der Eintragung angegebenen Betrag bestimmt.

(2) Auf eine nicht eingetragene Erhöhung der aus dem Handelsregister ersichtlichen Einlage können sich die Gläubiger nur berufen, wenn die Erhöhung in handelsüblicher Weise kundgemacht oder ihnen in anderer Weise von der Gesellschaft mitgeteilt worden ist.

(3) Eine Vereinbarung der Gesellschafter, durch die einem Kommanditisten die Einlage erlassen oder gestundet wird, ist den Gläubigern gegenüber unwirksam.

(4) Soweit die Einlage eines Kommanditisten zurückbezahlt wird, gilt sie den Gläubigern gegenüber als nicht geleistet. Das gleiche gilt, soweit ein Kommanditist Gewinnanteile entnimmt, während sein Kapitalanteil

§ 171 Liability of the limited partner

(1) The limited partner is directly liable to the creditors of the partnership up to the amount of his capital contribution; the liability is excluded to the extent that the capital contribution has been paid in.

(2) Where insolvency proceedings are commenced with respect to the assets of the partnership, the rights of the partnership's creditors pursuant to Subsection 1 will be exercised by the insolvency administrator or the property administrator during the course of the proceedings.

§ 172 Scope of liability

(1) With respect to the creditors of the partnership, the capital contribution of a limited partner will, after registration in the Commercial Register, be determined by the amount stated in the registration.

(2) The creditors may only claim reliance on an unregistered increase in the amount of the capital contribution if the increase is announced in a normal commercial way or has been communicated to them in some other way by the partnership.

(3) Any agreement of the partners by which one of the limited partners is released from making the capital contribution, or by which the obligation to make the capital contribution is deferred, is ineffective with respect to the creditors.

(4) To the extent that the capital contribution of a limited partner has been repaid, it is deemed not to have been made as far as the creditors are concerned. The same applies insofar as a limited partner withdraws his share of

durch Verlust unter den Betrag der geleisteten Einlage herabgemindert ist, oder soweit durch die Entnahme der Kapitalanteil unter den bezeichneten Betrag herabgemindert wird.

(5) Was ein Kommanditist auf Grund einer in gutem Glauben errichteten Bilanz in gutem Glauben als Gewinn bezieht, ist er in keinem Falle zurückzuzahlen verpflichtet.

(6) Gegenüber den Gläubigern einer Gesellschaft, bei der kein persönlich haftender Gesellschafter eine natürliche Person ist, gilt die Einlage eines Kommanditisten als nicht geleistet, soweit sie in Anteilen an den persönlich haftenden Gesellschaftern bewirkt ist. Dies gilt nicht, wenn zu den persönlich haftenden Gesellschaftern eine offene Handelsgesellschaft oder Kommanditgesellschaft gehört, bei der ein persönlich haftender Gesellschafter eine natürliche Person ist.

§ 172 a [Rückgewähr von Darlehen]

Bei einer Kommanditgesellschaft, bei der kein persönlich haftender Gesellschafter eine natürliche Person ist, gelten die §§ 32 a, 32 b des Gesetzes betreffend die Gesellschaften mit beschränkter Haftung sinngemäß mit der Maßgabe, daß an die Stelle der Gesellschafter der Gesellschaft mit beschränkter Haftung die Gesellschafter oder Mitglieder der persönlich haftenden Gesellschafter der Kommanditgesellschaft sowie die Kommanditisten treten. Dies gilt nicht, wenn zu den persönlich haftenden Gesellschaftern eine offene Handelsgesellschaft oder Kommanditgesellschaft gehört, bei der ein persönlich haftender Gesellschafter eine natürliche Person ist.

the profits in a period during which his capital share has been reduced through losses below the amount of the contribution paid in or would be so reduced as a result of the withdrawal.

(5) Whatever a limited partner receives in good faith as profits from a balance sheet prepared in good faith, he is in no case obligated to repay.

(6) Vis-à-vis the creditors of a partnership in which none of the general commercial partners is a natural person, the contribution of a limited partner is deemed not to have been made to the extent that it is made in shares of the general partners. This does not apply where one of the general partners is a general commercial partnership or limited partnership, of which one of the general partners is a natural person.

§ 172 a Repayment of loans

In a limited partnership, where none of the general partners is a natural person, §§ 32 a and 32 b of the Limited Liability Companies Act applies analogously, with the proviso that the shareholders of the limited liability company are replaced by the partners or members of the general partners of the limited partnership as well as the limited partners. This does not apply where one of the general partners is a general commercial partnership or limited partnership, of which one of the general partners is a natural person.

§ 173 [Haftung bei Eintritt als Kommanditist]

(1) Wer in eine bestehende Handelsgesellschaft als Kommanditist eintritt, haftet nach Maßgabe der §§ 171 und 172 für die vor seinem Eintritte begründeten Verbindlichkeiten der Gesellschaft, ohne Unterschied, ob die Firma eine Änderung erleidet oder nicht.

(2) Eine entgegenstehende Vereinbarung ist Dritten gegenüber unwirksam.

§ 174 [Herabsetzung der Einlage]

Eine Herabsetzung der Einlage eines Kommanditisten ist, solange sie nicht in das Handelsregister des Gerichts, in dessen Bezirke die Gesellschaft ihren Sitz hat, eingetragen ist, den Gläubigern gegenüber unwirksam; Gläubiger, deren Forderungen zur Zeit der Eintragung begründet waren, brauchen die Herabsetzung nicht gegen sich gelten zu lassen.

§ 175 [Anmeldung der Änderung einer Einlage]

Die Erhöhung sowie die Herabsetzung einer Einlage ist durch die sämtlichen Gesellschafter zur Eintragung in das Handelsregister anzumelden. § 162 Abs. 2 gilt entsprechend. Auf die Eintragung in das Handelsregister des Sitzes der Gesellschaft finden die Vorschriften des § 14 keine Anwendung.

§ 176 [Haftung vor Eintragung]

(1) Hat die Gesellschaft ihre Geschäfte begonnen, bevor sie in das Handelsregister des Gerichts, in

§ 173 Liability upon joining as a limited partner

(1) One who joins an existing partnership as a limited partner is liable pursuant to §§ 171 and 172 for partnership obligations incurred before he joined regardless of whether the firm name was changed.

(2) Any contrary agreement is ineffective with respect to third parties.

§ 174 Reduction of capital contribution

A reduction of the capital contribution of a limited partner is ineffective vis-à-vis the creditors so long as it is not registered in the Commercial Register of the court in whose district the partnership has its domicile; creditors whose claims were in existence at the time of the registration need not recognise such reduction.

§ 175 Filing for registration of change in capital contribution

Filing for registration in the Commercial Register of an increase or decrease of a capital contribution shall be made by all of the partners. § 162 Subsection 2 applies analogously. The provisions of § 14 do not apply to registration in the Commercial Register of the partnership's domicile.

§ 176 Liability prior to registration

(1) Where the partnership commences business prior to its registration in the Commercial Register of the court in

dessen Bezirke sie ihren Sitz hat, eingetragen ist, so haftet jeder Kommanditist, der dem Geschäftsbeginne zugestimmt hat, für die bis zur Eintragung begründeten Verbindlichkeiten der Gesellschaft gleich einem persönlich haftenden Gesellschafter, es sei denn, daß seine Beteiligung als Kommanditist dem Gläubiger bekannt war. Diese Vorschrift kommt nicht zur Anwendung, soweit sich aus § 2 oder § 105 Abs. 2 ein anderes ergibt.

(2) Tritt ein Kommanditist in eine bestehende Handelsgesellschaft ein, so findet die Vorschrift des Absatzes 1 Satz 1 für die in der Zeit zwischen seinem Eintritt und dessen Eintragung in das Handelsregister begründeten Verbindlichkeiten der Gesellschaft entsprechende Anwendung.

whose district it has its domicile, each limited partner who has agreed to the commencement of business is liable, in the same manner as a general partner, for business debts incurred prior to registration, unless his participation as a limited partner was known to the creditor. This provision does not apply to the extent that § 2 or § 105 Subsection 2 provides otherwise.

(2) Where a limited partner joins an existing commercial partnership, the provisions of Subsection 1 sentence 1, apply analogously for obligations of the partnership which arise during the period between his joining and its registration in the Commercial Register.

§ 177 [Tod des Kommanditisten]

Beim Tod eines Kommanditisten wird die Gesellschaft mangels abweichender vertraglicher Bestimmung mit den Erben fortgesetzt.

§ 177 Death of a limited partner

Upon the death of a limited partner, the partnership shall be continued with the heirs, unless the partnership agreement provides otherwise.

§ 177 a [Angaben auf Geschäftsbriefen; Antragspflicht bei Zahlungsunfähigkeit oder Überschuldung]

Die §§ 125 a, 130 a und 130 b gelten auch für die Gesellschaft, bei der ein Kommanditist eine natürliche Person ist, § 130 a jedoch mit der Maßgabe, daß anstelle des Absatzes 1 Satz 1 zweiter Halbsatz der § 172 Abs. 6 Satz 2 anzuwenden ist. Der in § 125 a Abs. 1 Satz 2 für die Gesellschafter vorgeschriebenen Angaben bedarf es nur für die persönlich haftenden Gesellschafter der Gesellschaft.

§ 177 a Information on business letters; duty to file a petition in the event of inability to meet obligations or insolvency

§§ 125 a, 130 a and 130 b also apply to a partnership in which a limited partner is a natural person, except that as to § 130 a, § 172 Subsection 6 sentence 2 shall apply instead of Subsection 1 sentence 1, second half-sentence. The information provided for in § 125 a Subsection 1 sentence 2 for the partners is only required for the general partners of the partnership.

§§ 178–229 *(aufgehoben)*

§§ 178–229 *(repealed)*

Dritter Abschnitt. Stille Gesellschaft

Part Three. Silent Partnership

§ 230 [Begriff und Wesen der stillen Gesellschaft]

(1) Wer sich als stiller Gesellschafter an dem Handelsgewerbe, das ein anderer betreibt, mit einer Vermögenseinlage beteiligt, hat die Einlage so zu leisten, daß sie in das Vermögen des Inhabers des Handelsgeschäfts übergeht.

(2) Der Inhaber wird aus den in dem Betriebe geschlossenen Geschäften allein berechtigt und verpflichtet.

§ 230 Definition and nature of the silent partnership

(1) One who participates as a silent partner by means of a capital contribution in a commercial enterprise operated by another must make his contribution in such a manner that it is transferred to the assets of the owner of the business.

(2) The owner alone has rights and obligations with respect to transactions concluded within the operation of the business.

§ 231 [Gewinn und Verlust]

(1) Ist der Anteil des stillen Gesellschafters am Gewinn und Verluste nicht bestimmt, so gilt ein den Umständen nach angemessener Anteil als bedungen.

(2) Im Gesellschaftsvertrage kann bestimmt werden, daß der stille Gesellschafter nicht am Verluste beteiligt sein soll; seine Beteiligung am Gewinne kann nicht ausgeschlossen werden.

§ 231 Profits and losses

(1) Where the share of the silent partner in the profits and losses has not been determined, a share which is reasonable under the circumstances is deemed to be required.

(2) The partnership agreement may provide that the silent partner shall not participate in losses; his share in profits cannot be excluded.

§ 232 [Gewinn- und Verlustrechnung]

(1) Am Schlusse jedes Geschäftsjahrs wird der Gewinn und Verlust berechnet und der auf den stillen Gesellschafter fallende Gewinn ihm ausbezahlt.

(2) Der stille Gesellschafter nimmt an dem Verluste nur bis zum Betrage seiner eingezahlten oder rückständigen Einlage teil. Er ist nicht verpflichtet,

§ 232 Calculation of profits and losses

(1) The profits and losses shall be calculated at the close of every fiscal year and the silent partner's share of the profits paid out to him.

(2) The silent partner participates in losses only up to the amount of his paid-in or outstanding capital contribution. He is not obligated, because of

den bezogenen Gewinn wegen späterer Verluste zurückzuzahlen; jedoch wird, solange seine Einlage durch Verlust vermindert ist, der jährliche Gewinn zur Deckung des Verlustes verwendet.

(3) Der Gewinn, welcher von dem stillen Gesellschafter nicht erhoben wird, vermehrt dessen Einlage nicht, sofern nicht ein anderes vereinbart ist.

§ 233 [Kontrollrecht des stillen Gesellschafters]

(1) Der stille Gesellschafter ist berechtigt, die abschriftliche Mitteilung des Jahresabschlusses zu verlangen und dessen Richtigkeit unter Einsicht der Bücher und Papiere zu prüfen.

(2) Die in § 716 des Bürgerlichen Gesetzbuchs dem von der Geschäftsführung ausgeschlossenen Gesellschafter eingeräumten weiteren Rechte stehen dem stillen Gesellschafter nicht zu.

(3) Auf Antrag des stillen Gesellschafters kann das Gericht, wenn wichtige Gründe vorliegen, die Mitteilung einer Bilanz und eines Jahresabschlusses oder sonstiger Aufklärungen sowie die Vorlegung der Bücher und Papiere jederzeit anordnen.

§ 234 [Kündigung der Gesellschaft; Tod des stillen Gesellschafters]

(1) Auf die Kündigung der Gesellschaft durch einen der Gesellschafter oder durch einen Gläubiger des stillen Gesellschafters finden die Vorschriften der §§ 132, 134 und 135 entsprechende Anwendung. Die Vorschriften des § 723 des Bürgerlichen Gesetzbuchs über das Recht, die Gesellschaft aus wichtigen Gründen ohne Einhaltung einer Frist zu kündigen, bleiben unberührt.

subsequent losses, to repay profits received; however, for so long as his contribution is reduced by losses, the annual profits shall be used to cover the losses.

(3) Profits not withdrawn by the silent partner shall not, without agreement to the contrary, increase his capital contribution.

§ 233 Inspection right of the silent partner

(1) The silent partner is entitled to request a copy of the annual financial statements and determine their accuracy by inspecting the books and records.

(2) The silent partner does not have the additional rights granted by § 716 of the Civil Code to a partner excluded from management of the business.

(3) The court may at any time, on application of the silent partner and recognition of important reasons therefore, order the communication of a balance sheet, annual financial statements or other clarifications, as well as the production of the books and records.

§ 234 Termination of the partnership; death of the silent partner

(1) The provisions of §§ 132, 134, and 135 apply analogously to the termination of the partnership by one of the partners or by a creditor of the silent partner. The provisions of § 723 of the Civil Code concerning the right to terminate the partnership for an important reason without compliance with a notice period remain unaffected.

Stille Gesellschaft §§ 234–237

(2) Durch den Tod des stillen Gesellschafters wird die Gesellschaft nicht aufgelöst.

(2) The partnership is not dissolved by the death of the silent partner.

§ 235 [Auseinandersetzung]

(1) Nach der Auflösung der Gesellschaft hat sich der Inhaber des Handelsgeschäfts mit dem stillen Gesellschafter auseinanderzusetzen und dessen Guthaben in Geld zu berichtigen.

(2) Die zur Zeit der Auflösung schwebenden Geschäfte werden von dem Inhaber des Handelsgeschäfts abgewickelt. Der stille Gesellschafter nimmt teil an dem Gewinn und Verluste, der sich aus diesen Geschäften ergibt.

(3) Er kann am Schlusse jedes Geschäftsjahrs Rechenschaft über die inzwischen beendigten Geschäfte, Auszahlung des ihm gebührenden Betrags und Auskunft über den Stand der noch schwebenden Geschäfte verlangen.

§ 235 Settlement following dissolution

(1) Following dissolution of the partnership, the owner of the business shall settle with the silent partner and pay his credit balance in money.

(2) Transactions pending at the time of dissolution shall be wound up by the owner of the business. The silent partner shall participate in the profits and losses resulting from these transactions.

(3) He may, at the close of every fiscal year, demand an accounting of the transactions concluded in the meantime, payment of the amount due to him and information concerning the status of pending transactions.

§ 236 [Insolvenz des Inhabers]

(1) Wird über das Vermögen des Inhabers des Handelsgeschäfts das Insolvenzverfahren eröffnet, so kann der stille Gesellschafter wegen der Einlage, soweit sie den Betrag des auf ihn fallenden Anteils am Verlust übersteigt, seine Forderung als Insolvenzgläubiger geltend machen.

(2) Ist die Einlage rückständig, so hat sie der stille Gesellschafter bis zu dem Betrage, welcher zur Deckung seines Anteils am Verlust erforderlich ist, zur Insolvenzmasse einzuzahlen.

§ 236 Insolvency of the business owner

(1) Where insolvency proceedings are commenced with respect to the business owner's assets, the silent partner, because of the capital contribution, can assert a claim as a creditor in insolvency to the extent that the amount of his capital contribution exceeds the amount of his share of losses.

(2) Where the capital contribution is in arrears, the silent partner shall pay it in to the insolvency estate, up to the amount necessary to cover his share of the losses.

§ 237 *(aufgehoben)*

§ 237 *(repealed)*

Drittes Buch. Handelsbücher

Erster Abschnitt. Vorschriften für alle Kaufleute

Erster Unterabschnitt. Buchführung. Inventar

§ 238 Buchführungspflicht

(1) Jeder Kaufmann ist verpflichtet, Bücher zu führen und in diesen seine Handelsgeschäfte und die Lage seines Vermögens nach den Grundsätzen ordnungsmäßiger Buchführung ersichtlich zu machen. Die Buchführung muß so beschaffen sein, daß sie einem sachverständigen Dritten innerhalb angemessener Zeit einen Überblick über die Geschäftsvorfälle und über die Lage des Unternehmens vermitteln kann. Die Geschäftsvorfälle müssen sich in ihrer Entstehung und Abwicklung verfolgen lassen.

(2) Der Kaufmann ist verpflichtet, eine mit der Urschrift übereinstimmende Wiedergabe der abgesandten Handelsbriefe (Kopie, Abdruck, Abschrift oder sonstige Wiedergabe des Wortlauts auf einem Schrift-, Bild- oder anderen Datenträger) zurückzubehalten.

§ 239 Führung der Handelsbücher

(1) Bei der Führung der Handelsbücher und bei den sonst erforderlichen Aufzeichnungen hat sich der Kaufmann einer lebenden Sprache zu bedienen. Werden Abkürzungen, Ziffern, Buchstaben oder Symbole verwendet, muß im Einzelfall deren Bedeutung eindeutig festliegen.

Book Three. Commercial Records

Part One. Regulations for all Merchants

First Subpart. Bookkeeping. Inventory

§ 238 Duty to keep books

(1) Every merchant is obligated to keep books and to show clearly in them his commercial transactions and his financial position pursuant to generally accepted accounting principles. The bookkeeping must be maintained in such a way that an outside expert can derive from it within a reasonable time an overview of the business operations and the position of the enterprise. The business operations must be comprehensible from their beginning to end.

(2) The merchant is obligated to retain copies of all mailed business correspondence that conform to the original (such as a copy, print, duplicate or other reproduction of the text on a written, photographic or other data storage device).

§ 239 Method of commercial bookkeeping

(1) In keeping the books and other required records, the merchant must employ a language in common use. Where abbreviations, numerals, letters or symbols are used, their meaning must be clearly determinable in each particular case.

(2) Die Eintragungen in Büchern und die sonst erforderlichen Aufzeichnungen müssen vollständig, richtig, zeitgerecht und geordnet vorgenommen werden.

(3) Eine Eintragung oder eine Aufzeichnung darf nicht in einer Weise verändert werden, daß der ursprüngliche Inhalt nicht mehr feststellbar ist. Auch solche Veränderungen dürfen nicht vorgenommen werden, deren Beschaffenheit es ungewiß läßt, ob sie ursprünglich oder erst später gemacht worden sind.

(4) Die Handelsbücher und die sonst erforderlichen Aufzeichnungen können auch in der geordneten Ablage von Belegen bestehen oder auf Datenträgern geführt werden, soweit diese Formen der Buchführung einschließlich des dabei angewandten Verfahrens den Grundsätzen ordnungsmäßiger Buchführung entsprechen. Bei der Führung der Handelsbücher und der sonst erforderlichen Aufzeichnungen auf Datenträgern muß insbesondere sichergestellt sein, daß die Daten während der Dauer der Aufbewahrungsfrist verfügbar sind und jederzeit innerhalb angemessener Frist lesbar gemacht werden können. Absätze 1 bis 3 gelten sinngemäß.

§ 240 Inventar

(1) Jeder Kaufmann hat zu Beginn seines Handelsgewerbes seine Grundstücke, seine Forderungen und Schulden, den Betrag seines baren Geldes sowie seine sonstigen Vermögensgegenstände genau zu verzeichnen und dabei den Wert der einzelnen Vermögensgegenstände und Schulden anzugeben.

(2) The entries in the books and other required records must be complete, correct, timely and orderly.

(3) An entry or recording may not be altered in such a way that the original meaning is no longer ascertainable. Also, alterations may not be made that leave unclear whether they were in the original or made at a later date.

(4) The commercial books and other required records can consist of the organized files of original documents or be kept on electronic data storage devices in so far as these bookkeeping methods, including the procedures used, comply with generally accepted accounting principles. In keeping the commercial books and other required records on electronic data storage devices, it must be especially guaranteed that the electronic data is retrievable during the statutory retention period and can be put into a legible form at any time within a reasonable period. Subsections 1 through 3 apply analogously.

§ 240 Inventory

(1) With the establishment of his business, every merchant must record precisely his real property, his receivables and liabilities, the amount of his cash on hand as well as his other assets and, in doing so, specify the value of the individual assets and liabilities.

(2) Er hat demnächst für den Schluß eines jeden Geschäftsjahrs ein solches Inventar aufzustellen. Die Dauer des Geschäftsjahres darf zwölf Monate nicht überschreiten. Die Aufstellung des Inventars ist innerhalb der einem ordnungsmäßigen Geschäftsgang entsprechenden Zeit zu bewirken.

(3) Vermögensgegenstände des Sachanlagevermögens sowie Roh-, Hilfs- und Betriebsstoffe können, wenn sie regelmäßig ersetzt werden und ihr Gesamtwert für das Unternehmen von nachrangiger Bedeutung ist, mit einer gleichbleibenden Menge und einem gleichbleibenden Wert angesetzt werden, sofern ihr Bestand in seiner Größe, seinem Wert und seiner Zusammensetzung nur geringen Veränderungen unterliegt. Jedoch ist in der Regel alle drei Jahre eine körperliche Bestandsaufnahme durchzuführen.

(4) Gleichartige Vermögensgegenstände des Vorratsvermögens sowie andere gleichartige oder annähernd gleichwertige bewegliche Vermögensgegenstände und Schulden können jeweils zu einer Gruppe zusammengefaßt und mit dem gewogenen Durchschnittswert angesetzt werden.

§ 241 Inventurvereinfachungsverfahren

(1) Bei der Aufstellung des Inventars darf der Bestand der Vermögensgegenstände nach Art, Menge und Wert auch mit Hilfe anerkannter mathematisch-statistischer Methoden auf Grund von Stichproben ermittelt werden. Das Verfahren muß den Grundsätzen ordnungsmäßiger Buchführung entsprechen. Der Aussagewert des auf diese Weise aufgestellten Inventars muß dem Aussagewert eines

(2) He must from then on prepare such an inventory for the close of every fiscal year. The length of the fiscal year may not exceed twelve months. The inventory shall be prepared within a period consistent with proper business practice.

(3) Fixed assets as well as raw materials, supplies and operating materials, if they are regularly replaced and their total value is of minor importance to the firm, may be assessed at a constant quantity and a constant value, so long as the size, value and composition of the inventory undergo only small changes. Nonetheless, as a rule, a physical inventory shall be taken every three years.

(4) Assets in inventory that are alike as well as other tangible assets and debts that are alike or of nearly equal value may from time to time be combined respectively into a single group and assessed at the weighted average value.

§ 241 Procedures for simplifying the keeping of inventory

(1) In preparing the inventory, the existence of business assets according to kind, quantity and value may be ascertained by means of recognised statistical methods based on random sampling. The procedure must be consistent with generally accepted accounting principles. The informative value of the inventory prepared by this method must be equivalent to the informative value of an inventory pre-

Vorschriften für alle Kaufleute § 241

auf Grund einer körperlichen Bestandsaufnahme aufgestellten Inventars gleichkommen.

(2) Bei der Aufstellung des Inventars für den Schluß eines Geschäftsjahrs bedarf es einer körperlichen Bestandsaufnahme der Vermögensgegenstände für diesen Zeitpunkt nicht, soweit durch Anwendung eines den Grundsätzen ordnungsmäßiger Buchführung entsprechenden anderen Verfahrens gesichert ist, daß der Bestand der Vermögensgegenstände nach Art, Menge und Wert auch ohne die körperliche Bestandsaufnahme für diesen Zeitpunkt festgestellt werden kann.

(3) In dem Inventar für den Schluß eines Geschäftsjahrs brauchen Vermögensgegenstände nicht verzeichnet zu werden, wenn

1. der Kaufmann ihren Bestand auf Grund einer körperlichen Bestandsaufnahme oder auf Grund eines nach Absatz 2 zulässigen anderen Verfahrens nach Art, Menge und Wert in einem besonderen Inventar verzeichnet hat, das für einen Tag innerhalb der letzten drei Monate vor oder der ersten beiden Monate nach dem Schluß des Geschäftsjahrs aufgestellt ist, und

2. auf Grund des besonderen Inventars durch Anwendung eines den Grundsätzen ordnungsmäßiger Buchführung entsprechenden Fortschreibungs- oder Rückrechnungsverfahrens gesichert ist, daß der am Schluß des Geschäftsjahrs vorhandene Bestand der Vermögensgegenstände für diesen Zeitpunkt ordnungsgemäß bewertet werden kann.

pared on the basis of a physical inventory.

(2) In preparing the inventory for the close of a fiscal year, a physical inventory check of business assets is not required at that time if the application of another procedure consistent with generally accepted accounting principles can ensure the determination of the current amount of the business assets according to the kind, quantity and value even without the physical inventory check.

(3) The assets of the business need not be listed in the inventory for the close of the fiscal year if:

1. the merchant has recorded, based on a physical inventory check or other procedure permissible pursuant to Subsection 2, their amount according to kind, quantity and value in a special inventory prepared for a day within the last three months before or the first two months after the close of the fiscal year, and

2. it is certain that, by means of a forward or backward projection consistent with generally accepted accounting principles which is based on the special inventory, the assets existing at the close of the fiscal year can be correctly valued for this point in time.

Zweiter Unterabschnitt. Eröffnungsbilanz. Jahresabschluß

Erster Titel. Allgemeine Vorschriften

§ 242 Pflicht zur Aufstellung

(1) Der Kaufmann hat zu Beginn seines Handelsgewerbes und für den Schluß eines jeden Geschäftsjahrs einen das Verhältnis seines Vermögens und seiner Schulden darstellenden Abschluß (Eröffnungsbilanz, Bilanz) aufzustellen. Auf die Eröffnungsbilanz sind die für den Jahresabschluß geltenden Vorschriften entsprechend anzuwenden, soweit sie sich auf die Bilanz beziehen.

(2) Er hat für den Schluß eines jeden Geschäftsjahrs eine Gegenüberstellung der Aufwendungen und Erträge des Geschäftsjahrs (Gewinn- und Verlustrechnung) aufzustellen.

(3) Die Bilanz und die Gewinn- und Verlustrechnung bilden den Jahresabschluß.

§ 243 Aufstellungsgrundsatz

(1) Der Jahresabschluß ist nach den Grundsätzen ordnungsmäßiger Buchführung aufzustellen.

(2) Er muß klar und übersichtlich sein.

(3) Der Jahresabschluß ist innerhalb der einem ordnungsmäßigen Geschäftsgang entsprechenden Zeit aufzustellen.

§ 244 Sprache. Währungseinheit

Der Jahresabschluß ist in deutscher Sprache und in Euro aufzustellen.

Second Subpart. Opening Balance Sheet. Annual Financial Statements

First Title. General Regulations

§ 242 Duty to prepare

(1) Upon the establishment of his business and at the close of every fiscal year, the merchant must prepare financial statements (opening balance sheet, balance sheet) showing his assets and liabilities. The provisions pertaining to the annual financial statements shall apply to the opening balance sheet insofar as they pertain to the balance sheet.

(2) For the close of every fiscal year he shall prepare a schedule of the expenses and revenues of that fiscal year (a profit and loss statement).

(3) The balance sheet and the profit and loss statement comprise the annual financial statements.

§ 243 Principle of preparation

(1) The annual financial statements shall be prepared according to generally accepted accounting principles.

(2) They must be clear and lucidly arranged.

(3) The annual financial statements shall be prepared within a time consistent with the proper conduct of business.

§ 244 Language. Currency

The annual financial statements shall be prepared in the German language and in Euro.

§ 245 Unterzeichnung

Der Jahresabschluß ist vom Kaufmann unter Angabe des Datums zu unterzeichnen. Sind mehrere persönlich haftende Gesellschafter vorhanden, so haben sie alle zu unterzeichnen.

Zweiter Titel. Ansatzvorschriften

§ 246 Vollständigkeit. Verrechnungsverbot

(1) Der Jahresabschluß hat sämtliche Vermögensgegenstände, Schulden, Rechnungsabgrenzungsposten, Aufwendungen und Erträge zu enthalten, soweit gesetzlich nichts anderes bestimmt ist. Vermögensgegenstände, die unter Eigentumsvorbehalt erworben oder an Dritte für eigene oder fremde Verbindlichkeiten verpfändet oder in anderer Weise als Sicherheit übertragen worden sind, sind in die Bilanz des Sicherungsgebers aufzunehmen. In die Bilanz des Sicherungsnehmers sind sie nur aufzunehmen, wenn es sich um Bareinlagen handelt.

(2) Posten der Aktivseite dürfen nicht mit Posten der Passivseite, Aufwendungen nicht mit Erträgen, Grundstücksrechte nicht mit Grundstückslasten verrechnet werden.

§ 247 Inhalt der Bilanz

(1) In der Bilanz sind das Anlage- und das Umlaufvermögen, das Eigenkapital, die Schulden sowie die Rechnungsabgrenzungsposten gesondert auszuweisen und hinreichend aufzugliedern.

(2) Beim Anlagevermögen sind nur die Gegenstände auszuweisen, die bestimmt sind, dauernd dem Geschäftsbetrieb zu dienen.

§ 245 Signature

The annual financial statements shall be signed and dated by the merchant. If there is more than one general partner, then they all must sign.

Second Title. Assessment Regulations

§ 246 Completeness. Prohibition of offset

(1) The annual financial statements must contain all assets, liabilities, accrued and deferred items, expenses and revenues, except as provided otherwise by law. Assets which have been acquired from a party who retains title thereto, or which have been pledged or otherwise transferred to a third party as security for debts of the pledgor or another, shall be included in the balance sheet of the party giving security. They shall be included in the balance sheet of the secured party only when they consist of cash deposits.

(2) Entries on the assets side may not be offset against entries on the liabilities side, nor expenses against revenues, nor rights in real property against encumbrances on real property.

§ 247 Contents of the balance sheet

(1) On the balance sheet, the fixed and current assets, the net worth and the liabilities as well as the accrued and deferred items shall be shown separately and classified adequately.

(2) Only those items that are intended to serve the business operations permanently shall be shown under fixed assets.

(3) Passivposten, die für Zwecke der Steuern vom Einkommen und vom Ertrag zulässig sind, dürfen in der Bilanz gebildet werden. Sie sind als Sonderposten mit Rücklageanteil auszuweisen und nach Maßgabe des Steuerrechts aufzulösen. Einer Rückstellung bedarf es insoweit nicht.

§ 248 Bilanzierungsverbote

(1) Aufwendungen für die Gründung des Unternehmens und für die Beschaffung des Eigenkapitals dürfen in die Bilanz nicht als Aktivposten aufgenommen werden.

(2) Für immaterielle Vermögensgegenstände des Anlagevermögens, die nicht entgeltlich erworben wurden, darf ein Aktivposten nicht angesetzt werden.

(3) Aufwendungen für den Abschluß von Versicherungsverträgen dürfen nicht aktiviert werden.

§ 249 Rückstellungen

(1) Rückstellungen sind für ungewisse Verbindlichkeiten und für drohende Verluste aus schwebenden Geschäften zu bilden. Ferner sind Rückstellungen zu bilden für

1. im Geschäftsjahr unterlassene Aufwendungen für Instandhaltung, die im folgenden Geschäftsjahr innerhalb von drei Monaten, oder für Abraumbeseitigung, die im folgenden Geschäftsjahr nachgeholt werden,

2. Gewährleistungen, die ohne rechtliche Verpflichtung erbracht werden.

(3) Liability entries, which are permissible for income and revenue tax purposes, may be made on the balance sheet. They shall be shown as special entries with a capital surplus portion and dissolved in accordance with the tax law. To that extent, an accrual is unneccessary.

§ 248 Prohibitions in balancing accounts

(1) Expenses for establishing the enterprise and procuring equity may not be included on the balance sheet as asset entries.

(2) An asset entry may not be made for intangible fixed assets that were not acquired for valuable consideration.

(3) Expenses for the conclusion of insurance contracts may not be included as asset entries.

§ 249 Accruals

(1) Accruals shall be made for uncertain liabilities and for threatened losses from pending transactions. Furthermore, accruals shall be made for the following:

1. expenses for maintenance that was omitted in the fiscal year but that will be completed in the next fiscal year within three months or for removal of earth and demolished buildings in the context of construction work that will be completed in the next fiscal year,

2. guarantees granted without required legal obligation.

| Vorschriften für alle Kaufleute | §§ 249, 250 |

Rückstellungen dürfen für unterlassene Aufwendungen für Instandhaltung auch gebildet werden, wenn die Instandhaltung nach Ablauf der Frist nach Satz 2 Nr. 1 innerhalb des Geschäftsjahrs nachgeholt wird.

(2) Rückstellungen dürfen außerdem für ihrer Eigenart nach genau umschriebene, dem Geschäftsjahr oder einem früheren Geschäftsjahr zuzuordnende Aufwendungen gebildet werden, die am Abschlußstichtag wahrscheinlich oder sicher, aber hinsichtlich ihrer Höhe oder des Zeitpunkts ihres Eintritts unbestimmt sind.

(3) Für andere als die in den Absätzen 1 und 2 bezeichneten Zwecke dürfen Rückstellungen nicht gebildet werden. Rückstellungen dürfen nur aufgelöst werden, soweit der Grund hierfür entfallen ist.

§ 250 Rechnungsabgrenzungsposten

(1) Als Rechnungsabgrenzungsposten sind auf der Aktivseite Ausgaben vor dem Abschlußstichtag auszuweisen, soweit sie Aufwand für eine bestimmte Zeit nach diesem Tag darstellen. Ferner dürfen ausgewiesen werden

1. als Aufwand berücksichtigte Zölle und Verbrauchsteuern, soweit sie auf am Abschlußstichtag auszuweisende Vermögensgegenstände des Vorratsvermögens entfallen,
2. als Aufwand berücksichtigte Umsatzsteuer auf am Abschlußstichtag auszuweisende oder von den Vorräten offen abgesetzte Anzahlungen.

(2) Auf der Passivseite sind als Rechnungsabgrenzungsposten Einnahmen vor dem Abschlußstichtag auszuwei-

Accruals may also be made for omitted maintenance expenses if the maintenance will be completed after the time period set forth in sentence 2 No. 1 above, but within the fiscal year.

(2) Accruals may be made furthermore for expenses that are precisely described according to their special characteristics and attributed to the fiscal year or an earlier fiscal year, and that are probable or certain at the close of the fiscal year, but are indeterminate with regard to the amount or the date of their occurrence.

(3) Accruals may not be made for purposes other than those designated in Subsections 1 and 2 above. Accruals may be dissolved only to the extent that the reason for them has disappeared.

§ 250 Accrued and deferred items

(1) Payments made before the close of the fiscal year shall be entered as prepaid expenses on the assets side to the extent that they represent expenses for a definite period of time after the close of the fiscal year. Furthermore, there may be entered

1. customs duties and excise taxes listed as expenses to the extent that they can be allocated to assets in the inventory to be shown at the close of the fiscal year,
2. turnover tax relating to payments on account which are to be disclosed or openly deducted from inventories at the close of the fiscal year listed as expenses.

(2) Receipts before the close of the fiscal year shall be entered as deferred income on the liability side if they repre-

sen, soweit sie Ertrag für eine bestimmte Zeit nach diesem Tag darstellen.

(3) Ist der Rückzahlungsbetrag einer Verbindlichkeit höher als der Ausgabebetrag, so darf der Unterschiedsbetrag in den Rechnungsabgrenzungsposten auf der Aktivseite aufgenommen werden. Der Unterschiedsbetrag ist durch planmäßige jährliche Abschreibungen zu tilgen, die auf die gesamte Laufzeit der Verbindlichkeit verteilt werden können.

§ 251 Haftungsverhältnisse

Unter der Bilanz sind, sofern sie nicht auf der Passivseite auszuweisen sind, Verbindlichkeiten aus der Begebung und Übertragung von Wechseln, aus Bürgschaften, Wechsel- und Scheckbürgschaften und aus Gewährleistungsverträgen sowie Haftungsverhältnisse aus der Bestellung von Sicherheiten für fremde Verbindlichkeiten zu vermerken; sie dürfen in einem Betrag angegeben werden. Haftungsverhältnisse sind auch anzugeben, wenn ihnen gleichwertige Rückgriffsforderungen gegenüberstehen.

Dritter Titel. Bewertungsvorschriften

§ 252 Allgemeine Bewertungsgrundsätze

(1) Bei der Bewertung der im Jahresabschluß ausgewiesenen Vermögensgegenstände und Schulden gilt insbesondere folgendes:

sent income for a definite period after the close of the fiscal year.

(3) If the amount of a liability's repayment is higher than the amount of the original outlay, then the difference in amounts may be included in prepaid expenses on the assets side. The difference in amounts shall be amortized by regularly scheduled annual charges that can be spread out over the entire lifetime of the liability.

§ 251 Contingencies and commitments

Liabilities arising from the issuance and transfer of bills of exchange, from suretyships, guarantees of bills of exchange and check guarantees, and from contracts of indemnity as well as contingencies and commitments arising from the creation of security for third-party liabilities shall be entered as below-the-line items on the financial statements to the extent that they shall not be entered on the liability side. These liabilities may be reported as one sum. Contingencies and commitments shall also be reported if they are matched by equivalent claims for recourse.

Third Title. Valuation Regulations

§ 252 General principles of valuation

(1) In valuing assets and liabilities entered in the annual financial statements the following applies in particular:

1. Die Wertansätze in der Eröffnungsbilanz des Geschäftsjahrs müssen mit denen der Schlußbilanz des vorhergehenden Geschäftsjahrs übereinstimmen.
2. Bei der Bewertung ist von der Fortführung der Unternehmenstätigkeit auszugehen, sofern dem nicht tatsächliche oder rechtliche Gegebenheiten entgegenstehen.
3. Die Vermögensgegenstände und Schulden sind zum Abschlußstichtag einzeln zu bewerten.
4. Es ist vorsichtig zu bewerten, namentlich sind alle vorhersehbaren Risiken und Verluste, die bis zum Abschlußstichtag entstanden sind, zu berücksichtigen, selbst wenn diese erst zwischen dem Abschlußstichtag und dem Tag der Aufstellung des Jahresabschlusses bekanntgeworden sind; Gewinne sind nur zu berücksichtigen, wenn sie am Abschlußstichtag realisiert sind.
5. Aufwendungen und Erträge des Geschäftsjahrs sind unabhängig von den Zeitpunkten der entsprechenden Zahlungen im Jahresabschluß zu berücksichtigen.
6. Die auf den vorhergehenden Jahresabschluß angewandten Bewertungsmethoden sollen beibehalten werden.

(2) Von den Grundsätzen des Absatzes 1 darf nur in begründeten Ausnahmefällen abgewichen werden.

§ 253 Wertansätze der Vermögensgegenstände und Schulden

(1) Vermögensgegenstände sind höchstens mit den Anschaffungs- oder Herstellungskosten, vermindert um Ab-

1. The valuations on the opening balance sheet of the fiscal year must match those on the closing balance sheet of the preceding fiscal year.
2. The valuation shall assume the continuation of the business operation unless the actual facts or legal situation indicates otherwise.
3. The assets and liabilities shall be valued individually as of the close of the fiscal year.
4. The valuation shall be undertaken cautiously. In particular, all foreseeable risks and losses that have emerged up to the close of the fiscal year shall be taken into account, even if these first become known between the close of the fiscal year and the day of preparation of the annual financial statements. Profits shall be taken into account only if they have been realized by the close of the fiscal year.
5. Expenses and revenues of the fiscal year shall be taken into account in the annual financial statements regardless of the time of the corresponding payments.
6. The method of valuation used in the preceding annual financial statements shall be retained.

(2) Deviations from the principles of Subsection 1 above are permissible only in justifiable exceptional cases.

§ 253 Valuation of assets and liabilities

(1) Assets shall be assessed at no higher than the cost of acquisition or production less depreciation pursu-

§ 253

schreibungen nach den Absätzen 2 und 3 anzusetzen. Verbindlichkeiten sind zu ihrem Rückzahlungsbetrag, Rentenverpflichtungen, für die eine Gegenleistung nicht mehr zu erwarten ist, zu ihrem Barwert und Rückstellungen nur in Höhe des Betrags anzusetzen, der nach vernünftiger kaufmännischer Beurteilung notwendig ist; Rückstellungen dürfen nur abgezinst werden, soweit die ihnen zugrundeliegenden Verbindlichkeiten einen Zinsanteil enthalten.

(2) Bei Vermögensgegenständen des Anlagevermögens, deren Nutzung zeitlich begrenzt ist, sind die Anschaffungs- oder Herstellungskosten um planmäßige Abschreibungen zu vermindern. Der Plan muß die Anschaffungs- oder Herstellungskosten auf die Geschäftsjahre verteilen, in denen der Vermögensgegenstand voraussichtlich genutzt werden kann. Ohne Rücksicht darauf, ob ihre Nutzung zeitlich begrenzt ist, können bei Vermögensgegenständen des Anlagevermögens außerplanmäßige Abschreibungen vorgenommen werden, um die Vermögensgegenstände mit dem niedrigeren Wert anzusetzen, der ihnen am Abschlußstichtag beizulegen ist; sie sind vorzunehmen bei einer voraussichtlich dauernden Wertminderung.

(3) Bei Vermögensgegenständen des Umlaufvermögens sind Abschreibungen vorzunehmen, um diese mit einem niedrigeren Wert anzusetzen, der sich aus einem Börsen- oder Marktpreis am Abschlußstichtag ergibt. Ist ein Börsen- oder Marktpreis nicht festzustellen und übersteigen die Anschaffungs- oder Herstellungskosten den Wert, der den Vermögensgegenständen am Abschlußstichtag beizulegen ist, so ist auf diesen Wert abzuschreiben. Außerdem dürfen Abschreibungen vorgenom-

Handelsbücher

ant to Subsections 2 and 3 below. Liabilities shall be assessed at their redemption amount, pension obligations (for which consideration is no longer expected) at their cash value and accruals only at the amount necessary according to reasonable business judgment; reserves may be discounted only to extent that their underlying obligations contain an interest component.

(2) The costs of acquisition or production of fixed assets with a limited useful life shall be depreciated according to a regular schedule. The schedule must spread the costs of acquisition and production out over the fiscal years in which the asset prospectively can be used. Without regard to whether the fixed assets have a limited useful life, extraordinary depreciation may be taken on fixed assets in order to assess the assets at the lower value that is ascribed to them on the close of the fiscal year. Such depreciation shall be taken on a prospective permanent reduction in value.

(3) Current assets shall be written down in order to ascribe to them a lower value resulting from an exchange or market price on the close of the fiscal year. If an exchange or market price cannot be determined and the costs of acquisition or production exceed the value ascribed to the assets on the close of the fiscal year, then they shall be written down to this value. In addition, write-downs may be made as deemed necessary according to reasonable business judgment

| Vorschriften für alle Kaufleute | §§ 253–255 |

men werden, soweit diese nach vernünftiger kaufmännischer Beurteilung notwendig sind, um zu verhindern, daß in der nächsten Zukunft der Wertansatz dieser Vermögensgegenstände auf Grund von Wertschwankungen geändert werden muß.

(4) Abschreibungen sind außerdem im Rahmen vernünftiger kaufmännischer Beurteilung zulässig.

(5) Ein niedrigerer Wertansatz nach Absatz 2 Satz 3, Absatz 3 oder 4 darf beibehalten werden, auch wenn die Gründe dafür nicht mehr bestehen.

§ 254 Steuerrechtliche Abschreibungen

Abschreibungen können auch vorgenommen werden, um Vermögensgegenstände des Anlage- oder Umlaufvermögens mit dem niedrigeren Wert anzusetzen, der auf einer nur steuerrechtlich zulässigen Abschreibung beruht. § 253 Abs. 5 ist entsprechend anzuwenden.

§ 255 Anschaffungs- und Herstellungskosten

(1) Anschaffungskosten sind die Aufwendungen, die geleistet werden, um einen Vermögensgegenstand zu erwerben und ihn in einen betriebsbereiten Zustand zu versetzen, soweit sie dem Vermögensgegenstand einzeln zugeordnet werden können. Zu den Anschaffungskosten gehören auch die Nebenkosten sowie die nachträglichen Anschaffungskosten. Anschaffungspreisminderungen sind abzusetzen.

(2) Herstellungskosten sind die Aufwendungen, die durch den Verbrauch von Gütern und die Inanspruchnahme von Diensten für die Herstellung ei-

to avoid having to adjust the valuation of these assets in the near future because of value fluctuations.

(4) Depreciation is also permissible within the boundaries of reasonable business judgment.

(5) A lower valuation made pursuant to Subsection 2 sentence 3 or Subsection 3 or 4 above may be retained even if the reasons for it no longer exist.

§ 254 Depreciation under tax law

Depreciation may also be taken in order to assess fixed and current assets at the lower value based exclusively on depreciation permissible under tax law. Subsection 5 of § 253 shall apply analogously.

§ 255 Costs of acquisition and production

(1) Costs of acquisition are the expenditures made in order to purchase an asset and to put it into business-operating condition to the extent that these costs can be separately allocated to the asset. The costs of acquisition also include incidental expenses as well as subsequent costs of acquisition. Any reductions in the acquisition price shall be deducted.

(2) Costs of production are the expenditures arising out of goods consumed and services used in producing an asset, enlarging it or substantially im-

nes Vermögensgegenstands, seine Erweiterung oder für eine über seinen ursprünglichen Zustand hinausgehende wesentliche Verbesserung entstehen. Dazu gehören die Materialkosten, die Fertigungskosten und die Sonderkosten der Fertigung. Bei der Berechnung der Herstellungskosten dürfen auch angemessene Teile der notwendigen Materialgemeinkosten, der notwendigen Fertigungsgemeinkosten und des Wertverzehrs des Anlagevermögens, soweit er durch die Fertigung veranlaßt ist, eingerechnet werden. Kosten der allgemeinen Verwaltung sowie Aufwendungen für soziale Einrichtungen des Betriebs, für freiwillige soziale Leistungen und für betriebliche Altersversorgung brauchen nicht eingerechnet zu werden. Aufwendungen im Sinne der Sätze 3 und 4 dürfen nur insoweit berücksichtigt werden, als sie auf den Zeitraum der Herstellung entfallen. Vertriebskosten dürfen nicht in die Herstellungskosten einbezogen werden.

(3) Zinsen für Fremdkapital gehören nicht zu den Herstellungskosten. Zinsen für Fremdkapital, das zur Finanzierung der Herstellung eines Vermögensgegenstands verwendet wird, dürfen angesetzt werden, soweit sie auf den Zeitraum der Herstellung entfallen; in diesem Falle gelten sie als Herstellungskosten des Vermögensgegenstands.

(4) Als Geschäfts- oder Firmenwert darf der Unterschiedsbetrag angesetzt werden, um den die für die Übernahme eines Unternehmens bewirkte Gegenleistung den Wert der einzelnen Vermögensgegenstände des Unternehmens abzüglich der Schulden im Zeitpunkt der Übernahme übersteigt. Der Betrag ist in jedem folgenden Geschäftsjahr zu mindestens einem Viertel durch Abschreibungen

proving it beyond its original condition. That includes the costs of materials, the manufacturing costs and special manufacturing costs. In calculating the costs of production, appropriate portions of the necessary material overhead, necessary production overhead and depreciation in value of assets, to the extent brought about in the course of manufacturing, may also be taken into account. Costs of general administration as well as expenditures for the business's social welfare arrangements, for voluntary social benefits and for the business's old age pension scheme need not be taken into account. Expenditures falling within the meaning of sentences 3 and 4 may be considered only to the extent that they fall within the time frame of production. Selling expenses may not be included in the costs of production.

(3) Interest on borrowed capital is not part of the costs of production. Interest on borrowed capital that is used for financing the production of an asset may be assessed to the extent that it falls within the time frame of production. In this case it is deemed to be a cost of production of the asset.

(4) The goodwill of the business or firm may be assessed at the amount by which the consideration paid for acquiring an enterprise exceeds the value of the enterprise's separate assets less its liabilities at the time of acquisition. The amount shall be amortized in each following fiscal year by at least one-fourth. The amortization of the business's or firm's goodwill may also be spread out according to a

Vorschriften für alle Kaufleute §§ 255–257

zu tilgen. Die Abschreibung des Geschäfts- oder Firmenwerts kann aber auch planmäßig auf die Geschäftsjahre verteilt werden, in denen er voraussichtlich genutzt wird.

regular schedule among the fiscal years in which it prospectively will be used.

§ 256 Bewertungsvereinfachungsverfahren

Soweit es den Grundsätzen ordnungsmäßiger Buchführung entspricht, kann für den Wertansatz gleichartiger Vermögensgegenstände des Vorratsvermögens unterstellt werden, daß die zuerst oder daß die zuletzt angeschafften oder hergestellten Vermögensgegenstände zuerst oder in einer sonstigen bestimmten Folge verbraucht oder veräußert worden sind. § 240 Abs. 3 und 4 ist auch auf den Jahresabschluß anwendbar.

§ 256 Procedures for simplifying valuation

So long as in conformity with generally accepted accounting principles, it can be assumed in valuing like assets in inventory that either the first or last asset acquired or produced was consumed or sold first or in another specificed sequence. Subsections 3 and 4 of § 240 also apply to the annual financial statements.

Dritter Unterabschnitt. Aufbewahrung und Vorlage

Third Subpart. Retention and Production

§ 257 Aufbewahrung von Unterlagen. Aufbewahrungsfristen

(1) Jeder Kaufmann ist verpflichtet, die folgenden Unterlagen geordnet aufzubewahren:

1. Handelsbücher, Inventare, Eröffnungsbilanzen, Jahresabschlüsse, Lageberichte, Konzernabschlüsse, Konzernlageberichte sowie die zu ihrem Verständnis erforderlichen Arbeitsanweisungen und sonstigen Organisationsunterlagen,

2. die empfangenen Handelsbriefe,

3. Wiedergaben der abgesandten Handelsbriefe,

§ 257 Retention of records; time periods of retention

(1) Every merchant is obligated to retain the following documents in an orderly fashion:

1. commercial business records, inventories, opening balance sheets, annual financial statements, management reports, consolidated financial statements, consolidated statements of affairs as well as procedural instructions and other organizational documents necessary for interpreting such documents,

2. incoming business correspondence,

3. copies of mailed business correspondence and

151

§ 257 — Handelsbücher

4. Belege für Buchungen in den von ihm nach § 238 Abs. 1 zu führenden Büchern (Buchungsbelege).

(2) Handelsbriefe sind nur Schriftstücke, die ein Handelsgeschäft betreffen.

(3) Mit Ausnahme der Eröffnungsbilanzen, Jahresabschlüsse und der Konzernabschlüsse können die in Absatz 1 aufgeführten Unterlagen auch als Wiedergabe auf einem Bildträger oder auf anderen Datenträgern aufbewahrt werden, wenn dies den Grundsätzen ordnungsmäßiger Buchführung entspricht und sichergestellt ist, daß die Wiedergabe oder die Daten

1. mit den empfangenen Handelsbriefen und den Buchungsbelegen bildlich und mit den anderen Unterlagen inhaltlich übereinstimmen, wenn sie lesbar gemacht werden,

2. während der Dauer der Aufbewahrungsfrist verfügbar sind und jederzeit innerhalb angemessener Frist lesbar gemacht werden können.

Sind Unterlagen auf Grund des § 239 Abs. 4 Satz 1 auf Datenträgern hergestellt worden, können statt des Datenträgers die Daten auch ausgedruckt aufbewahrt werden; die ausgedruckten Unterlagen können auch nach Satz 1 aufbewahrt werden.

(4) Die in Absatz 1 Nr. 1 und 4 aufgeführten Unterlagen sind zehn Jahre, die sonstigen in Absatz 1 aufgeführten Unterlagen sechs Jahre aufzubewahren.

(5) Die Aufbewahrungsfrist beginnt mit dem Schluß des Kalenderjahrs, in dem die letzte Eintragung in das Handelsbuch gemacht, das Inventar aufgestellt, die Eröffnungsbilanz oder der Jahresabschluß festgestellt, der Konzernabschluß aufgestellt, der Han-

4. the original records underlying the entries made in the books to be kept by him pursuant to § 238 Subsection 1 (accounting records).

(2) Business correspondence comprises only such documents as pertain to a commercial transaction.

(3) Except for the opening balance sheets, annual financial statements and consolidated financial statements, the documents listed in Subsection 1 may also be stored as photographic reproductions or on other electronic data storage devices if this complies with generally accepted accounting principles and it is assured that the reproduction or data

1. provides a picture-perfect duplicate of the incoming business correspondence and accounting records and exactly reproduces the content of the other documents whenever they are put into a legible form and

2. is accessible during the period of retention and can be put into a legible form at any time within a reasonable period.

If records are placed in an electronic data storage device on the basis of § 239 Subsection 4 sentence 1, the data may also be stored in print-out form instead of in the electronic data storage device. The printed records may also be retained pursuant to sentence 1.

(4) The records listed in Subsection 1 Nos. 1 and 4 shall be retained for ten years, and the other records listed in Subsection 1 shall be retained for six years.

(5) The period of retention begins upon the close of the calendar year in which the last entry in the commercial record was made, the inventory prepared, the opening balance sheet or the annual financial statements determined, the consolidated financial

Vorschriften für alle Kaufleute §§ 257–261

delsbrief empfangen oder abgesandt worden oder der Buchungsbeleg entstanden ist.

§ 258 Vorlegung im Rechtsstreit

(1) Im Laufe eines Rechtsstreits kann das Gericht auf Antrag oder von Amts wegen die Vorlegung der Handelsbücher einer Partei anordnen.

(2) Die Vorschriften der Zivilprozeßordnung über die Verpflichtung des Prozeßgegners zur Vorlegung von Urkunden bleiben unberührt.

§ 259 Auszug bei Vorlegung im Rechtsstreit

Werden in einem Rechtsstreit Handelsbücher vorgelegt, so ist von ihrem Inhalt, soweit er den Streitpunkt betrifft, unter Zuziehung der Parteien Einsicht zu nehmen und geeignetenfalls ein Auszug zu fertigen. Der übrige Inhalt der Bücher ist dem Gericht insoweit offenzulegen, als es zur Prüfung ihrer ordnungsmäßigen Führung notwendig ist.

§ 260 Vorlegung bei Auseinandersetzungen

Bei Vermögensauseinandersetzungen, insbesondere in Erbschafts-, Gütergemeinschafts- und Gesellschaftsteilungssachen, kann das Gericht die Vorlegung der Handelsbücher zur Kenntnisnahme von ihrem ganzen Inhalt anordnen.

§ 261 Vorlegung von Unterlagen auf Bild- oder Datenträgern

Wer aufzubewahrende Unterlagen nur in der Form einer Wiedergabe auf einem Bildträger oder auf anderen Da-

statements prepared, the business correspondence received or mailed out or the accounting records originated.

§ 258 Production during litigation

(1) In the course of litigation the court may order on application or on its own motion the production of the commercial records of one of the parties.

(2) The provisions of the Code of Civil Procedure with respect to the duty of the adverse party to produce documents remain unaffected.

§ 259 Excerpts from materials produced during litigation

If commercial records are produced during litigation, their content shall be inspected to the extent that it concerns the issue in contention among the parties present. In appropriate cases an excerpt shall be made. The remaining content of the books shall be revealed to the court to the extent necessary to determine that the books were properly kept.

§ 260 Production of documents for distribution of assets

In the event of distribution of assets, especially in probate, common property and partnership division matters, the court can order the production of commercial records in order to take notice of their entire contents.

§ 261 Production of documents from film or data storage devices

One who can produce stored documents only in the form of a reproduction from film or other data storage de-

tenträgern vorlegen kann, ist verpflichtet, auf seine Kosten diejenigen Hilfsmittel zur Verfügung zu stellen, die erforderlich sind, um die Unterlagen lesbar zu machen; soweit erforderlich, hat er die Unterlagen auf seine Kosten auszudrucken oder ohne Hilfsmittel lesbare Reproduktionen beizubringen.

vice is obligated to make available at his own expense the devices necessary to put the documents into a legible form. To the extent necessary, he must, at his own expense, print out the records or furnish reproductions which can be read without auxiliary devices.

Vierter Unterabschnitt. Landesrecht

§ 262 *(aufgehoben)*

§ 263 Vorbehalt landesrechtlicher Vorschriften

Unberührt bleiben bei Unternehmen ohne eigene Rechtspersönlichkeit einer Gemeinde, eines Gemeindeverbands oder eines Zweckverbands landesrechtliche Vorschriften, die von den Vorschriften dieses Abschnitts abweichen.

Fourth Subpart. State Law

§ 262 *(repealed)*

§ 263 Reservation of state law regulations

This Part's regulations shall not affect regulations of state law pertaining to enterprises without a separate juridical personality in a municipality, an association of local governments or a special purpose association (linking local authorities for joint performance of certain tasks) that deviate from this Part's regulations.

Zweiter Abschnitt. Ergänzende Vorschriften für Kapitalgesellschaften (Aktiengesellschaften, Kommanditgesellschaften auf Aktien und Gesellschaften mit beschränkter Haftung) sowie bestimmte Personenhandelsgesellschaften

Part Two. Additional Regulations for Corporations (Stock Corporations, Corporations Limited by Shares but having one or more General Partners and Limited Liability Companies) as well as certain Business Partnerships

Erster Unterabschnitt. Jahresabschluß der Kapitalgesellschaft und Lagebericht

First Subpart. Annual Financial Statements of the Corporation and Management Reports

Erster Titel. Allgemeine Vorschriften

First Title. General Regulations

§ 264 Pflicht zur Aufstellung

(1) Die gesetzlichen Vertreter einer Kapitalgesellschaft haben den Jahresabschluß (§ 242) um einen Anhang zu erweitern, der mit der Bilanz und der Gewinn- und Verlustrechnung eine Einheit bildet, sowie einen Lagebe-

§ 264 Duty to prepare

(1) The legal representatives of a corporation must supplement the annual financial statements (§ 242) with notes, which together with the balance sheet and profit and loss statement comprises a whole, and must

Ergänzende Vorschriften für Kapitalgesellschaften § 264

richt aufzustellen. Der Jahresabschluß und der Lagebericht sind von den gesetzlichen Vertretern in den ersten drei Monaten des Geschäftsjahrs für das vergangene Geschäftsjahr aufzustellen. Kleine Kapitalgesellschaften (§ 267 Abs. 1) brauchen den Lagebericht nicht aufzustellen; sie dürfen den Jahresabschluß auch später aufstellen, wenn dies einem ordnungsgemäßen Geschäftsgang entspricht, jedoch innerhalb der ersten sechs Monate des Geschäftsjahres.

(2) Der Jahresabschluß der Kapitalgesellschaft hat unter Beachtung der Grundsätze ordnungsmäßiger Buchführung ein den tatsächlichen Verhältnissen entsprechendes Bild der Vermögens-, Finanz- und Ertragslage der Kapitalgesellschaft zu vermitteln. Führen besondere Umstände dazu, daß der Jahresabschluß ein den tatsächlichen Verhältnissen entsprechendes Bild im Sinne des Satzes 1 nicht vermittelt, so sind im Anhang zusätzliche Angaben zu machen.

(3) Eine Kapitalgesellschaft, die Tochterunternehmen eines nach § 290 zur Aufstellung eines Konzernabschlusses verpflichteten Mutterunternehmens ist, braucht die Vorschriften dieses Unterabschnitts und des Dritten und Vierten Unterabschnitts dieses Abschnitts nicht anzuwenden, wenn

1. alle Gesellschafter des Tochterunternehmens der Befreiung für das jeweilige Geschäftsjahr zugestimmt haben und der Beschluß nach § 325 offengelegt worden ist,
2. das Mutterunternehmen zur Verlustübernahme nach § 302 des Aktiengesetzes verpflichtet ist oder eine solche Verpflichtung freiwillig übernommen hat und diese Erklärung nach § 325 offengelegt worden ist,

prepare a management report. The annual financial statements and the management report shall be prepared by the legal representatives in the first three months of the fiscal year for the preceding fiscal year. Small corporations (§ 267 Subsection 1) need not prepare the management report; they may also prepare the annual financial statements later, if that conforms to proper conduct of business, but in any event within the first six months of the fiscal year.

(2) The corporation's annual financial statements must present a factually accurate picture of the corporation's net assets, financing and results of operations according to generally accepted accounting principles. If, as a result of special circumstances, the annual financial statements do not present a factually accurate picture within the meaning of the first sentence, then supplementary information must be provided in the notes.

(3) A corporation which is the subsidiary of a parent which must prepare consolidated financial statements pursuant to § 290 need not apply the provisions of this Subpart or the Third and Fourth Subparts if

1. all shareholders of the subsidiary have approved the exemption for the respective fiscal year and the resolution has been disclosed pursuant to § 325,
2. the parent is obligated to assume the losses pursuant to § 302 of the Stock Corporation Act or has voluntarily assumed such an obligation and this declaration has been disclosed pursuant to § 325,

3. das Tochterunternehmen in den Konzernabschluß nach den Vorschriften dieses Abschnitts einbezogen worden ist,
4. die Befreiung des Tochterunternehmens im Anhang des von dem Mutterunternehmen aufgestellten Konzernabschlusses angegeben wird und
5. die von dem Mutterunternehmen nach den Vorschriften über die Konzernrechnungslegung gemäß § 325 offenzulegenden Unterlagen auch zum Handelsregister des Sitzes der die Befreiung in Anspruch nehmenden Kapitalgesellschaft eingereicht worden sind.

(4) Absatz 3 ist auf Kapitalgesellschaften, die Tochterunternehmen eines nach § 11 des Publizitätsgesetzes zur Aufstellung eines Konzernabschlusses verpflichteten Mutterunternehmens sind, entsprechend anzuwenden, soweit in diesem Konzernabschluss von dem Wahlrecht des § 13 Abs. 3 Satz 1 des Publizitätsgesetzes nicht Gebrauch gemacht worden ist.

§ 264 a Anwendung auf bestimmte offene Handelsgesellschaften und Kommanditgesellschaften

(1) Die Vorschriften des Ersten bis Fünften Unterabschnitts des Zweiten Abschnitts sind auch anzuwenden auf offene Handelsgesellschaften und Kommanditgesellschaften, bei denen nicht wenigstens ein persönlich haftender Gesellschafter

1. eine natürliche Person oder
2. eine offene Handelsgesellschaft, Kommanditgesellschaft oder andere Personengesellschaft mit einer natürlichen Person als persönlich haftendem Gesellschafter

3. the subsidiary has been included in the consolidated financial statements pursuant to the provisions of this part,
4. the exemption of the subsidiary is indicated in the notes to the consolidated financial statements prepared by the parent and
5. the records which the parent must disclose pursuant to the provisions concerning the consolidated accounting according to § 325 have also been submitted to the Commercial Register of the domicile of the corporation claiming exemption.

(4) Subsection 3 applies analogously to corporations which are the subsidiary of a parent which pursuant to § 11 of the Publicity Law is obligated to prepare consolidated financial statements, to the extent that in the consolidated financial statements no use has been made of the option right under § 13 Subsection 3 sentence 1 of the Publicity Law.

§ 264 a Application to certain general commercial partnerships and limited partnerships

(1) The regulations of the First through Fifth Subpart of the Second Part shall also apply to general commercial partnerships and limited partnerships where not at least one general partner is

1. a natural person
2. a general commercial partnership, limited partnership or other business partnership with a natural person as general partner

ist, oder sich die Verbindung von Gesellschaften in dieser Art fortsetzt.

(2) In den Vorschriften dieses Abschnitts gelten als gesetzliche Vertreter einer offenen Handelsgesellschaft und Kommanditgesellschaft nach Absatz 1 die Mitglieder des vertretungsberechtigten Organs der vertretungsberechtigten Gesellschaften.

§ 264 b Befreiung von der Pflicht zur Aufstellung eines Jahresabschlusses nach den für Kapitalgesellschaften geltenden Vorschriften

Eine Personenhandelsgesellschaft im Sinne des § 264 a Abs. 1 ist von der Verpflichtung befreit, einen Jahresabschluss und einen Lagebericht nach den Vorschriften dieses Abschnittes aufzustellen, prüfen zu lassen und offen zu legen, wenn

1. sie in den Konzernabschluss eines Mutterunternehmens mit Sitz in einem Mitgliedstaat der Europäischen Union oder einem anderen Vertragsstaat des Abkommens über den Europäischen Wirtschaftsraum oder in den Konzernabschluss eines anderen Unternehmens, das persönlich haftender Gesellschafter dieser Personenhandelsgesellschaft ist, einbezogen ist;

2. der Konzernabschluss sowie der Konzernlagebericht im Einklang mit der Richtlinie 83/349/EWG des Rates vom 13. Juni 1983 auf Grund von Artikel 54 Abs. 3 Buchstabe g des Vertrages über den konsolidierten Abschluss (ABl. EG Nr. L 193 S 1) und der Richtlinie 84/253/EWG des Rates vom 10. April 1984 über die Zulassung der mit der Pflichtprüfung der Rechnungs-

or the association of companies continues itself in this way.

(2) For the regulations of this Part the members of the bodies legally representing the companies which in turn legally represent the partnerships shall be deemed to be the legal representives of a general commercial partnership or limited partnership under Subsection 1.

§ 264 b Exemption from the duty to prepare annual financial statements pursuant to the regulations applicable to corporations

A business partnership within the meaning of § 264a Subsection 1 is exempt from the duty to prepare, have audited and disclose annual financial statements and management reports pursuant to this Subsection if

1. it is included in the consolidated financial statements of a parent company with its domicile in a member state of the European Union or another contracting state of the Treaty on the European Economic Area or in the consolidated financial statements of another enterprise which is the general partner of this business partnership;

2. the consolidated financial statements and consolidated management report are prepared, audited by a certified accountant and disclosed pursuant to the governing law for the enterprise preparing the consolidated financial statements in accordance with the Directive 83/349/EEC of the Commission of June 13, 1983 on the basis of Article 54 Subsection 3 Letter g of the

legungsunterlagen beauftragten Personen (ABl. EG Nr. L 126 S. 20) nach dem für das den Konzernabschluss aufstellende Unternehmen maßgeblichen Recht aufgestellt, von einem zugelassenen Abschlussprüfer geprüft und offen gelegt worden ist;

3. das den Konzernabschluss aufstellende Unternehmen die offen zu legenden Unterlagen in deutscher Sprache auch zum Handelsregister des Sitzes der Personenhandelsgesellschaft eingereicht hat und

4. die Befreiung der Personenhandelsgesellschaft im Anhang des Konzernabschlusses angegeben ist.

§ 264 c Besondere Bestimmungen für offene Handelsgesellschaften und Kommanditgesellschaften im Sinne des § 264 a

(1) Ausleihungen, Forderungen und Verbindlichkeiten gegenüber Gesellschaftern sind in der Regel als solche jeweils gesondert auszuweisen oder im Anhang anzugeben. Werden sie unter anderen Posten ausgewiesen, so muss diese Eigenschaft vermerkt werden.

(2) § 266 Abs. 3 Buchstabe A ist mit der Maßgabe anzuwenden, dass als Eigenkapital die folgenden Posten gesondert auszuweisen sind:

I. Kapitalanteile
II. Rücklagen
III. Gewinnvortrag/Verlustvortrag
IV. Jahresüberschuss/Jahresfehlbetrag.

Anstelle des Postens „Gezeichnetes Kapital" sind die Kapitalanteile der persönlich haftenden Gesellschafter auszuweisen; sie dürfen auch zusammengefasst ausgewiesen werden. Der

Agreement on Consolidated Financial Statements (OJ EC No. L 193, p. 1) and the Directive 84/253/EEC of the Commission of April 10, 1984 pertaining to the Certification of Persons charged with the Mandatory Audit of Accounting Records (OJ EC No. L 126, p. 20);

3. the enterprise preparing the consolidated financial statements has submitted the documents requiring disclosure in German to the commercial register also where the business partnership has its domicile and

4. the exemption of the business partnership is stated in the notes of the consolidated financial statements.

§ 264 c Special provisions for general commercial partnerships and limited partnerships within the meaning of § 264 a

(1) Loans, receivables and payables vis-á-vis partners shall, as a rule, be shown as such separately in each case or stated in the notes. If they are shown under other entries this feature must be noted.

(2) § 266 Subsection 3 Letter A shall apply, provided that the following entries are shown separately as shareholder's equity:

I. Capital shares
II. Reserves
III. Profits and losses carried forward
IV. Annual surplus/Annual deficit

Capital shares of the general partners shall be shown in the place of the entry "Subscribed capital"; they may also be shown collectively. The loss allocable to the capital share of a general partner

auf den Kapitalanteil eines persönlich haftenden Gesellschafters für das Geschäftsjahr entfallende Verlust ist von dem Kapitalanteil abzuschreiben. Soweit der Verlust den Kapitalanteil übersteigt, ist er auf der Aktivseite unter der Bezeichnung „Einzahlungsverpflichtungen persönlich haftender Gesellschafter" unter den Forderungen gesondert auszuweisen, soweit eine Zahlungsverpflichtung besteht. Besteht keine Zahlungsverpflichtung, so ist der Betrag als „Nicht durch Vermögenseinlagen gedeckter Verlustanteil persönlich haftender Gesellschafter" zu bezeichnen und gemäß § 268 Abs. 3 auszuweisen. Die Sätze 2 bis 5 sind auf die Einlagen von Kommanditisten entsprechend anzuwenden, wobei diese insgesamt gesondert gegenüber den Kapitalanteilen der persönlich haftenden Gesellschafter auszuweisen sind. Eine Forderung darf jedoch nur ausgewiesen werden, soweit eine Einzahlungsverpflichtung besteht; dasselbe gilt, wenn ein Kommanditist Gewinnanteile entnimmt, während sein Kapitalanteil durch Verlust unter den Betrag der geleisteten Einlage herabgemindert ist, oder soweit durch die Entnahme der Kapitalanteil unter den bezeichneten Betrag herabgemindert wird. Als Rücklagen sind nur solche Beträge auszuweisen, die auf Grund einer gesellschaftsrechtlichen Vereinbarung gebildet worden sind. Im Anhang ist der Betrag der im Handelsregister gemäß § 172 Abs. 1 eingetragenen Einlagen anzugeben, soweit diese nicht geleistet sind.

(3) Das sonstige Vermögen der Gesellschafter (Privatvermögen) darf nicht in die Bilanz und die auf das Privatvermögen entfallenden Aufwendungen und Erträge dürfen nicht in die Gewinn- und Verlustrechnung aufgenommen werden. In der Gewinn- und Verlust-

for the fiscal year shall be deducted from the capital share. To the extent the loss exceeds the capital share, it shall be shown separately on the assets side under "Receivables" and be designated "Obligations to make Contributions of General Partners" to the extent there is a duty to pay. If there is no duty to pay, the amount shall be designated "Share in Loss of General Partners not covered by Capital Contribution" and shall be shown in accordance with § 268 Subsection 2 through 5. Sentences 2 to 5 shall apply analogously to the capital contributions of limited partners, whereby these shall be shown collectively separately from the capital shares of the general partners. A receivable may only be shown to the extent a duty to pay exists; the same applies if a limited partner withdraws profit shares while his capital shares is reduced by losses to an amount less than the capital contribution made or to the extent reduced by the withdrawal of capital share to an amount less than the designated amount. Only those amounts which are established on the basis of a partnership agreement shall be shown as reserves. The amount of the capital contributions which have been registered in the Commercial Register in accordance with § 172 Subsection 1 shall be stated in the notes, to the extent that these have not been paid in.

(3) The other assets of the partners (private assets) may not be included in the balance sheet and the expenses and income allocable to the private assets may not be included in the profit and loss statement. Nevertheless, a tax expense corresponding to the tax

rechnung darf jedoch nach dem Posten „Jahresüberschuss/Jahresfehlbetrag" ein dem Steuersatz der Komplementärgesellschaft entsprechender Steueraufwand der Gesellschafter offen abgesetzt oder hinzugerechnet werden.

(4) Anteile an Komplementärgesellschaften sind in der Bilanz auf der Aktivseite unter den Posten A. III. 1 oder A. III. 3 auszuweisen. § 272 Abs. 4 ist mit der Maßgabe anzuwenden, dass für diese Anteile in Höhe des aktivierten Betrags nach dem Posten „Eigenkapital" ein Sonderposten unter der Bezeichnung „Ausgleichsposten für aktivierte eigene Anteile" zu bilden ist. §§ 269, 274 Abs. 2 sind mit der Maßgabe anzuwenden, dass nach dem Posten „Eigenkapital" ein Sonderposten in Höhe der aktivierten Bilanzierungshilfen anzusetzen ist.

rate of the company which is the general partner may be openly deducted or added in the profit and loss statements under the entry „Annual surplus, Annual deficit".

(4) Shares in companies which are general partners shall be shown on the asset side of the balance sheet under the entry A.III.1 or A.III.3. § 272 Subsection 4 shall apply, provided that a special entry designated „Adjustment entry for capitalized treasury shares" is made for these shares in the amount of the capitalized sum under the entry „Shareholder's equity". §§ 269, 274 Subsection 2 shall apply, provided that after the entry „Shareholder's equity" a special item is shown in the amount of the capitalized balance sheet support shown on the assets side.

§ 265 Allgemeine Grundsätze für die Gliederung

(1) Die Form der Darstellung, insbesondere die Gliederung der aufeinanderfolgenden Bilanzen und Gewinn- und Verlustrechnungen, ist beizubehalten, soweit nicht in Ausnahmefällen wegen besonderer Umstände Abweichungen erforderlich sind. Die Abweichungen sind im Anhang anzugeben und zu begründen.

(2) In der Bilanz sowie in der Gewinn- und Verlustrechnung ist zu jedem Posten der entsprechende Betrag des vorhergehenden Geschäftsjahrs anzugeben. Sind die Beträge nicht vergleichbar, so ist dies im Anhang anzugeben und zu erläutern. Wird der Vorjahresbetrag angepaßt, so ist auch dies im Anhang anzugeben und zu erläutern.

§ 265 General principles of classification

(1) The form of the statement, especially the arrangement of successive balance sheets and profit and loss statements shall be retained, unless the special circumstances of exceptional situations make deviations necessary. Such deviations shall be reported in the notes and justified.

(2) For every entry on the balance sheet as well as in the profit and loss statement, the corresponding amount from the preceding fiscal year shall be specified. If the amounts are not comparable, then that shall be reported and discussed in the notes. If the amount from the previous year is adjusted, then that shall also be reported and discussed in the notes.

Ergänzende Vorschriften für Kapitalgesellschaften § 265

(3) Fällt ein Vermögensgegenstand oder eine Schuld unter mehrere Posten der Bilanz, so ist die Mitzugehörigkeit zu anderen Posten bei dem Posten, unter dem der Ausweis erfolgt ist, zu vermerken oder im Anhang anzugeben, wenn dies zur Aufstellung eines klaren und übersichtlichen Jahresabschlusses erforderlich ist. Eigene Anteile dürfen unabhängig von ihrer Zweckbestimmung nur unter dem dafür vorgesehenen Posten im Umlaufvermögen ausgewiesen werden.

(4) Sind mehrere Geschäftszweige vorhanden und bedingt dies die Gliederung des Jahresabschlusses nach verschiedenen Gliederungsvorschriften, so ist der Jahresabschluß nach der für einen Geschäftszweig vorgeschriebenen Gliederung aufzustellen und nach der für die anderen Geschäftszweige vorgeschriebenen Gliederung zu ergänzen. Die Ergänzung ist im Anhang anzugeben und zu begründen.

(5) Eine weitere Untergliederung der Posten ist zulässig; dabei ist jedoch die vorgeschriebene Gliederung zu beachten. Neue Posten dürfen hinzugefügt werden, wenn ihr Inhalt nicht von einem vorgeschriebenen Posten gedeckt wird.

(6) Gliederung und Bezeichnung der mit arabischen Zahlen versehenen Posten der Bilanz und der Gewinn- und Verlustrechnung sind zu ändern, wenn dies wegen Besonderheiten der Kapitalgesellschaft zur Aufstellung eines klaren und übersichtlichen Jahresabschlusses erforderlich ist.

(7) Die mit arabischen Zahlen versehenen Posten der Bilanz und der Gewinn- und Verlustrechnung können,

(3) If an asset or a liability appears under several entries on the balance sheet, then the relationship of the other entries to the entry under which the identification is made shall be either noted or reported in the notes if necessary for the preparation of clear and lucidly arranged annual financial statements. Treasury shares held may be shown only under the entries in current assets provided for them regardless of their intended purpose.

(4) If there are several lines of business and the annual financial statements' classification should be different depending upon the classification regulations applicable to the respective line of business, then the annual financial statements shall be prepared according to the classification regulations prescribed for one line of business and supplemented according to the classification regulations required for the other lines of business. The supplementary information shall be reported and justified in the notes.

(5) A further subclassification of the entries is permissible so long as the prescribed classification is observed. New entries may be added if their contents are not already covered by a prescribed entry.

(6) The classification and designation of the entries of the balance sheet and the profit and loss statement with Arabic numbers shall be changed if necessary because of peculiarities of the corporation in preparing clear and lucidly arranged annual financial statements.

(7) The entries with Arabic numbers on the balance sheet and the profit and loss statement may be shown summa-

161

wenn nicht besondere Formblätter vorgeschrieben sind, zusammengefaßt ausgewiesen werden, wenn

1. sie einen Betrag enthalten, der für die Vermittlung eines den tatsächlichen Verhältnissen entsprechenden Bildes im Sinne des § 264 Abs. 2 nicht erheblich ist, oder

2. dadurch die Klarheit der Darstellung vergrößert wird; in diesem Falle müssen die zusammengefaßten Posten jedoch im Anhang gesondert ausgewiesen werden.

(8) Ein Posten der Bilanz oder der Gewinn- und Verlustrechnung, der keinen Betrag ausweist, braucht nicht aufgeführt zu werden, es sei denn, daß im vorhergehenden Geschäftsjahr unter diesem Posten ein Betrag ausgewiesen wurde.

Zweiter Titel. Bilanz

§ 266 Gliederung der Bilanz

(1) Die Bilanz ist in Kontoform aufzustellen. Dabei haben große und mittelgroße Kapitalgesellschaften (§ 267 Abs. 3, 2) auf der Aktivseite die in Absatz 2 und auf der Passivseite die in Absatz 3 bezeichneten Posten gesondert und in der vorgeschriebenen Reihenfolge auszuweisen. Kleine Kapitalgesellschaften (§ 267 Abs. 1) brauchen nur eine verkürzte Bilanz aufzustellen, in die nur die in den Absätzen 2 und 3 mit Buchstaben und römischen Zahlen bezeichneten Posten gesondert und in der vorgeschriebenen Reihenfolge aufgenommen werden.

rised together if no special forms are required and if

1. they contain a sum that is not significant for providing a factually accurate picture within the meaning of § 264 Subsection 2 or

2. by so doing the clarity of the statement is enhanced. In this case, the summarised entries must still be shown separately in the notes.

(8) An entry on the balance sheet or the profit and loss statement that does not show an amount need not be made, unless an amount was shown under this entry in the preceding fiscal year.

Second Title. The Balance Sheet

§ 266 Classification of the balance sheet

(1) The balance sheet shall be prepared in the form of an account. In doing so, large and medium-sized corporations (§ 267 Subsections 3 and 2) shall show separately and in the prescribed order entries designated in Subsection 2 below on the assets side and entries designated in Subsection 3 below on the liabilities side. Small corporations (§ 267 Subsection 1) need prepare only an abridged balance sheet that includes separately and in the prescribed order only the entries designated with letters and Roman numerals in Subsections 2 and 3 below.

B. Rückstellungen:
1. Rückstellungen für Pensionen und ähnliche Verpflichtungen;
2. Steuerrückstellungen;
3. sonstige Rückstellungen.

C. Verbindlichkeiten:
1. Anleihen,
davon konvertibel;
2. Verbindlichkeiten gegenüber Kreditinstituten;
3. erhaltene Anzahlungen auf Bestellungen;
4. Verbindlichkeiten aus Lieferungen und Leistungen;
5. Verbindlichkeiten aus der Annahme gezogener Wechsel und der Ausstellung eigener Wechsel;
6. Verbindlichkeiten gegenüber verbundenen Unternehmen;
7. Verbindlichkeiten gegenüber Unternehmen, mit denen ein Beteiligungsverhältnis besteht;
8. sonstige Verbindlichkeiten,
davon aus Steuern,
davon im Rahmen der sozialen Sicherheit.

D. Rechnungsabgrenzungsposten.

B. Accruals:
1. Accruals for pensions and similar obligations;
2. Accrued taxes;
3. Other accruals.

C. Liabilities:
1. Debentures,
noting the amount for convertible ones;
2. Payables due to commercial banks;
3. Advance payments received;
4. Trade payables;
5. Payables from the acceptance of drafts and the issuance of promissory notes;
6. Payables due to related enterprises;
7. Payables due to enterprises in which there is a participating interest;
8. Other liabilities,
noting the amount for taxes;
noting the amount for social insurance.

D. Deferred Income.

§ 267 Umschreibung der Größenklassen

(1) Kleine Kapitalgesellschaften sind solche, die mindestens zwei der drei nachstehenden Merkmale nicht überschreiten:

1. 3 438 000 Euro Bilanzsumme nach Abzug eines auf der Aktivseite aus-

§ 267 Definition of class sizes

(1) Small corporations are those that do not exceed at least two of the following three criteria:

1. A balance sheet total of 3 438 000 EUR after deducting any deficit

gewiesenen Fehlbetrags (§ 268 Abs. 3).

2. 6 875 000 Euro Umsatzerlöse in den zwölf Monaten vor dem Abschlußstichtag.

3. Im Jahresdurchschnitt fünfzig Arbeitnehmer.

(2) Mittelgroße Kapitalgesellschaften sind solche, die mindestens zwei der drei in Absatz 1 bezeichneten Merkmale überschreiten und jeweils mindestens zwei der drei nachstehenden Merkmale nicht überschreiten:

1. 13 750 000 Euro Bilanzsumme nach Abzug eines auf der Aktivseite ausgewiesenen Fehlbetrags (§ 268 Abs. 3).

2. 27 500 000 Euro Umsatzerlöse in den zwölf Monaten vor dem Abschlußstichtag.

3. Im Jahresdurchschnitt zweihundertfünfzig Arbeitnehmer.

(3) Große Kapitalgesellschaften sind solche, die mindestens zwei der drei in Absatz 2 bezeichneten Merkmale überschreiten. Eine Kapitalgesellschaft gilt stets als große, wenn sie einen organisierten Markt im Sinne des § 2 Abs. 5 des Wertpapierhandelsgesetzes durch von ihr ausgegebene Wertpapiere im Sinne des § 2 Abs. 1 Satz 1 des Wertpapierhandelsgesetzes in Anspruch nimmt oder die Zulassung zum Handel an einem organisierten Markt beantragt worden ist.

(4) Die Rechtsfolgen der Merkmale nach den Absätzen 1 bis 3 Satz 1 treten nur ein, wenn sie an den Abschlußstichtagen von zwei aufeinanderfolgenden Geschäftsjahren über- oder unterschritten werden. Im Falle der Umwandlung oder Neugründung treten die Rechtsfolgen schon ein, wenn die Voraussetzungen des Absat-

shown on the assets side (§ 268 Subsection 3).

2. 6 875 000 EUR in turnover proceeds in the twelve months preceding the close of the fiscal year.

3. An average of fifty employees during the year.

(2) Medium-sized corporations are those that exceed at least two of the three criteria in Subsection 1 but at any given time do not exceed at least two of the three following criteria:

1. A balance sheet total of 13 750 000 EUR after deducting any deficit shown on the assets side (§ 268 Subsection 3).

2. 27 500 000 EUR in sales proceeds in the twelve months preceding the close of the fiscal year.

3. An average of two hundred fifty employees during the year.

(3) Large corporations are those that exceed at least two of the three criteria in Subsection 2. A corporation is always deemed to be large if it makes use of an organized exchange within the meaning of § 2 Subsection 5 of the Securities Trading Act by means of issued securities within the meaning of section 2 Subsection 1 sentence 1 of the Securities Trading Act or has applied for admission to trading to an organized exchange.

(4) The legal consequences of the criteria pursuant to Subsections 1 through 3, sentence 1 take effect only if they are exceeded or not exceeded on the close of the fiscal year for two consecutive fiscal years. In the case of restructuring or new formation, the legal consequences of Subsections 1, 2 or 3 take effect if their preconditions

Ergänzende Vorschriften für Kapitalgesellschaften §§ 267, 268

zes 1, 2 oder 3 am ersten Abschlußstichtag nach der Umwandlung oder Neugründung vorliegen.

(5) Als durchschnittliche Zahl der Arbeitnehmer gilt der vierte Teil der Summe aus den Zahlen der jeweils am 31. März, 30. Juni, 30. September und 31. Dezember beschäftigten Arbeitnehmer einschließlich der im Ausland beschäftigten Arbeitnehmer, jedoch ohne die zu ihrer Berufsausbildung Beschäftigten.

(6) Informations- und Auskunftsrechte der Arbeitnehmervertretungen nach anderen Gesetzen bleiben unberührt.

§ 268 Vorschriften zu einzelnen Posten der Bilanz. Bilanzvermerke

(1) Die Bilanz darf auch unter Berücksichtigung der vollständigen oder teilweisen Verwendung des Jahresergebnisses aufgestellt werden. Wird die Bilanz unter Berücksichtigung der teilweisen Verwendung des Jahresergebnisses aufgestellt, so tritt an die Stelle der Posten „Jahresüberschuß/Jahresfehlbetrag" und „Gewinnvortrag/Verlustvortrag" der Posten „Bilanzgewinn/Bilanzverlust"; ein vorhandener Gewinn- oder Verlustvortrag ist in den Posten „Bilanzgewinn/Bilanzverlust" einzubeziehen und in der Bilanz oder im Anhang gesondert anzugeben.

(2) In der Bilanz oder im Anhang ist die Entwicklung der einzelnen Posten des Anlagevermögens und des Postens „Aufwendungen für die Ingangsetzung und Erweiterung des Geschäftsbetriebs" darzustellen. Dabei sind, ausgehend von den gesamten Anschaffungs- und Herstellungskosten,

are met on the first close of the fiscal year after the restructuring or new formation.

(5) The average number of employees is deemed to be one-quarter of the sum of the number of employees employed on March 31, June 30, September 30 and December 31, respectively, including those employees employed abroad but excluding those in apprenticeship for their professional training.

(6) The rights of bodies representing employees to obtain information pursuant to other laws shall remain unaffected.

§ 268 Regulations as to particular entries on the balance sheet; balance sheet notations

(1) The balance sheet may be prepared to take into consideration the complete or partial appropriation of the annual earnings. If the balance sheet is prepared taking into consideration the partial appropriation of annual earnings, then in place of the entry "Annual Surplus/Annual Deficit" and "Profits carried forward/Losses carried forward" shall appear the entry "Balance sheet profits/Balance sheet losses." Any profits or losses carried forward shall be included under the entry "Balance sheet profits/Balance sheet losses" and shall be reported separately on the balance sheet or in the notes.

(2) The development of the individual items of the fixed assets and of the entries "Expenses related to the Formation and Expansion of the Business Operation" shall be shown on the balance sheet or in the notes. Proceeding from the total acquisition and production costs, the additions, retirements,

die Zugänge, Abgänge, Umbuchungen und Zuschreibungen des Geschäftsjahrs sowie die Abschreibungen in ihrer gesamten Höhe gesondert aufzuführen. Die Abschreibungen des Geschäftsjahrs sind entweder in der Bilanz bei dem betreffenden Posten zu vermerken oder im Anhang in einer der Gliederung des Anlagevermögens entsprechenden Aufgliederung anzugeben.

(3) Ist das Eigenkapital durch Verluste aufgebraucht und ergibt sich ein Überschuß der Passivposten über die Aktivposten, so ist dieser Betrag am Schluß der Bilanz auf der Aktivseite gesondert unter der Bezeichnung „Nicht durch Eigenkapital gedeckter Fehlbetrag" auszuweisen.

(4) Der Betrag der Forderungen mit einer Restlaufzeit von mehr als einem Jahr ist bei jedem gesondert ausgewiesenen Posten zu vermerken. Werden unter dem Posten „sonstige Vermögensgegenstände" Beträge für Vermögensgegenstände ausgewiesen, die erst nach dem Abschlußstichtag rechtlich entstehen, so müssen Beträge, die einen größeren Umfang haben, im Anhang erläutert werden.

(5) Der Betrag der Verbindlichkeiten mit einer Restlaufzeit bis zu einem Jahr ist bei jedem gesondert ausgewiesenen Posten zu vermerken. Erhaltene Anzahlungen auf Bestellungen sind, soweit Anzahlungen auf Vorräte nicht von dem Posten „Vorräte" offen abgesetzt werden, unter den Verbindlichkeiten gesondert auszuweisen. Sind unter dem Posten „Verbindlichkeiten" Beträge für Verbindlichkeiten ausgewiesen, die erst nach dem Abschlußstichtag rechtlich entstehen, so müssen Beträge, die einen größeren Umfang haben, im Anhang erläutert werden.

transfers of entries and write-ups during the fiscal year as well as the total amount of depreciation shall be set forth separately. The depreciation of the fiscal year shall either be noted on the balance sheet under the appropriate entries or be reported in the notes, broken down according to the classification of fixed assets.

(3) If the shareholder's equity has been used up by losses and there is an excess of liabilities over assets, then this sum shall be shown separately at the end of the balance sheet on the assets side under the heading "Deficit not covered by shareholder's equity".

(4) The amount of receivables with a term of more than a year shall be noted with each separately shown entry. If under the entry for "Other Assets" amounts of assets are shown that become legally existent only after the close of the fiscal year, then of those amounts such as are larger must be discussed in the notes.

(5) The amount of liabilities due within one year shall be noted with each separately shown entry. Down payments received on account of orders shall be shown separately under receivables to the extent that payments for inventory are not openly deducted from the entry "Inventory". If under the entry "Liabilities" amounts are shown that become legally existent only after the close of the fiscal year, then of those amounts such as are larger must be discussed in the notes.

(6) Ein nach § 250 Abs. 3 in den Rechnungsabgrenzungsposten auf der Aktivseite aufgenommener Unterschiedsbetrag ist in der Bilanz gesondert auszuweisen oder im Anhang anzugeben.

(7) Die in § 251 bezeichneten Haftungsverhältnisse sind jeweils gesondert unter der Bilanz oder im Anhang unter Angabe der gewährten Pfandrechte und sonstigen Sicherheiten anzugeben; bestehen solche Verpflichtungen gegenüber verbundenen Unternehmen, so sind sie gesondert anzugeben.

§ 269 Aufwendungen für die Ingangsetzung und Erweiterung des Geschäftsbetriebs

Die Aufwendungen für die Ingangsetzung des Geschäftsbetriebs und dessen Erweiterung dürfen, soweit sie nicht bilanzierungsfähig sind, als Bilanzierungshilfe aktiviert werden; der Posten ist in der Bilanz unter der Bezeichnung „Aufwendungen für die Ingangsetzung und Erweiterung des Geschäftsbetriebs" vor dem Anlagevermögen auszuweisen und im Anhang zu erläutern. Werden solche Aufwendungen in der Bilanz ausgewiesen, so dürfen Gewinne nur ausgeschüttet werden, wenn die nach der Ausschüttung verbleibenden jederzeit auflösbaren Gewinnrücklagen zuzüglich eines Gewinnvortrags und abzüglich eines Verlustvortrags dem angesetzten Betrag mindestens entsprechen.

§ 270 Bildung bestimmter Posten

(1) Einstellungen in die Kapitalrücklage und deren Auflösung sind bereits bei der Aufstellung der Bilanz vorzunehmen. Satz 1 ist auf Einstellungen

(6) The difference in amounts entered on the assets side under prepaid expenses pursuant to § 250 Subsection 3 shall be shown separately on the balance sheet or reported in the notes.

(7) The contingencies and commitments listed in § 251 shall be reported separately as a below-the-line entry on the balance sheet or in the notes with indications of the liens or other forms of security given. If such liabilities exist vis-à-vis related enterprises, they shall be reported separately.

§ 269 Expenses related to the formation and expansion of the business operation

To the extent that they cannot be capitalized, the expenses related to the formation and expansion of the business operation may, as an aid in formulating the balance sheet, be carried forward. The entry shall be shown on the balance sheet before fixed assets under the heading "Expenditures for Starting up and Expanding the Business" and shall be discussed in the notes. If such expenditures are shown on the balance sheet, then profits may be distributed only if after the profits distribution the remaining earnings reserves that are liquidatable at any time plus any profits carried forward less any losses carried forward equal at least the capitalized amount.

§ 270 Setting up certain entries

(1) Allocations to capital reserves and their liquidation shall be made even as the balance sheet is being prepared. Sentence 1 shall be applied to the allo-

in den Sonderposten mit Rücklageanteil und dessen Auflösung anzuwenden.

(2) Wird die Bilanz unter Berücksichtigung der vollständigen oder teilweisen Verwendung des Jahresergebnisses aufgestellt, so sind Entnahmen aus Gewinnrücklagen sowie Einstellungen in Gewinnrücklagen, die nach Gesetz, Gesellschaftsvertrag oder Satzung vorzunehmen sind oder auf Grund solcher Vorschriften beschlossen worden sind, bereits bei der Aufstellung der Bilanz zu berücksichtigen.

§ 271 Beteiligungen. Verbundene Unternehmen

(1) Beteiligungen sind Anteile an anderen Unternehmen, die bestimmt sind, dem eigenen Geschäftsbetrieb durch Herstellung einer dauernden Verbindung zu jenen Unternehmen zu dienen. Dabei ist es unerheblich, ob die Anteile in Wertpapieren verbrieft sind oder nicht. Als Beteiligung gelten im Zweifel Anteile an einer Kapitalgesellschaft, die insgesamt den fünften Teil des Nennkapitals dieser Gesellschaft überschreiten. Auf die Berechnung ist § 16 Abs. 2 und 4 des Aktiengesetzes entsprechend anzuwenden. Die Mitgliedschaft in einer eingetragenen Genossenschaft gilt nicht als Beteiligung im Sinne dieses Buches.

(2) Verbundene Unternehmen im Sinne dieses Buches sind solche Unternehmen, die als Mutter- oder Tochterunternehmen (§ 290) in den Konzernabschluß eines Mutterunternehmens nach den Vorschriften über die Vollkonsolidierung einzubeziehen sind, das als oberstes Mutterunternehmen den am weitestgehenden

cations to special entries in the capital surplus section and their liquidation.

(2) If the balance sheet is prepared taking into consideration the use of all or part of the annual profits or losses, then withdrawals from as well as allocations to the earnings reserves – which are undertaken pursuant to law, the articles of association or by-laws or which were resolved on the basis of such provisions – shall be taken into account in the preparation of the balance sheet.

§ 271 Participations; related enterprises

(1) Participations are shares in other enterprises whose purpose is to promote one's own business by developing a lasting relationship with that other enterprise. In that regard it is irrelevant whether or not the shares are evidenced by a document of title. In case of doubt, participations include shares in a corporation in excess of one-fifth of the nominal value of the corporation. In making the calculation, § 16 Subsections 2 and 4 of the Stock Corporation Act shall apply analogously. Membership in a registered co-operative is not deemed to be a participation interest within the meaning of this Book.

(2) Related enterprises within the meaning of this Book are those enterprises that shall be included as parents or subsidiaries (§ 290) in a parent's consolidated financial statements pursuant to the regulations pertaining to the full consolidation which, as highest parent, must prepare the most comprehensive consolidated financial

Konzernabschluß nach dem Zweiten Unterabschnitt aufzustellen hat, auch wenn die Aufstellung unterbleibt, oder das einen befreienden Konzernabschluß nach § 291 oder nach einer nach § 292 erlassenen Rechtsverordnung aufstellt oder aufstellen könnte; Tochterunternehmen, die nach § 295 oder § 296 nicht einbezogen werden, sind ebenfalls verbundene Unternehmen.

statements pursuant to the Second Subpart, even if the preparation remains undone, or which prepares or could prepare exempt consolidated financial statements pursuant to § 291 or to a regulation issued pursuant to § 292. Subsidiaries that are not included pursuant to § 295 or § 296 are also related enterprises.

§ 272 Eigenkapital

(1) Gezeichnetes Kapital ist das Kapital, auf das die Haftung der Gesellschafter für die Verbindlichkeiten der Kapitalgesellschaft gegenüber den Gläubigern beschränkt ist. Die ausstehenden Einlagen auf das gezeichnete Kapital sind auf der Aktivseite vor dem Anlagevermögen gesondert auszuweisen und entsprechend zu bezeichnen; die davon eingeforderten Einlagen sind zu vermerken. Die nicht eingeforderten ausstehenden Einlagen dürfen auch von dem Posten „Gezeichnetes Kapital" offen abgesetzt werden; in diesem Falle ist der verbleibende Betrag als Posten „Eingefordertes Kapital" in der Hauptspalte der Passivseite auszuweisen und ist außerdem der eingeforderte, aber noch nicht eingezahlte Betrag unter den Forderungen gesondert auszuweisen und entsprechend zu bezeichnen. Der Nennbetrag oder, falls ein solcher nicht vorhanden ist, der rechnerische Wert von nach § 71 Abs. 1 Nr. 6 oder 8 des Aktiengesetzes zur Einziehung erworbenen Aktien ist in der Vorspalte offen von dem Posten „Gezeichnetes Kapital" als Kapitalrückzahlung abzusetzen. Ist der Erwerb der Aktien nicht zur Einziehung erfolgt, ist Satz 4 auch anzuwenden, soweit in dem Beschluß über den

§ 272 Shareholder's equity

(1) Subscribed capital is that capital to which the liability of the shareholders for the obligations of the corporation to creditors is limited. The outstanding contributions to the subscribed capital shall be shown separately on the assets side before the fixed assets and designated accordingly. The capital called in therefrom shall be specified. The unclaimed outstanding contributions may also be openly deducted from the entry "Subscribed capital". In this case, the remaining amount shall be shown under the entry "Called-in capital" in the main column of the liabilities side and furthermore the called-in but not yet paid-in amount shall be shown separately under receivables and designated accordingly. The nominal value or, in absence of such, the proportional share of nominal share capital of shares acquired for redemption pursuant to § 71 Subsection 1 No. 6 or 8 of the Stock Corporation Act shall be deducted clearly in the preliminary column from the entry "Subscribed capital" as repayment of capital. If the shares have not been acquired for redemption, sentence 4 shall also apply to the extent that, in the resolution concerning the acquisition of the company's treasury shares, the subse-

Rückkauf die spätere Veräußerung von einem Beschluß der Hauptversammlung in entsprechender Anwendung des § 182 Abs. 1 Satz 1 des Aktiengesetzes abhängig gemacht worden ist. Wird der Nennbetrag oder der rechnerische Wert von Aktien nach Satz 4 abgesetzt, ist der Unterschiedsbetrag dieser Aktien zwischen ihrem Nennbetrag oder dem rechnerischen Wert und ihrem Kaufpreis mit den anderen Gewinnrücklagen (§ 266 Abs. 3 A.III.4.) zu verrechnen; weitergehende Anschaffungskosten sind als Aufwand des Geschäftsjahres zu berücksichtigen.

(2) Als Kapitalrücklage sind auszuweisen

1. der Betrag, der bei der Ausgabe von Anteilen einschließlich von Bezugsanteilen über den Nennbetrag oder, falls ein Nennbetrag nicht vorhanden ist, über den rechnerischen Wert hinaus erzielt wird;

2. der Betrag, der bei der Ausgabe von Schuldverschreibungen für Wandlungsrechte und Optionsrechte zum Erwerb von Anteilen erzielt wird;

3. der Betrag von Zuzahlungen, die Gesellschafter gegen Gewährung eines Vorzugs für ihre Anteile leisten;

4. der Betrag von anderen Zuzahlungen, die Gesellschafter in das Eigenkapital leisten.

(3) Als Gewinnrücklagen dürfen nur Beträge ausgewiesen werden, die im Geschäftsjahr oder in einem früheren Geschäftsjahr aus dem Ergebnis gebildet worden sind. Dazu gehören aus dem Ergebnis zu bildende gesetzliche oder auf Gesellschaftsvertrag oder Satzung beruhende Rücklagen und andere Gewinnrücklagen.

quent sale has been made contingent upon a resolution of the shareholders' meeting by analogous application of § 182 Subsection 1 sentence 1 of the Stock Corporation Act. Where the nominal value or the proportional share of nominal share capital of shares is deducted pursuant to sentence 4, the difference between the nominal value or the proportional share of nominal share capital and the sales price of these shares shall be set off against the "Other earnings reserves" (§ 266 Subsection 3 A. III. 4.); further costs of acquisition shall be taken into account as expenses of the fiscal year.

(2) The following shall be shown as capital reserves:

1. The amount realised by the issuance of shares, including subscription rights, above and beyond the nominal value or, in the absence of such a nominal value, the amount above and beyond the proportional share of nominal share capital;

2. the amount realized pursuant to a sale of conversion rights and option rights for share acquisition in connection with the issuance of bonds;

3. the amount of additional payments made by shareholders for a guaranteed preference for their shares;

4. the amount of other additional payments made by shareholders into shareholder's equity.

(3) Only those amounts may be shown as earnings reserves that resulted from the returns of the fiscal year or an earlier fiscal year. This includes statutory reserves or reserves based on the articles of association formed from the returns and other earnings reserves.

(4) In eine Rücklage für eigene Anteile ist ein Betrag einzustellen, der dem auf der Aktivseite der Bilanz für die eigenen Anteile anzusetzenden Betrag entspricht. Die Rücklage darf nur aufgelöst werden, soweit die eigenen Anteile ausgegeben, veräußert oder eingezogen werden oder soweit nach § 253 Abs. 3 auf der Aktivseite ein niedrigerer Betrag angesetzt wird. Die Rücklage, die bereits bei der Aufstellung der Bilanz vorzunehmen ist, darf aus vorhandenen Gewinnrücklagen gebildet werden, soweit diese frei verfügbar sind. Die Rücklage nach Satz 1 ist auch für Anteile eines herrschenden oder eines mit Mehrheit beteiligten Unternehmens zu bilden.

§ 273 Sonderposten mit Rücklageanteil

Der Sonderposten mit Rücklageanteil (§ 247 Abs. 3) darf nur insoweit gebildet werden, als das Steuerrecht die Anerkennung des Wertansatzes bei der steuerrechtlichen Gewinnermittlung davon abhängig macht, daß der Sonderposten in der Bilanz gebildet wird. Er ist auf der Passivseite vor den Rückstellungen auszuweisen; die Vorschriften, nach denen er gebildet worden ist, sind in der Bilanz oder im Anhang anzugeben.

§ 274 Steuerabgrenzung

(1) Ist der dem Geschäftsjahr und früheren Geschäftsjahren zuzurechnende Steueraufwand zu niedrig, weil der nach den steuerrechtlichen Vorschriften zu versteuernde Gewinn niedriger als das handelsrechtliche Ergebnis ist, und gleicht sich der zu niedrige Steueraufwand des Geschäftsjahrs und früherer Geschäftsjahre in späteren Ge-

(4) An amount shall be allocated to a reserve for treasury shares that corresponds to the amount of treasury shares assessed on the assets side of the balance sheet. The reserves may be dissolved only to the extent that the treasury shares are issued, sold or withdrawn or to the extent that a lower amount is assessed on the assets side pursuant to § 253 Subsection 3. The reserves, which shall proceed even as the balance sheet is being prepared, may be formed from available earnings reserves to the extent that these are freely available. A reserve pursuant to sentence 1 shall also be set up for shares in a controlling enterprise or a participating enterprise with a majority interest.

§ 273 Special entries in capital surplus

The special entry in capital surplus (§ 247 Subsection 3) may be set up only to the extent that tax law makes the recognition of valuation for computing taxable profits dependent upon the special entry's being set up on the balance sheet. It shall be shown on the liabilities side before accruals. The provision under which it was set up shall be reported on the balance sheet or in the notes.

§ 274 Tax deferrals

(1) If the tax expenses attributable to the fiscal year or earlier fiscal years are too low because the profits taxable pursuant to the provisions of the tax law are lower than the commercial earnings, and if the tax expenses of the fiscal year and the earlier fiscal year that are too low will prospectively balance out in upcoming fiscal years,

schäftsjahren voraussichtlich aus, so ist in Höhe der voraussichtlichen Steuerbelastung nachfolgender Geschäftsjahre eine Rückstellung nach § 249 Abs. 1 Satz 1 zu bilden und in der Bilanz oder im Anhang gesondert anzugeben. Die Rückstellung ist aufzulösen, sobald die höhere Steuerbelastung eintritt oder mit ihr voraussichtlich nicht mehr zu rechnen ist.

(2) Ist der dem Geschäftsjahr und früheren Geschäftsjahren zuzurechnende Steueraufwand zu hoch, weil der nach den steuerrechtlichen Vorschriften zu versteuernde Gewinn höher als das handelsrechtliche Ergebnis ist, und gleicht sich der zu hohe Steueraufwand des Geschäftsjahrs und früherer Geschäftsjahre in späteren Geschäftsjahren voraussichtlich aus, so darf in Höhe der voraussichtlichen Steuerentlastung nachfolgender Geschäftsjahre ein Abgrenzungsposten als Bilanzierungshilfe auf der Aktivseite der Bilanz gebildet werden. Dieser Posten ist unter entsprechender Bezeichnung gesondert auszuweisen und im Anhang zu erläutern. Wird ein solcher Posten ausgewiesen, so dürfen Gewinne nur ausgeschüttet werden, wenn die nach der Ausschüttung verbleibenden jederzeit auflösbaren Gewinnrücklagen zuzüglich eines Gewinnvortrags und abzüglich eines Verlustvortrags dem angesetzten Betrag mindestens entsprechen. Der Betrag ist aufzulösen, sobald die Steuerentlastung eintritt oder mit ihr voraussichtlich nicht mehr zu rechnen ist.

then an accrual pursuant to § 249 Subsection 1 sentence 1 shall be formed in the amount of the prospective tax burden of the upcoming fiscal years and shall be reported separately on the balance sheet or in the notes. The accrual shall be dissolved as soon as the higher tax burden occurs or is no longer expected.

(2) If the tax expenses attributable to the fiscal year or earlier fiscal years are too high because the profits taxable pursuant to provisions of the tax law are higher than commercial earnings, and if the excessive tax expenses of the fiscal year and earlier fiscal years will prospectively balance out in upcoming fiscal years, then a deferral entry in the amount of the prospective tax relief for following fiscal years may be formed as an aid in formulating the balance sheet on the assets side of the balance sheet. The entry shall be shown separately under the appropriate heading and discussed in the notes. If such an entry is shown, then profits may be distributed only if after the distribution, the earnings reserves remaining which are liquidatable at any time plus any profits carried forward less any losses carried forward at least equal the appropriated amount. The amount shall be dissolved as soon as the tax relief occurs or is no longer expected.

§ 274 a Größenabhängige Erleichterungen

Kleine Kapitalgesellschaften sind von der Anwendung der folgenden Vorschriften befreit:

§ 274 a Size-related relief

Small corporations are exempted from the application of the following provisions:

Ergänzende Vorschriften für Kapitalgesellschaften §§ 274a, 275

1. § 268 Abs. 2 über die Aufstellung eines Anlagegitters,
2. § 268 Abs. 4 Satz 2 über die Pflicht zur Erläuterung bestimmter Forderungen im Anhang,
3. § 268 Abs. 5 Satz 3 über die Erläuterung bestimmter Verbindlichkeiten im Anhang,
4. § 268 Abs. 6 über den Rechnungsabgrenzungsposten nach § 250 Abs. 3,
5. § 269 Satz 1 insoweit, als die Aufwendungen für die Ingangsetzung und Erweiterung des Geschäftsbetriebs im Anhang erläutert werden müssen.

1. § 268 Subsection 2 on preparing of facility plan,
2. § 268 Subsection 4 sentence 2 on the duty to explain certain claims in the notes,
3. § 268 Subsection 5 sentence 3 on the explanation of certain obligations in the notes,
4. § 268 Subsection 6 on accrued and deferred items according to § 250 Subsection 3,
5. § 269 sentence 1 to the extent that expenses related to the formation and expansion of the business operation must be explained in the notes.

Dritter Titel. Gewinn- und Verlustrechnung

§ 275 Gliederung

(1) Die Gewinn- und Verlustrechnung ist in Staffelform nach dem Gesamtkostenverfahren oder dem Umsatzkostenverfahren aufzustellen. Dabei sind die in Absatz 2 oder 3 bezeichneten Posten in der angegebenen Reihenfolge gesondert auszuweisen.

(2) Bei Anwendung des Gesamtkostenverfahrens sind auszuweisen:

1. Umsatzerlöse
2. Erhöhung oder Verminderung des Bestands an fertigen und unfertigen Erzeugnissen
3. andere aktivierte Eigenleistungen
4. sonstige betriebliche Erträge
5. Materialaufwand:
   a) Aufwendungen für Roh-, Hilfs- und Betriebsstoffe und für bezogene Waren
   b) Aufwendungen für bezogene Leistungen

Third Title. Profit and Loss Statement

§ 275 Presentation

(1) The profit and loss statement shall be prepared in a vertical format according to the total cost procedure or the sales cost procedure. In so doing, the entries designated in Subsection 2 or 3 shall be shown separately in the sequence given there.

(2) In using the total cost procedure, the following shall be shown:

1. Sales proceeds
2. Increase or decrease in the inventory of finished products and work in progress
3. Other capitalized own work
4. Other operating income
5. Material costs:
   a) Costs of raw material, supplies, operating materials and acquired goods
   b) Costs of acquired services

6. Personalaufwand:
   a) Löhne und Gehälter
   b) soziale Abgaben und Aufwendungen für Altersversorgung und für Unterstützung, davon für Altersversorgung
7. Abschreibungen:
   a) auf immaterielle Vermögensgegenstände des Anlagevermögens und Sachanlagen sowie auf aktivierte Aufwendungen für die Ingangsetzung und Erweiterung des Geschäftsbetriebs
   b) auf Vermögensgegenstände des Umlaufvermögens, soweit diese die in der Kapitalgesellschaft üblichen Abschreibungen überschreiten
8. sonstige betriebliche Aufwendungen
9. Erträge aus Beteiligungen, davon aus verbundenen Unternehmen
10. Erträge aus anderen Wertpapieren und Ausleihungen des Finanzanlagevermögens,
    davon aus verbundenen Unternehmen
11. sonstige Zinsen und ähnliche Erträge,
    davon aus verbundenen Unternehmen
12. Abschreibungen auf Finanzanlagen und auf Wertpapiere des Umlaufvermögens
13. Zinsen und ähnliche Aufwendungen,
    davon an verbundene Unternehmen
14. Ergebnis der gewöhnlichen Geschäftstätigkeit
15. außerordentliche Erträge
16. außerordentliche Aufwendungen
17. außerordentliches Ergebnis

6. Personnel costs:
   a) Wages and salaries
   b) Social security and expenses for old age pensions and support, noting the amount for old age pensions
7. Depreciation and Amortization:
   a) For intangible fixed assets and tangible assets as well as capitalized expenditures for starting up or expanding the business
   b) For current assets to the extent that they exceed the corporation's usual depreciation or amortization
8. Other operating expenses
9. Income from participations, noting the amount from related enterprises
10. Income from other securities and long-term loans,
    noting the amount from related enterprises
11. Other interest and similar income,
    noting the amount from related enterprises
12. Amortization of financial assets and of securities included in current assets
13. Interest and similar expenses,
    noting the amount to related enterprises
14. Results from ordinary business operations
15. Extraordinary income
16. Extraordinary expenses
17. Extraordinary results

Ergänzende Vorschriften für Kapitalgesellschaften § 275

18. Steuern vom Einkommen und vom Ertrag	18. Taxes on income and revenue
19. sonstige Steuern	19. Other taxes
20. Jahresüberschuß/Jahresfehlbetrag.	20. Annual surplus/annual deficit.
(3) Bei Anwendung des Umsatzkostenverfahrens sind auszuweisen:	(3) In using the sales cost method, the following shall be shown:
1. Umsatzerlöse	1. Sales proceeds
2. Herstellungskosten der zur Erzielung der Umsatzerlöse erbrachten Leistungen	2. Production costs for performance provided in achieving the sales proceeds
3. Bruttoergebnis vom Umsatz	3. Gross earnings from sales
4. Vertriebskosten	4. Selling expenses
5. allgemeine Verwaltungskosten	5. General administrative expenses
6. sonstige betriebliche Erträge	6. Other operating income
7. sonstige betriebliche Aufwendungen	7. Other operating expenses
8. Erträge aus Beteiligungen, davon aus verbundenen Unternehmen	8. Revenues from participations, noting the amount from related enterprises
9. Erträge aus anderen Wertpapieren und Ausleihungen des Finanzanlagevermögens, davon aus verbundenen Unternehmen	9. Income from other securities and long-term loans, noting the amount from related enterprises
10. sonstige Zinsen und ähnliche Erträge, davon aus verbundenen Unternehmen	10. Other interest and similar income, noting the amount from related enterprises
11. Abschreibungen auf Finanzanlagen und auf Wertpapiere des Umlaufvermögens	11. Amortization of financial assets and of securities included in current assets
12. Zinsen und ähnliche Aufwendungen, davon an verbundene Unternehmen	12. Interest and similar expenses, noting the amount to related enterprises
13. Ergebnis der gewöhnlichen Geschäftstätigkeit	13. Results of ordinary business operations
14. außerordentliche Erträge	14. Extraordinary income
15. außerordentliche Aufwendungen	15. Extraordinary expenses
16. außerordentliches Ergebnis	16. Extraordinary results

17. Steuern vom Einkommen und vom Ertrag

18. sonstige Steuern

19. Jahresüberschuß/Jahresfehlbetrag.

(4) Veränderungen der Kapital- und Gewinnrücklagen dürfen in der Gewinn- und Verlustrechnung erst nach dem Posten „Jahresüberschuß/Jahresfehlbetrag" ausgewiesen werden.

§ 276 Größenabhängige Erleichterungen

Kleine und mittelgroße Kapitalgesellschaften (§ 267 Abs. 1, 2) dürfen die Posten § 275 Abs. 2 Nr. 1 bis 5 oder Abs. 3 Nr. 1 bis 3 und 6 zu einem Posten unter der Bezeichnung „Rohergebnis" zusammenfassen. Kleine Kapitalgesellschaften brauchen außerdem die in § 277 Abs. 4 Satz 2 und 3 verlangten Erläuterungen zu den Posten „außerordentliche Erträge" und „außerordentliche Aufwendungen" nicht zu machen.

§ 277 Vorschriften zu einzelnen Posten der Gewinn- und Verlustrechnung

(1) Als Umsatzerlöse sind die Erlöse aus dem Verkauf und der Vermietung oder Verpachtung von für die gewöhnliche Geschäftstätigkeit der Kapitalgesellschaft typischen Erzeugnissen und Waren sowie aus von für die gewöhnliche Geschäftstätigkeit der Kapitalgesellschaft typischen Dienstleistungen nach Abzug von Erlösschmälerungen und der Umsatzsteuer auszuweisen.

(2) Als Bestandsveränderungen sind sowohl Änderungen der Menge als auch solche des Wertes zu berücksichtigen; Abschreibungen jedoch nur, so-

17. Taxes on income and revenue

18. Other taxes

19. Annual surplus/annual deficit.

(4) Changes in the capital and earnings reserves may be shown in the profit and loss statement only after the entries "Annual surplus/annual deficit".

§ 276 Size-related relief

Small and medium-sized companies (§ 267 Subsections 1 and 2) may combine the entries § 275 Subsection 2 Nos. 1 through 5 or Subsection 3 Nos. 1 through 3 and 6 into a single entry under the heading "Gross Results". Moreover, small corporations need not render the explanations required in § 277 Subsection 4 sentences 2 and 3 on "extraordinary yields" and "extraordinary expenses" entries.

§ 277 Regulations for particular entries in the profit and loss statement

(1) Turnover proceeds shall include the proceeds from the sale and the renting or leasing of products and goods typical of the corporation's usual business operations as well as from the services typical of the corporation's usual business operations after deducting sales reductions and the sales turnover tax.

(2) For inventory changes, changes in amount as well as value shall be taken into consideration, but depreciation only to the extent that it does not ex-

weit diese die in der Kapitalgesellschaft sonst üblichen Abschreibungen nicht überschreiten.

(3) Außerplanmäßige Abschreibungen nach § 253 Abs. 2 Satz 3 sowie Abschreibungen nach § 253 Abs. 3 Satz 3 sind jeweils gesondert auszuweisen oder im Anhang anzugeben. Erträge und Aufwendungen aus Verlustübernahme und auf Grund einer Gewinngemeinschaft, eines Gewinnabführungs- oder eines Teilgewinnabführungsvertrags erhaltene oder abgeführte Gewinne sind jeweils gesondert unter entsprechender Bezeichnung auszuweisen.

(4) Unter den Posten „außerordentliche Erträge" und „außerordentliche Aufwendungen" sind Erträge und Aufwendungen auszuweisen, die außerhalb der gewöhnlichen Geschäftstätigkeit der Kapitalgesellschaft anfallen. Die Posten sind hinsichtlich ihres Betrags und ihrer Art im Anhang zu erläutern, soweit die ausgewiesenen Beträge für die Beurteilung der Ertragslage nicht von untergeordneter Bedeutung sind. Satz 2 gilt auch für Erträge und Aufwendungen, die einem anderen Geschäftsjahr zuzurechnen sind.

ceed the corporation's normal depreciation.

(3) Extraordinary depreciation pursuant to § 253 Subsection 2 sentence 3 as well as depreciation pursuant to § 253 Subsection 3 sentence 3 shall each be shown separately or reported in the notes. Proceeds and expenses from the assumption of losses or on the basis of profits received or transferred from a profit pool, a profit transfer agreement or a partial profit transfer agreement shall each be shown separately under the appropriate heading.

(4) Income and expenses arising outside the corporation's normal business operations shall be shown under the entries "Extraordinary Income" and "Extraordinary Expenses". The entries shall be discussed in the notes with regard to their amount and their kind to the extent that the amounts shown are not of minor importance for evaluating the income situation. Sentence 2 also applies to income and expenses attributable to another fiscal year.

§ 278 Steuern

Die Steuern vom Einkommen und vom Ertrag sind auf der Grundlage des Beschlusses über die Verwendung des Ergebnisses zu berechnen; liegt ein solcher Beschluß im Zeitpunkt der Feststellung des Jahresabschlusses nicht vor, so ist vom Vorschlag über die Verwendung des Ergebnisses auszugehen. Weicht der Beschluß über die Verwendung des Ergebnisses vom Vorschlag ab, so braucht der Jahresabschluß nicht geändert zu werden.

§ 278 Taxes

Taxation of income and revenues shall be calculated on the basis of the resolution on the use of the results. If there is no such resolution at the time of the determination of the annual financial statements, then the proposal on the use of the results shall be used. If the resolution on the use of the results varies from the proposal, the annual financial statements need not be changed.

Vierter Titel. Bewertungsvorschriften

§ 279 Nichtanwendung von Vorschriften. Abschreibungen

(1) § 253 Abs. 4 ist nicht anzuwenden. § 253 Abs. 2 Satz 3 darf, wenn es sich nicht um eine voraussichtlich dauernde Wertminderung handelt, nur auf Vermögensgegenstände, die Finanzanlagen sind, angewendet werden.

(2) Abschreibungen nach § 254 dürfen nur insoweit vorgenommen werden, als das Steuerrecht ihre Anerkennung bei der steuerrechtlichen Gewinnermittlung davon abhängig macht, daß sie sich aus der Bilanz ergeben.

§ 280 Wertaufholungsgebot

(1) Wird bei einem Vermögensgegenstand eine Abschreibung nach § 253 Abs. 2 Satz 3 oder Abs. 3 oder § 254 Satz 1 vorgenommen und stellt sich in einem späteren Geschäftsjahr heraus, daß die Gründe dafür nicht mehr bestehen, so ist der Betrag dieser Abschreibung im Umfang der Werterhöhung unter Berücksichtigung der Abschreibungen, die inzwischen vorzunehmen gewesen wären, zuzuschreiben. § 253 Abs. 5, § 254 Satz 2 sind insoweit nicht anzuwenden.

(2) Von der Zuschreibung nach Absatz 1 kann abgesehen werden, wenn der niedrigere Wertansatz bei der steuerrechtlichen Gewinnermittlung beibehalten werden kann und wenn Voraussetzung für die Beibehaltung ist, daß der niedrigere Wertansatz auch in der Bilanz beibehalten wird.

Fourth Title. Regulations as to Valuation

§ 279 Inapplicability of regulations; depreciation

(1) § 253 Subsection 4 is inapplicable. Except when a permanent diminution in value is expected, § 253 Subsection 2 sentence 3 may be applied only to assets that are financial assets.

(2) Depreciation pursuant to § 254 may be taken only when the tax law makes its recognition in computing taxable profits dependent upon its appearing on the balance sheet.

§ 280 Obligation to recover original value

(1) If an asset is depreciated pursuant to § 253 Subsection 2 sentence 3 or Subsection 3 or § 254 sentence 1, and if in a later fiscal year it turns out that the reasons for the depreciation no longer exist, then the amount of this depreciation shall be credited to the extent of the increase in value, with consideration given to the depreciation which would have been taken in the meantime. In this regard, § 253 Subsection 5 and § 254 sentence 2 are inapplicable.

(2) The crediting of depreciation pursuant to Subsection 1 may be disregarded if the lower valuation can be retained for computing taxable profits and if the condition for retaining the lower valuation is that it will also be retained on the balance sheet.

(3) Im Anhang ist der Betrag der im Geschäftsjahr aus steuerrechtlichen Gründen unterlassenen Zuschreibungen anzugeben und hinreichend zu begründen.

§ 281 Berücksichtigung steuerrechtlicher Vorschriften

(1) Die nach § 254 zulässigen Abschreibungen dürfen auch in der Weise vorgenommen werden, daß der Unterschiedsbetrag zwischen der nach § 253 in Verbindung mit § 279 und der nach § 254 zulässigen Bewertung in den Sonderposten mit Rücklageanteil eingestellt wird. In der Bilanz oder im Anhang sind die Vorschriften anzugeben, nach denen die Wertberichtigung gebildet worden ist. Unbeschadet steuerrechtlicher Vorschriften über die Auflösung ist die Wertberichtigung insoweit aufzulösen, als die Vermögensgegenstände, für die sie gebildet worden ist, aus dem Vermögen ausscheiden oder die steuerrechtliche Wertberichtigung durch handelsrechtliche Abschreibungen ersetzt wird.

(2) Im Anhang ist der Betrag der im Geschäftsjahr allein nach steuerrechtlichen Vorschriften vorgenommenen Abschreibungen, getrennt nach Anlage- und Umlaufvermögen, anzugeben, soweit er sich nicht aus der Bilanz oder der Gewinn- und Verlustrechnung ergibt, und hinreichend zu begründen. Erträge aus der Auflösung des Sonderpostens mit Rücklageanteil sind in dem Posten „sonstige betriebliche Erträge", Einstellungen in den Sonderposten mit Rücklageanteil sind in dem Posten „sonstige betriebliche Aufwendungen" der Gewinn- und Verlustrechnung gesondert auszuweisen oder im Anhang anzugeben.

(3) The amount of depreciation credits omitted for the fiscal year for tax reasons shall be reported in the notes and adequately justified.

§ 281 Consideration of tax regulations

(1) The depreciation permitted pursuant to § 254 may also be brought about in such a way that the difference between the valuation permitted pursuant to § 253 in conjunction with § 279 and the valuation permitted pursuant to § 254 will be allocated to special entries in the capital surplus Section. The provisions according to which the allowance for depreciation was formed shall be reported on the balance sheet or in the notes. Without prejudice to tax regulations pertaining to dissolution, the allowance for depreciation shall be dissolved to the extent that the assets for which it was formed are eliminated from the total assets or that the tax allowance for depreciation is replaced by commercial depreciation.

(2) The amount of depreciation taken in the fiscal year exclusively pursuant to tax regulations shall be reported in the notes, separated as to fixed and current assets, to the extent that it does not appear on the balance sheet or profit and loss statement, and shall be adequately explained. Income from the dissolution of the special reserves in capital surplus shall be shown separately or reported in the notes of the profit and loss statement under the entry "Other Operating Income" and allocations to special reserves in capital surplus under the entry "Other Operating Expenses".

§ 282 Abschreibung der Aufwendungen für die Ingangsetzung und Erweiterung des Geschäftsbetriebs

Für die Ingangsetzung und Erweiterung des Geschäftsbetriebs ausgewiesene Beträge sind in jedem folgenden Geschäftsjahr zu mindestens einem Viertel durch Abschreibungen zu tilgen.

§ 283 Wertansatz des Eigenkapitals

Das gezeichnete Kapital ist zum Nennbetrag anzusetzen.

Fünfter Titel. Anhang

§ 284 Erläuterung der Bilanz und der Gewinn- und Verlustrechnung

(1) In den Anhang sind diejenigen Angaben aufzunehmen, die zu den einzelnen Posten der Bilanz oder der Gewinn- und Verlustrechnung vorgeschrieben oder die im Anhang zu machen sind, weil sie in Ausübung eines Wahlrechts nicht in die Bilanz oder in die Gewinn- und Verlustrechnung aufgenommen wurden.

(2) Im Anhang müssen

1. die auf die Posten der Bilanz und der Gewinn- und Verlustrechnung angewandten Bilanzierungs- und Bewertungsmethoden angegeben werden;

2. die Grundlagen für die Umrechnung in Euro angegeben werden, soweit der Jahresabschluß Posten enthält, denen Beträge zugrunde liegen, die auf fremde Währung lauten oder ursprünglich auf fremde Währung lauteten;

§ 282 Amortization of expenses relating to the formation and expansion of the business operation

At least one-fourth of expenses shown to be related to the formation and expansion of the business operation shall be amortized in each following fiscal year.

§ 283 Valuation of equity capital

Subscribed capital shall be assessed at face value.

Fifth Title. Notes

§ 284 Explanation of the balance sheet and the profit and loss statement

(1) The notes shall include those disclosures that are prescribed for the individual entries on the balance sheet or the profit and loss statement or shall be made in the notes because, in exercising an option permitted by law, they were not included on the balance sheet or the profit and loss statement.

(2) In the notes

1. the accounting and valuation principles used for the entries on the balance sheet and the profit and loss statement must be reported;

2. the basis for conversion into Euro must be indicated to the extent that the annual financial statements contain entries in which the underlying amounts are in foreign currency or originally were in foreign currency;

3. Abweichungen von Bilanzierungs- und Bewertungsmethoden angegeben und begründet werden; deren Einfluß auf die Vermögens-, Finanz- und Ertragslage ist gesondert darzustellen;

4. bei Anwendung einer Bewertungsmethode nach § 240 Abs. 4, § 256 Satz 1 die Unterschiedsbeträge pauschal für die jeweilige Gruppe ausgewiesen werden, wenn die Bewertung im Vergleich zu einer Bewertung auf der Grundlage des letzten vor dem Abschlußstichtag bekannten Börsenkurses oder Marktpreises einen erheblichen Unterschied aufweist;

5. Angaben über die Einbeziehung von Zinsen für Fremdkapital in die Herstellungskosten gemacht werden.

§ 285 Sonstige Pflichtangaben

Ferner sind im Anhang anzugeben:

1. zu den in der Bilanz ausgewiesenen Verbindlichkeiten

   a) der Gesamtbetrag der Verbindlichkeiten mit einer Restlaufzeit von mehr als fünf Jahren,

   b) der Gesamtbetrag der Verbindlichkeiten, die durch Pfandrechte oder ähnliche Rechte gesichert sind, unter Angabe von Art und Form der Sicherheiten;

2. die Aufgliederung der in Nummer 1 verlangten Angaben für jeden Posten der Verbindlichkeiten nach dem vorgeschriebenen Gliederungsschema, sofern sich diese Angaben nicht aus der Bilanz ergeben;

3. der Gesamtbetrag der sonstigen finanziellen Verpflichtungen, die nicht in der Bilanz erscheinen und

3. variations from the accounting and valuation principles must be reported and justified, and their effect on the net assets, financing and results of operations shall be shown separately;

4. when using a method of valuation pursuant to § 240 Subsection 4 and § 256 sentence 1, the amount of difference must be shown in a lump sum for the respective groups if the valuation shows a substantial difference when compared to a valuation based on the last known exchange rate or market price before the close of the fiscal year; and

5. disclosures must be made in regard to the inclusion of interest on borrowed capital in the costs of production.

§ 285 Other mandatory disclosures

The following shall also be reported in the notes:

1. in regard to the liabilities shown on the balance sheet

   a) the total amount of liabilities with a remaining term of more than five years,

   b) the total amount of liabilities that are secured by liens or similar rights, with disclosure of the type and form of the security;

2. a classification of the disclosures required in No. 1 for every liability entry according to the prescribed classification scheme to the extent that these disclosures do not appear on the balance sheet;

3. the total amount of other financial liabilities that do not appear on the balance sheet and also need not be

auch nicht nach § 251 anzugeben sind, sofern diese Angabe für die Beurteilung der Finanzlage von Bedeutung ist; davon sind Verpflichtungen gegenüber verbundenen Unternehmen gesondert anzugeben;

4. die Aufgliederung der Umsatzerlöse nach Tätigkeitsbereichen sowie nach geographisch bestimmten Märkten, soweit sich, unter Berücksichtigung der Organisation des Verkaufs von für die gewöhnliche Geschäftstätigkeit der Kapitalgesellschaft typischen Erzeugnissen und der für die gewöhnliche Geschäftstätigkeit der Kapitalgesellschaft typischen Dienstleistungen, die Tätigkeitsbereiche und geographisch bestimmten Märkte untereinander erheblich unterscheiden;

5. das Ausmaß, in dem das Jahresergebnis dadurch beeinflußt wurde, daß bei Vermögensgegenständen im Geschäftsjahr oder in früheren Geschäftsjahren Abschreibungen nach § 254, 280 Abs. 2 auf Grund steuerrechtlicher Vorschriften vorgenommen oder beibehalten wurden oder ein Sonderposten nach § 273 gebildet wurde; ferner das Ausmaß erheblicher künftiger Belastungen, die sich aus einer solchen Bewertung ergeben;

6. in welchem Umfang die Steuern vom Einkommen und vom Ertrag das Ergebnis der gewöhnlichen Geschäftstätigkeit und das außerordentliche Ergebnis belasten;

7. die durchschnittliche Zahl der während des Geschäftsjahrs beschäftigten Arbeitnehmer getrennt nach Gruppen;

8. bei Anwendung des Umsatzkostenverfahrens (§ 275 Abs. 3)

reported pursuant to § 251 to the extent that this disclosure is important for evaluating the financial situation; of these, liabilities to related enterprises shall be reported separately;

4. a breakdown of the turnover proceeds according to lines of business as well as according to geographically determined markets to the extent that the lines of business and geographically determined markets are substantially different from one another, with regard given to the organization of the sales of products typical of the corporation's usual business and of services typical of the corporation's usual business;

5. the extent to which the annual results were affected by depreciation taken or maintained on assets in the fiscal year or previous fiscal years pursuant to § 254 or § 280 Subsection 2 based on tax regulations or a separate entry was set up pursuant to § 273; further, the extent of substantial future burdens that will result from such a valuation;

6. to what extent the taxes on income and earnings burden the results of the ordinary business operations and the extraordinary results;

7. the average number of employees employed during the fiscal year, divided by groups;

8. when using the turnover cost method (§ 275 Subsection 3)

a) der Materialaufwand des Geschäftsjahrs, gegliedert nach § 275 Abs. 2 Nr. 5,
b) der Personalaufwand des Geschäftsjahrs, gegliedert nach § 275 Abs. 2 Nr. 6;
9. für die Mitglieder des Geschäftsführungsorgans, eines Aufsichtsrats, eines Beirats oder einer ähnlichen Einrichtung jeweils für jede Personengruppe
   a) die für die Tätigkeit im Geschäftsjahr gewährten Gesamtbezüge (Gehälter, Gewinnbeteiligungen, Bezugsrechte und sonstige aktienbasierte Vergütungen, Aufwandsentschädigungen, Versicherungsentgelte, Provisionen und Nebenleistungen jeder Art). In die Gesamtbezüge sind auch Bezüge einzurechnen, die nicht ausgezahlt, sondern in Ansprüche anderer Art umgewandelt oder zur Erhöhung anderer Ansprüche verwendet werden. Außer den Bezügen für das Geschäftsjahr sind die weiteren Bezüge anzugeben, die im Geschäftsjahr gewährt, bisher aber in keinem Jahresabschluß angegeben worden sind;
   b) die Gesamtbezüge (Abfindungen, Ruhegehälter, Hinterbliebenenbezüge und Leistungen verwandter Art) der früheren Mitglieder der bezeichneten Organe und ihrer Hinterbliebenen. Buchstabe a Satz 2 und 3 ist entsprechend anzuwenden. Ferner ist der Betrag der für diese Personengruppe gebildeten Rückstellungen für laufende Pensionen und Anwartschaften auf Pensionen und der Betrag der für diese Verpflichtungen nicht gebildeten Rückstellungen anzugeben;

a) the cost of material for the fiscal year, classified pursuant to § 275 Subsection 2 No. 5, and
b) the cost of personnel for the fiscal year, classified pursuant to § 275 Subsection 2 No. 6;
9. for the members of the management organ, a supervisory board, an advisory board or a similar body, separately for each respective group of people
   a) total remuneration (salaries, profit, participations, options and other stock based compensation, expense allowances, insurance payments, commissions and fringe benefits of every kind) granted for activities in the fiscal year. Total remuneration shall also include such remuneration that is not paid out but converted into claims of another kind or is used to increase other claims. Besides the remuneration for the fiscal year, the further remuneration shall be reported that was granted in the fiscal year but not yet reported in any annual financial statements;
   b) the total remuneration (severance pay, pensions, survivors' benefits and similar payments) of the previous members of the noted organs and their survivors. Letter a sentences 2 and 3 shall apply analogously. Further, the amount of accruals for current pensions and expectancies of pensions set up for this group of people and the amount of accruals not set up for these liabilities shall be reported;

c) die gewährten Vorschüsse und Kredite unter Angabe der Zinssätze, der wesentlichen Bedingungen und der gegebenenfalls im Geschäftsjahr zurückgezahlten Beträge sowie die zugunsten dieser Personen eingegangenen Haftungsverhältnisse;

10. alle Mitglieder des Geschäftsführungsorgans und eines Aufsichtsrats, auch wenn sie im Geschäftsjahr oder später ausgeschieden sind, mit dem Familiennamen und mindestens einem ausgeschriebenen Vornamen, einschließlich des ausgeübten Berufs und bei börsennotierten Gesellschaften auch der Mitgliedschaft in Aufsichtsräten und anderen Kontrollgremien im Sinne des § 125 Abs. 1 Satz 3 des Aktiengesetzes. Der Vorsitzende eines Aufsichtsrats, seine Stellvertreter und ein etwaiger Vorsitzender des Geschäftsführungsorgans sind als solche zu bezeichnen;

11. Name und Sitz anderer Unternehmen, von denen die Kapitalgesellschaft oder eine für Rechnung der Kapitalgesellschaft handelnde Person mindestens den fünften Teil der Anteile besitzt; außerdem sind die Höhe des Anteils am Kapital, das Eigenkapital und das Ergebnis des letzten Geschäftsjahrs dieser Unternehmen anzugeben, für das ein Jahresabschluß vorliegt; auf die Berechnung der Anteile ist § 16 Abs. 2 und 4 des Aktiengesetzes entsprechend anzuwenden; ferner sind von börsennotierten Kapitalgesellschaften zusätzlich alle Beteiligungen an großen Kapitalgesellschaften anzugeben, die fünf vom Hundert der Stimmrechte überschreiten;

c) the advances and credits granted, with disclosure of the interest rates, the material terms and, where applicable, the amounts paid back in the fiscal year as well as contingencies and commitments entered into for the benefit of these people;

10. all members of the management organ and a supervisory board, even if they withdrew during the fiscal year or thereafter, with the last name and at least one full first name including the exercised profession and in case of companies quoted on the stock exchange also the membership in supervisory boards and other control organs within the meaning of § 125 Subsection 1 sentence 3 of the Stock Corporation Act. The chairman of a supervisory board, his representative and a chairman of the management organ, if applicable, shall be noted as such;

11. the name and domicile of other enterprises of which the corporation or a person acting on behalf of the corporation owns at least one-fifth of the shares. Furthermore, the amount of the interest in the capital, the shareholder's equity and the results of the last fiscal year shall be reported for these enterprises for which annual financial statements are available. For assessing the shares, § 16 Subsections 2 and 4 of the Stock Corporation Act shall apply analogously; corporations quoted on the exchange shall also disclose all holdings of large corporations which exceed five percent of the voting rights;

11 a. Name, Sitz und Rechtsform der Unternehmen, deren unbeschränkt haftender Gesellschafter die Kapitalgesellschaft ist;	11 a. the name, domicile and legal form of the enterprises whose general partner is the corporation;
12. Rückstellungen, die in der Bilanz unter dem Posten „sonstige Rückstellungen" nicht gesondert ausgewiesen werden, sind zu erläutern, wenn sie einen nicht unerheblichen Umfang haben;	12. accruals that are not shown separately on the balance sheet under the entry "Other Accruals" shall be discussed if their size is not insubstantial;
13. bei Anwendung des § 255 Abs. 4 Satz 3 die Gründe für die planmäßige Abschreibung des Geschäfts- oder Firmenwerts;	13. in applying § 255 Subsection 4 sentence 3, the reasons for the scheduled depreciation of the goodwill;
14. Name und Sitz des Mutterunternehmens der Kapitalgesellschaft, das den Konzernabschluß für den größten Kreis von Unternehmen aufstellt, und ihres Mutterunternehmens, das den Konzernabschluß für den kleinsten Kreis von Unternehmen aufstellt, sowie im Falle der Offenlegung der von diesen Mutterunternehmen aufgestellten Konzernabschlüsse der Ort, wo diese erhältlich sind;	14. the name and domicile of the corporation's parent, which prepares the consolidated annual financial statements for the largest group of enterprises, and of its parent, which prepares the consolidated annual financial statements for the smallest group of enterprises, as well as the place where the consolidated annual financial statements prepared by these parents are available if such statements are published;
15. soweit es sich um den Anhang des Jahresabschlusses einer Personenhandelsgesellschaft im Sinne des § 264 a Abs. 1 handelt, Name und Sitz der Gesellschaften, die persönlich haftende Gesellschafter sind, sowie deren gezeichnetes Kapital;	15. to the extent that it relates to the notes of the annual financial statements of a business partnership within the meaning of § 264 a Subsection 1, the name and domicile of the companies who are general partners and their registered capital contributions;
16. dass die nach § 161 des Aktiengesetzes vorgeschriebene Erklärung abgegeben und den Aktionären zugänglich gemacht worden ist.	16. that the statement required under § 161 of the Stock Corporation Act (Aktiengesetz) has been made and has been made available to the shareholders.

§ 286 Unterlassen von Angaben

(1) Die Berichterstattung hat insoweit zu unterbleiben, als es für das Wohl der

§ 286 Omission of disclosures

(1) Reporting must be left undone to the extent that it is necessary for the

Bundesrepublik Deutschland oder eines ihrer Länder erforderlich ist.

(2) Die Aufgliederung der Umsatzerlöse nach § 285 Nr. 4 kann unterbleiben, soweit die Aufgliederung nach vernünftiger kaufmännischer Beurteilung geeignet ist, der Kapitalgesellschaft oder einem Unternehmen, von dem die Kapitalgesellschaft mindestens den fünften Teil der Anteile besitzt, einen erheblichen Nachteil zuzufügen.

(3) Die Angaben nach § 285 Nr. 11 und 11a können unterbleiben, soweit sie

1. für die Darstellung der Vermögens-, Finanz- und Ertragslage der Kapitalgesellschaft nach § 264 Abs. 2 von untergeordneter Bedeutung sind oder

2. nach vernünftiger kaufmännischer Beurteilung geeignet sind, der Kapitalgesellschaft oder dem anderen Unternehmen einen erheblichen Nachteil zuzufügen.

Die Angabe des Eigenkapitals und des Jahresergebnisses kann unterbleiben, wenn das Unternehmen, über das zu berichten ist, seinen Jahresabschluß nicht offenzulegen hat und die berichtende Kapitalgesellschaft weniger als die Hälfte der Anteile besitzt. Satz 1 Nr. 2 findet keine Anwendung, wenn eine Kapitalgesellschaft einen organisierten Markt im Sinne des § 2 Abs. 5 des Wertpapierhandelsgesetzes durch von ihr oder einem ihrer Tochterunternehmen (§ 290 Abs. 1, 2) ausgegebene Wertpapiere im Sinne des § 2 Abs. 1 Satz 1 des Wertpapierhandelsgesetzes in Anspruch nimmt oder wenn die Zulassung solcher Wertpapiere zum Handel an einem organisierten Markt beantragt worden ist.

good of the Federal Republic of Germany or any of its states.

(2) The classification of the sales proceeds pursuant to § 285 No. 4 may be left undone to the extent that, according to reasonable business judgment, the classification tends to inflict substantial disadvantage on the corporation or an enterprise of which the corporation owns at least one-fifth of the shares.

(3) The disclosures pursuant to § 285 No. 11 and 11 a may be omitted to the extent that they

1. are of minor importance for describing the state of the net assets, financing and results of operation of the corporation pursuant to § 264 Subsection 2, or

2. according to reasonable business judgment, tend to inflict substantial disadvantage on the corporation or the other enterprise.

Disclosure of the shareholder's equity and of results may be omitted if the enterprise, which is the subject of the reporting, need not disclose its annual financial statements and the corporation that is reporting owns less than one-half of its shares. Sentence 1 No. 2 shall not apply if a stock corporation makes use of an organized market within the meaning of § 2 Subsection 5 of the Securities Trading Act (*Wertpapierhandelsgesetz*) for securities within the meaning of § 2 Subsection 1 sentence 1 of the Securities Trading Act issued by it or one of its subsidiaries (§ 290 Subsection 1, 2) or if an application has been filed for the admission of such securities to trading on an organized market. In addition, the use

Im Übrigen ist die Anwendung der Ausnahmeregelung nach Satz 1 Nr. 2 im Anhang anzugeben.

(4) Die in § 285 Nr. 9 Buchstabe a und b verlangten Angaben über die Gesamtbezüge der dort bezeichneten Personen können unterbleiben, wenn sich anhand dieser Angaben die Bezüge eines Mitglieds dieser Organe feststellen lassen.

§ 287 Aufstellung des Anteilsbesitzes

Die in § 285 Nr. 11 und 11 a verlangten Angaben dürfen statt im Anhang auch in einer Aufstellung des Anteilsbesitzes gesondert gemacht werden. Die Aufstellung ist Bestandteil des Anhangs. Auf die besondere Aufstellung nach Satz 1 und den Ort ihrer Hinterlegung ist im Anhang hinzuweisen.

§ 288 Größenabhängige Erleichterungen

Kleine Kapitalgesellschaften im Sinne des § 267 Abs. 1 brauchen die Angaben nach § 284 Abs. 2 Nr. 4, § 285 Nr. 2 bis 8 Buchstabe a, Nr. 9 Buchstabe a und b und Nr. 12 nicht zu machen. Mittelgroße Kapitalgesellschaften im Sinne des § 267 Abs. 2 brauchen die Angaben nach § 285 Nr. 4 nicht zu machen.

Sechster Titel. Lagebericht

§ 289

(1) Im Lagebericht sind zumindest der Geschäftsverlauf und die Lage der Kapitalgesellschaft so darzustellen, daß ein den tatsächlichen Verhältnissen

of the statutory exception pursuant to sentence 1 No. 2 shall be disclosed in the notes.

(4) The disclosures required in § 285 No. 9 Letters a and b of aggregate remuneration of the persons specified there can be omitted if the remuneration of a member of such organs can be determined by means of such disclosures.

§ 287 List of share ownership

The disclosures required pursuant to § 285 No. 11 and 11 a may be made separately in a list of shareholdings instead of in the notes. The list is a part of the notes. The special list under sentence 1 and the place of its filing shall be pointed out in the notes.

§ 288 Size-related relief

Small corporations within the meaning of § 267 Subsection 1 need not make the disclosures pursuant to § 284 Subsection 2 No. 4, § 285 Nos. 2 to 8 Letter a, No. 9 Letters a and b and No. 12. Medium-sized corporations within the meaning of § 267 Subsection 2 need not make the disclosures pursuant to § 285 No. 4.

Sixth Title. Management Report

§ 289

(1) The management report shall at least describe the course of business and the state of the corporation in such a way that it presents a factually

entsprechendes Bild vermittelt wird; dabei ist auch auf die Risiken der künftigen Entwicklung einzugehen.

(2) Der Lagebericht soll auch eingehen auf:

1. Vorgänge von besonderer Bedeutung, die nach dem Schluß des Geschäftsjahrs eingetreten sind;
2. die voraussichtliche Entwicklung der Kapitalgesellschaft;
3. den Bereich Forschung und Entwicklung;
4. bestehende Zweigniederlassungen der Gesellschaft.

**Zweiter Unterabschnitt.
Konzernabschluß und
Konzernlagebericht**

Erster Titel. Anwendungsbereich

§ 290 Pflicht zur Aufstellung

(1) Stehen in einem Konzern die Unternehmen unter der einheitlichen Leitung einer Kapitalgesellschaft (Mutterunternehmen) mit Sitz im Inland und gehört dem Mutterunternehmen eine Beteiligung nach § 271 Abs. 1 an dem oder den anderen unter der einheitlichen Leitung stehenden Unternehmen (Tochterunternehmen), so haben die gesetzlichen Vertreter des Mutterunternehmens in den ersten fünf Monaten des Konzerngeschäftsjahrs für das vergangene Konzerngeschäftsjahr einen Konzernabschluß und einen Konzernlagebericht aufzustellen.

(2) Eine Kapitalgesellschaft mit Sitz im Inland ist stets zur Aufstellung eines Konzernabschlusses und eines Konzernlageberichts verpflichtet (Mutterunternehmen), wenn ihr bei einem Unternehmen (Tochterunternehmen)

accurate picture; the risks of the future developments shall be dealt with as well.

(2) The management report should also deal with:

1. events of special importance that took place after the end of the fiscal year;
2. the anticipated development of the corporation;
3. the field of research and development;
4. existing branches of the company.

**Second Subpart. The Consolidated
Financial Statements and Consolidated Management Report**

First Title. Area of Application

§ 290 Duty to prepare

(1) If in a consolidated group of companies the enterprises are under the unified control of a corporation (parent) domiciled within the country and if the parent owns a participation pursuant to § 271 Subsection 1 in one or the other of the enterprises (subsidiaries) under the unified control, then the legal representatives of the parent shall prepare within the first five months of the group of companies' fiscal year consolidated financial statements and a consolidated management report for the preceding fiscal year.

(2) A corporation domiciled within the country (parent) is always obligated to prepare consolidated financial statements and a consolidated management report if it has in an enterprise (subsidiary)

Ergänzende Vorschriften für Kapitalgesellschaften § 290

1. die Mehrheit der Stimmrechte der Gesellschafter zusteht,
2. das Recht zusteht, die Mehrheit der Mitglieder des Verwaltungs-, Leitungs- oder Aufsichtsorgans zu bestellen oder abzuberufen, und sie gleichzeitig Gesellschafter ist oder
3. das Recht zusteht, einen beherrschenden Einfluß auf Grund eines mit diesem Unternehmen geschlossenen Beherrschungsvertrags oder auf Grund einer Satzungsbestimmung dieses Unternehmens auszuüben.

(3) Als Rechte, die einem Mutterunternehmen nach Absatz 2 zustehen, gelten auch die einem Tochterunternehmen zustehenden Rechte und die den für Rechnung des Mutterunternehmens oder von Tochterunternehmen handelnden Personen zustehenden Rechte. Den einem Mutterunternehmen an einem anderen Unternehmen zustehenden Rechten werden die Rechte hinzugerechnet, über die es oder ein Tochterunternehmen auf Grund einer Vereinbarung mit anderen Gesellschaftern dieses Unternehmens verfügen kann. Abzuziehen sind Rechte, die

1. mit Anteilen verbunden sind, die von dem Mutterunternehmen oder von Tochterunternehmen für Rechnung einer anderen Person gehalten werden, oder
2. mit Anteilen verbunden sind, die als Sicherheit gehalten werden, sofern diese Rechte nach Weisung des Sicherungsgebers oder, wenn ein Kreditinstitut die Anteile als Sicherheit für ein Darlehen hält, im Interesse des Sicherungsgebers ausgeübt werden.

(4) Welcher Teil der Stimmrechte einem Unternehmen zusteht, bestimmt sich für die Berechnung der Mehrheit

1. the majority of the shareholders' voting rights,
2. the right to appoint or dismiss the majority of the members of the administrative, management or supervisory organ and is at the same time a shareholder, or
3. the right to exercise a controlling influence by reason of a control agreement concluded with this enterprise or by reason of a provision of this enterprise's by-laws.

(3) Rights that belong to a parent pursuant to Subsection 2 include the rights belonging to a subsidiary and the rights belonging to persons acting for the account of the parent or subsidiary. To the rights of a parent in another company will be added the rights which the parent or a subsidiary has at its disposal on the basis of an agreement with other shareholders of this enterprise. Rights shall be deducted that

1. are connected with shares that are held by the parent or a subsidiary for the account of another person, or
2. are connected with shares that are held as security, to the extent that these rights are exercised according to instructions of the person providing the security or, if a credit institution holds the shares as security for a loan, in the interest of the person providing the security.

(4) For calculating the majority pursuant to Subsection 2 No. 1, the portion of voting rights belonging to an enter-

nach Absatz 2 Nr. 1 nach dem Verhältnis der Zahl der Stimmrechte, die es aus den ihm gehörenden Anteilen ausüben kann, zur Gesamtzahl aller Stimmrechte. Von der Gesamtzahl aller Stimmrechte sind die Stimmrechte aus eigenen Anteilen abzuziehen, die dem Tochterunternehmen selbst, einem seiner Tochterunternehmen oder einer anderen Person für Rechnung dieser Unternehmen gehören.

prise shall be determined by the proportion of the number of voting rights that it can exercise from the shares belonging to it to the total number of all voting rights. From the total number of all voting rights shall be deducted the voting rights from treasury shares that belong to the subsidiary itself, one of its subsidiaries or another person for the account of these enterprises.

§ 291 Befreiende Wirkung von EU/EWR-Konzernabschlüssen

§ 291 Exemptive effect of EU/EEA consolidated financial statements

(1) Ein Mutterunternehmen, das zugleich Tochterunternehmen eines Mutterunternehmens mit Sitz in einem Mitgliedstaat der Europäischen Union oder in einem anderen Vertragsstaat des Abkommens über den Europäischen Wirtschaftsraum ist, braucht einen Konzernabschluß und einen Konzernlagebericht nicht aufzustellen, wenn ein den Anforderungen des Absatzes 2 entsprechender Konzernabschluß und Konzernlagebericht seines Mutterunternehmens einschließlich des Bestätigungsvermerks oder des Vermerks über dessen Versagung nach den für den entfallenden Konzernabschluß und Konzernlagebericht maßgeblichen Vorschriften in deutscher Sprache offengelegt wird. Ein befreiender Konzernabschluß und ein befreiender Konzernlagebericht können von jedem Unternehmen unabhängig von seiner Rechtsform und Größe aufgestellt werden, wenn das Unternehmen als Kapitalgesellschaft mit Sitz in einem Mitgliedstaat der Europäischen Union oder in einem anderen Vertragsstaat des Abkommens über den Europäischen Wirt-

(1) A parent that is also a subsidiary of a parent domiciled in a member state of the European Union or in another contracting state of the European Economic Area Agreement need not prepare consolidated financial statements or a consolidated management report if disclosure is made in the German language of consolidated financial statements and a consolidated management report of its parent, meeting the requirements of Subsection 2, including the certification of the financial statements or a statement refusing certification and according to the regulations governing the omitted consolidated financial statements and consolidated management report. Exemptive consolidated financial statements and an exemptive consolidated management report may be prepared by any enterprise regardless of its legal form and size if the enterprise would be obligated as a corporation domiciled in a member state of the European Union or in another contracting state of the European Economic Area Agreement to prepare consolidated financial statements in-

schaftsraum zur Aufstellung eines Konzernabschlusses unter Einbeziehung des zu befreienden Mutterunternehmens und seiner Tochterunternehmen verpflichtet wäre.

(2) Der Konzernabschluß und Konzernlagebericht eines Mutterunternehmens mit Sitz in einem Mitgliedstaat der Europäischen Union oder in einem anderen Vertragsstaat des Abkommens über den Europäischen Wirtschaftsraum haben befreiende Wirkung, wenn

1. das zu befreiende Mutterunternehmen und seine Tochterunternehmen in den befreienden Konzernabschluß unbeschadet der §§ 295, 296 einbezogen worden sind,

2. der befreiende Konzernabschluß und der befreiende Konzernlagebericht im Einklang mit der Richtlinie 83/349/EWG des Rates vom 13. Juni 1983 über den konsolidierten Abschluß (ABl. EG Nr. L 193 S. 1) und der Richtlinie 84/253/EWG des Rates vom 10. April 1984 über die Zulassung der mit der Pflichtprüfung der Rechnungslegungsunterlagen beauftragten Personen (ABl. EG Nr. L 126 S. 20) nach dem für das aufstellende Mutterunternehmen maßgeblichen Recht aufgestellt und von einem zugelassenen Abschlußprüfer geprüft worden sind,

3. der Anhang des Jahresabschlusses des zu befreienden Unternehmens folgende Angaben enthält:

   a) Name und Sitz des Mutterunternehmens, das den befreienden Konzernabschluß und Konzernlagebericht aufstellt,

cluding the parent and its subsidiary, which are to be exempted.

(2) The consolidated financial statements and consolidated management report of a parent domiciled in a member state of the European Union or in another contracting state of the European Economic Area Agreement have exemptive effect if

1. the parent to be exempted and its subsidiaries are included in the exemptive consolidated financial statements notwithstanding §§ 295 and 296,

2. the exemptive consolidated financial statements and the exemptive consolidated management report have been prepared pursuant to the law applicable to the preparing parent in accordance with the Directive 83/349/EEC of the Commission of June 13, 1983 concerning the consolidated financial statements (OJ EC No. L 193, p. 1) and the Directive 84/253/EEC of the Commission of April 10, 1984 pertaining to the admission of the persons charged with the mandatory audit of the accounting records (OJ EC No. L 126, p. 20) and have been examined by a licensed auditor.

3. the notes to the annual financial statements of the enterprise to be exempted includes the following information:

   a) name and domicile of the parent that is preparing the exemptive consolidated financial statements and a consolidated management report,

b) einen Hinweis auf die Befreiung von der Verpflichtung, einen Konzernabschluß und einen Konzernlagebericht aufzustellen, und

c) eine Erläuterung der im befreienden Konzernabschluß vom deutschen Recht abweichend angewandten Bilanzierungs-, Bewertungs- und Konsolidierungsmethoden.

Satz 1 gilt für Kreditinstitute und Versicherungsunternehmen entsprechend; unbeschadet der übrigen Voraussetzungen in Satz 1 hat die Aufstellung des befreienden Konzernabschlusses und des befreienden Konzernlageberichts bei Kreditinstituten im Einklang mit der Richtlinie 86/635/EWG des Rates vom 8. Dezember 1986 über den Jahresabschluß und den konsolidierten Abschluß von Banken und anderen Finanzinstituten (ABl. EG Nr. L 372 S. 1) und bei Versicherungsunternehmen im Einklang mit der Richtlinie 91/674/EWG des Rates vom 19. Dezember 1991 über den Jahresabschluß und den konsolidierten Jahresabschluß von Versicherungsunternehmen (ABl. EG Nr. L 374 S. 7) zu erfolgen.

(3) Die Befreiung nach Absatz 1 kann trotz Vorliegens der Voraussetzungen nach Absatz 2 von einem Mutterunternehmen nicht in Anspruch genommen werden, wenn

1. das zu befreiende Mutterunternehmen eine Aktiengesellschaft ist, deren Aktien zum Handel im amtlichen Markt zugelassen sind, oder

2. Gesellschafter, denen bei Aktiengesellschaften und Kommanditgesellschaften auf Aktien mindestens 10 vom Hundert und bei Ge-

b) an indication of the exemption from the duty to prepare consolidated financial statements and a consolidated management report, and

c) an explanation of the balance sheet, valuation and consolidation methods used preparing in the exemptive consolidated financial statements which deviate from German law.

Sentence 1 applies analogously to credit institutions and insurance companies; notwithstanding the other requirements in sentence 1, the preparation of exemptive consolidated financial statements and the exemptive consolidated management report for credit institutions has to be in accordance with the Directive 86/635/EEC of the Commission of December 8, 1986 concerning the annual financial statements and the consolidated financial statements of banks and other financial institutions (OJ EC No. L 372, p. 1), and in case of insurance companies, in accordance with the Directive 91/674/EEC of the Commission of December 19, 1991 concerning the annual financial statements and the consolidated financial statements of insurance companies (OJ EC No. 374, p. 7).

(3) Notwithstanding the satisfaction of the requirements under Subsection 2, a parent can not make use of the exemption under Subsection 1 if

1. the parent to be exempted is a stock corporation whose shares are admitted to trading on the official market, or

2. shareholders who own, in the case of stock corporations and partnerships limited by shares, at least 10% and, in the case of limited lia-

sellschaften mit beschränkter Haftung mindestens 20 vom Hundert der Anteile an dem zu befreienden Mutterunternehmen gehören, spätestens sechs Monate vor dem Ablauf des Konzerngeschäftsjahrs die Aufstellung eines Konzernabschlusses und eines Konzernlageberichts beantragt haben. Gehören dem Mutterunternehmen mindestens 90 vom Hundert der Anteile an dem zu befreienden Mutterunternehmen, so kann Absatz 1 nur angewendet werden, wenn die anderen Gesellschafter der Befreiung zugestimmt haben

bility companies, at least 20% of the shares of the parent to be exempted have applied for the preparation of consolidated financial statements and a consolidated management report no later than six months before the expiration of the group of companies' fiscal year. If the parent owns at least 90% of the shares of the parent to be exempted, then Subsection 1 may be used only if the other shareholders have approved the exemption.

§ 292 Rechtsverordnungsermächtigung für befreiende Konzernabschlüsse und Konzernlageberichte

(1) Das Bundesministerium der Justiz wird ermächtigt, im Einvernehmen mit dem Bundesministerium der Finanzen und dem Bundesministerium für Wirtschaft und Technologie durch Rechtsverordnung, die nicht der Zustimmung des Bundesrates bedarf, zu bestimmen, daß § 291 auf Konzernabschlüsse und Konzernlageberichte von Mutterunternehmen mit Sitz in einem Staat, der nicht Mitglied der Europäischen Union und auch nicht Vertragsstaat des Abkommens über den Europäischen Wirtschaftsraum ist, mit der Maßgabe angewendet werden darf, daß der befreiende Konzernabschluß und der befreiende Konzernlagebericht nach dem mit den Anforderungen der Richtlinie 83/349/EWG übereinstimmenden Recht eines Mitgliedstaates der Europäischen Union oder eines anderen Vertragsstaates des Abkommens über den Europäischen Wirtschaftsraum aufgestellt worden oder einem nach diesem Recht eines Mitgliedstaa-

§ 292 Enabling rule for the exemptive consolidated financial statements and consolidated management reports

(1) The Federal Ministry of Justice is authorized, with the agreement of the Federal Ministry of Finance and the Federal Ministry for Economics and Technology, to set rules, which do not require the approval of the Federal upper house of Parliament, that § 291 may be used for consolidated financial statements and consolidated management reports of a parent domiciled in a state that is not a member of the European Union and also not a contracting state of the European Economic Area Agreement, with the proviso that the exemptive consolidated financial statements and the exemptive consolidated management report have been prepared pursuant to the law of a member state of the European Union or another contracting state of the European Economic Area Agreement conforming to the requirements of the Directive 83/349/EEC or must be equivalent to consolidated financial statements or a consolidated manage-

tes der Europäischen Union oder eines anderen Vertragsstaates des Abkommens über den Europäischen Wirtschaftsraum aufgestellten Konzernabschluß und Konzernlagebericht gleichwertig sein müssen. Das Recht eines anderen Mitgliedstaates der Europäischen Union oder Vertragsstaates des Abkommens über den Europäischen Wirtschaftsraum kann einem befreienden Konzernabschluß und einem befreienden Konzernlagebericht jedoch nur zugrunde gelegt oder für die Herstellung der Gleichwertigkeit herangezogen werden, wenn diese Unterlagen in dem anderen Mitgliedstaat oder Vertragsstaat anstelle eines sonst nach dem Recht dieses Mitgliedstaates oder Vertragsstaates vorgeschriebenen Konzernabschlusses und Konzernlageberichts offengelegt werden. Die Anwendung dieser Vorschrift kann in der Rechtsverordnung nach Satz 1 davon abhängig gemacht werden, daß die nach diesem Unterabschnitt aufgestellten Konzernabschlüsse und Konzernlageberichte in dem Staat, in dem das Mutterunternehmen seinen Sitz hat, als gleichwertig mit den dort für Unternehmen mit entsprechender Rechtsform und entsprechendem Geschäftszweig vorgeschriebenen Konzernabschlüssen und Konzernlageberichten angesehen werden.

(2) Ist ein nach Absatz 1 zugelassener Konzernabschluß nicht von einem in Übereinstimmung mit den Vorschriften der Richtlinie 84/253/EWG zugelassenen Abschlußprüfer geprüft worden, so kommt ihm befreiende Wirkung nur zu, wenn der Abschlußprüfer eine den Anforderungen dieser Richtlinie gleichwertige Befähigung hat und der Konzernabschluß in einer den Anforderungen des Dritten Unterabschnitts entsprechenden Weise geprüft worden ist.

ment report prepared pursuant to such a law of a member state of the European Union or another contracting state of the European Economic Area Agreement. The law of another member state of the European Union or of a contracting state of the European Economic Area Agreement, however, may form the basis of exemptive consolidated financial statements and an exemptive consolidated management report or be called upon for the preparation of the equivalent only if these records are disclosed in the other member state or contracting state instead of consolidated financial statements and a consolidated management report otherwise prescribed by the law of this member state or contracting state. In the rule pursuant to sentence 1, the use of this provision may be made conditional on the consolidated financial statements and consolidated management reports prepared pursuant to this Subpart being viewed in the state in which the parent has its domicile as equivalent to the consolidated financial statements and the consolidated management reports prescribed there for thc enterprises with a corresponding legal form and a corresponding line of business.

(2) If consolidated financial statements permitted pursuant to Subsection 1 have not been examined by an accountant certified in accordance with the provisions of the Directive 84/253/EEC, then it has the exemptive effect only if the accountant has qualifications equivalent to those required by the Directives and the consolidated financial statements have been examined in a manner conforming to the requirements of the Third Subpart.

Ergänzende Vorschriften für Kapitalgesellschaften § 292

(3) In einer Rechtsverordnung nach Absatz 1 kann außerdem bestimmt werden, welche Voraussetzungen Konzernabschlüsse und Konzernlageberichte von Mutterunternehmen mit Sitz in einem Staat, der nicht Mitglied der Europäischen Union und auch nicht Vertragsstaat des Abkommens über den Europäischen Wirtschaftsraum ist, im einzelnen erfüllen müssen, um nach Absatz 1 gleichwertig zu sein, und wie die Befähigung von Abschlußprüfern beschaffen sein muß, um nach Absatz 2 gleichwertig zu sein. In der Rechtsverordnung können zusätzliche Angaben und Erläuterungen zum Konzernabschluß vorgeschrieben werden, soweit diese erforderlich sind, um die Gleichwertigkeit dieser Konzernabschlüsse und Konzernlageberichte mit solchen nach diesem Unterabschnitt oder dem Recht eines anderen Mitgliedstaates der Europäischen Union oder Vertragsstaates des Abkommens über den Europäischen Wirtschaftsraum herzustellen.

(4) Die Rechtsverordnung ist vor Verkündung dem Bundestag zuzuleiten. Sie kann durch Beschluß des Bundestages geändert oder abgelehnt werden. Der Beschluß des Bundestages wird dem Bundesministerium der Justiz zugeleitet. Das Bundesministerium der Justiz ist bei der Verkündung der Rechtsverordnung an den Beschluß gebunden. Hat sich der Bundestag nach Ablauf von drei Sitzungswochen seit Eingang einer Rechtsverordnung nicht mit ihr befaßt, so wird die unveränderte Rechtsverordnung dem Bundesministerium der Justiz zur Verkündung zugeleitet. Der Bundestag befaßt sich mit der Rechtsverordnung auf Antrag von so vielen Mitgliedern des Bundestages, wie zur Bildung einer Fraktion erforderlich sind.

(3) An administrative rule pursuant to Subsection 1 may also determine what conditions consolidated financial statements and consolidated management reports of a parent domiciled in a state that is not a member of the European Union and also not a contracting state of the European Economic Area Agreement must meet in particular to be equivalent pursuant to Subsection 1, and how the auditors must be qualified to be equivalent pursuant to Subsection 2. The rule can prescribe additional disclosures and explanations in the consolidated financial statements to the extent that these are necessary to establish the equivalence of the consolidated financial statements and consolidated management reports with those pursuant to this Subpart or the law of another member state of the European Union or of a contracting state of the European Economic Area Agreement.

(4) The legal rule shall be brought before the Federal lower house of Parliament (Bundestag) before its promulgation. It can be amended or rejected by a resolution of the Federal lower house of Parliament (Bundestag). The resolution of the Federal lower house of Parliament (Bundestag) shall be brought to the Federal Ministry of Justice. The Federal Ministry of Justice is bound by the resolution in promulgating the administrative order. If the Federal lower house of Parliament (Bundestag) has not dealt with the administrative order after the expiration of three weeks in session since its receipt, then the administrative order will be brought unchanged to the Federal Ministry of Justice for promulgation. The Federal lower house of Parliament will deal with the legal rule upon the applica-

197

tion of as many members of the Federal lower house of Parliament as are necessary for the formation of a parliamentary political group.

§ 292 a Befreiung von der Aufstellungspflicht[1]

§ 292 a Exemption from the duty to prepare consolidated financial statements and a consolidated management report[1]

(1) Ein Mutterunternehmen, das einen organisierten Markt im Sinne des § 2 Abs. 5 des Wertpapierhandelsgesetzes durch von ihm oder einem seiner Tochterunternehmen ausgegebene Wertpapiere im Sinne des § 2 Abs. 1 Satz 1 des Wertpapierhandelsgesetzes in Anspruch nimmt, braucht einen Konzernabschluß und einen Konzernlagebericht nach den Vorschriften dieses Unterabschnitts nicht aufzustellen, wenn es einen den Anforderungen des Absatzes 2 entsprechenden Konzernabschluß und Konzernlagebericht aufstellt und ihn in deutscher Sprache und Euro nach den §§ 325, 328 offenlegt. Satz 1 gilt auch, wenn die Zulassung zum Handel an einem organisierten Markt beantragt worden ist. Bei der Offenlegung der befreienden Unterlagen ist ausdrücklich darauf hinzuweisen, daß es sich um einen nicht nach deutschem Recht aufgestellten Konzernabschluß und Konzernlagebericht handelt.

(1) A parent which makes use of an organized exchange within the meaning of § 2 Subsection 5 of the Securities Trading Act through securities, within the meaning of § 2 Subsection 1 sentence 1 of the Securities Trading Act, issued by it or a subsidiary need not prepare consolidated financial statements and a consolidated management report pursuant to the provisions of this Subpart, provided it prepares consolidated financial statements and a consolidated management report conforming to the requirements of Subsection 2 and discloses it in the German language and in Euro pursuant to §§ 325 and 328. Sentence 1 also applies where admission to trading on a organized exchange has been applied for. In disclosing the exemptive records it must be expressly indicated that these are not consolidated financial statements and a consolidated management report prepared pursuant to German law.

(2) Der Konzernabschluß und der Konzernlagebericht haben befreiende Wirkung, wenn

(2) The consolidated financial statements and the consolidated management report have exemptive effect where

1. das Mutterunternehmen und seine Tochterunternehmen in den be-

1. the parent and its subsidiaries have been included in the exemp-

---

[1] § 292 a tritt am 31. 12. 2004 außer Kraft (Art. 5 des Kapitalaufnahmeerleichterungsgesetzes, BGBl. I 1998 S. 707).

[1] § 292 a will be repealed on December 31, 2004 (Article 5 of the Capital Raising Simplification Act (*Kapitalaufnahmeerleichterungsgesetz*), BGBl. I, 1998, page 707).

Ergänzende Vorschriften für Kapitalgesellschaften § 292a

freienden Konzernabschluß unbeschadet der §§ 295, 296 einbezogen worden sind,

2. der Konzernabschluß und der Konzernlagebericht

   a) nach international anerkannten Rechnungslegungsgrundsätzen aufgestellt worden sind,
   b) im Einklang mit der Richtlinie 83/349/EWG und gegebenenfalls den für Kreditinstitute und Versicherungsunternehmen in § 291 Abs. 2 Satz 2 bezeichneten Richtlinien stehen,

3. die Aussagekraft der danach aufgestellten Unterlagen der Ausagekraft eines nach den Vorschriften dieses Unterabschnitts aufgestellten Konzernabschlusses und Konzernlageberichts gleichwertig ist,

4. der Anhang oder die Erläuterungen zum Konzernabschluß die folgenden Angaben enthält:

   a) die Bezeichnung der angewandten Rechnungslegungsgrundsätze,
   b) eine Erläuterung der vom deutschen Recht abweichenden Bilanzierungs-, Bewertungs- und Konsolidierungsmethoden, und

5. die befreienden Unterlagen von dem nach § 318 bestellten Abschlußprüfer geprüft worden sind und von dem Abschlußprüfer außerdem bestätigt worden ist, daß die Bedingungen für die Befreiung erfüllt sind.

(3) Das Bundesministerium der Justiz kann im Einvernehmen mit dem Bundesministerium der Finanzen und dem Bundesministerium für Wirtschaft und Technologie durch Rechts-

tive consolidated financial statements without prejudice to §§ 295 and 296,

2. the consolidated financial reports and the consolidated management report

   a) have been prepared pursuant to internationally accepted accounting principles,
   b) are in accordance with the Directive 83/349/EEC and, as the case may be, the directives for credit institutions and insurance companies indicated in § 291 Subsection 2 sentence 2,

3. the informative value of the statements prepared thereunder is equivalent to the informative value of consolidated financial statements and a consolidated management report prepared under the provisions of this Subpart,

4. the notes or the explanations to the consolidated financial statements contain the following information:

   a) the description of the accounting principles applied,
   b) an explanation of the balance sheet, valuation and consolidating methods which deviate from German law, and

5. the exemptive records have been examined by an auditor appointed pursuant to § 318 and the auditor has also certified that the requirements for the exemption are met.

(3) The Federal Ministry of Justice is authorized, with the agreement of the Federal Ministry of Finance and the Federal Ministry for Economics and Technology, to determine by statu-

verordnung bestimmen, welche Voraussetzungen Konzernabschlüsse und Konzernlageberichte von Mutterunternehmen im einzelnen erfüllen müssen, um nach Absatz 2 Nr. 3 gleichwertig zu sein. Dies kann auch in der Weise geschehen, daß Rechnungslegungsgrundsätze bezeichnet werden, bei deren Anwendung die Gleichwertigkeit gegeben ist.

§ 293 Größenabhängige Befreiungen

(1) Ein Mutterunternehmen ist von der Pflicht, einen Konzernabschluß und einen Konzernlagebericht aufzustellen, befreit, wenn

1. am Abschlußstichtag seines Jahresabschlusses und am vorhergehenden Abschlußstichtag mindestens zwei der drei nachstehenden Merkmale zutreffen:

   a) Die Bilanzsummen in den Bilanzen des Mutterunternehmens und der Tochterunternehmen, die in den Konzernabschluß einzubeziehen wären, übersteigen insgesamt nach Abzug von in den Bilanzen auf der Aktivseite ausgewiesenen Fehlbeträgen nicht 16 500 000 Euro.

   b) Die Umsatzerlöse des Mutterunternehmens und der Tochterunternehmen, die in den Konzernabschluß einzubeziehen wären, übersteigen in den zwölf Monaten vor dem Abschlußstichtag insgesamt nicht 33 000 000 Euro.

   c) Das Mutterunternehmen und die Tochterunternehmen, die in den Konzernabschluß einzubeziehen wären, haben in den zwölf Monaten vor dem Abschlußstichtag im Jahresdurch-

tory order which requirements must be met specifically by consolidated financial statements and consolidated management reports of parents in order to be equivalent pursuant to Subsection 2 No. 3. This can also be done by designating accounting principles the application of which results in the records being equivalent.

§ 293 Size-related exemptions

(1) A parent is exempted from the duty to prepare consolidated financial statements and a consolidated management report if

1. at least two of the following three criteria are met on the close of the fiscal year of its annual financial statement and on the preceding close of the fiscal year:

   a) the balance sheet totals in the balance sheets of the parent and the subsidiary that would be included in the consolidated financial statement do not exceed in total, after deducting the deficits shown on the assets side of the balance sheets, 16 500 000 EUR;

   b) the sales revenue of the parent and the subsidiary that would be included in the consolidated financial statements does not exceed in total in the twelve months before the the close of the fiscal year 33 000 000 EUR;

   c) the parent and the subsidiary that would be included in the consolidated financial statements did not employ on the average more than 250 employees in the twelve months before the

schnitt nicht mehr als 250 Arbeitnehmer beschäftigt; oder

2. am Abschlußstichtag eines von ihm aufzustellenden Konzernabschlusses und am vorhergehenden Abschlußstichtag mindestens zwei der drei nachstehenden Merkmale zutreffen:

   a) Die Bilanzsumme übersteigt nach Abzug eines auf der Aktivseite ausgewiesenen Fehlbetrags nicht 13 750 000 Euro.

   b) Die Umsatzerlöse in den zwölf Monaten vor dem Abschlußstichtag übersteigen nicht 27 500 000 Euro.

   c) Das Mutterunternehmen und die in den Konzernabschluß einbezogenen Tochterunternehmen haben in den zwölf Monaten vor dem Abschlußstichtag im Jahresdurchschnitt nicht mehr als 250 Arbeitnehmer beschäftigt.

Auf die Ermittlung der durchschnittlichen Zahl der Arbeitnehmer ist § 267 Abs. 5 anzuwenden.

(2) *(aufgehoben)*

(3) *(aufgehoben)*

(4) Außer in den Fällen des Absatzes 1 ist ein Mutterunternehmen von der Pflicht zur Aufstellung des Konzernabschlusses und des Konzernlageberichts befreit, wenn die Voraussetzungen des Absatzes 1 nur am Abschlußstichtag oder nur am vorhergehenden Abschlußstichtag erfüllt sind und das Mutterunternehmen am vorhergehenden Abschlußstichtag von der Pflicht zur Aufstellung des Konzernabschlusses und des Konzernlageberichts befreit war.

(5) Die Absätze 1 und 4 sind nicht anzuwenden, wenn das Mutterunternehmen oder ein in den Konzernab-

close of the fiscal year; or

2. at least two of the following three criteria are met by consolidated financial statements to be prepared by it on the close of the fiscal year and on the preceding close of the fiscal year:

   a) the balance sheet total does not exceed after deducting any deficit shown on the assets side 13 750 000 EUR;

   b) the turnover revenue in the twelve months before the close of the fiscal year does not exceed 27 500 000 EUR;

   c) the parent and the subsidiary included in the consolidated financial statements did not employ on the average more than 250 employees in the twelve months before the close of the fiscal year.

§ 267 Subsection 5 shall be applied for ascertaining the average number of employees.

(2) *(repealed)*

(3) *(repealed)*

(4) Besides the cases of Subsection 1, a parent is exempted from the duty to prepare the consolidated financial statements and the consolidated management report if the conditions of Subsection 1 are met only on the close of the fiscal year or only on the preceding close of the fiscal year, and on the preceding close of the fiscal year the parent was exempted from the duty to prepare the consolidated financial statements and the consolidated management report.

(5) Subsections 1 and 4 do not apply where the parent or a subsidiary included in the consolidated financial

§§ 293, 294 | Handelsbücher

schluss des Mutterunternehmens einbezogenes Tochterunternehmen am Abschlussstichtag einen organisierten Markt im Sinne des § 2 Abs. 5 des Wertpapierhandelsgesetzes durch von ihm ausgegebene Wertpapiere im Sinne des § 2 Abs. 1 Satz 1 des Wertpapierhandelsgesetzes in Anspruch nimmt oder die Zulassung zum Handel an einem organisierten Markt beantragt worden ist.

statements of the parent at the close of the fiscal year makes use of an organized exchange within the meaning of § 2 Subsection 5 of the Securities Trading Act through securities within the meaning of § 2 Subsection 1 Sentence 1 of the Securities Trading Act issued by it or admission to trading on an organized exchange has been applied for.

Zweiter Titel. Konsolidierungskreis

§ 294 Einzubeziehende Unternehmen. Vorlage- und Auskunftspflichten

(1) In den Konzernabschluß sind das Mutterunternehmen und alle Tochterunternehmen ohne Rücksicht auf den Sitz der Tochterunternehmen einzubeziehen, sofern die Einbeziehung nicht nach den §§ 295, 296 unterbleibt.

(2) Hat sich die Zusammensetzung der in den Konzernabschluß einbezogenen Unternehmen im Laufe des Geschäftsjahrs wesentlich geändert, so sind in den Konzernabschluß Angaben aufzunehmen, die es ermöglichen, die aufeinanderfolgenden Konzernabschlüsse sinnvoll zu vergleichen. Dieser Verpflichtung kann auch dadurch entsprochen werden, daß die entsprechenden Beträge des vorhergehenden Konzernabschlusses an die Änderung angepaßt werden.

(3) Die Tochterunternehmen haben dem Mutterunternehmen ihre Jahresabschlüsse, Lageberichte, Konzernabschlüsse, Konzernlageberichte und, wenn eine Prüfung des Jahresabschlusses oder des Konzernabschlusses stattgefunden hat, die Prüfungsberichte sowie, wenn ein Zwischenabschluß

Second Title. Consolidated Group

§ 294 Enterprises to be included; duty to produce and inform

(1) The parent and all subsidiaries, without regard to the domicile of the subsidiaries, shall be included in the consolidated financial statements, to the extent that the inclusion is not omitted pursuant to §§ 295 and 296.

(2) If the composition of the enterprises included in the consolidated financial statements has substantially changed in the course of the fiscal year, then the consolidated financial statements shall include information that facilitates a reasonable comparison among the successive consolidated financial statements. This obligation may also be met by conforming the appropriate amounts in the previous consolidated financial statements to the change.

(3) The subsidiaries shall provide to the parent without undue delay their annual financial statements, management reports, consolidated financial statements, consolidated management reports and, if an audit of the annual financial statements or the consolidated financial statements has

Ergänzende Vorschriften für Kapitalgesellschaften §§ 294, 295

aufzustellen ist, einen auf den Stichtag des Konzernabschlusses aufgestellten Abschluß unverzüglich einzureichen. Das Mutterunternehmen kann von jedem Tochterunternehmen alle Aufklärungen und Nachweise verlangen, welche die Aufstellung des Konzernabschlusses und des Konzernlageberichts erfordert.

taken place, the audit reports, as well as, if intermediate financial statements shall be prepared, financial statements prepared on the close of the fiscal year of the consolidated financial statements. The parent may demand from each subsidiary all explanations and supporting documents that are necessary for preparing the consolidated financial statements and the consolidated management report.

§ 295 Verbot der Einbeziehung

(1) Ein Tochterunternehmen darf in den Konzernabschluß nicht einbezogen werden, wenn sich seine Tätigkeit von der Tätigkeit der anderen einbezogenen Unternehmen derart unterscheidet, daß die Einbeziehung in den Konzernabschluß mit der Verpflichtung, ein den tatsächlichen Verhältnissen entsprechendes Bild der Vermögens-, Finanz- und Ertragslage des Konzerns zu vermitteln, unvereinbar ist; § 311 über die Einbeziehung von assoziierten Unternehmen bleibt unberührt.

(2) Absatz 1 ist nicht allein deshalb anzuwenden, weil die in den Konzernabschluß einbezogenen Unternehmen teils Industrie-, teils Handels- und teils Dienstleistungsunternehmen sind oder weil diese Unternehmen unterschiedliche Erzeugnisse herstellen, mit unterschiedlichen Erzeugnissen Handel treiben oder Dienstleistungen unterschiedlicher Art erbringen.

(3) Die Anwendung des Absatzes 1 ist im Konzernanhang anzugeben und zu begründen. Wird der Jahresabschluß oder der Konzernabschluß eines nach Absatz 1 nicht einbezogenen Unternehmens im Geltungsbereich dieses Gesetzes nicht offengelegt, so ist er

§ 295 Prohibition of inclusion

(1) A subsidiary shall not be included in the consolidated financial statements if its activities differ from the activities of the other included enterprises in such a way that its inclusion in the consolidated financial statements is not reconcilable with the obligation to convey a factually accurate picture of the state of the net assets, financing and results of operations of the consolidated company. § 311, in regard to the inclusion of associated enterprises, is unaffected.

(2) Subsection 1 shall not be applied simply because the enterprises included in the consolidated financial statements are in part industrial enterprises, in part trade enterprises and in part service enterprises or because these enterprises manufacture different products, conduct trade with different products or provide services of different types.

(3) The application of Subsection 1 shall be reported and justified in the consolidated notes. If the annual financial statements or the consolidated financial statements of an enterprise not included pursuant to Subsection 1 are not disclosed within the

gemeinsam mit dem Konzernabschluß zum Handelsregister einzureichen.

§ 296 Verzicht auf die Einbeziehung

(1) Ein Tochterunternehmen braucht in den Konzernabschluß nicht einbezogen zu werden, wenn

1. erhebliche und andauernde Beschränkungen die Ausübung der Rechte des Mutterunternehmens in bezug auf das Vermögen oder die Geschäftsführung dieses Unternehmens nachhaltig beeinträchtigen,

2. die für die Aufstellung des Konzernabschlusses erforderlichen Angaben nicht ohne unverhältnismäßig hohe Kosten oder Verzögerungen zu erhalten sind oder

3. die Anteile des Tochterunternehmens ausschließlich zum Zwecke ihrer Weiterveräußerung gehalten werden.

(2) Ein Tochterunternehmen braucht in den Konzernabschluß nicht einbezogen zu werden, wenn es für die Verpflichtung, ein den tatsächlichen Verhältnissen entsprechendes Bild der Vermögens-, Finanz- und Ertragslage des Konzerns zu vermitteln, von untergeordneter Bedeutung ist. Entsprechen mehrere Tochterunternehmen der Voraussetzung des Satzes 1, so sind diese Unternehmen in den Konzernabschluß einzubeziehen, wenn sie zusammen nicht von untergeordneter Bedeutung sind.

(3) Die Anwendung der Absätze 1 und 2 ist im Konzernanhang zu begründen.

geographical scope of this law, then it shall be filed in the Commercial Register together with the consolidated financial statements.

§ 296 Waiver of the inclusion

(1) A subsidiary need not be included in the consolidated financial statements if

1. substantial and persistent limitations permanently impair the exercise of the parent's rights in regard to the property or the business management of this subsidiary,

2. the information necessary for the preparation of the consolidated financial statements is not available without disproportionately high costs or delays, or

3. the shares in the subsidiary are held exclusively for the purpose of their further sale.

(2) A subsidiary need not be included in the consolidated financial statements if it is of minor importance in regard to the obligation to provide a factually accurate picture of the net assets, financing and results of operations of the consolidated group of companies. If several subsidiaries meet the conditions of sentence 1, these subsidiaries shall be included in the consolidated financial statements if taken together they are not of minor importance.

(3) The application of Subsections 1 and 2 shall be justified in the consolidated notes.

Ergänzende Vorschriften für Kapitalgesellschaften § 297

Dritter Titel. Inhalt und Form des Konzernabschlusses

§ 297 Inhalt

(1) Der Konzernabschluß besteht aus der Konzernbilanz, der Konzern-Gewinn- und Verlustrechnung und dem Konzernanhang, die eine Einheit bilden. Nimmt ein Mutterunternehmen einen organisierten Markt im Sinne des § 2 Abs. 5 des Wertpapierhandelsgesetzes durch von ihm oder einem seiner Tochterunternehmen ausgegebene Wertpapiere im Sinne des § 2 Abs. 1 Satz 1 des Wertpapierhandelsgesetzes in Anspruch oder ist die Zulassung solcher Wertpapiere zum Handel an einem organisierten Markt beantragt worden, so besteht der Konzernabschluss außerdem aus einer Kapitalflussrechnung, einer Segmentberichterstattung sowie einem Eigenkapitalspiegel.

(2) Der Konzernabschluß ist klar und übersichtlich aufzustellen. Er hat unter Beachtung der Grundsätze ordnungsmäßiger Buchführung ein den tatsächlichen Verhältnissen entsprechendes Bild der Vermögens-, Finanz- und Ertragslage des Konzerns zu vermitteln. Führen besondere Umstände dazu, daß der Konzernabschluß ein den tatsächlichen Verhältnissen entsprechendes Bild im Sinne des Satzes 2 nicht vermittelt, so sind im Konzernanhang zusätzliche Angaben zu machen.

(3) Im Konzernabschluß ist die Vermögens-, Finanz- und Ertragslage der einbezogenen Unternehmen so darzustellen, als ob diese Unternehmen insgesamt ein einziges Unternehmen wären. Die auf den vorhergehenden Konzernabschluß angewandten Kon-

Third Title. Content and Form of the Consolidated Financial Statements

§ 297 Content

(1) The consolidated financial statements shall consist of the consolidated balance sheet, the consolidated profit and loss statement and the consolidated notes, which taken together comprise a whole. If a parent company makes use of an organized market within the meaning of § 2 Subsection 5 of the Securities Trading Act (*Wertpapierhandelsgesetz*) for securities within the meaning of § 2 Subsection 1 sentence 1 of the Securities Trading Act issued by it or one of its subsidiaries or if an application has been filed for the admission of such securities to trading on an organized market, then the consolidated financial statements shall also include a cash-flow calculation, a market segment report as well as a reflection of shareholders' equity

(2) The consolidated financial statements shall be prepared so as to be clear and easily understandable. They shall provide a factually accurate picture of the net assets, financing and results of operations of the group of companies in accordance with generally accepted accounting principles. If special circumstances lead to the result that the consolidated financial statements do not provide a factually accurate picture within the meaning of sentence 2, then additional information shall be provided in the consolidated notes.

(3) In the consolidated financial statements, the net assets, financing and results of operations of the included enterprises shall be presented as if these enterprises together were a single enterprise. The consolidation methods used for the preceding con-

205

solidierungsmethoden sollen beibehalten werden. Abweichungen von Satz 2 sind in Ausnahmefällen zulässig. Sie sind im Konzernanhang anzugeben und zu begründen. Ihr Einfluß auf die Vermögens-, Finanz- und Ertragslage des Konzerns ist anzugeben.

§ 298 Anzuwendende Vorschriften. Erleichterungen

(1) Auf den Konzernabschluß sind, soweit seine Eigenart keine Abweichung bedingt oder in den folgenden Vorschriften nichts anderes bestimmt ist, die §§ 244 bis 247 Abs. 1 und 2, §§ 248 bis 253, 255, 256, 265, 266, 268 bis 272, 274, 275, 277 bis 279 Abs. 1, § 280 Abs. 1, §§ 282 und 283 über den Jahresabschluß und die für die Rechtsform und den Geschäftszweig der in den Konzernabschluß einbezogenen Unternehmen mit Sitz im Geltungsbereich dieses Gesetzes geltenden Vorschriften, soweit sie für große Kapitalgesellschaften gelten, entsprechend anzuwenden.

(2) In der Gliederung der Konzernbilanz dürfen die Vorräte in einem Posten zusammengefaßt werden, wenn deren Aufgliederung wegen besonderer Umstände mit einem unverhältnismäßigen Aufwand verbunden wäre.

(3) Der Konzernanhang und der Anhang des Jahresabschlusses des Mutterunternehmens dürfen zusammengefaßt werden. In diesem Falle müssen der Konzernabschluß und der Jahresabschluß des Mutterunternehmens gemeinsam offengelegt werden. Bei Anwendung des Satzes 1 dürfen auch die Prüfungsberichte und die Bestätigungsvermerke jeweils zusammengefaßt werden.

solidated financial statements shall be retained. Deviations from sentence 2 are permissible in exceptional situations. They shall be reported and justified in the consolidated notes. Their effect on the net assets, financing and results of operations of the group of companies shall be reported.

§ 298 Applicable regulations; relief

(1) §§ 244 through 247 Subsections 1 and 2, §§ 248 through 253, 255, 256, 265, 266, 268 through 272, 274, 275, 277 through 279 Subsection 1, § 280 Subsection 1, §§ 282 and 283 on the annual financial statements and the regulations applicable to the legal form and lines of business of enterprises included in the consolidated financial statements domiciled in the geographical area of this law's applicability apply analogously to the consolidated financial statements to the extent that they apply to large companies, unless its special characteristics require a deviation or the preceding provisions provide otherwise.

(2) In the classification of the consolidated balance sheet, items in inventory may be incorporated into one entry if breaking them down would involve disproportionate expense and effort because of special circumstances.

(3) The consolidated notes and the notes of the parent's annual financial statements may be combined. In this case, the consolidated financial statements and the parent's financial statements must be disclosed together. Upon application of sentence 1, the auditing reports and the certification of the annual financial statements may each be combined.

§ 299 Stichtag für die Aufstellung

(1) Der Konzernabschluß ist auf den Stichtag des Jahresabschlusses des Mutterunternehmens aufzustellen.

(2) Die Jahresabschlüsse der in den Konzernabschluß einbezogenen Unternehmen sollen auf den Stichtag des Konzernabschlusses aufgestellt werden. Liegt der Abschlußstichtag eines Unternehmens um mehr als drei Monate vor dem Stichtag des Konzernabschlusses, so ist dieses Unternehmen auf Grund eines auf den Stichtag und den Zeitraum des Konzernabschlusses aufgestellten Zwischenabschlusses in den Konzernabschluß einzubeziehen.

(3) Wird bei abweichenden Abschlußstichtagen ein Unternehmen nicht auf der Grundlage eines auf den Stichtag und den Zeitraum des Konzernabschlusses aufgestellten Zwischenabschlusses in den Konzernabschluß einbezogen, so sind Vorgänge von besonderer Bedeutung für die Vermögens-, Finanz- und Ertragslage eines in den Konzernabschluß einbezogenen Unternehmens, die zwischen dem Abschlußstichtag dieses Unternehmens und dem Abschlußstichtag des Konzernabschlusses eingetreten sind, in der Konzernbilanz und der Konzern-Gewinn- und Verlustrechnung zu berücksichtigen oder im Konzernanhang anzugeben.

§ 299 Closing day for the preparation

(1) The consolidated financial statements shall be prepared as of the close of the fiscal year of the parent.

(2) The annual financial statements of the enterprises included in the consolidated financial statements should be prepared on the close of the fiscal year of the consolidated financial statements. If an enterprise's close of the fiscal year is more than three months before the close of the fiscal year of the consolidated financial statements, then this enterprise shall be included in the consolidated financial statements on the basis of interim financial statements prepared for the close of the fiscal year and the time period of the consolidated financial statements.

(3) If an enterprise with a different close of the fiscal year is not included in the consolidated financial statements on the basis of interim financial statements prepared for the close of the fiscal year and the time period of the consolidated financial statements, then the transactions of substantial importance for net assets, financing and results of operations of an enterprise included in the consolidated financial statements, which took place between the close of the fiscal year of this enterprise and the close of the fiscal year of the consolidated financial statements, shall be taken into account in the consolidated balance sheet and the consolidated profit and loss statement and reported in the consolidated notes.

§ 300

Vierter Titel. Vollkonsolidierung

§ 300 Konsolidierungsgrundsätze. Vollständigkeitsgebot

(1) In dem Konzernabschluß ist der Jahresabschluß des Mutterunternehmens mit den Jahresabschlüssen der Tochterunternehmen zusammenzufassen. An die Stelle der dem Mutterunternehmen gehörenden Anteile an den einbezogenen Tochterunternehmen treten die Vermögensgegenstände, Schulden, Rechnungsabgrenzungsposten, Bilanzierungshilfen und Sonderposten der Tochterunternehmen, soweit sie nach dem Recht des Mutterunternehmens bilanzierungsfähig sind und die Eigenart des Konzernabschlusses keine Abweichungen bedingt oder in den folgenden Vorschriften nichts anderes bestimmt ist.

(2) Die Vermögensgegenstände, Schulden und Rechnungsabgrenzungsposten sowie die Erträge und Aufwendungen der in den Konzernabschluß einbezogenen Unternehmen sind unabhängig von ihrer Berücksichtigung in den Jahresabschlüssen dieser Unternehmen vollständig aufzunehmen, soweit nach dem Recht des Mutterunternehmens nicht ein Bilanzierungsverbot oder ein Bilanzierungswahlrecht besteht. Nach dem Recht des Mutterunternehmens zulässige Bilanzierungswahlrechte dürfen im Konzernabschluß unabhängig von ihrer Ausübung in den Jahresabschlüssen der in den Konzernabschluß einbezogenen Unternehmen ausgeübt werden. Ansätze, die auf der Anwendung von für Kreditinstitute oder Versicherungsunternehmen wegen der Besonderheiten des Geschäftszweigs geltenden Vorschriften beruhen, dürfen beibehalten

Fourth Title. Full Consolidation

§ 300 Principles of consolidation; requirement of completeness

(1) In the consolidated financial statements, the parent's annual financial statements shall be combined with the subsidiaries' annual financial statements. In place of the shares in the included subsidiaries belonging to the parent, the assets, liabilities, accrued and deferred items, aids in formulating the balance sheet and special entries of the subsidiaries shall be entered to the extent that they are capable of being included in the balance sheet pursuant to the law applicable to the parent and to the extent that special characteristics of the consolidated financial statements do not require any deviations or the following regulations do not provide to the contrary.

(2) The assets, liabilities and accrued and deferred items as well as the revenues and expenses of the enterprises included in the consolidated financial statements shall be included in full regardless of their being taken into account in the annual financial statements of these enterprises to the extent that pursuant to the law applicable to the parent, a prohibition of inclusion in the balance sheet or an optional accounting treatment does not exist. Optional accounting treatments permitted pursuant to the law applicable to the parent may be exercised in the consolidated financial statements regardless of their use in the annual financial statements of the enterprises included in the consolidated financial statements. Book values based on the application of provisions applying to credit institutions or insurance companies because of the

werden; auf die Anwendung dieser Ausnahme ist im Konzernanhang hinzuweisen.

§ 301 Kapitalkonsolidierung

(1) Der Wertansatz der dem Mutterunternehmen gehörenden Anteile an einem in den Konzernabschluß einbezogenen Tochterunternehmen wird mit dem auf diese Anteile entfallenden Betrag des Eigenkapitals des Tochterunternehmens verrechnet. Das Eigenkapital ist anzusetzen

1. entweder mit dem Betrag, der dem Buchwert der in den Konzernabschluß aufzunehmenden Vermögensgegenstände, Schulden, Rechnungsabgrenzungsposten, Bilanzierungshilfen und Sonderposten, gegebenenfalls nach Anpassung der Wertansätze nach § 308 Abs. 2, entspricht, oder

2. mit dem Betrag, der dem Wert der in den Konzernabschluß aufzunehmenden Vermögensgegenstände, Schulden, Rechnungsabgrenzungsposten, Bilanzierungshilfen und Sonderposten entspricht, der diesen an dem für die Verrechnung nach Absatz 2 gewählten Zeitpunkt beizulegen ist.

Bei Ansatz mit dem Buchwert nach Satz 2 Nr. 1 ist ein sich ergebender Unterschiedsbetrag den Wertansätzen von in der Konzernbilanz anzusetzenden Vermögensgegenständen und Schulden des jeweiligen Tochterunternehmens insoweit zuzuschreiben oder mit diesen zu verrechnen, als deren Wert höher oder niedriger ist als der bisherige Wertansatz. Die angewandte Methode ist im Konzernanhang anzugeben.

special characteristics of the line of business can be kept; the consolidated notes shall indicate the application of this exception.

§ 301 Capital consolidation

(1) The valuation of the shares belonging to the parent of a subsidiary included in the consolidated financial statements shall be charged against the amount attributable to these shares in the shareholder's equity of the subsidiary. The shareholder's equity shall be established either

1. at the amount that corresponds to the book value of the assets, debts, accrued and deferred items, aids in formulating the balance sheet and special entries included in the consolidated financial statements, where appropriate after adjustments in the valuations pursuant to § 308 Subsection 2, or

2. at the amount that corresponds to the value of the assets, debts, accrued and deferred items, aids in formulating the balance sheet and special entries included in the consolidated financial statements, which amount shall be allocated to these items at the point in time elected for the setoff pursuant to Subsection 2.

Upon electing the book value pursuant to sentence 2 No. 1, any resultant difference in amounts shall be credited to or set off against the valuation of the assets or debts established in the consolidated balance sheet of the respective subsidiary to the extent that their value is higher or lower than the previous valuation. The method used shall be reported in the consolidated notes.

(2) Die Verrechnung nach Absatz 1 wird auf der Grundlage der Wertansätze zum Zeitpunkt des Erwerbs der Anteile oder der erstmaligen Einbeziehung des Tochterunternehmens in den Konzernabschluß oder, beim Erwerb der Anteile zu verschiedenen Zeitpunkten, zu dem Zeitpunkt, zu dem das Unternehmen Tochterunternehmen geworden ist, durchgeführt. Der gewählte Zeitpunkt ist im Konzernanhang anzugeben.

(3) Ein bei der Verrechnung nach Absatz 1 Satz 2 Nr. 2 entstehender oder ein nach Zuschreibung oder Verrechnung nach Absatz 1 Satz 3 verbleibender Unterschiedsbetrag ist in der Konzernbilanz, wenn er auf der Aktivseite entsteht, als Geschäfts- oder Firmenwert und, wenn er auf der Passivseite entsteht, als Unterschiedsbetrag aus der Kapitalkonsolidierung auszuweisen. Der Posten und wesentliche Änderungen gegenüber dem Vorjahr sind im Anhang zu erläutern. Werden Unterschiedsbeträge der Aktivseite mit solchen der Passivseite verrechnet, so sind die verrechneten Beträge im Anhang anzugeben.

(4) Absatz 1 ist nicht auf Anteile an dem Mutterunternehmen anzuwenden, die dem Mutterunternehmen oder einem in den Konzernabschluß einbezogenen Tochterunternehmen gehören. Solche Anteile sind der Konzernbilanz als eigene Anteile im Umlaufvermögen gesondert auszuweisen.

§ 302 Kapitalkonsolidierung bei Interessenzusammenführung

(1) Ein Mutterunternehmen darf die in § 301 Abs. 1 vorgeschriebene Verrechnung der Anteile unter den folgenden Voraussetzungen auf das gezeichnete Kapital des Tochterunternehmens beschränken:

(2) The setoff pursuant to Subsection 1 will be carried out on the basis of the valuation at the time of the purchase of the shares or the first inclusion of the subsidiary in the consolidated financial statements, or, with the purchase of shares at different times, at the time when the enterprise became a subsidiary. The point in time chosen shall be reported in the consolidated notes.

(3) A difference in amounts arising out of the setoff pursuant to Subsection 1 sentence 2 No. 2 or remaining after the attribution or setoff pursuant to Subsection 1 sentence 3 shall be shown in the consolidated balance sheet as goodwill if arising on the assets side and as a difference in amounts from the capital consolidation if arising on the liabilities side. This entry and material changes from the previous year shall be discussed in the notes. If differences in amounts on the assets side are set off against such differences on the liabilities side, then the amounts set off shall be reported in the notes.

(4) Subsection 1 shall not apply to shares in the parent that belong to the parent or a subsidiary included in the consolidated financial statements. Such shares shall be shown separately on the consolidated balance sheet as treasury shares under current assets.

§ 302 Capital consolidation using the pooling-of-interest method

(1) A parent may limit the setoff of shares, prescribed in § 301 Subsection 1, to the subscribed capital of the subsidiary under the following conditions:

1. die zu verrechnenden Anteile betragen mindestens neunzig vom Hundert des Nennbetrags oder, falls ein Nennbetrag nicht vorhanden ist, des rechnerischen Wertes der Anteile des Tochterunternehmens, die nicht eigene Anteile sind,
2. die Anteile sind auf Grund einer Vereinbarung erworben worden, die die Ausgabe von Anteilen eines in den Konzernabschluß einbezogenen Unternehmens vorsieht, und
3. eine in der Vereinbarung vorgesehene Barzahlung übersteigt nicht zehn vom Hundert des Nennbetrags oder, falls ein Nennbetrag nicht vorhanden ist, des rechnerischen Wertes der ausgegebenen Anteile.

(2) Ein sich nach Absatz 1 ergebender Unterschiedsbetrag ist, wenn er auf der Aktivseite entsteht, mit den Rücklagen zu verrechnen oder, wenn er auf der Passivseite entsteht, den Rücklagen hinzuzurechnen.

(3) Die Anwendung der Methode nach Absatz 1 und die sich daraus ergebenden Veränderungen der Rücklagen sowie Name und Sitz des Unternehmens sind im Konzernanhang anzugeben.

§ 303 Schuldenkonsolidierung

(1) Ausleihungen und andere Forderungen, Rückstellungen und Verbindlichkeiten zwischen den in den Konzernabschluß einbezogenen Unternehmen sowie entsprechende Rechnungsabgrenzungsposten sind wegzulassen.

(2) Absatz 1 braucht nicht angewendet zu werden, wenn die wegzulassenden Beträge für die Vermittlung eines den tatsächlichen Verhältnissen entsprechenden Bildes der Vermögens-, Finanz- und Ertragslage des Konzerns nur von untergeordneter Bedeutung sind.

1. the shares to be set off amount to at least ninety percent of the nominal value, or if a nominal value is not available, of the calculated value of the shares of the subsidiary that are not treasury shares,
2. the shares were purchased on the basis of an agreement that provided for the issuance of shares of an enterprise included in the consolidated financial statements, and
3. a cash payment provided for in the agreement does not exceed ten percent of the nominal value, or if a nominal value is not available, the calculated value of the issued shares.

(2) A difference in amounts resulting from Subsection 1 shall be set off against reserves if it arises on the assets side, or credited to reserves if it arises on the liabilities side.

(3) The use of the method pursuant to Subsection 1 and the changes in reserves resulting therefrom, as well as the enterprise's name and domicile, shall be reported in the consolidated notes.

§ 303 Debt consolidation

(1) Loans and other claims, accruals and liabilities between enterprises included in the consolidated financial statements as well as corresponding accrued and deferred items shall be omitted.

(2) Subsection 1 need not be applied if the amounts to be omitted are of only minor importance for presentation of a factually accurate picture of the net assets, financing and results of operations of the group of companies.

§ 304 Behandlung der Zwischenergebnisse

(1) In den Konzernabschluß zu übernehmende Vermögensgegenstände, die ganz oder teilweise auf Lieferungen oder Leistungen zwischen in den Konzernabschluß einbezogenen Unternehmen beruhen, sind in der Konzernbilanz mit einem Betrag anzusetzen, zu dem sie in der auf den Stichtag des Konzernabschlusses aufgestellten Jahresbilanz dieses Unternehmens angesetzt werden könnten, wenn die in den Konzernabschluß einbezogenen Unternehmen auch rechtlich ein einziges Unternehmen bilden würden.

(2) Absatz 1 braucht nicht angewendet zu werden, wenn die Behandlung der Zwischenergebnisse nach Absatz 1 für die Vermittlung eines den tatsächlichen Verhältnissen entsprechenden Bildes der Vermögens-, Finanz- und Ertragslage des Konzerns nur von untergeordneter Bedeutung ist.

§ 305 Aufwands- und Ertragskonsolidierung

(1) In der Konzern-Gewinn- und Verlustrechnung sind

1. bei den Umsatzerlösen, die Erlöse aus Lieferungen und Leistungen zwischen den in den Konzernabschluß einbezogenen Unternehmen mit den auf sie entfallenden Aufwendungen zu verrechnen, soweit sie nicht als Erhöhung des Bestands an fertigen und unfertigen Erzeugnissen oder als andere aktivierte Eigenleistungen auszuweisen sind,

2. andere Erträge aus Lieferungen und Leistungen zwischen den in den Konzernabschluß einbezogenen

§ 304 Treatment of interim results

(1) The assets to be included in the consolidated financial statements that involve in whole or in part deliveries or services between enterprises included in the consolidated financial statements shall be fixed in the consolidated balance sheet at an amount at which they could be set in this enterprise's annual balance sheet prepared for the close of the fiscal year of the consolidated financial statements if the enterprises included in the consolidated financial statements formed a single legal enterprise.

(2) Subsection 1 need not be applied if the treatment of the interim results pursuant to Subsection 1 is of only minor importance for conveying a factually accurate picture of the net assets, financing and results of operations of the group of companies.

§ 305 Consolidation of expenses and revenues

(1) In the consolidated profit and loss statement

1. in sales revenues, the proceeds from deliveries and services between enterprises included in the consolidated financial statements shall be set off against the corresponding expenses to the extent that they are not shown as increases in the inventory of finished products and work-in-progress or as other capitalized company-manufactured fixed assets and supplies, and

2. other revenues from deliveries and services between enterprises included in the consolidated financial

Unternehmen mit den auf sie entfallenden Aufwendungen zu verrechnen, soweit sie nicht als andere aktivierte Eigenleistungen auszuweisen sind.

(2) Aufwendungen und Erträge brauchen nach Absatz 1 nicht weggelassen zu werden, wenn die wegzulassenden Beträge für die Vermittlung eines den tatsächlichen Verhältnissen entsprechenden Bildes der Vermögens-, Finanz- und Ertragslage des Konzerns nur von untergeordneter Bedeutung sind.

§ 306 Steuerabgrenzung

Ist das im Konzernabschluß ausgewiesene Jahresergebnis auf Grund von Maßnahmen, die nach den Vorschriften dieses Titels durchgeführt worden sind, niedriger oder höher als die Summe der Einzelergebnisse der in den Konzernabschluß einbezogenen Unternehmen, so ist der sich für das Geschäftsjahr und frühere Geschäftsjahre ergebende Steueraufwand, wenn er im Verhältnis zum Jahresergebnis zu hoch ist, durch Bildung eines Abgrenzungspostens auf der Aktivseite oder, wenn er im Verhältnis zum Jahresergebnis zu niedrig ist, durch Bildung einer Rückstellung nach § 249 Abs. 1 Satz 1 anzupassen, soweit sich der zu hohe oder der zu niedrige Steueraufwand in späteren Geschäftsjahren voraussichtlich ausgleicht. Der Posten ist in der Konzernbilanz oder im Konzernanhang gesondert anzugeben. Er darf mit den Posten nach § 274 zusammengefaßt werden.

§ 307 Anteile anderer Gesellschafter

(1) In der Konzernbilanz ist für nicht dem Mutterunternehmen gehörende Anteile an in den Konzernabschluß

statements shall be set off against the corresponding expenses to the extent that they are not shown as other capitalized company-manufactured fixed assets and supplies.

(2) Expenses and revenues need not be omitted pursuant to Subsection 1 if the amounts to be omitted are of minor importance for conveying a factually accurate picture of the net assets, financing and results of operations of the group of companies.

§ 306 Tax deferral

If the annual results shown in the consolidated financial statements are lower or higher than the sum of the individual results of the enterprises included in the consolidated financial statements because of measures that were taken pursuant to this Title's regulations, then the tax expenses resulting from the fiscal year or preceding fiscal years shall be adjusted by making a deferral on the assets side if they are too high in relation to the annual results or by making an accrual pursuant to § 249 Subsection 1 sentence 1 if they are too low in relation to the annual results, to the extent that the tax expenses, which are either too high or too low, are expected to be offset in later fiscal years. The entry shall be shown separately on the consolidated balance sheet or in the consolidated notes. It may be combined with the entries pursuant to § 274.

§ 307 Shares of other shareholders

(1) For shares not belonging to the parent in subsidiaries included in the consolidated financial statements, the

einbezogenen Tochterunternehmen ein Ausgleichsposten für die Anteile der anderen Gesellschafter in Höhe ihres Anteils am Eigenkapital unter entsprechender Bezeichnung innerhalb des Eigenkapitals gesondert auszuweisen. In den Ausgleichsposten sind auch die Beträge einzubeziehen, die bei Anwendung der Kapitalkonsolidierungsmethode nach § 301 Abs. 1 Satz 2 Nr. 2 dem Anteil der anderen Gesellschafter am Eigenkapital entsprechen.

(2) In der Konzern-Gewinn- und Verlustrechnung ist der im Jahresergebnis enthaltene, anderen Gesellschaftern zustehende Gewinn und der auf sie entfallende Verlust nach dem Posten „Jahresüberschuß/Jahresfehlbetrag" unter entsprechender Bezeichnung gesondert auszuweisen.

Fünfter Titel. Bewertungsvorschriften

§ 308 Einheitliche Bewertung

(1) Die in den Konzernabschluß nach § 300 Abs. 2 übernommenen Vermögensgegenstände und Schulden der in den Konzernabschluß einbezogenen Unternehmen sind nach den auf den Jahresabschluß des Mutterunternehmens anwendbaren Bewertungsmethoden einheitlich zu bewerten. Nach dem Recht des Mutterunternehmens zulässige Bewertungswahlrechte können im Konzernabschluß unabhängig von ihrer Ausübung in den Jahresabschlüssen der in den Konzernabschluß einbezogenen Unternehmen ausgeübt werden. Abweichungen von den auf den Jahresabschluß des Mutterunternehmens angewandten Bewertungsmethoden sind im Konzernanhang anzugeben und zu begründen.

consolidated balance sheet shall show separately with an appropriate designation within shareholder's equity an adjusting entry for the shares of the other shareholders in the amount of their shares in the shareholder's equity. The adjusting entries shall also include the amounts that correspond to the shares of the other shareholders in shareholder's equity when using the capital consolidation method pursuant to § 301 Subsection 1 sentence 2 No. 2.

(2) The consolidated profit and loss statement shall show separately in the annual results the profits attributable to other shareholders and the losses applicable to them under the entries "Annual Surplus/Annual Deficit" with an appropriate designation.

Fifth Title. Valuation Regulations

§ 308 Uniform valuation

(1) The assets and liabilities included in the consolidated financial statements pursuant to § 300 Subsection 2 of the enterprises included in the consolidated financial statements shall be valued uniformly according to the valuation methods applicable to the annual financial statements of the parent. Valuation method options permissible pursuant to the law governing the parent may be used in the consolidated financial statements regardless of their use in the annual financial statements of the enterprises included in the consolidated financial statements. Deviations from the valuation methods used in the parent's annual financial statements shall be reported and justified in the consolidated notes.

(2) Sind in den Konzernabschluß aufzunehmende Vermögensgegenstände oder Schulden des Mutterunternehmens oder der Tochterunternehmen in den Jahresabschlüssen dieser Unternehmen nach Methoden bewertet worden, die sich von denen unterscheiden, die auf den Konzernabschluß anzuwenden sind oder die von den gesetzlichen Vertretern des Mutterunternehmens in Ausübung von Bewertungswahlrechten auf den Konzernabschluß angewendet werden, so sind die abweichend bewerteten Vermögensgegenstände oder Schulden nach den auf den Konzernabschluß angewandten Bewertungsmethoden neu zu bewerten und mit den neuen Wertansätzen in den Konzernabschluß zu übernehmen. Wertansätze, die auf der Anwendung von für Kreditinstitute oder Versicherungsunternehmen wegen der Besonderheiten des Geschäftszweigs geltenden Vorschriften beruhen, dürfen beibehalten werden; auf die Anwendung dieser Ausnahme ist im Konzernanhang hinzuweisen. Eine einheitliche Bewertung nach Satz 1 braucht nicht vorgenommen zu werden, wenn ihre Auswirkungen für die Vermittlung eines den tatsächlichen Verhältnissen entsprechenden Bildes der Vermögens-, Finanz- und Ertragslage des Konzerns nur von untergeordneter Bedeutung sind. Darüber hinaus sind Abweichungen in Ausnahmefällen zulässig; sie sind im Konzernanhang anzugeben und zu begründen.

§ 309 Behandlung des Unterschiedsbetrags

(1) Ein nach § 301 Abs. 3 auszuweisender Geschäfts- oder Firmenwert ist in jedem folgenden Geschäftsjahr zu

(2) If assets or liabilities of the parent or the subsidiaries to be included in the consolidated financial statements are assessed in the annual financial statements of these enterprises according to methods that are different from those that must be used in the consolidated financial statements or from those that are used by the parent's legal representatives in carrying out the right to elect a valuation method in the consolidated financial statements, then the differently valued assets or liabilities shall be valued anew according to the valuation methods applied in the consolidated financial statements and shall be adopted with the new valuations in the consolidated financial statements. Valuations that are based on the use of regulations applicable to credit institutions or insurance companies because of the peculiarities of these lines of business may be retained. The use of this exception shall be indicated in the consolidated notes. A uniform valuation pursuant to sentence 1 need not be undertaken if its effect on the communication of a factually accurate picture of the net assets, financing and results of operations of the group of companies is of only minor importance. In addition, deviations in exceptional cases are permissible; they shall be reported and justified in the consolidated notes.

§ 309 Treatment of difference in amounts

(1) A business's goodwill shown pursuant to § 301 Subsection 3 shall be amortized by at least one-fourth in

§§ 309, 310

mindestens einem Viertel durch Abschreibungen zu tilgen. Die Abschreibung des Geschäfts- oder Firmenwerts kann aber auch planmäßig auf die Geschäftsjahre verteilt werden, in denen er voraussichtlich genutzt werden kann. Der Geschäfts- oder Firmenwert darf auch offen mit den Rücklagen verrechnet werden.

(2) Ein nach § 301 Abs. 3 auf der Passivseite auszuweisender Unterschiedsbetrag darf ergebniswirksam nur aufgelöst werden, soweit

1. eine zum Zeitpunkt des Erwerbs der Anteile oder der erstmaligen Konsolidierung erwartete ungünstige Entwicklung der künftigen Ertragslage des Unternehmens eingetreten ist oder zu diesem Zeitpunkt erwartete Aufwendungen zu berücksichtigen sind oder

2. am Abschlußstichtag feststeht, daß er einem realisierten Gewinn entspricht.

Sechster Titel. Anteilmäßige Konsolidierung

§ 310

(1) Führt ein in einen Konzernabschluß einbezogenes Mutter- oder Tochterunternehmen ein anderes Unternehmen gemeinsam mit einem oder mehreren nicht in den Konzernabschluß einbezogenen Unternehmen, so darf das andere Unternehmen in den Konzernabschluß entsprechend den Anteilen am Kapital einbezogen werden, die dem Mutterunternehmen gehören.

(2) Auf die anteilmäßige Konsolidierung sind die §§ 297 bis 301, §§ 303 bis 306, 308, 309 entsprechend anzuwenden.

every subsequent fiscal year. The amortization of the business's goodwill may also be systematically allocated to the fiscal years in which it prospectively can be used. The business's goodwill may also be openly set off against reserves.

(2) A difference in amounts shown on the liabilities side pursuant to § 301 Subsection 3 may be dissolved for profits accumulation only to the extent that

1. an unfavorable development in the future state of the enterprise's revenues anticipated at the time of the purchase of the shares or the first consolidation has occurred, or expenditures anticipated at this point in time must be taken into account, or

2. it is determined on the close of the fiscal year that it corresponds to a realized profit.

Sixth Title. Proportionate Consolidation

§ 310

(1) If a parent or subsidiary included in consolidated financial statements manages another enterprise together with one or more enterprises not included in the consolidated financial statements, then the other enterprise may be included in the consolidated financial statements in proportion to the shares of capital belonging to the parent.

(2) §§ 297 through 301, §§ 303 through 306, 308, and 309 apply analogously to the proportionate consolidation.

Siebenter Titel. Assoziierte Unternehmen

§ 311 Definition. Befreiung

(1) Wird von einem in den Konzernabschluß einbezogenen Unternehmen ein maßgeblicher Einfluß auf die Geschäfts- und Finanzpolitik eines nicht einbezogenen Unternehmens, an dem das Unternehmen nach § 271 Abs. 1 beteiligt ist, ausgeübt (assoziiertes Unternehmen), so ist diese Beteiligung in der Konzernbilanz unter einem besonderen Posten mit entsprechender Bezeichnung auszuweisen. Ein maßgeblicher Einfluß wird vermutet, wenn ein Unternehmen bei einem anderen Unternehmen mindestens den fünften Teil der Stimmrechte der Gesellschafter innehat.

(2) Auf eine Beteiligung an einem assoziierten Unternehmen brauchen Absatz 1 und § 312 nicht angewendet zu werden, wenn die Beteiligung für die Vermittlung eines den tatsächlichen Verhältnissen entsprechenden Bildes der Vermögens-, Finanz- und Ertragslage des Konzerns von untergeordneter Bedeutung ist.

§ 312 Wertansatz der Beteiligung und Behandlung des Unterschiedsbetrags

(1) Eine Beteiligung an einem assoziierten Unternehmen ist in der Konzernbilanz

1. entweder mit dem Buchwert oder
2. mit dem Betrag, der dem anteiligen Eigenkapital des assoziierten Unternehmens entspricht,

anzusetzen. Bei Ansatz mit dem Buchwert nach Satz 1 Nr. 1 ist der Unterschiedsbetrag zwischen diesem Wert und dem anteiligen Eigenkapital

Seventh Title. Associated Enterprises

§ 311 Definition; exemption

(1) If an enterprise included in the consolidated financial statements exercises a controlling influence on the business and financial policies of an enterprise not so included and in which the enterprise participates pursuant to § 271 Subsection 1 (an "associated enterprise"), then this participation shall be shown on the consolidated balance sheet under a special entry with an appropriate designation. A substantial influence is presumed if an enterprise holds at least one-fifth of the shareholders' voting rights in another enterprise.

(2) Subsection 1 and § 312 need not be applied to a participation in an associated enterprise if the participation is of minor importance for conveying a factually accurate picture of the consolidated company's net assets, financing and results of operations.

§ 312 Valuation of the participation and treatment of the difference in amounts

(1) A participation in an associated enterprise shall be fixed in the consolidated balance sheet at either

1. the book value, or
2. the amount that corresponds to the proportionate equity capital of the associated enterprise.

In using the book value pursuant to sentence 1 No. 1, the difference in amounts between this value and the proportion of equity capital of the as-

des assoziierten Unternehmens bei erstmaliger Anwendung an der Konzernbilanz zu vermerken oder im Konzernanhang anzugeben. Bei Ansatz mit dem anteiligen Eigenkapital nach Satz 1 Nr. 2 ist das Eigenkapital mit dem Betrag anzusetzen, der sich ergibt, wenn die Vermögensgegenstände, Schulden, Rechnungsabgrenzungsposten, Bilanzierungshilfen und Sonderposten des assoziierten Unternehmens mit dem Wert angesetzt werden, der ihnen an dem nach Absatz 3 gewählten Zeitpunkt beizulegen ist, jedoch darf dieser Betrag die Anschaffungskosten für die Anteile an dem assoziierten Unternehmen nicht überschreiten; der Unterschiedsbetrag zwischen diesem Wertansatz und dem Buchwert der Beteiligung ist bei erstmaliger Anwendung in der Konzernbilanz gesondert auszuweisen oder im Konzernanhang anzugeben. Die angewandte Methode ist im Konzernanhang anzugeben.

(2) Der Unterschiedsbetrag nach Absatz 1 Satz 2 ist den Wertansätzen von Vermögensgegenständen und Schulden des assoziierten Unternehmens insoweit zuzuordnen, als deren Wert höher oder niedriger ist als der bisherige Wertansatz. Der nach Satz 1 zugeordnete oder der sich nach Absatz 1 Satz 1 Nr. 2 ergebende Betrag ist entsprechend der Behandlung der Wertansätze dieser Vermögensgegenstände und Schulden im Jahresabschluß des assoziierten Unternehmens im Konzernabschluß fortzuführen, abzuschreiben oder aufzulösen. Auf einen nach Zuordnung nach Satz 1 verbleibenden Unterschiedsbetrag und einen Unterschiedsbetrag nach Absatz 1 Satz 3 zweiter Halbsatz ist § 309 entsprechend anzuwenden.

sociated enterprise shall, the first time that it is used, be noted on the consolidated balance sheet or reported in the consolidated notes. In using the proportionate equity capital pursuant to sentence 1 No. 2, the equity capital shall be fixed at the amount that results if the assets, liabilities, deferred and accrued items, aids in formulating the balance sheet and special entries of the associated enterprise are fixed at the value that is attributed to them at the selected time pursuant to Subsection 3; this amount, however, may not exceed the acquisition costs of the shares in the associated enterprise. The difference in amounts between this valuation and the book value of the participation shall be shown separately upon its first use on the consolidated balance sheet or shall be reported in the consolidated notes. The method employed shall be reported in the consolidated notes.

(2) The difference in amounts pursuant to Subsection 1 sentence 2 shall be attributed to the valuations of the assets and liabilities of the associated enterprise to the extent that their value is higher or lower than the present valuation. The amount attributed pursuant to sentence 1 or resulting pursuant to Subsection 1 sentence 1 No. 2 shall be retained, depreciated or dissolved in the consolidated financial statements in conformity with the treatment of the valuation of these assets and liabilities in the associated enterprise's annual financial statements. § 309 shall apply analogously to a difference in amounts remaining after an attribution pursuant to sentence 1 and a difference in amounts pursuant to Subsection 1 sentence 3, second half of the sentence.

Ergänzende Vorschriften für Kapitalgesellschaften § 312

(3) Der Wertansatz der Beteiligung und die Unterschiedsbeträge werden auf der Grundlage der Wertansätze zum Zeitpunkt des Erwerbs der Anteile oder der erstmaligen Einbeziehung des assoziierten Unternehmens in den Konzernabschluß oder beim Erwerb der Anteile zu verschiedenen Zeitpunkten zu dem Zeitpunkt, zu dem das Unternehmen assoziiertes Unternehmen geworden ist, ermittelt. Der gewählte Zeitpunkt ist im Konzernanhang anzugeben.

(4) Der nach Absatz 1 ermittelte Wertansatz einer Beteiligung ist in den Folgejahren um den Betrag der Eigenkapitalveränderungen, die den dem Mutterunternehmen gehörenden Anteilen am Kapital des assoziierten Unternehmens entsprechen, zu erhöhen oder zu vermindern; auf die Beteiligung entfallende Gewinnausschüttungen sind abzusetzen. In der Konzern-Gewinn- und Verlustrechnung ist das auf assoziierte Beteiligungen entfallende Ergebnis unter einem gesonderten Posten auszuweisen.

(5) Wendet das assoziierte Unternehmen in seinem Jahresabschluß vom Konzernabschluß abweichende Bewertungsmethoden an, so können abweichend bewertete Vermögensgegenstände oder Schulden für die Zwecke der Absätze 1 bis 4 nach den auf den Konzernabschluß angewandten Bewertungsmethoden bewertet werden. Wird die Bewertung nicht angepaßt, so ist dies im Konzernanhang anzugeben. § 304 über die Behandlung der Zwischenergebnisse ist entsprechend anzuwenden, soweit die für die Beurteilung maßgeblichen Sachverhalte bekannt oder zugänglich sind. Die Zwischenergebnisse dürfen auch

(3) The valuation of the participation and the difference in amounts will be ascertained on the basis of the valuation at the time of the acquisition of the shares or the first inclusion of the associated enterprises in the consolidated financial statements or, upon acquisition of the shares at different times, at the time at which the enterprise became an associated enterprise. The time chosen shall be reported in the consolidated notes.

(4) The valuation of a participation ascertained pursuant to Subsection 1 shall be increased or decreased in the following years by the amount of the changes in equity capital that corresponds to the shares of capital of the associated enterprise belonging to the parent. Profit distributions allotted to the participation shall be deducted. The results allotted to associated participations shall be shown under a separate entry in the consolidated profit and loss statement.

(5) If the associated enterprise uses valuation methods in its annual financial statements differing from those in the consolidated financial statements, then differently valued assets or liabilities may be valued for the purposes of Subsections 1 through 4 according to the valuation methods used in the consolidated financial statements. If the valuation is not adjusted, then this shall be reported in the consolidated notes. § 304 on the treatment of interim results shall apply analogously to the extent that the facts needed to make the judgment are known or accessible. The interim results may also be omitted in proportion to the shares

anteilig entsprechend den dem Mutterunternehmen gehörenden Anteilen am Kapital des assoziierten Unternehmens weggelassen werden.

(6) Es ist jeweils der letzte Jahresabschluß des assoziierten Unternehmens zugrunde zu legen. Stellt das assoziierte Unternehmen einen Konzernabschluß auf, so ist von diesem und nicht vom Jahresabschluß des assoziierten Unternehmens auszugehen.

in the associated enterprise's capital belonging to the parent.

(6) The basis shall be in each case the associated enterprise's last annual financial statements. If the associated enterprise draws up consolidated financial statements, then these and not the associated enterprise's annual financial statements shall be used.

Achter Titel. Konzernanhang

§ 313 Erläuterung der Konzernbilanz und der Konzern-Gewinn- und Verlustrechnung. Angaben zum Beteiligungsbesitz

(1) In den Konzernanhang sind diejenigen Angaben aufzunehmen, die zu einzelnen Posten der Konzernbilanz oder der Konzern-Gewinn- und Verlustrechnung vorgeschrieben oder die im Konzernanhang zu machen sind, weil sie in Ausübung eines Wahlrechts nicht in die Konzernbilanz oder in die Konzern-Gewinn- und Verlustrechnung aufgenommen wurden. Im Konzernanhang müssen

1. die auf die Posten der Konzernbilanz und der Konzern-Gewinn- und Verlustrechnung angewandten Bilanzierungs- und Bewertungsmethoden angegeben werden;
2. die Grundlagen für die Umrechnung in Euro angegeben werden, sofern der Konzernabschluß Posten enthält, denen Beträge zugrunde liegen, die auf fremde Währung lauten oder ursprünglich auf fremde Währung lauteten;
3. Abweichungen von Bilanzierungs-, Bewertungs- und Konsolidierungsmethoden angegeben und begründet werden; deren Einfluß auf die

Eighth Title. Consolidated Notes

§ 313 Discussion of the consolidated balance sheet and the consolidated profit and loss statement; reports on participations

(1) The consolidated notes shall include that information that is prescribed for particular entries on the consolidated balance sheet or the consolidated profit and loss statement or that is to be made in the consolidated notes because, in the exercise of an option right, it was not included in the consolidated balance sheet or in the consolidated profit and loss statement. The consolidated notes

1. must report the accounting and valuation methods used for the entries on the consolidated balance sheet and the consolidated profit and loss statement;
2. must report the bases for the conversion to Euro to the extent that the consolidated financial statements include entries that are based upon amounts denominated in foreign currency or originally denominated in foreign currency;
3. must report and justify deviations from the accounting, valuation and consolidation methods; their influence upon the net assets, fi-

Vermögens-, Finanz- und Ertragslage des Konzerns ist gesondert darzustellen.

(2) Im Konzernanhang sind außerdem anzugeben:

1. Name und Sitz der in den Konzernabschluß einbezogenen Unternehmen, der Anteil am Kapital der Tochterunternehmen, der dem Mutterunternehmen und den in den Konzernabschluß einbezogenen Tochterunternehmen gehört oder von einer für Rechnung dieser Unternehmen handelnden Person gehalten wird, sowie der zur Einbeziehung in den Konzernabschluß verpflichtende Sachverhalt, sofern die Einbeziehung nicht auf einer der Kapitalbeteiligung entsprechenden Mehrheit der Stimmrechte beruht. Diese Angaben sind auch für Tochterunternehmen zu machen, die nach den §§ 295, 296 nicht einbezogen worden sind;

2. Name und Sitz der assoziierten Unternehmen, der Anteil am Kapital der assoziierten Unternehmen, der dem Mutterunternehmen und den in den Konzernabschluß einbezogenen Tochterunternehmen gehört oder von einer für Rechnung dieser Unternehmen handelnden Person gehalten wird. Die Anwendung des § 311 Abs. 2 ist jeweils anzugeben und zu begründen;

3. Name und Sitz der Unternehmen, die nach § 310 nur anteilmäßig in den Konzernabschluß einbezogen worden sind, der Tatbestand, aus dem sich die Anwendung dieser Vorschrift ergibt, sowie der Anteil am Kapital dieser Unternehmen, der dem Mutterunternehmen und den in den Konzernabschluß einbezogenen Tochterunternehmen ge-

nancing and results of operations of the group of companies shall be indicated separately.

(2) The consolidated notes shall furthermore report:

1. the name and domicile of the enterprises included in the consolidated financial statements, the share in the subsidiaries' capital that belongs to the parent and the subsidiaries included in the consolidated financial statements or is held by a person acting on behalf of these enterprises, as well as the circumstances requiring inclusion in the consolidated financial statements, provided that the inclusion is not based upon a majority of the voting rights corresponding to the capital participation. This information shall also be given for subsidiaries that were not included pursuant to §§ 295 and 296;

2. the name and domicile of associated enterprises, the share in the associated enterprises' capital that belongs to the parent and the subsidiaries included in the consolidated financial statements or is held by a person acting on behalf of these enterprises. The application of § 311 Subsection 2 shall be reported and justified in every case;

3. the name and domicile of the enterprises that were only proportionately included in the consolidated financial statements pursuant to § 310, the circumstances from which the use of this regulation resulted, as well as the share in these enterprises' capital that belongs to the parent or to the subsidiaries included in the consoli-

hört oder von einer für Rechnung dieser Unternehmen handelnden Person gehalten wird;

4. Name und Sitz anderer als der unter den Nummern 1 bis 3 bezeichneten Unternehmen, bei denen das Mutterunternehmen, ein Tochterunternehmen oder eine für Rechnung eines dieser Unternehmen handelnde Person mindestens den fünften Teil der Anteile besitzt, unter Angabe des Anteils am Kapital sowie der Höhe des Eigenkapitals und des Ergebnisses des letzten Geschäftsjahrs, für das ein Abschluß aufgestellt worden ist. Ferner sind anzugeben alle Beteiligungen an großen Kapitalgesellschaften, die andere als die in Nummer 1 bis 3 bezeichneten Unternehmen sind, wenn sie von einem börsennotierten Mutterunternehmen, einem börsennotierten Tochterunternehmen oder einer für Rechnung eines dieser Unternehmen handelnden Person gehalten werden und fünf vom Hundert der Stimmrechte überschreiten. Diese Angaben brauchen nicht gemacht zu werden, wenn sie für die Vermittlung eines den tatsächlichen Verhältnissen entsprechenden Bildes der Vermögens-, Finanz- und Ertragslage des Konzerns von untergeordneter Bedeutung sind. Das Eigenkapital und das Ergebnis brauchen nicht angegeben zu werden, wenn das in Anteilsbesitz stehende Unternehmen seinen Jahresabschluß nicht offenzulegen hat und das Mutterunternehmen, das Tochterunternehmen oder die Person weniger als die Hälfte der Anteile an diesem Unternehmen besitzt.

dated financial statements or is held by a person acting on behalf of these enterprises;

4. the name and domicile of enterprises other than those designated under Nos. 1 through 3 in which the parent, a subsidiary or a person acting on behalf of one of these enterprises possesses at least one-fifth of the shares, specifying the shares in capital as well as the amount of the equity capital and the results of the preceding fiscal year for which financial statements were prepared. In addition, all participations in large corporations which are not the same as those enterprises designated in Nos. 1 through 3 must be reported if they are held by a parent listed on an exchange, a subsidiary listed on an exchange or a person acting on behalf of such enterprises and exceed five percent of the voting rights. These specifications need not be made if they are of minor importance for presenting a factually accurate picture of the consolidated company's net assets, financing and results of operations. The equity capital and the results need not be reported if the enterprise whose shares are owned does not have to disclose its annual financial statements and the parent, the subsidiary or the person owns less than one-half of this enterprise's shares.

(3) Die in Absatz 2 verlangten Angaben brauchen insoweit nicht gemacht zu werden, als nach vernünftiger kaufmännischer Beurteilung damit gerechnet werden muß, daß durch die Angaben dem Mutterunternehmen, einem Tochterunternehmen oder einem anderen in Absatz 2 bezeichneten Unternehmen erhebliche Nachteile entstehen können. Die Anwendung der Ausnahmeregelung ist im Konzernanhang anzugeben. Satz 1 gilt nicht, wenn ein Mutterunternehmen einen organisierten Markt im Sinne des § 2 Abs. 5 des Wertpapierhandelsgesetzes durch von ihm oder einem seiner Tochterunternehmen ausgegebene Wertpapiere im Sinne des § 2 Abs. 1 Satz 1 des Wertpapierhandelsgesetzes in Anspruch nimmt oder wenn die Zulassung solcher Wertpapiere zum Handel an einem organisierten Markt beantragt worden ist.

(4) Die in Absatz 2 verlangten Angaben dürfen statt im Anhang auch in einer Aufstellung des Anteilsbesitzes gesondert gemacht werden. Die Aufstellung ist Bestandteil des Anhangs. Auf die besondere Aufstellung des Anteilsbesitzes und den Ort ihrer Hinterlegung ist im Anhang hinzuweisen.

§ 314 Sonstige Pflichtangaben

(1) Im Konzernanhang sind ferner anzugeben:

1. der Gesamtbetrag der in der Konzernbilanz ausgewiesenen Verbindlichkeiten mit einer Restlaufzeit von mehr als fünf Jahren sowie der Gesamtbetrag der in der Konzernbilanz ausgewiesenen Verbindlichkeiten, die von in den Konzernabschluß einbezogenen Unternehmen durch Pfandrechte oder

(3) The information required pursuant to Subsection 2 need not be disclosed if according to reasonable business judgment one would expect that such information can cause substantial harm to the parent, the subsidiary or another enterprise designated in Subsection 2. The use of this exception provision shall be reported in the consolidated notes. Sentence 1 shall not apply if the parent makes use of an organized market within the meaning of § 2 Subsection 5 of the Securities Trading Act (*Wertpapierhandelsgesetz*) for securities within the meaning of § 2 Subsection 1 sentence 1 of the Securities Trading Act issued by it or of its subsidiaries or if an application has been filed for the admission of such securities to trading on an organized market.

(4) The information required pursuant to Subsection 2 may also be disclosed separately in a list of the share ownership instead of in the notes. The list shall be a part of the notes. The notes shall indicate the special list of the share ownership and the place of its filing.

§ 314 Other mandatory disclosures

(1) The consolidated notes shall report further:

1. the total amount of liabilities shown in the consolidated balance sheet with a remaining term of more than five years as well as the total amount of liabilities shown in the consolidated balance sheet that are secured by liens or similar rights by enterprises included in the consolidated financial state-

ähnliche Rechte gesichert sind, unter Angabe von Art und Form der Sicherheiten;

2. der Gesamtbetrag der sonstigen finanziellen Verpflichtungen, die nicht in der Konzernbilanz erscheinen oder nicht nach § 298 Abs. 1 in Verbindung mit § 251 anzugeben sind, sofern diese Angabe für die Beurteilung der Finanzlage des Konzerns von Bedeutung ist; davon und von den Haftungsverhältnissen nach § 251 sind Verpflichtungen gegenüber Tochterunternehmen, die nicht in den Konzernabschluß einbezogen werden, jeweils gesondert anzugeben;

3. die Aufgliederung der Umsatzerlöse nach Tätigkeitsbereichen sowie nach geographisch bestimmten Märkten, soweit sich, unter Berücksichtigung der Organisation des Verkaufs von für die gewöhnliche Geschäftstätigkeit des Konzerns typischen Erzeugnissen und der für die gewöhnliche Geschäftstätigkeit des Konzerns typischen Dienstleistungen, die Tätigkeitsbereiche und geographisch bestimmten Märkte untereinander erheblich unterscheiden;

4. die durchschnittliche Zahl der Arbeitnehmer der in den Konzernabschluß einbezogenen Unternehmen während des Geschäftsjahrs, getrennt nach Gruppen, sowie der in dem Geschäftsjahr verursachte Personalaufwand, sofern er nicht gesondert in der Konzern-Gewinn- und Verlustrechnung ausgewiesen ist; die durchschnittliche Zahl der Arbeitnehmer von nach § 310 nur anteilmäßig einbezogenen Unternehmen ist gesondert anzugeben;

ments, specifying the type and form of the security interests;

2. the total amount of other financial obligations that do not appear in the consolidated balance sheet or are not reported pursuant to § 298 Subsection 1 in connection with § 251, to the extent that these reports are important for evaluating the financial state of the group of companies. Of these and of the contingencies and commitments pursuant to § 251, obligations to subsidiaries that are not included in the consolidated financial statements shall be reported separately in every case;

3. the classification of the sales volume according to lines of business as well as geographically determined markets to the extent that the lines of business and geographically determined markets differ considerably from one another with regard to the sales organization of the typical products and the typical services of the usual business of the group of companies;

4. the average number of employees of the enterprises included in the consolidated financial statements during the fiscal year, separated according to groups, as well as personnel expenses incurred during the fiscal year to the extent that it is not shown separately in the consolidated profit and loss statement. The average number of employees of enterprises included only proportionately pursuant to § 310 shall be reported separately;

Ergänzende Vorschriften für Kapitalgesellschaften § 314

5 (aufgehoben)

6. für die Mitglieder des Geschäftsführungsorgans, eines Aufsichtsrats, eines Beirats oder einer ähnlichen Einrichtung des Mutterunternehmens, jeweils für jede Personengruppe:

 a) die für die Wahrnehmung ihrer Aufgaben im Mutterunternehmen und den Tochterunternehmen im Geschäftsjahr gewährten Gesamtbezüge (Gehälter, Gewinnbeteiligungen, Bezugsrechte und sonstige aktienbasierte Vergütungen, Aufwandsentschädigungen, Versicherungsentgelte, Provisionen und Nebenleistungen jeder Art). In die Gesamtbezüge sind auch Bezüge einzurechnen, die nicht ausgezahlt, sondern in Ansprüche anderer Art umgewandelt oder zur Erhöhung anderer Ansprüche verwendet werden. Außer den Bezügen für das Geschäftsjahr sind die weiteren Bezüge anzugeben, die im Geschäftsjahr gewährt, bisher aber in keinem Konzernabschluß angegeben worden sind;

 b) die für die Wahrnehmung ihrer Aufgaben im Mutterunternehmen und den Tochterunternehmen gewährten Gesamtbezüge (Abfindungen, Ruhegehälter, Hinterbliebenenbezüge und Leistungen verwandter Art) der früheren Mitglieder der bezeichneten Organe und ihrer Hinterbliebenen; Buchstabe a Satz 2 und 3 ist entsprechend anzuwenden. Ferner ist der Betrag der für diese Personengruppe gebildeten Rückstellungen für laufende Pensionen und

5. (repealed)

6. for members of the business management organ, a supervisory board, an advisory board or a similar body of the parent, separately by each group of persons:

 a) total remuneration (salaries, profit participations, subscription rights and other stock based compensation, reimbursement of expenses, insurance payments, commissions and fringe benefits of every kind) granted for the performance of their duties in the parent and subsidiaries during the fiscal year. Total remuneration shall also include such remuneration that is not paid out but converted into claims of another type or used to increase other claims. Besides the remuneration for the fiscal year, further remuneration shall be reported that was granted in the fiscal year but was not yet reported in any consolidated financial statements;

 b) the total remuneration (severance pay, pensions, survivors' benefits and similar payments) that was granted to former members of the organs described for the performance of duties in the parent and subsidiaries and to their survivors. Letter a sentences 2 and 3 shall apply analogously. Furthermore, the amount of the accruals set up for these groups of persons for current pensions and expectancies of pensions and the amount of accruals which have

225

§§ 314, 315   Handelsbücher

Anwartschaften auf Pensionen und der Betrag der für diese Verpflichtungen nicht gebildeten Rückstellungen anzugeben;

c) die vom Mutterunternehmen und den Tochterunternehmen gewährten Vorschüsse und Kredite unter Angabe der Zinssätze, der wesentlichen Bedingungen und der gegebenenfalls im Geschäftsjahr zurückgezahlten Beträge sowie die zugunsten dieser Personengruppen eingegangenen Haftungsverhältnisse;

7. der Bestand an Anteilen an dem Mutterunternehmen, die das Mutterunternehmen oder ein Tochterunternehmen oder ein anderer für Rechnung eines in den Konzernabschluß einbezogenen Unternehmens erworben oder als Pfand genommen hat; dabei sind die Zahl und der Nennbetrag oder rechnerische Wert dieser Anteile sowie deren Anteil am Kapital anzugeben;

8. für jedes in den Konzernabschluss einbezogene börsennotierte Unternehmen, dass die nach § 161 des Aktiengesetzes vorgeschriebene Erklärung abgegeben und den Aktionären zugänglich gemacht worden ist.

(2) Mutterunternehmen, die den Konzernabschluss um eine Segmentberichterstattung gemäß § 297 Abs. 1 zu erweitern haben oder dies freiwillig tun, sind von der Angabepflicht gemäß § 314 Abs. 1 Nr. 3 befreit.

Neunter Titel. Konzernlagebericht

§ 315

(1) Im Konzernlagebericht sind zumindest der Geschäftsverlauf und die Lage des Konzerns so darzustellen,

not been set up for these obligations shall be reported;

c) the advances and credits granted by the parent and the subsidiaries specifying the interest rates, the material conditions and, where applicable, the amounts paid back in the fiscal year as well as the contingencies and commitments entered into for the benefit of these groups of persons;

7. the amount of shares in the parent purchased by or taken as security by the parent or a subsidiary or a third party for the account of another enterprise included in the consolidated financial statements; the number and face value of these shares as well as their share in the capital shall be reported along with the above;

8. For each quoted company included in the consolidated financial statements that the statement required under § 161 of the Stock Corporation Act (*Aktiengesetz*) has been made and has been made available to the shareholders.

(2) Parents which have to include a market segment report in the consolidated financial statements pursuant to § 297 Subsection 1 or do so voluntarily are exempted from the disclosure pursuant to § 314 Subsection 1 No. 3

Ninth Title. Consolidated Management Report

§ 315

(1) The consolidated management report shall at least present the course of business and the state of the group of

daß ein den tatsächlichen Verhältnissen entsprechendes Bild vermittelt wird; dabei ist auch auf die Risiken der künftigen Entwicklung einzugehen.

(2) Der Konzernlagebericht soll auch eingehen auf:

1. Vorgänge von besonderer Bedeutung, die nach dem Schluß des Konzerngeschäftsjahrs eingetreten sind;
2. die voraussichtliche Entwicklung des Konzerns;
3. den Bereich Forschung und Entwicklung des Konzerns.

(3) § 298 Abs. 3 über die Zusammenfassung von Konzernanhang und Anhang ist entsprechend anzuwenden.

Dritter Unterabschnitt. Prüfung

§ 316 Pflicht zur Prüfung

(1) Der Jahresabschluß und der Lagebericht von Kapitalgesellschaften, die nicht kleine im Sinne des § 267 Abs. 1 sind, sind durch einen Abschlußprüfer zu prüfen. Hat keine Prüfung stattgefunden, so kann der Jahresabschluß nicht festgestellt werden.

(2) Der Konzernabschluß und der Konzernlagebericht von Kapitalgesellschaften sind durch einen Abschlußprüfer zu prüfen. Hat keine Prüfung stattgefunden, so kann der Konzernabschluss nicht gebilligt werden.

(3) Werden der Jahresabschluß, der Konzernabschluß, der Lagebericht oder der Konzernlagebericht nach Vorlage des Prüfungsberichts geändert, so hat der Abschlußprüfer diese Unterlagen erneut zu prüfen, soweit es die Änderung erfordert. Über das Ergebnis der Prüfung ist zu berichten;

companies so that a factually accurate picture is presented. The risks of the future developments shall be dealt with as well.

(2) The consolidated management report should also go into:

1. events of special importance that took place after the close of the group of companies' fiscal year;
2. the anticipated development of the group of companies;
3. the research and development field of the group of companies.

(3) § 298 Subsection 3 on the summary of the consolidated notes and the notes shall apply analogously.

Third Subpart. Audit

§ 316 Duty to audit

(1) The annual financial statements and the management report of companies, which are not small within the meaning of § 267 Subsection 1, shall be examined by an auditor. If no examination has taken place, then the annual financial statements cannot be adopted.

(2) The consolidated financial statements and consolidated management report of companies shall be examined by an auditor. If no examination has been made, then the consolidated financial statements can not be approved.

(3) If the annual financial statements, consolidated financial statements, management report or consolidated management report is changed after the presentation of the accountant's report, then the auditor shall examine these records again to the extent that the changes require. The results of the

der Bestätigungsvermerk ist entsprechend zu ergänzen.

§ 317 Gegenstand und Umfang der Prüfung

(1) In die Prüfung des Jahresabschlusses ist die Buchführung einzubeziehen. Die Prüfung des Jahresabschlusses und des Konzernabschlusses hat sich darauf zu erstrecken, ob die gesetzlichen Vorschriften und sie ergänzende Bestimmungen des Gesellschaftsvertrags oder der Satzung beachtet worden sind. Die Prüfung ist so anzulegen, daß Unrichtigkeiten und Verstöße gegen die in Satz 2 aufgeführten Bestimmungen, die sich auf die Darstellung des sich nach § 264 Abs. 2 ergebenden Bildes der Vermögens-, Finanz- und Ertragslage des Unternehmens wesentlich auswirken, bei gewissenhafter Berufsausübung erkannt werden.

(2) Der Lagebericht und der Konzernlagebericht sind darauf zu prüfen, ob der Lagebericht mit dem Jahresabschluß und der Konzernlagebericht mit dem Konzernabschluß sowie mit den bei der Prüfung gewonnenen Erkenntnissen des Abschlußprüfers in Einklang stehen und ob der Lagebericht insgesamt eine zutreffende Vorstellung von der Lage des Unternehmens und der Konzernlagebericht insgesamt eine zutreffende Vorstellung von der Lage des Konzerns vermittelt. Dabei ist auch zu prüfen, ob die Risiken der künftigen Entwicklung zutreffend dargestellt sind.

examination shall be reported; the certification of the annual financial statements shall be correspondingly revised.

§ 317 Subject matter and extent of the audit

(1) The accounting records shall be included in the examination of the annual financial statements. The examination of the annual financial statements and the consolidated financial statements shall encompass whether the legal regulations and the supplementing provisions of the articles of association have been observed. The examination shall be prepared such that errors and violations of the provisions set forth in sentence 2 which materially affect the presentation of the net assets, financing and results of operations of the enterprise pursuant to § 264 Subsection 2 will be recognised if professional diligence is exercised.

(2) The management report and the consolidated management report shall be examined as to whether the management report is in accordance with the annual financial statements and the consolidated management report with the consolidated financial statements as well as with the findings of the auditor gained during the examination and whether the management report as a whole conveys a valid picture of the state of the enterprise and the consolidated management report as a whole a picture of the state of the group of companies. It shall also be examined whether the risks of the future developments have been accurately represented.

(3) Der Abschlußprüfer des Konzernabschlusses hat auch die im Konzernabschluß zusammengefaßten Jahresabschlüsse, insbesondere die konsolidierungsbedingten Anpassungen, in entsprechender Anwendung des Absatzes 1 zu prüfen. Dies gilt nicht für Jahresabschlüsse, die aufgrund gesetzlicher Vorschriften nach diesem Unterabschnitt oder die ohne gesetzliche Verpflichtungen nach den Grundsätzen dieses Unterabschnitts geprüft worden sind. Satz 2 ist entsprechend auf die Jahresabschlüsse von in den Konzernabschluß einbezogenen Tochterunternehmen mit Sitz im Ausland anzuwenden; sind diese Jahresabschlüsse nicht von einem in Übereinstimmung mit den Vorschriften der Richtlinie 84/253/EWG zugelassenen Abschlußprüfer geprüft worden, so gilt dies jedoch nur, wenn der Abschlußprüfer eine den Anforderungen dieser Richtlinie gleichwertige Befähigung hat und der Jahresabschluß in einer den Anforderungen dieses Unterabschnitts entsprechenden Weise geprüft worden ist.

(4) Bei einer börsennotierten Aktiengesellschaft ist außerdem im Rahmen der Prüfung zu beurteilen, ob der Vorstand die ihm nach § 91 Abs. 2 des Aktiengesetzes obliegenden Maßnahmen in einer geeigneten Form getroffen hat und ob das danach einzurichtende Überwachungssystem seine Aufgaben erfüllen kann.

(3) The auditor of the consolidated financial statements shall also examine, in analogous application of Subsection 1, the annual financial statements consolidated in the consolidated financial statements, especially the adjustments necessitated by consolidation. This does not apply to annual financial statements that were examined pursuant to this Subpart based on statutory provisions or that were examined pursuant to the principles of this Subpart without legal obligations. Sentence 2 shall apply analogously to the annual financial statements of the subsidiaries with domicile abroad included in the consolidated financial statements; if these annual financial statements are not examined by an auditor certified in accordance with the provisions of the Directive 84/253/EEC, then this applies only if the auditor has a qualification equivalent to the requirements of this Directive and the annual financial statements have been examined in a manner conforming to the requirements of this Subpart.

(4) In the case of a quoted stock corporation, it shall also be determined in the scope of the examination whether the managing board has taken the measures imposed on it pursuant to § 91 Subsection 2 of the Stock Corporation Act in a suitable form and whether the internal control system which is to be installed thereunder can fulfil its duties.

§ 318 Bestellung und Abberufung des Abschlußprüfers

(1) Der Abschlußprüfer des Jahresabschlusses wird von den Gesellschaftern gewählt; den Abschlußprüfer des Konzernabschlusses wählen die Ge-

§ 318 Retaining and terminating the auditor

(1) The auditor for the annual financial statements will be chosen by the shareholders. The parent's shareholders shall choose the auditor for the

sellschafter des Mutterunternehmens. Bei Gesellschaften mit beschränkter Haftung und bei offenen Handelsgesellschaften und Kommanditgesellschaften im Sinne des § 264 a Abs. 1 kann der Gesellschaftsvertrag etwas anderes bestimmen. Der Abschlußprüfer soll jeweils vor Ablauf des Geschäftsjahrs gewählt werden, auf das sich seine Prüfungstätigkeit erstreckt. Die gesetzlichen Vertreter, bei Zuständigkeit des Aufsichtsrats dieser, haben unverzüglich nach der Wahl den Prüfungsauftrag zu erteilen. Der Prüfungsauftrag kann nur widerrufen werden, wenn nach Absatz 3 ein anderer Prüfer bestellt worden ist.

(2) Als Abschlußprüfer des Konzernabschlusses gilt, wenn kein anderer Prüfer bestellt wird, der Prüfer als bestellt, der für die Prüfung des in den Konzernabschluß einbezogenen Jahresabschlusses des Mutterunternehmens bestellt worden ist. Erfolgt die Einbeziehung auf Grund eines Zwischenabschlusses, so gilt, wenn kein anderer Prüfer bestellt wird, der Prüfer als bestellt, der für die Prüfung des letzten vor dem Konzernabschlußstichtag aufgestellten Jahresabschlusses des Mutterunternehmens bestellt worden ist.

(3) Auf Antrag der gesetzlichen Vertreter, des Aufsichtsrats oder von Gesellschaftern, bei Aktiengesellschaften und Kommanditgesellschaften auf Aktien jedoch nur, wenn die Anteile dieser Gesellschafter zusammen den zehnten Teil des Grundkapitals oder den anteiligen Betrag in Höhe von einer Million Euro erreichen, hat das Gericht nach Anhörung der Beteiligten und des gewählten Prüfers einen anderen Abschlußprüfer zu bestellen, wenn dies aus einem in der Person des

consolidated financial statements. The articles of association for limited liability companies and for general commercial partnerships and limited partnerships within the meaning of § 264 a Subsection 1 can provide otherwise. The auditor should be chosen annually before the end of the fiscal year to which his examination activity applies. After the choice is made, the legal representatives, or where the supervisory board is responsible, the supervisory board, shall issue the examination mandate without undue delay. The examination mandate may be revoked only if another auditor is retained pursuant to Subsection 3.

(2) If no other auditor is retained, the auditor of the consolidated financial statements shall be deemed to be the auditor retained to examine the annual financial statements of the parent included in the consolidated financial statements. If the inclusion takes place on the basis of interim financial statements, then, if no other auditor is retained, the auditor who was retained to examine the last annual financial statements of the parent prepared before the close of the fiscal year of the consolidated financial statements shall be deemed to have been retained.

(3) Upon the application of the legal representatives, supervisory board or shareholders, in case of stock corporations or partnerships limited by shares, however, only if the shares of these shareholders together amount to one-tenth of the capital stock or to the proportionate amount of one million Euro, the court shall appoint another auditor after hearing the interested parties and the chosen auditor if this seems necessary for reasons pertaining to the person of the chosen au-

gewählten Prüfers liegenden Grund geboten erscheint, insbesondere wenn Besorgnis der Befangenheit besteht. Der Antrag ist binnen zwei Wochen seit dem Tage der Wahl des Abschlußprüfers zu stellen; Aktionäre können den Antrag nur stellen, wenn sie gegen die Wahl des Abschlußprüfers bei der Beschlußfassung Widerspruch erklärt haben. Stellen Aktionäre den Antrag, so haben sie glaubhaft zu machen, daß sie seit mindestens drei Monaten vor dem Tage der Hauptversammlung Inhaber der Aktien sind. Zur Glaubhaftmachung genügt eine eidesstattliche Versicherung vor einem Notar. Unterliegt die Gesellschaft einer staatlichen Aufsicht, so kann auch die Aufsichtsbehörde den Antrag stellen. Gegen die Entscheidung ist die sofortige Beschwerde zulässig.

(4) Ist der Abschlußprüfer bis zum Ablauf des Geschäftsjahrs nicht gewählt worden, so hat das Gericht auf Antrag der gesetzlichen Vertreter, des Aufsichtsrats oder eines Gesellschafters den Abschlußprüfer zu bestellen. Gleiches gilt, wenn ein gewählter Abschlußprüfer die Annahme des Prüfungsauftrags abgelehnt hat, weggefallen ist oder am rechtzeitigen Abschluß der Prüfung verhindert ist und ein anderer Abschlußprüfer nicht gewählt worden ist. Die gesetzlichen Vertreter sind verpflichtet, den Antrag zu stellen. Gegen die Entscheidung des Gerichts findet die sofortige Beschwerde statt; die Bestellung des Abschlußprüfers ist unanfechtbar.

(5) Der vom Gericht bestellte Abschlußprüfer hat Anspruch auf Ersatz angemessener barer Auslagen und auf Vergütung für seine Tätigkeit. Die Auslagen und die Vergütung setzt das Gericht fest. Gegen die Entscheidung ist die sofortige Beschwerde zulässig.

ditor, especially if concern as to prejudice exists. The application shall be made within two weeks from the day of the choice of the auditor; shareholders may make the application only if they lodged objections to the choice of the auditor upon the adoption of the resolution. If shareholders make the application, then they must present prima facie evidence that they owned the shares at least three months before the day of the shareholders' meeting. An affidavit sworn to before a notary suffices as prima facie evidence. If the company is subject to state supervision, then the supervisory officials may also make the application. An immediate appeal against the decision is permissible.

(4) If the auditor has not been chosen by the end of the fiscal year, then the court shall appoint the auditor upon the application of the legal representatives, the supervisory board or a shareholder. The same applies if a chosen auditor has refused to take on the examination mandate, becomes unavailable or is prevented from the timely completion of the examination and another auditor has not been chosen. The legal representatives are obligated to make the application. An immediate appeal may be made against the court's decision; the appointment of the auditor is final.

(5) An auditor appointed by the court is entitled to reimbursement for appropriate cash expenses and to remuneration for his work. The court shall determine the expenses and remuneration. An immediate appeal against the decision is permissible. A further

§§ 318, 319	Handelsbücher

Die weitere Beschwerde ist ausgeschlossen. Aus der rechtskräftigen Entscheidung findet die Zwangsvollstreckung nach der Zivilprozeßordnung statt.

(6) Ein von dem Abschlußprüfer angenommener Prüfungsauftrag kann von dem Abschlußprüfer nur aus wichtigem Grund gekündigt werden. Als wichtiger Grund ist es nicht anzusehen, wenn Meinungsverschiedenheiten über den Inhalt des Bestätigungsvermerks, seine Einschränkung oder Versagung bestehen. Die Kündigung ist schriftlich zu begründen. Der Abschlußprüfer hat über das Ergebnis seiner bisherigen Prüfung zu berichten; § 321 ist entsprechend anzuwenden.

(7) Kündigt der Abschlußprüfer den Prüfungsauftrag nach Absatz 6, so haben die gesetzlichen Vertreter die Kündigung dem Aufsichtsrat, der nächsten Hauptversammlung oder bei Gesellschaften mit beschränkter Haftung den Gesellschaftern mitzuteilen. Den Bericht des bisherigen Abschlußprüfers haben die gesetzlichen Vertreter unverzüglich dem Aufsichtsrat vorzulegen. Jedes Aufsichtsratsmitglied hat das Recht, von dem Bericht Kenntnis zu nehmen. Der Bericht ist auch jedem Aufsichtsratsmitglied oder, soweit der Aufsichtsrat dies beschlossen hat, den Mitgliedern eines Ausschusses auszuhändigen. Ist der Prüfungsauftrag vom Aufsichtsrat erteilt worden, obliegen die Pflichten der gesetzlichen Vertreter dem Aufsichtsrat einschließlich der Unterrichtung der gesetzlichen Vertreter.

§ 319 Auswahl der Abschlußprüfer

(1) Abschlußprüfer können Wirtschaftsprüfer und Wirtschaftsprüfungsgesellschaften sein. Abschlußprüfer

appeal is excluded. Enforcement of the legal decision shall take place pursuant to the Code of Civil Procedure.

(6) An examination mandate accepted by an auditor may be terminated by the auditor only for an important reason. Differences of opinion as to the content of the certification of the financial statements, their qualification or rejection shall not be viewed as an important reason. Termination shall be justified in writing. The auditor must report the results of his examination up to that point; § 321 shall apply analogously.

(7) If the auditor terminates the examination mandate pursuant to Subsection 6, then the legal representatives must report the termination to the supervisory board, the next shareholders' meeting, or in the case of a limited liability company, to the shareholders. The legal representatives must present the report of the former auditor to the supervisory board without undue delay. Every supervisory board member has the right to inspect the report. The report shall be distributed to every supervisory board member, or where the supervisory board has so resolved, to the members of a committee. Where the examination mandate has been issued by the supervisory board, it shall be subject to the duties of the legal representatives, including informing the legal representatives.

§ 319 Choice of the auditors

(1) Auditors may be qualified auditors and qualified auditing firms. Auditors of the annual financial statements and

Ergänzende Vorschriften für Kapitalgesellschaften § 319

von Jahresabschlüssen und Lageberichten mittelgroßer Gesellschaften mit beschränkter Haftung (§ 267 Abs. 2) oder von mittelgroßen Personenhandelsgesellschaften im Sinne des § 264 a Abs. 1 können auch vereidigte Buchprüfer und Buchprüfungsgesellschaften sein.

(2) Ein Wirtschaftsprüfer oder vereidigter Buchprüfer darf nicht Abschlußprüfer sein, wenn er oder eine Person, mit der er seinen Beruf gemeinsam ausübt,

1. Anteile an der zu prüfenden Kapitalgesellschaft besitzt;
2. gesetzlicher Vertreter oder Mitglied des Aufsichtsrats oder Arbeitnehmer der zu prüfenden Kapitalgesellschaft ist oder in den letzten drei Jahren vor seiner Bestellung war;
3. gesetzlicher Vertreter oder Mitglied des Aufsichtsrats einer juristischen Person, Gesellschafter einer Personengesellschaft oder Inhaber eines Unternehmens ist, sofern die juristische Person, die Personengesellschaft oder das Einzelunternehmen mit der zu prüfenden Kapitalgesellschaft verbunden ist oder von dieser mehr als zwanzig vom Hundert der Anteile besitzt;
4. Arbeitnehmer eines Unternehmens ist, das mit der zu prüfenden Kapitalgesellschaft verbunden ist oder an dieser mehr als zwanzig vom Hundert der Anteile besitzt, oder Arbeitnehmer einer natürlichen Person ist, die an der zu prüfenden Kapitalgesellschaft mehr als zwanzig vom Hundert der Anteile besitzt;
5. bei der Führung der Bücher oder der Aufstellung des zu prüfenden Jahresabschlusses der Kapitalgesellschaft über die Prüfungstätigkeit hinaus mitgewirkt hat;

management reports of medium-sized limited liability companies (§ 267 Subsection 2) or of medium-sized business partnerships within the meaning of § 264 section 1 may also be certified accountants or certified accounting firms.

(2) A qualified auditor or certified accountant may not be an auditor if he or a person with whom he jointly practices his profession,

1. owns shares in the corporation to be examined;
2. is a legal representative or member of the supervisory board or employee of the corporation to be examined or was one within the three years before being retained;
3. is a legal representative or member of the supervisory board of a juridical person, shareholder of a partnership or owner of an enterprise to the extent that the juridical person, the partnership or the sole enterprise is related to the corporation to be examined or owns more than twenty percent of its shares;
4. is an employee of an enterprise that is related to the corporation to be examined or owns more than twenty percent of its shares, or is an employee of a natural person who owns more than twenty percent of the shares of the corporation to be examined;
5. has worked on keeping the books or preparing the annual financial statements of the corporation to be examined in capacities beyond the task of examination;

233

§ 319 Handelsbücher

6. gesetzlicher Vertreter, Arbeitnehmer, Mitglied des Aufsichtsrats oder Gesellschafter einer juristischen oder natürlichen Person oder einer Personengesellschaft oder Inhaber eines Unternehmens ist, sofern die juristische oder natürliche Person, die Personengesellschaft oder einer ihrer Gesellschafter oder das Einzelunternehmen nach Nummer 5 nicht Abschlußprüfer der zu prüfenden Kapitalgesellschaft sein darf;

7. bei der Prüfung eine Person beschäftigt, die nach den Nummern 1 bis 6 nicht Abschlußprüfer sein darf;

8. in den letzten fünf Jahren jeweils mehr als dreißig vom Hundert der Gesamteinnahmen aus seiner beruflichen Tätigkeit aus der Prüfung und Beratung der zu prüfenden Kapitalgesellschaft und von Unternehmen, an denen die zu prüfende Kapitalgesellschaft mehr als zwanzig vom Hundert der Anteile besitzt, bezogen hat und dies auch im laufenden Geschäftsjahr zu erwarten ist; zur Vermeidung von Härtefällen kann die Wirtschaftsprüferkammer befristete Ausnahmegenehmigungen erteilen.

Ein Wirtschaftsprüfer oder vereidigter Buchprüfer darf ferner nicht Abschlussprüfer sein, wenn er

1. in entsprechender Anwendung von Absatz 3 Nr. 6 ausgeschlossen wäre;

2. über keine wirksame Bescheinigung über die Teilnahme an der Qualitätskontrolle nach § 57a der Wirtschaftsprüferordnung verfügt und die Wirtschaftsprüferkammer keine Ausnahmegenehmigung erteilt hat.

(3) Eine Wirtschaftsprüfungsgesellschaft oder Buchprüfungsgesellschaft darf nicht Abschlußprüfer sein, wenn

6. is a legal representative, employee, supervisory board member or shareholder of a juridical or natural person or of a partnership or an owner of an enterprise to the extent that the juridical or natural person, the partnership or one of its shareholders or the sole enterprise may not be the auditor of the corporation to be examined pursuant to No. 5;

7. employs a person in the examination who may not be the auditor pursuant to Nos. 1 through 6;

8. has received in each of the last five years more than thirty percent of his total income for his professional activity from examining and advising the corporation to be examined and enterprises in which the corporation to be examined owns more than twenty percent of the shares and this is also expected to be the case in the current fiscal year. To avoid hardship, the Association of Certified Accountants may issue exceptional approvals for a limited time.

A certified accountant sworn auditor may not also be an auditor where he

1. would be disqualified by analogous application of Subsection 3 No. 6;

2. does not possess a valid certificate of participation in quality control pursuant to § 57 a of the Certified Accountants Code and the Chamber of Certified Accountants has not granted an exemption.

(3) A certified accounting firm or an auditing firm may not be an auditor if

Ergänzende Vorschriften für Kapitalgesellschaften § 319

1. sie Anteile an der zu prüfenden Kapitalgesellschaft besitzt oder mit dieser verbunden ist oder wenn ein mit ihr verbundenes Unternehmen an der zu prüfenden Kapitalgesellschaft mehr als zwanzig vom Hundert der Anteile besitzt oder mit dieser verbunden ist;
2. sie nach Absatz 2 Nr. 6 als Gesellschafter einer juristischen Person oder einer Personengesellschaft oder nach Absatz 2 Nr. 5, 7 oder 8 nicht Abschlußprüfer sein darf,
3. bei einer Wirtschaftsprüfungsgesellschaft oder Buchprüfungsgesellschaft, die juristische Person ist, ein gesetzlicher Vertreter oder ein Gesellschafter, der fünfzig vom Hundert oder mehr der den Gesellschaftern zustehenden Stimmrechte besitzt, oder bei anderen Wirtschaftsprüfungsgesellschaften oder Buchprüfungsgesellschaften ein Gesellschafter nach Absatz 2 Nr. 1 bis 4 nicht Abschlußprüfer sein darf;
4. einer ihrer gesetzlichen Vertreter oder einer ihrer Gesellschafter nach Absatz 2 Nr. 5 oder 6 nicht Abschlußprüfer sein darf;
5. eines ihrer Aufsichtsratsmitglieder nach Absatz 2 Nr. 2 oder 5 nicht Abschlußprüfer sein darf oder
6. sie bei der Prüfung einer Aktiengesellschaft, deren Aktien zum Handel im amtlichen Markt zugelassen sind, einen Wirtschaftsprüfer beschäftigt, der in den dem zu prüfenden Geschäftsjahr vorhergehenden zehn Jahren den Bestätigungsvermerk nach § 322 über die Prüfung der Jahres- oder Konzernabschlüsse der Kapitalgesellschaft in mehr als sechs Fällen gezeichnet hat;

1. it owns shares in the corporation to be examined or is related to it or if an enterprise related to it owns more than twenty percent of the shares of the corporation to be examined or is related to it;
2. it may not be the auditor pursuant to Subsection 2 No. 6 as the shareholder of a juridical person or a partnership or pursuant to Subsection 2 Nos. 5, 7 or 8;
3. in the case of a certified accounting firm or an auditing firm that is a juridical person, a legal representative or a shareholder who owns fifty percent or more of the voting rights belonging to the shareholders, or in the case of other certified accounting firms or auditing firms, a shareholder may not be the auditor pursuant to Subsection 2 Nos. 1 through 4;
4. one of its legal representatives or shareholders may not be the auditor pursuant to Subsection 2 No. 5 or 6;
5. one of its supervisory board members may not be the auditor pursuant to Subsection 2 No. 2 or 5; or
6. it employs for the examination of a stock corporation whose shares are admitted to trading on the official market a certified accountant who has signed the certification of the financial statements pursuant to § 322 concerning the examination of the annual financial statements or the consolidated financial statements of the corporation more than six times in the ten years prior to the fiscal year to be examined;

235

7. sie über keine wirksame Bescheinigung über die Teilnahme an der Qualitätskontrolle nach § 57 a der Wirtschaftsprüferordnung verfügt und die Wirtschaftsprüferkammer keine Ausnahmegenehmigung erteilt hat.

(4) Die Absätze 2 und 3 sind auf den Abschlußprüfer des Konzernabschlusses entsprechend anzuwenden.

§ 320 Vorlagepflicht. Auskunftsrecht

(1) Die gesetzlichen Vertreter der Kapitalgesellschaft haben dem Abschlußprüfer den Jahresabschluß und den Lagebericht unverzüglich nach der Aufstellung vorzulegen. Sie haben ihm zu gestatten, die Bücher und Schriften der Kapitalgesellschaft sowie die Vermögensgegenstände und Schulden, namentlich die Kasse und die Bestände an Wertpapieren und Waren, zu prüfen.

(2) Der Abschlußprüfer kann von den gesetzlichen Vertretern alle Aufklärungen und Nachweise verlangen, die für eine sorgfältige Prüfung notwendig sind. Soweit es die Vorbereitung der Abschlußprüfung erfordert, hat der Abschlußprüfer die Rechte nach Absatz 1 Satz 2 und nach Satz 1 auch schon vor Aufstellung des Jahresabschlusses. Soweit es für eine sorgfältige Prüfung notwendig ist, hat der Abschlußprüfer die Rechte nach den Sätzen 1 und 2 auch gegenüber Mutter- und Tochterunternehmen.

(3) Die gesetzlichen Vertreter einer Kapitalgesellschaft, die einen Konzernabschluß aufzustellen hat, haben dem Abschlußprüfer des Konzernabschlusses den Konzernabschluß, den Konzernlagebericht, die Jahresabschlüsse,

7. it does not possess a valid certificate of participation in quality control pursuant to section 57a of the Certified Accountants Code and the Chamber of Certified Accountants has not granted an exemption.

(4) Subsections 2 and 3 shall apply analogously to the auditor of the consolidated financial statements.

§ 320 Duty to produce; right to information

(1) The corporation's legal representatives shall present the annual financial statements and the management report to the auditor without undue delay after their preparation. They shall permit him to examine the corporation's books and records as well as its assets and debts, in particular cash and the holdings of securities and goods.

(2) The auditor may ask the legal representatives for all explanations and supporting documents that are necessary for a careful examination. To the extent required for preparing for the examination of the financial statements, the auditor has the rights pursuant to Subsection 1 sentence 2 and pursuant to sentence 1, even before the preparation of the annual financial statements. To the extent necessary for a careful examination, the auditor also has the rights pursuant to sentences 1 and 2 vis-à-vis parent companies and subsidiaries.

(3) The legal representatives of a corporation that must prepare consolidated financial statements shall present to the auditor of the consolidated financial statements the consolidated financial statements, consoli-

Lageberichte und, wenn eine Prüfung stattgefunden hat, die Prüfungsberichte des Mutterunternehmens und der Tochterunternehmen vorzulegen. Der Abschlußprüfer hat die Rechte nach Absatz 1 Satz 2 und nach Absatz 2 bei dem Mutterunternehmen und den Tochterunternehmen, die Rechte nach Absatz 2 auch gegenüber den Abschlußprüfern des Mutterunternehmens und der Tochterunternehmen.

§ 321 Prüfungsbericht

(1) Der Abschlußprüfer hat über Art und Umfang sowie über das Ergebnis der Prüfung schriftlich und mit der gebotenen Klarheit zu berichten. Im Bericht ist vorweg zu der Beurteilung der Lage des Unternehmens oder Konzerns durch die gesetzlichen Vertreter Stellung zu nehmen, wobei insbesondere auf die Beurteilung des Fortbestandes und der künftigen Entwicklung des Unternehmens unter Berücksichtigung des Lageberichts und bei der Prüfung des Konzernabschlusses von Mutterunternehmen auch des Konzerns unter Berücksichtigung des Konzernlageberichts einzugehen ist, soweit die geprüften Unterlagen und der Lagebericht oder der Konzernlagebericht eine solche Beurteilung erlauben. Außerdem hat der Abschlussprüfer über bei Durchführung der Prüfung festgestellte Unrichtigkeiten oder Verstöße gegen gesetzliche Vorschriften sowie Tatsachen zu berichten, die den Bestand des geprüften Unternehmens oder des Konzerns gefährden oder seine Entwicklung wesentlich beeinträchtigen können oder die schwerwiegende Verstöße der gesetzlichen Vertreter oder von Arbeitnehmern gegen Gesetz, Gesellschaftsvertrag oder die Satzung erkennen lassen.

dated management report, annual financial statements, management reports and, if an examination has taken place, auditing reports of the parent and subsidiaries. The auditor has the rights pursuant to Subsection 1 sentence 2 and pursuant to Subsection 2 in regard to the parent and subsidiaries, and the rights pursuant to Subsection 2 also with respect to the auditors of the parent and subsidiaries.

§ 321 Audit report

(1) The auditor shall report in writing and with the necessary clarity on the kind and scope as well as on the results of his examination. In the audit report, there shall at the outset be a comment on the opinion by the legal representatives as to the state of the enterprise or the group of companies, especially an assessment of the continuity and the future development of the enterprise taking into consideration the management report and, in case of the examination of consolidated financial statements of parent companies, an assessment of the group of companies taking into consideration the consolidated management report, insofar as the audited records and the management report or the consolidated management report permit such an assessment. In addition, the auditor shall report any irregularities determined in carrying out the examination or violations of statutory provisions as well as facts that jeopardize the existence of the examined enterprise or the group of companies or can substantially harm its development or show serious violations of the law or the articles of association by legal representatives or employees.

§ 321

(2) Im Hauptteil des Prüfungsberichts ist festzustellen, ob die Buchführung und die weiteren geprüften Unterlagen, der Jahresabschluss, der Lagebericht, der Konzernabschluss und der Konzernlagebericht den gesetzlichen Vorschriften und den ergänzenden Bestimmungen des Gesellschaftsvertrags oder der Satzung entsprechen. In diesem Rahmen ist auch über Beanstandungen zu berichten, die nicht zur Einschränkung oder Versagung des Bestätigungsvermerks geführt haben, soweit dies für die Überwachung der Geschäftsführung und des geprüften Unternehmens von Bedeutung ist. Es ist auch darauf einzugehen, ob der Abschluss insgesamt unter Beachtung der Grundsätze ordnungsgemäßer Buchführung ein den tatsächlichen Verhältnissen entsprechendes Bild der Vermögens-, Finanz- und Ertragslage der Kapitalgesellschaft oder des Konzerns vermittelt. Dazu ist auch auf wesentliche Bewertungsgrundlagen sowie darauf einzugehen, welchen Einfluss Änderungen in den Bewertungsgrundlagen einschließlich der Ausübung von Bilanzierungs- und Bewertungswahlrechten und der Ausnutzung von Ermessensspielräumen sowie sachverhaltsgestaltende Maßnahmen insgesamt auf die Darstellung der Vermögens-, Finanz- und Ertragslage haben. Hierzu sind die Posten des Jahres- und des Konzernabschlusses aufzugliedern und ausreichend zu erläutern, soweit diese Angaben nicht im Anhang enthalten sind. Es ist darzustellen, ob die gesetzlichen Vertreter die verlangten Aufklärungen und Nachweise erbracht haben.

(3) In einem besonderen Abschnitt des Prüfungsberichts sind Gegenstand, Art und Umfang der Prüfung zu erläutern.

(2) In the main part of the audit report it shall be determined whether the bookkeeping records and the other audited records, the annual financial statements, the management report, the consolidated financial statements and the consolidated management report conform to the statutory provisions and the supplementary provisions of the articles of association. In this scope there shall also be reported any objections that have not lead to a restriction or denial of the audit opinion to the extent that this of importance for the supervision of the management and of the examined enterprise. It shall also be discussed whether the financial statements as a whole, pursuant to generally accepted accounting principals, present a factually accurate picture of the net assets, financing and results of operations of the corporation. Substantial bases for valuation shall be discussed as well as what influence changes in the bases of evaluation including the exercise of elections for accounting and valuation principles and the use of discretion as well as measures to structure the facts have as a whole on the presentation of the net assets, financing and results of operations of the corporation. The items in the annual financial statements and the consolidated financial statements shall be broken down and adequately explained to the extent that this information is not contained in the notes. It shall be explained whether the legal representatives have supplied the required explanations and substantiation.

(3) The subject, kind and scope of the examination shall be explained in a special section of the audit report.

Ergänzende Vorschriften für Kapitalgesellschaften§§ 321, 322

(4) Ist im Rahmen der Prüfung eine Beurteilung nach § 317 Abs. 4 abgegeben worden, so ist deren Ergebnis in einem besonderen Teil des Prüfungsberichts darzustellen. Es ist darauf einzugehen, ob Maßnahmen erforderlich sind, um das interne Überwachungssystem zu verbessern.

(5) Der Abschlußprüfer hat den Bericht zu unterzeichnen und den gesetzlichen Vertretern vorzulegen. Hat der Aufsichtsrat den Auftrag erteilt, so ist der Bericht ihm vorzulegen; dem Vorstand ist vor Zuleitung Gelegenheit zur Stellungnahme zu geben.

§ 322 Bestätigungsvermerk

(1) Der Abschlußprüfer hat das Ergebnis der Prüfung in einem Bestätigungsvermerk zum Jahresabschluß und zum Konzernabschluß zusammenzufassen. Der Bestätigungsvermerk hat neben einer Beschreibung von Gegenstand, Art und Umfang der Prüfung auch eine Beurteilung des Prüfungsergebnisses zu enthalten. Sind vom Abschlußprüfer keine Einwendungen zu erheben, so hat er in seinem Bestätigungsvermerk zu erklären, daß die von ihm nach § 317 durchgeführte Prüfung zu keinen Einwendungen geführt hat und daß der von den gesetzlichen Vertretern der Gesellschaft aufgestellte Jahres- oder Konzernabschluß aufgrund der bei der Prüfung gewonnenen Erkenntnisse des Abschlußprüfers nach seiner Beurteilung unter Beachtung der Grundsätze ordnungsmäßiger Buchführung ein den tatsächlichen Verhältnissen entsprechendes Bild der Vermögens-, Finanz- und Ertragslage des Unternehmens oder des Konzerns vermittelt.

(4) If in the scope of the examination an assessment pursuant to § 317 Subsection 4 has been made, the result thereof shall be presented in a special part of the audit report. It shall be discussed whether measures are necessary to improve the internal control system.

(5) The auditor shall sign the report and present it to the legal representatives. Where the supervisory board has issued the examination mandate, the report shall be presented to the supervisory board; the managing board shall have an opportunity to comment on the report before it is presented to the supervisory board.

§ 322 Certification of the financial statements

(1) The auditor shall summarise the result of the examination in a certification of the annual financial statements and of the consolidated financial statements. The certification shall contain, in addition to a description of the subject, kind and scope of the examination, also an assessment of the results of the examination. If the auditor does not have any objections to raise, he shall declare in his certification that the examination conducted by him pursuant to § 317 has not led to any objections and that the annual financial statements or consolidated financial statements prepared by the legal representatives of the company based on the findings of the auditor gained during the examination in his judgment pursuant to generally accepted accounting principles present a factually accurate picture of the net assets, financing and results of operations of the enterprise or the group of companies.

(2) Die Beurteilung des Prüfungsergebnisses soll allgemeinverständlich und problemorientiert unter Berücksichtigung des Umstandes erfolgen, daß die gesetzlichen Vertreter den Abschluß zu verantworten haben. Auf Risiken, die den Fortbestand des Unternehmens gefährden, ist gesondert einzugehen.

(3) Im Bestätigungsvermerk ist auch darauf einzugehen, ob der Lagebericht und der Konzernlagebericht insgesamt nach der Beurteilung des Abschlußprüfers eine zutreffende Vorstellung von der Lage des Unternehmens oder des Konzerns vermittelt. Dabei ist auch darauf einzugehen, ob die Risiken der künftigen Entwicklung zutreffend dargestellt sind.

(4) Sind Einwendungen zu erheben, so hat der Abschlußprüfer seine Erklärung nach Absatz 1 Satz 3 einzuschränken oder zu versagen. Die Versagung ist in den Vermerk, der nicht mehr als Bestätigungsvermerk zu bezeichnen ist, aufzunehmen. Die Einschränkung und die Versagung sind zu begründen. Einschränkungen sind so darzustellen, daß deren Tragweite erkennbar wird.

(5) Der Abschlußprüfer hat den Bestätigungsvermerk oder den Vermerk über seine Versagung unter Angabe von Ort und Tag zu unterzeichnen. Der Bestätigungsvermerk oder der Vermerk über seine Versagung ist auch in den Prüfungsbericht aufzunehmen.

§ 323 Verantwortlichkeit des Abschlußprüfers

(1) Der Abschlußprüfer, seine Gehilfen und die bei der Prüfung mitwirkenden gesetzlichen Vertreter einer Prüfungsgesellschaft sind zur gewissenhaften

(2) The assessment of the result of the examination should be generally intelligible and directed to problems, taking into consideration the fact that the legal representatives are responsible for the financial statements. Risks which endanger the continuity of the enterprise are to be discussed separately.

(3) The certification shall also treat the questions whether the management report and the consolidated management report as a whole, in the opinion of the auditor, present an accurate picture of the state of the enterprise or the group of companies. It shall also be discussed whether the risks of the future developments have been described correctly.

(4) If objections are to be raised, then the auditor must limit his declaration pursuant to Subsection 1 sentence 3 or must refuse to give such a declaration. The refusal shall be contained in the notation which shall no longer be designated as a certification of the financial statements. The limitation or the refusal shall be justified. Limitations shall be presented in such a way that their scope is clearly recognisable.

(5) The auditor shall sign the certification or the notation concerning his refusal, giving the place and day. The certification or the notation of the auditor's refusal shall also be included in the audit report.

§ 323 The auditor's responsibilities

(1) The auditor, his assistants and the legal representatives of an auditing firm assisting in the examination are obligated to make a conscientious and

Ergänzende Vorschriften für Kapitalgesellschaften § 323

und unparteiischen Prüfung und zur Verschwiegenheit verpflichtet; § 57 b der Wirtschaftsprüferordnung bleibt unberührt. Sie dürfen nicht unbefugt Geschäfts- und Betriebsgeheimnisse verwerten, die sie bei ihrer Tätigkeit erfahren haben. Wer vorsätzlich oder fahrlässig seine Pflichten verletzt, ist der Kapitalgesellschaft und, wenn ein verbundenes Unternehmen geschädigt worden ist, auch diesem zum Ersatz des daraus entstehenden Schadens verpflichtet. Mehrere Personen haften als Gesamtschuldner.

(2) Die Ersatzpflicht von Personen, die fahrlässig gehandelt haben, beschränkt sich auf eine Million Euro für eine Prüfung. Bei Prüfung einer Aktiengesellschaft, deren Aktien zum Handel im amtlichen Markt zugelassen sind, beschränkt sich die Ersatzpflicht von Personen, die fahrlässig gehandelt haben, abweichend von Satz 1 auf vier Millionen Euro für eine Prüfung. Dies gilt auch, wenn an der Prüfung mehrere Personen beteiligt gewesen oder mehrere zum Ersatz verpflichtende Handlungen begangen worden sind, und ohne Rücksicht darauf, ob andere Beteiligte vorsätzlich gehandelt haben.

(3) Die Verpflichtung zur Verschwiegenheit besteht, wenn eine Prüfungsgesellschaft Abschlußprüfer ist, auch gegenüber dem Aufsichtsrat und den Mitgliedern des Aufsichtsrats der Prüfungsgesellschaft.

(4) Die Ersatzpflicht nach diesen Vorschriften kann durch Vertrag weder ausgeschlossen noch beschränkt werden.

(5) Die Ansprüche aus diesen Vorschriften verjähren in fünf Jahren.

impartial examination and to maintain confidentiality; § 57 b of the Certified Accountants Code shall not be affected. They may not exploit without authorization business secrets learned in their work. Whoever intentionally or negligently violates his duties is obligated to compensate the company for the damages incurred, and, if a related enterprise is damaged, that one as well. If there is more than one person, they are liable as joint and several debtors.

(2) The liability for damages of persons who have acted negligently is limited to one million EUR per examination. Where a stock corporation whose shares are admitted to trading on the official market is audited, the liability for damages of persons who have acted negligently is limited, deviating from sentence 1, to four million EUR per examination. This also applies if several persons participated in the examination or several acts giving rise to liability for damages were commited, and this is so without regard to whether other participants acted intentionally.

(3) If an auditing firm is the auditor, the obligation to maintain confidentiality also exists vis-à-vis the auditing supervisory board and the members of the firm's supervisory board.

(4) The liability for damages pursuant to these regulations may be neither excluded nor limited by contract.

(5) The claims based on these regulations are subject to a five-year statute of limitations.

§ 324 Meinungsverschiedenheiten zwischen Kapitalgesellschaft und Abschlußprüfer

(1) Bei Meinungsverschiedenheiten zwischen dem Abschlußprüfer und der Kapitalgesellschaft über die Auslegung und Anwendung der gesetzlichen Vorschriften sowie von Bestimmungen des Gesellschaftsvertrags oder der Satzung über den Jahresabschluß, Lagebericht, Konzernabschluß oder Konzernlagebericht entscheidet auf Antrag des Abschlußprüfers oder der gesetzlichen Vertreter der Kapitalgesellschaft ausschließlich das Landgericht.

(2) Auf das Verfahren ist das Gesetz über die Angelegenheiten der freiwilligen Gerichtsbarkeit anzuwenden. Das Landgericht entscheidet durch einen mit Gründen versehenen Beschluß. Die Entscheidung wird erst mit der Rechtskraft wirksam. Gegen die Entscheidung findet die sofortige Beschwerde statt, wenn das Landgericht sie in der Entscheidung zugelassen hat. Es soll sie nur zulassen, wenn dadurch die Klärung einer Rechtsfrage von grundsätzlicher Bedeutung zu erwarten ist. Die Beschwerde kann nur durch Einreichung einer von einem Rechtsanwalt unterzeichneten Beschwerdeschrift eingelegt werden. Über sie entscheidet das Oberlandesgericht; § 28 Abs. 2 und 3 des Gesetzes über die Angelegenheiten der freiwilligen Gerichtsbarkeit ist entsprechend anzuwenden. Die weitere Beschwerde ist ausgeschlossen. Die Landesregierung kann durch Rechtsverordnung die Entscheidung über die Beschwerde für die Bezirke mehrerer Oberlandesgerichte einem der Oberlandesgerichte oder dem Obersten Landesgericht übertragen, wenn dies der Sicherung einer einheitlichen

§ 324 Differences of opinion between corporation and auditor

(1) In cases of differences of opinion between the auditor and the corporation as to the interpretation and application of legal regulations as well as to the terms of the articles of association as to the annual financial statements, management report, consolidated financial statements or consolidated management report, the District Court, upon the application of the auditor or the corporation's legal representatives, shall make the exclusive decision.

(2) The Law concerning Administrative Acts of the Judiciary shall be applied in the proceedings. The District Court shall make a decision in a ruling supported by reasons. The decision will take effect only upon becoming final. An immediate appeal against the decision can be taken if the District Court so permits in its decision. It should only so permit if that could lead to clarification of a legal question of fundamental importance. The appeal may be lodged only by the filing of an appellate brief signed by an attorney. The Regional State Court of Appeals shall make a decision on it. § 28 Subsections 2 and 3 of the Law concerning Administrative Acts of the Judiciary shall apply analogously. Further appeals are precluded. The state government can promulgate an administrative order assigning the decision as to appeals from the districts of several Regional State Court of Appeals to one of the Regional State Courts of Appeals or the High State Courts of Appeals if this serves to secure the uniform administration of justice. The state government may delegate such power by an administra-

| Ergänzende Vorschriften für Kapitalgesellschaften | §§ 324, 325 |

Rechtsprechung dient. Die Landesregierung kann die Ermächtigung durch Rechtsverordnung auf die Landesjustizverwaltung übertragen.

(3) Für die Kosten des Verfahrens gilt die Kostenordnung. Für das Verfahren des ersten Rechtszugs wird das Doppelte der vollen Gebühr erhoben. Für den zweiten Rechtszug wird die gleiche Gebühr erhoben; dies gilt auch dann, wenn die Beschwerde Erfolg hat. Wird der Antrag oder die Beschwerde zurückgenommen, bevor es zu einer Entscheidung kommt, so ermäßigt sich die Gebühr auf die Hälfte. Der Geschäftswert ist von Amts wegen festzusetzen. Er bestimmt sich nach § 30 Abs. 2 der Kostenordnung. Der Abschlußprüfer ist zur Leistung eines Kostenvorschusses nicht verpflichtet. Schuldner der Kosten ist die Kapitalgesellschaft. Die Kosten können jedoch ganz oder zum Teil dem Abschlußprüfer auferlegt werden, wenn dies der Billigkeit entspricht.

Vierter Unterabschnitt. Offenlegung (Einreichung zu einem Register, Bekanntmachung im Bundesanzeiger). Veröffentlichung und Vervielfältigung. Prüfung durch das Registergericht.

§ 325 Offenlegung

(1) Die gesetzlichen Vertreter von Kapitalgesellschaften haben den Jahresabschluß unverzüglich nach seiner Vorlage an die Gesellschafter, jedoch spätestens vor Ablauf des zwölften Monats des dem Abschlußstichtag nachfolgenden Geschäftsjahrs, mit dem Bestätigungsvermerk oder dem Vermerk über dessen Versagung zum Handelsregister des Sitzes der Kapitalgesellschaft einzureichen; gleichzei-

tive order to the state Ministry of Justice.

(3) The Fee Ordinance applies to the costs of the proceedings. Double the full fees will be collected for the proceedings before the first instance. The same fees will be collected for the second instance. This also applies if the appeal is successful. If the application or appeal is withdrawn before a decision is rendered, the fees shall be reduced by one-half. The amount in controversy shall be set by the court on its own motion. It shall be determined pursuant to § 30 Subsection 2 of the Fee Ordinance. The auditor is not obligated to make an advance on costs. The party liable for costs is the corporation. The costs can nonetheless be imposed upon the auditor in whole or in part if justice so requires.

Fourth Subpart. Disclosure (Filing in the Register, Publication in the Federal Gazette). Publication and Reproduction. Examination by the Registry Court

§ 325 Disclosure

(1) The legal representatives of corporations must file at the Commercial Register of the corporation's domicile the annual financial statements with the certification of the financial statements or the notation as to refusal without undue delay after their presentation to the shareholders, but at the latest prior to the expiration of the twelfth month of the fiscal year following the close of the fiscal year. At

243

§ 325

tig sind der Lagebericht, der Bericht des Aufsichtsrats und, soweit sich der Vorschlag für die Verwendung des Ergebnisses und der Beschluß über seine Verwendung aus dem eingereichten Jahresabschluß nicht ergeben, der Vorschlag für die Verwendung des Ergebnisses und der Beschluß über seine Verwendung unter Angabe des Jahresüberschusses oder Jahresfehlbetrags sowie die nach § 161 des Aktiengesetzes vorgeschriebene Erklärung einzureichen; Angaben über die Ergebnisverwendung brauchen von Gesellschaften mit beschränkter Haftung nicht gemacht zu werden, wenn sich anhand dieser Angaben die Gewinnanteile von natürlichen Personen feststellen lassen, die Gesellschafter sind. Die gesetzlichen Vertreter haben unverzüglich nach der Einreichung der in Satz 1 bezeichneten Unterlagen im Bundesanzeiger bekanntzumachen, bei welchem Handelsregister und unter welcher Nummer diese Unterlagen eingereicht worden sind. Werden zur Wahrung der Frist nach Satz 1 der Jahresabschluß und der Lagebericht ohne die anderen Unterlagen eingereicht, so sind der Bericht und der Vorschlag nach ihrem Vorliegen, die Beschlüsse nach der Beschlußfassung und der Vermerk nach der Erteilung unverzüglich einzureichen; wird der Jahresabschluß bei nachträglicher Prüfung oder Feststellung geändert, so ist auch die Änderung nach Satz 1 einzureichen.

(2) Absatz 1 ist auf große Kapitalgesellschaften (§ 267 Abs. 3) mit der Maßgabe anzuwenden, daß die in Absatz 1 bezeichneten Unterlagen zunächst im Bundesanzeiger bekanntzumachen sind und die Bekanntmachung unter Beifügung der bezeichneten Unterlagen zum Handelsregister des Sitzes der Kapitalgesellschaft einzureichen ist;

the same time, the management report, report of the supervisory board and, to the extent that the proposal for the use of the results and the resolution as to its use are not apparent from the filed annual financial statements, the proposal for the use of the results and the resolution as to their use, specifying the annual surplus or annual deficit as well as the statement required under § 161 of the Stock Corporation Act (*Aktiengesetz*), shall be filed; limited liability companies need not make disclosures as to use of the results if such disclosures can serve to determine profit shares of natural persons who are shareholders. The legal representatives shall announce in the Federal Gazette without undue delay after filing the records designated in sentence 1 at which Commercial Register and under which number these records have been filed. If in order to meet the time limit set in sentence 1 the annual financial statements and management report are filed without the other records, then the report and proposal shall be filed without undue delay after their availability, the resolutions after their adoption and the notation after its issuance. If the annual financial statements are changed after subsequent examination or determinations, then that change shall also be filed pursuant to sentence 1.

(2) Subsection 1 shall be applied to large corporations (§ 267 Subsection 3), subject to the proviso that the records designated in Subsection 1 shall first be published in the Federal Gazette and the publication shall be filed at the Commercial Register at the corporation's domicile with the enclosure of the designated records.

Ergänzende Vorschriften für Kapitalgesellschaften § 325

die Bekanntmachung nach Absatz 1 Satz 2 entfällt. Die Aufstellung des Anteilsbesitzes (§ 287) braucht nicht im Bundesanzeiger bekannt gemacht zu werden.

(3) Die gesetzlichen Vertreter einer Kapitalgesellschaft, die einen Konzernabschluß aufzustellen hat, haben den Konzernabschluß unverzüglich nach seiner Vorlage an die Gesellschafter, jedoch spätestens vor Ablauf des zwölften Monats des dem Konzernabschlußstichtag nachfolgenden Geschäftsjahrs, mit dem Bestätigungsvermerk oder dem Vermerk über dessen Versagung und den Konzernlagebericht sowie den Bericht des Aufsichtsrats im Bundesanzeiger bekanntzumachen und die Bekanntmachung unter Beifügung der bezeichneten Unterlagen zum Handelsregister des Sitzes der Kapitalgesellschaft einzureichen. Ist die Berichterstattung des Aufsichtsrats über Konzernabschluss und Konzernlagebericht in einem nach Absatz 2 Satz 1 erster Halbsatz in Verbindung mit Absatz 1 Satz 1 zweiter Halbsatz offen gelegten Bericht des Aufsichtsrats enthalten, so kann die Bekanntmachung des Berichts nach Satz 1 durch einen Hinweis auf die frühere oder gleichzeitige Bekanntmachung nach Absatz 2 Satz 1 erster Halbsatz ersetzt werden. Die Aufstellung des Anteilsbesitzes (§ 313 Abs. 4) braucht nicht im Bundesanzeiger bekannt gemacht zu werden. Absatz 1 Satz 3 ist entsprechend anzuwenden.

(4) Bei Anwendung der Absätze 2 und 3 ist für die Wahrung der Fristen nach Absatz 1 Satz 1 und Absatz 3 Satz 1 der Zeitpunkt der Einreichung der Unterlagen beim Bundesanzeiger maßgebend.

The publication pursuant to Subsection 1 sentence 2 shall be omitted. The list of share ownership (§ 287) need not be published in the Federal Gazette.

(3) The legal representatives of a corporation which must prepare consolidated financial statements must publish the consolidated financial statements, along with the certification of the financial statements or the notation as to its refusal, and the consolidated management report as well as the report of the supervisory board (Aufsichtsrat) in the Federal Gazette without undue delay after their presentation to the shareholders, but at the latest prior to the expiration of the twelfth month of the fiscal year following the close of the fiscal year of the consolidated financial statements and shall file the publication at the Commercial Register at the corporation's domicile with the enclosure of the designated records. If the reporting of the supervisory board regarding the consolidated financial statements and the consolidated management report is contained in a report published pursuant to Subsection 2 sentence 1 first half-sentence in connection with Subsection 1 sentence 2 second half-sentence, then the publication of the report under sentence 1 can be replaced by a reference to the earlier or concurrent publication pursuant to Subsection 2 sentence 1 first half-sentence. The list of share ownership (§ 313 Subsection 4) need not be published in the Federal Gazette. Subsection 1 sentence 3 shall apply analogously.

(4) In applying Subsections 2 and 3, the time of the filing of the records in the Federal Gazette governs the observance of the time period pursuant to Subsection 1 sentence 1 and Subsection 3 sentence 1.

(5) Auf Gesetz, Gesellschaftsvertrag oder Satzung beruhende Pflichten der Gesellschaft, den Jahresabschluß, Lagebericht, Konzernabschluß oder Konzernlagebericht in anderer Weise bekanntzumachen, einzureichen oder Personen zugänglich zu machen, bleiben unberührt.

§ 325 a Zweigniederlassungen von Kapitalgesellschaften mit Sitz im Ausland

(1) Bei inländischen Zweigniederlassungen von Kapitalgesellschaften mit Sitz in einem anderen Mitgliedstaat der Europäischen Wirtschaftsgemeinschaft oder Vertragsstaat des Abkommens über den Europäischen Wirtschaftsraum haben die in § 13 e Abs. 2 Satz 4 Nr. 3 genannten Personen oder, wenn solche nicht angemeldet sind, die gesetzlichen Vertreter der Gesellschaft die Unterlagen der Rechnungslegung der Hauptniederlassung, die nach dem für die Hauptniederlassung maßgeblichen Recht erstellt, geprüft und offengelegt worden sind, nach den §§ 325, 328, 329 Abs. 1 offenzulegen. Die Unterlagen sind zu dem Handelsregister am Sitz der Zweigniederlassung einzureichen; bestehen mehrere inländische Zweigniederlassungen derselben Gesellschaft, brauchen die Unterlagen nur zu demjenigen Handelsregister eingereicht zu werden, zu dem gemäß § 13 e Abs. 5 die Satzung oder der Gesellschaftsvertrag eingereicht wurde. Die Unterlagen sind in deutscher Sprache einzureichen. Soweit dies nicht die Amtssprache am Sitz der Hauptniederlassung ist, können die Unterlagen auch in englischer Sprache oder in einer von dem Register der Hauptniederlassung beglaubigten Abschrift eingereicht werden; von der Beglaubigung des Registers ist eine beglaubigte Über-

(5) The company's obligations pursuant to law or the articles of association to differently publish, file or make accessible to persons the annual financial statements, management report, consolidated financial statements or the consolidated management report remain unaffected.

§ 325 a Branches of corporations with foreign domicile

(1) In the case of domestic branches of corporations with domicile in another member state of the European Union or contracting state of the European Economic Area Agreement the persons named in § 13 e Subsection 2 sentence 4 No. 3, or, if such have not been entered, the legal representatives of the company shall, pursuant to §§ 325, 328 and 329 Subsection 1, disclose the financial statements for the head office which have been prepared, audited and disclosed according to the law applicable to the head office. The documents shall be submitted to the Commercial Register at the domicile of the branch; in the event that several domestic branches of the same company exist, the documents need be submitted only to the Commercial Register to which the articles of association were submitted pursuant to § 13 e Subsection 5. The documents shall be submitted in the German language. To the extent that this is not the official language at the domicile of the head office, the documents may also be submitted in the English language or in a translation certified by the Commercial Register of the head office; a certified German translation of the certification of the Commercial Register shall be submitted. § 325 Subsection 2 shall only apply if the

Ergänzende Vorschriften für Kapitalgesellschaften §§ 325a–327

setzung in deutscher Sprache einzureichen. § 325 Abs. 2 ist nur anzuwenden, wenn die Merkmale für große Kapitalgesellschaften (§ 267 Abs. 3) von der Zweigniederlassung überschritten werden.

(2) Diese Vorschrift gilt nicht für Zweigniederlassungen, die von Kreditinstituten im Sinne des § 340 oder von Versicherungsunternehmen im Sinne des § 341 errichtet werden.

criteria for large corporations (§ 267 Subsection 3) are not exceeded by the domestic branch.

(2) This provision shall not apply to branches established by financial institutions within the meaning of § 340 or by insurance companies within the meaning of § 341.

§ 326 Größenabhängige Erleichterungen für kleine Kapitalgesellschaften bei der Offenlegung

Auf kleine Kapitalgesellschaften (§ 267 Abs. 1) ist § 325 Abs. 1 mit der Maßgabe anzuwenden, daß die gesetzlichen Vertreter nur die Bilanz und den Anhang einzureichen haben. Der Anhang braucht die die Gewinn- und Verlustrechnung betreffenden Angaben nicht zu enthalten.

§ 326 Size-related relief for disclosures by small corporations

§ 325 Subsection 1 shall be applied to small corporations (§ 267 Subsection 1) with the proviso that the legal representatives must submit only the balance sheet and the notes. The notes need not contain the information relating to the profit and loss statement.

§ 327 Größenabhängige Erleichterungen für mittelgroße Kapitalgesellschaften bei der Offenlegung

Auf mittelgroße Kapitalgesellschaften (§ 267 Abs. 2) ist § 325 Abs. 1 mit der Maßgabe anzuwenden, daß die gesetzlichen Vertreter

1. die Bilanz nur in der für kleine Kapitalgesellschaften nach § 266 Abs. 1 Satz 3 vorgeschriebenen Form zum Handelsregister einreichen müssen. In der Bilanz oder im Anhang sind jedoch die folgenden Posten des § 266 Abs. 2 und 3 zusätzlich gesondert anzugeben:

§ 327 Size-related relief for disclosures by medium-sized corporations

§ 325 Subsection 1 shall be applied to medium-sized corporations (§ 267 Subsection 2) with the proviso that the legal representatives

1. must file the balance sheet at the Commercial Register only in the form prescribed for small companies pursuant to § 266 Subsection 1 sentence 3. The balance sheet or the notes, however, shall in addition show separately the following entries from § 266 Subsections 2 and 3:

Auf der Aktivseite
- A I 2 Geschäfts- oder Firmenwert;
- A II 1 Grundstücke, grundstücksgleiche Rechte und Bauten einschließlich der Bauten auf fremden Grundstücken;
- A II 2 technische Anlagen und Maschinen;
- A II 3 andere Anlagen, Betriebs- und Geschäftsausstattung;
- A II 4 geleistete Anzahlungen und Anlagen im Bau;
- A III 1 Anteile an verbundenen Unternehmen;
- A III 2 Ausleihungen an verbundene Unternehmen;
- A III 3 Beteiligungen;
- A III 4 Ausleihungen an Unternehmen, mit denen ein Beteiligungsverhältnis besteht;
- B II 2 Forderungen gegen verbundene Unternehmen;
- B II 3 Forderungen gegen Unternehmen, mit denen ein Beteiligungsverhältnis besteht;
- B III 1 Anteile an verbundenen Unternehmen;
- B III 2 eigene Anteile.

Auf der Passivseite
- C 1 Anleihen, davon konvertibel;
- C 2 Verbindlichkeiten gegenüber Kreditinstituten;
- C 6 Verbindlichkeiten gegenüber verbundenen Unternehmen;
- C 7 Verbindlichkeiten gegenüber Unternehmen, mit denen ein Beteiligungsverhältnis besteht;

2. den Anhang ohne die Angaben nach § 285 Nr. 2, 5 und 8 Buchstabe a, Nr. 12 zum Handelsregister einreichen dürfen.

On the assets side
- A I 2 goodwill;
- A II 1 real property, rights similar to those in real property and buildings, including buildings on real property of third parties;
- A II 2 technical installations and machines;
- A II 3 other installations and business and office equipment;
- A II 4 payments made and installations under construction;
- A III 1 shares in related enterprises;
- A III 2 loans to related enterprises;
- A III 3 participations;
- A III 4 loans to enterprises in which participations exist;
- B II 2 claims against related enterprises;
- B II 3 claims against enterprises in which participations exist;
- B III 1 shares in related enterprises; and
- B III 2 treasury shares.

On the liabilities side
- C 1 loans, noting the amount for convertibles;
- C 2 liabilities to credit institutions;
- C 6 liabilities to related enterprises; and
- C 7 liabilities to related enterprises;

2. may file the notes at the Commercial Register without the information pursuant to § 285, Nos. 2, 5 and 8, Letter a and No. 12.

§ 328 Form und Inhalt der Unterlagen bei der Offenlegung, Veröffentlichung und Vervielfältigung

(1) Bei der vollständigen oder teilweisen Offenlegung des Jahresabschlusses und des Konzernabschlusses und bei der Veröffentlichung oder Vervielfältigung in anderer Form auf Grund des Gesellschaftsvertrags oder der Satzung sind die folgenden Vorschriften einzuhalten:

1. Der Jahresabschluß und der Konzernabschluß sind so wiederzugeben, daß sie den für ihre Aufstellung maßgeblichen Vorschriften entsprechen, soweit nicht Erleichterungen nach §§ 326, 327 in Anspruch genommen werden; sie haben in diesem Rahmen vollständig und richtig zu sein. Das Datum der Feststellung ist anzugeben, sofern der Jahresabschluß festgestellt worden ist. Wurde der Jahresabschluß oder der Konzernabschluß auf Grund gesetzlicher Vorschriften durch einen Abschlußprüfer geprüft, so ist jeweils der vollständige Wortlaut des Bestätigungsvermerks oder des Vermerks über dessen Versagung wiederzugeben; wird der Jahresabschluß wegen der Inanspruchnahme von Erleichterungen nur teilweise offengelegt und bezieht sich der Bestätigungsvermerk auf den vollständigen Jahresabschluß, so ist hierauf hinzuweisen.

2. Werden der Jahresabschluß oder der Konzernabschluß zur Wahrung der gesetzlich vorgeschriebenen Fristen über die Offenlegung vor der Prüfung oder Feststellung, sofern diese gesetzlich vorgeschrieben sind, oder nicht gleichzeitig mit beizufügenden Unterlagen of-

§ 328 Form and content of records upon disclosure, publication and reproduction

(1) Upon the full or partial disclosure of the annual financial statements and consolidated financial statements and upon their publication or reproduction in another form by reason of the articles of association, the following regulations shall be adhered to:

1. The annual financial statements and consolidated financial statements shall be presented in such a way that they conform to the regulations governing their preparation to the extent that relief cannot be claimed pursuant to §§ 326 and 327; within these guidelines they must be complete and correct. The date of approval shall be given to the extent that the annual financial statements have been approved. If the annual financial statements or the consolidated financial statements were examined by an auditor based on legal regulations, then the complete text of the financial statements' certification or of the notation of its refusal shall be provided. If the annual financial statements are only partly disclosed because of the use of exemptive provisions and if the certification of the financial statements refers to the entire annual financial statements, this fact shall be indicated.

2. If, in order to preserve the legally prescribed period of time for disclosure, the annual financial statements or the consolidated financial statements are disclosed before the audit or approval, to the extent that these are legally prescribed, or are not disclosed simul-

fengelegt, so ist hierauf bei der Offenlegung hinzuweisen.

(2) Werden der Jahresabschluß oder der Konzernabschluß in Veröffentlichungen und Vervielfältigungen, die nicht durch Gesetz, Gesellschaftsvertrag oder Satzung vorgeschrieben sind, nicht in der nach Absatz 1 vorgeschriebenen Form wiedergegeben, so ist jeweils in einer Überschrift darauf hinzuweisen, daß es sich nicht um eine der gesetzlichen Form entsprechende Veröffentlichung handelt. Ein Bestätigungsvermerk darf nicht beigefügt werden. Ist jedoch auf Grund gesetzlicher Vorschriften eine Prüfung durch einen Abschlußprüfer erfolgt, so ist anzugeben, ob der Abschlußprüfer den in gesetzlicher Form erstellten Jahresabschluß oder den Konzernabschluß bestätigt hat oder ob er die Bestätigung eingeschränkt oder versagt hat. Ferner ist anzugeben, bei welchem Handelsregister und in welcher Nummer des Bundesanzeigers die Offenlegung erfolgt ist oder daß die Offenlegung noch nicht erfolgt ist.

(3) Absatz 1 Nr. 1 ist auf den Lagebericht, den Konzernlagebericht, den Vorschlag für die Verwendung des Ergebnisses und den Beschluß über seine Verwendung sowie auf die Aufstellung des Anteilsbesitzes entsprechend anzuwenden. Werden die in Satz 1 bezeichneten Unterlagen nicht gleichzeitig mit dem Jahresabschluß oder dem Konzernabschluß offengelegt, so ist bei ihrer nachträglichen Offenlegung jeweils anzugeben, auf welchen Abschluß sie sich beziehen und wo dieser offengelegt worden ist; dies gilt auch für die nachträgliche Offenlegung des Bestätigungsvermerks oder des Vermerks über seine Versagung.

(4) *(aufgehoben)*

taneously with the accompanying records, this shall be indicated upon the disclosure.

(2) If in publications and reproductions that are not prescribed by law or the articles of association, the annual financial statements or the consolidated financial statements are not provided in the form prescribed pursuant to Subsection 1, then a heading shall indicate that this is not a publication conforming to the legally prescribed form. A certification of the financial statements may not be included. If for reason of legal regulations an examination by an auditor has taken place nonetheless, then it shall be indicated whether the auditor certified the annual financial statements or the consolidated financial statements prepared in the legal form or whether the certification was limited or refused. It shall be further indicated at which Commercial Register and in which number of the Federal Gazette the disclosure appeared or that the disclosure has not yet been made.

(3) Subsection 1 No. 1 shall apply analogously to the management report, the consolidated management report, the proposal for the use of the results and the resolution on their use as well as to the list of share ownership. If the records described in sentence 1 are not disclosed simultaneously with the annual financial statements or the consolidated financial statements, then it shall be indicated upon their later disclosure to which financial statements they relate and where this was disclosed; this applies also to the later disclosure of the certification of the financial statements or the notation of its refusal.

(4) *(repealed)*

§ 329 Prüfungspflicht des Registergerichts

(1) Das Gericht prüft, ob die vollständig oder teilweise zum Handelsregister einzureichenden Unterlagen vollzählig sind und, sofern vorgeschrieben, bekanntgemacht worden sind.

(2) Gibt die Prüfung nach Absatz 1 Anlaß zu der Annahme, daß von der Größe der Kapitalgesellschaft abhängige Erleichterungen nicht hätten in Anspruch genommen werden dürfen, so kann das Gericht zu seiner Unterrichtung von der Kapitalgesellschaft innerhalb einer angemessenen Frist die Mitteilung der Umsatzerlöse (§ 277 Abs. 1) und der durchschnittlichen Zahl der Arbeitnehmer (§ 267 Abs. 5), in den Fällen des § 325 a Abs. 1 Satz 5 zusätzlich die Bilanzsumme der Zweigniederlassung und in den Fällen des § 340 l Abs. 2 in Verbindung mit Abs. 4 Satz 1 die Bilanzsumme der Zweigstelle des Kreditinstituts verlangen. Unterläßt die Kapitalgesellschaft die fristgemäße Mitteilung, so gelten die Erleichterungen als zu Unrecht in Anspruch genommen.

(3) In den Fällen des § 325 a Abs. 1 Satz 4, § 340 l Abs. 2 Satz 4 kann das Gericht im Einzelfall die Vorlage einer Übersetzung in die deutsche Sprache verlangen.

**Fünfter Unterabschnitt.
Verordnungsermächtigung für Formblätter und andere Vorschriften**

§ 330

(1) Das Bundesministerium der Justiz wird ermächtigt, im Einvernehmen mit dem Bundesministerium der Finanzen und dem Bundesministerium

§ 329 Examination duty of the registry court of the Commercial Register

(1) The court shall examine whether the records to be filed in whole or in part at the Commercial Register are complete and were published to the extent prescribed.

(2) If the examination pursuant to Subsection 1 gives cause for the assumption that relief contingent upon the size of the corporation was not allowed to have been claimed, then within an appropriate period of time the court may request the corporation to provide for the court's information the sales proceeds (§ 277 Subsection 1) and the average number of employees (§ 267 Subsection 5), in the cases of § 325 a Subsection 1 sentence 5 also the balance sheet total of the domestic branch and in the cases of § 340 l Subsection 2 in connection with Subsection 4 sentence 1 the balance sheet total of the branch of the financial institution. If the corporation fails to provide the information within the appropriate period of time, then the relief shall be deemed to have been claimed wrongfully.

(3) In the cases of § 325 a Subsection 1 sentence 4, § 340 l Subsection 2 sentence 4, the court may in the individual case request the submission of a translation in the German language.

Fifth Subpart. Enabling Rule for Printed Forms and Other Regulations

§ 330

(1) The Federal Ministry of Justice is authorized, in consultation with the Federal Ministry of Finance and the Federal Ministry for Economics and

für Wirtschaft und Technologie durch Rechtsverordnung, die nicht der Zustimmung des Bundesrates bedarf, für Kapitalgesellschaften Formblätter vorzuschreiben oder andere Vorschriften für die Gliederung des Jahresabschlusses oder des Konzernabschlusses oder den Inhalt des Anhangs, des Konzernanhangs, des Lageberichts oder des Konzernlageberichts zu erlassen, wenn der Geschäftszweig eine von den §§ 266, 275 abweichende Gliederung des Jahresabschlusses oder des Konzernabschlusses oder von den Vorschriften des Ersten Abschnitts und des Ersten und Zweiten Unterabschnitts des Zweiten Abschnitts abweichende Regelungen erfordert. Die sich aus den abweichenden Vorschriften ergebenden Anforderungen an die in Satz 1 bezeichneten Unterlagen sollen den Anforderungen gleichwertig sein, die sich für große Kapitalgesellschaften (§ 267 Abs. 3) aus den Vorschriften des Ersten Abschnitts und des Ersten und Zweiten Unterabschnitts des Zweiten Abschnitts sowie den für den Geschäftszweig geltenden Vorschriften ergeben. Über das geltende Recht hinausgehende Anforderungen dürfen nur gestellt werden, soweit sie auf Rechtsakten des Rates der Europäischen Union beruhen.

(2) Absatz 1 ist auf Kreditinstitute im Sinne des § 1 Abs. 1 des Gesetzes über das Kreditwesen, soweit sie nach dessen § 2 Abs. 1, 4 oder 5 von der Anwendung nicht ausgenommen sind, und auf Finanzdienstleistungsinstitute im Sinne von § 1 Abs. 1 a des Gesetzes über das Kreditwesen, soweit sie nach dessen § 2 Abs. 6 oder 10 von der Anwendung nicht ausgenommen sind, nach Maßgabe der Sätze 3 und 4 ungeachtet ihrer Rechtsform anzuwenden. Satz 1 ist auch auf Zweigstel-

Technology, to prescribe by administrative order which does not require the approval of the Federal upper house of Parliament printed forms for stock corporations, or to issue other regulations for the classification of the annual financial statements or the consolidated financial statements or the content of the notes, the consolidated notes, the management report or the consolidated management report, if the line of business requires classification of the annual financial statements or the consolidated financial statements deviating from § 266 or § 275 or deviating from the regulations of the First Part or of the First and Second Subparts of the Second Part. The requirements resulting from the deviating provisions for the records described in sentence 1 should be equivalent to the requirements for large corporations (§ 267 Subsection 3), resulting from the regulations of the First Part and the First and Second Subparts of the Second Part as well as the regulations applying to the line of business. Requirements going beyond currently valid law may be made only to the extent that they rest upon legal acts of the Council of the European Union.

(2) Subsection 1 shall be applied to credit institutions within the meaning of § 1 Subsection 1 of the Banking Law (Gesetz über das Kreditwesen), to the extent that they are not exempted by § 2 Subsections 1, 4 or 5 thereof, and to financial service institutions within the meaning of § 1 Subsection 1 a of the Banking Law, to the extent that they are not exempted by § 2 Subsections 6 or 10 thereof, according to sentences 3 and 4 without regard to their legal form. Sentence 1 shall also

len von Unternehmen mit Sitz in einem Staat anzuwenden, der nicht Mitglied der Europäischen Gemeinschaft und auch nicht Vertragsstaat des Abkommens über den Europäischen Wirtschaftsraum ist, sofern die Zweigstelle nach § 53 Abs. 1 des Gesetzes über das Kreditwesen als Kreditinstitut oder als Finanzinstitut gilt. Die Rechtsverordnung bedarf nicht der Zustimmung des Bundesrates; sie ist im Einvernehmen mit dem Bundesministerium der Finanzen und im Benehmen mit der Deutschen Bundesbank zu erlassen. In die Rechtsverordnung nach Satz 1 können auch nähere Bestimmungen über die Aufstellung des Jahresabschlusses und des Konzernabschlusses im Rahmen der vorgeschriebenen Formblätter für die Gliederung des Jahresabschlusses und des Konzernabschlusses sowie des Zwischenabschlusses gemäß § 340 a Abs. 3 und des Konzernzwischenabschlusses gemäß § 340 i Abs. 4 aufgenommen werden, soweit dies zur Erfüllung der Aufgaben des Bundesaufsichtsamts für das Kreditwesen oder der Deutschen Bundesbank erforderlich ist, insbesondere um einheitliche Unterlagen zur Beurteilung der von den Kreditinstituten und Finanzdienstleistungsinstituten durchgeführten Bankgeschäfte und erbrachten Finanzdienstleistungen zu erhalten.

(3) Absatz 1 ist auf Versicherungsunternehmen nach Maßgabe der Sätze 3 und 4 ungeachtet ihrer Rechtsform anzuwenden. Satz 1 ist auch auf Niederlassungen im Geltungsbereich dieses Gesetzes von Versicherungsunternehmen mit Sitz in einem anderen Staat anzuwenden, wenn sie zum Betrieb des Direktversicherungsge-

be applied to branch offices of businesses domiciled in a country which is not a member of the European Union and is also not a contracting state of the European Economic Area Agreement to the extent that the branch office constitutes a credit or financial institution under § 53 Subsection 1 of the Banking Law. The administrative order shall not require the approval of the Federal upper house of Parliament; it shall be issued after consultation with the Federal Ministry of Finance and in consultation with the German Federal Bank. In the administrative order under sentence 1, more detailed provisions may be included concerning the preparation of annual financial statements and consolidated financial statements in the context of the prescribed forms for the presentation of the annual financial statements and consolidated financial statements as well as of the interim financial statements pursuant to § 340 a Subsection 3 and the interim consolidated financial statements pursuant to § 340 i Subsection 4, to the extent that this is required to fulfil the duties of the Federal Supervisory Authority for Financial Institutions or the German Federal Bank, particularly in order to obtain uniform documentation for evaluation of the banking transactions carried out and financial services rendered by the credit institutions and financial service institutions.

(3) Subsection 1 is to be applied to insurance companies according to sentences 3 and 4 without regard to their legal form. Within this Law's area of applicability, sentence 1 is also to be applied to branches of insurance companies domiciled in another country if they require permission of the German Insurance Supervisory Author-

schäfts der Erlaubnis durch die deutsche Versicherungsaufsichtsbehörde bedürfen. Die Rechtsverordnung bedarf der Zustimmung des Bundesrates und ist im Einvernehmen mit dem Bundesministerium der Finanzen zu erlassen. In die Rechtsverordnung nach Satz 1 können auch nähere Bestimmungen über die Aufstellung des Jahresabschlusses und des Konzernabschlusses im Rahmen der vorgeschriebenen Formblätter für die Gliederung des Jahresabschlusses und des Konzernabschlusses sowie Vorschriften über den Ansatz und die Bewertung von versicherungstechnischen Rückstellungen, insbesondere die Näherungsverfahren, aufgenommen werden.

(4) In der Rechtsverordnung nach Absatz 1 in Verbindung mit Absatz 3 kann bestimmt werden, daß Versicherungsunternehmen, auf die die Richtlinie 91/674/EWG nach deren Artikel 2 in Verbindung mit Artikel 3 der Richtlinie 73/239/EWG oder in Verbindung mit Artikel 2 Nr. 2 oder 3 oder Artikel 3 der Richtlinie 79/267/EWG nicht anzuwenden ist, von den Regelungen des Zweiten Unterabschnitts des Vierten Abschnitts ganz oder teilweise befreit werden, soweit dies erforderlich ist, um eine im Verhältnis zur Größe der Versicherungsunternehmen unangemessene Belastung zu vermeiden; Absatz 1 Satz 2 ist insoweit nicht anzuwenden. In der Rechtsverordnung dürfen diesen Versicherungsunternehmen auch für die Gliederung des Jahresabschlusses und des Konzernabschlusses, für die Erstellung von Anhang und Lagebericht und Konzernanhang und Konzernlagebericht sowie für die Offenlegung ihrer Größe angemessene Vereinfachungen gewährt werden.

ity to conduct direct insurance business. The administrative order requires the consent of the federal and is to be issued in coordination with the Federal Ministry of Finance. Additional provisions on preparation of the annual financial statements and of the consolidated financial statements within the framework of the prescribed forms for the presentation of the annual financial statements and the consolidated financial statements and regulations on the estimate and the valuation of actuarial reserves, especially the approximation procedure, can be included in the administrative order pursuant to sentence 1.

(4) The administrative order pursuant to Subsection 1 in conjunction with Subsection 3 can determine that insurance companies not subject to Directive 91/674/EEC, pursuant to its Article 2 in conjunction with Article 3 of Directive 73/239/EEC or in conjunction with Article 2 No. 2 or 3 or Article 3 of Directive 79/267/EEC, shall be exempted in whole or in part from the provisions of the Second Subpart of Part Four to the extent that this is necessary to avoid a burden inappropriate to the size of the insurance company; Subsection 1 sentence 2 is to this extent not to be applied. The administrative rule may allow these insurance companies appropriate simplifications for the presentation of the annual financial statements and of the consolidated financial statements, for the preparation of the notes and the management report and the consolidated notes and the consolidated management report and for the disclosure of their size.

(5) Die Absätze 3 und 4 sind auf Pensionsfonds (§ 112 Abs. 1 des Versicherungsaufsichtsgesetzes) entsprechend anzuwenden.

Sechster Unterabschnitt. Straf- und Bußgeldvorschriften. Zwangsgelder

§ 331 Unrichtige Darstellung

Mit Freiheitsstrafe bis zu drei Jahren oder mit Geldstrafe wird bestraft, wer

1. als Mitglied des vertretungsberechtigten Organs oder des Aufsichtsrats einer Kapitalgesellschaft die Verhältnisse der Kapitalgesellschaft in der Eröffnungsbilanz, im Jahresabschluß, im Lagebericht oder im Zwischenabschluß nach § 340 a Abs. 3 unrichtig wiedergibt oder verschleiert,

2. als Mitglied des vertretungsberechtigten Organs oder des Aufsichtsrats einer Kapitalgesellschaft die Verhältnisse des Konzerns im Konzernabschluß, im Konzernlagebericht oder im Konzernzwischenabschluß nach § 340 i Abs. 4 unrichtig wiedergibt oder verschleiert,

3. als Mitglied des vertretungsberechtigten Organs einer Kapitalgesellschaft zum Zwecke der Befreiung nach den §§ 291, 292 a oder einer nach § 292 erlassenen Rechtsverordnung einen Konzernabschluß oder Konzernlagebericht, in dem die Verhältnisse des Konzerns unrichtig wiedergegeben oder verschleiert worden sind, vorsätzlich oder leichtfertig offenlegt oder

4. als Mitglied des vertretungsberechtigten Organs einer Kapitalgesellschaft oder als Mitglied des ver-

(5) Subsections 3 and 4 shall apply analogously to Pension Funds (§ 112 Subsection 1 of the Act on Supervision of Insurance Companies).

Sixth Subpart. Criminal Law and Civil Penalty Provisions. Coercive Fines

§ 331 False presentation

A term of imprisonment of up to three years or a monetary fine will be imposed upon anyone who

1. as a member of the body legally representing the corporation or the supervisory board falsely reports or conceals the corporation's conditions in the opening balance sheet, in the annual financial statements, in the management report or in the interim financial statements pursuant to § 340 a Subsection 3,

2. as a member of the body legally representing the corporation or the supervisory board falsely reports or conceals the group of companies' conditions in the consolidated financial statements, consolidated management report or in the interim consolidated financial statements pursuant to § 340 i Subsection 4,

3. as a member of the body legally representing the corporation intentionally or recklessly discloses consolidated financial statements or a consolidated management report, in which the group of companies' conditions were falsely reported or concealed, in order to claim the exemptions pursuant to §§ 291, 292 a or an administrative order issued pursuant to § 292, or

4. as a member of the body legally representing the corporation or as a member of the body legally rep-

tretungsberechtigten Organs oder als vertretungsberechtigter Gesellschafter eines ihrer Tochterunternehmen (§ 290 Abs. 1, 2) in Aufklärungen oder Nachweisen, die nach § 320 einem Abschlußprüfer der Kapitalgesellschaft, eines verbundenen Unternehmens oder des Konzerns zu geben sind, unrichtige Angaben macht oder die Verhältnisse der Kapitalgesellschaft, eines Tochterunternehmens oder des Konzerns unrichtig wiedergibt oder verschleiert.

§ 332 Verletzung der Berichtspflicht

(1) Mit Freiheitsstrafe bis zu drei Jahren oder mit Geldstrafe wird bestraft, wer als Abschlußprüfer oder Gehilfe eines Abschlußprüfers über das Ergebnis der Prüfung eines Jahresabschlusses, eines Lageberichts, eines Konzernabschlusses, eines Konzernlageberichts einer Kapitalgesellschaft oder eines Zwischenabschlusses nach § 340 a Abs. 3 oder eines Konzernzwischenabschlusses gemäß § 340 i Abs. 4 unrichtig berichtet, im Prüfungsbericht (§ 321) erhebliche Umstände verschweigt oder einen inhaltlich unrichtigen Bestätigungsvermerk (§ 322) erteilt.

(2) Handelt der Täter gegen Entgelt oder in der Absicht, sich oder einen anderen zu bereichern oder einen anderen zu schädigen, so ist die Strafe Freiheitsstrafe bis zu fünf Jahren oder Geldstrafe.

§ 333 Verletzung der Geheimhaltungspflicht

(1) Mit Freiheitsstrafe bis zu einem Jahr oder mit Geldstrafe wird bestraft, wer ein Geheimnis der Kapitalgesell-

resenting one of its subsidiaries or as a shareholder with power of representation of one of its subsidiaries (§ 290 Subsections 1 and 2) gives false information, or falsely reports or conceals the conditions of the corporation, a subsidiary or the group of companies in explanations or supporting documents that must be given pursuant to § 320 to an auditor of the corporation, of a related enterprise or of the group of companies.

§ 332 Violation of the duty to report

(1) A term of imprisonment of up to three years or a monetary fine shall be imposed on anyone who as an auditor or auditor's assistant falsely reports the examination results of a corporation's annual financial statements, management report, consolidated financial statements, consolidated management report or interim financial statements pursuant to § 340 a Subsection 3 or interim consolidated statements pursuant to § 340 i Subsection 4, conceals significant circumstances in the audit report (§ 321) or issues a sfpaubstantively false certification of the financial statements (§ 322).

(2) If the perpetrator acts for pay or with the intent to enrich himself or another or to harm another, then the punishment shall be a term of imprisonment of up to five years or a monetary fine.

§ 333 Violation of the duty of confidentiality

(1) A term of imprisonment of up to one year or a monetary fine shall be imposed on anyone who without authori-

schaft, eines Tochterunternehmens (§ 290 Abs. 1, 2), eines gemeinsam geführten Unternehmens (§ 310) oder eines assoziierten Unternehmens (§ 311), namentlich ein Betriebs- oder Geschäftsgeheimnis, das ihm in seiner Eigenschaft als Abschlußprüfer oder Gehilfe eines Abschlußprüfers bei Prüfung des Jahresabschlusses oder des Konzernabschlusses bekannt geworden ist, unbefugt offenbart.

(2) Handelt der Täter gegen Entgelt oder in der Absicht, sich oder einen anderen zu bereichern oder einen anderen zu schädigen, so ist die Strafe Freiheitsstrafe bis zu zwei Jahren oder Geldstrafe. Ebenso wird bestraft, wer ein Geheimnis der in Absatz 1 bezeichneten Art, namentlich ein Betriebs- oder Geschäftsgeheimnis, das ihm unter den Voraussetzungen des Absatzes 1 bekannt geworden ist, unbefugt verwertet.

(3) Die Tat wird nur auf Antrag der Kapitalgesellschaft verfolgt.

§ 334 Bußgeldvorschriften

(1) Ordnungswidrig handelt, wer als Mitglied des vertretungsberechtigten Organs oder des Aufsichtsrats einer Kapitalgesellschaft

1. bei der Aufstellung oder Feststellung des Jahresabschlusses einer Vorschrift
    a) des § 243 Abs. 1 oder 2, der §§ 244, 245, 246, 247, 248, 249 Abs. 1 Satz 1 oder Abs. 3, des § 250 Abs. 1 Satz 1 oder Abs. 2, des § 251 oder des § 264 Abs. 2 über Form oder Inhalt,

zation discloses a secret of the corporation, a subsidiary (§ 290 Subsections 1 and 2), a jointly run enterprise (§ 310) or an associated enterprise (§ 311), especially a trade or business secret that became known to him in his capacity as an auditor or auditor's assistant while examining the annual financial statements or the consolidated financial statements.

(2) If the perpetrator acts for pay or with the intent to enrich himself or another or to harm another, then the punishment shall be a term of imprisonment of up to two years or a monetary fine. The same punishment shall be imposed on anyone who without authorization exploits a secret in the way described in Subsection 1, especially a trade or business secret that became known to him under the conditions described in Subsection 1.

(3) The action will only be prosecuted upon the application of the corporation.

§ 334 Civil penalty provisions

(1) An administrative offense is committed by anyone who, as a member of a body legally representing a corporation or the supervisory board, contravenes

1. upon the preparation or adoption of the annual financial statements a provision
    a) on form or content of § 243 Subsections 1 or 2, of §§ 244, 245, 246, 247, 248 or 249 Subsection 1 sentence 1 or Subsection 3, of § 250 Subsection 1 sentence 1 or Subsection 2, of § 251 or of § 264 Subsection 2,

b) des § 253 Abs. 1 Satz 1 in Verbindung mit § 255 Abs. 1 oder 2 Satz 1, 2 oder 6, des § 253 Abs. 1 Satz 2 oder Abs. 2 Satz 1, 2 oder 3, dieser in Verbindung mit § 279 Abs. 1 Satz 2, des § 253 Abs. 3 Satz 1 oder 2, des § 280 Abs. 1, des § 282 oder des § 283 über die Bewertung,

c) des § 265 Abs. 2, 3, 4 oder 6, der §§ 266, 268 Abs. 2, 3, 4, 5, 6 oder 7, der §§ 272, 273, 274 Abs. 1, des § 275 oder des § 277 über die Gliederung oder

d) des § 280 Abs. 3, des § 281 Abs. 1 Satz 2 oder 3 oder Abs. 2 Satz 1, des § 284 oder des § 285 über die in der Bilanz oder im Anhang zu machenden Angaben,

2. bei der Aufstellung des Konzernabschlusses einer Vorschrift

a) des § 294 Abs. 1 über den Konsolidierungskreis,

b) des § 297 Abs. 2 oder 3 oder des § 298 Abs. 1 in Verbindung mit den § 244, 245, 246, 247, 248, 249 Abs. 1 Satz 1 oder Abs. 3, dem § 250 Abs. 1 Satz 1 oder Abs. 2 oder dem § 251 über Inhalt oder Form,

c) des § 300 über die Konsolidierungsgrundsätze oder das Vollständigkeitsgebot,

d) des § 308 Abs. 1 Satz 1 in Verbindung mit den in Nummer 1 Buchstabe b bezeichneten Vorschriften oder des § 308 Abs. 2 über die Bewertung,

b) on valuation of § 253 Subsection 1 sentence 1 in connection with § 255 Subsection 1 or 2 sentence 1, 2 or 6, of § 253 Subsection 1 sentence 2 or Subsection 2 sentence 1, 2, or 3, the latter in connection with § 279 Subsection 1 sentence 2, of § 253 Subsection 3 sentence 1 or 2, of § 280 Subsection 1, of § 282 or of § 283,

c) on classification of § 265 Subsection 2, 3, 4 or 6, of §§ 266, 268 Subsection 2, 3, 4, 5, 6 or 7, of § 277, §§ 272, 273, 274 Subsection 1, § 275 or § 277 or

d) on the information to be provided in the balance sheet or notes of § 280 Subsection 3, of § 281 Subsection 1 sentence 2 or 3 or Subsection 2 sentence 1, of § 284 or § 285,

2. upon the preparation of the consolidated financial statements a provision

a) on the consolidated group, of § 294 Subsection 1,

b) on content or form of § 297 Subsection 2 or 3 or of § 298 Subsection 1 in connection with §§ 244, 245, 246, 247, 248 or 249 Subsection 1 sentence 1 or Subsection 3, of § 250 Subsection 1 sentence 1 or Subsection 2 or of § 251,

c) on the consolidation principles or requirements for completeness of § 300,

d) on valuation of § 308 Subsection 1 sentence 1 in connection with the provisions described in No. 1, Letter b) or of § 308 Subsection 2,

e) des § 311 Abs. 1 Satz 1 in Verbindung mit § 312 über die Behandlung assoziierter Unternehmen oder

f) des § 308 Abs. 1 Satz 3, des § 313 oder des § 314 über die im Anhang zu machenden Angaben,

3. bei der Aufstellung des Lageberichts einer Vorschrift des § 289 Abs. 1 über den Inhalt des Lageberichts,

4. bei der Aufstellung des Konzernlageberichts einer Vorschrift des § 315 Abs. 1 über den Inhalt des Konzernlageberichts,

5. bei der Offenlegung, Veröffentlichung oder Vervielfältigung einer Vorschrift des § 328 über Form oder Inhalt oder

6. einer auf Grund des § 330 Abs. 1 Satz 1 erlassenen Rechtsverordnung, soweit sie für einen bestimmten Tatbestand auf diese Bußgeldvorschrift verweist, zuwiderhandelt.

(2) Ordnungswidrig handelt auch, wer zu einem Jahresabschluß oder einem Konzernabschluß, der auf Grund gesetzlicher Vorschriften zu prüfen ist, einen Vermerk nach § 322 erteilt, obwohl nach § 319 Abs. 2 er oder nach § 319 Abs. 3 die Wirtschaftsprüfungsgesellschaft oder Buchprüfungsgesellschaft, für die er tätig wird, nicht Abschlußprüfer sein darf.

(3) Die Ordnungswidrigkeit kann mit einer Geldbuße bis zu fünfundzwanzigtausend Euro geahndet werden.

(4) Die Absätze 1 bis 3 sind auf Kreditinstitute im Sinne des § 340 und auf Versicherungsunternehmen im Sinne des § 341 Abs. 1 nicht anzuwenden.

e) on the treatment of associated enterprises of § 311 Subsection 1 sentence 1 in connection with § 312, or

f) on the information to be provided in the notes of § 308 Subsection 1 sentence 3, of § 313 or of § 314,

3. upon the preparation of the management report a provision on the content of the management report of § 289 Subsection 1,

4. upon the preparation of the consolidated management report a provision on the content of the consolidated management report of § 315 Subsection 1,

5. upon the disclosure, publication or reproduction of a provision on form or content of § 328, or

6. an administrative order issued on the basis of § 330 Subsection 1 sentence 1, to the extent that it refers to this penalty provision for the elements of a particular act.

(2) An administrative offense is also committed by anyone who issues a certification pursuant to § 322 for annual financial statements or consolidated financial statements that must be examined pursuant to legal regulations, even though pursuant to § 319 Subsection 2 he, or pursuant to § 319 Subsection 3, the certified accounting firm or the auditing firm for which he is acting, may not be the auditor.

(3) An administrative offense can be punished with a fine of up to twenty-five thousand EUR.

(4) Subsections 1 through 3 shall not be applied to financial institutions within the meaning of § 340 and to insurance companies within the meaning of § 341 Subsection 1.

§ 335 Festsetzung von Zwangsgeld

Mitglieder des vertretungsberechtigten Organs einer Kapitalgesellschaft, die

1. § 242 Abs. 1 und 2, § 264 Abs. 1 über die Pflicht zur Aufstellung eines Jahresabschlusses und eines Lageberichts,
2. § 290 Abs. 1 und 2 über die Pflicht zur Aufstellung eines Konzernabschlusses und eines Konzernlageberichts,
3. § 318 Abs. 1 Satz 4 über die Pflicht zur unverzüglichen Erteilung des Prüfungsauftrags,
4. § 318 Abs. 4 Satz 3 über die Pflicht, den Antrag auf gerichtliche Bestellung des Abschlussprüfers zu stellen oder
5. § 320 über die Pflichten gegenüber dem Abschlussprüfer

nicht befolgen, sind hierzu vom Registergericht durch Festsetzung von Zwangsgeld nach § 140 a Abs. 1 des Gesetzes über die Angelegenheiten der freiwilligen Gerichtsbarkeit anzuhalten. Das Registergericht schreitet jedoch nur auf Antrag ein; § 14 ist insoweit nicht anzuwenden. Das einzelne Zwangsgeld darf den Betrag von fünftausend Euro nicht übersteigen.

§ 335a Festsetzung von Ordnungsgeld

Gegen die Mitglieder des vertretungsberechtigten Organs einer Kapitalgesellschaft, die

1. § 325 über die Pflicht zur Offenlegung des Jahresabschlusses, des Lageberichts, des Konzernabschlusses, des Konzernlageberichts und anderer Unterlagen der Rechnungslegung oder

§ 335 Setting of a coercive fine

Members of the body legally representing a corporation who do not comply with

1. § 242 Subsection 1 and 2 or § 264 Subsection 1 on the duty to prepare annual financial statements and a management report,
2. § 290 Subsections 1 and 2 on the duty to prepare consolidated financial statements and a consolidated management report,
3. § 318 Subsection 1 sentence 4 on the duty to issue the examination mandate without undue delay,
4. § 318 Subsection 4 sentence 3 on the duty to make an application for court appointment of an auditor,
5. § 320 on the duties vis-à-vis the auditor,

shall be induced to do so by the registry court by means of a coercive fine pursuant to § 140 a of the Law concerning Administrative Acts of the Judiciary. The registry court shall, however, intervene only upon application; § 14 shall not apply in this regard. An individual fine may not exceed the amount of five thousand Euro.

§ 335a Setting of administrative fines

Members of the body legally representing a corporation who do not comply with

1. § 325 on the duty to disclose the annual financial statements, the management report, the consolidated financial statement, the consolidated management report and other documents for the rendering of accounts or

2. § 325 a über die Pflicht der Offenlegung der Rechnungslegungsunterlagen der Hauptniederlassung

nicht befolgen, ist wegen des pflichtwidrigen Unterlassens der rechtzeitigen Offenlegung vom Registergericht ein Ordnungsgeld nach § 140 a Abs. 2 des Gesetzes über die Angelegenheiten der freiwilligen Gerichtsbarkeit festzusetzen; im Falle der Nummer 2 treten die in § 13 e Abs. 2 Satz 4 Nr. 3 genannten Personen, sobald sie angemeldet sind, an die Stelle der Mitglieder des vertretungsberechtigten Organs der Kapitalgesellschaft. Einem Verfahren nach Satz 1 steht nicht entgegen, dass eine in § 335 Satz 1 bezeichnete Pflicht noch nicht erfüllt ist. Das Registergericht schreitet jedoch nur auf Antrag ein; § 14 ist insoweit nicht anzuwenden. Das Ordnungsgeld beträgt mindestens zweitausendfünfhundert und höchstens fünfundzwanzigtausend Euro; § 140 a Abs. 2 Satz 4 des Gesetzes über die Angelegenheiten der freiwilligen Gerichtsbarkeit bleibt unberührt.

2. § 325 a concerning the duty to disclose the financial statements of the head office

shall be subject to an administrative fine imposed by the registry court pursuant to § 140 a Subsection 2 of the Law concerning Administrative Acts of the Judiciary for failure to timely disclose in violation of the duty; in the case of No. 2 those persons named in § 13 e Subsection 2 Sentence 4 No. 3, as soon as they are registered, shall take the place of the members of the body legally representing the corporation. The nonfulfillment of a duty designated in § 335 Sentence 1 shall not prevent a proceeding pursuant to sentence 1. The registry court shall, however, intervene only upon application; to this extent § 14 does not apply. An administrative fine shall not be less than 2500 Euro nor exceed 25 000 Euro; Section 140a Subsection 2 Sentence 4 of the Law concerning Administrative Acts of the Judiciary shall not be affected.

§ 335 b Anwendung der Straf- und Bußgeldvorschriften sowie der Zwangs- und Ordnungsgeldvorschriften auf bestimmte offene Handelsgesellschaften und Kommanditgesellschaften

Die Strafvorschriften der §§ 331 bis 333, die Bußgeldvorschriften des § 334, die Zwangs- und Ordnungsgeldvorschriften der §§ 335, 335 a gelten auch für offene Handelsgesellschaften und Kommanditgesellschaften im Sinne des § 264 a Abs. 1.

§ 335 b Application of criminal and civil penalty provisions and coercive and administrative fine provisions to certain general commercial partnerships and limited partnerships

The criminal penalty provisions of §§ 331 through 333, the civil penalty provisions of § 334, the coercive and administrative fine provisions of §§ 335, 335 a also apply to general commercial partnerships and limited partnerships within the meaning of § 264 a Subsection 1.

Dritter Abschnitt. Ergänzende Vorschriften für eingetragene Genossenschaften

§ 336 Pflicht zur Aufstellung von Jahresabschluß und Lagebericht

(1) Der Vorstand einer Genossenschaft hat den Jahresabschluß (§ 242) um einen Anhang zu erweitern, der mit der Bilanz und der Gewinn- und Verlustrechnung eine Einheit bildet, sowie einen Lagebericht aufzustellen. Der Jahresabschluß und der Lagebericht sind in den ersten fünf Monaten des Geschäftsjahrs für das vergangene Geschäftsjahr aufzustellen.

(2) Auf den Jahresabschluß und den Lagebericht sind, soweit in den folgenden Vorschriften nichts anderes bestimmt ist, § 264 Abs. 1 Satz 3 Halbsatz 1, Abs. 2, §§ 265 bis 289 über den Jahresabschluß und den Lagebericht entsprechend anzuwenden; § 277 Abs. 3 Satz 1, §§ 279, 280, 281 Abs. 2 Satz 1, § 285 Nr. 5, 6 brauchen jedoch nicht angewendet zu werden. Sonstige Vorschriften, die durch den Geschäftszweig bedingt sind, bleiben unberührt.

(3) § 330 Abs. 1 über den Erlaß von Rechtsverordnungen ist entsprechend anzuwenden.

§ 337 Vorschriften zur Bilanz

(1) An Stelle des gezeichneten Kapitals ist der Betrag der Geschäftsguthaben der Genossen auszuweisen. Dabei ist der Betrag der Geschäftsguthaben der mit Ablauf des Geschäftsjahrs ausgeschiedenen Genossen gesondert an-

Part Three. Supplementary Provisions for Registered Co-operative Associations

§ 336 Duty to prepare annual financial statements and a management report

(1) The managing board of a co-operative association shall enlarge the annual financial statements (§ 242) with notes that form a whole with the balance sheet and the profit and loss statement as well as prepare a management report. The annual financial statements and the management report shall be prepared in the first five months of the fiscal year for the preceding fiscal year.

(2) To the extent that the following provisions do not provide otherwise, § 264 Subsection 1 sentence 3 first half sentence, Subsection 2 and §§ 265 through 289 on the annual financial statements and the management report shall apply analogously to the annual financial statements and the management report; § 277 Subsection 3 sentence 1 and §§ 279, 280, 281 Subsection 2 sentence 1 and § 285 No. 5 and 6, however, need not be applied. Other regulations that are contingent on the line of business remain unaffected.

(3) § 330 Subsection 1, on the issuance of administrative orders shall apply analogously.

§ 337 Provisions as to the balance sheet

(1) In place of the subscribed capital, the amount of the credit balance of the co-operative members shall be shown. With that, the amount of the credit balance of co-operative members who have withdrawn upon the expiration

zugeben. Werden rückständige fällige Einzahlungen auf Geschäftsanteile in der Bilanz als Geschäftsguthaben ausgewiesen, so ist der entsprechende Betrag auf der Aktivseite unter der Bezeichnung „Rückständige fällige Einzahlungen auf Geschäftsanteile" einzustellen. Werden rückständige fällige Einzahlungen nicht als Geschäftsguthaben ausgewiesen, so ist der Betrag bei dem Posten „Geschäftsguthaben" zu vermerken. In beiden Fällen ist der Betrag mit dem Nennwert anzusetzen.

(2) An Stelle der Gewinnrücklagen sind die Ergebnisrücklagen auszuweisen und wie folgt aufzugliedern:

1. Gesetzliche Rücklage;
2. andere Ergebnisrücklagen; die Ergebnisrücklage nach § 73 Abs. 3 des Gesetzes betreffend die Erwerbs- und Wirtschaftsgenossenschaften und die Beträge, die aus dieser Ergebnisrücklage an ausgeschiedene Genossen auszuzahlen sind, müssen vermerkt werden.

(3) Bei den Ergebnisrücklagen sind in der Bilanz oder im Anhang gesondert aufzuführen:

1. Die Beträge, welche die Generalversammlung aus dem Bilanzgewinn des Vorjahrs eingestellt hat;
2. die Beträge, die aus dem Jahresüberschuß des Geschäftsjahrs eingestellt werden;
3. die Beträge, die für das Geschäftsjahr entnommen werden.

§ 338 Vorschriften zum Anhang

(1) Im Anhang sind auch Angaben zu machen über die Zahl der im Laufe des Geschäftsjahrs eingetretenen oder ausgeschiedenen sowie die Zahl der am Schluß des Geschäftsjahrs der Ge-

of the fiscal year shall be reported separately. If payments due in arrears for shares in the business are shown on the balance sheet as credit balances, then the corresponding amount shall be allocated to the assets side with the designation "Payments Due in Arrears for Business Shares". If payments due in arrears are not shown as credit balances, then the amount shall be noted under the entry "Credit Balances". In both cases the amount shall be assessed at face value.

(2) In place of the retained income, the earnings reserves shall be shown and classified as follows:

1. legal reserves;
2. other earnings reserves. The earnings reserves pursuant to § 73 Subsection 3 of the Law Pertaining to Trade and Industrial Co-operatives and the amounts that shall be paid out from these earnings reserves to co-operative members who have withdrawn must be noted.

(3) The earnings reserves shall set forth separately in the balance sheet or the notes:

1. the amounts that the general assembly allocated from the balance sheet profits of the preceding year;
2. the amounts that are allocated from the annual surplus of the fiscal year; and
3. the amounts that are withdrawn for the fiscal year.

§ 338 Provisions as to notes

(1) The notes shall provide information on the number of co-operative members who joined or withdrew during the fiscal year as well as the number belonging to the co-operative

nossenschaft angehörenden Genossen. Ferner sind der Gesamtbetrag, um welchen in diesem Jahr die Geschäftsguthaben sowie die Haftsummen der Genossen sich vermehrt oder vermindert haben, und der Betrag der Haftsummen anzugeben, für welche am Jahresschluß alle Genossen zusammen aufzukommen haben.

(2) Im Anhang sind ferner anzugeben:

1. Name und Anschrift des zuständigen Prüfungsverbandes, dem die Genossenschaft angehört;

2. alle Mitglieder des Vorstands und des Aufsichtsrats, auch wenn sie im Geschäftsjahr oder später ausgeschieden sind, mit dem Familiennamen und mindestens einem ausgeschriebenen Vornamen; ein etwaiger Vorsitzender des Aufsichtsrats ist als solcher zu bezeichnen.

(3) An Stelle der in § 285 Nr. 9 vorgeschriebenen Angaben über die an Mitglieder von Organen geleisteten Bezüge, Vorschüsse und Kredite sind lediglich die Forderungen anzugeben, die der Genossenschaft gegen Mitglieder des Vorstands oder Aufsichtsrats zustehen. Die Beträge dieser Forderungen können für jedes Organ in einer Summe zusammengefaßt werden.

§ 339 Offenlegung

(1) Der Vorstand hat unverzüglich nach der Generalversammlung über den Jahresabschluß, jedoch spätestens vor Ablauf des zwölften Monats des dem Abschlussstichtag nachfolgenden Geschäftsjahrs, den festgestellten Jahresabschluß, den Lagebericht und den Bericht des Aufsichtsrats zum Genossenschaftsregister des Sitzes der Genossenschaft einzureichen. Ist die Erteilung eines Bestätigungsvermerks nach § 58 Abs. 2 des Gesetzes betref-

at the close of the fiscal year. Furthermore, the total amount by which the credit balances as well as the liability sums of the co-operative members have increased or decreased in this year and the amount of the liability sums shall be reported for which all co-operative members together shall be liable at the close of the fiscal year.

(2) The notes shall indicate further:

1. the name and address of the responsible auditing association to which the co-operative belongs; and

2. all members of the managing board and the supervisory board, even if they withdrew in the fiscal year or subsequently, with the family name and at least one full first name. Any chairman of the supervisory board shall be designated as such.

(3) In place of the information prescribed in § 285 No. 9 on remunerations, advances and credits granted to members of organs, only those claims shall be reported that the co-operative has against members of the managing board or the supervisory board. The amounts of these claims may be combined into one sum for each organ.

§ 339 Disclosure

(1) Without undue delay after the general assembly on the annual financial statements, but at the latest prior to the expiration of the twelfth month of the fiscal year following the balance sheet date, the managing board shall file the adopted annual financial statements, the management report and the supervisory board's report in the Co-operative Association Register of the co-operative's domicile. If the issuance of a certification of the finan-

fend die Erwerbs- und Wirtschaftsgenossenschaften vorgeschrieben, so ist dieser mit dem Jahresabschluß einzureichen; hat der Prüfungsverband die Bestätigung des Jahresabschlusses versagt, so muß dies auf dem eingereichten Jahresabschluß vermerkt und der Vermerk vom Prüfungsverband unterschrieben sein. Ist die Prüfung des Jahresabschlusses im Zeitpunkt der Einreichung der Unterlagen nach Satz 1 nicht abgeschlossen, so ist der Bestätigungsvermerk oder der Vermerk über seine Versagung unverzüglich nach Abschluß der Prüfung einzureichen. Wird der Jahresabschluß oder der Lagebericht nach der Einreichung geändert, so ist auch die geänderte Fassung einzureichen.

(2) Der Vorstand einer Genossenschaft, die die Größenmerkmale des § 267 Abs. 3 erfüllt, hat ferner unverzüglich nach der Generalversammlung über den Jahresabschluß, jedoch spätestens vor Ablauf des zwölften Monats des dem Abschlussstichtag nachfolgenden Geschäftsjahrs, den festgestellten Jahresabschluß mit dem Bestätigungsvermerk in den für die Bekanntmachungen der Genossenschaft bestimmten Blättern bekanntzumachen und die Bekanntmachung zu dem Genossenschaftsregister des Sitzes der Genossenschaft einzureichen. Ist die Prüfung des Jahresabschlusses im Zeitpunkt der Generalversammlung nicht abgeschlossen, so hat die Bekanntmachung nach Satz 1 unverzüglich nach dem Abschluß der Prüfung, jedoch spätestens vor Ablauf des zwölften Monats des dem Abschlussstichtag nachfolgenden Geschäftsjahrs, zu erfolgen.

cial statements is prescribed pursuant to § 58 Subsection 2 of the Law in regard to Trade and Industrial Co-operatives, then this shall be filed with the annual financial statements. If the auditing association refused the certification of the annual financial statements, then this must be noted on the filed annual financial statements and the notation signed by the auditing association. If the examination of the annual financial statement has not been completed by the time of the filing of the records pursuant to sentence 1, then the certification of the financial statements or the notation of its refusal shall be filed without undue delay after the completion of the examination. If the annual financial statements or the management report is changed after the filing, then this changed version shall be filed as well.

(2) The managing board of a co-operative that meets the size criteria of § 267 Subsection 3 must further without undue delay after the general assembly on the annual financial statements, but at the latest prior to the expiration of the twelfth month of the fiscal year following the balance sheet date publish the completed annual financial statements with the certification of the financial statements in the journals meant for the publications of co-operatives and must file the publication at the Co-operative Association Register at the co-operative's domicile. If the examination of the annual financial statements has not been completed by the time of the general assembly, then the publication must take place pursuant to sentence 1 without undue delay after the completion of the examination, but at the latest prior to the expiration of the twelfth month of the fiscal year following the balance sheet date.

(3) Die §§ 326 bis 329 über die größenabhängigen Erleichterungen bei der Offenlegung, über Form und Inhalt der Unterlagen bei der Offenlegung, Veröffentlichung und Vervielfältigung sowie über die Prüfungspflicht des Registergerichts sind entsprechend anzuwenden.

(3) §§ 326 through 329 on size-related relief for disclosure, on the form and content of records upon disclosure, publication and reproduction as well as on the registry court's duty of examination shall apply analogously.

Vierter Abschnitt. Ergänzende Vorschriften für Unternehmen bestimmter Geschäftszweige

Part Four. Supplementary Provisions for Enterprises of Certain Branches

Erster Unterabschnitt. Ergänzende Vorschriften für Kreditinstitute und Finanzdienstleistungsinstitute

First Subpart. Supplementary Provisions for Credit Institutions and Financial Service Institutions

Erster Titel. Anwendungsbereich

First Title. Area of Application

§ 340

§ 340

(1) Dieser Unterabschnitt ist auf Kreditinstitute im Sinne des § 1 Abs. 1 des Gesetzes über das Kreditwesen anzuwenden, soweit sie nach dessen § 2 Abs. 1, 4 oder 5 von der Anwendung nicht ausgenommen sind, sowie auf Zweigstellen von Unternehmen mit Sitz in einem Staat, der nicht Mitglied der Europäischen Gemeinschaft und auch nicht Vertragsstaat des Abkommens über den Europäischen Wirtschaftsraum ist, sofern die Zweigstelle nach § 53 Abs. 1 des Gesetzes über das Kreditwesen als Kreditinstitut gilt. § 340 l Abs. 2 bis 4 ist außerdem auf Zweigstellen im Sinne des § 53 b Abs. 1 Satz 1 und Abs. 7 des Gesetzes über das Kreditwesen, auch in Verbindung mit einer Rechtsverordnung nach § 53 c Nr. 1 dieses Gesetzes, anzuwenden, sofern diese Zweigstellen Bankgeschäfte im Sinne des § 1 Abs. 1 Satz 2 Nr. 1 bis 5 und 7 bis 12 dieses Gesetzes betreiben. Zusätzliche Anforderungen auf Grund von Vorschriften, die wegen der

(1) This Subpart shall apply to financial institutions within the meaning of § 1 Subsection 1 of the Banking Law to the extent that they do not fall within the exemptions contained in § 2 Subsections 1, 4 or 5 thereof; it shall also apply to branches of enterprises domiciled in a country which is not a member state of the European Union and is also not a contracting state of the European Economic Area Agreement, to the extent that such branch is considered a financial institution pursuant to § 53 Subsection 1 of the Banking Law. § 340 l Subsections 2 through 4 shall also apply to branches within the meaning of § 53 b Subsection 1 sentence 1 and Subsection 7 of the Banking Law also in conjunction with an ordinance pursuant to § 53 c No. 1 of this law to the extent that these branches conduct banking transactions within the meaning of § 1 Subsection 1 sentence 2 Nos. 1 through 5 and 7 through 12 of this law. Additional requirements by

Ergänzende Vorschriften für bestimmte Unternehmen § 340

Rechtsform oder für Zweigstellen bestehen, bleiben unberührt.

(2) Dieser Unterabschnitt ist auf Unternehmen der in § 2 Abs. 1 Nr. 4 und 5 des Gesetzes über das Kreditwesen bezeichneten Art insoweit ergänzend anzuwenden, als sie Bankgeschäfte betreiben, die nicht zu den ihnen eigentümlichen Geschäften gehören.

(3) Dieser Unterabschnitt ist auf Wohnungsunternehmen mit Spareinrichtung nicht anzuwenden.

(4) Dieser Unterabschnitt ist auch auf Finanzdienstleistungsinstitute im Sinne des § 1 Abs. 1 a des Gesetzes über das Kreditwesen anzuwenden, soweit sie nicht nach dessen § 2 Abs. 6 oder 10 von der Anwendung ausgenommen sind, sowie auf Zweigstellen von Unternehmen mit Sitz in einem anderen Staat, der nicht Mitglied der Europäischen Gemeinschaft und auch nicht Vertragsstaat des Abkommens über den Europäischen Wirtschaftsraum ist, sofern die Zweigstelle nach § 53 Abs. 1 des Gesetzes über das Kreditwesen als Finanzdienstleistungsinstitut gilt. § 340 c Abs. 1 ist nicht anzuwenden auf Finanzdienstleistungsinstitute und Kreditinstitute, soweit letztere Skontroführer im Sinne des § 24 Satz 1 des Börsengesetzes und nicht Einlagenkreditinstitute im Sinne des § 1 Abs. 3 d Satz 1 des Gesetzes über das Kreditwesen sind. § 340 l ist nur auf Finanzdienstleistungsinstitute anzuwenden, die Kapitalgesellschaften sind. Zusätzliche Anforderungen auf Grund von Vorschriften, die wegen der Rechtsform oder für Zweigstellen bestehen, bleiben unberührt.

reason of provisions which exist because of a certain legal form or for branches remain unaffected hereby.

(2) This Subpart shall additionally apply to those institutions defined in § 2 Subsection 1, Nos. 4 and 5 of the Banking Law to the extent that such institutions carry on banking activities which are not part of their usual and proper transactions.

(3) This Subpart shall not apply to housing companies with savings facilities.

(4) This Subpart shall also apply to financial service institutions within the meaning of § 1 Subsection 1 a of the Banking Law to the extent that they do not fall within the exemptions contained in § 2 Subsection 6 or 10; it shall also apply to branches of enterprises domiciled in another country which is not a member state of the European Union and also is not a contracting state of the European Economic Area Agreement to the extent that such branch is considered to be a financial service institution pursuant to the Banking Law. § 340 c Subsection 1 shall not be applied to financial service institutions and credit institutions to the extent that the latter are lead clearing agents within the meaning of § 24 sentence 1 of the Stock Exchange Law and not credit institutions taking deposits within the meaning of § 1 Subsection 3 d sentence 1 of the Banking Law. § 340 l shall only be applied to financial service institutions which are corporations. Additional requirements based on provisions which exist as a result of the legal form or for branches shall not be affected.

Zweiter Titel. Jahresabschluß. Lagebericht. Zwischenabschluß

§ 340 a Anzuwendende Vorschriften

(1) Kreditinstitute, auch wenn sie nicht in der Rechtsform einer Kapitalgesellschaft betrieben werden, haben auf ihren Jahresabschluß die für große Kapitalgesellschaften geltenden Vorschriften des Ersten Unterabschnitts des Zweiten Abschnitts anzuwenden, soweit in den Vorschriften dieses Unterabschnitts nichts anderes bestimmt ist; Kreditinstitute haben außerdem einen Lagebericht nach § 289 aufzustellen.

(2) § 265 Abs. 6 und 7, §§ 267, 268 Abs. 4 Satz 1, Abs. 5 Satz 1 und 2, §§ 276, 277 Abs. 1, 2, 3 Satz 1, § 279 Abs. 1 Satz 2, § 284 Abs. 2 Nr. 4, § 285 Nr. 8 und 12, § 288 sind nicht anzuwenden. An Stelle von § 247 Abs. 1, §§ 251, 266, 268 Abs. 2 und 7, §§ 275, 285 Nr. 1, 2, 4 und 9 Buchstabe c sind die durch Rechtsverordnung erlassenen Formblätter und anderen Vorschriften anzuwenden. § 246 Abs. 2 ist nicht anzuwenden, soweit abweichende Vorschriften bestehen. § 264 Abs. 3 und § 264b sind mit der Maßgabe anzuwenden, daß das Kreditinstitut unter den genannten Voraussetzungen die Vorschriften des Vierten Unterabschnitts des Zweiten Abschnitts nicht anzuwenden braucht.

(3) Sofern Kreditinstitute Zwischenabschlüsse zur Ermittlung von Zwischenergebnissen im Sinne des § 10 Abs. 3 des Gesetzes über das Kreditwesen aufstellen, gelten die Bestimmungen über den Jahresabschluß und § 340 k über die Prüfung entsprechend.

Second Title. Annual Financial Statements. Management Report. Interim Financial Statements

§ 340 a Applicable provisions

(1) Except as provided otherwise in this Subpart, financial institutions shall apply to their annual financial statements the provisions applicable to large corporations contained in the First Subpart of the Second Part, even if such financial institutions are not operated in corporate form; in addition, financial institutions shall prepare a management report pursuant to § 289.

(2) § 265 Subsections 6 and 7, §§ 267, 268 Subsection 4 sentence 1, Subsection 5 sentences 1 and 2, §§ 276, 277 Subsections 1, 2, 3 sentence 1, § 279 Subsection 1 sentence 2, § 284 Subsection 2 No. 4, § 285, Nos. 8 and 12, and § 288 are not applicable. Instead of § 247 Subsection 1, § 251, 266, 268 Subsections 2 and 7, §§ 275, 285, Nos. 1, 2, 4, and 9 Letter c, the forms and other provisions stipulated by regulations are to be applied. § 246 Subsection 2 shall not be applied to the extent that contrary provisions exist. § 264 Subsection 3 and § 264 b shall apply with the proviso that the credit institution under the conditions mentioned above does not need to apply the provisions of the Fourth Subpart of the Second Part.

(3) To the extent that financial institutions prepare interim financial statements in order to determine interim results within the meaning of § 10 Subsection 3 of the Banking Law, the provisions concerning the annual financial statements and § 340 k concerning the examination apply analogously.

Ergänzende Vorschriften für bestimmte Unternehmen	§§ 340a, b

(4) Zusätzlich haben Kreditinstitute im Anhang zum Jahresabschluß anzugeben:

1. alle Mandate in gesetzlich zu bildenden Aufsichtsgremien von großen Kapitalgesellschaften (§ 267 Abs. 3), die von gesetzlichen Vertretern oder anderen Mitarbeitern wahrgenommen werden;

2. alle Beteiligungen an großen Kapitalgesellschaften, die fünf vom Hundert der Stimmwerte überschreiten.

§ 340 b Pensionsgeschäfte

(1) Pensionsgeschäfte sind Verträge, durch die ein Kreditinstitut oder der Kunde eines Kreditinstituts (Pensionsgeber) ihm gehörende Vermögensgegenstände einem anderen Kreditinstitut oder einem seiner Kunden (Pensionsnehmer) gegen Zahlung eines Betrags überträgt und in denen gleichzeitig vereinbart wird, daß die Vermögensgegenstände später gegen Entrichtung des empfangenen oder eines im voraus vereinbarten anderen Betrags an den Pensionsgeber zurückübertragen werden müssen oder können.

(2) Übernimmt der Pensionsnehmer die Verpflichtung, die Vermögensgegenstände zu einem bestimmten oder vom Pensionsgeber zu bestimmenden Zeitpunkt zurückzuübertragen, so handelt es sich um ein echtes Pensionsgeschäft.

(3) Ist der Pensionsnehmer lediglich berechtigt, die Vermögensgegenstände zu einem vorher bestimmten oder von ihm noch zu bestimmenden Zeitpunkt zurückzuübertragen, so handelt es sich um ein unechtes Pensionsgeschäft.

(4) In addition, financial institutions have to declare in the notes to the annual financial statements:

1. all seats on supervisory bodies of large corporations (§ 267 Subsection 3) to be established by law which are held by legal representatives or other employees;

2. all holdings in large corporations which exceed five percent of the voting rights.

§ 340 b Cash sale coupled with a contract for subsequent repurchase

(1) "Pension Transactions" are contracts by means of which a financial institution or the customer of a financial institution (pledgor) transfers, in exchange for payment of an amount, certain assets belonging to it to another financial institution or one of its customers (creditor), and in which contracts it is simultaneously agreed that such assets shall or may be later retransferred to the pledgor upon payment of the amount received or another amount agreed to in advance.

(2) If the creditor assumes the obligation to retransfer the assets at a particular time or at a time to be determined by the pledgor, a "genuine cash sale coupled with a contract for subsequent repurchase" (Genuine Pension Transaction) is involved.

(3) If the creditor is only entitled to retransfer the assets at a previously agreed upon time or at a time which is to be determined by it, a "non-genuine cash sale coupled with a contract for subsequent repurchase" (Non-Genuine Pension Transaction) is involved.

§§ 340b, c — Handelsbücher

(4) Im Falle von echten Pensionsgeschäften sind die übertragenen Vermögensgegenstände in der Bilanz des Pensionsgebers weiterhin auszuweisen. Der Pensionsgeber hat in Höhe des für die Übertragung erhaltenen Betrags eine Verbindlichkeit gegenüber dem Pensionsnehmer auszuweisen. Ist für die Rückübertragung ein höherer oder ein niedrigerer Betrag vereinbart, so ist der Unterschiedsbetrag über die Laufzeit des Pensionsgeschäfts zu verteilen. Außerdem hat der Pensionsgeber den Buchwert der in Pension gegebenen Vermögensgegenstände im Anhang anzugeben. Der Pensionsnehmer darf die ihm in Pension gegebenen Vermögensgegenstände nicht in seiner Bilanz ausweisen; er hat in Höhe des für die Übertragung gezahlten Betrags eine Forderung an den Pensionsgeber in seiner Bilanz auszuweisen. Ist für die Rückübertragung ein höherer oder ein niedrigerer Betrag vereinbart, so ist der Unterschiedsbetrag über die Laufzeit des Pensionsgeschäfts zu verteilen.

(5) Im Falle von unechten Pensionsgeschäften sind die Vermögensgegenstände nicht in der Bilanz des Pensionsgebers, sondern in der Bilanz des Pensionsnehmers auszuweisen. Der Pensionsgeber hat unter der Bilanz den für den Fall der Rückübertragung vereinbarten Betrag anzugeben.

(6) Devisentermingeschäfte, Finanztermingeschäfte und ähnliche Geschäfte sowie die Ausgabe eigener Schuldverschreibungen auf abgekürzte Zeit gelten nicht als Pensionsgeschäfte im Sinne dieser Vorschrift.

§ 340 c Vorschriften zur Gewinn- und Verlustrechnung und zum Anhang

(1) Als Ertrag oder Aufwand aus Finanzgeschäften ist der Unterschieds-

(4) In the case of a Genuine Pension Transaction, the transferred assets are to be carried on the balance sheet of the pledgor. The pledgor shall show in its balance sheet in favor of the creditor an obligation in the amount of the sum received pursuant to the transfer. If a higher or lower amount is agreed upon for the retransfer, the difference is to be apportioned over the term of the transaction. The pledgor shall additionally state in the notes the book value of the assets involved. The creditor may not state in its balance sheet the assets transferred to it for purposes of the transaction; it must show in its balance sheet a claim against the pledgor in the amount of the sum transferred. In the event that a higher or lower amount is agreed upon for retransfer, the difference shall be apportioned over the term of the transaction.

(5) In the event of a Non-Genuine Pension Transaction, the assets are to be shown not in the balance sheet of the pledgor but rather in the balance sheet of the creditor. The pledgor shall state beneath its balance sheet the amount agreed upon in case of retransfer.

(6) Dealing in foreign exchange or futures and similar transactions, as well as issuance of bonds with short maturities are not considered to be transactions within the meaning of this provision.

§ 340 c Provisions concerning the profit and loss statement and the notes

(1) The difference between income and expenses from transactions with

betrag der Erträge und Aufwendungen aus Geschäften mit Wertpapieren des Handelsbestands, Finanzinstrumenten, Devisen und Edelmetallen sowie der Erträge aus Zuschreibungen und der Aufwendungen aus Abschreibungen bei diesen Vermögensgegenständen auszuweisen. In die Verrechnung sind außerdem die Aufwendungen für die Bildung von Rückstellungen für drohende Verluste aus den in Satz 1 bezeichneten Geschäften und die Erträge aus der Auflösung dieser Rückstellungen einzubeziehen.

(2) Die Aufwendungen aus Abschreibungen auf Beteiligungen, Anteile an verbundenen Unternehmen und wie Anlagevermögen behandelte Wertpapiere dürfen mit den Erträgen aus Zuschreibungen zu solchen Vermögensgegenständen verrechnet und in einem Aufwand- oder Ertragsposten ausgewiesen werden. In die Verrechnung nach Satz 1 dürfen auch die Aufwendungen und Erträge aus Geschäften mit solchen Vermögensgegenständen einbezogen werden.

(3) Kreditinstitute, die dem haftenden Eigenkapital nicht realisierte Reserven nach § 10 Abs. 2 b Satz 1 Nr. 6 oder 7 des Gesetzes über das Kreditwesen zurechnen, haben den Betrag, mit dem diese Reserven dem haftenden Eigenkapital zugerechnet werden, im Anhang zur Bilanz und zur Gewinn- und Verlustrechnung anzugeben.

§ 340 d Fristengliederung

Die Forderungen und Verbindlichkeiten sind im Anhang nach der Fristigkeit zu gliedern. Für die Gliederung nach der Fristigkeit ist die Restlaufzeit am Bilanzstichtag maßgebend.

securities in existing holdings, with financial instruments, foreign exchange and precious metals, as well as income from write-ups and expenses from depreciation shall be shown as income or expense for these assets. Expenses for the building of reserves for threatened losses arising from transactions described in sentence 1 and income from the cancellation of such reserves shall be included in the calculation.

(2) Expenses from depreciation of participations, shares in associated enterprises, and securities treated as capital assets, may be set off from income from write-ups to such assets and may be set forth in a single expense or income item. Expenses and income from transactions with such assets may also be included in the set-off pursuant to sentence 1.

(3) Financial institutions which allocate unrealised reserves to the exposed share capital pursuant to § 10 Subsection 2 b sentence 1 No. 6 or 7 of the Banking Act must denote the amount with which these reserves are allocated to the exposed share capital in the notes to the balance sheet and in the profit and loss statement.

§ 340 d Classification by due date

Claims and liabilities shall be classified in the notes according to due date. For such classification according to due date, the remaining term as of the close of the fiscal year of the balance sheet is determinative.

Dritter Titel. Bewertungsvorschriften

§ 340 e Bewertung von Vermögensgegenständen

(1) Kreditinstitute haben Beteiligungen einschließlich der Anteile an verbundenen Unternehmen, Konzessionen, gewerbliche Schutzrechte und ähnliche Rechte und Werte sowie Lizenzen an solchen Rechten und Werten, Grundstücke, grundstücksgleiche Rechte und Bauten einschließlich der Bauten auf fremden Grundstücken, technische Anlagen und Maschinen, andere Anlagen, Betriebs- und Geschäftsausstattung sowie Anlagen im Bau nach den für das Anlagevermögen geltenden Vorschriften zu bewerten, es sei denn, daß sie nicht dazu bestimmt sind, dauernd dem Geschäftsbetrieb zu dienen; in diesem Falle sind sie nach Satz 2 zu bewerten. Andere Vermögensgegenstände, insbesondere Forderungen und Wertpapiere, sind nach den für das Umlaufvermögen geltenden Vorschriften zu bewerten, es sei denn, daß sie dazu bestimmt werden, dauernd dem Geschäftsbetrieb zu dienen; in diesem Falle sind sie nach Satz 1 zu bewerten. § 253 Abs. 2 Satz 3 darf auf die in Satz 1 bezeichneten Vermögensgegenstände mit Ausnahme der Beteiligungen und der Anteile an verbundenen Unternehmen nur angewendet werden, wenn es sich um eine voraussichtlich dauernde Wertminderung handelt.

(2) Abweichend von § 253 Abs. 1 Satz 1 dürfen Hypothekendarlehen und andere Forderungen mit ihrem Nennbetrag angesetzt werden, soweit der Unterschiedsbetrag zwischen dem Nennbetrag und dem Auszahlungsbetrag oder den Anschaffungskosten Zinscharakter hat. Ist der Nennbetrag höher als der Auszahlungsbetrag oder

Third Title. Valuation Provisions

§ 340 e Valuation of assets

(1) Financial institutions shall value participations, including shares in associated enterprises, licences, industrial property rights and similar rights and assets as well as licences to such rights and assets, real property, rights equivalent to real property rights and buildings, including buildings on real estate owned by third parties, technical equipment and machines, other equipment, industrial and business assets as well as capital assets under construction, according to the provisions applicable to capital assets, unless such items are not intended to serve a permanent business purpose; in such case they shall be valued according to sentence 2. Other assets, particularly claims and securities, shall be valued according to the provisions applicable to current assets, unless such items are intended to serve a permanent business purpose; in such case they shall be valued according to sentence 1. § 253 Subsection 2 sentence 3 may be applied to the assets described in sentence 1, with the exception of participations and shares in associated enterprises, only if there is a probable permanent loss in value.

(2) In derogation of § 253 Subsection 1 sentence 1, mortgage loans and other claims may be stated according to their face amounts to the extent that the difference between the face amount and the amount actually paid or the acquisition costs is in the nature of interest. If the stated amount is higher than the amount actually paid

die Anschaffungskosten, so ist der Unterschiedsbetrag in den Rechnungsabgrenzungsposten auf der Passivseite aufzunehmen; er ist planmäßig aufzulösen und in seiner jeweiligen Höhe in der Bilanz oder im Anhang gesondert anzugeben. Ist der Nennbetrag niedriger als der Auszahlungsbetrag oder die Anschaffungskosten, so darf der Unterschiedsbetrag in den Rechnungsabgrenzungsposten auf der Aktivseite aufgenommen werden; er ist planmäßig aufzulösen und in seiner jeweiligen Höhe in der Bilanz oder im Anhang gesondert anzugeben.

or the acquisition costs, the amount of the difference shall be included in deferred income and accrued expenses; such items shall be cancelled according to plan and set forth separately in the current amount in the balance sheet or in the notes. If the stated value is lower than the amount paid or the acquisition costs, the amount of the difference may be included in deferred expenses and accrued income; they shall be cancelled according to plan and separately stated in the current amount in the balance sheet or in the notes.

§ 340 f Vorsorge für allgemeine Bankrisiken

(1) Kreditinstitute dürfen Forderungen an Kreditinstitute und Kunden, Schuldverschreibungen und andere festverzinsliche Wertpapiere sowie Aktien und andere nicht festverzinsliche Wertpapiere, die weder wie Anlagevermögen behandelt werden noch Teil des Handelsbestands sind, mit einem niedrigeren als dem nach § 253 Abs. 1 Satz 1, Abs. 3 vorgeschriebenen oder zugelassenen Wert ansetzen, soweit dies nach vernünftiger kaufmännischer Beurteilung zur Sicherung gegen die besonderen Risiken des Geschäftszweigs der Kreditinstitute notwendig ist. Der Betrag der auf diese Weise gebildeten Vorsorgereserven darf vier vom Hundert des Gesamtbetrags der in Satz 1 bezeichneten Vermögensgegenstände, der sich bei deren Bewertung nach § 253 Abs. 1 Satz 1, Abs. 3 ergibt, nicht übersteigen.

(2) Ein niedrigerer Wertansatz nach Absatz 1 darf beibehalten werden; § 280 ist auf die in Absatz 1 bezeichneten Vermögensgegenstände nicht anzuwenden. In der Bilanz oder im Anhang brauchen die in § 281 Abs. 1

§ 340 f Provision for general bank risks

(1) Financial institutions may set forth claims against other financial institutions and clients, bonds and other fixed-interest securities as well as shares in publicly held corporations and other non-fixed-interest securities, which are neither treated as capital assets nor are part of commercial inventory, at a lower amount than that stipulated or allowed by § 253 Subsection 1 sentence 1, Subsection 3, to the extent that this is necessary according to reasonable commercial judgment as security against the special risks attendant on financial institutions in their line of business. The aggregate amount of reserves formed in this manner may not exceed four percent of the total amount of assets described in sentence 1 as computed pursuant to § 253 Subsection 1 sentence 1, Subsection 3.

(2) A lower valuation according to Subsection 1 may be retained; § 280 shall not be applied to assets described in Subsection 1. The information and classifications required by § 281 Subsection 1 sentence 2, Subsection 2, are

Satz 2, Abs. 2 verlangten Angaben und Aufgliederungen nicht gemacht zu werden, soweit Satz 1 angewendet wird.

(3) Aufwendungen und Erträge aus der Anwendung von Absatz 1 und aus Geschäften mit in Absatz 1 bezeichneten Wertpapieren und Aufwendungen aus Abschreibungen sowie Erträge aus Zuschreibungen zu diesen Wertpapieren dürfen mit den Aufwendungen aus Abschreibungen auf Forderungen, Zuführungen zu Rückstellungen für Eventualverbindlichkeiten und für Kreditrisiken sowie mit den Erträgen aus Zuschreibungen zu Forderungen oder aus deren Eingang nach teilweiser oder vollständiger Abschreibung und aus Auflösungen von Rückstellungen für Eventualverbindlichkeiten und für Kreditrisiken verrechnet und in der Gewinn- und Verlustrechnung in einem Aufwand- oder Ertragsposten ausgewiesen werden.

(4) Angaben über die Bildung und Auflösung von Vorsorgereserven nach Absatz 1 sowie über vorgenommene Verrechnungen nach Absatz 3 brauchen im Jahresabschluß, Lagebericht, Konzernabschluß und Konzernlagebericht nicht gemacht zu werden.

§ 340 g Sonderposten für allgemeine Bankrisiken

(1) Kreditinstitute dürfen auf der Passivseite ihrer Bilanz zur Sicherung gegen allgemeine Bankrisiken einen Sonderposten „Fonds für allgemeine Bankrisiken" bilden, soweit dies nach vernünftiger kaufmännischer Beurteilung wegen der besonderen Risiken des Geschäftszweigs der Kreditinstitute notwendig ist.

not required to be included in the balance sheet or in the notes to the extent that sentence 1 is applied.

(3) Expenses and income arising out of the application of Subsection 1 and out of transactions in securities described in Subsection 1, along with expenses from depreciation and income from write-ups of such securities, may be set off against expenses from write-offs of claims, allocations to reserves for contingent liabilities and for credit risks, as well as against income from write-ups concerning claims or from the receipt of such claims after partial or total write-offs, and from cancellation of reserves for contingent liabilities and for credit risks, and may be set forth in the profit and loss statement in a single expense or income item.

(4) No statements need be made in the annual financial statements, management report, consolidated financial statements or consolidated management report concerning the formation or cancellation of reserves pursuant to Subsection 1 or concerning calculations undertaken pursuant to Subsection 3.

§ 340 g Special items for general bank risks

(1) Financial institutions may form on the liabilities side of the balance sheet a special item "fund for general bank risks" as security against general bank risks, to the extent necessary according to reasonable commercial judgment because of the special risks attendant on financial institutions in their line of business.

(2) Die Zuführungen zum Sonderposten oder die Erträge aus der Auflösung des Sonderpostens sind in der Gewinn- und Verlustrechnung gesondert auszuweisen.

(2) The additions to such special items or the income arising from cancellation of the same shall be separately set forth in the profit and loss statement.

Vierter Titel. Währungsumrechnung

§ 340 h

(1) Auf ausländische Währung lautende Vermögensgegenstände, die wie Anlagevermögen behandelt werden, sind, soweit sie weder durch Verbindlichkeiten noch durch Termingeschäfte in derselben Währung besonders gedeckt sind, mit ihrem Anschaffungskurs in Euro umzurechnen. Andere auf ausländische Währung lautende Vermögensgegenstände und Schulden sowie am Bilanzstichtag nicht abgewickelte Kassageschäfte sind mit dem Kassakurs am Bilanzstichtag in Euro umzurechnen. Nicht abgewickelte Termingeschäfte sind zum Terminkurs am Bilanzstichtag umzurechnen.

(2) Aufwendungen, die sich aus der Währungsumrechnung ergeben, sind in der Gewinn- und Verlustrechnung zu berücksichtigen. Erträge, die sich aus der Währungsumrechnung ergeben, sind in der Gewinn- und Verlustrechnung zu berücksichtigen, soweit die Vermögensgegenstände, Schulden oder Termingeschäfte durch Vermögensgegenstände, Schulden oder andere Termingeschäfte in derselben Währung besonders gedeckt sind. Liegt keine besondere Deckung vor, aber eine Deckung in derselben Währung, so dürfen Erträge nach Satz 2 berücksichtigt werden, soweit sie einen nur vorübergehend wirksamen Auf-

Fourth Title. Currency Conversion

§ 340 h

(1) Assets denominated in foreign currency which are treated as capital assets shall, to the extent that they are not specially covered by futures contracts or liabilities in the same currency, be converted into Euro at the acquisition exchange rate. Other assets and liabilities, as well as cash transactions not settled as of the close of the fiscal year of the balance sheet, and which are denominated in foreign currency, shall be converted into Euro at the spot rate in effect on the close of the fiscal year of the balance sheet. Futures contracts not yet settled shall be converted according to the futures rate in effect on the close of the fiscal year of the balance sheet.

(2) Expenses which arise out of such currency conversion shall be included in the profit and loss statement. Income arising from such currency conversion shall be included in the profit and loss statement to the extent that the assets, debts or futures transactions are specifically covered by assets, debts or other futures transactions in the same currency. If no specific covering item exists, but a covering item in the same currency does exist, income according to sentence 2 shall be included to the extent that it balances an expense which is only temporarily effective out of the covering transactions. In all other cases in-

wand aus den zur Deckung dienenden Geschäften ausgleichen. In allen anderen Fällen dürfen Erträge aus der Währungsumrechnung nicht berücksichtigt werden; sie dürfen auch mit Aufwendungen nach Satz 1 nicht verrechnet werden.

come from currency conversion shall not be included; it may also not be set off against expenses pursuant to sentence 1.

Fünfter Titel. Konzernabschluß. Konzernlagebericht. Konzernzwischenabschluß

Fifth Title. Consolidated Financial Statements. Consolidated Management Report. Interim Consolidated Financial Statements

§ 340 i Pflicht zur Aufstellung

§ 340 i Duty to prepare

(1) Kreditinstitute, auch wenn sie nicht in der Rechtsform einer Kapitalgesellschaft betrieben werden, haben unabhängig von ihrer Größe einen Konzernabschluß und einen Konzernlagebericht nach den Vorschriften des Zweiten Unterabschnitts des Zweiten Abschnitts über den Konzernabschluß und Konzernlagebericht aufzustellen, soweit in den Vorschriften dieses Abschnitts nichts anderes bestimmt ist. Zusätzliche Anforderungen auf Grund von Vorschriften, die wegen der Rechtsform bestehen, bleiben unberührt.

(1) Financial institutions, independent of size and regardless of whether they are conducted in the legal form of a corporation, shall prepare consolidated financial statements and a consolidated management report according to the provisions of the Second Subpart of the Second Part concerning consolidated financial statements and consolidated management reports, to the extent not otherwise required in the provisions of this Part. Additional requirements contained in provisions which exist because of the legal form of the business remain unaffected hereby.

(2) Auf den Konzernabschluß sind, soweit seine Eigenart keine Abweichung bedingt, die §§ 340 a bis 340 g über den Jahresabschluß und die für die Rechtsform und den Geschäftszweig der in den Konzernabschluß einbezogenen Unternehmen mit Sitz im Geltungsbereich dieses Gesetzes geltenden Vorschriften entsprechend anzuwenden, soweit sie für große Kapitalgesellschaften gelten. Die §§ 293, 298 Abs. 1 und 2, § 314 Abs. 1 Nr. 1, 3, 6 Buchstabe c sind nicht anzuwenden.

(2) §§ 340 a through 340 g concerning annual financial statements, and the provisions applicable to the legal form and line of business of the institutions domiciled within the territory in which this law is in force and which are included in the consolidated financial statements, shall, to the extent that they are effective for large corporations, be applied to the consolidated financial statements, insofar as the uniqueness thereof does not require departure from such provisions. §§ 293, 298 Subsections 1 and 2, § 314 Subsection 1 No. 1, 3, 6 Letter c shall not be applied.

(3) Als Kreditinstitute im Sinne dieses Titels gelten auch Mutterunternehmen, deren einziger Zweck darin besteht, Beteiligungen an Tochterunternehmen zu erwerben sowie die Verwaltung und Verwertung dieser Beteiligungen wahrzunehmen, sofern diese Tochterunternehmen ausschließlich oder überwiegend Kreditinstitute sind.

(4) Sofern Kreditinstitute Konzernzwischenabschlüsse zur Ermittlung von Konzernzwischenergebnissen im Sinne des § 10 a Abs. 1 Satz 2 in Verbindung mit § 10 Abs. 3 des Gesetzes über das Kreditwesen aufstellen, gelten die Bestimmungen über den Konzernabschluß und § 340 k über die Prüfung entsprechend.

§ 340 j Einzubeziehende Unternehmen

(1) Eine unterschiedliche Tätigkeit im Sinne des § 295 Abs. 1 liegt nicht vor, wenn das Tochterunternehmen eines Kreditinstituts eine Tätigkeit ausübt, die eine unmittelbare Verlängerung der Banktätigkeit oder eine Hilfstätigkeit für das Mutterunternehmen darstellt.

(2) Bezieht ein Kreditinstitut ein Tochterunternehmen, das Kreditinstitut ist, nach § 296 Abs. 1 Nr. 3 in seinen Konzernabschluß nicht ein und ist der vorübergehende Besitz von Aktien oder Anteilen dieses Unternehmens auf eine finanzielle Stützungsaktion zur Sanierung oder Rettung des genannten Unternehmens zurückzuführen, so hat es den Jahresabschluß dieses Unternehmens seinem Konzernabschluß beizufügen und im Konzernanhang zusätzliche Angaben über die Art und die Bedingungen der finanziellen Stützungsaktion zu machen.

(3) Parent companies whose sole purpose is to acquire, administer and utilise shares in subsidiaries are considered to be financial institutions within the meaning of this Title to the extent that the subsidiaries are exclusively or predominantly financial institutions.

(4) To the extent that financial institutions prepare consolidated interim financial statements for determining consolidated interim results within the meaning of § 10 a Subsection 1 sentence 2 in conjunction with § 10 Subsection 3 of the Banking Act, the provisions regarding the consolidated financial statements and § 340 k concerning the audit apply analogously.

§ 340 j Includable enterprises

(1) A "differing activity" within the meaning of § 295 Subsection 1 does not exist when the subsidiary of a financial institution engages in an activity which represents a direct continuation of banking activity or an activity which assists the parent corporation.

(2) In the event that a financial institution does not include a subsidiary financial institution in its consolidated financial statements according to § 296 Subsection 1 No. 3, and the temporary possession of publicly or closely held shares of the subsidiary is to be attributed to financial support measures for reorganization or rehabilitation of such institution, the parent financial institution shall attach to its consolidated financial statements the annual financial statements of such enterprise and include in its consolidated notes information concerning the type and conditions of the financial rehabilitation measures.

§ 340k | Handelsbücher

Sechster Titel. Prüfung

§ 340 k

(1) Kreditinstitute haben unabhängig von ihrer Größe ihren Jahresabschluß und Lagebericht sowie ihren Konzernabschluß und Konzernlagebericht unbeschadet der Vorschriften der §§ 28 und 29 des Gesetzes über das Kreditwesen nach den Vorschriften des Dritten Unterabschnitts des Zweiten Abschnitts über die Prüfung prüfen zu lassen; § 319 Abs. 1 Satz 2 ist nicht anzuwenden. Die Prüfung ist spätestens vor Ablauf des fünften Monats des dem Abschlußstichtag nachfolgenden Geschäftsjahres vorzunehmen. Der Jahresabschluß ist nach der Prüfung unverzüglich festzustellen.

(2) Ist das Kreditinstitut eine Genossenschaft oder ein rechtsfähiger wirtschaftlicher Verein, so ist die Prüfung abweichend von § 319 Abs. 1 Satz 1 von dem Prüfungsverband durchzuführen, dem das Kreditinstitut als Mitglied angehört, sofern mehr als die Hälfte der geschäftsführenden Mitglieder des Vorstands dieses Prüfungsverbands Wirtschaftsprüfer sind. Hat der Prüfungsverband nur zwei Vorstandsmitglieder, so muß einer von ihnen Wirtschaftsprüfer sein. § 319 Abs. 2 und 3 ist entsprechend anzuwenden; § 319 Abs. 3 Nr. 5 ist nicht anzuwenden, sofern sichergestellt ist, daß der Abschlußprüfer die Prüfung unabhängig von den Weisungen durch das Aufsichtsorgan des Prüfungsverbands durchführen kann. Ist das Mutterunternehmen eine Genossenschaft, so ist der Prüfungsverband, dem die Genossenschaft angehört, unter den Voraussetzungen der Sätze 1 bis 3 auch Abschlußprüfer des Kon-

Sixth Title. Audit

§ 340 k

(1) Financial institutions, without regard to their size, shall, without prejudice to the provisions of §§ 28 and 29 of the Banking Law, have their annual financial statements and management reports, as well as their consolidated financial statements and consolidated management reports, audited pursuant to the provisions of the Third Subpart of the Second Part; § 319 Subsection 1 sentence 2 shall not be applied. The audit shall be conducted at the latest prior to the expiration of the fifth month of the fiscal year following the closing of the fiscal year. The annual financial statements shall be adopted without undue delay following such audit.

(2) In the event the financial institution is a co-operative association or an incorporated association, the audit, deviating from § 319 Subsection 1 sentence 1, shall be carried out by the auditors' association in which the financial institution is a member, to the extent that more than one-half of the executive members of the managing board of such auditing association are certified accountants. In the event the auditing association has only two members of the managing board, one of them must be a certified accountant. § 319 Subsections 2 and 3 shall apply analogously; § 319 Subsection 3 No. 5 shall not be applied to the extent that it can be ensured that the auditor can carry out the audit independent of instructions from the supervisory body of the auditing association. If the parent institution is a co-operative association, the auditing association to which the co-operative association belongs is also, provided

zernabschlusses und des Konzernlageberichts.

(3) Ist das Kreditinstitut eine Sparkasse, so dürfen die nach Absatz 1 vorgeschriebenen Prüfungen abweichend von § 319 Abs. 1 Satz 1 von der Prüfungsstelle eines Sparkassen- und Giroverbands durchgeführt werden. Die Prüfung darf von der Prüfungsstelle jedoch nur durchgeführt werden, wenn der Leiter der Prüfungsstelle die Voraussetzungen des § 319 erfüllt. Außerdem muß sichergestellt sein, daß der Abschlußprüfer die Prüfung unabhängig von den Weisungen der Organe des Sparkassen- und Giroverbands durchführen kann. Soweit das Landesrecht nichts anderes vorsieht, findet § 319 Abs. 2 Satz 2 Nr. 2 mit der Maßgabe Anwendung, dass die Bescheinigung der Prüfungsstelle erteilt worden sein muss.

(4) Finanzdienstleistungsinstitute, deren Bilanzsumme am Stichtag 150 Millionen Euro nicht übersteigt, dürfen auch von den in § 319 Abs. 1 Satz 2 genannten Personen geprüft werden.

Siebenter Titel. Offenlegung

§ 340 l

(1) Kreditinstitute haben den Jahresabschluß und den Lagebericht sowie den Konzernabschluß und den Konzernlagebericht und die anderen in § 325 bezeichneten Unterlagen nach § 325 Abs. 2 bis 5, §§ 328, 329 Abs. 1 offenzulegen. Kreditinstitute, die nicht Zweigstellen sind, haben die in Satz 1 bezeichneten Unterlagen außerdem in jedem anderen Mitgliedstaat der Europäischen Gemeinschaft

the requirements of sentences 1 through 3 are met, the auditor of the consolidated financial statements and the consolidated management report.

(3) If the financial institution is a savings bank, the audits required by Subsection 1 may, deviating from § 319 Subsection 1 sentence 1, be performed by the examining board of a savings bank association. The audit may only be carried out by such examining board if the head of the examining board fulfils the requirements of § 319. In addition, it must be ensured that the auditor can carry out the audit independent of the instructions of the savings bank association. To the extent that the state (Land) laws do not provide otherwise, § 319 Subsection 2 sentence 2 No. 2 applies, provided that the certificate of the examining board must have been issued.

(4) Financial service institutions whose balance sheet total does not exceed 150 million EUR on the close of the fiscal year may also be examined by the persons mentioned in § 319 Subsection 1 sentence 2.

Seventh Title. Disclosure

§ 340 l

(1) Financial institutions must disclose the annual financial statements and the management report, the consolidated financial statements and the consolidated management report and the other documents described in § 325 pursuant to § 325 Subsections 2 through 5, §§ 328, 329 Subsection 1. Financial institutions which are not branches shall additionally disclose the documents described in sentence

§ 340l

und in jedem anderen Vertragsstaat des Abkommens über den Europäischen Wirtschaftsraum offenzulegen, in dem sie eine Zweigstelle errichtet haben. Die Offenlegung (Einreichung zu einem Register, Bekanntmachung in einem Amtsblatt) richtet sich nach dem Recht des jeweiligen Mitgliedstaats oder Vertragsstaats.

(2) Zweigstellen im Geltungsbereich dieses Gesetzes von Unternehmen mit Sitz in einem anderen Staat haben die in Absatz 1 Satz 1 bezeichneten Unterlagen ihrer Hauptniederlassung, die nach deren Recht aufgestellt und geprüft worden sind, nach § 325 Abs. 2 bis 5, §§ 328, 329 Abs. 1 offenzulegen. Zweigstellen im Geltungsbereich dieses Gesetzes von Unternehmen mit Sitz in einem Staat, der nicht Mitglied der Europäischen Gemeinschaft und auch nicht Vertragsstaat des Abkommens über den Europäischen Wirtschaftsraum ist, brauchen auf ihre eigene Geschäftätigkeit bezogene gesonderte Rechnungslegungsunterlagen nach Absatz 1 Satz 1 nicht offenzulegen, sofern die nach Satz 1 offenzulegenden Unterlagen nach einem an die Richtlinie 86/635/EWG angepaßten Recht aufgestellt und geprüft worden oder den nach einem dieser Rechte aufgestellten Unterlagen gleichwertig sind. Die Unterlagen sind in deutscher Sprache einzureichen. Soweit dies nicht die Amtssprache am Sitz der Hauptniederlassung ist, können die Unterlagen der Hauptniederlassung auch in englischer Sprache oder in einer von dem Register der Hauptniederlassung beglaubigten Abschrift eingereicht werden; von der Beglaubigung des Registers ist eine beglaubigte Übersetzung in deutscher Sprache einzureichen.

Handelsbücher

1 in every other member state of the European Union and in every other contracting state of the European Economic Area Agreement in which they have established a branch office. Such disclosure (filing with a registry court, publication in an official periodical) shall be conducted according to the law of the applicable member state or contracting state.

(2) Branch offices within the territory to which this Law applies which are branches of enterprises domiciled in another state shall disclose the documents described in Subsection 1 sentence 1, pertaining to their head office, which documents shall be prepared and audited according to the law applicable to these enterprises according to § 325 Subsections 2 through 5, §§ 328, 329 Subsection 1. Branches within the territory to which this Law applies of institutions domiciled in another state which is not a member of the European Union and is also not a contracting state of the European Economic Area Agreement shall not be obligated to disclose special financial records which refer to their own business activity according to Subsection 1 sentence 1, to the extent that the documents to be disclosed pursuant to sentence 1 were prepared and audited according to a law corresponding to Directive 86/635/EEC, or which are substantially equivalent to documents prepared according to one of these laws. The documents shall be submitted in the German language. To the extent that this is not the official language at the domicile of the head office, the documents of the head office may also be submitted in the English language or in a copy certified by the Commercial Register of the head office; a certified German translation of the certification of the Commercial Register shall be submitted.

(3) Ist das Kreditinstitut eine Genossenschaft, so tritt an die Stelle des Handelsregisters das Genossenschaftsregister. § 339 ist auf Kreditinstitute, die Genossenschaften sind, nicht anzuwenden.

(4) Kreditinstitute oder Zweigstellen im Sinne des Absatzes 2, deren Bilanzsumme am Bilanzstichtag 200 Millionen Euro nicht übersteigt, dürfen anstelle von § 325 Abs. 2 auf die Offenlegung § 325 Abs. 1 anwenden.

Achter Titel. Straf- und Bußgeldvorschriften. Zwangsgelder

§ 340 m Strafvorschriften

Die Strafvorschriften der §§ 331 bis 333 sind auch auf nicht in der Rechtsform einer Kapitalgesellschaft betriebene Kreditinstitute sowie auf Finanzdienstleistungsinstitute im Sinne des § 340 Abs. 4 Satz 1 anzuwenden. § 331 ist darüber hinaus auch anzuwenden auf die Verletzung von Pflichten durch den Geschäftsleiter (§ 1 Abs. 2 Satz 1 des Gesetzes über das Kreditwesen) eines nicht in der Rechtsform einer Kapitalgesellschaft betriebenen Kreditinstituts oder Finanzdienstleistungsinstituts im Sinne des § 340 Abs. 4 Satz 1, durch den Inhaber eines in der Rechtsform des Einzelkaufmanns betriebenen Kreditinstituts oder Finanzdienstleistungsinstituts im Sinne des § 340 Abs. 4 Satz 1 oder durch den Geschäftsleiter im Sinne des § 53 Abs. 2 Nr. 1 des Gesetzes über das Kreditwesen.

§ 340 n Bußgeldvorschriften

(1) Ordnungswidrig handelt, wer als Geschäftsleiter im Sinne des § 1 Abs. 2 Satz 1 oder des § 53 Abs. 2

(3) If the financial institution is a co-operative association, the Co-operative Association Register shall replace the Commercial Register. § 339 shall be applied to financial institutions which are co-operative associations.

(4) Financial institutions or branch offices within the meaning of Subsection 2, whose balance sheet totals as of the close of the fiscal year of such balance sheet do not exceed 200 million EUR may apply § 325 a Subsection 1 to their disclosure instead of § 325 Subsection 2.

Eighth Title. Criminal Law and Civil Penalty. Provisions, Coercive Fines

§ 340 m Criminal law provisions

The criminal law provisions of §§ 331 through 333 shall also apply to financial institutions and to financial service institutions within the meaning of § 340 Subsection 4 sentence 1 which are not conducted in the legal form of a corporation. § 331 further applies to breaches of obligations by the manager (§ 1 Subsection 2 sentence 1 of the Banking Law) of a financial institution or financial service institution within the meaning of § 340 Subsection 4 sentence 1 which is not conducted in the form of a corporation, by the owner of a financial institution or financial service institution within the meaning of § 340 Subsection 4 sentence 1 conducted in the legal form of a sole proprietorship, or by the manager within the meaning of § 53 Subsection 2 No. 1 of the Banking Law.

§ 340 n Civil penalty provisions

(1) It shall be an administrative offence for a manager within the meaning of § 1 Subsection 2 sentence 1 or

§ 340n   Handelsbücher

Nr. 1 des Gesetzes über das Kreditwesen oder als Inhaber eines in der Rechtsform des Einzelkaufmanns betriebenen Kreditinstituts oder Finanzdienstleistungsinstituts im Sinne des § 340 Abs. 4 Satz 1 oder als Mitglied des Aufsichtsrats

1. bei der Aufstellung oder Feststellung des Jahresabschlusses oder bei der Aufstellung des Zwischenabschlusses gemäß § 340 a Abs. 3 einer Vorschrift

   a) des § 243 Abs. 1 oder 2, der §§ 244, 245, 246 Abs. 1 oder 2, dieser in Verbindung mit § 340 a Abs. 2 Satz 3, des § 247 Abs. 2 oder 3, der §§ 248, 249 Abs. 1 Satz 1 oder Abs. 3, des § 250 Abs. 1 Satz 1 oder Abs. 2, des § 264 Abs. 2, des § 340 b Abs. 4 oder 5 oder des § 340 c Abs. 1 über Form oder Inhalt,

   b) des § 253 Abs. 1 Satz 1 in Verbindung mit § 255 Abs. 1 oder 2 Satz 1, 2 oder 6, des § 253 Abs. 1 Satz 2 oder Abs. 2 Satz 1, 2 oder 3, dieser in Verbindung mit § 340 e Abs. 1 Satz 3, des § 253 Abs. 3 Satz 1 oder 2, des § 280 Abs. 1 in Verbindung mit § 340 f Abs. 2, der §§ 282, 283, des § 340 e Abs. 1, des § 340 f Abs. 1 Satz 2 oder des § 340 g Abs. 2 über die Bewertung,

   c) des § 265 Abs. 2, 3 oder 4, des § 268 Abs. 3 oder 6, der §§ 272, 273, 274 Abs. 1 oder des § 277 Abs. 3 Satz 2 oder Abs. 4 über die Gliederung,

§ 53 Subsection 2 No. 1 of the Banking Law, or the owner of a financial institution or financial service institution within the meaning of § 340 Subsection 4 sentence 1 conducted in the legal form of a sole proprietorship, or for a member of the supervisory board to violate:

1. in preparation or adoption of the annual financial statements or in preparation of the interim financial statements under § 340 a Subsection 3, a provision of

   a) § 243 Subsection 1 or 2, §§ 244, 245, 246 Subsection 1 or 2, the latter in conjunction with § 340 a Subsection 2 sentence 3, § 247 Subsection 2 or 3, §§ 248, 249 Subsection 1 sentence 1 or Subsection 3, § 250 Subsection 1 sentence 1 or Subsection 2, § 264 Subsection 2, § 340 b Subsection 4 or 5, or § 340 c Subsection 1, concerning form or content,

   b) § 253 Subsection 1 sentence 1 in conjunction with § 255 Subsection 1 or 2 sentence 1, 2 or 6, § 253 Subsection 1 sentence 2, or Subsection 2 sentence 1, 2 or 3, the latter in conjunction with § 340 e Subsection 1 sentence 3, § 253 Subsection 3 sentence 1 or 2, § 280 Subsection 1 in conjunction with § 340 f Subsection 2, §§ 282, 283, § 340 e Subsection 1, § 340 f Subsection 1 sentence 2 or § 340 g Subsection 2, concerning valuation,

   c) § 265 Subsection 2, 3 or 4, § 268 Subsection 3 or 6, §§ 272, 273, 274 Subsection 1, or § 277 Subsection 3 sentence 2 or Subsection 4, concerning classification,

Ergänzende Vorschriften für bestimmte Unternehmen § 340n

d) des § 280 Abs. 3, des § 281 Abs. 1 Satz 2, dieser in Verbindung mit § 340 f Abs. 2 Satz 2, oder des § 281 Abs. 1 Satz 3 oder Abs. 2 Satz 1, dieser in Verbindung mit § 340 f Abs. 2 Satz 2, des § 284 Abs. 1, 2 Nr. 1, 3 oder 5 oder des § 285 Nr. 3, 5 bis 7, 9 Buchstabe a oder b, Nr. 10, 11, 13 oder 14 über die in der Bilanz oder im Anhang zu machenden Angaben oder

2. bei der Aufstellung des Konzernabschlusses oder des Konzernzwischenabschlusses gemäß § 340 i Abs. 4 einer Vorschrift

   a) des § 294 Abs. 1 über den Konsolidierungskreis,

   b) des § 297 Abs. 2 oder 3 oder des § 340 i Abs. 2 Satz 1 in Verbindung mit einer der in Nummer 1 Buchstabe a bezeichneten Vorschriften über Form oder Inhalt,

   c) des § 300 über die Konsolidierungsgrundsätze oder das Vollständigkeitsgebot,

   d) des § 308 Abs. 1 Satz 1 in Verbindung mit den in Nummer 1 Buchstabe b bezeichneten Vorschriften oder des § 308 Abs. 2 über die Bewertung,

   e) des § 311 Abs. 1 Satz 1 in Verbindung mit § 312 über die Behandlung assoziierter Unternehmen oder

   f) des § 308 Abs. 1 Satz 3, des § 313 oder des § 314 über die im Anhang zu machenden Angaben,

d) § 280 Subsection 3, § 281 Subsection 1 sentence 2, the latter in conjunction with § 340 f Subsection 2 sentence 2, or § 281 Subsection 1 sentence 3 or Subsection 2 sentence 1, the latter in conjunction with § 340 f Subsection 2 sentence 2, § 284 Subsections 1, 2 No. 1, 3 or 5, or § 285 Nos. 3, 5 through 7, 9 Letter a or b, No. 10, 11, 13 or 14, concerning the information to be stated in the balance sheet or in the notes, or

2. in preparation of the consolidated financial statements or the interim consolidated financial statements under § 340 i Subsection 4 a provision of

   a) § 294 Subsection 1, concerning the scope of consolidation,

   b) § 297 Subsection 2 or 3, or § 340 i Subsection 2 sentence 1 in conjunction with one of the provisions referred to in No. 1 Letter a, concerning form or content,

   c) § 300, concerning principles of consolidation or the requirement of completeness,

   d) § 308 Subsection 1 sentence 1 in conjuction with one of the provisions referred to in No. 1 Letter b or of § 308 Subsection 2, concerning valuation,

   e) § 311 Subsection 1 sentence 1 in conjunction with § 312, concerning the treatment of related enterprises, or

   f) § 308 Subsection 1 sentence 3, § 313 or § 314, concerning the information to be included in the notes,

3. bei der Aufstellung des Lageberichts einer Vorschrift des § 289 Abs. 1 über den Inhalt des Lageberichts,
4. bei der Aufstellung des Konzernlageberichts einer Vorschrift des § 315 Abs. 1 über den Inhalt des Konzernlageberichts,
5. bei der Offenlegung, Veröffentlichung oder Vervielfältigung einer Vorschrift des § 328 über Form oder Inhalt oder
6. einer auf Grund des § 330 Abs. 2 in Verbindung mit Abs. 1 Satz 1 erlassenen Rechtsverordnung, soweit sie für einen bestimmten Tatbestand auf diese Bußgeldvorschrift verweist,

zuwiderhandelt.

(2) Ordnungswidrig handelt auch, wer zu einem Jahresabschluß oder einem Konzernabschluß, der auf Grund gesetzlicher Vorschriften zu prüfen ist, einen Vermerk nach § 322 erteilt, obwohl nach § 319 Abs. 2 er, nach § 319 Abs. 3 die Wirtschaftsprüfungsgesellschaft oder nach § 340 k Abs. 2 oder 3 der Prüfungsverband, für die oder für den er tätig wird, nicht Abschlußprüfer sein darf.

(3) Die Ordnungswidrigkeit kann mit einer Geldbuße bis zu fünfundzwanzigtausend Euro geahndet werden.

§ 340 o Festsetzung von Zwangs- und Ordnungsgeld

Personen, die

1. als Geschäftsleiter im Sinne des § 1 Abs. 2 Satz 1 des Gesetzes über das Kreditwesen eines Kreditinstituts oder Finanzdienstleistungsinsti-

3. in preparation of the management report, a provision of § 289 Subsection 1, concerning the contents of the management report,
4. in preparation of the consolidated management report, a provision of § 315 Subsection 1, concerning the contents of the consolidated management report,
5. in disclosure, publication or reproduction, a provision of § 328, concerning the form or contents, or
6. a regulation issued on the basis of § 330 Subsection 2 in conjunction with Subsection 1 sentence 1, to the extent that the same refers to these civil penalty provisions for particular elements of an offence.

(2) It shall also be an administrative offense for anyone to issue an opinion according to § 322 with regard to annual financial statements or consolidated financial statements which must legally be audited, despite the fact that, according to § 319 Subsection 2, he and, according to § 319 Subsection 3, the auditing firm or, according to § 340 k Subsection 2 or 3, the auditing association, respectively, for which he is working are not allowed to audit such annual financial statements.

(3) The violation can be punished with a fine of up to twenty-five thousand EUR.

§ 340 o Setting of a coercive and administrative fine

Persons who

1. as managers, within the meaning of § 1 Subsection 2 sentence 1 of the Banking Law, of a financial institution or financial service institution,

tuts im Sinne des § 340 Abs. 4 Satz 1, das nicht Kapitalgesellschaft ist, oder als Inhaber eines in der Rechtsform des Einzelkaufmanns betriebenen Kreditinstituts oder Finanzdienstleistungsinstituts im Sinne des § 340 Abs. 4 Satz 1

a) eine der in § 335 Satz 1 Nr. 1, 3 bis 5 bezeichneten Vorschriften,

b) § 325 über die Pflicht zur Offenlegung des Jahresabschlusses, des Lageberichts, des Konzernabschlusses, des Konzernlageberichts und anderer Unterlagen der Rechnungslegung oder

c) § 340 i Abs. 1 Satz 1 oder

2. als Geschäftsleiter von Zweigstellen im Sinne des § 53 Abs. 1 des Gesetzes über das Kreditwesen § 340 l Abs. 1 oder 2 über die Offenlegung der Rechnungslegungsunterlagen

nicht befolgen, sind hierzu vom Registergericht in den Fällen der Nummer 1 Buchstabe a und c durch Festsetzung von Zwangsgeld nach § 335 und in den Fällen der Nummer 1 Buchstabe b und der Nummer 2 durch Festsetzung von Ordnungsgeld nach § 335 a anzuhalten.

within the meaning of § 340 Subsection 4 sentence 1, which is not a corporation, or as owners of a financial institution, or financial service institution within the meaning of § 340 Subsection 4 sentence 1, operated in the legal form of a sole proprietorship, do not adhere to

a) one of the provisions described in § 335 sentence 1 Nos. 1, 3 through 5,

b) § 325 on the duty to disclose the annual financial statements, the management report, the consolidated statements, the consolidated management report and other accounting working papers or

c) § 340 i Subsection 1 sentence 1, or

2. as managers of a branch, within the meaning of § 53 Subsection 1 of the Banking Law, do not adhere to § 340 l Subsection 1 or 2, concerning disclosure of accounting working papers,

shall, in the case of No. 1 Letter a and c, be induced to do so by the registry court of the Commercial Register by means of a coercive fine pursuant to § 335 and in the cases of No. 1 Letter b and No. 2 by means of an administrative fine pursuant to § 335a.

Zweiter Unterabschnitt. Ergänzende Vorschriften für Versicherungsunternehmen und Pensionsfonds

Erster Titel. Anwendungsbereich

§ 341

(1) Dieser Unterabschnitt ist, soweit nichts anderes bestimmt ist, auf Unternehmen, die den Betrieb von Versi-

Second Subpart. Supplementary Rules for Insurance Companies and Pension Funds

First Title. Area of Application

§ 341

(1) This Subpart, unless otherwise provided, is to be applied to enterprises having as their business pur-

§ 341

cherungsgeschäften zum Gegenstand haben und nicht Träger der Sozialversicherung sind (Versicherungsunternehmen), anzuwenden. Dies gilt nicht für solche Versicherungsunternehmen, die auf Grund von Gesetz, Tarifvertrag oder Satzung ausschließlich für ihre Mitglieder oder die durch Gesetz oder Satzung begünstigten Personen Leistungen erbringen oder als nicht rechtsfähige Einrichtungen ihre Aufwendungen im Umlageverfahren decken, es sei denn, sie sind Aktiengesellschaften, Versicherungsvereine auf Gegenseitigkeit oder rechtsfähige kommunale Schadenversicherungsunternehmen.

(2) Versicherungsunternehmen im Sinne des Absatzes 1 sind auch Niederlassungen im Geltungsbereich dieses Gesetzes von Versicherungsunternehmen mit Sitz in einem anderen Staat, wenn sie zum Betrieb des Direktversicherungsgeschäfts der Erlaubnis durch die deutsche Versicherungsaufsichtsbehörde bedürfen.

(3) Zusätzliche Anforderungen auf Grund von Vorschriften, die wegen der Rechtsform oder für Niederlassungen bestehen, bleiben unberührt.

(4) Die Vorschriften des Ersten bis Siebenten Titels dieses Unterabschnitts sind mit Ausnahme von Absatz 1 Satz 2 auf Pensionsfonds (§ 112 Abs. 1 des Versicherungsaufsichtsgesetzes) entsprechend anzuwenden. § 341 d ist mit der Maßgabe anzuwenden, dass Kapitalanlagen für Rechnung und Risiko von Arbeitnehmern und Arbeitgebern mit dem Zeitwert unter Berücksichtigung des Grundsatzes der Vorsicht zu bewerten sind; §§ 341 b, 341 c sind insoweit nicht anzuwenden.

pose the operation of insurance businesses and which are not social security agencies (insurance companies). This does not apply to such insurance companies which by operation of law, union wage agreement or articles of association provide services exclusively for their members or which provide services by statute or articles of association to benefited persons or which, as non-incorporated associations, cover their expenses by an adjustable contributions procedure unless they are stock corporations, mutual insurance associations or incorporated municipal indemnity insurance companies.

(2) Insurance companies within the meaning of Subsection 1 are also branches within the area of applicability of this Law of insurance companies domiciled in another country if they require permission from the German Insurance Supervisory Authority to conduct direct insurance business.

(3) Additional requirements based on provisions which exist because of the legal form or for branches remain unaffected.

(4) The provisions of the First through Seventh Titles of this Subpart shall, with the exception of Subsection 1 sentence 2, apply analogously to pension funds (§112 Subsection. 1 of Insurance Supervisory Law). § 341d shall apply with the proviso that capital assets for the account and risk of employees and employers are to be valued at present value with regard to the principle of conservatism; to this extent §§ 341 b, 341 c shall not apply.

Zweiter Titel. Jahresabschluß, Lagebericht

§ 341 a Anzuwendende Vorschriften

(1) Versicherungsunternehmen haben einen Jahresabschluß und einen Lagebericht nach den für große Kapitalgesellschaften geltenden Vorschriften des Ersten Unterabschnitts des Zweiten Abschnitts in den ersten vier Monaten des Geschäftsjahres für das vergangene Geschäftsjahr aufzustellen und dem Abschlußprüfer zur Durchführung der Prüfung vorzulegen; die Frist des § 264 Abs. 1 Satz 2 gilt nicht.

(2) § 265 Abs. 6, §§ 267, 268 Abs. 4 Satz 1, Abs. 5 Satz 1 und 2, §§ 276, 277 Abs. 1 und 2, § 279 Abs. 1 Satz 2, § 285 Nr. 8 Buchstabe a und § 288 sind nicht anzuwenden. Anstelle von § 247 Abs. 1, §§ 251, 265 Abs. 7, §§ 266, 268 Abs. 2 und 7, §§ 275, 281 Abs. 2 Satz 2, § 285 Nr. 4 und 8 Buchstabe b sowie § 286 Abs. 2 sind die durch Rechtsverordnung erlassenen Formblätter und anderen Vorschriften anzuwenden. § 246 Abs. 2 ist nicht anzuwenden, soweit abweichende Vorschriften bestehen. § 264 Abs. 3 und § 264 b sind mit der Maßgabe anzuwenden, daß das Versicherungsunternehmen unter den genannten Voraussetzungen die Vorschriften des Vierten Unterabschnitts des Zweiten Abschnitts nicht anzuwenden braucht. § 285 Nr. 3 gilt mit der Maßgabe, daß die Angaben für solche finanzielle Verpflichtungen nicht zu machen sind, die im Rahmen des Versicherungsgeschäfts entstehen.

(3) Auf Krankenversicherungsunternehmen, die das Krankenversicherungsgeschäft ausschließlich oder überwiegend nach Art der Lebensversicherung betreiben, sind die für die

Second Title. Annual Financial Statements, Management Report

§ 341 a Applicable provisions

(1) Insurance companies are to prepare annual financial statements and a management report pursuant to the provisions applying to large corporations of the First Subpart of Part Two in the first four months of the fiscal year for the previous fiscal year and to submit same to the auditor of the annual financial statements for the performance of the audit; the time period of § 264 Subsection 1 sentence 2 does not apply.

(2) § 265 Subsection 6, §§ 267, 268 Subsection 4 sentence 1, Subsection 5 sentences 1 and 2, §§ 276, 277 Subsections 1 and 2, § 279 Subsection 1 sentence 2, § 285 No. 8 Letter a and § 288 are not to be applied. Printed forms prescribed by administrative order and other provisions are to be applied in place of § 247 Subsection 1, §§ 251, 265 Subsection 7, §§ 266, 268 Subsections 2 and 7, §§ 275, 281 Subsection 2 sentence 2, § 285 Nos. 4 and 8 Letter b and § 286 Subsection 2. § 246 Subsection 2 is not to be applied to the extent that provisions varying therefrom exist. § 264 Subsection 3 and § 264 b shall be applied with the proviso that the insurance company under the conditions mentioned above need not apply the provisions of the Fourth Subpart of the Second Part. § 285 No. 3 applies with the proviso that disclosures for financial obligations which arise in the context of the insurance business are not to be made.

(3) Provisions that apply to accounting methods of life insurance companies are to be analogously applied to health insurance companies that exclusively or predominantly conduct

Rechnungslegung der Lebensversicherungsunternehmen geltenden Vorschriften entsprechend anzuwenden.

(4) Auf Versicherungsunternehmen, die nicht Aktiengesellschaften, Kommanditgesellschaften auf Aktien oder kleinere Vereine sind, sind § 152 Abs. 2 und 3 sowie die §§ 170 bis 176 des Aktiengesetzes entsprechend anzuwenden; § 160 des Aktiengesetzes ist entsprechend anzuwenden, soweit er sich auf Genußrechte bezieht.

(5) Bei Versicherungsunternehmen, die ausschließlich die Rückversicherung betreiben oder deren Beiträge aus in Rückdeckung übernommenen Versicherungen die übrigen Beiträge übersteigen, verlängert sich die in Absatz 1 erster Halbsatz genannte Frist von vier Monaten auf zehn Monate, sofern das Geschäftsjahr mit dem Kalenderjahr übereinstimmt; die Hauptversammlung oder die Versammlung der obersten Vertretung, die den Jahresabschluß entgegennimmt oder festzustellen hat, muß abweichend von § 175 Abs. 1 Satz 2 des Aktiengesetzes spätestens 14 Monate nach dem Ende des vergangenen Geschäftsjahres stattfinden.

Dritter Titel. Bewertungsvorschriften

§ 341 b Bewertung von Vermögensgegenständen

(1) Versicherungsunternehmen haben immaterielle Vermögensgegenstände, soweit sie entgeltlich erworben wurden, Grundstücke, grundstücksgleiche Rechte und Bauten einschließlich der Bauten auf fremden Grundstücken, technische Anlagen und Maschinen, andere Anlagen, Betriebs- und Geschäftsausstattung, Anlagen im Bau

health insurance business in the manner of life insurance.

(4) § 152 Subsections 2 and 3 and §§ 170 through 176 of the Stock Corporation Act are to be analogously applied to insurance companies which are not stock corporations, limited partnerships on shares or small associations; § 160 of the Stock Corporation Act is to be analogously applied to the extent that it refers to option certificates.

(5) The time period specified in Subsection 1, first half-sentence of four months shall be lengthened to ten months to the extent that the fiscal year coincides with the calendar year in the case of insurance companies which conduct only reinsurance business or whose premiums from the reinsurance business exceed the remaining premiums; deviating from § 175 Subsection 1 sentence 2 of the Stock Corporation Act, the shareholders' meeting or the meeting of highest representation which accepts or adopts the annual financial statements must be held at the latest fourteen months after the end of the previous fiscal year.

Third Title. Valuation provisions

§ 341 b Valuation of assets

(1) Insurance companies are to value intangible assets to the extent that they were acquired for pay, real estate, rights similar to real estate, structures including structures on real estate owned by third parties, technical facilities and machines, other facilities, operational and business equipment, facilities under construction and sup-

Ergänzende Vorschriften für bestimmte Unternehmen § 341b

und Vorräte nach den für das Anlagevermögen geltenden Vorschriften zu bewerten. Satz 1 ist vorbehaltlich Absatz 2 und § 341 c auch auf Kapitalanlagen anzuwenden, soweit es sich hierbei um Beteiligungen, Anteile an verbundenen Unternehmen, Ausleihungen an verbundene Unternehmen oder an Unternehmen, mit denen ein Beteiligungsverhältnis besteht, Namensschuldverschreibungen, Hypothekendarlehen und andere Forderungen und Rechte, sonstige Ausleihungen und Depotforderungen aus dem in Rückdeckung übernommenen Versicherungsgeschäft handelt. § 253 Abs. 2 Satz 3 darf, wenn es sich nicht um eine voraussichtlich dauernde Wertminderung handelt, nur auf die in Satz 2 bezeichneten Vermögensgegenstände angewendet werden.

(2) Auf Kapitalanlagen, soweit es sich hierbei um Aktien einschließlich der eigenen Anteile, Investmentanteile sowie sonstige festverzinsliche und nicht festverzinsliche Wertpapiere handelt, sind die für das Umlaufvermögen geltenden § 253 Abs. 1 Satz 1, Abs. 3, §§ 254, 256, 279 Abs. 1 Satz 1, Abs. 2, § 280 anzuwenden, es sei denn, dass sie dazu bestimmt werden, dauernd dem Geschäftsbetrieb zu dienen; in diesem Fall sind sie nach den für das Anlagevermögen geltenden Vorschriften zu bewerten. Pensions- und Sterbekassen, die nach § 5 Abs. 1 Nr. 3 des Körperschaftsteuergesetzes von der Körperschaftsteuer befreit sind, brauchen § 280 Abs. 1 Satz 1 nicht anzuwenden.

(3) § 256 Satz 2 in Verbindung mit § 240 Abs. 3 über die Bewertung zum Festwert ist auf Grundstücke, Bauten und im Bau befindliche Anlagen nicht anzuwenden.

plies pursuant to provisions applying to fixed assets. Sentence 1 is also to be applied to capital assets except where Subsection 2 and § 341 c apply, to the extent that these are participations, shares in affiliated enterprises, loans to affiliated enterprises or to enterprises with which there exists a participating relationship, registered bonds, mortgage loans and other claims and rights, other loans and deposit claims from the insurance business assumed as covering security. § 253 Subsection 2 sentence 3 may be applied only to assets specified in sentence 2 if it is not a matter of a foreseeably durable reduction in value.

(2) § 253 Subsection 1 sentence 1, Subsection 3, §§ 254, 256, 279 Subsection 1 sentence 1, Subsection 2 and § 280 applying to current assets are to be applied to capital assets to the extent that these are stocks including treasury shares, investment shares and other fixed-interest and variable-interest securities, unless they are intended to continuously serve the business operations; in this case they shall be valued in accordance with the provisions applicable to long-term assets. Pension and burial funds, which are exempted from corporate tax pursuant to § 5 Subsection 1 No. 3 of the Corporate Tax Act, need not apply § 280 Subsection 1 sentence 1.

(3) § 256 sentence 2 in conjunction with § 240 Subsection 3 concerning valuation of fixed value assets is not to be applied to real estate, structures and facilities under construction.

289

§ 341 c Namensschuldverschreibungen, Hypothekendarlehen und andere Forderungen

(1) Abweichend von § 253 Abs. 1 Satz 1 dürfen Namensschuldverschreibungen, Hypothekendarlehen und andere Forderungen mit ihrem Nennbetrag angesetzt werden.

(2) Ist der Nennbetrag höher als die Anschaffungskosten, so ist der Unterschiedsbetrag in den Rechnungsabgrenzungsposten auf der Passivseite aufzunehmen, planmäßig aufzulösen und in seiner jeweiligen Höhe in der Bilanz oder im Anhang gesondert anzugeben. Ist der Nennbetrag niedriger als die Anschaffungskosten, darf der Unterschiedsbetrag in den Rechnungsabgrenzungsposten auf der Aktivseite aufgenommen werden; er ist planmäßig aufzulösen und in seiner jeweiligen Höhe in der Bilanz oder im Anhang gesondert anzugeben.

§ 341 d Anlagestock der fondsgebundenen Lebensversicherung

Kapitalanlagen für Rechnung und Risiko von Inhabern von Lebensversicherungen, für die ein Anlagestock nach § 54 b des Versicherungsaufsichtsgesetzes zu bilden ist, sind mit dem Zeitwert unter Berücksichtigung des Grundsatzes der Vorsicht zu bewerten; die §§ 341 b, 341 c sind nicht anzuwenden.

§ 341 c Registered bonds, mortgage loans and other claims

(1) Deviating from § 253 Subsection 1 sentence 1, registered bonds, mortgage loans and other claims may be assessed at their nominal amounts.

(2) If the nominal amount is higher than the acquisition costs, then the difference in amounts is to be entered among the deferred accrued items on the liabilities side, is to be liquidated according to plan and is to be separately listed in its respective amount on the balance sheet or in the notes. If the nominal amount is lower than the acquisition costs, then the difference in amounts may be entered on the assets side among the deferred and accrued items; it is to be liquidated according to plan and separately listed in its respective amount on the balance sheet or in the notes.

§ 341 d Investment holdings of life insurance bound to a fund

Capital assets for the account and risk of owners of life insurances, for which investment holdings are to be formed pursuant to § 54 b of the Insurance Supervisory Act, are to be valued at present value with regard to the principle of conservatism; §§ 341 b, 341 c are not to be applied.

Vierter Titel. Versicherungstechnische Rückstellungen

§ 341 e Allgemeine Bilanzierungsgrundsätze

(1) Versicherungsunternehmen haben versicherungstechnische Rückstellungen auch insoweit zu bilden, wie dies nach vernünftiger kaufmännischer Beurteilung notwendig ist, um die dauernde Erfüllbarkeit der Verpflichtungen aus den Versicherungsverträgen sicherzustellen. Dabei sind die im Interesse der Versicherten erlassenen aufsichtsrechtlichen Vorschriften über die bei der Berechnung der Rückstellungen zu verwendenden Rechnungsgrundlagen einschließlich des dafür anzusetzenden Rechnungszinsfußes und über die Zuweisung bestimmter Kapitalerträge zu den Rückstellungen zu berücksichtigen.

(2) Versicherungstechnische Rückstellungen sind außer in den Fällen der §§ 341 f bis 341 h insbesondere zu bilden

1. für den Teil der Beiträge, der Ertrag für eine bestimmte Zeit nach dem Abschlußstichtag darstellt (Beitragsüberträge);
2. für erfolgsabhängige und erfolgsunabhängige Beitragsrückerstattungen, soweit die ausschließliche Verwendung der Rückstellung zu diesem Zweck durch Gesetz, Satzung, geschäftsplanmäßige Erklärung oder vertragliche Vereinbarung gesichert ist (Rückstellung für Beitragsrückerstattung);
3. für Verluste, mit denen nach dem Abschlußstichtag aus bis zum Ende des Geschäftsjahres geschlossenen Verträgen zu rechnen ist (Rückstellung für drohende Verluste aus dem Versicherungsgeschäft).

Fourth Title. Actuarial Reserves

§ 341 e General balance sheet principles

(1) Insurance companies are to form actuarial reserves also to the extent that this is necessary, according to reasonable business judgment, in order to ensure lasting performability of obligations arising from the insurance contracts. Supervisory provisions issued for the benefit of the insured parties and concerning the accounting principles to be applied in calculating the reserves, including the accounting interest rate to be assessed and the assignment of certain capital yields, are to be observed hereby.

(2) In addition to the cases of §§ 341 f through 341 h, actuarial reserves are to be formed especially

1. for that part of the premiums which constitutes yield for a certain time after the execution date (premium carry-forwards);
2. for success-dependent and success-independent premium returns, to the extent that statute, articles of association, declaration according to the business plan or contractual agreement secures exclusive use of the reserve for this purpose (reserve for premium return);
3. for losses anticipated after the close of the fiscal year out of contracts concluded up to the end of the fiscal year (reserve for threatened losses from insurance business).

(3) Soweit eine Bewertung nach § 252 Abs. 1 Nr. 3 oder § 240 Abs. 4 nicht möglich ist oder der damit verbundene Aufwand unverhältnismäßig wäre, können die Rückstellungen auf Grund von Näherungsverfahren geschätzt werden, wenn anzunehmen ist, daß diese zu annähernd gleichen Ergebnissen wie Einzelberechnungen führen.

§ 341 f Deckungsrückstellung

(1) Deckungsrückstellungen sind für die Verpflichtungen aus dem Lebensversicherungs- und dem nach Art der Lebensversicherung betriebenen Versicherungsgeschäft in Höhe ihres versicherungsmathematisch errechneten Wertes einschließlich bereits zugeteilter Überschußanteile mit Ausnahme der verzinslich angesammelten Überschußanteile und nach Abzug des versicherungsmathematisch ermittelten Barwerts der künftigen Beiträge zu bilden (prospektive Methode). Ist eine Ermittlung des Wertes der künftigen Verpflichtungen und der künftigen Beiträge nicht möglich, hat die Berechnung auf Grund der aufgezinsten Einnahmen und Ausgaben der vorangegangenen Geschäftsjahre zu erfolgen (retrospektive Methode).

(2) Bei der Bildung der Deckungsrückstellung sind auch gegenüber den Versicherten eingegangene Zinssatzverpflichtungen zu berücksichtigen, sofern die derzeitigen oder zu erwartenden Erträge der Vermögenswerte des Unternehmens für die Deckung dieser Verpflichtungen nicht ausreichen.

(3) In der Krankenversicherung, die nach Art der Lebensversicherung betrieben wird, ist als Deckungsrückstellung eine Alterungsrückstellung zu bilden; hierunter fallen auch der

(3) To the extent that a valuation pursuant to § 252 Subsection 1 No. 3 or § 240 Subsection 4 is not possible or the expense associated therewith would be disproportionate, the reserves can be estimated on the basis of approximation procedures if it can be assumed that they will lead to approximately the same results as individual calculations.

§ 341 f Covering reserve

(1) Covering reserves are to be formed for the obligations arising from life insurance business and insurance business operated as life insurance in the amount of their actuarially calculated value including surplus shares already assigned with the exception of interest-bearing accumulated surplus shares and after deduction of the actuarially calculated cash value of the future premiums (prospective method). If calculating the value of the future obligations and of the future premiums is not possible, then the calculation shall be performed on the basis of accrued interest receipts and outlays of the previous fiscal years (retrospective method).

(2) In forming the covering reserve, the interest rate obligations incurred in respect of the insured parties are also to be considered to the extent that current or expected asset yields of the enterprise are not sufficient to cover such obligations.

(3) In health insurance operated as life insurance, an aging reserve is to be formed as covering reserve; the amounts from the premium returns reserve previously allocated to the re-

Rückstellung bereits zugeführte Beträge aus der Rückstellung für Beitragsrückerstattung sowie Zuschreibungen, die dem Aufbau einer Anwartschaft auf Beitragsermäßigung im Alter dienen. Bei der Berechnung sind die für die Berechnung der Prämien geltenden aufsichtsrechtlichen Bestimmungen zu berücksichtigen.

§ 341 g Rückstellung für noch nicht abgewickelte Versicherungsfälle

(1) Rückstellungen für noch nicht abgewickelte Versicherungsfälle sind für die Verpflichtungen aus den bis zum Ende des Geschäftsjahres eingetretenen, aber noch nicht abgewickelten Versicherungsfällen zu bilden. Hierbei sind die gesamten Schadenregulierungsaufwendungen zu berücksichtigen.

(2) Für bis zum Abschlußstichtag eingetretene, aber bis zur inventurmäßigen Erfassung noch nicht gemeldete Versicherungsfälle ist die Rückstellung pauschal zu bewerten. Dabei sind die bisherigen Erfahrungen in bezug auf die Anzahl der nach dem Abschlußstichtag gemeldeten Versicherungsfälle und die Höhe der damit verbundenen Aufwendungen zu berücksichtigen.

(3) Bei Krankenversicherungsunternehmen ist die Rückstellung anhand eines statistischen Näherungsverfahrens zu ermitteln. Dabei ist von den in den ersten Monaten des nach dem Abschlußstichtag folgenden Geschäftsjahres erfolgten Zahlungen für die bis zum Abschlußstichtag eingetretenen Versicherungsfälle auszugehen.

(4) Bei Mitversicherungen muß die Rückstellung der Höhe nach anteilig

serve are also included and as well as subscriptions serving to create a vested interest in old age premiums reduction. Supervisory provisions applying to calculation of premiums are to be observed in the calculation.

§ 341 g Reserve for insurance cases not yet settled

(1) Reserves for insurance cases not yet settled are to be formed for the obligations that have arisen up to the end of the fiscal year and which are not yet settled insurance cases. All expenses connected with the handling of the loss are to be considered.

(2) For insurance cases which have arisen by the close of the fiscal year but which have not yet been reported in inventory capture, the reserve is to be assessed as a lump sum. Previous experience relative to the number of the insurance cases reported after the close of the fiscal year and the extent of the expenses associated therewith is to be considered.

(3) In the case of health insurance companies, the reserve is to be calculated with the help of a statistical approximation procedure. Payments which were made in the first months of the fiscal year following the closing day of the fiscal year for insurance cases that arose up to the closing day of the fiscal year are to serve as the basis.

(4) In the case of coinsurances, the reserve must proportionately corre-

zumindest derjenigen entsprechen, die der führende Versicherer nach den Vorschriften oder der Übung in dem Land bilden muß, von dem aus er tätig wird.

(5) Sind die Versicherungsleistungen auf Grund rechtskräftigen Urteils, Vergleichs oder Anerkenntnisses in Form einer Rente zu erbringen, so müssen die Rückstellungsbeträge nach anerkannten versicherungsmathematischen Methoden berechnet werden.

§ 341 h Schwankungsrückstellung und ähnliche Rückstellungen

(1) Schwankungsrückstellungen sind zum Ausgleich der Schwankungen im Schadenverlauf künftiger Jahre zu bilden, wenn insbesondere

1. nach den Erfahrungen in dem betreffenden Versicherungszweig mit erheblichen Schwankungen der jährlichen Aufwendungen für Versicherungsfälle zu rechnen ist,

2. die Schwankungen nicht jeweils durch Beiträge ausgeglichen werden und

3. die Schwankungen nicht durch Rückversicherungen gedeckt sind.

(2) Für Risiken gleicher Art, bei denen der Ausgleich von Leistung und Gegenleistung wegen des hohen Schadenrisikos im Einzelfall nach versicherungsmathematischen Grundsätzen nicht im Geschäftsjahr, sondern nur in einem am Abschlußstichtag nicht bestimmbaren Zeitraum gefunden werden kann, ist eine Rückstellung zu bilden und in der Bilanz als „ähnliche Rückstellung" unter den Schwankungsrückstellungen auszuweisen.

spond in amount at least to the reserve that the leading insurer, in accordance with provisions or practice, must form in that country from which such leading insurer is active.

(5) If the insurance payments are to be rendered in the form of a pension because of a final judgment, settlement or recognition, then the reserve amounts must be calculated in accordance with recognized actuarial methods.

§ 341 h Loss equalization reserve and similar reserves

(1) Loss equalization reserves are to be formed to compensate for variations in future loss experience especially if

1. experience in the relevant insurance branch indicates that considerable variations in annual expenses for insurance cases should be expected,

2. the respective variations cannot be compensated for by means of premiums, and

3. the variations are not covered by reinsurances.

(2) For risks of the same type and by which the balance of performance and counterperformance, because of the high risk of damage in the individual case, can be found only in a time period as yet unknown on the closing day of the fiscal year as opposed to during the fiscal year according to actuarial principles, a reserve is to be formed and shown in the balance sheet as "similar reserve" among the loss equalization reserves.

Fünfter Titel. Konzernabschluß, Konzernlagebericht

§ 341 i Aufstellung, Fristen

(1) Versicherungsunternehmen, auch wenn sie nicht in der Rechtsform einer Kapitalgesellschaft betrieben werden, haben unabhängig von ihrer Größe einen Konzernabschluß und einen Konzernlagebericht aufzustellen. Zusätzliche Anforderungen auf Grund von Vorschriften, die wegen der Rechtsform bestehen, bleiben unberührt.

(2) Als Versicherungsunternehmen im Sinne dieses Titels gelten auch Mutterunternehmen, deren einziger oder hauptsächlicher Zweck darin besteht, Beteiligungen an Tochterunternehmen zu erwerben, diese Beteiligungen zu verwalten und rentabel zu machen, sofern diese Tochterunternehmen ausschließlich oder überwiegend Versicherungsunternehmen sind.

(3) Die gesetzlichen Vertreter eines Mutterunternehmens haben den Konzernabschluß und den Konzernlagebericht abweichend von § 290 Abs. 1 innerhalb von zwei Monaten nach Ablauf der Aufstellungsfrist für den zuletzt aufzustellenden und in den Konzernabschluß einzubeziehenden Abschluß, spätestens jedoch innerhalb von zwölf Monaten nach dem Stichtag des Konzernabschlusses, für das vergangene Konzerngeschäftsjahr aufzustellen und dem Abschlußprüfer des Konzernabschlusses vorzulegen. § 299 Abs. 2 Satz 2 ist mit der Maßgabe anzuwenden, daß der Stichtag des Jahresabschlusses eines Unternehmens nicht länger als sechs Monate vor dem Stichtag des Konzernabschlusses liegen darf.

Fifth Title. Consolidated Annual Financial Statements, Consolidated Management Report

§ 341 i Preparation, deadlines

(1) Insurance companies, including those operated in other than the legal form of a corporation, are to prepare consolidated annual financial statements and a consolidated management report regardless of their size. Additional requirements based on provisions which exist by virtue of the legal form remain unaffected.

(2) Within the meaning of this Title, parent companies whose only or main purpose consists of acquiring holdings in subsidiaries, administering such holdings and rendering them profitable are also deemed to be insurance companies to the extent that such subsidiaries are exclusively or predominantly insurance companies.

(3) Legal representatives of a parent company are to prepare the consolidated annual financial statements and the consolidated management report deviating from § 290 Subsection 1 within two months after expiration of the preparatory deadline for the last financial statements to be prepared and included in the consolidated annual financial statements, at the latest, however, within twelve months after the closing day of the consolidated annual financial statements for the for the group of companies' previous fiscal year, and are to submit them to the auditor of the consolidated annual financial statements. § 299 Subsection 2 sentence 2 is to be applied with the proviso that the deadline between the closing day of an enterprise's annual financial statements may not precede the closing day of the group of compa-

§§ 341i, j   Handelsbücher

(4) Der Konzernabschluß und der Konzernlagebericht sind abweichend von § 337 Abs. 2 des Aktiengesetzes spätestens der nächsten nach Ablauf der Aufstellungsfrist für den Konzernabschluß und Konzernlagebericht einzuberufenden Hauptversammlung, die einen Jahresabschluß des Mutterunternehmens entgegennimmt oder festzustellen hat, vorzulegen.	nies' annual financial statements by more than six months. (4) The consolidated annual financial statements and the consolidated management report, deviating from § 337 Subsection 2 of the Stock Corporation Act, are to be submitted at the latest at the first shareholders' meeting to be convened after expiration of the preparatory deadline for the consolidated annual statements and the consolidated management report and which shareholders' meeting is either to accept or to adopt annual financial statements of the parent company.
§ 341 j Anzuwendende Vorschriften	**§ 341 j Applicable provisions**
(1) Auf den Konzernabschluß und den Konzernlagebericht sind die Vorschriften des Zweiten Unterabschnitts des Zweiten Abschnitts über den Konzernabschluß und den Konzernlagebericht und, soweit die Eigenart des Konzernabschlusses keine Abweichungen bedingt, die §§ 341 a bis 341 h über den Jahresabschluß sowie die für die Rechtsform und den Geschäftszweig der in den Konzernabschluß einbezogenen Unternehmen mit Sitz im Geltungsbereich dieses Gesetzes geltenden Vorschriften entsprechend anzuwenden, soweit sie für große Kapitalgesellschaften gelten. Die §§ 293, 298 Abs. 1 und 2 sowie § 314 Abs. 1 Nr. 3 sind nicht anzuwenden. § 314 Abs. 1 Nr. 2 gilt mit der Maßgabe, daß die Angaben für solche finanziellen Verpflichtungen nicht zu machen sind, die im Rahmen des Versicherungsgeschäfts entstehen.	(1) The provisions of the Second Subpart of Part Two on the consolidated annual financial statements and the consolidated management report are to be analogously applied to the consolidated annual financial statements and the consolidated management report and, to the extent that the uniqueness of the consolidated annual financial statements requires no variances, §§ 341 a through 341 h on the annual financial statements and the provisions on the legal form and the line of business of enterprises domiciled in this Law's area of applicability and included in the consolidated annual financial statements apply analogously to the extent that they apply to large corporations. §§ 293, 298 Subsections 1 and 2 and § 314 Subsection 1 No. 3 are not to be applied. § 314 Subsection 1 No. 2 applies with the proviso that disclosures for such financial obligations as arise within the context of the insurance business are not to be made.
(2) § 304 Abs. 1 braucht nicht angewendet zu werden, wenn die Lieferungen oder Leistungen zu üblichen Marktbe-	(2) § 304 Subsection 2 does not need to be used if the deliveries and services have been performed under the usual

Ergänzende Vorschriften für bestimmte Unternehmen §§ 341j–l

dingungen vorgenommen worden sind und Rechtsansprüche der Versicherungsnehmer begründet haben.

(3) Auf Versicherungsunternehmen, die nicht Aktiengesellschaften, Kommanditgesellschaften auf Aktien oder kleinere Vereine sind, ist § 337 Abs. 1 des Aktiengesetzes entsprechend anzuwenden.

Sechster Titel. Prüfung

§ 341 k

(1) Versicherungsunternehmen haben unabhängig von ihrer Größe ihren Jahresabschluß und Lagebericht sowie ihren Konzernabschluß und Konzernlagebericht nach den Vorschriften des Dritten Unterabschnitts des Zweiten Abschnitts prüfen zu lassen. § 319 Abs. 1 Satz 2 ist nicht anzuwenden. Hat keine Prüfung stattgefunden, so kann der Jahresabschluß nicht festgestellt werden.

(2) § 318 Abs. 1 Satz 1 ist mit der Maßgabe anzuwenden, daß der Abschlußprüfer des Jahresabschlusses und des Konzernabschlusses vom Aufsichtsrat bestimmt wird. § 318 Abs. 1 Satz 3 und 4 gilt entsprechend.

(3) In den Fällen des § 321 Abs. 1 Satz 3 hat der Abschlußprüfer die Aufsichtsbehörde unverzüglich zu unterrichten.

Siebenter Titel. Offenlegung

§ 341 l

(1) Versicherungsunternehmen haben den Jahresabschluß und den Lagebericht sowie den Konzernabschluß

market conditions and the legal claims of the insured parties have been substantiated.

(3) § 337 Subsection 1 of the Stock Corporation Act applies analogously to insurance companies which are not stock corporations, limited partnerships on shares or small associations.

Sixth Title. Audit

§ 341 k

(1) Independent of their size, insurance companies are to have their annual financial statements and management report as well as their consolidated annual financial statements and consolidated management report audited according to the provisions of the Third Subpart of Part Two. § 319 Subsection 1 sentence 2 is not to be applied. If no audit has taken place, then the annual financial statements cannot be adopted.

(2) § 318 Subsection 1 sentence 1 is to be applied with the proviso that the supervisory board shall choose the report auditor of the annual financial statements and the consolidated annual financial statements. § 318 Subsection 1 sentence 3 and 4 applies analogously.

(3) In cases of § 321 Subsection 1 sentence 3, the annual financial statement auditor is to inform the supervisory authority without undue delay.

Seventh Title. Disclosure

§ 341 l

(1) Insurance companies are to disclose the annual financial statements and the management report and the con-

und den Konzernlagebericht und die anderen in § 325 bezeichneten Unterlagen nach § 325 Abs. 2 bis 5, §§ 328, 329 Abs. 1 offenzulegen. Von den in § 341 a Abs. 5 genannten Versicherungsunternehmen ist § 325 Abs. 2 Satz 1 mit der Maßgabe anzuwenden, daß die Frist für die Einreichung der Unterlagen beim Bundesanzeiger 15 Monate beträgt.

(2) Ist das Versicherungsunternehmen nicht in das Handelsregister eingetragen, so sind die Unterlagen bei dem für den Sitz des Unternehmens zuständigen Registergericht einzureichen.

(3) Die gesetzlichen Vertreter eines Mutterunternehmens haben abweichend von § 325 Abs. 3 unverzüglich nach der Hauptversammlung oder der dieser entsprechenden Versammlung der obersten Vertretung, welcher der Konzernabschluß und der Konzernlagebericht vorzulegen sind, jedoch spätestens vor Ablauf des dieser Versammlung folgenden Monats den Konzernabschluß mit dem Bestätigungsvermerk oder dem Vermerk über dessen Versagung und den Konzernlagebericht mit Ausnahme der Aufstellung des Anteilsbesitzes im Bundesanzeiger bekanntzumachen und die Bekanntmachung unter Beifügung der bezeichneten Unterlagen zum Handelsregister des Sitzes des Mutterunternehmens einzureichen.

solidated annual financial statements and the consolidated management report and the other documents specified in § 325 pursuant to § 325 Subsections 2 through 5, §§ 328, 329 Subsection 1. The insurance companies specified in § 341 a Subsection 5 are to apply § 325 Subsection 2 sentence 1 with the proviso that the time period for submitting the documents to the Federal Gazette shall be fifteen months.

(2) If the insurance company is not entered in the Commercial Register, then the documents are to be submitted to the registry court with jurisdiction over the domicile of the enterprise.

(3) The legal representatives of the parent enterprise shall, deviating from § 325 Subsection 3, without undue delay after the shareholders' meeting, or after the first corresponding meeting of the highest representatives to whom the consolidated annual financial statements and the consolidated management report are to be submitted and at the latest before expiration of the month following such meeting, publish the consolidated annual financial statements, with the certification or the notation of its refusal and the consolidated management report, with the exception of the list of share ownership, in the Federal Gazette and are to submit the publication accompanied by the specified documents to the Commercial Register at the domicile of the parent company.

Achter Titel. Straf- und Bußgeldvorschriften. Zwangsgelder

§ 341 m Strafvorschriften

Die Strafvorschriften der §§ 331 bis 333 sind auch auf nicht in der Rechtsform einer Kapitalgesellschaft betriebene Versicherungsunternehmen und

Eighth Title. Criminal Law and Civil Penalty Provisions. Coercive Fines

§ 341 m Criminal law provisions

The criminal law provisions of §§ 331 through 333 also apply to insurance companies and pension funds which are not conducted in the legal form of

Pensionsfonds anzuwenden. § 331 ist darüber hinaus auch anzuwenden auf die Verletzung von Pflichten durch den Hauptbevollmächtigten (§ 106 Abs. 3 des Versicherungsaufsichtsgesetzes).

a corporation. § 331 further applies to breaches of duties by the chief authorized agent (§ 106 Subsection 3 of the Insurance Supervisory Act).

§ 341 n Bußgeldvorschriften

(1) Ordnungswidrig handelt, wer als Mitglied des vertretungsberechtigten Organs oder des Aufsichtsrats eines Versicherungsunternehmens oder eines Pensionsfonds oder als Hauptbevollmächtigter (§ 106 Abs. 3 des Versicherungsaufsichtsgesetzes)

1. bei der Aufstellung oder Feststellung des Jahresabschlusses einer Vorschrift

    a) des § 243 Abs. 1 oder 2, der §§ 244, 245, 246 Abs. 1 oder 2, dieser in Verbindung mit § 341 a Abs. 2 Satz 3, des § 247 Abs. 3, der §§ 248, 249 Abs. 1 Satz 1 oder Abs. 3, des § 250 Abs. 1 Satz 1 oder Abs. 2, des § 264 Abs. 2, des § 341 e Abs. 1 oder 2 oder der §§ 341 f, 341 g oder 341 h über Form oder Inhalt,

    b) des § 253 Abs. 1 Satz 1 in Verbindung mit § 255 Abs. 1 oder 2 Satz 1, 2 oder 6, des § 253 Abs. 1 Satz 2 oder Abs. 2 Satz 1, 2 oder 3, dieser in Verbindung mit § 341 b Abs. 1 Satz 3, des § 253 Abs. 3 Satz 1 oder 2, des § 280 Abs. 1, der §§ 282, 283, des § 341 b Abs. 1 Satz 1 oder des § 341 d über die Bewertung,

    c) des § 265 Abs. 2, 3 oder 4, des § 268 Abs. 3 oder 6, der §§ 272, 273, 274 Abs. 1 oder des § 277

§ 341 n Civil penalty provisions

(1) It shall be an administrative offense for a member of the organ entitled to represent, or a member of the supervisory board of an insurance company or of a pension fund, or for a chief authorized agent (§ 106 Subsection 3 of the Insurance Supervisory Act) to violate,

1. in preparation or adoption of the annual financial statements, a provision

    a) of § 243 Subsection 1 or 2, §§ 244, 245, 246 Subsection 1 or 2, the latter in conjunction with § 341 a Subsection 2 sentence 3, § 247 Subsection 3, §§ 248, 249 Subsection 1 sentence 1 or Subsection 3, of § 250 Subsection 1 sentence 1 or Subsection 2, of § 264 Subsection 2, of § 341 e Subsection 1 or 2 or §§ 341 f, 341 g or 341 h as to form or content,

    b) of § 253 Subsection 1 sentence 1 in conjunction with § 255 Subsection 1 or 2 sentence 1, 2 or 6, of § 253 Subsection 1 sentence 2 or Subsection 2 sentence 1, 2 or 3, the latter in conjunction with § 341 b Subsection 1 sentence 3, of § 253 Subsection 3 sentence 1 or 2, of § 280 Subsection 1, of §§ 282, 283, § 341 b Subsection 1 sentence 1 or § 341 d as to the valuation,

    c) of § 265 Subsection 2, 3 or 4, of § 268 Subsection 3 or 6, of §§ 272, 273, 274 Subsection 1 or

Abs. 3 Satz 2 oder Abs. 4 über die Gliederung,

d) des § 280 Abs. 3, des § 281 Abs. 1 Satz 2 oder 3 oder Abs. 2 Satz 1, des § 284 oder des § 285 Nr. 1, 2 oder 3 in Verbindung mit § 341 a Abs. 2 Satz 4, § 285 Nr. 5 bis 7, 9 bis 14 über die in der Bilanz oder im Anhang zu machenden Angaben oder

2. bei der Aufstellung des Konzernabschlusses einer Vorschrift

   a) des § 294 Abs. 1 über den Konsolidierungskreis,

   b) des § 297 Abs. 2 oder 3 oder des § 341 j Abs. 1 Satz 1 in Verbindung mit einer der in Nummer 1 Buchstabe a bezeichneten Vorschriften über Form oder Inhalt,

   c) des § 300 über die Konsolidierungsgrundsätze oder das Vollständigkeitsgebot,

   d) des § 308 Abs. 1 Satz 1 in Verbindung mit den in Nummer 1 Buchstabe b bezeichneten Vorschriften oder des § 308 Abs. 2 über die Bewertung,

   e) des § 311 Abs. 1 Satz 1 in Verbindung mit § 312 über die Behandlung assoziierter Unternehmen oder

   f) des § 308 Abs. 1 Satz 3, des § 313 oder des § 314 in Verbindung mit § 341 j Abs. 1 Satz 2 oder 3 über die im Anhang zu machenden Angaben,

3. bei der Aufstellung des Lageberichts einer Vorschrift des § 289 Abs. 1 über den Inhalt des Lageberichts,

of § 277 Subsection 3 sentence 2 or Subsection 4 as to organization,

d) of § 280 Subsection 3 or of § 281 Subsection 1 sentence 2 or 3 or Subsection 2 sentence 1, of § 284 or of § 285 No. 1, 2 or 3 in conjunction with § 341 a Subsection 2 sentence 4, § 285 Nos. 5 through 7, 9 through 14 as to the disclosures to be made in the balance sheet or in the notes, or

2. in preparing the consolidated annual financial statements, a provision

   a) of § 294 Subsection 1 as to extent of consolidation,

   b) of § 297 Subsection 2 or 3 or of § 341 j Subsection 1 sentence 1 in conjunction with one of the provisions specified in No. 1 Letter a as to form or content,

   c) of § 300 as to consolidation principles or requirement of completeness,

   d) of § 308 Subsection 1 sentence 1 in conjunction with the provisions specified in No. 1 Letter b or of § 308 Subsection 2 as to valuation,

   e) of § 311 Subsection 1 sentence 1 in conjunction with § 312 as to treatment of associated enterprises, or

   f) of § 308 Subsection 1 sentence 3, of § 313 or of § 314 in conjunction with § 341 j Subsection 1 sentence 2 or 3 as to the disclosures to be made in the notes,

3. in preparing the management report, a provision of § 289 Subsection 1 as to the contents of the management report,

4. bei der Aufstellung des Konzernlageberichts einer Vorschrift des § 315 Abs. 1 über den Inhalt des Konzernlageberichts,

5. bei der Offenlegung, Veröffentlichung oder Vervielfältigung einer Vorschrift des § 328 über Form oder Inhalt oder

6. einer auf Grund des § 330 Abs. 3 und 4 in Verbindung mit Abs. 1 Satz 1 erlassenen Rechtsverordnung, soweit sie für einen bestimmten Tatbestand auf diese Bußgeldvorschrift verweist,

zuwiderhandelt.

(2) Ordnungswidrig handelt auch, wer zu einem Jahresabschluß oder einem Konzernabschluß, der auf Grund gesetzlicher Vorschriften zu prüfen ist, einen Vermerk nach § 322 erteilt, obwohl nach § 319 Abs. 2 er oder nach § 319 Abs. 3 die Wirtschaftsprüfungsgesellschaft, für die er tätig wird, nicht Abschlußprüfer sein darf.

(3) Die Ordnungswidrigkeit kann mit einer Geldbuße bis zu fünfundzwanzigtausend Euro geahndet werden.

(4) Verwaltungsbehörde im Sinne des § 36 Abs. 1 Nr. 1 des Gesetzes über Ordnungswidrigkeiten ist bei Ordnungswidrigkeiten nach den Absätzen 1 und 2 das Bundesaufsichtsamt für das Versicherungswesen für die seiner Aufsicht unterliegenden Versicherungsunternehmen und Pensionsfonds. Unterliegt ein Versicherungsunternehmen und Pensionsfonds der Aufsicht einer Landesbehörde, so ist diese zuständig.

4. in preparing the consolidated management report, a provision of § 315 Subsection 1 as to the contents of the consolidated management report,

5. in disclosing, publishing or reproducing a provision of § 328 as to the form or contents, or

6. an administrative order issued on the basis of § 330 Subsection 3 and 4 in conjunction with Subsection 1 sentence 1, to the extent that the same refers to these civil provisions for particular elements of an offence.

(2) Anyone who issues a certification pursuant to § 322 for annual financial statements or for consolidated annual statements which must be audited by virtue of statutory provisions although, pursuant to § 319 Subsection 2 such person or pursuant to § 319 Subsection 3, the certified accounting firm for which such person works may not be an annual financial statement auditor, commits an administrative offense.

(3) The administrative offense can be prosecuted with a monetary penalty of up to twenty-five thousand EUR.

(4) Administrative authority within the meaning of § 36 Subsection 1 No. 1 of the Administrative offenses Act is, in the event of administrative offense according to Subsections 1 and 2, the Federal Supervisory Agency for Insurance for the insurance company and pension fund subject to its supervision. If an insurance company and pension fund is subject to the supervision of a state authority, then such authority has jurisdiction.

§ 341 o Festsetzung von Zwangs- und Ordnungsgeld

Personen, die

1. als Mitglieder des vertretungsberechtigten Organs eines Versicherungsunternehmens oder eines Pensionsfonds, die nicht Kapitalgesellschaften sind,
   a) eine der in § 335 Satz 1 Nr. 1, 3 bis 5 bezeichneten Vorschriften,
   b) § 325 über die Pflicht zur Offenlegung des Jahresabschlusses, des Lageberichts, des Konzernabschlusses, des Konzernlageberichts und anderer Unterlagen der Rechnungslegung oder
   c) § 341 i Abs. 1 Satz 1 oder
2. als Hauptbevollmächtigter (§ 106 Abs. 3 des Versicherungsaufsichtsgesetzes) § 341 l Abs. 1 über die Offenlegung der Rechnungslegungsunterlagen

nicht befolgen, sind hierzu vom Registergericht in den Fällen der Nummer 1 Buchstabe a und c durch Festsetzung von Zwangsgeld nach § 335 und in den Fällen der Nummer 1 Buchstabe b und der Nummer 2 durch Festsetzung von Ordnungsgeld nach § 335a anzuhalten.

§ 341 p Anwendung der Straf- und Bußgeldvorschriften sowie der Zwangs- und Ordnungsgeldvorschriften auf Pensionsfonds

Die Strafvorschriften des § 341 m, die Bußgeldvorschriften des § 341 n sowie die Zwangs- und Ordnungsgeldvorschriften des § 341 o gelten auch

§ 341 o Setting of coercive and administrative fines

Persons who

1. as members of the organ legally authorized to represent an insurance company or a pension fund which are not corporations do not observe
   a) one of the provisions specified in § 335 sentence 1 No. 1, 3 through 5,
   b) § 325 on the duty to disclose the annual financial statements, the management report, the consolidated annual financial statements, the consolidated management report and other accounting working papers or
   c) § 341 i Subsection 1 sentence 1 or
2. as chief authorized agent (§ 106 Subsection 3 of the Insurance Supervisory Act) do not observe § 341 l Subsection 1 as to the disclosure of the accounting documents,

shall be induced to do so by the registry court of the Commercial Register in cases No. 1 Letter a and c by means of a coercive fine pursuant to § 335 and in cases No. 1 Letter b and No. 2 by means of an administrative fine pursuant to § 335 a.

§ 341 p Application of the Criminal Law and Civil Penalty Provisions as well as the Coercive and Administrative Fine Provisions to Pension Funds

The criminal law penalty provisions of § 341 m, the civil law penalty provisions of § 341 n as well as the coercive and administrative fine provisions of

für Pensionsfonds im Sinne des § 341 Abs. 4 Satz 1.

§ 341 o also apply to pension funds within the meaning of § 341 Subsection 4 sentence 1.

Fünfter Abschnitt. Privates Rechnungslegungsgremium; Rechnungslegungsbeirat

Part Five. Private Accounting Panel; Accounting Board

§ 342 Privates Rechnungslegungsgremium

§ 342 Private accounting panel

(1) Das Bundesministerium der Justiz kann eine privatrechtlich organisierte Einrichtung durch Vertrag anerkennen und ihr folgende Aufgaben übertragen:

(1) The Federal Ministry of Justice can recognise a privately organized institution by contract and transfer to it the following duties:

1. Entwicklung von Empfehlungen zur Anwendung der Grundsätze über die Konzernrechnungslegung,

2. Beratung des Bundesministeriums der Justiz bei Gesetzgebungsvorhaben zu Rechnungslegungsvorschriften und

3. Vertretung der Bundesrepublik Deutschland in internationalen Standardisierungsgremien.

1. development of recommendations for application of the principles concerning consolidated accounting,

2. advising the Federal Ministry of Justice in connection with legislative projects concerning accounting rules,

3. representing the Federal Republic of Germany in international bodies dealing with standardisation of accounting rules.

Es darf jedoch nur eine solche Einrichtung anerkannt werden, die aufgrund ihrer Satzung gewährleistet, daß die Empfehlungen unabhängig und ausschließlich von Rechnungslegern in einem Verfahren entwickelt und beschlossen werden, das die fachlich interessierte Öffentlichkeit einbezieht. Soweit Unternehmen oder Organisationen von Rechnungslegern Mitglied einer solchen Einrichtung sind, dürfen die Mitgliedschaftsrechte nur von Rechnungslegern ausgeübt werden.

Only such an institution, however, may be recognised which by its articles of association warrants that the recommendations will be developed and resolved independently and exclusively by accounting practitioners in a proceeding which includes the professionally interested public. To the extent that enterprises or organizations of accounting practitioners are members of such an institution, the membership rights may be exercised only by accounting practitioners.

(2) Die Beachtung der die Konzernrechnungslegung betreffenden Grundsätze ordnungsmäßiger Buchführung wird vermutet, soweit vom Bundes-

(2) It shall be presumed that the principles of proper bookkeeping relating to consolidated accounting have been applied to the extent that the recom-

ministerium der Justiz bekanntgemachte Empfehlungen einer nach Absatz 1 Satz 1 anerkannten Einrichtung beachtet worden sind.

§ 342 a Rechnungslegungsbeirat

(1) Beim Bundesministerium der Justiz wird vorbehaltlich Absatz 9 ein Rechnungslegungsbeirat mit den Aufgaben nach § 342 Abs. 1 Satz 1 gebildet.

(2) Der Rechnungslegungsbeirat setzt sich zusammen aus

1. einem Vertreter des Bundesministeriums der Justiz als Vorsitzendem sowie je einem Vertreter des Bundesministeriums der Finanzen und des Bundesministeriums für Wirtschaft und Technologie,
2. vier Vertretern von Unternehmen,
3. vier Vertretern der wirtschaftsprüfenden Berufe,
4. zwei Vertretern der Hochschulen.

(3) Die Mitglieder des Rechnungslegungsbeirats werden durch das Bundesministerium der Justiz berufen. Als Mitglieder sollen nur Rechnungsleger berufen werden.

(4) Die Mitglieder des Rechnungslegungsbeirats sind unabhängig und nicht weisungsgebunden. Ihre Tätigkeit im Beirat ist ehrenamtlich.

(5) Das Bundesministerium der Justiz kann eine Geschäftsordnung für den Beirat erlassen.

(6) Der Beirat kann für bestimmte Sachgebiete Fachausschüsse und Arbeitskreise einsetzen.

(7) Der Beirat, seine Fachausschüsse und Arbeitskreise sind beschlußfähig, wenn mindestens zwei Drittel der Mitglieder anwesend sind. Bei Ab-

mendations of an institution recognised pursuant to Subsection 1 sentence 1, published by the Federal Ministry of Justice have been applied.

§ 342 a Accounting board

(1) Subject to Subsection 9, an accounting board shall be established at the Federal Ministry of Justice with the duties pursuant to § 342 Subsection 1 sentence 1.

(2) The accounting board is composed of

1. a representative of the Federal Ministry of Justice as chairman as well as one representative each of the Federal Ministry of Finance and the Federal Ministry for Economics and Technology,
2. four representatives of enterprises,
3. four representatives of the auditing profession,
4. two representatives of universities.

(3) The members of the accounting board shall be appointed by the Federal Ministry of Justice. Only accounting practitioners shall be appointed as members.

(4) The members of the accounting board are independent and not subject to instructions. Their activity on the accounting board is honorary.

(5) The Federal Ministry of Justice can issue rules of order for the accounting board.

(6) The accounting board can nominate specialised committees and working groups for certain subjects.

(7) The accounting board, its specialised committees and working groups shall have a quorum if at least two-thirds of the members are present. In

stimmungen entscheidet die Stimmenmehrheit, bei Stimmengleichheit die Stimme des Vorsitzenden.

(8) Für die Empfehlungen des Rechnungslegungsbeirats gilt § 342 Abs. 2 entsprechend.

(9) Die Bildung eines Rechnungslegungsbeirats nach Absatz 1 unterbleibt, soweit das Bundesministerium der Justiz eine Einrichtung nach § 342 Abs. 1 anerkennt.

case of voting, the majority of votes shall decide; in case of a tie, the vote of the chairman shall decide.

(8) § 341 Subsection 2 applies analogously to the recommendations of the accounting board.

(9) No accounting board pursuant to Subsection 1 shall be established to the extent that the Federal Ministry of Justice recognises an institution pursuant to § 342 Subsection 1.

Viertes Buch. Handelsgeschäfte

Erster Abschnitt. Allgemeine Vorschriften

§ 343 [Begriff der Handelsgeschäfte]

(1) Handelsgeschäfte sind alle Geschäfte eines Kaufmanns, die zum Betriebe seines Handelsgewerbes gehören.

(2) *(aufgehoben)*

§ 344 [Vermutung für das Handelsgeschäft]

(1) Die von einem Kaufmanne vorgenommenen Rechtsgeschäfte gelten im Zweifel als zum Betriebe seines Handelsgewerbes gehörig.

(2) Die von einem Kaufmanne gezeichneten Schuldscheine gelten als im Betriebe seines Handelsgewerbes gezeichnet, sofern nicht aus der Urkunde sich das Gegenteil ergibt.

§ 345 [Einseitige Handelsgeschäfte]

Auf ein Rechtsgeschäft, das für einen der beiden Teile ein Handelsgeschäft ist, kommen die Vorschriften über Handelsgeschäfte für beide Teile gleichmäßig zur Anwendung, soweit nicht aus diesen Vorschriften sich ein anderes ergibt.

§ 346 [Handelsbräuche]

Unter Kaufleuten ist in Ansehung der Bedeutung und Wirkung von Handlungen und Unterlassungen auf die im Handelsverkehr geltenden Gewohnheiten und Gebräuche Rücksicht zu nehmen.

Book Four. Commercial Transactions

Part One. General Provisions

§ 343 Definition of commercial transactions

(1) Commercial transactions are all transactions of a merchant which relate to the operation of his business.

(2) *(repealed)*

§ 344 Presumption of a commercial transaction

(1) Legal transactions undertaken by a merchant are deemed, in case of doubt, to be related to the operation of his business.

(2) Promissory notes signed by a merchant are deemed to have been signed in the course of the operation of his business insofar as a contrary result does not arise from the document.

§ 345 Unilateral commercial transactions

The provisions concerning commercial transactions apply in the same manner for both parties to a legal transaction that is a commercial transaction for at least one of the two parties, to the extent that these provisions do not provide otherwise.

§ 346 Commercial practices

Due consideration shall be given to prevailing commercial customs and usages concerning the meaning and effect of acts and omissions among merchants.

Allgemeine Vorschriften §§ 347–350

§ 347 [Sorgfaltspflicht]

(1) Wer aus einem Geschäfte, das auf seiner Seite ein Handelsgeschäft ist, einem anderen zur Sorgfalt verpflichtet ist, hat für die Sorgfalt eines ordentlichen Kaufmanns einzustehen.

(2) Unberührt bleiben die Vorschriften des Bürgerlichen Gesetzbuchs, nach welchen der Schuldner in bestimmten Fällen nur grobe Fahrlässigkeit zu vertreten oder nur für diejenige Sorgfalt einzustehen hat, welche er in eigenen Angelegenheiten anzuwenden pflegt.

§ 348 [Vertragsstrafe]

Eine Vertragsstrafe, die von einem Kaufmann im Betriebe seines Handelsgewerbes versprochen ist, kann nicht auf Grund der Vorschriften des § 343 des Bürgerlichen Gesetzbuchs herabgesetzt werden.

§ 349 [Keine Einrede der Vorausklage]

Dem Bürgen steht, wenn die Bürgschaft für ihn ein Handelsgeschäft ist, die Einrede der Vorausklage nicht zu. Das gleiche gilt unter der bezeichneten Voraussetzung für denjenigen, welcher aus einem Kreditauftrag als Bürge haftet.

§ 350 [Formfreiheit]

Auf eine Bürgschaft, ein Schuldversprechen oder ein Schuldanerkenntnis finden, sofern die Bürgschaft auf

§ 347 Duty of care

(1) One who, by reason of a transaction that is for him a commercial transaction, is obligated to observe a certain standard of care with regard to another person, shall meet the standard of care of a prudent merchant.

(2) The provisions of the Civil Code, according to which the obligor in certain cases is only liable for gross negligence or only has to exercise the care he normally applies to his own affairs, remain unaffected.

§ 348 Contract penalty

A contract penalty which a merchant has promised in the operation of his business cannot be reduced by reason of the provisions of § 343 of the Civil Code.

§ 349 No defense by a guarantor that the creditor must first unsuccessfully try to execute his claim on the debtor

If the guaranty is a commercial transaction for the guarantor, he is not entitled to raise the defense that the creditor must first unsuccessfully try to execute his claim on the debtor. The same applies, under the conditions stated, to anyone who is liable as a guarantor under a financing agreement.

§ 350 Freedom from formal requirements

The formal requirements of § 766 sentence 1 and 2, § 780 and § 781 sentence 1 and 2, of the Civil Code do not

§§ 350–354 Handelsgeschäfte

der Seite des Bürgen, das Versprechen oder das Anerkenntnis auf der Seite des Schuldners ein Handelsgeschäft ist, die Formvorschriften des § 766 Satz 1 und 2, des § 780 und des § 781 Satz 1 und 2 des Bürgerlichen Gesetzbuchs keine Anwendung.

apply to a guaranty, an admission of liability or a debt acknowledgement to the extent that the guaranty, for the guarantor, or the admission of liability or debt acknowledgment, for the debtor, is a commercial transaction.

§ 351 *(aufgehoben)*

§ 351 *(repealed)*

§ 352 [Gesetzlicher Zinssatz]

(1) Die Höhe der gesetzlichen Zinsen, mit Ausnahme der Verzugszinsen, ist bei beiderseitigen Handelsgeschäften fünf vom Hundert für das Jahr. Das gleiche gilt, wenn für eine Schuld aus einem solchen Handelsgeschäfte Zinsen ohne Bestimmung des Zinsfußes versprochen sind.

(2) Ist in diesem Gesetzbuche die Verpflichtung zur Zahlung von Zinsen ohne Bestimmung der Höhe ausgesprochen, so sind darunter Zinsen zu fünf vom Hundert für das Jahr zu verstehen.

§ 352 Statutory interest rate

(1) Interest, with the exeption of interest due as a consequence of default, is five per cent per annum for bilateral commercial transactions. The same applies if interest has been promised with respect to a debt relating to such a commercial transaction without specification of a rate of interest.

(2) Where an interest obligation is established by this Commercial Code without specification of the rate, interest of five per cent per annum shall be understood.

§ 353 [Fälligkeitszinsen]

Kaufleute untereinander sind berechtigt, für ihre Forderungen aus beiderseitigen Handelsgeschäften vom Tage der Fälligkeit an Zinsen zu fordern. Zinsen von Zinsen können auf Grund dieser Vorschrift nicht gefordert werden.

§ 353 Interest from the date due

Merchants are entitled, with respect to claims arising out of bilateral commercial transactions, to demand interest from one another beginning with the due date of the respective claims. Interest on interest may not be demanded by reason of this provision.

§ 354 [Provision; Lagergeld; Zinsen]

(1) Wer in Ausübung seines Handelsgewerbes einem anderen Geschäfte besorgt oder Dienste leistet, kann dafür auch ohne Verabredung Provision

§ 354 Commission; storage charges; interest

(1) One who, in the conduct of his business, solicits or transacts business or renders services for another, may demand commission therefor

Allgemeine Vorschriften §§ 354–355

und, wenn es sich um Aufbewahrung handelt, Lagergeld nach den an dem Orte üblichen Sätzen fordern.

(2) Für Darlehen, Vorschüsse, Auslagen und andere Verwendungen kann er vom Tage der Leistung an Zinsen berechnen.

§ 354 a [Wirksamkeit der Abtretung einer Geldforderung]

Ist die Abtretung einer Geldforderung durch Vereinbarung mit dem Schuldner gemäß § 399 des Bürgerlichen Gesetzbuchs ausgeschlossen und ist das Rechtsgeschäft, das diese Forderung begründet hat, für beide Teile ein Handelsgeschäft, oder ist der Schuldner eine juristische Person des öffentlichen Rechts oder ein öffentlich-rechtliches Sondervermögen, so ist die Abtretung gleichwohl wirksam. Der Schuldner kann jedoch mit befreiender Wirkung an den bisherigen Gläubiger leisten. Abweichende Vereinbarungen sind unwirksam.

§ 355 [Laufende Rechnung, Kontokorrent]

(1) Steht jemand mit einem Kaufmanne derart in Geschäftsverbindung, daß die aus der Verbindung entspringenden beiderseitigen Ansprüche und Leistungen nebst Zinsen in Rechnung gestellt und in regelmäßigen Zeitabschnitten durch Verrechnung und Feststellung des für den einen oder anderen Teil sich ergebenden Überschusses ausgeglichen werden (laufende Rechnung, Kontokorrent), so kann derjenige, welchem bei dem Rechnungsabschluß ein Überschuß gebührt, von dem Tage des Abschlusses an Zinsen

even absent an express agreement. If such business or services consist of storage, he may demand storage charges at rates which are customary in the area.

(2) He may charge interest from the date of performance for loans, advances, expenses and other financial outlays.

§ 354 a **Effectiveness of transfer of monetary claim**

If the transfer of a monetary claim by agreement with the debtor pursuant to § 399 of the Civil Code is precluded and if the legal transaction underlying this claim is a commercial transaction for both parties or if the debtor is a public law juridical person or a special public law asset agency, then the transfer is effective despite the preclusion. The debtor can, however, render performance to the previous creditor with discharging effect. Deviating agreements are invalid.

§ 355 **Revolving account, current account**

(1) Where someone has a business relationship with a merchant such that bilateral claims and payments (along with interest) arising from the relationship are placed on account and balanced at regular intervals by charging, and determining the balance for, one or the other of the parties (revolving account, current account), the person to whom a balance is due on the balance date, may demand interest on the balance due from the balance date even if interest is included in the account.

309

§§ 355–357 Handelsgeschäfte

von dem Überschusse verlangen, auch soweit in der Rechnung Zinsen enthalten sind.

(2) Der Rechnungsabschluß geschieht jährlich einmal, sofern nicht ein anderes bestimmt ist.

(3) Die laufende Rechnung kann im Zweifel auch während der Dauer einer Rechnungsperiode jederzeit mit der Wirkung gekündigt werden, daß derjenige, welchem nach der Rechnung ein Überschuß gebührt, dessen Zahlung beanspruchen kann.

§ 356 [Sicherheiten]

(1) Wird eine Forderung, die durch Pfand, Bürgschaft oder in anderer Weise gesichert ist, in die laufende Rechnung aufgenommen, so wird der Gläubiger durch die Anerkennung des Rechnungsabschlusses nicht gehindert, aus der Sicherheit insoweit Befriedigung zu suchen, als sein Guthaben aus der laufenden Rechnung und die Forderung sich decken.

(2) Haftet ein Dritter für eine in die laufende Rechnung aufgenommene Forderung als Gesamtschuldner, so findet auf die Geltendmachung der Forderung gegen ihn die Vorschrift des Absatzes 1 entsprechende Anwendung.

§ 357 [Pfändung des Saldos]

Hat der Gläubiger eines Beteiligten die Pfändung und Überweisung des Anspruchs auf dasjenige erwirkt, was seinem Schuldner als Überschuß aus der laufenden Rechnung zukommt, so können dem Gläubiger gegenüber Schuldposten, die nach der Pfändung durch neue Geschäfte entstehen, nicht in Rechnung gestellt werden.

(2) Accounts shall be balanced annually, absent an agreement to the contrary.

(3) In case of doubt, the revolving account may also be terminated during the term of an accounting period with the effect that the person to whom a balance is due following balancing of the account may demand payment thereof.

§ 356 Security interests

(1) Where an outstanding debt secured by pledge, guaranty or otherwise is included in the revolving account, the creditor is not, by acknowledgement of the account balance, hindered from seeking satisfaction of such debt out of the collateral to the extent that the debt does not exceed the balance due him on the revolving account.

(2) Where a third party is liable as joint debtor for a debt included in the revolving account, the provisions of Subsection 1 apply analogously in the assertion of the debt against him.

§ 357 Execution on the account balance

Where a third-party creditor of one of the parties has executed on, and effected transfer to himself of, the balance of the revolving account due to his debtor, the creditor's claim cannot be reduced by debit items which arise from new transactions following such execution. Transactions which have been undertaken by reason of a right

Geschäfte, die auf Grund eines schon vor der Pfändung bestehenden Rechtes oder einer schon vor diesem Zeitpunkte bestehenden Verpflichtung des Drittschuldners vorgenommen werden, gelten nicht als neue Geschäfte im Sinne dieser Vorschrift.

§ 358 [Zeit der Leistung]

Bei Handelsgeschäften kann die Leistung nur während der gewöhnlichen Geschäftszeit bewirkt und gefordert werden.

§ 359 [Vereinbarte Zeit der Leistung; „acht Tage"]

(1) Ist als Zeit der Leistung das Frühjahr oder der Herbst oder ein in ähnlicher Weise bestimmter Zeitpunkt vereinbart, so entscheidet im Zweifel der Handelsgebrauch des Ortes der Leistung.

(2) Ist eine Frist von acht Tagen vereinbart, so sind hierunter im Zweifel volle acht Tage zu verstehen.

§ 360 [Gattungsschuld]

Wird eine nur der Gattung nach bestimmte Ware geschuldet, so ist Handelsgut mittlerer Art und Güte zu leisten.

§ 361 [Maß, Gewicht, Währung, Zeitrechnung und Entfernungen]

Maß, Gewicht, Währung, Zeitrechnung und Entfernungen, die an dem Orte gelten, wo der Vertrag erfüllt werden soll, sind im Zweifel als die vertragsmäßigen zu betrachten.

existing prior to the execution, or by reason of an obligation of the debtor existing before this point in time, are not considered to be new transactions within the meaning of this provision.

§ 358 Time of performance

Performance of commercial transactions may only be made and demanded during normal business hours.

§ 359 Agreed time for performance; "eight days"

(1) In case of doubt, local custom of the place of performance shall be determinative for the time of performance where the time agreed is "spring", "autumn" or a point in time defined in a similar manner.

(2) In case of doubt, eight full days are to be understood where a period of "eight days" is agreed.

§ 360 Obligation to deliver merchandise specified only by generic characteristics

Where merchandise specified only by the generic characteristics is to be provided, merchandise of average kind and quality shall be tendered.

§ 361 Measure, weight, currency, computation of time, distance

Measure, weight, currency, computation of time and distance which are customary at the location where the contract is to be fulfilled are, in case of doubt, to be considered as contractually agreed upon.

§ 362 [Schweigen des Kaufmanns auf Anträge]

(1) Geht einem Kaufmanne, dessen Gewerbebetrieb die Besorgung von Geschäften für andere mit sich bringt, ein Antrag über die Besorgung solcher Geschäfte von jemand zu, mit dem er in Geschäftsverbindung steht, so ist er verpflichtet, unverzüglich zu antworten; sein Schweigen gilt als Annahme des Antrags. Das gleiche gilt, wenn einem Kaufmann ein Antrag über die Besorgung von Geschäften von jemand zugeht, dem gegenüber er sich zur Besorgung solcher Geschäfte erboten hat.

(2) Auch wenn der Kaufmann den Antrag ablehnt, hat er die mitgesendeten Waren auf Kosten des Antragstellers, soweit er für diese Kosten gedeckt ist und soweit es ohne Nachteil für ihn geschehen kann, einstweilen vor Schaden zu bewahren.

§ 363 [Kaufmännische Orderpapiere]

(1) Anweisungen, die auf einen Kaufmann über die Leistung von Geld, Wertpapieren oder anderen vertretbaren Sachen ausgestellt sind, ohne daß darin die Leistung von einer Gegenleistung abhängig gemacht ist, können durch Indossament übertragen werden, wenn sie an Order lauten. Dasselbe gilt von Verpflichtungsscheinen, die von einem Kaufmann über Gegenstände der bezeichneten Art an Order ausgestellt sind, ohne daß darin die Leistung von einer Gegenleistung abhängig gemacht ist.

(2) Ferner können Konnossemente der Verfrachter, Ladescheine der Frachtführer, Lagerscheine sowie Transport-

§ 362 Silence of merchant as to offers

(1) Where an offer is made to a merchant whose business includes solicitation or conclusion of business transactions for others, and such offer is from someone with whom the merchant has a business relationship and concerns solicitation or conclusion of such transactions on behalf of the offeror, the merchant is obligated to reply immediately; his silence will be deemed to be acceptance of the offer. The same applies where the merchant receives an offer to conclude transactions from someone to whom he has offered his services in concluding such transactions.

(2) Even if the merchant rejects the offer, he is obligated temporarily to protect from damage the goods sent to him at the offeror's expense, insofar as he is covered for these expenses and insofar as it can be done without disadvantage to him.

§ 363 Commercial negotiable instruments

(1) Orders issued to a merchant with regard to the payment of money, the provision of securities or other fungible items, without the performance or provision being made dependent on consideration, may be negotiated by indorsement if they are made payable to order. The same applies to certificates of obligation (with respect to items of the kind described) issued to order by a merchant without the performance being made dependent on consideration.

(2) Further, shipper's bills of lading, carrier's bills of lading, warehouse receipts, as well as transportation insur-

Allgemeine Vorschriften §§ 363–365

versicherungspolicen durch Indossament übertragen werden, wenn sie an Order lauten.

ance policies, may be negotiated by indorsement if they are made payable to order.

§ 364 [Indossament]

(1) Durch das Indossament gehen alle Rechte aus dem indossierten Papier auf den Indossatar über.

(2) Dem legitimierten Besitzer der Urkunde kann der Schuldner nur solche Einwendungen entgegensetzen, welche die Gültigkeit seiner Erklärung in der Urkunde betreffen oder sich aus dem Inhalte der Urkunde ergeben oder ihm unmittelbar gegen den Besitzer zustehen.

(3) Der Schuldner ist nur gegen Aushändigung der quittierten Urkunde zur Leistung verpflichtet.

§ 364 Indorsement

(1) All rights arising from the indorsed instrument are transferred by indorsement to the indorsee.

(2) Against the holder legitimated by indorsement, the debtor may raise only such defenses which concern the validity of his declaration in the document, which arise from the contents of the document, or which he may assert directly against the holder.

(3) The debtor is obligated to perform only against surrender of the document marked "paid".

§ 365 [Anwendung des Wechselrechts; Aufgebotsverfahren]

(1) In betreff der Form des Indossaments, in betreff der Legitimation des Besitzers und der Prüfung der Legitimation sowie in betreff der Verpflichtung des Besitzers zur Herausgabe, finden die Vorschriften der Artikel 11 bis 13, 36, 74 der Wechselordnung[1] entsprechende Anwendung.

(2) Ist die Urkunde vernichtet oder abhanden gekommen, so unterliegt sie der Kraftloserklärung im Wege des Aufgebotsverfahrens. Ist das Aufgebotsverfahren eingeleitet, so kann der

§ 365 Applicability of the law governing bills of exchange; cancellation proceedings by public advertisement

(1) With respect to the form of indorsement, the establishment of the holder's legal title and the examination thereof as well as the obligation of the holder to surrender the document, the provisions of Articles 11 through 13, 36, 74 of the Law governing Bills of Exchange[1] apply analogously.

(2) Where the document is destroyed or mislaid, it is subject to cancellation by public cancellation proceedings. Where public cancellation proceedings are begun, the authorized party

---

[1] Jetzt Art. 13, 14 Abs. 2, 16, 40 Abs. 3 Satz 2 Wechselgesetz.

[1] Now articles 13, 14 Subsection 2, 16 and 40 Subsection 3 sentence 2 of (new) Law governing Bills of Exchange according to article 3 Subsection 1 of Law of June 21, 1933 (RGBl. 1/409).

Berechtigte, wenn er bis zur Kraftloserklärung Sicherheit bestellt, Leistung nach Maßgabe der Urkunde von dem Schuldner verlangen.

§ 366 [Gutgläubiger Erwerb von beweglichen Sachen]

(1) Veräußert oder verpfändet ein Kaufmann im Betriebe seines Handelsgewerbes eine ihm nicht gehörige bewegliche Sache, so finden die Vorschriften des Bürgerlichen Gesetzbuchs zugunsten derjenigen, welche Rechte von einem Nichtberechtigten herleiten, auch dann Anwendung, wenn der gute Glaube des Erwerbers die Befugnis des Veräußerers oder Verpfänders, über die Sache für den Eigentümer zu verfügen, betrifft.

(2) Ist die Sache mit dem Rechte eines Dritten belastet, so finden die Vorschriften des Bürgerlichen Gesetzbuchs zugunsten derjenigen, welche Rechte von einem Nichtberechtigten herleiten, auch dann Anwendung, wenn der gute Glaube die Befugnis des Veräußerers oder Verpfänders, ohne Vorbehalt des Rechtes über die Sache zu verfügen, betrifft.

(3) Das gesetzliche Pfandrecht des Kommissionärs, des Frachtführers, des Spediteurs und des Lagerhalters steht hinsichtlich des Schutzes des guten Glaubens einem gemäß Absatz 1 durch Vertrag erworbenen Pfandrecht gleich, das gesetzliche Pfandrecht des Frachtführers, des Spediteurs und des Lagerhalters an Gut, das nicht Gegenstand des Vertrages ist, aus dem die durch das Pfandrecht zu sichernde Forderung herrührt, jedoch nur insoweit, als der gute Glaube des Erwerbers das Eigentum des Vertragspartners betrifft.

can demand payment by the debtor pursuant to the terms of the document if the authorized party provides security before the cancellation.

§ 366 Good faith acquisition of tangible property

(1) Where a merchant in the operation of his business sells or pledges tangible property that does not belong to him, the provisions of the Civil Code which apply for the benefit of persons whose rights are derived from an unauthorized party also apply if the good faith of the purchaser relates to the authority of the seller or pledgor to dispose of the item on behalf of the owner.

(2) Where the property is burdened by the rights of a third party, the provisions of the Civil Code which apply for the benefit of persons whose rights are derived from an unauthorized party also apply if the good faith of the purchaser relates to the authority of the seller or pledgor to dispose of the item without reservation of the third-party right.

(3) With respect to the protection of the good faith position, the statutory lien of the commission agent, the carrier, the forwarding agent and the warehouseman is equivalent to the lien acquired under Subsection 1 by contract, the statutory lien of the carrier, the forwarding agent and the warehouseman pertaining to goods which are not the subject of the contract which gives rise to the claim to be secured by the lien, however, only to the extent that the good faith of the purchaser relates to the title of the other contracting party.

Allgemeine Vorschriften §§ 367, 368

§ 367 [Gutgläubiger Erwerb gewisser Wertpapiere]

(1) Wird ein Inhaberpapier, das dem Eigentümer gestohlen worden, verlorengegangen oder sonst abhanden gekommen ist, an einen Kaufmann, der Bankier- oder Geldwechslergeschäfte betreibt, veräußert oder verpfändet, so gilt dessen guter Glaube als ausgeschlossen, wenn zur Zeit der Veräußerung oder Verpfändung der Verlust des Papiers im Bundesanzeiger bekanntgemacht und seit dem Ablauf des Jahres, in dem die Veröffentlichung erfolgt ist, nicht mehr als ein Jahr verstrichen war. Inhaberpapieren stehen an Order lautende Anleiheschuldverschreibungen sowie Namensaktien, Zwischenscheine und Reichsbankanteilscheine gleich, falls sie mit einem Blankoindossament versehen sind.

(2) Der gute Glaube des Erwerbers wird durch die Veröffentlichung im Bundesanzeiger nicht ausgeschlossen, wenn der Erwerber die Veröffentlichung infolge besonderer Umstände nicht kannte und seine Unkenntnis nicht auf grober Fahrlässigkeit beruht.

(3) Auf Zins-, Renten- und Gewinnanteilscheine, die nicht später als in dem nächsten auf die Veräußerung oder Verpfändung folgenden Einlösungstermin fällig werden, auf unverzinsliche Inhaberpapiere, die auf Sicht zahlbar sind, und auf Banknoten sind diese Vorschriften nicht anzuwenden.

§ 368 [Pfandverkauf]

(1) Bei dem Verkauf eines Pfandes tritt, wenn die Verpfändung auf der Seite des Pfandgläubigers und des Verpfänders ein Handelsgeschäft ist, an die Stelle der in § 1234 des Bürgerlichen Gesetzbuchs bestimmten Frist von einem Monat eine solche von einer Woche.

§ 367 Good faith acquisition of certain securities

(1) Where a bearer instrument that has been stolen from the owner, lost or otherwise misplaced, is sold or pledged to a merchant in the banking or currency exchange business, good faith is deemed to be excluded if, at the time of the sale or pledge, loss of the instrument had been published in the Federal Gazette and not more than one year had elapsed since the expiration of the year in which publication was made. Debenture bonds payable to order, registered shares, interim certificates and Reichsbank shares, provided that they have been indorsed in blank, are equivalent to bearer instruments.

(2) The purchaser's good faith is not excluded by publication in the Federal Gazette if the purchaser, as a result of special circumstances, did not know of the publication, and his lack of knowledge is not due to gross negligence.

(3) These provisions are not applicable to interest, annuity or dividend coupons which become due no later than at the next redemption date following the sale or pledge, to non-interest-bearing bearer instruments payable at sight, or to bank notes.

§ 368 Sale of pledged items

(1) With respect to the sale of a pledged item, where the pledge was a commercial transaction for both the pledgee and pledgor, a period of one week shall replace the period of one month specified in § 1234 of the Civil Code.

(2) Diese Vorschrift findet auf das gesetzliche Pfandrecht des Kommissionärs, des Spediteurs, des Lagerhalters und des Frachtführers entsprechende Anwendung, auf das Pfandrecht des Spediteurs und des Frachtführers auch dann, wenn nur auf ihrer Seite der Speditions- oder Frachtvertrag ein Handelsgeschäft ist.

(2) This provision is also applicable to the statutory lien of the commission agent, forwarding agent, warehouseman and freight carrier. It applies to the lien of the forwarding agent and freight carrier even where the applicable contract is a commercial transaction only for them.

§ 369 [Kaufmännisches Zurückbehaltungsrecht]

§ 369 Merchant's right of retention

(1) Ein Kaufmann hat wegen der fälligen Forderungen, welche ihm gegen einen anderen Kaufmann aus den zwischen ihnen geschlossenen beiderseitigen Handelsgeschäften zustehen, ein Zurückbehaltungsrecht an den beweglichen Sachen und Wertpapieren des Schuldners, welche mit dessen Willen auf Grund von Handelsgeschäften in seinen Besitz gelangt sind, sofern er sie noch im Besitze hat, insbesondere mittels Konnossements, Ladescheins oder Lagerscheins darüber verfügen kann. Das Zurückbehaltungsrecht ist auch dann begründet, wenn das Eigentum an dem Gegenstande von dem Schuldner auf den Gläubiger übergegangen oder von einem Dritten für den Schuldner auf den Gläubiger übertragen, aber auf den Schuldner zurückzuübertragen ist.

(1) A merchant has, on the basis of claims due him from another merchant which arise out of bilateral commercial transactions concluded between them, a right of retention with regard to tangible property and securities of the debtor which have come into his possession with the debtor's consent by reason of commercial transactions, to the extent that he still has possession of them, particularly where he has the power of disposition over them by means of bills of lading, inland bills of lading and warehouse receipts. The right of retention also arises where ownership of the item has passed from the debtor to the creditor or has been transferred by a third party for the debtor to the creditor, but is to be re-transferred to the debtor.

(2) Einem Dritten gegenüber besteht das Zurückbehaltungsrecht insoweit, als dem Dritten die Einwendungen gegen den Anspruch des Schuldners auf Herausgabe des Gegenstandes entgegengesetzt werden können.

(2) The right of retention exists as against third parties to the extent that defenses against the debtor's restitution rights can be asserted against the third party.

(3) Das Zurückbehaltungsrecht ist ausgeschlossen, wenn die Zurückbehaltung des Gegenstandes der von dem Schuldner vor oder bei der Übergabe erteilten Anweisung oder der von dem Gläubiger übernommenen Ver-

(3) The right of retention is excluded if retention of the item conflicts with the instructions given by the debtor before or upon delivery thereof or with the creditor's duty to deal with the item in a specific manner.

Allgemeine Vorschriften §§ 369–371

pflichtung, in einer bestimmten Weise mit dem Gegenstande zu verfahren, widerstreitet.

(4) Der Schuldner kann die Ausübung des Zurückbehaltungsrechts durch Sicherheitsleistung abwenden. Die Sicherheitsleistung durch Bürgen ist ausgeschlossen.

§ 370 *(aufgehoben)*

§ 371 **[Befriedigungsrecht]**

(1) Der Gläubiger ist kraft des Zurückbehaltungsrechts befugt, sich aus dem zurückbehaltenen Gegenstande für seine Forderung zu befriedigen. Steht einem Dritten ein Recht an dem Gegenstande zu, gegen welches das Zurückbehaltungsrecht nach § 369 Abs. 2 geltend gemacht werden kann, so hat der Gläubiger in Ansehung der Befriedigung aus dem Gegenstande den Vorrang.

(2) Die Befriedigung erfolgt nach den für das Pfandrecht geltenden Vorschriften des Bürgerlichen Gesetzbuchs. An die Stelle der in § 1234 des Bürgerlichen Gesetzbuchs bestimmten Frist von einem Monate tritt eine solche von einer Woche.

(3) Sofern die Befriedigung nicht im Wege der Zwangsvollstreckung stattfindet, ist sie erst zulässig, nachdem der Gläubiger einen vollstreckbaren Titel für sein Recht auf Befriedigung gegen den Eigentümer oder, wenn der Gegenstand ihm selbst gehört, gegen den Schuldner erlangt hat; in dem letzteren Falle finden die den Eigentümer betreffenden Vorschriften des Bürgerlichen Gesetzbuchs über die Befriedigung auf den Schuldner entsprechende Anwendung. In Ermangelung des vollstreckbaren Titels ist der Verkauf des Gegenstandes nicht rechtmäßig.

(4) The debtor may prevent exercise of the right of retention by providing security. The provision of security by guarantors is excluded.

§ 370 *(repealed)*

§ 371 **Right to satisfaction**

(1) By virtue of the right of retention, the creditor is entitled to satisfy his claims out of the item retained. Where a third party has a right to the item against which the right of retention may be asserted pursuant to § 369 Subsection 2, the creditor has a superior right with regard to satisfaction out of the item.

(2) Satisfaction shall be effected pursuant to the provisions of the Civil Code applicable to liens. A period of one week shall replace the period of one month specified in § 1234 of the Civil Code.

(3) Satisfaction is only allowable, insofar as it is not accomplished by means of execution, after the creditor has acquired an enforceable title for his right to satisfaction against the owner, or if the item belongs to him, against the debtor; in the latter case, the satisfaction-related provisions of the Civil Code pertaining to the owner apply analogously to the debtor. In the absence of an enforceable title, the sale of the item is not legally valid.

(4) Die Klage auf Gestattung der Befriedigung kann bei dem Gericht, in dessen Bezirke der Gläubiger seinen allgemeinen Gerichtsstand oder den Gerichtsstand der Niederlassung hat, erhoben werden.

§ 372 [Eigentumsfiktion und Rechtskraftwirkung bei Befriedigungsrecht]

(1) In Ansehung der Befriedigung aus dem zurückbehaltenen Gegenstande gilt zugunsten des Gläubigers der Schuldner, sofern er bei dem Besitzerwerbe des Gläubigers der Eigentümer des Gegenstandes war, auch weiter als Eigentümer, sofern nicht der Gläubiger weiß, daß der Schuldner nicht mehr Eigentümer ist.

(2) Erwirbt ein Dritter nach dem Besitzerwerbe des Gläubigers von dem Schuldner das Eigentum, so muß er ein rechtskräftiges Urteil, das in einem zwischen dem Gläubiger und dem Schuldner wegen Gestattung der Befriedigung geführten Rechtsstreit ergangen ist, gegen sich gelten lassen, sofern nicht der Gläubiger bei dem Eintritte der Rechtshängigkeit gewußt hat, daß der Schuldner nicht mehr Eigentümer war.

Zweiter Abschnitt. Handelskauf

§ 373 [Annahmeverzug des Käufers]

(1) Ist der Käufer mit der Annahme der Ware im Verzuge, so kann der Verkäufer die Ware auf Gefahr und Kosten des Käufers in einem öffentlichen Lagerhaus oder sonst in sicherer Weise hinterlegen.

(4) An action for permission to seek satisfaction may be brought at the court for the district where the creditor has his place of general jurisdiction or which is the place of jurisdiction for the offices of the business.

§ 372 Fictive ownership and effect of final judgment pertaining to the right to satisfaction

(1) With regard to satisfaction out of the item retained, the debtor is deemed to continue his status as owner of the item, for the creditor's benefit, if he was the owner of the item at the time the creditor acquired possession, unless the creditor knows the debtor is no longer the owner.

(2) Where a third party acquires ownership after the creditor acquired possession from the debtor, the third party must recognise a final judgment issued in litigation conducted between the creditor and the debtor for permission to seek satisfaction, unless the creditor knew at the time of entering into litigation that the debtor was no longer the owner.

Part Two. Commercial Sale of Goods

§ 373 Default in acceptance by the buyer

(1) Where the buyer of goods is in default as regards taking delivery, the seller may deposit the goods at the buyer's risk and expense in a public warehouse or in some other secure manner.

(2) Er ist ferner befugt, nach vorgängiger Androhung die Ware öffentlich versteigern zu lassen; er kann, wenn die Ware einen Börsen- oder Marktpreis hat, nach vorgängiger Androhung den Verkauf auch aus freier Hand durch einen zu solchen Verkäufen öffentlich ermächtigten Handelsmakler oder durch eine zur öffentlichen Versteigerung befugte Person zum laufenden Preise bewirken. Ist die Ware dem Verderb ausgesetzt und Gefahr im Verzuge, so bedarf es der vorgängigen Androhung nicht; dasselbe gilt, wenn die Androhung aus anderen Gründen untunlich ist.

(3) Der Selbsthilfeverkauf erfolgt für Rechnung des säumigen Käufers.

(4) Der Verkäufer und der Käufer können bei der öffentlichen Versteigerung mitbieten.

(5) Im Falle der öffentlichen Versteigerung hat der Verkäufer den Käufer von der Zeit und dem Orte der Versteigerung vorher zu benachrichtigen; von dem vollzogenen Verkaufe hat er bei jeder Art des Verkaufs dem Käufer unverzüglich Nachricht zu geben. Im Falle der Unterlassung ist er zum Schadensersatze verpflichtet. Die Benachrichtigungen dürfen unterbleiben, wenn sie untunlich sind.

§ 374 [Vorschriften des BGB über Annahmeverzug]

Durch die Vorschriften des § 373 werden die Befugnisse nicht berührt, welche dem Verkäufer nach dem Bürgerlichen Gesetzbuche zustehen, wenn der Käufer im Verzuge der Annahme ist.

(2) He is furthermore authorized after prior warning to have the goods sold at public auction; he may, if the goods have an exchange or market price, following prior warning, also have the sale conducted on the open market at the current price by a broker officially authorized to conduct such sales or by a public auctioneer. If the goods are perishable and there is risk in delay, prior warning is not required; the same applies if the warning is impracticable for other reasons.

(3) The self-help sale is made for the account of the defaulting buyer.

(4) Both the seller and the buyer may bid at the public auction.

(5) In the event of a public auction, the seller must inform the buyer beforehand as to the time and place of the auction; he must immediately inform the buyer of the execution of any kind of sale. In the case of failure to do this, he is liable for damages. Notifications may be omitted if they are impracticable.

§ 374 Provisions of the Civil Code with respect to default in taking delivery

The rights of the seller pursuant to the Civil Code where a buyer defaults in taking delivery will not be affected by the provisions of § 373.

§ 375 [Bestimmungskauf]

(1) Ist bei dem Kaufe einer beweglichen Sache dem Käufer die nähere Bestimmung über Form, Maß oder ähnliche Verhältnisse vorbehalten, so ist der Käufer verpflichtet, die vorbehaltene Bestimmung zu treffen.

(2) Ist der Käufer mit der Erfüllung dieser Verpflichtung in Verzug, so kann der Verkäufer die Bestimmung statt des Käufers vornehmen oder gemäß den §§ 280, 281 des Bürgerlichen Gesetzbuchs Schadensersatz statt der Leistung verlangen oder gemäß § 323 des Bürgerlichen Gesetzbuchs vom Vertrag zurücktreten. Im ersteren Falle hat der Verkäufer die von ihm getroffene Bestimmung dem Käufer mitzuteilen und ihm zugleich eine angemessene Frist zur Vornahme einer anderweitigen Bestimmung zu setzen. Wird eine solche innerhalb der Frist von dem Käufer nicht vorgenommen, so ist die von dem Verkäufer getroffene Bestimmung maßgebend.

§ 375 Sale where the buyer specifies the item

(1) Where, with respect to the sale of tangible property, specific determinations are reserved to the buyer with respect to form, size or similar conditions, the buyer is obligated to make the determinations thus reserved.

(2) Where the buyer defaults in fulfilling this duty, the seller may make the determination instead of the buyer, or demand damages instead of the performance pursuant to §§ 280, 281 of the Civil Code or rescind the contract pursuant to § 323 of the Civil Code. In the first case, the seller must inform the buyer of the determination made by him and at the same time set a reasonable period for him to make a contrary determination. Where a determination is not made by the buyer within the period, the determination made by the seller shall prevail.

§ 376 [Fixhandelskauf]

(1) Ist bedungen, daß die Leistung des einen Teiles genau zu einer festbestimmten Zeit oder innerhalb einer festbestimmten Frist bewirkt werden soll, so kann der andere Teil, wenn die Leistung nicht zu der bestimmten Zeit oder nicht innerhalb der bestimmten Frist erfolgt, von dem Vertrage zurücktreten oder, falls der Schuldner im Verzug ist, statt der Erfüllung Schadensersatz wegen Nichterfüllung verlangen. Erfüllung kann er nur beanspruchen, wenn er sofort nach dem Ablaufe der Zeit oder der Frist dem Gegner anzeigt, daß er auf Erfüllung bestehe.

§ 376 Sale to be performed at a fixed point in time

(1) Where it is stipulated that performance by one of the parties should be effected at an exact time or within a specific period, the other party may rescind the contract if performance is not made at the exact time or within the period specified, or in the event that the debtor has defaulted, demand payment of damages for non-performance in lieu of performance of the contract. He may only demand performance if he indicates to the other party, immediately following expiration of the time or the period, that he insists on performance.

(2) Wird Schadensersatz wegen Nichterfüllung verlangt und hat die Ware einen Börsen- oder Marktpreis, so kann der Unterschied des Kaufpreises und des Börsen- oder Marktpreises zur Zeit und am Orte der geschuldeten Leistung gefordert werden.

(3) Das Ergebnis eines anderweit vorgenommenen Verkaufs oder Kaufes kann, falls die Ware einen Börsen- oder Marktpreis hat, dem Ersatzanspruche nur zugrunde gelegt werden, wenn der Verkauf oder Kauf sofort nach dem Ablaufe der bedungenen Leistungszeit oder Leistungsfrist bewirkt ist. Der Verkauf oder Kauf muß, wenn er nicht in öffentlicher Versteigerung geschieht, durch einen zu solchen Verkäufen oder Käufen öffentlich ermächtigten Handelsmakler oder eine zur öffentlichen Versteigerung befugte Person zum laufenden Preise erfolgen.

(4) Auf den Verkauf mittels öffentlicher Versteigerung findet die Vorschrift des § 373 Abs. 4 Anwendung. Von dem Verkauf oder Kaufe hat der Gläubiger den Schuldner unverzüglich zu benachrichtigen; im Falle der Unterlassung ist er zum Schadensersatze verpflichtet.

§ 377 [Untersuchungs- und Rügepflicht]

(1) Ist der Kauf für beide Teile ein Handelsgeschäft, so hat der Käufer die Ware unverzüglich nach der Ablieferung durch den Verkäufer, soweit dies nach ordnungsmäßigem Geschäftsgange tunlich ist, zu untersuchen und, wenn sich ein Mangel zeigt, dem Verkäufer unverzüglich Anzeige zu machen.

(2) Where damages are demanded for non-performance and the goods have an exchange or market price, the difference between the purchase price and the exchange or market price at the time and place of the performance due can be demanded.

(3) The result of another sale or purchase can, in the case where the goods have an exchange or market price, only be taken as the basis for the damage claim if the sale or purchase is effected immediately after the performance time or performance deadline has elapsed. If it does not occur at a public auction, the sale or purchase must be carried out at the current price by a broker officially authorized to conduct such sales or by a public auctioneer.

(4) The provision of § 373 Subsection 4 applies to the sale at public auction. The creditor must promptly notify the debtor of the sale or purchase; in case of failure to do this, he is liable for damages.

§ 377 Duty to examine and object to defects

(1) Where the sale is a commercial transaction for both parties, the buyer must examine the goods promptly following delivery by the seller insofar as this is practicable in the proper course of business, and if a defect becomes apparent, promptly advise the seller.

(2) Unterläßt der Käufer die Anzeige, so gilt die Ware als genehmigt, es sei denn, daß es sich um einen Mangel handelt, der bei der Untersuchung nicht erkennbar war.

(3) Zeigt sich später ein solcher Mangel, so muß die Anzeige unverzüglich nach der Entdeckung gemacht werden; anderenfalls gilt die Ware auch in Ansehung dieses Mangels als genehmigt.

(4) Zur Erhaltung der Rechte des Käufers genügt die rechtzeitige Absendung der Anzeige.

(5) Hat der Verkäufer den Mangel arglistig verschwiegen, so kann er sich auf diese Vorschriften nicht berufen.

§ 378 *(aufgehoben)*

§ 379 [Einstweilige Aufbewahrung; Notverkauf]

(1) Ist der Kauf für beide Teile ein Handelsgeschäft, so ist der Käufer, wenn er die ihm von einem anderen Orte übersendete Ware beanstandet, verpflichtet, für ihre einstweilige Aufbewahrung zu sorgen.

(2) Er kann die Ware, wenn sie dem Verderb ausgesetzt und Gefahr im Verzug ist, unter Beobachtung der Vorschriften des § 373 verkaufen lassen.

§ 380 [Taragewicht]

(1) Ist der Kaufpreis nach dem Gewichte der Ware zu berechnen, so kommt das Gewicht der Verpackung (Taragewicht) in Abzug, wenn nicht aus dem Vertrag oder dem Handelsgebrauche des Ortes, an welchem der Verkäufer zu erfüllen hat, sich ein anderes ergibt.

(2) If the buyer fails to advise the seller, the goods are deemed to have been approved, unless there is a defect which was not apparent during the examination.

(3) Where such a defect becomes apparent at a later time, notice must be given promptly following the discovery; otherwise, the goods are to be deemed approved, also with regard to this defect.

(4) The timely dispatch of notice suffices to preserve the buyer's rights.

(5) Where the seller has maliciously concealed the defect, he may not assert these provisions.

§ 378 *(repealed)*

§ 379 Temporary storage; forced sale

(1) Where the sale is a commercial transaction for both parties, a buyer who refuses to accept goods shipped to him from another location is obligated to provide temporary storage for them.

(2) He may have the goods sold, under observance of the provisions of § 373, if they are perishable and there is risk in delay.

§ 380 Tare weight

(1) Where the purchase price is calculated according to the weight of the merchandise, the weight of the packaging (tare weight) is to be subtracted unless the contract or the trade custom of the place at which the seller is to perform provides otherwise.

(2) Ob und in welcher Höhe das Taragewicht nach einem bestimmten Ansatz oder Verhältnisse statt nach genauer Ausmittelung abzuziehen ist, sowie ob und wieviel als Gutgewicht zugunsten des Käufers zu berechnen ist oder als Vergütung für schadhafte oder unbrauchbare Teile (Refaktie) gefordert werden kann, bestimmt sich nach dem Vertrag oder dem Handelsgebrauchs des Ortes, an welchem der Verkäufer zu erfüllen hat.

(2) Whether and to what extent the tare weight is to be subtracted pursuant to a specific rate or ratio in lieu of an exact weight, as well as whether and how much is to be calculated as weight for the buyer's benefit or can be claimed as compensation for defective or useless parts (allowance for loss, breakage, shrinkage, etc.) shall be determined by the contract or the trade custom of the place at which the seller is obligated to perform.

§ 381 [Kauf von Wertpapieren; Werklieferungsvertrag]

§ 381 Sale of securities

(1) Die in diesem Abschnitte für den Kauf von Waren getroffenen Vorschriften gelten auch für den Kauf von Wertpapieren.

(1) The provisions set forth in this Part for the sale of goods also apply to the sale of securities.

(2) Sie finden auch auf einen Vertrag Anwendung, der die Lieferung herzustellender oder zu erzeugender beweglicher Sachen zum Gegenstand hat.

(2) They shall also apply to a contract which has as its subject the delivery of nonfungible tangible goods to be manufactured or produced.

§ 382 *(aufgehoben)*

§ 382 *(repealed)*

Dritter Abschnitt. Kommissionsgeschäft

Part Three. Transactions on a Commission Basis

§ 383 [Kommissionär; Kommissionsvertrag]

§ 383 Commission agent; contract concluded by a commission agent

(1) Kommissionär ist, wer es gewerbsmäßig übernimmt, Waren oder Wertpapiere für Rechnung eines anderen (des Kommittenten) in eigenem Namen zu kaufen oder zu verkaufen.

(1) A commission agent is one who professionally undertakes to buy and sell goods or securities in his own name for the account of another (principal).

(2) Die Vorschriften dieses Abschnittes finden auch Anwendung, wenn das Unternehmen des Kommissionärs nach Art oder Umfang einen in kaufmännischer Weise eingerichteten Ge-

(2) The provisions of this Part apply where the enterprise of the commission agent by type and volume does not require a commercially organized business operation and the firm name

schäftsbetrieb nicht erfordert und die Firma des Unternehmens nicht nach § 2 in das Handelsregister eingetragen ist. In diesem Fall finden in Ansehung des Kommissionsgeschäfts auch die Vorschriften des Ersten Abschnitts des Vierten Buches mit Ausnahme der §§ 348 bis 350 Anwendung.

of the enterprise is not registered in the Commercial Register pursuant to § 2. In this case the provisions of the First Part of the Fourth Book, with the exception of §§ 348 to 350, also apply with respect to the commission business.

§ 384 [Pflichten des Kommissionärs]

(1) Der Kommissionär ist verpflichtet, das übernommene Geschäft mit der Sorgfalt eines ordentlichen Kaufmanns auszuführen; er hat hierbei das Interesse des Kommittenten wahrzunehmen und dessen Weisungen zu befolgen.

(2) Er hat dem Kommittenten die erforderlichen Nachrichten zu geben, insbesondere von der Ausführung der Kommissson unverzüglich Anzeige zu machen; er ist verpflichtet, dem Kommittenten über das Geschäft Rechenschaft abzulegen und ihm dasjenige herauszugeben, was er aus der Geschäftsbesorgung erlangt hat.

(3) Der Kommissionär haftet dem Kommittenten für die Erfüllung des Geschäfts, wenn er ihm nicht zugleich mit der Anzeige von der Ausführung der Kommission den Dritten namhaft macht, mit dem er das Geschäft abgeschlossen hat.

§ 384 Duties of the commission agent

(1) The commission agent is obligated to carry out the transaction undertaken with the care of a prudent merchant; in so doing he must protect the principal's interests and follow with his instructions.

(2) He must give the principal the necessary information, especially prompt notice as to the conclusion of the transaction; he is obligated to account to the principal for the transaction and deliver to him anything obtained from the business commissioned.

(3) The commission agent is liable to the principal for performance of the transaction if he does not, simultaneously with notice of conclusion of the transaction, name the third party with whom he concluded the transaction.

§ 385 [Weisungen des Kommittenten]

(1) Handelt der Kommissionär nicht gemäß den Weisungen des Kommittenten, so ist er diesem zum Ersatze des Schadens verpflichtet; der Kommittent braucht das Geschäft nicht für seine Rechnung gelten zu lassen.

§ 385 Instructions of the principal

(1) Where the commission agent does not act in accordance with the principal's instructions, he is liable to him for damages; the principal need not accept the transaction for his account.

(2) Die Vorschriften des § 665 des Bürgerlichen Gesetzbuchs bleiben unberührt.

§ 386 [Preisgrenzen]

(1) Hat der Kommissionär unter dem ihm gesetzten Preise verkauft oder hat er den ihm für den Einkauf gesetzten Preis überschritten, so muß der Kommittent, falls er das Geschäft als nicht für seine Rechnung abgeschlossen zurückweisen will, dies unverzüglich auf die Anzeige von der Ausführung des Geschäfts erklären; anderenfalls gilt die Abweichung von der Preisbestimmung als genehmigt.

(2) Erbietet sich der Kommissionär zugleich mit der Anzeige von der Ausführung des Geschäfts zur Deckung des Preisunterschieds, so ist der Kommittent zur Zurückweisung nicht berechtigt. Der Anspruch des Kommittenten auf den Ersatz eines den Preisunterschied übersteigenden Schadens bleibt unberührt.

§ 387 [Vorteilhafterer Abschluß]

(1) Schließt der Kommissionär zu vorteilhaften Bedingungen ab, als sie ihm von dem Kommittenten gesetzt worden sind, so kommt dies dem Kommittenten zustatten.

(2) Dies gilt insbesondere, wenn der Preis, für welchen der Kommissionär verkauft, den von dem Kommittenten bestimmten niedrigsten Preis übersteigt oder wenn der Preis, für welchen er einkauft, den von dem Kommittenten bestimmten höchsten Preis nicht erreicht.

(2) The provisions of § 665 of the Civil Code remain unaffected.

§ 386 Buying and selling price limitations

(1) Where the commission agent has sold for less than the price set for him or has exceeded the price set for the purchase, the principal, in the event he desires to reject the transaction as not having been concluded for his account, must give notice thereof promptly upon receiving notification of the conclusion of the transaction; otherwise, the deviation from the price stipulation is deemed to have been consented to.

(2) Where the commission agent, simultaneously with notice of conclusion of the transaction, offers to cover the price differential, the principal may not reject the transaction. The principal's right to damages which exceed the price differential remains unaffected.

§ 387 More profitable conclusion of business

(1) Where the commission agent concludes the transaction on more favorable terms than were stipulated for him by the principal, the resulting benefit shall accrue to the principal.

(2) This applies particularly where the price at which the commission agent sold exceeded the lowest price specified by the principal or where the price at which he bought did not reach the highest price specified by the principal.

§ 388 [Beschädigtes oder mangelhaftes Kommissionsgut]

(1) Befindet sich das Gut, welches dem Kommissionär zugesendet ist, bei der Ablieferung in einem beschädigten oder mangelhaften Zustande, der äußerlich erkennbar ist, so hat der Kommissionär die Rechte gegen den Frachtführer oder Schiffer zu wahren, für den Beweis des Zustandes zu sorgen und dem Kommittenten unverzüglich Nachricht zu geben; im Falle der Unterlassung ist er zum Schadensersatze verpflichtet.

(2) Ist das Gut dem Verderb ausgesetzt oder treten später Veränderungen an dem Gute ein, die dessen Entwertung befürchten lassen, und ist keine Zeit vorhanden, die Verfügung des Kommittenten einzuholen, oder ist der Kommittent in der Erteilung der Verfügung säumig, so kann der Kommissionär den Verkauf des Gutes nach Maßgabe der Vorschriften des § 373 bewirken.

§ 389 [Hinterlegung; Selbsthilfeverkauf]

Unterläßt der Kommittent über das Gut zu verfügen, obwohl er dazu nach Lage der Sache verpflichtet ist, so hat der Kommissionär die nach § 373 dem Verkäufer zustehenden Rechte.

§ 390 [Haftung des Kommissionärs für das Gut]

(1) Der Kommissionär ist für den Verlust und die Beschädigung des in seiner Verwahrung befindlichen Gutes verantwortlich, es sei denn, daß der Verlust oder die Beschädigung auf Umständen beruht, die durch die Sorgfalt eines ordentlichen Kaufmanns nicht abgewendet werden konnten.

§ 388 Damaged or defective goods on commission

(1) Where the goods sent to the commission agent are in a damaged or defective condition apparent at the time of delivery, the commission agent is obligated to reserve all rights against the carrier or shipper, make arrangements to preserve proof of the condition and notify the principal promptly; where he fails to do this, he is liable for damages.

(2) Where the goods are perishable or subsequent changes therein cause concern that they will depreciate and there is no time to obtain instructions from the principal, or the principal delays in responding with instructions, the commission agent may have the goods sold according to the provisions of § 373.

§ 389 Deposit; self-help sale

Where the principal fails to dispose of the merchandise although obligated to do so under the circumstances, the commission agent has the rights of a seller pursuant to § 373.

§ 390 The commission agent's liability for the goods

(1) The commission agent is responsible for loss of and damage to goods in his custody unless the loss or damage is due to circumstances which could not have been avoided by use of the care of a prudent merchant.

(2) Der Kommissionär ist wegen der Unterlassung der Versicherung des Gutes nur verantwortlich, wenn er von dem Kommittenten angewiesen war, die Versicherung zu bewirken.

(2) The commission agent is responsible for failure to insure the goods only if he was instructed by the principal to obtain the insurance.

§ 391 [Untersuchungs- und Rügepflicht; Aufbewahrung; Notverkauf]

Ist eine Einkaufskommission erteilt, die für beide Teile ein Handelsgeschäft ist, so finden in bezug auf die Verpflichtung des Kommittenten, das Gut zu untersuchen und dem Kommissionär von den entdeckten Mängeln Anzeige zu machen, sowie in bezug auf die Sorge für die Aufbewahrung des beanstandeten Gutes und auf den Verkauf bei drohendem Verderbe die für den Käufer geltenden Vorschriften der §§ 377 bis 379 entsprechende Anwendung. Der Anspruch des Kommittenten auf Abtretung der Rechte, die dem Kommissionär gegen den Dritten zustehen, von welchem er das Gut für Rechnung des Kommittenten gekauft hat, wird durch eine verspätete Anzeige des Mangels nicht berührt.

§ 391 Duty to examine and object; storage; forced sale

Where the commission to purchase is a commercial transaction for both parties, the provisions of §§ 377 through 379 applicable to the buyer are analogously applicable to the principal's duty to examine the goods and give notice to the commission agent of defects discovered, as well as to the duty of storage for the rejected goods and the sale of perishable goods. The right of the principal to assignment of the rights of the commission agent against third parties from whom he bought the goods for the principal's account will not be affected by late notification of defects.

§ 392 [Forderungen aus dem Kommissionsgeschäft]

(1) Forderungen aus einem Geschäfte, das der Kommissionär abgeschlossen hat, kann der Kommittent dem Schuldner gegenüber erst nach der Abtretung geltend machen.

(2) Jedoch gelten solche Forderungen, auch wenn sie nicht abgetreten sind, im Verhältnisse zwischen dem Kommittenten und dem Kommissionär oder dessen Gläubigern als Forderungen des Kommittenten.

§ 392 Claims arising from transactions on a commission basis

(1) Claims arising from a transaction concluded by the commission agent may be asserted by the principal against the debtor only after assignment.

(2) Such claims are deemed, however, even if they are not assigned, to be claims of the principal in the relationship between the principal and the commission agent or his creditors.

§ 393 [Vorschuß; Kredit]

(1) Wird von dem Kommissionär ohne Zustimmung des Kommittenten einem Dritten ein Vorschuß geleistet oder Kredit gewährt, so handelt der Kommissionär auf eigene Gefahr.

(2) Insoweit jedoch der Handelsgebrauch am Orte des Geschäfts die Stundung des Kaufpreises mit sich bringt, ist in Ermangelung einer anderen Bestimmung des Kommittenten auch der Kommissionär dazu berechtigt.

(3) Verkauft der Kommissionär unbefugt auf Kredit, so ist er verpflichtet, dem Kommittenten sofort als Schuldner des Kaufpreises die Zahlung zu leisten. Wäre beim Verkaufe gegen bar der Preis geringer gewesen, so hat der Kommissionär nur den geringeren Preis und, wenn dieser niedriger ist als der ihm gesetzte Preis, auch den Unterschied nach § 386 zu vergüten.

§ 394 [Delkredere]

(1) Der Kommissionär hat für die Erfüllung der Verbindlichkeit des Dritten, mit dem er das Geschäft für Rechnung des Kommittenten abschließt, einzustehen, wenn dies von ihm übernommen oder am Orte seiner Niederlassung Handelsgebrauch ist.

(2) Der Kommissionär, der für den Dritten einzustehen hat, ist dem Kommittenten für die Erfüllung im Zeitpunkte des Verfalls unmittelbar insoweit verhaftet, als die Erfüllung aus dem Vertragsverhältnisse gefordert werden kann. Er kann eine besondere Vergütung (Delkredereprovision) beanspruchen.

§ 393 Advance; credit

(1) Where an advance is paid or credit is given to a third party by the commission agent without the principal's consent, the commission agent acts at his own risk.

(2) To the extent, however, that commercial usage at the location of the transaction includes a grace period for payment of the purchase price, the commission agent is authorized to grant such extension in the absence of a contrary instruction by the principal.

(3) Where the commission agent sells on credit without authorization, he is obligated, as the party liable for the purchase price, to pay the principal immediately. If the price for a cash sale would have been lower, the commission agent is obligated to pay only the lower price plus the difference pursuant to § 386 if the lower price is even lower than the price set by the principal.

§ 394 *Del credere* commission

(1) The commission agent shall be responsible for performance by the third party with whom he concludes the transaction for the account of the principal if this is undertaken by him or is commercially customary at the location of his establishment.

(2) The commission agent who is responsible for third-party performance is directly liable to the principal for performance at the time of the breach insofar as performance can be demanded on the basis of the contractual relationship. He may demand special remuneration (*del credere* commission).

§ 395 [Wechselindossament]

Ein Kommissionär, der den Ankauf eines Wechsels übernimmt, ist verpflichtet, den Wechsel, wenn er ihn indossiert, in üblicher Weise und ohne Vorbehalt zu indossieren.

§ 396 [Provision des Kommissionärs; Ersatz von Aufwendungen]

(1) Der Kommissionär kann die Provision fordern, wenn das Geschäft zur Ausführung gekommen ist. Ist das Geschäft nicht zur Ausführung gekommen, so hat er gleichwohl den Anspruch auf die Auslieferungsprovision, sofern eine solche ortsgebräuchlich ist; auch kann er die Provision verlangen, wenn die Ausführung des von ihm abgeschlossenen Geschäfts nur aus einem in der Person des Kommittenten liegenden Grunde unterblieben ist.

(2) Zu dem von dem Kommittenten für Aufwendungen des Kommissionärs nach den §§ 670 und 675 des Bürgerlichen Gesetzbuchs zu leistenden Ersatze gehört auch die Vergütung für die Benutzung der Lagerräume und der Beförderungsmittel des Kommissionärs.

§ 397 [Gesetzliches Pfandrecht]

Der Kommissionär hat an dem Kommissionsgute, sofern er es im Besitze hat, insbesondere mittels Konnossements, Ladescheins oder Lagerscheins darüber verfügen kann, ein Pfandrecht wegen der auf das Gut verwendeten Kosten, der Provision, der auf das Gut gegebenen Vorschüsse und Darlehen, der mit Rücksicht auf das Gut gezeichneten Wechsel oder in anderer

§ 395 Bill of exchange indorsement

A commission agent who undertakes to purchase a bill of exchange is obligated to indorse the same, if at all, in the customary manner and without reservation.

§ 396 Commission agent's commission; reimbursement for expenditures

(1) The commission agent may demand the commission when the transaction has been performed. Where the transaction has not been performed, he nevertheless has the right to a delivery commission to the extent that one is customary within the area; he may also demand the commission if the performance of the transaction concluded by him does not take place solely because of a personal reason related to the principal.

(2) Included within the amount to be reimbursed by the principal for the commission agent's expenditures pursuant to §§ 670 and 675 of the Civil Code are expenditures for the use of the storage areas and the commission agent's means of transport.

§ 397 Statutory lien

The commission agent has a statutory lien on the commission goods in his possession, especially where he has the power of disposition over them by means of a bill of lading, inland bill of lading or warehouse receipt, for advances made on the goods, the commission, advances and loans given on the goods, bills of exchange signed with respect to the goods, or obliga-

Weise eingegangenen Verbindlichkeiten sowie wegen aller Forderungen aus laufender Rechnung in Kommissionsgeschäften.

§ 398 [Befriedigung aus eigenem Kommissionsgut]

Der Kommissionär kann sich, auch wenn er Eigentümer des Kommissionsguts ist, für die in § 397 bezeichneten Ansprüche nach Maßgabe der für das Pfandrecht geltenden Vorschriften aus dem Gute befriedigen.

§ 399 [Befriedigung aus Forderungen]

Aus den Forderungen, welche durch das für Rechnung des Kommittenten geschlossene Geschäft begründet sind, kann sich der Kommissionär für die in § 397 bezeichneten Ansprüche vor dem Kommittenten und dessen Gläubigern befriedigen.

§ 400 [Selbsteintritt des Kommissionärs]

(1) Die Kommission zum Einkauf oder zum Verkaufe von Waren, die einen Börsen- oder Marktpreis haben, sowie von Wertpapieren, bei denen ein Börsen- oder Marktpreis amtlich festgestellt wird, kann, wenn der Kommittent nicht ein anderes bestimmt hat, von dem Kommissionär dadurch ausgeführt werden, daß er das Gut, welches er einkaufen soll, selbst als Verkäufer liefert oder das Gut, welches er verkaufen soll, selbst als Käufer übernimmt.

(2) Im Falle einer solchen Ausführung der Kommission beschränkt sich die

tions entered into in another way, as well as all claims arising on open account from commission transactions.

§ 398 Satisfaction from one's own commission goods

The commission agent may satisfy himself for the claims listed in § 397, according to the provisions applicable to liens, out of the goods, even if he is the legal owner of the commission goods.

§ 399 Satisfaction out of claims

The commission agent may satisfy himself ahead of the principal and the principal's creditors for the claims listed in § 397 out of claims (against third parties) arising from the transaction concluded for the principal's account.

§ 400 Commission agent's substitution of himself for the third party he would otherwise deal with on the principal's behalf

(1) The commission to buy or sell goods at an exchange or market price or securities for which an exchange or market price is officially determined may be performed by the commission agent such that, where the principal has not otherwise instructed he himself delivers as seller the goods which he is to buy or accepts as buyer the goods which he is to sell.

(2) Where the commission has been performed in such a manner, the com-

Pflicht des Kommissionärs, Rechenschaft über die Abschließung des Kaufes oder Verkaufs abzulegen, auf den Nachweis, daß bei dem berechneten Preise der zur Zeit der Ausführung der Kommission bestehende Börsen- oder Marktpreis eingehalten ist. Als Zeit der Ausführung gilt der Zeitpunkt, in welchem der Kommissionär die Anzeige von der Ausführung zur Absendung an den Kommittenten abgegeben hat.

(3) Ist bei einer Kommission, die während der Börsen- oder Marktzeit auszuführen war, die Ausführungsanzeige erst nach dem Schlusse der Börse oder des Marktes zur Absendung abgegeben, so darf der berechnete Preis für den Kommittenten nicht ungünstiger sein als der Preis, der am Schlusse der Börse oder des Marktes bestand.

(4) Bei einer Kommission, die zu einem bestimmten Kurse (erster Kurs, Mittelkurs, letzter Kurs) ausgeführt werden soll, ist der Kommissionär ohne Rücksicht auf den Zeitpunkt der Absendung der Ausführungsanzeige berechtigt und verpflichtet, diesen Kurs dem Kommittenten in Rechnung zu stellen.

(5) Bei Wertpapieren und Waren, für welche der Börsen- oder Marktpreis amtlich festgestellt wird, kann der Kommissionär im Falle der Ausführung der Kommission durch Selbsteintritt dem Kommittenten keinen ungünstigeren Preis als den amtlich festgestellten in Rechnung stellen.

§ 401 [Deckungsgeschäft]

(1) Auch im Falle der Ausführung der Kommission durch Selbsteintritt hat

mission agent's duty to account for the conclusion of the purchase or sale is limited to furnishing proof that, with respect to the price charged, the existing exchange or market price at the time of performance of the commission was adhered to. Time of performance is deemed to be the time at which the commission agent sent the notice of performance to the principal.

(3) Where the notice of performance of a commission which was to be performed during the time the exchange or market was open is sent after the close of the exchange or market, the price charged may not be less favorable for the principal than the price existing at the close of the exchange or market.

(4) With respect to a commission which was to be performed at a specific rate (opening rate, mean rate, closing rate), the commission agent is authorized and obligated to charge this rate to the principal without regard to the time at which the notice of performance was sent.

(5) With respect to securities and goods for which the exchange or market price is officially determined, the commission agent cannot, where he performs the commission by substituting himself for the third party he would otherwise deal with on the principal's behalf, charge the principal a price less favorable than the officially established price.

§ 401 Covering transactions

(1) Even if the commission agent has performed the commission by substi-

der Kommissionär, wenn er bei Anwendung pflichtmäßiger Sorgfalt die Kommission zu einem günstigeren als dem nach § 400 sich ergebenden Preise ausführen konnte, dem Kommittenten den günstigeren Preis zu berechnen.

(2) Hat der Kommissionär vor der Absendung der Ausführungsanzeige aus Anlaß der erteilten Kommission an der Börse oder am Markte ein Geschäft mit einem Dritten abgeschlossen, so darf er dem Kommittenten keinen ungünstigeren als den hierbei vereinbarten Preis berechnen.

§ 402 [Unabdingbarkeit]

Die Vorschriften des § 400 Abs. 2 bis 5 und des § 401 können nicht durch Vertrag zum Nachteile des Kommittenten abgeändert werden.

§ 403 [Provision bei Selbsteintritt]

Der Kommissionär, der das Gut selbst als Verkäufer liefert oder als Käufer übernimmt, ist zu der gewöhnlichen Provision berechtigt und kann die bei Kommissionsgeschäften sonst regelmäßig vorkommenden Kosten berechnen.

§ 404 [Gesetzliches Pfandrecht]

Die Vorschriften der §§ 397 und 398 finden auch im Falle der Ausführung der Kommission durch Selbsteintritt Anwendung.

tuting himself for the third party he would otherwise deal with on the principal's behalf, he must charge the principal the more favorable price if by the exercise of due care he could have obtained a more favorable price than the one resulting from the application of § 400.

(2) Where the commission agent has, on the basis of the commission, concluded a transaction with a third party on the exchange or on the market before sending the notice of performance, he may not charge the principal a less advantageous price than the price agreed.

§ 402 Unalterable rights

The provisions of § 400 Subsections 2 through 5 and § 401 cannot be altered contractually to the principal's disadvantage.

§ 403 Commission for entry of the commission agent simultaneously as third party

The commission agent who has delivered goods himself as the seller or accepted goods as the buyer may charge the customary commission and the costs which regularly occur in conjunction with commission transactions.

§ 404 Statutory lien

The provisions of §§ 397 and 398 also apply where the commission is performed by the commission agent substituting himself for the third party he would otherwise deal with on the principal's behalf.

Kommissionsgeschäft §§ 405, 406

§ 405 [Ausführungsanzeige und Selbsteintritt; Widerruf der Kommission]

(1) Zeigt der Kommissionär die Ausführung der Kommission an, ohne ausdrücklich zu bemerken, daß er selbst eintreten wolle, so gilt dies als Erklärung, daß die Ausführung durch Abschluß des Geschäfts mit einem Dritten für Rechnung des Kommittenten erfolgt sei.

(2) Eine Vereinbarung zwischen dem Kommittenten und dem Kommissionär, daß die Erklärung darüber, ob die Kommission durch Selbsteintritt oder durch Abschluß mit einem Dritten ausgeführt sei, später als am Tage der Ausführungsanzeige abgegeben werden dürfe, ist nichtig.

(3) Widerruft der Kommittent die Kommission und geht der Widerruf dem Kommissionär zu, bevor die Ausführungsanzeige zur Absendung abgegeben ist, so steht dem Kommissionär das Recht des Selbsteintritts nicht mehr zu.

§ 406 [Ähnliche Geschäfte]

(1) Die Vorschriften dieses Abschnitts kommen auch zur Anwendung, wenn ein Kommissionär im Betriebe seines Handelsgewerbes ein Geschäft anderer als der in § 383 bezeichneten Art für Rechnung eines anderen in eigenem Namen zu schließen übernimmt. Das gleiche gilt, wenn ein Kaufmann, der nicht Kommissionär ist, im Betriebe seines Handelsgewerbes ein Geschäft in der bezeichneten Weise zu schließen übernimmt.

§ 405 Notice of performance and substitution of commission agent for the third party he would otherwise deal with on the principal's behalf; revocation of the commission

(1) Where the commission agent gives notice of performance of the commission without expressly noting that he plans to enter simultaneously as the third party, this shall be deemed to be a statement that performance has been made through conclusion of the transaction with a third party for the principal's account.

(2) Any agreement between the principal and the commission agent, pursuant to which the statement specifying whether the commission has been performed by the commission agent's entry simultaneously as the third party or by a transaction with a third party may be sent later than the date of the notice of completion, is void.

(3) In the event that the principal revokes the commission and the revocation reaches the commission agent before notice of performance has been sent, the commission agent is no longer entitled to enter simultaneously as the third party.

§ 406 Similar transactions

(1) The provisions of this Part also apply if a commission agent agrees, within the context of the operation of his business, to conclude a transaction other than the type set out in § 383 in his own name for the account of another. The same applies if a merchant who is not a commission agent agrees to conclude a transaction within the operation of his business in the manner described.

(2) Als Einkaufs- und Verkaufskommission im Sinne dieses Abschnitts gilt auch eine Kommission, welche die Lieferung einer nicht vertretbaren beweglichen Sache, die aus einem von dem Unternehmer zu beschaffenden Stoffe herzustellen ist, zum Gegenstande hat.

(2) A commission which relates to the delivery of a non-fungible tangible good to be made out of material to be procured by the manufacturer is also deemed to be a buying and selling commission within the meaning of this Part.

Vierter Abschnitt. Frachtgeschäft

Part Four. Carrier Business

Erster Unterabschnitt. Allgemeine Vorschriften

First Subpart. General Provisions

§ 407 Frachtvertrag

§ 407 Freight agreement

(1) Durch den Frachtvertrag wird der Frachtführer verpflichtet, das Gut zum Bestimmungsort zu befördern und dort an den Empfänger abzuliefern.

(1) The freight agreement obligates the carrier to transport the goods to the place of destination and to deliver them there to the consignee.

(2) Der Absender wird verpflichtet, die vereinbarte Fracht zu zahlen.

(2) The shipper is obligated to pay the freight charges agreed upon.

(3) Die Vorschriften dieses Unterabschnitts gelten, wenn

(3) The provisions of this Subpart apply where

1. das Gut zu Lande, auf Binnengewässern oder mit Luftfahrzeugen befördert werden soll und

2. die Beförderung zum Betrieb eines gewerblichen Unternehmens gehört.

1. the goods are to be transported by land, on inland waterways or by aircraft and

2. the shipment is part of the operation of a commercial enterprise.

Erfordert das Unternehmen nach Art oder Umfang einen in kaufmännischer Weise eingerichteten Geschäftsbetrieb nicht und ist die Firma des Unternehmens auch nicht nach § 2 in das Handelsregister eingetragen, so sind in Ansehung des Frachtgeschäfts auch insoweit die Vorschriften des Ersten Abschnitts des Vierten Buches ergänzend anzuwenden; dies gilt jedoch nicht für die §§ 348 bis 350.

Where the enterprise by type and volume does not require a commercially organized business operation and the firm name of the enterprise is not registered in the Commercial Register pursuant to § 2, the provisions of the First Part of the Fourth Book shall apply supplementally with respect to the freight business; this, however, does not apply for §§ 348 to 350.

Frachtgeschäft

§ 408

§ 408 Frachtbrief

(1) Der Frachtführer kann die Ausstellung eines Frachtbriefs mit folgenden Angaben verlangen:

1. Ort und Tag der Ausstellung;
2. Name und Anschrift des Absenders;
3. Name und Anschrift des Frachtführers;
4. Stelle und Tag der Übernahme des Gutes sowie die für die Ablieferung vorgesehene Stelle;
5. Name und Anschrift des Empfängers und eine etwaige Meldeadresse;
6. die übliche Bezeichnung der Art des Gutes und die Art der Verpackung, bei gefährlichen Gütern ihre nach den Gefahrgutvorschriften vorgesehene, sonst ihre allgemein anerkannte Bezeichnung;
7. Anzahl, Zeichen und Nummern der Frachtstücke;
8. das Rohgewicht oder die anders angegebene Menge des Gutes;
9. die vereinbarte Fracht und die bis zur Ablieferung anfallenden Kosten sowie einen Vermerk über die Frachtzahlung;
10. den Betrag einer bei der Ablieferung des Gutes einzuziehenden Nachnahme;
11. Weisungen für die Zoll- und sonstige amtliche Behandlung des Gutes;
12. eine Vereinbarung über die Beförderung in offenem, nicht mit Planen gedecktem Fahrzeug oder auf Deck.

§ 408 Waybill

(1) The carrier may require issuance of a waybill with the following data:

1. place and date of issuance;
2. name and address of the shipper;
3. name and address of the carrier;
4. place and date of acceptance of the goods as well as the place foreseen for delivery;
5. name and address of the consignee and any registered address;
6. the customary description of the type of goods and the type of packaging, in case of dangerous goods the description pursuant to the statutory provisions relating to dangerous goods or otherwise the generally accepted description;
7. quantity, identifying marks and numbers of the packages;
8. the gross weight or the other designated quantity of the goods;
9. the agreed freight charges and the costs which will be incurred up to the time of delivery as well as a notation concerning the payment of the freight charges;
10. the amount of any charges to be collected upon delivery of the goods;
11. instructions for the customs and other official handling of the goods;
12. an agreement concerning the shipment in open vehicles not covered by tarps or on deck.

In den Frachtbrief können weitere Angaben eingetragen werden, die die Parteien für zweckmäßig halten.

(2) Der Frachtbrief wird in drei Originalausfertigungen ausgestellt, die vom Absender unterzeichnet werden. Der Absender kann verlangen, daß auch der Frachtführer den Frachtbrief unterzeichnet. Nachbildungen der eigenhändigen Unterschriften durch Druck oder Stempel genügen. Eine Ausfertigung ist für den Absender bestimmt, eine begleitet das Gut, eine behält der Frachtführer.

§ 409 Beweiskraft des Frachtbriefs

(1) Der von beiden Parteien unterzeichnete Frachtbrief dient bis zum Beweis des Gegenteils als Nachweis für Abschluß und Inhalt des Frachtvertrages sowie für die Übernahme des Gutes durch den Frachtführer.

(2) Der von beiden Parteien unterzeichnete Frachtbrief begründet ferner die Vermutung, daß das Gut und seine Verpackung bei der Übernahme durch den Frachtführer in äußerlich gutem Zustand waren und daß die Anzahl der Frachtstücke und ihre Zeichen und Nummern mit den Angaben im Frachtbrief übereinstimmen. Der Frachtbrief begründet diese Vermutung jedoch nicht, wenn der Frachtführer einen begründeten Vorbehalt in den Frachtbrief eingetragen hat; der Vorbehalt kann auch damit begründet werden, daß dem Frachtführer keine angemessenen Mittel zur Verfügung standen, die Richtigkeit der Angaben zu überprüfen.

(3) Ist das Rohgewicht oder die anders angegebene Menge des Gutes oder der Inhalt der Frachtstücke vom Frachtführer überprüft und das Ergebnis der

Further data which the parties consider to be useful can be included in the waybill.

(2) The waybill shall be issued in three counterparts which are to be signed by the shipper. The shipper may require that the carrier also sign the waybill. Facsimiles of the signatures by print or stamp suffice. One counterpart is intended for the shipper, one accompanies the goods and one is retained by the carrier.

§ 409 Evidentiary value of the waybill

(1) The waybill signed by both parties serves as evidence for the conclusion and contents of the freight agreement as well as for the acceptance of the goods by the carrier until the contrary has been proven.

(2) The waybill signed by both parties also establishes the presumption that the goods and their packaging were externally in good condition upon the acceptance by the carrier and that the quantity of packages and their identifying marks and numbers corresponded to the data in the waybill. The waybill, however, does not establish this presumption if the carrier entered a justified reservation in the waybill; the reservation can also be justified by the fact that the carrier did not have appropriate means available to check the correctness of the data.

(3) If the gross weight or the other designated quantity of the goods or the contents of the packages have been examined by the carrier and the result of

Überprüfung in den von beiden Parteien unterzeichneten Frachtbrief eingetragen worden, so begründet dieser auch die Vermutung, daß Gewicht, Menge oder Inhalt mit den Angaben im Frachtbrief übereinstimmt. Der Frachtführer ist verpflichtet, Gewicht, Menge oder Inhalt zu überprüfen, wenn der Absender dies verlangt und dem Frachtführer angemessene Mittel zur Überprüfung zur Verfügung stehen; der Frachtführer hat Anspruch auf Ersatz seiner Aufwendungen für die Überprüfung.

the examination has been entered in the waybill signed by both parties, then this also establishes the presumption that weight, quantity or contents correspond to the data in the waybill. The carrier is obligated to examine weight, quantity or contents where the shipper so requests and the carrier has appropriate means for examination available; the carrier is entitled to reimbursement of his costs for the examination.

§ 410 Gefährliches Gut

(1) Soll gefährliches Gut befördert werden, so hat der Absender dem Frachtführer rechtzeitig in Textform die genaue Art der Gefahr und, soweit erforderlich, zu ergreifende Vorsichtsmaßnahmen mitzuteilen.

(2) Der Frachtführer kann, sofern ihm nicht bei Übernahme des Gutes die Art der Gefahr bekannt war oder jedenfalls mitgeteilt worden ist,

1. gefährliches Gut ausladen, einlagern, zurückbefördern oder, soweit erforderlich, vernichten oder unschädlich machen, ohne dem Absender deshalb ersatzpflichtig zu werden, und
2. vom Absender wegen dieser Maßnahmen Ersatz der erforderlichen Aufwendungen verlangen.

§ 410 Dangerous goods

(1) Where dangerous goods are to be transported, the shipper shall inform the carrier in timely manner and in written form about the exact type of danger and, as far as necessary, the precautions to be taken.

(2) The carrier may to the extent that the type of danger was unknown to him or in any case was not communicated to him upon acceptance of the goods

1. unload, warehouse, return or, to the extent necessary, destroy or render harmless the dangerous goods without becoming liable to the shipper for damages therefor, and
2. demand from the shipper reimbursement of the costs necessitated by these measures.

§ 411 Verpackung. Kennzeichnung

Der Absender hat das Gut, soweit dessen Natur unter Berücksichtigung der vereinbarten Beförderung eine Verpackung erfordert, so zu verpacken, daß es vor Verlust und Beschädigung

§ 411 Packaging; labelling

The shipper shall package the goods, to the extent that the nature of the goods requires packaging, taking into consideration the agreed shipment, in such manner that they are protected

geschützt ist und daß auch dem Frachtführer keine Schäden entstehen. Der Absender hat das Gut ferner, soweit dessen vertragsgemäße Behandlung dies erfordert, zu kennzeichnen.

§ 412 Verladen und Entladen

(1) Soweit sich aus den Umständen oder der Verkehrssitte nicht etwas anderes ergibt, hat der Absender das Gut beförderungssicher zu laden, zu stauen und zu befestigen (verladen) sowie zu entladen. Der Frachtführer hat für die betriebssichere Verladung zu sorgen.

(2) Für die Lade- und Entladezeit, die sich mangels abweichender Vereinbarung nach einer den Umständen des Falles angemessenen Frist bemißt, kann keine besondere Vergütung verlangt werden.

(3) Wartet der Frachtführer auf Grund vertraglicher Vereinbarung oder aus Gründen, die nicht seinem Risikobereich zuzurechnen sind, über die Lade- oder Entladezeit hinaus, so hat er Anspruch auf eine angemessene Vergütung (Standgeld).

(4) Das Bundesministerium der Justiz wird ermächtigt, im Einvernehmen mit dem Bundesministerium für Verkehr, Bau- und Wohnungswesen durch Rechtsverordnung, die nicht der Zustimmung des Bundesrates bedarf, für die Binnenschiffahrt unter Berücksichtigung der Art der zur Beförderung bestimmten Fahrzeuge, der Art und Menge der umzuschlagenden Güter, der beim Güterumschlag zur Verfügung stehenden technischen Mittel und der Erfordernisse eines beschleunigten Verkehrsablaufs die Voraussetzungen für den Beginn der Lade-

against loss and damage and also such that no damages arise to the carrier. The shipper shall also label the goods to the extent that the agreed-upon handling requires this.

§ 412 Loading and unloading

(1) To the extent that nothing different follows from the circumstances or the trade usage, the shipper shall load, stow, secure (off-load) as well as unload the goods so that they can be transported safely. The carrier is responsible for the safe off-loading.

(2) No special remuneration can be requested for the time of loading and unloading which, absent a differing agreement, is determined according to a period reasonable for the circumstances of the case.

(3) The carrier is entitled to reasonable remuneration (demurrage) if he waits beyond the time for loading or unloading on the basis of a contractual agreement or for reasons which are not attributable to his sphere of risks.

(4) The Federal Ministry of Justice is authorized, in agreement with the Federal Ministry of Transportation, Construction and Housing, to determine by administrative order which does not require the consent of the Federal upper house of Parliament the requirements for the commencement of the times for loading and unloading, their duration and the amount of demurrage for the inland waterway carriers, taking into consideration the types of vehicles designated for shipment, the kind and quantity of the goods to be transshipped, the technical means

Frachtgeschäft §§ 412–414

und Entladezeit, deren Dauer sowie die Höhe des Standgeldes zu bestimmen.

§ 413 Begleitpapiere

(1) Der Absender hat dem Frachtführer Urkunden zur Verfügung zu stellen und Auskünfte zu erteilen, die für eine amtliche Behandlung, insbesondere eine Zollabfertigung, vor der Ablieferung des Gutes erforderlich sind.

(2) Der Frachtführer ist für den Schaden verantwortlich, der durch Verlust oder Beschädigung der ihm übergebenen Urkunden oder durch deren unrichtige Verwendung verursacht worden ist, es sei denn, daß der Verlust, die Beschädigung oder die unrichtige Verwendung auf Umständen beruht, die der Frachtführer nicht vermeiden und deren Folgen er nicht abwenden konnte. Seine Haftung ist jedoch auf den Betrag begrenzt, der bei Verlust des Gutes zu zahlen wäre.

§ 414 Verschuldensunabhängige Haftung des Absenders in besonderen Fällen

(1) Der Absender hat, auch wenn ihn kein Verschulden trifft, dem Frachtführer Schäden und Aufwendungen zu ersetzen, die verursacht werden durch

1. ungenügende Verpackung oder Kennzeichnung,

2. Unrichtigkeit oder Unvollständigkeit der in den Frachtbrief aufgenommenen Angaben,

3. Unterlassen der Mitteilung über die Gefährlichkeit des Gutes oder

available for transshipping the goods and the requirements of expedited traffic operations.

§ 413 Documents accompanying the goods

(1) The shipper shall make documents available to the carrier and give him the information necessary for an official handling prior to delivery of the goods, especially a customs clearance.

(2) The carrier is responsible for the damage which is caused through loss of or damage to the documents handed over to him or their incorrect use unless the loss, the damage or the incorrect use is caused by circumstances which the carrier could not avoid and which consequences he could not prevent. His liability, however, is limited to the amount which would have to be paid in case of loss of the goods.

§ 414 Strict liability of the shipper in special cases

(1) The shipper, even if he is not at fault, has to reimburse the carrier for damages and expenditures which are caused by the following circumstances:

1. Insufficient packaging or labelling,

2. incorrectness or incompleteness of the data contained in the waybill,

3. omission of the information concerning the dangerous nature of the goods,

339

4. Fehlen, Unvollständigkeit oder Unrichtigkeit der in § 413 Abs. 1 genannten Urkunden oder Auskünfte.

Für Schäden hat der Absender jedoch nur bis zu einem Betrag von 8,33 Rechnungseinheiten für jedes Kilogramm des Rohgewichts der Sendung Ersatz zu leisten; § 431 Abs. 4 und die §§ 434 bis 436 sind entsprechend anzuwenden.

(2) Hat bei der Verursachung der Schäden oder Aufwendungen ein Verhalten des Frachtführers mitgewirkt, so hängen die Verpflichtung zum Ersatz sowie der Umfang des zu leistenden Ersatzes davon ab, inwieweit dieses Verhalten zu den Schäden und Aufwendungen beigetragen hat.

(3) Ist der Absender ein Verbraucher, so hat er dem Frachtführer Schäden und Aufwendungen nach den Absätzen 1 und 2 nur zu ersetzen, soweit ihn ein Verschulden trifft.

(4) *(aufgehoben)*

§ 415 Kündigung durch den Absender

(1) Der Absender kann den Frachtvertrag jederzeit kündigen.

(2) Kündigt der Absender, so kann der Frachtführer entweder

1. die vereinbarte Fracht, das etwaige Standgeld sowie zu ersetzende Aufwendungen unter Anrechnung dessen, was er infolge der Aufhebung des Vertrages an Aufwendungen erspart oder anderweitig erwirbt oder zu erwerben böswillig unterläßt, oder

2. ein Drittel der vereinbarten Fracht (Fautfracht)

4. lack, incompleteness or incorrectness of the documents or information mentioned in § 413 Subsection 1.

The shipper shall, however, be liable only up to an amount of 8.33 units of account for each kilogram of the gross weight of the shipment; § 431 Subsection 4 and §§ 434 to 436 apply analogously.

(2) Where conduct of the carrier contributed to the cause of the damages or expenditures, the obligation to pay damages and the amount of the damages to be paid depend on the extent to which this conduct has contributed to the damages and expenditures.

(3) If the shipper is a consumer, he only has to reimburse the carrier for damages and expenditures pursuant Subsections 1 and 2 to the extent that he is at fault.

(4) *(repealed)*.

§ 415 Termination by the shipper

(1) The shipper can terminate the freight agreement at any time.

(2) In case of termination by the shipper, the carrier can request either

1. the agreed freight charges, demurrage, if any, as well as expenditures to be reimbursed taking into account the amounts he saves on expenditures because of the termination of the agreement, the amounts he earns otherwise or the amounts he maliciously neglects to earn, or

2. one-third of the agreed freight charges (dead freight).

Frachtgeschäft	§§ 415, 416

verlangen. Beruht die Kündigung auf Gründen, die dem Risikobereich des Frachtführers zuzurechnen sind, so entfällt der Anspruch auf Fautfracht nach Satz 1 Nr. 2; in diesem Falle entfällt auch der Anspruch nach Satz 1 Nr. 1, soweit die Beförderung für den Absender nicht von Interesse ist.

(3) Wurde vor der Kündigung bereits Gut verladen, so kann der Frachtführer auf Kosten des Absenders Maßnahmen entsprechend § 419 Abs. 3 Satz 2 bis 4 ergreifen oder vom Absender verlangen, daß dieser das Gut unverzüglich entlädt. Der Frachtführer braucht das Entladen des Gutes nur zu dulden, soweit dies ohne Nachteile für seinen Betrieb und ohne Schäden für die Absender oder Empfänger anderer Sendungen möglich ist. Beruht die Kündigung auf Gründen, die dem Risikobereich des Frachtführers zuzurechnen sind, so ist abweichend von den Sätzen 1 und 2 der Frachtführer verpflichtet, das Gut, das bereits verladen wurde, unverzüglich auf eigene Kosten zu entladen.

§ 416 Anspruch auf Teilbeförderung

Wird nur ein Teil der vereinbarten Ladung verladen, so kann der Absender jederzeit verlangen, daß der Frachtführer mit der Beförderung der unvollständigen Ladung beginnt. In diesem Fall gebührt dem Frachtführer die volle Fracht, das etwaige Standgeld sowie Ersatz der Aufwendungen, die ihm infolge der Unvollständigkeit der Ladung entstehen; von der vollen Fracht kommt jedoch die Fracht für dasjenige Gut in Abzug, welches der Frachtführer mit demselben Beförderungsmittel anstelle des nicht verladenen Gutes befördert. Der Frachtführer ist außerdem berechtigt, soweit

If the termination is caused by reasons which are attributable to the sphere of risks of the carrier, the claim to dead freight pursuant to sentence 1 No. 2 is dropped; in this case, the claim pursuant to sentence 1 No. 1 is also dropped to the extent that the shipment is not of interest for the shipper.

(3) Where goods have already been loaded before the termination, the carrier can take measures according to § 419 Subsection 3 sentences 2 to 4 at the expense of the shipper or he can request that the shipper unload the goods without undue delay. The carrier only has to tolerate the unloading of the goods to the extent that this is possible without disadvantages to his operations and without damages for the shippers or consignees of other shipments. If the termination is caused by reasons which are attributable to the sphere of risks of the carrier, he is obligated, deviating from sentences 1 and 2, to unload goods which have already been loaded without undue delay at his own expense.

§ 416 Claim to partial shipment

If only part of the cargo agreed upon is loaded, the shipper can request at any time that the carrier start with the shipment of the incomplete cargo. In this case the carrier is entitled to the full freight charges, the demurrage, if any, as well as reimbursement of the expenditures which he incurs because of the incompleteness of the cargo; the freight charges for the goods which the carrier transports with the same means of shipment in place of the goods not loaded shall, however, be deducted from the full freight charges. The carrier is also entitled to request that other security be furnished to the

ihm durch die Unvollständigkeit der Ladung die Sicherheit für die volle Fracht entgeht, die Bestellung einer anderweitigen Sicherheit zu fordern. Beruht die Unvollständigkeit der Verladung auf Gründen, die dem Risikobereich des Frachtführers zuzurechnen sind, so steht diesem der Anspruch nach den Sätzen 2 und 3 nur insoweit zu, als tatsächlich Ladung befördert wird.

§ 417 Rechte des Frachtführers bei Nichteinhaltung der Ladezeit

(1) Verlädt der Absender das Gut nicht innerhalb der Ladezeit oder stellt er, wenn er zur Verladung nicht verpflichtet ist, das Gut nicht innerhalb der Ladezeit zur Verfügung, so kann ihm der Frachtführer eine angemessene Frist setzen, innerhalb derer das Gut verladen oder zur Verfügung gestellt werden soll.

(2) Wird bis zum Ablauf der nach Absatz 1 gesetzten Frist keine Ladung verladen oder zur Verfügung gestellt, so kann der Frachtführer den Vertrag kündigen und die Ansprüche nach § 415 Abs. 2 geltend machen.

(3) Wird bis zum Ablauf der nach Absatz 1 gesetzten Frist nur ein Teil der vereinbarten Ladung verladen oder zur Verfügung gestellt, so kann der Frachtführer mit der Beförderung der unvollständigen Ladung beginnen und die Ansprüche nach § 416 Satz 2 und 3 geltend machen.

(4) Dem Frachtführer stehen die Rechte nicht zu, wenn die Nichteinhaltung der Ladezeit auf Gründen beruht, die seinem Risikobereich zuzurechnen sind.

extent that he does not obtain security for the full freight charges due to the incompleteness of the cargo. Where the incompleteness of the loading is caused by reasons which are attributable to the sphere of risks of the carrier, he is entitled to the claim pursuant to sentences 2 and 3 only to the extent that cargo is actually transported.

§ 417 Rights of the carrier in case of non-observance of the loading time

(1) If the shipper does not load the goods within the loading time or, where he is not obligated to load, he does not make the goods available within the loading time, then the carrier can set a reasonable time limit within which the goods should be loaded or made available.

(2) Where upon expiry of the time limit set pursuant to Subsection 1 no cargo has been loaded or made available, the carrier may terminate the freight agreement and assert the claims pursuant to § 415 Subsection 2.

(3) Where upon expiry of the time limit set pursuant to Subsection 1 only part of the cargo agreed upon has been loaded or made available, the carrier may start with the shipment of the incomplete cargo and assert the claims pursuant to § 416 sentences 2 and 3.

(4) The carrier is not entitled to the claims if the non-observance of the loading time is caused by reasons which are attributable to his sphere of risks.

Frachtgeschäft § 418

§ 418 Nachträgliche Weisungen

(1) Der Absender ist berechtigt, über das Gut zu verfügen. Er kann insbesondere verlangen, daß der Frachtführer das Gut nicht weiterbefördert oder es an einem anderen Bestimmungsort, an einer anderen Ablieferungsstelle oder an einen anderen Empfänger abliefert. Der Frachtführer ist nur insoweit zur Befolgung solcher Weisungen verpflichtet, als deren Ausführung weder Nachteile für den Betrieb seines Unternehmens noch Schäden für die Absender oder Empfänger anderer Sendungen mit sich zu bringen droht. Er kann vom Absender Ersatz seiner durch die Ausführung der Weisung entstehenden Aufwendungen sowie eine angemessene Vergütung verlangen; der Frachtführer kann die Befolgung der Weisung von einem Vorschuß abhängig machen.

(2) Das Verfügungsrecht des Absenders erlischt nach Ankunft des Gutes an der Ablieferungsstelle. Von diesem Zeitpunkt an steht das Verfügungsrecht nach Absatz 1 dem Empfänger zu. Macht der Empfänger von diesem Recht Gebrauch, so hat er dem Frachtführer die entstehenden Mehraufwendungen zu ersetzen sowie eine angemessene Vergütung zu zahlen; der Frachtführer kann die Befolgung der Weisung von einem Vorschuß abhängig machen.

(3) Hat der Empfänger in Ausübung seines Verfügungsrechts die Ablieferung des Gutes an einen Dritten angeordnet, so ist dieser nicht berechtigt, seinerseits einen anderen Empfänger zu bestimmen.

(4) Ist ein Frachtbrief ausgestellt und von beiden Parteien unterzeichnet worden, so kann der Absender sein Verfügungsrecht nur gegen Vorlage

§ 418 Subsequent instructions

(1) The shipper is entitled to dispose of the goods. He can in particular request that the carrier discontinue to transport the goods or deliver them to another place of destination, another delivery point or to another consignee. The carrier is only obligated to follow such instructions to the extent that carrying them out does not threaten to bring about disadvantages for the operations of his enterprise or damages for the shippers or consignees of other shipments. He can request from the shipper reimbursement of his expenditures incurred in carrying out the instructions as well as reasonable remuneration. The carrier can make his compliance with the instructions conditional upon the payment of an advance.

(2) The shipper's right of disposition terminates when the goods have arrived at the point of delivery. From this time on, the right of disposition pursuant to Subsection 1 belongs to the consignee. Where the consignee makes use of this right, he has to reimburse the carrier for any additional expenditures incurred and to pay him reasonable remuneration; the carrier can make his compliance with the instructions conditional upon the payment of an advance.

(3) Where in exercising his right of disposition the consignee has instructed the carrier to deliver the goods to a third party, such third party is not entitled on his part to designate another consignee.

(4) Where a waybill has been issued and signed by both parties, the shipper can exercise his right of disposition only upon presentation of the ship-

der Absenderausfertigung des Frachtbriefs ausüben, sofern dies im Frachtbrief vorgeschrieben ist.

(5) Beabsichtigt der Frachtführer, eine ihm erteilte Weisung nicht zu befolgen, so hat er denjenigen, der die Weisung gegeben hat, unverzüglich zu benachrichtigen.

(6) Ist die Ausübung des Verfügungsrechts von der Vorlage des Frachtbriefs abhängig gemacht worden und führt der Frachtführer eine Weisung aus, ohne sich die Absenderausfertigung des Frachtbriefs vorlegen zu lassen, so haftet er dem Berechtigten für den daraus entstehenden Schaden. Die Vorschriften über die Beschränkung der Haftung finden keine Anwendung.

§ 419 Beförderungs- und Ablieferungshindernisse

(1) Wird vor Ankunft des Gutes an der für die Ablieferung vorgesehenen Stelle erkennbar, daß die Beförderung nicht vertragsgemäß durchgeführt werden kann, oder bestehen nach Ankunft des Gutes an der Ablieferungsstelle Ablieferungshindernisse, so hat der Frachtführer Weisungen des nach § 418 Verfügungsberechtigten einzuholen. Ist der Empfänger verfügungsberechtigt und ist er nicht zu ermitteln oder verweigert er die Annahme des Gutes, so ist Verfügungsberechtigter nach Satz 1 der Absender; ist die Ausübung des Verfügungsrechts von der Vorlage eines Frachtbriefs abhängig gemacht worden, so bedarf es in diesem Fall der Vorlage des Frachtbriefs nicht. Der Frachtführer ist, wenn ihm Weisungen erteilt worden sind und das Hindernis nicht seinem Risikobereich zuzurechnen ist, be-

per's counterpart of the waybill, to the extent that this has been required in the waybill.

(5) Where the carrier does not intend to comply with instructions issued to him, he shall without undue delay so inform the party which has given the instructions.

(6) If the exercise of the right of disposition has been made contingent on the presentation of the waybill and the carrier follows instructions without having the shipper's counterpart of the waybill presented to him, he is liable to the entitled party for the damage resulting therefrom. The provisions concerning the limitation of the liability do not apply.

§ 419 Hindrances to shipment and delivery

(1) The carrier shall ask for instructions from the party entitled to the right of disposition pursuant to § 418 where prior to arrival of the goods at the point provided for delivery it becomes discernible that the shipment cannot be carried out according to the freight agreement or, after arrival of the goods at the point of delivery, there exist hindrances to delivery. If the consignee has the right of disposition and he cannot be located or refuses to accept the goods, then the party entitled to the right of disposition pursuant to sentence 1 is the shipper; where the exercise of the right of disposition has been made subject to presentation of a waybill, the presentation of the waybill in this case is not required. The carrier is entitled to assert claims pursuant to § 418 Subsection 1 sentence 4 if in-

rechtigt, Ansprüche nach § 418 Abs. 1 Satz 4 geltend zu machen.

(2) Tritt das Beförderungs- oder Ablieferungshindernis ein, nachdem der Empfänger auf Grund seiner Verfügungsbefugnis nach § 418 die Weisung erteilt hat, das Gut an einen Dritten abzuliefern, so nimmt bei der Anwendung des Absatzes 1 der Empfänger die Stelle des Absenders und der Dritte die des Empfängers ein.

(3) Kann der Frachtführer Weisungen, die er nach § 418 Abs. 1 Satz 3 befolgen müßte, innerhalb angemessener Zeit nicht erlangen, so hat er die Maßnahmen zu ergreifen, die im Interesse des Verfügungsberechtigten die besten zu sein scheinen. Er kann etwa das Gut entladen und verwahren, für Rechnung des nach § 418 Abs. 1 bis 4 Verfügungsberechtigten einem Dritten zur Verwahrung anvertrauen oder zurückbefördern; vertraut der Frachtführer das Gut einem Dritten an, so haftet er nur für die sorgfältige Auswahl des Dritten. Der Frachtführer kann das Gut auch gemäß § 373 Abs. 2 bis 4 verkaufen lassen, wenn es sich um verderbliche Ware handelt oder der Zustand des Gutes eine solche Maßnahme rechtfertigt oder wenn die andernfalls entstehenden Kosten in keinem angemessenen Verhältnis zum Wert des Gutes stehen. Unverwertbares Gut darf der Frachtführer vernichten. Nach dem Entladen des Gutes gilt die Beförderung als beendet.

(4) Der Frachtführer hat wegen der nach Absatz 3 ergriffenen Maßnahmen Anspruch auf Ersatz der erforderlichen Aufwendungen und auf angemessene Vergütung, es sei denn, daß das Hindernis seinem Risikobereich zuzurechnen ist.

structions have been given to him and the hindrance is not attributable to his sphere of risks.

(2) Where the hindrance to shipment or delivery occurs after the consignee has given instructions, based on his right of disposition pursuant to § 418, to deliver the goods to a third party, the consignee replaces the shipper and the third party replaces the consignee in applying Subsection 1.

(3) Where the freight carrier cannot within a reasonable period of time obtain instructions which he would have to follow pursuant to § 418 Subsection 1 sentence 3, he shall take the measures which seem to be in the best interests of the party entitled to the right of disposition. He may, e. g., unload the goods and store them, hand them over to a third party for safekeeping for the account of the party entitled to the right of disposition pursuant to § 418 Subsections 1 to 4, or return them; where the carrier hands over the goods to a third party, he is only liable for the careful selection of the third party. The carrier may have the goods sold under § 373 Subsections 2 to 4 if the goods are perishable, or if the condition of the goods justifies such a measure, or if the costs which would otherwise arise do not bear a reasonable relationship to the value of the goods. The carrier may destroy goods which are unsalable. After unloading of the goods, the shipment is deemed to have been completed.

(4) The carrier is entitled to reimbursement of the necessary expenditures incurred in connection with the measures taken pursuant to Subsection 3 and to reasonable remuneration unless the hindrance is attributable to his sphere of risks.

§ 420 Zahlung. Frachtberechnung

(1) Die Fracht ist bei Ablieferung des Gutes zu zahlen. Der Frachtführer hat über die Fracht hinaus einen Anspruch auf Ersatz von Aufwendungen, soweit diese für das Gut gemacht wurden und er sie den Umständen nach für erforderlich halten durfte.

(2) Wird die Beförderung infolge eines Beförderungs- oder Ablieferungshindernisses vorzeitig beendet, so gebührt dem Frachtführer die anteilige Fracht für den zurückgelegten Teil der Beförderung. Ist das Hindernis dem Risikobereich des Frachtführers zuzurechnen, steht ihm der Anspruch nur insoweit zu, als die Beförderung für den Absender von Interesse ist.

(3) Tritt nach Beginn der Beförderung und vor Ankunft an der Ablieferungsstelle eine Verzögerung ein und beruht die Verzögerung auf Gründen, die dem Risikobereich des Absenders zuzurechnen sind, so gebührt dem Frachtführer neben der Fracht eine angemessene Vergütung.

(4) Ist die Fracht nach Zahl, Gewicht oder anders angegebener Menge des Gutes vereinbart, so wird für die Berechnung der Fracht vermutet, daß Angaben hierzu im Frachtbrief oder Ladeschein zutreffen; dies gilt auch dann, wenn zu diesen Angaben ein Vorbehalt eingetragen ist, der damit begründet ist, daß keine angemessenen Mittel zur Verfügung standen, die Richtigkeit der Angaben zu überprüfen.

§ 421 Rechte des Empfängers. Zahlungspflicht

(1) Nach Ankunft des Gutes an der Ablieferungsstelle ist der Empfänger be-

§ 420 Payment; computation of freight charges

(1) Freight charges are payable upon delivery of the goods. The carrier has, in addition to the freight charges, a claim for reimbursement of his expenditures to the extent that these were made for the goods and he could deem them to be necessary according to the circumstances.

(2) Where the shipment is terminated prematurely because of a hindrance to shipment or delivery, the carrier is entitled to the pro rata freight charges for the part of the shipment which has been made. Where the hindrance is attributable to the sphere of risks of the carrier, he is entitled to the claim only to the extent that the shipment is of interest to the shipper.

(3) If after the start of the shipment and before arrival at the point of delivery a delay occurs and is caused by reasons which are attributable to the sphere of risks of the shipper, the carrier is entitled to reasonable remuneration in addition to the freight charges.

(4) If the freight charges have been agreed upon according to the number, weight or other designated quantity of the goods, it shall be presumed for the computation of the freight charges that the pertinent data in the waybill or the bill of lading are accurate. This also applies if with respect to the data a reservation has been entered which is justified by the fact that no reasonable means were available to check the correctness of the data.

§ 421 Rights of the consignee; payment obligation

(1) Upon arrival of the goods at the point of delivery the consignee is enti-

rechtigt, vom Frachtführer zu verlangen, ihm das Gut gegen Erfüllung der Verpflichtungen aus dem Frachtvertrag abzuliefern. Ist das Gut beschädigt oder verspätet abgeliefert worden oder verlorengegangen, so kann der Empfänger die Ansprüche aus dem Frachtvertrag im eigenen Namen gegen den Frachtführer geltend machen; der Absender bleibt zur Geltendmachung dieser Ansprüche befugt. Dabei macht es keinen Unterschied, ob Empfänger oder Absender im eigenen oder fremden Interesse handeln.

(2) Der Empfänger, der sein Recht nach Absatz 1 Satz 1 geltend macht, hat die noch geschuldete Fracht bis zu dem Betrag zu zahlen, der aus dem Frachtbrief hervorgeht. Ist ein Frachtbrief nicht ausgestellt oder dem Empfänger nicht vorgelegt worden oder ergibt sich aus dem Frachtbrief nicht die Höhe der zu zahlenden Fracht, so hat der Empfänger die mit dem Absender vereinbarte Fracht zu zahlen, soweit diese nicht unangemessen ist.

(3) Der Empfänger, der sein Recht nach Absatz 1 Satz 1 geltend macht, hat ferner ein Standgeld oder eine Vergütung nach § 420 Abs. 3 zu zahlen, ein Standgeld wegen Überschreitung der Ladezeit und eine Vergütung nach § 420 Abs. 3 jedoch nur, wenn ihm der geschuldete Betrag bei Ablieferung des Gutes mitgeteilt worden ist.

(4) Der Absender bleibt zur Zahlung der nach dem Vertrag geschuldeten Beträge verpflichtet.

§ 422 Nachnahme

(1) Haben die Parteien vereinbart, daß das Gut nur gegen Einziehung einer Nachnahme an den Empfänger abge-

tled to request that the carrier deliver the goods against performance of the obligations arising out of the freight agreement. If the goods have been damaged or delivered late or have been lost, the consignee may assert the claims arising out of the freight agreement in his own name against the carrier; the shipper remains entitled to assert these claims. It makes no difference whether the consignee or the shipper acts in his own or in a third party's interest.

(2) The consignee who asserts his rights pursuant to Subsection 1 sentence 1 still has to pay the freight charges due up to the amount which results from the waybill. If a waybill has not been issued or has not been presented to the consignee, or if the amount of the freight charges payable is not shown on the waybill, the consignee shall pay the freight charges agreed with the shipper unless these are not reasonable.

(3) The consignee who asserts his rights pursuant to Subsection 1 sentence 1 also has to pay demurrage or remuneration pursuant to § 420 Subsection 3; demurrage because of exceeding the loading time and remuneration pursuant to § 420 Subsection 3, however, only where he has been informed of the amount due upon delivery of the goods.

(4) The shipper remains obligated to pay the amounts due pursuant to the agreement.

§ 422 Cash due on delivery

(1) If the parties have agreed that the goods may be delivered to the consignee only against collection of pay-

liefert werden darf, so ist anzunehmen, daß der Betrag in bar oder in Form eines gleichwertigen Zahlungsmittels einzuziehen ist.

(2) Das auf Grund der Einziehung Erlangte gilt im Verhältnis zu den Gläubigern des Frachtführers als auf den Absender übertragen.

(3) Wird das Gut dem Empfänger ohne Einziehung der Nachnahme abgeliefert, so haftet der Frachtführer, auch wenn ihn kein Verschulden trifft, dem Absender für den daraus entstehenden Schaden, jedoch nur bis zur Höhe des Betrages der Nachnahme.

§ 423 Lieferfrist

Der Frachtführer ist verpflichtet, das Gut innerhalb der vereinbarten Frist oder mangels Vereinbarung innerhalb der Frist abzuliefern, die einem sorgfältigen Frachtführer unter Berücksichtigung der Umstände vernünftigerweise zuzubilligen ist (Lieferfrist).

§ 424 Verlustvermutung

(1) Der Anspruchsberechtigte kann das Gut als verloren betrachten, wenn es weder innerhalb der Lieferfrist noch innerhalb eines weiteren Zeitraums abgeliefert wird, der der Lieferfrist entspricht, mindestens aber zwanzig Tage, bei einer grenzüberschreitenden Beförderung dreißig Tage beträgt.

(2) Erhält der Anspruchsberechtigte eine Entschädigung für den Verlust des Gutes, so kann er bei deren Empfang verlangen, daß er unverzüglich benachrichtigt wird, wenn das Gut wiederaufgefunden wird.

(3) Der Anspruchsberechtigte kann innerhalb eines Monats nach Emp-

ment, then it is presumed that the amount is to be collected in cash or in form of an equivalent means of payment.

(2) In the relationship to the creditors of the carrier, the amount collected is deemed to have been transferred to the shipper.

(3) Where the goods are delivered to the consignee without collecting the payment, the carrier is liable to the shipper for the resulting damage even if he is not at fault, but only up to the amount of the payment to be collected.

§ 423 Term for delivery

The carrier is obligated to deliver the goods within the term agreed upon or, absent such agreement, within the time period which is to be reasonably granted to a careful carrier taking the circumstances into consideration.

§ 424 Presumption of loss

(1) The beneficiary can consider the goods to be lost if they are not delivered within the term for delivery or within a further period which is equal to the term for delivery, but at least twenty days, or in the case of a transborder shipment, thirty days.

(2) If the beneficiary receives an indemnification for the loss of the goods, he can request upon its receipt that he be informed without undue delay if the goods reappear.

(3) The beneficiary may request, within one month after receipt of the

fang der Benachrichtigung von dem Wiederauffinden des Gutes verlangen, daß ihm das Gut Zug um Zug gegen Erstattung der Entschädigung, gegebenenfalls abzüglich der in der Entschädigung enthaltenen Kosten, abgeliefert wird. Eine etwaige Pflicht zur Zahlung der Fracht sowie Ansprüche auf Schadenersatz bleiben unberührt.

(4) Wird das Gut nach Zahlung einer Entschädigung wiederaufgefunden und hat der Anspruchsberechtigte eine Benachrichtigung nicht verlangt oder macht er nach Benachrichtigung seinen Anspruch auf Ablieferung nicht geltend, so kann der Frachtführer über das Gut frei verfügen.

§ 425 Haftung für Güter- und Verspätungsschäden. Schadensteilung

(1) Der Frachtführer haftet für den Schaden, der durch Verlust oder Beschädigung des Gutes in der Zeit von der Übernahme zur Beförderung bis zur Ablieferung oder durch Überschreitung der Lieferfrist entsteht.

(2) Hat bei der Entstehung des Schadens ein Verhalten des Absenders oder des Empfängers oder ein besonderer Mangel des Gutes mitgewirkt, so hängen die Verpflichtung zum Ersatz sowie der Umfang des zu leistenden Ersatzes davon ab, inwieweit diese Umstände zu dem Schaden beigetragen haben.

§ 426 Haftungsausschluß

Der Frachtführer ist von der Haftung befreit, soweit der Verlust, die Beschädigung oder die Überschreitung der Lieferfrist auf Umständen beruht, die der Frachtführer auch bei größter

notification of the goods having been found again, that the goods be delivered to him against reimbursement of the indemnification less the costs contained in the indemnification, if any. Any obligation to pay the freight charges as well as claims for payment of damages shall not be affected.

(4) Where the goods have been found after payment of an indemnification and where the beneficiary has not requested to be notified or where he does not assert his claim for delivery after notification, the carrier may freely dispose of the goods.

§ 425 Liability for damages to goods and for delay; partition of damages

(1) The carrier is liable for the damage which arises from loss of or damage to the goods from the time they are accepted for shipment until delivery, or from exceeding the term for delivery.

(2) Where the conduct of the shipper or the consignee or a special defect of the goods has contributed to the cause of the damages, the obligation to pay damages and the amount of the damages to be paid depend on the extent to which these circumstances have contributed to the damage.

§ 426 Exclusion of liability

The carrier is exempted from the liability to the extent that the loss, the damage or the failure to meet the agreed deadline for delivery is caused by circumstances which the carrier

Sorgfalt nicht vermeiden und deren Folgen er nicht abwenden konnte.

§ 427 Besondere Haftungsausschlußgründe

(1) Der Frachtführer ist von seiner Haftung befreit, soweit der Verlust, die Beschädigung oder die Überschreitung der Lieferfrist auf eine der folgenden Gefahren zurückzuführen ist:

1. vereinbarte oder der Übung entsprechende Verwendung von offenen, nicht mit Planen gedeckten Fahrzeugen oder Verladung auf Deck;
2. ungenügende Verpackung durch den Absender;
3. Behandeln, Verladen oder Entladen des Gutes durch den Absender oder den Empfänger;
4. natürliche Beschaffenheit des Gutes, die besonders leicht zu Schäden, insbesondere durch Bruch, Rost, inneren Verderb, Austrocknen, Auslaufen, normalen Schwund, führt;
5. ungenügende Kennzeichnung der Frachtstücke durch den Absender;
6. Beförderung lebender Tiere.

(2) Ist ein Schaden eingetreten, der nach den Umständen des Falles aus einer der in Absatz 1 bezeichneten Gefahren entstehen konnte, so wird vermutet, daß der Schaden aus dieser Gefahr entstanden ist. Diese Vermutung gilt im Falle des Absatzes 1 Nr. 1 nicht bei außergewöhnlich großem Verlust.

(3) Der Frachtführer kann sich auf Absatz 1 Nr. 1 nur berufen, soweit der Verlust, die Beschädigung oder die Überschreitung der Lieferfrist nicht darauf zurückzuführen ist, daß der

could not avoid even with the utmost care and which consequences he could not prevent.

§ 427 Special grounds for exclusion of liability

(1) The carrier is exempted from his liability to the extent that the loss, the damage or the failure to meet the agreed deadline for delivery is attributable to one of the following risks:

1. Utilisation of open vehicles not covered by tarps or loading on deck as agreed upon or according to trade custom;
2. inadequate packaging by the shipper;
3. handling, loading or unloading of the goods by the shipper or the consignee;
4. natural condition of the goods which leads especially easily to damages, especially by breakage, rust, inner spoilage, drying up, leaking out, normal shrinkage;
5. insufficient labelling of the freight pieces by the shipper;
6. shipment of living animals.

(2) Where damage has occurred which according to the circumstances of the case could arise from a designated risk described in Subsection 1, it shall be presumed that the damage has arisen from this risk. This presumption does not apply in case of Subsection 1 No. 1 where the loss is extraordinarily large.

(3) The carrier can only rely on Subsection 1 No. 1 to the extent that the loss, the damage or exceeding the term for delivery is not attributable to the fact that the carrier has disre-

Frachtführer besondere Weisungen des Absenders im Hinblick auf die Beförderung des Gutes nicht beachtet hat.

(4) Ist der Frachtführer nach dem Frachtvertrag verpflichtet, das Gut gegen die Einwirkung von Hitze, Kälte, Temperaturschwankungen, Luftfeuchtigkeit, Erschütterungen oder ähnlichen Einflüssen besonders zu schützen, so kann er sich auf Absatz 1 Nr. 4 nur berufen, wenn er alle ihm nach den Umständen obliegenden Maßnahmen, insbesondere hinsichtlich der Auswahl, Instandhaltung und Verwendung besonderer Einrichtungen, getroffen und besondere Weisungen beachtet hat.

(5) Der Frachtführer kann sich auf Absatz 1 Nr. 6 nur berufen, wenn er alle ihm nach den Umständen obliegenden Maßnahmen getroffen und besondere Weisungen beachtet hat.

§ 428 Haftung für andere

Der Frachtführer hat Handlungen und Unterlassungen seiner Leute in gleichem Umfange zu vertreten wie eigene Handlungen und Unterlassungen, wenn die Leute in Ausübung ihrer Verrichtungen handeln. Gleiches gilt für Handlungen und Unterlassungen anderer Personen, deren er sich bei Ausführung der Beförderung bedient.

§ 429 Wertersatz

(1) Hat der Frachtführer für gänzlichen oder teilweisen Verlust des Gutes Schadenersatz zu leisten, so ist der Wert am Ort und zur Zeit der Übernahme zur Beförderung zu ersetzen.

garded special instructions of the shipper with regard to the shipment of the goods.

(4) Where the carrier is obligated pursuant to the freight agreement to specially protect the goods against the effects of heat, cold, fluctuations of temperature, humidity, vibrations or similar influences, he can only rely on Subsection 1 No. 4 if he has taken all measures he was supposed to take under the circumstances, especially with regard to the selection, maintenance and use of special equipment, and has followed special instructions.

(5) The carrier can only rely on Subsection 1 No. 6 if he has taken all measures he was supposed to take under the circumstances and has followed special instructions.

§ 428 Liability for others

The carrier is liable for the acts and omissions of his employees to the same extent as for his own acts and omissions where the employees act in performance of their duties. The same applies for acts and omissions of other persons he uses in carrying out the shipment.

§ 429 Compensation for lost value

(1) Where the carrier has to pay damages for the total or partial loss of the goods, the value at the place and at the time of acceptance for shipment must be compensated.

§§ 429–431   Handelsgeschäfte

(2) Bei Beschädigung des Gutes ist der Unterschied zwischen dem Wert des unbeschädigten Gutes am Ort und zur Zeit der Übernahme zur Beförderung und dem Wert zu ersetzen, den das beschädigte Gut am Ort und zur Zeit der Übernahme gehabt hätte. Es wird vermutet, daß die zur Schadensminderung und Schadensbehebung aufzuwendenden Kosten dem nach Satz 1 zu ermittelnden Unterschiedsbetrag entsprechen.

(3) Der Wert des Gutes bestimmt sich nach dem Marktpreis, sonst nach dem gemeinen Wert von Gütern gleicher Art und Beschaffenheit. Ist das Gut unmittelbar vor Übernahme zur Beförderung verkauft worden, so wird vermutet, daß der in der Rechnung des Verkäufers ausgewiesene Kaufpreis abzüglich darin enthaltener Beförderungskosten der Marktpreis ist.

§ 430 Schadensfeststellungskosten

Bei Verlust oder Beschädigung des Gutes hat der Frachtführer über den nach § 429 zu leistenden Ersatz hinaus die Kosten der Feststellung des Schadens zu tragen.

§ 431 Haftungshöchstbetrag

(1) Die nach den §§ 429 und 430 zu leistende Entschädigung wegen Verlust oder Beschädigung der gesamten Sendung ist auf einen Betrag von 8,33 Rechnungseinheiten für jedes Kilogramm des Rohgewichts der Sendung begrenzt.

(2) Sind nur einzelne Frachtstücke der Sendung verloren oder beschädigt worden, so ist die Haftung des Fracht-

(2) Where the goods have been damaged, the difference between the value of the undamaged goods at the place and at the time of the acceptance for shipment and the value which the damaged goods would have had at the place and time of acceptance must be compensated. It is presumed that the costs incurred to minimise or repair the damage correspond to the difference in amounts to be computed according to sentence 1.

(3) The value of the goods is determined by the market price and otherwise the common value of goods of the same kind and condition. If the goods have been sold immediately before acceptance for shipment, it shall be presumed that the market price is the purchase price shown in the invoice of the seller less the costs of shipment contained therein.

§ 430 Costs of determining the damage

Where goods have been lost or damaged, the carrier shall, in addition to the Compensation to be paid pursuant to § 429, also bear the costs of the determination of the damage.

§ 431 Maximum liability

(1) The indemnification to be paid pursuant to §§ 429 and 430 because of loss of or damage to the entire shipment is limited to an amount of 8.33 accounting units for each kilogram of the gross weight of the shipment.

(2) Where only individual freight pieces of the shipment have been lost or damaged, the liability of the carrier

führers begrenzt auf einen Betrag von 8,33 Rechnungseinheiten für jedes Kilogramm des Rohgewichts

1. der gesamten Sendung, wenn die gesamte Sendung entwertet ist,

2. des entwerteten Teils der Sendung, wenn nur ein Teil der Sendung entwertet ist.

(3) Die Haftung des Frachtführers wegen Überschreitung der Lieferfrist ist auf den dreifachen Betrag der Fracht begrenzt.

(4) Die in den Absätzen 1 und 2 genannte Rechnungseinheit ist das Sonderziehungsrecht des Internationalen Währungsfonds. Der Betrag wird in Deutsche Mark entsprechend dem Wert der Deutschen Mark gegenüber dem Sonderziehungsrecht am Tag der Übernahme des Gutes zur Beförderung oder an dem von den Parteien vereinbarten Tag umgerechnet. Der Wert der Deutschen Mark gegenüber dem Sonderziehungsrecht wird nach der Berechnungsmethode ermittelt, die der Internationale Währungsfonds an dem betreffenden Tag für seine Operationen und Transaktionen anwendet.

§ 432 Ersatz sonstiger Kosten

Haftet der Frachtführer wegen Verlust oder Beschädigung, so hat er über den nach den §§ 429 bis 431 zu leistenden Ersatz hinaus die Fracht, öffentliche Abgaben und sonstige Kosten aus Anlaß der Beförderung des Gutes zu erstatten, im Fall der Beschädigung jedoch nur in dem nach § 429 Abs. 2 zu ermittelnden Wertverhältnis. Weiteren Schaden hat er nicht zu ersetzen.

is limited to an amount of 8.33 accounting units for each kilogram of the gross weight

1. of the total shipment if the total shipment has been devalued;

2. of the devalued part of the shipment, if only part of the shipment has been devalued.

(3) The liability of the carrier because of exceeding the agreed term for delivery is limited to three times the amount of the freight charges.

(4) The accounting unit mentioned in Subsections 1 and 2 is the special drawing right of the International Monetary Fund. The amount will be converted to German Mark according to the value of the German Mark as compared to the special drawing right on the day of the acceptance of the goods for shipment or on the day agreed upon by the parties. The value of the German Mark as compared to the special drawing rights shall be determined pursuant to the conversion method which the International Monetary Fund uses for its operations and transactions on the relevant day.

§ 432 Reimbursement of other costs

Where the carrier is liable because of loss or damage, he shall, in addition to the compensation payable pursuant to §§ 429 to 431, reimburse the freight charges, the public levies and other costs incurred in connection with the shipment of the goods, in case of damage, however, only in the value relationship to be determined pursuant to § 429 Subsection 2. He is not obligated to compensate further damage.

§ 433 Haftungshöchstbetrag bei sonstigen Vermögensschäden

Haftet der Frachtführer wegen der Verletzung einer mit der Ausführung der Beförderung des Gutes zusammenhängenden vertraglichen Pflicht für Schäden, die nicht durch Verlust oder Beschädigung des Gutes oder durch Überschreitung der Lieferfrist entstehen, und handelt es sich um andere Schäden als Sach- oder Personenschäden, so ist auch in diesem Falle die Haftung begrenzt, und zwar auf das Dreifache des Betrages, der bei Verlust des Gutes zu zahlen wäre.

§ 434 Außervertragliche Ansprüche

(1) Die in diesem Unterabschnitt und im Frachtvertrag vorgesehenen Haftungsbefreiungen und Haftungsbegrenzungen gelten auch für einen außervertraglichen Anspruch des Absenders oder des Empfängers gegen den Frachtführer wegen Verlust oder Beschädigung des Gutes oder wegen Überschreitung der Lieferfrist.

(2) Der Frachtführer kann auch gegenüber außervertraglichen Ansprüchen Dritter wegen Verlust oder Beschädigung des Gutes die Einwendungen nach Absatz 1 geltend machen. Die Einwendungen können jedoch nicht geltend gemacht werden, wenn

1. der Dritte der Beförderung nicht zugestimmt hat und der Frachtführer die fehlende Befugnis des Absenders, das Gut zu versenden, kannte oder fahrlässig nicht kannte oder

2. das Gut vor Übernahme zur Beförderung dem Dritten oder einer Person, die von diesem ihr Recht zum Besitz ableitet, abhanden gekommen ist.

§ 433 Maximum amount of liability in case of other pecuniary loss

Where the carrier because of the violation of a contractual duty connected with carrying out the shipment of goods is liable for damages which do not arise out of loss of or damage to the goods or exceeding the term for delivery, and if the damages are other than damages to property or persons, the liability in this case is also limited to three times the amount which would be payable upon loss of the goods.

§ 434 Non-contractual claims

(1) The exemptions from and limitations of liability provided for in this Subpart and in the freight agreement also apply to non-contractual claims of the shipper or the consignee against the carrier because of loss of or damage to the goods or because of exceeding the term for delivery.

(2) The carrier can also assert the objections pursuant to Subsection 1 against non-contractual claims of third parties because of loss of or damage to the goods. The objections can, however, not be asserted where

1. the third party has not consented to the shipment and the carrier was aware, or negligently was not aware, of the lack of authority of the shipper to ship the goods;

2. the goods have been lost prior to acceptance for shipment by the third party or a person who derives his right to possess the goods from the third party.

§ 435 Wegfall der Haftungsbefreiungen und -begrenzungen

Die in diesem Unterabschnitt und im Frachtvertrag vorgesehenen Haftungsbefreiungen und Haftungsbegrenzungen gelten nicht, wenn der Schaden auf eine Handlung oder Unterlassung zurückzuführen ist, die der Frachtführer oder eine in § 428 genannte Person vorsätzlich oder leichtfertig und in dem Bewußtsein, daß ein Schaden mit Wahrscheinlichkeit eintreten werde, begangen hat.

§ 436 Haftung der Leute

Werden Ansprüche aus außervertraglicher Haftung wegen Verlust oder Beschädigung des Gutes oder wegen Überschreitung der Lieferfrist gegen einen der Leute des Frachtführers erhoben, so kann sich auch jener auf die in diesem Unterabschnitt und im Frachtvertrag vorgesehenen Haftungsbefreiungen und -begrenzungen berufen. Dies gilt nicht, wenn er vorsätzlich oder leichtfertig und in dem Bewußtsein, daß ein Schaden mit Wahrscheinlichkeit eintreten werde, gehandelt hat.

§ 437 Ausführender Frachtführer

(1) Wird die Beförderung ganz oder teilweise durch einen Dritten ausgeführt (ausführender Frachtführer), so haftet dieser für den Schaden, der durch Verlust oder Beschädigung des Gutes oder durch Überschreitung der Lieferfrist während der durch ihn ausgeführten Beförderung entsteht, in gleicher Weise wie der Frachtführer. Vertragliche Vereinbarungen mit dem Absender oder Empfänger, durch die der Frachtführer seine Haftung erwei-

§ 435 Loss of exemptions from and limitations of liability

The exemptions from and limitations of liability provided for in this subpart and in the freight agreement do not apply if the damage is caused by an act or an omission which the carrier or a person mentioned in § 428 has committed or has omitted wilfully or recklessly with the knowledge that damage would probably occur.

§ 436 Liability of employees

Where claims are asserted against an employee of the carrier based on non-contractual liability because of loss of or damage to the goods or because of exceeding the term for delivery, such employee can also invoke the exemptions from and limitations of liability provided for in this Subpart and with the freight agreement. This does not apply if he has acted wilfully or recklessly the knowledge that damage would probably occur.

§ 437 Acting carrier

(1) Where the shipment is carried out totally or partially by a third party (acting carrier); this acting carrier is liable in the same way as the carrier for the damage which arises out of loss of or damage to the goods or exceeding the term for delivery during the shipment carried out by him. Contractual agreements with the shipper or the consignee by which the carrier expands his liability are effective against the acting carrier only to the extent

§§ 437, 438   Handelsgeschäfte

tert, wirken gegen den ausführenden Frachtführer nur, soweit er ihnen schriftlich zugestimmt hat.

(2) Der ausführende Frachtführer kann alle Einwendungen geltend machen, die dem Frachtführer aus dem Frachtvertrag zustehen.

(3) Frachtführer und ausführender Frachtführer haften als Gesamtschuldner.

(4) Werden die Leute des ausführenden Frachtführers in Anspruch genommen, so gilt für diese § 436 entsprechend.

§ 438 Schadensanzeige

(1) Ist ein Verlust oder eine Beschädigung des Gutes äußerlich erkennbar und zeigt der Empfänger oder der Absender dem Frachtführer Verlust oder Beschädigung nicht spätestens bei Ablieferung des Gutes an, so wird vermutet, daß das Gut in vertragsgemäßem Zustand abgeliefert worden ist. Die Anzeige muß den Schaden hinreichend deutlich kennzeichnen.

(2) Die Vermutung nach Absatz 1 gilt auch, wenn der Verlust oder die Beschädigung äußerlich nicht erkennbar war und nicht innerhalb von sieben Tagen nach Ablieferung angezeigt worden ist.

(3) Ansprüche wegen Überschreitung der Lieferfrist erlöschen, wenn der Empfänger dem Frachtführer die Überschreitung der Lieferfrist nicht innerhalb von einundzwanzig Tagen nach Ablieferung anzeigt.

(4) Eine Schadensanzeige nach Ablieferung ist in Textform zu erstatten. Zur Wahrung der Frist genügt die rechtzeitige Absendung.

(5) Werden Verlust, Beschädigung oder Überschreitung der Lieferfrist bei

that he has consented to these in writing.

(2) The acting carrier can assert all the defenses which the carrier could assert based on the freight agreement.

(3) Carrier and acting carrier are jointly and severally liable.

(4) Where claims are asserted against employees of the acting carrier, § 436 applies to them analogously.

§ 438 Notification of damage

(1) If loss or damage to the goods is externally visible and the consignee or the shipper does not notify the carrier of the loss or damage before or at the time of delivery of the goods, it shall be presumed that the goods have been delivered in condition in conformity with the contract. The notification shall characterise the damage with adequate clarity.

(2) The presumption pursuant to Subsection 1 shall apply also where the loss or the damage was not externally visible and notice has not been given within seven days after delivery.

(3) Claims based on exceeding the term for delivery expire where the consignee does not notify the carrier within twenty-one days after delivery that he has exceeding the term for delivery.

(4) Notification of damages after delivery shall be made in written form. Timely dispatch is sufficient to comply with the time limit.

(5) Where notice of loss, damage or exceeding the term for delivery is given

Ablieferung angezeigt, so genügt die Anzeige gegenüber demjenigen, der das Gut abliefert.

§ 439 Verjährung

(1) Ansprüche aus einer Beförderung, die den Vorschriften dieses Unterabschnitts unterliegt, verjähren in einem Jahr. Bei Vorsatz oder bei einem dem Vorsatz nach § 435 gleichstehenden Verschulden beträgt die Verjährungsfrist drei Jahre.

(2) Die Verjährung beginnt mit Ablauf des Tages, an dem das Gut abgeliefert wurde. Ist das Gut nicht abgeliefert worden, beginnt die Verjährung mit dem Ablauf des Tages, an dem das Gut hätte abgeliefert werden müssen. Abweichend von den Sätzen 1 und 2 beginnt die Verjährung von Rückgriffsansprüchen mit dem Tag des Eintritts der Rechtskraft des Urteils gegen den Rückgriffsgläubiger oder, wenn kein rechtskräftiges Urteil vorliegt, mit dem Tag, an dem der Rückgriffsgläubiger den Anspruch befriedigt hat, es sei denn, der Rückgriffsschuldner wurde nicht innerhalb von drei Monaten, nachdem der Rückgriffsgläubiger Kenntnis von dem Schaden und der Person des Rückgriffsschuldners erlangt hat, über diesen Schaden unterrichtet.

(3) Die Verjährung eines Anspruchs gegen den Frachtführer wird durch eine schriftliche Erklärung des Absenders oder Empfängers, mit der dieser Ersatzansprüche erhebt, bis zu dem Zeitpunkt gehemmt, in dem der Frachtführer die Erfüllung des Anspruchs schriftlich ablehnt. Eine weitere Erklärung, die denselben Ersatzanspruch zum Gegenstand hat, hemmt die Verjährung nicht erneut.

upon delivery, the notification is sufficient if it is given to the party delivering the goods.

§ 439 Statute of limitations

(1) The statute of limitations for claims resulting from a shipment which is subject to the provisions of this Subpart is one year. In case of wilfulness or fault equal to wilfulness pursuant to § 435, the statute of limitations is three years.

(2) The statute of limitations begins to run upon expiration of the day on which the goods were delivered. If the goods have not been delivered, the statute of limitations begins to run upon expiration of the day on which the goods should have been delivered. Deviating from sentences 1 and 2, the statute of limitations for claims of recourse begins to run on the day the judgment against the recourse creditor becomes final, or where there is no final judgment, on the day on which the recourse creditor has paid the claim unless the recourse debtor has not been informed about the damage within three months after the recourse creditor became aware of the damage and of the identity of the recourse debtor.

(3) The statute of limitations for a claim against the carrier shall be suspended by a declaration in writing of the shipper or the consignee by which he asserts claims for damages until such point in time in which the carrier refuses in writing to pay the claim. A further declaration dealing with the same claims for indemnification does not suspend the statute of limitations anew.

(4) Die Verjährung kann nur durch Vereinbarung, die im einzelnen ausgehandelt ist, auch wenn sie für eine Mehrzahl von gleichartigen Verträgen zwischen denselben Vertragsparteien getroffen ist, erleichtert oder erschwert werden.

§ 440 Gerichtsstand

(1) Für Rechtsstreitigkeiten aus einer Beförderung, die den Vorschriften dieses Unterabschnitts unterliegt, ist auch das Gericht zuständig, in dessen Bezirk der Ort der Übernahme des Gutes oder der für die Ablieferung des Gutes vorgesehene Ort liegt.

(2) Eine Klage gegen den ausführenden Frachtführer kann auch in dem Gerichtsstand des Frachtführers, eine Klage gegen den Frachtführer auch in dem Gerichtsstand des ausführenden Frachtführers erhoben werden.

§ 441 Pfandrecht

(1) Der Frachtführer hat wegen aller durch den Frachtvertrag begründeten Forderungen sowie wegen unbestrittener Forderungen aus anderen mit dem Absender abgeschlossenen Fracht-, Speditions- oder Lagerverträgen ein Pfandrecht an dem Gut. Das Pfandrecht erstreckt sich auf die Begleitpapiere.

(2) Das Pfandrecht besteht, solange der Frachtführer das Gut in seinem Besitz hat, insbesondere solange er mittels Konnossements, Ladescheins oder Lagerscheins darüber verfügen kann.

(3) Das Pfandrecht besteht auch nach der Ablieferung fort, wenn der Frachtführer es innerhalb von drei Tagen nach der Ablieferung gerichtlich geltend macht und das Gut noch im Besitz des Empfängers ist.

(4) The statute of limitations can only be facilitated or impeded by an agreement negotiated in detail, even if it applies to a number of similar contracts between the same parties.

§ 440 Place of jurisdiction

(1) For lawsuits resulting from a shipment which is subject to the provisions of this Subpart, the court for the district in which lies the place for acceptance of shipment of the goods, or the place for delivery of the goods, shall also be competent.

(2) A legal action against the acting carrier can also be brought at the place of jurisdiction of the carrier, and an action against the carrier also at the place of jurisdiction of the acting carrier.

§ 441 Lien

(1) The carrier shall have a lien on the goods for all claims arising out of the freight agreement as well as for undisputed claims arising out of other freight, forwarding agency or warehouse contracts concluded with the shipper. The lien also extends to the accompanying documents.

(2) The lien exists as long as the carrier has the goods in his possession, especially as long as he can dispose of them by means of bill of lading, inland bill of lading or warehouse receipt.

(3) The lien continues to exist even after delivery if the carrier has asserted the lien in court within three days after delivery of the goods and the goods are still in the consignee's possession.

(4) Die in § 1234 Abs. 1 des Bürgerlichen Gesetzbuchs bezeichnete Androhung des Pfandverkaufs sowie die in den §§ 1237 und 1241 des Bürgerlichen Gesetzbuchs vorgesehenen Benachrichtigungen sind an den Empfänger zu richten. Ist dieser nicht zu ermitteln oder verweigert er die Annahme des Gutes, so haben die Androhung und die Benachrichtigung gegenüber dem Absender zu erfolgen.

§ 442 Nachfolgender Frachtführer

(1) Hat im Falle der Beförderung durch mehrere Frachtführer der letzte bei der Ablieferung die Forderungen der vorhergehenden Frachtführer einzuziehen, so hat er die Rechte der vorhergehenden Frachtführer, insbesondere auch das Pfandrecht, auszuüben. Das Pfandrecht jedes vorhergehenden Frachtführers bleibt so lange bestehen wie das Pfandrecht des letzten Frachtführers.

(2) Wird ein vorhergehender Frachtführer von einem nachgehenden befriedigt, so gehen Forderung und Pfandrecht des ersteren auf den letzteren über.

(3) Die Absätze 1 und 2 gelten auch für die Forderungen und Rechte eines Spediteurs, der an der Beförderung mitgewirkt hat.

§ 443 Rang mehrerer Pfandrechte

(1) Bestehen an demselben Gut mehrere nach den §§ 397, 441, 464, 475 b und 623 begründete Pfandrechte, so geht unter denjenigen Pfandrechten, die durch die Versendung oder durch die Beförderung des Gutes entstanden sind, das später entstandene dem früher entstandenen vor.

(4) The warning of a foreclosure sale described in § 1234 Subsection 1 of the Civil Code, as well as the notice provided for in §§ 1237 and 1241 of the Civil Code, is to be addressed to the consignee. Where he cannot be located or refuses to accept the goods, the warning and notice must be given to the shipper.

§ 442 Subsequent carrier

(1) Where in case of shipment by more than one carrier the last carrier has to collect the claims of the prior carriers upon delivery, he shall exercise the rights of the prior carriers and in particular the lien right. The lien right of each prior carrier continues to exist as long as the lien right of the last carrier.

(2) Where a preceding carrier is paid by a subsequent carrier, his claim and lien right are transferred to the latter.

(3) Subsections 1 and 2 apply also to the claims and rights of a forwarding agent who has been involved in the shipment.

§ 443 Priority among multiple liens

(1) Where more than one lien exists on the same goods by reason of §§ 397, 441, 464, 475 b and 623, among the liens existing by reason of the forwarding or shipment of the goods, the later lien has priority over the earlier lien.

(2) Diese Pfandrechte haben Vorrang vor dem nicht aus der Versendung entstandenen Pfandrecht des Kommissionärs und des Lagerhalters sowie vor dem Pfandrecht des Spediteurs, des Frachtführers und des Verfrachters für Vorschüsse.

(2) These liens have priority over the liens of the commission agent and warehouseman not arising from the forwarding of the goods as well as over the liens of the forwarding agent, the carrier and the charterer for advances.

§ 444 Ladeschein

(1) Über die Verpflichtung zur Ablieferung des Gutes kann von dem Frachtführer ein Ladeschein ausgestellt werden, der die in § 408 Abs. 1 genannten Angaben enthalten soll. Der Ladeschein ist vom Frachtführer zu unterzeichnen; eine Nachbildung der eigenhändigen Unterschrift durch Druck oder durch Stempel genügt.

(2) Ist der Ladeschein an Order gestellt, so soll er den Namen desjenigen enthalten, an dessen Order das Gut abgeliefert werden soll. Wird der Name nicht angegeben, so ist der Ladeschein als an Order des Absenders gestellt anzusehen.

(3) Der Ladeschein ist für das Rechtsverhältnis zwischen dem Frachtführer und dem Empfänger maßgebend. Er begründet insbesondere die widerlegliche Vermutung, daß die Güter wie im Ladeschein beschrieben übernommen sind; § 409 Abs. 2, 3 Satz 1 gilt entsprechend. Ist der Ladeschein einem gutgläubigen Dritten übertragen worden, so ist die Vermutung nach Satz 2 unwiderleglich.

(4) Für das Rechtsverhältnis zwischen dem Frachtführer und dem Absender bleiben die Bestimmungen des Frachtvertrages maßgebend.

§ 444 Bill of lading

(1) An inland bill of lading, which should contain the data mentioned in § 408 Subsection 1, may be issued by the carrier with respect to the obligation for delivery of the goods. The inland bill of lading shall be signed by the carrier; a facsimile of the signature by print or by stamp is sufficient.

(2) If the inland bill of lading is issued to order, it shall contain the name of the party to the order of whom the goods are to be delivered. If the name is not mentioned, the inland bill of lading is to be deemed to have been issued to the order of the shipper.

(3) The inland bill of lading governs the legal relationship between the carrier and the consignee of the goods. It establishes especially the rebuttable presumption that the goods have been accepted for shipment as described in the inland bill of lading; § 409 Subsections 2, 3 sentence 1 applies analogously. If the inland bill of lading has been transferred to a bona fide third party, the presumption according to sentence 2 is irrebuttable.

(4) The terms of the freight agreement continue to govern the legal relationship between the carrier and the shipper.

| Frachtgeschäft | §§ 445–448 |

§ 445 Ablieferung gegen Rückgabe des Ladescheins

Der Frachtführer ist zur Ablieferung des Gutes nur gegen Rückgabe des Ladescheins, auf dem die Ablieferung bescheinigt ist, verpflichtet.

§ 446 Legitimation durch Ladeschein

(1) Zum Empfang des Gutes legitimiert ist derjenige, an den das Gut nach dem Ladeschein abgeliefert werden soll oder auf den der Ladeschein, wenn er an Order lautet, durch Indossament übertragen ist.

(2) Dem zum Empfang Legitimierten steht das Verfügungsrecht nach § 418 zu. Der Frachtführer braucht den Weisungen wegen Rückgabe oder Ablieferung des Gutes an einen anderen als den durch den Ladeschein legitimierten Empfänger nur Folge zu leisten, wenn ihm der Ladeschein zurückgegeben wird.

§ 447 Ablieferung und Weisungsbefolgung ohne Ladeschein

Der Frachtführer haftet dem rechtmäßigen Besitzer des Ladescheins für den Schaden, der daraus entsteht, daß er das Gut abliefert oder einer Weisung wegen Rückgabe oder Ablieferung Folge leistet, ohne sich den Ladeschein zurückgeben zu lassen. Die Haftung ist auf den Betrag begrenzt, der bei Verlust des Gutes zu zahlen wäre.

§ 448 Traditionspapier

Die Übergabe des Ladescheins an denjenigen, den der Ladeschein zum Empfang des Gutes legitimiert, hat, wenn

§ 445 Delivery against return of the bill of lading

The carrier is obligated to deliver the goods only against return of the inland bill of lading on which the delivery is acknowledged.

§ 446 Identification by means of the bill of lading

(1) Anyone to whom the goods are to be delivered pursuant to the inland bill of lading or to whom the inland bill of lading, if it is made to order, is transferred by endorsement is entitled to take delivery of the goods.

(2) The person entitled to take delivery has the right of disposition pursuant to § 418. The carrier only has to follow instructions to return or deliver the goods to someone other than the person identified as consignee by the inland bill of lading if the inland bill of lading is returned to him.

§ 447 Delivery and compliance with instructions without inland bill of lading

The carrier is liable to the rightful holder of the inland bill of lading for the damage which arises from delivering, or complying with an instruction to return or deliver, the goods without having the inland bill of lading returned to him. The liability is limited to the amount which would be payable upon loss of the goods.

§ 448 Negotiable document of title

Delivery of the inland bill of lading to someone whom the inland bill of lading authorizes to accept delivery of

das Gut von dem Frachtführer übernommen ist, für den Erwerb von Rechten an dem Gut dieselben Wirkungen wie die Übergabe des Gutes.

§ 449 Abweichende Vereinbarungen

(1) Ist der Absender ein Verbraucher, so kann nicht zu dessen Nachteil von § 413 Abs. 2, den §§ 414, 418 Abs. 6, § 422 Abs. 3, den §§ 425 bis 438 und 447 abgewichen werden, es sei denn, der Frachtvertrag hat die Beförderung von Briefen oder briefähnlichen Sendungen zum Gegenstand. § 418 Abs. 6 und § 447 können nicht zu Lasten gutgläubiger Dritter abbedungen werden.

(2) In allen anderen als den in Absatz 1 Satz 1 genannten Fällen kann, soweit der Frachtvertrag nicht die Beförderung von Briefen oder briefähnlichen Sendungen zum Gegenstand hat, von den in Absatz 1 Satz 1 genannten Vorschriften nur durch Vereinbarung abgewichen werden, die im einzelnen ausgehandelt ist, auch wenn sie für eine Mehrzahl von gleichartigen Verträgen zwischen denselben Vertragsparteien getroffen ist. Die vom Frachtführer zu leistende Entschädigung wegen Verlust oder Beschädigung des Gutes kann jedoch auch durch vorformulierte Vertragsbedingungen auf einen anderen als den in § 431 Abs. 1 und 2 vorgesehenen Betrag begrenzt werden, wenn dieser Betrag

1. zwischen zwei und vierzig Rechnungseinheiten liegt und in drucktechnisch deutlicher Gestaltung besonders hervorgehoben ist oder

2. für den Verwender der vorformulierten Vertragsbedingungen ungünstiger ist als der in § 431 Abs. 1 und 2 vorgesehene Betrag.

the goods has, if the goods have been accepted by the carrier, the same effect with respect to the acquisition of rights in the goods as the delivery of the goods.

§ 449 Deviating agreements

(1) Where the shipper is a consumer, § 413 Subsection 2, §§ 414, 418 Subsection 6, § 422 Subsection 3, §§ 425 to 438 and § 447 cannot be deviated from to the detriment of the shipper unless the subject of the freight agreement is the shipment of letters or letter-like consignments. It cannot be agreed, to the detriment of bona fide third parties, that § 418 Subsection 6 and § 447 shall not apply.

(2) In all cases other than those mentioned in Subsection 1 sentence 1, to the extent that the subject of the freight agreement is not the shipment of letters or letter-like consignments one may deviate from the provisions mentioned in Subsection 1 sentence 1 only by an agreement which has been negotiated in detail even if it applies to a number of similar contracts between the same parties. The indemnification to be paid by the carrier because of loss of or damage to the goods may, however, be limited to an amount other than the amount provided for in § 431 Subsections 1 and 2 by pre-formulated contractual provisions, provided that this amount

1. lies between two and forty accounting units and has been especially highlighted by textual modification, or

2. is less advantageous to the user of the pre-formulated contractual provisions than the amount provided for in § 431 Subsections 1 and 2.

Gleiches gilt für die vom Absender nach § 414 zu leistende Entschädigung.

(3) Unterliegt der Frachtvertrag ausländischem Recht, so sind die Absätze 1 und 2 gleichwohl anzuwenden, wenn nach dem Vertrag der Ort der Übernahme und der Ort der Ablieferung des Gutes im Inland liegen.

§ 450 Anwendung von Seefrachtrecht

Hat der Frachtvertrag die Beförderung des Gutes ohne Umladung sowohl auf Binnen- als auch auf Seegewässern zum Gegenstand, so ist auf den Vertrag Seefrachtrecht anzuwenden, wenn

1. ein Konnossement ausgestellt ist oder
2. die auf Seegewässern zurückzulegende Strecke die größere ist.

Zweiter Unterabschnitt. Beförderung von Umzugsgut

§ 451 Umzugsvertrag

Hat der Frachtvertrag die Beförderung von Umzugsgut zum Gegenstand, so sind auf den Vertrag die Vorschriften des Ersten Unterabschnitts anzuwenden, soweit die folgenden besonderen Vorschriften oder anzuwendende internationale Übereinkommen nichts anderes bestimmen.

§ 451 a Pflichten des Frachtführers

(1) Die Pflichten des Frachtführers umfassen auch das Ab- und Aufbauen der Möbel sowie das Ver- und Entla-

The same applies for the indemnification which the shipper has to pay pursuant to § 414.

(3) If the freight agreement is subject to foreign law, Subsections 1 and 2 are still applicable if, according to the agreement, the place of acceptance for shipping and the place for delivery of the goods are in Germany.

§ 450 Application of maritime shipping law

Where the freight agreement deals with the shipment of the goods without transshipment both by inland waterways and by sea, maritime shipping law shall apply to the contract where

1. a bill of lading has been issued; or
2. the distance to be covered by sea is the longer one.

Second Subpart. Shipment of Personal and Household Goods in Course of Relocation

§ 451 Relocation agreement

Where the freight agreement provides for the shipment of personal and household goods in the course of relocation, the provisions of the First Subpart shall apply to the agreement to the extent that the following special provisions or applicable international conventions do not provide otherwise.

§ 451 a Duties of the carrier

(1) The duties of the carrier also include the dismantling and assembling of the furniture as well as the loading

den des Umzugsgutes.

(2) Ist der Absender ein Verbraucher, so zählt zu den Pflichten des Frachtführers ferner die Ausführung sonstiger auf den Umzug bezogener Leistungen wie die Verpackung und Kennzeichnung des Umzugsgutes.

§ 451 b Frachtbrief. Gefährliches Gut. Begleitpapiere. Mitteilungs- und Auskunftspflichten

(1) Abweichend von § 408 ist der Absender nicht verpflichtet, einen Frachtbrief auszustellen.

(2) Zählt zu dem Umzugsgut gefährliches Gut und ist der Absender ein Verbraucher, so ist er abweichend von § 410 lediglich verpflichtet, den Frachtführer über die von dem Gut ausgehende Gefahr allgemein zu unterrichten; die Unterrichtung bedarf keiner Form. Der Frachtführer hat den Absender über dessen Pflicht nach Satz 1 zu unterrichten.

(3) Der Frachtführer hat den Absender, wenn dieser ein Verbraucher ist, über die zu beachtenden Zoll- und sonstigen Verwaltungsvorschriften zu unterrichten. Er ist jedoch nicht verpflichtet zu prüfen, ob vom Absender zur Verfügung gestellte Urkunden und erteilte Auskünfte richtig und vollständig sind.

§ 451 c Haftung des Absenders in besonderen Fällen

Abweichend von § 414 Abs. 1 Satz 2 hat der Absender dem Frachtführer für Schäden nur bis zu einem Betrag von

and unloading of the personal and household goods.

(2) Where the shipper is a consumer, the carrier is also has the duty to perform other services pertaining to the relocation, such as the packaging and labelling of the personal and household goods.

§ 451 b Waybill. Dangerous goods. Accompanying documents; duties to notify and inform

(1) Deviating from § 408, the shipper is not obligated to issue a waybill.

(2) If there are dangerous goods among the personal and household goods in the course of relocation and if the shipper is a consumer, he is, deviating from § 410, only obligated to inform the carrier in a general way about the danger emanating from the goods. The information does not require any particular form. The carrier shall notify the shipper concerning his duties pursuant to sentence 1.

(3) The carrier shall advise the shipper, if he is a consumer, concerning the customs and other administrative regulations which have to be complied with. He is, however, not obligated to check whether the documents submitted and information given by the shipper are correct and complete.

§ 451 c Liability of the shipper in special cases

Deviating from § 414 Subsection 1 sentence 2, the shipper has to indemnify the carrier for damages only up to

600 EUR je Kubikmeter Laderaum, der zur Erfüllung des Vertrages benötigt wird, Ersatz zu leisten.	an amount of 600 EUR per cubic meter of cargo space necessary for carrying out the freight agreement.
§ 451 d Besondere Haftungsausschlußgründe	**§ 451 d Special reasons for exemption from liability**
(1) Abweichend von § 427 ist der Frachtführer von seiner Haftung befreit, soweit der Verlust oder die Beschädigung auf eine der folgenden Gefahren zurückzuführen ist:	(1) Deviating from § 427, the carrier is exempted from his liability to the extent that the loss or the damage is attributable to one of the following risks:
1. Beförderung von Edelmetallen, Juwelen, Edelsteinen, Geld, Briefmarken, Münzen, Wertpapieren oder Urkunden;	1. Shipment of precious metals, jewels, gems, money, stamps, coins, securities or official documents;
2. ungenügende Verpackung oder Kennzeichnung durch den Absender;	2. insufficient packaging or labelling by the shipper;
3. Behandeln, Verladen oder Entladen des Gutes durch den Absender;	3. handling, loading or unloading of the goods by the shipper;
4. Beförderung von nicht vom Frachtführer verpacktem Gut in Behältern;	4. shipment of goods in containers not packaged by the carrier;
5. Verladen oder Entladen von Gut, dessen Größe oder Gewicht den Raumverhältnissen an der Ladestelle oder Entladestelle nicht entspricht, sofern der Frachtführer den Absender auf die Gefahr einer Beschädigung vorher hingewiesen und der Absender auf der Durchführung der Leistung bestanden hat;	5. loading or unloading of goods whose volume or weight does not correspond to the space conditions at the point of loading or unloading, provided the carrier has indicated the risk of damage in advance and the shipper has insisted on the service being carried out;
6. Beförderung lebender Tiere oder von Pflanzen;	6. shipment of living animals or plants;
7. natürliche oder mangelhafte Beschaffenheit des Gutes, der zufolge es besonders leicht Schäden, insbesondere durch Bruch, Funktionsstörungen, Rost, inneren Verderb oder Auslaufen, erleidet.	7. natural or defective condition of the goods as the result of which they suffer especially easily damage, especially by breakage, disfunctioning, rust, inner spoilage or leaking out.
(2) Ist ein Schaden eingetreten, der nach den Umständen des Falles aus einer der in Absatz 1 bezeichneten	(2) Where damage has occurred which according to the circumstances of the case could arise from a risk designated

Gefahren entstehen konnte, so wird vermutet, daß der Schaden aus dieser Gefahr entstanden ist.

(3) Der Frachtführer kann sich auf Absatz 1 nur berufen, wenn er alle ihm nach den Umständen obliegenden Maßnahmen getroffen und besondere Weisungen beachtet hat.

§ 451 e Haftungshöchstbetrag

Abweichend von § 431 Abs. 1 und 2 ist die Haftung des Frachtführers wegen Verlust oder Beschädigung auf einen Betrag von 600 EUR je Kubikmeter Laderaum, der zur Erfüllung des Vertrages benötigt wird, beschränkt.

§ 451 f Schadensanzeige

Abweichend von § 438 Abs. 1 und 2 erlöschen Ansprüche wegen Verlust oder Beschädigung des Gutes,

1. wenn der Verlust oder die Beschädigung des Gutes äußerlich erkennbar war und dem Frachtführer nicht spätestens am Tag nach der Ablieferung angezeigt worden ist,
2. wenn der Verlust oder die Beschädigung äußerlich nicht erkennbar war und dem Frachtführer nicht innerhalb von vierzehn Tagen nach Ablieferung angezeigt worden ist.

§ 451 g Wegfall der Haftungsbefreiungen und -begrenzungen

Ist der Absender ein Verbraucher, so kann sich der Frachtführer oder eine in § 428 genannte Person

in Subsection 1, it shall be presumed that the damage has arisen from this risk.

(3) The carrier can rely on Subsection 1 only if he has taken all measures he was supposed to take according to the circumstances and has followed to special instructions.

§ 451 e Maximum amount of liability

Deviating from § 431 Subsections 1 and 2, the liability of the carrier because of loss or damage is limited to an amount of 600 EUR per cubic meter of cargo space necessary to carry out the freight agreement.

§ 451 f Notification of damage

Deviating from § 438 Subsections 1 and 2, claims for losses or damage of the goods lapse where

1. the loss or the damage of the goods was externally visible and notice has not been given to the carrier at the latest on the day after the delivery,
2. the loss or the damage was not externally visible and notice has not been given to the carrier within fourteen days after delivery.

§ 451 g Loss of the exemptions from and limitations of liability

Where the shipper is a consumer, the carrier or a person designated in § 428 cannot

1. auf die in den §§ 451 d und 451 e sowie in dem Ersten Unterabschnitt vorgesehenen Haftungsbefreiungen und Haftungsbegrenzungen nicht berufen, soweit der Frachtführer es unterläßt, den Absender bei Abschluß des Vertrages über die Haftungsbestimmungen zu unterrichten und auf die Möglichkeiten hinzuweisen, eine weitergehende Haftung zu vereinbaren oder das Gut zu versichern,

2. auf § 451 f in Verbindung mit § 438 nicht berufen, soweit der Frachtführer es unterläßt, den Empfänger spätestens bei der Ablieferung des Gutes über die Form und Frist der Schadensanzeige sowie die Rechtsfolgen bei Unterlassen der Schadensanzeige zu unterrichten.

Die Unterrichtung nach Satz 1 Nr. 1 muß in drucktechnisch deutlicher Gestaltung besonders hervorgehoben sein.

§ 451 h Abweichende Vereinbarungen

(1) Ist der Absender ein Verbraucher, so kann von den die Haftung des Frachtführers und des Absenders regelnden Vorschriften dieses Unterabschnitts sowie den danach auf den Umzugsvertrag anzuwendenden Vorschriften des Ersten Unterabschnitts nicht zum Nachteil des Absenders abgewichen werden.

(2) In allen anderen als den in Absatz 1 genannten Fällen kann von den darin genannten Vorschriften nur durch Vereinbarung abgewichen werden, die im einzelnen ausgehandelt ist, auch

1. rely on the exemptions from and limitations of liability provided for in §§ 451 d and 451 e as well as in the First Subpart to the extent that the carrier omits to inform the shipper upon conclusion of the contract about the provisions pertaining to liability and of the possibilities to agree on an extended liability or to insure the goods,

2. rely on § 451 f in conjunction with § 438 to the extent that the carrier omits to inform the consignee not later than upon delivery of the goods of the form and time period for the notification of damage as well as of the legal consequences if the notification of damage is omitted.

The information pursuant to sentence 1 No. 1, shall be especially highlighted by textual modification.

§ 451 h Deviating agreements

(1) Where the shipper is a consumer, the provisions of this subpart regulating the liability of the carrier and the shipper cannot be deviated from to the detriment of the shipper; the same applies to the provisions of the First Subpart to be applied thereunder to the relocation contract for personal and household goods.

(2) In all cases other than those mentioned in Subsection 1, one may deviate from the provisions mentioned therein only by an agreement which has been negotiated in detail even if it

wenn sie für eine Mehrzahl von gleichartigen Verträgen zwischen denselben Vertragsparteien getroffen ist. Die vom Frachtführer zu leistende Entschädigung wegen Verlust oder Beschädigung des Gutes kann jedoch auch durch vorformulierte Vertragsbedingungen auf einen anderen als den in § 451 e vorgesehenen Betrag begrenzt werden. Gleiches gilt für die vom Absender nach § 414 in Verbindung mit § 451 c zu leistende Entschädigung. Die in den vorformulierten Vertragsbedingungen enthaltene Bestimmung ist jedoch unwirksam, wenn sie nicht in drucktechnisch deutlicher Gestaltung besonders hervorgehoben ist.

(3) Unterliegt der Umzugsvertrag ausländischem Recht, so sind die Absätze 1 und 2 gleichwohl anzuwenden, wenn nach dem Vertrag der Ort der Übernahme und der Ort der Ablieferung des Gutes im Inland liegen.

Dritter Unterabschnitt. Beförderung mit verschiedenartigen Beförderungsmitteln

§ 452 Frachtvertrag über eine Beförderung mit verschiedenartigen Beförderungsmitteln

Wird die Beförderung des Gutes auf Grund eines einheitlichen Frachtvertrags mit verschiedenartigen Beförderungsmitteln durchgeführt und wären, wenn über jeden Teil der Beförderung mit jeweils einem Beförderungsmittel (Teilstrecke) zwischen den Vertragsparteien ein gesonderter Vertrag abgeschlossen worden wäre, mindestens zwei dieser Verträge verschiedenen Rechtsvorschriften unterworfen, so sind auf den Vertrag die Vorschriften des Ersten Unterabschnitts anzuwen-

applies to a number of similar contracts between the same parties. The indemnification to be paid by the carrier because of loss of or damage to the goods may, however, be limited to an amount other than the one provided for in § 451 e by pre-formulated contractual provisions. The same applies to the indemnification to be paid by the shipper pursuant to § 414 in conjunction with § 451 c. The provision contained in the pre-formulated contractual provisions is, however, invalid unless it is especially highlighted by textual modification.

(3) If the relocation contract is subject to foreign law, Subsections 1 and 2 are still applicable if, according to the contract, the place of acceptance and the place of delivery of the goods are in Germany.

Third Subpart. Shipment by Different Means of Transportation

§ 452 Freight agreement pertaining to a shipment by different means of transportation

Where, based on a uniform freight agreement, the shipment of the goods is carried out by different means of transportation and where, if a separate agreement had been made between the parties pertaining to each part of the shipment one means of shipment from time to time (partial route), at least two of these agreements would have been subject to different legal regulations, the provisions of the First Subpart are to be applied to the agreement to the extent that the following

den, soweit die folgenden besonderen Vorschriften oder anzuwendende internationale Übereinkommen nichts anderes bestimmen. Dies gilt auch dann, wenn ein Teil der Beförderung zur See durchgeführt wird.

§ 452 a Bekannter Schadensort

Steht fest, daß der Verlust, die Beschädigung oder das Ereignis, das zu einer Überschreitung der Lieferfrist geführt hat, auf einer bestimmten Teilstrecke eingetreten ist, so bestimmt sich die Haftung des Frachtführers abweichend von den Vorschriften des Ersten Unterabschnitts nach den Rechtsvorschriften, die auf einen Vertrag über eine Beförderung auf dieser Teilstrecke anzuwenden wären. Der Beweis dafür, daß der Verlust, die Beschädigung oder das zu einer Überschreitung der Lieferfrist führende Ereignis auf einer bestimmten Teilstrecke eingetreten ist, obliegt demjenigen, der dies behauptet.

§ 452 b Schadensanzeige. Verjährung

(1) § 438 ist unabhängig davon anzuwenden, ob der Schadensort unbekannt ist, bekannt ist oder später bekannt wird. Die für die Schadensanzeige vorgeschriebene Form und Frist ist auch gewahrt, wenn die Vorschriften eingehalten werden, die auf einen Vertrag über eine Beförderung auf der letzten Teilstrecke anzuwenden wären.

(2) Für den Beginn der Verjährung des Anspruchs wegen Verlust, Beschädigung oder Überschreitung der Lieferfrist ist, wenn auf den Ablieferungszeitpunkt abzustellen ist, der Zeitpunkt der Ablieferung an den Empfänger maßgebend. Der Anspruch verjährt

special provisions or applicable international conventions do not provide otherwise. This also applies if a part of the shipment is carried out on sea.

§ 452 a Identified place where damage occurred

Where it is certain that the loss, the damage or the incident which led to the term for delivery being exceeded has occurred on a particular partial route, the liability of the carrier is determined, deviating from the provisions of the First Subpart, according to the legal regulations which would be applicable to a contract pertaining to a shipment on this partial route. The proof pertaining to the question whether the loss, the damage or the event leading to exceeding the delivery deadline occurred on a particular partial route is incumbent upon the person who asserts it.

§ 452 b Notification of damage. Statute of limitations

(1) Section 438 shall be applied regardless of whether the place where the damage occurred is unknown, known or becomes known later. Form and time period for the notification of damage are also complied with where the provisions which apply to a freight agreement on the last partial route are complied with.

(2) The point in time of delivery to the consignee governs for the beginning of the statute of limitations pertaining to the claims for losses, damage or exceeding the term for delivery if the point in time of delivery is to be taken into account. The claim expires at the

§§ 452b–d

auch bei bekanntem Schadensort frühestens nach Maßgabe des § 439.

§ 452 c Umzugsvertrag über eine Beförderung mit verschiedenartigen Beförderungsmitteln

Hat der Frachtvertrag die Beförderung von Umzugsgut mit verschiedenartigen Beförderungsmitteln zum Gegenstand, so sind auf den Vertrag die Vorschriften des Zweiten Unterabschnitts anzuwenden. § 452 a ist nur anzuwenden, soweit für die Teilstrecke, auf der der Schaden eingetreten ist, Bestimmungen eines für die Bundesrepublik Deutschland verbindlichen internationalen Übereinkommens gelten.

§ 452 d Abweichende Vereinbarungen

(1) Von der Regelung des § 452 b Abs. 2 Satz 1 kann nur durch Vereinbarung abgewichen werden, die im einzelnen ausgehandelt ist, auch wenn diese für eine Mehrzahl von gleichartigen Verträgen zwischen denselben Vertragsparteien getroffen ist. Von den übrigen Regelungen dieses Unterabschnitts kann nur insoweit durch vertragliche Vereinbarung abgewichen werden, als die darin in Bezug genommenen Vorschriften abweichende Vereinbarungen zulassen.

(2) Abweichend von Absatz 1 kann jedoch auch durch vorformulierte Vertragsbedingungen vereinbart werden, daß sich die Haftung bei bekanntem Schadensort (§ 452 a)

1. unabhängig davon, auf welcher Teilstrecke der Schaden eintreten wird, oder

Handelsgeschäfte

earliest according to § 439 even if the place where the damage occurred is known.

§ 452 c Relocation agreement pertaining to shipment by different means of transportation

Where the freight agreement provides for the shipment of the personal and household goods in course of relocation with different means of transportation, the provisions of the Second Subpart apply. Section 452 a applies only to the extent that provisions of an international convention binding for the Federal Republic of Germany apply for the partial route where the damage occurred.

§ 452 d Deviating agreements

(1) One may deviate from the provisions of § 452 b Subsection 2 sentence 1 only by an agreement which has been negotiated in detail even if such agreement applies to a number of similar contracts between the same parties. One may deviate from the other provisions of this Subpart by contractual agreements only to the extent that the pertinent provisions permit deviating agreements.

(2) Deviating from Subsection 1, it can be agreed, however, also by pre-formulated contractual provisions that the liability in case the place of damage is known (§ 452 a) is regulated by the provisions of the First Subpart

1. irrespective of on which partial route the damage occurred, or

2. für den Fall des Schadenseintritts auf einer in der Vereinbarung genannten Teilstrecke

nach den Vorschriften des Ersten Unterabschnitts bestimmt.

(3) Vereinbarungen, die die Anwendung der für eine Teilstrecke zwingend geltenden Bestimmungen eines für die Bundesrepublik Deutschland verbindlichen internationalen Übereinkommens ausschließen, sind unwirksam.

Fünfter Abschnitt. Speditionsgeschäft

§ 453 Speditionsvertrag

(1) Durch den Speditionsvertrag wird der Spediteur verpflichtet, die Versendung des Gutes zu besorgen.

(2) Der Versender wird verpflichtet, die vereinbarte Vergütung zu zahlen.

(3) Die Vorschriften dieses Abschnitts gelten nur, wenn die Besorgung der Versendung zum Betrieb eines gewerblichen Unternehmens gehört. Erfordert das Unternehmen nach Art oder Umfang einen in kaufmännischer Weise eingerichteten Geschäftsbetrieb nicht und ist die Firma des Unternehmens auch nicht nach § 2 in das Handelsregister eingetragen, so sind in Ansehung des Speditionsgeschäfts auch insoweit die Vorschriften des Ersten Abschnitts des Vierten Buches ergänzend anzuwenden; dies gilt jedoch nicht für die §§ 348 bis 350.

§ 454 Besorgung der Versendung

(1) Die Pflicht, die Versendung zu besorgen, umfaßt die Organisation der Beförderung, insbesondere

2. in case of the occurrence of the damage on a partial route mentioned in the agreement.

(3) Agreements which exclude the applicability of provisions of an international convention binding for the Federal Republic of Germany which are mandatory for a partial route are invalid.

Part Five. The Forwarding Business

§ 453 Forwarding agreement

(1) The forwarding agreement obligates the forwarding agent to handle the shipment of the goods.

(2) The shipper is obligated to pay the agreed remuneration.

(3) The provisions of this part apply only if the handling of the shipment is part of the operation of a commercial enterprise. Where the type and volume of the business not require a commercially organized business operation and where the firm name of the enterprise is not registered in the Commercial Register pursuant to § 2, the provisions of the First Part of the Fourth Book are to be applied supplementally with respect to the forwarding business; this does not apply, however, to §§ 348 to 350.

§ 454 Handling the shipment

(1) The obligation to handle the shipment includes the organization of the shipment, in particular

1. die Bestimmung des Beförderungsmittels und des Beförderungsweges,

2. die Auswahl ausführender Unternehmer, den Abschluß der für die Versendung erforderlichen Fracht-, Lager- und Speditionsverträge sowie die Erteilung von Informationen und Weisungen an die ausführenden Unternehmer und

3. die Sicherung von Schadenersatzansprüchen des Versenders.

(2) Zu den Pflichten des Spediteurs zählt ferner die Ausführung sonstiger vereinbarter auf die Beförderung bezogener Leistungen wie die Versicherung und Verpackung des Gutes, seine Kennzeichnung und die Zollbehandlung. Der Spediteur schuldet jedoch nur den Abschluß der zur Erbringung dieser Leistungen erforderlichen Verträge, wenn sich dies aus der Vereinbarung ergibt.

(3) Der Spediteur schließt die erforderlichen Verträge im eigenen Namen oder, sofern er hierzu bevollmächtigt ist, im Namen des Versenders ab.

(4) Der Spediteur hat bei Erfüllung seiner Pflichten das Interesse des Versenders wahrzunehmen und dessen Weisungen zu befolgen.

§ 455 Behandlung des Gutes. Begleitpapiere. Mitteilungs- und Auskunftspflichten

(1) Der Versender ist verpflichtet, das Gut, soweit erforderlich, zu verpacken und zu kennzeichnen und Urkunden zur Verfügung zu stellen sowie alle Auskünfte zu erteilen, deren der Spediteur zur Erfüllung seiner Pflichten bedarf. Soll gefährliches Gut

1. the determination of the means of shipment and the route of shipment,

2. the selection of the enterprises to carry out the shipment, the conclusion of the freight, warehouse and forwarding contracts necessary for the shipment as well as the giving of information and instructions to the enterprises which carry out the shipment, and

3. securing claims for damages of the shipper.

(2) Among the obligations of the forwarding agent are also the carrying out of other services agreed upon and pertaining to the shipment, such as the insurance and packaging of the goods, their labelling and customs handling. The forwarding agent is, however, only obligated to conclude the contracts necessary to procure these services where this follows from the forwarding agreement.

(3) The forwarding agent concludes the necessary contracts in his own name or, to the extent that he has been authorized to do so, in the name of the shipper.

(4) The forwarding agent shall in fulfilling his duties protect the interests of the shipper and follow his instructions.

§ 455 Handling of the goods; accompanying documents; duties to notify and inform

(1) The shipper shall, to the extent that necessary, package and label the goods, make documents available and provide all the information which the forwarding agent needs to discharge his duties. Where dangerous goods are to be shipped, the shipper shall inform

| Speditionsgeschäft | §§ 455–457 |

versendet werden, so hat der Versender dem Spediteur rechtzeitig in Textform die genaue Art der Gefahr und, soweit erforderlich, zu ergreifende Vorsichtsmaßnahmen mitzuteilen.	the forwarding agent in a timely manner and in written form about the specific kind of danger and, if necessary, the precautions to be taken.
(2) Der Versender hat, auch wenn ihn kein Verschulden trifft, dem Spediteur Schäden und Aufwendungen zu ersetzen, die verursacht werden durch	(2) The shipper shall, even if he is not at fault, reimburse the forwarding agent for damages and expenditures which are caused by the following circumstances:
1. ungenügende Verpackung oder Kennzeichnung,	1. Insufficient packaging or labelling,
2. Unterlassen der Mitteilung über die Gefährlichkeit des Gutes oder	2. failure to make notification as to the dangerous nature of the goods,
3. Fehlen, Unvollständigkeit oder Unrichtigkeit der Urkunden oder Auskünfte, die für eine amtliche Behandlung des Gutes erforderlich sind.	3. lack, incompleteness or incorrectness of the documents or information which is required for official handling of the goods.
§ 414 Abs. 1 Satz 2 und Abs. 2 ist entsprechend anzuwenden.	Section 414 Subsection 1 sentence 2 and Subsection 2 apply accordingly.
(3) Ist der Versender ein Verbraucher, so hat er dem Spediteur Schäden und Aufwendungen nach Absatz 2 nur zu ersetzen, soweit ihn ein Verschulden trifft.	(3) Where the shipper is a consumer, he shall reimburse the forwarding agent for damages and expenditures pursuant to Subsection 2 only to the extent that he is at fault.

§ 456 Fälligkeit der Vergütung

§ 456 Due date of the remuneration

Die Vergütung ist zu zahlen, wenn das Gut dem Frachtführer oder Verfrachter übergeben worden ist.	The remuneration is due when the goods have been handed over to the carrier or the charterer.

§ 457 Forderungen des Versenders

§ 457 Claims of the shipper

Der Versender kann Forderungen aus einem Vertrag, den der Spediteur für Rechnung des Versenders im eigenen Namen abgeschlossen hat, erst nach der Abtretung geltend machen. Solche Forderungen sowie das in Erfüllung solcher Forderungen Erlangte gelten jedoch im Verhältnis zu den Gläubi-	The shipper can assert claims resulting from an agreement which the forwarding agent has concluded in his own name for the account of the shipper only after it has been assigned to him. In the relationship to the creditors of the forwarding agent, however, such claims as well as what has been

gern des Spediteurs als auf den Versender übertragen.

§ 458 Selbsteintritt

Der Spediteur ist befugt, die Beförderung des Gutes durch Selbsteintritt auszuführen. Macht er von dieser Befugnis Gebrauch, so hat er hinsichtlich der Beförderung die Rechte und Pflichten eines Frachtführers oder Verfrachters. In diesem Fall kann er neben der Vergütung für seine Tätigkeit als Spediteur die gewöhnliche Fracht verlangen.

§ 459 Spedition zu festen Kosten

Soweit als Vergütung ein bestimmter Betrag vereinbart ist, der Kosten für die Beförderung einschließt, hat der Spediteur hinsichtlich der Beförderung die Rechte und Pflichten eines Frachtführers oder Verfrachters. In diesem Fall hat er Anspruch auf Ersatz seiner Aufwendungen nur, soweit dies üblich ist.

§ 460 Sammelladung

(1) Der Spediteur ist befugt, die Versendung des Gutes zusammen mit Gut eines anderen Versenders auf Grund eines für seine Rechnung über eine Sammelladung geschlossenen Frachtvertrages zu bewirken.

(2) Macht der Spediteur von dieser Befugnis Gebrauch, so hat er hinsichtlich der Beförderung in Sammelladung die Rechte und Pflichten eines

obtained in fulfilment of such claims are deemed to have been transferred to the shipper.

§ 458 The forwarding agent's right to substitute himself for the third party he would otherwise deal with on the principal's behalf

The forwarding agent is authorized to carry out the shipment of the goods by substituting himself for the third party he would otherwise deal with on the principal's behalf. If he makes use of this right, he has the rights and obligations of a carrier or a charterer pertaining to the shipment. In this case he can claim, in addition to the remuneration for his activity as forwarding agent, the normal freight charges.

§ 459 Forwarding at fixed costs

To the extent that a fixed amount has been agreed upon as remuneration which includes the cost of the shipment, the forwarding agent has the rights and obligations of a carrier or a charterer pertaining to the shipment. In this case he has a claim for reimbursement of his expenditures only to the extent that this is customary.

§ 460 Mixed Consignment

(1) The forwarding agent is authorized to effect the shipping of the goods together with goods of another shipper by reason of a forwarding agreement concerning a mixed consignment concluded for his account.

(2) Where the forwarding agent makes use of this right, he has the rights and duties of a carrier or a charterer pertaining to the shipping in a mixed con-

Frachtführers oder Verfrachters. In diesem Fall kann der Spediteur eine den Umständen nach angemessene Vergütung verlangen, höchstens aber die für die Beförderung des einzelnen Gutes gewöhnliche Fracht.

§ 461 Haftung des Spediteurs

(1) Der Spediteur haftet für den Schaden, der durch Verlust oder Beschädigung des in seiner Obhut befindlichen Gutes entsteht. Die §§ 426, 427, 429, 430, 431 Abs. 1, 2 und 4, die §§ 432, 434 bis 436 sind entsprechend anzuwenden.

(2) Für Schaden, der nicht durch Verlust oder Beschädigung des in der Obhut des Spediteurs befindlichen Gutes entstanden ist, haftet der Spediteur, wenn er eine ihm nach § 454 obliegende Pflicht verletzt. Von dieser Haftung ist er befreit, wenn der Schaden durch die Sorgfalt eines ordentlichen Kaufmanns nicht abgewendet werden konnte.

(3) Hat bei der Entstehung des Schadens ein Verhalten des Versenders oder ein besonderer Mangel des Gutes mitgewirkt, so hängen die Verpflichtung zum Ersatz sowie der Umfang des zu leistenden Ersatzes davon ab, inwieweit diese Umstände zu dem Schaden beigetragen haben.

§ 462 Haftung für andere

Der Spediteur hat Handlungen und Unterlassungen seiner Leute in gleichem Umfang zu vertreten wie eigene Handlungen und Unterlassungen, wenn die Leute in Ausübung ihrer Verrichtungen handeln. Gleiches gilt für Handlungen und Unterlassungen

signment. In this case the forwarding agent may claim remuneration reasonable according to the circumstances, but not more than the customary freight charges for the shipping of the individual goods.

§ 461 Liability of the forwarding agent

(1) The forwarding agent is liable for the damage which arises from loss of or damage to goods in his custody. Sections 426, 427, 429, 430, 431 Subsections 1, 2 and 4, §§ 432, 434 to 436 apply analogously.

(2) For damage which does not arise from loss of or damage to the goods in the custody of the forwarding agent, the forwarding agent is liable if he violates a duty incumbent on him pursuant to § 454. He is exempted from this liability if the damage could not have been averted by the care of a prudent merchant.

(3) If a conduct of the shipper or a special defect of the goods has contributed to the origin of the damage, then the obligation to pay damages as well as the amount of the damages to be paid depends on the extent to which these circumstances have contributed to the damage.

§ 462 Liability for others

The forwarding agent is liable for the acts and omissions of his employees to the same extent as for his own acts and omissions where the employees act in performance of their duties. The same applies for actions and omissions of other persons he uses in ful-

anderer Personen, deren er sich bei Erfüllung seiner Pflicht, die Versendung zu besorgen, bedient.

§ 463 Verjährung

Auf die Verjährung der Ansprüche aus einer Leistung, die den Vorschriften dieses Abschnitts unterliegt, ist § 439 entsprechend anzuwenden.

§ 464 Pfandrecht

Der Spediteur hat wegen aller durch den Speditionsvertrag begründeten Forderungen sowie wegen unbestrittener Forderungen aus anderen mit dem Versender abgeschlossenen Speditions-, Fracht- und Lagerverträgen ein Pfandrecht an dem Gut. § 441 Abs. 1 Satz 2 bis Abs. 4 ist entsprechend anzuwenden.

§ 465 Nachfolgender Spediteur

(1) Wirkt an einer Beförderung neben dem Frachtführer auch ein Spediteur mit und hat dieser die Ablieferung zu bewirken, so ist auf den Spediteur § 442 Abs. 1 entsprechend anzuwenden.

(2) Wird ein vorhergehender Frachtführer oder Spediteur von einem nachfolgenden Spediteur befriedigt, so gehen Forderung und Pfandrecht des ersteren auf den letzteren über.

§ 466 Abweichende Vereinbarungen

(1) Ist der Versender ein Verbraucher, so kann nicht zu dessen Nachteil von § 461 Abs. 1, den §§ 462 und 463 abgewichen werden, es sei denn, der Spedi-

filling his duty to carry out the shipment.

§ 463 Statute of limitations

Section 439 applies analogously to the statute of limitations for claims arising from a service which is subject to the provisions of this Part.

§ 464 Lien

The forwarding agent shall have a lien on the goods for all claims arising out of the forwarding agency agreement as well as for undisputed claims arising out of other forwarding agency, freight and warehouse contracts concluded with the shipper. Section 441 Subsection 1 sentence 2 to Subsection 4 applies analogously.

§ 465 Subsequent forwarding agent

(1) If, in addition to the carrier, also a forwarding agent is involved in the shipment and he is responsible for the delivery, § 442 Subsection 1 shall apply analogously to the forwarding agent.

(2) If a preceding carrier or forwarding agent is paid by a subsequent forwarding agent, the claim and lien right of the former are transferred to the latter.

§ 466 Deviating agreements

(1) Where the shipper is a consumer, § 461 Subsection 1, §§ 462 and 463 cannot be deviated from to the detriment of the shipper unless the subject

tionsvertrag hat die Versendung von Briefen oder briefähnlichen Sendungen zum Gegenstand.

(2) In allen anderen als den in Absatz 1 genannten Fällen kann, soweit der Speditionsvertrag nicht die Versendung von Briefen oder briefähnlichen Sendungen zum Gegenstand hat, von den in Absatz 1 genannten Vorschriften nur durch Vereinbarung abgewichen werden, die im einzelnen ausgehandelt ist, auch wenn sie für eine Mehrzahl von gleichartigen Verträgen zwischen denselben Vertragsparteien getroffen ist. Die vom Spediteur zu leistende Entschädigung wegen Verlust oder Beschädigung des Gutes kann jedoch auch durch vorformulierte Vertragsbedingungen auf einen anderen als den in § 431 Abs. 1 und 2 vorgesehenen Betrag begrenzt werden, wenn dieser Betrag

1. zwischen zwei und vierzig Rechnungseinheiten liegt und in drucktechnisch deutlicher Gestaltung besonders hervorgehoben ist oder

2. für den Verwender der vorformulierten Vertragsbedingungen ungünstiger ist als der in § 431 Abs. 1 und 2 vorgesehene Betrag.

(3) Von § 458 Satz 2, § 459 Satz 1, § 460 Abs. 2 Satz 1 kann nur insoweit durch vertragliche Vereinbarung abgewichen werden, als die darin in Bezug genommenen Vorschriften abweichende Vereinbarungen zulassen.

(4) Unterliegt der Speditionsvertrag ausländischem Recht, so sind die Absätze 1 bis 3 gleichwohl anzuwenden, wenn nach dem Vertrag der Ort der Übernahme und der Ort der Ablieferung des Gutes im Inland liegen.

of the forwarding agreement is the shipment of letters or letter-like consignments.

(2) In all cases other than those mentioned in Subsection 1, to the extent that the subject of the forwarding agreement is not the shipment of letters or letter-like consignments, one may deviate from the provisions mentioned in Subsection 1 only by an agreement which has been negotiated in detail even if it applies to a number of similar contracts between the same parties. The indemnification to be paid by the forwarding agent because of loss of or damage to the goods may, however, be limited to an amount other than the amount provided for in § 431 Subsections 1 and 2 by pre-formulated contractual provisions, provided that this amount

1. lies between two and forty accounting units and has been especially highlighted by textual modification, or

2. is less advantageous for the user of the pre-formulated contractual provisions than the amount provided for in § 431 Subsections 1 and 2.

(3) One may deviate from § 458 sentence 2, § 459 sentence 1 and § 460 Subsection 2 sentence 1 by contractual agreement only to the extent that the pertinent provisions permit deviating agreements.

(4) If the forwarding agency agreement is subject to foreign law, Subsections 1 to 3 are still applicable if, according to the agreement, the place of acceptance of the goods and the place of delivery of the goods are in Germany.

Sechster Abschnitt. Lagergeschäft

§ 467 Lagervertrag

(1) Durch den Lagervertrag wird der Lagerhalter verpflichtet, das Gut zu lagern und aufzubewahren.

(2) Der Einlagerer wird verpflichtet, die vereinbarte Vergütung zu zahlen.

(3) Die Vorschriften dieses Abschnitts gelten nur, wenn die Lagerung und Aufbewahrung zum Betrieb eines gewerblichen Unternehmens gehören. Erfordert das Unternehmen nach Art oder Umfang einen in kaufmännischer Weise eingerichteten Geschäftsbetrieb nicht und ist die Firma des Unternehmens auch nicht nach § 2 in das Handelsregister eingetragen, so sind in Ansehung des Lagergeschäfts auch insoweit die Vorschriften des Ersten Abschnitts des Vierten Buches ergänzend anzuwenden; dies gilt jedoch nicht für die §§ 348 bis 350.

§ 468 Behandlung des Gutes. Begleitpapiere. Mitteilungs- und Auskunftspflichten

(1) Der Einlagerer ist verpflichtet, dem Lagerhalter, wenn gefährliches Gut eingelagert werden soll, rechtzeitig in Textform die genaue Art der Gefahr und, soweit erforderlich, zu ergreifende Vorsichtsmaßnahmen mitzuteilen. Er hat ferner das Gut, soweit erforderlich, zu verpacken und zu kennzeichnen und Urkunden zur Verfügung zu stellen sowie alle Auskünfte zu erteilen, die der Lagerhalter zur Erfüllung seiner Pflichten benötigt.

(2) Ist der Einlagerer ein Verbraucher, so ist abweichend von Absatz 1

Part Six. Warehousing

§ 467 Warehousing contract

(1) The warehousing contract obligates the warehouseman to warehouse and store the goods.

(2) The person storing the goods is obligated to pay the agreed remuneration.

(3) The provisions of this part apply only if warehousing and storage are part of the operation of a commercial enterprise. Where the type and volume of the business do not require a commercially organized business operation and where the firm name is not registered in the Commercial Register pursuant to § 2, the provisions of the First Part of the Fourth Book are to be applied supplementally with respect to the warehousing business; this does not apply, however, to §§ 348 to 350.

§ 468 Handling of the goods; accompanying documents; duties to notify and inform

(1) Where dangerous goods are to be warehoused, the person storing the goods shall inform the warehouseman in a timely manner and in written form about the specific kind of danger and, if necessary, the precautions to be taken. He shall also, to the extent necessary, package and label the goods, make documents available and provide all the information which the warehouseman needs in order to discharge his duties.

(2) Where the person storing the goods is a consumer, then deviating from Subsection 1

1. der Lagerhalter verpflichtet, das Gut, soweit erforderlich, zu verpacken und zu kennzeichnen,	1. the warehouseman is obligated, to the extent necessary, to package and label the goods,
2. der Einlagerer lediglich verpflichtet, den Lagerhalter über die von dem Gut ausgehende Gefahr allgemein zu unterrichten; die Unterrichtung bedarf keiner Form.	2. the person storing the goods is merely obligated to advise the warehouseman about the danger emanating from the goods in a general way; the information does not require any special form.
Der Lagerhalter hat in diesem Falle den Einlagerer über dessen Pflicht nach Satz 1 Nr. 2 sowie über die von ihm zu beachtenden Verwaltungsvorschriften über eine amtliche Behandlung des Gutes zu unterrichten.	The warehouseman shall in this case advise the person storing the goods about his duty according to sentence 1 No. 2 as well as about the administrative regulations pertaining to official handling of the goods to be complied with by him.
(3) Der Einlagerer hat, auch wenn ihn kein Verschulden trifft, dem Lagerhalter Schäden und Aufwendungen zu ersetzen, die verursacht werden durch	(3) The person storing the goods shall – even if he is not at fault – reimburse the warehouseman for damages and expenditures which are caused by
1. ungenügende Verpackung oder Kennzeichnung,	1. insufficient packaging or labelling,
2. Unterlassen der Mitteilung über die Gefährlichkeit des Gutes oder	2. failure to make notification of the dangerous nature of the goods, or
3. Fehlen, Unvollständigkeit oder Unrichtigkeit der in § 413 Abs. 1 genannten Urkunden oder Auskünfte.	3. lack, incompleteness or incorrectness of the documents or information mentioned in § 413 Subsection 1.
§ 414 Abs. 1 Satz 2 und Abs. 2 ist entsprechend anzuwenden.	Section 414 Subsection 1 sentence 2 and Subsection 2 apply analogously.
(4) Ist der Einlagerer ein Verbraucher, so hat er dem Lagerhalter Schäden und Aufwendungen nach Absatz 3 nur zu ersetzen, soweit ihn ein Verschulden trifft.	(4) Where the person storing the goods is a consumer, he shall reimburse the warehouseman for damages and expenditures pursuant to Subsection 3 only to the extent that he is at fault.

§ 469 Sammellagerung

(1) Der Lagerhalter ist nur berechtigt, vertretbare Sachen mit anderen Sachen gleicher Art und Güte zu vermischen, wenn die beteiligten Einlagerer ausdrücklich einverstanden sind.

§ 469 Mixed deposit storage

(1) The warehouseman is entitled to commingle fungible goods with goods of the same kind and quality only where the participating persons storing goods have expressly permitted him to do so.

(2) Ist der Lagerhalter berechtigt, Gut zu vermischen, so steht vom Zeitpunkt der Einlagerung ab den Eigentümern der eingelagerten Sachen Miteigentum nach Bruchteilen zu.

(3) Der Lagerhalter kann jedem Einlagerer den ihm gebührenden Anteil ausliefern, ohne daß er hierzu der Genehmigung der übrigen Beteiligten bedarf.

§ 470 Empfang des Gutes

Befindet sich Gut, das dem Lagerhalter zugesandt ist, beim Empfang in einem beschädigten oder mangelhaften Zustand, der äußerlich erkennbar ist, so hat der Lagerhalter Schadenersatzansprüche des Einlagerers zu sichern und dem Einlagerer unverzüglich Nachricht zu geben.

§ 471 Erhaltung des Gutes

(1) Der Lagerhalter hat dem Einlagerer die Besichtigung des Gutes, die Entnahme von Proben und die zur Erhaltung des Gutes notwendigen Handlungen während der Geschäftsstunden zu gestatten. Er ist jedoch berechtigt und im Falle der Sammellagerung auch verpflichtet, die zur Erhaltung des Gutes erforderlichen Arbeiten selbst vorzunehmen.

(2) Sind nach dem Empfang Veränderungen an dem Gut entstanden oder zu befürchten, die den Verlust oder die Beschädigung des Gutes oder Schäden des Lagerhalters erwarten lassen, so hat der Lagerhalter dies dem Einlagerer oder, wenn ein Lagerschein ausgestellt ist, dem letzten ihm bekanntgewordenen legitimierten Besitzer des Scheins unverzüglich anzuzeigen und dessen Weisungen einzuholen. Kann der Lagerhalter innerhalb angemesse-

(2) Where the warehouseman is entitled to commingle goods, the owners of the warehoused goods, from the point in time of the warehousing onwards, have fractional co-ownership.

(3) The warehouseman can deliver to each person storing goods the share due him without needing the consent of the other participants therefor.

§ 470 Acceptance of the goods

If upon acceptance the goods which have been sent to the warehouseman are in a damaged or defective condition which is externally visible, the warehouseman shall secure claims for damages of the person storing the goods and notify the person storing the goods without undue delay.

§ 471 Maintenance of the goods

(1) The warehouseman must permit the person storing the goods, during business hours, to inspect the goods, to take samples and to perform acts necessary for the maintenance of the goods. He is, however, entitled and in case of mixed deposit storage also obligated to perform the work necessary for the maintenance of the goods himself.

(2) If after acceptance changes of the goods have arisen or are to be feared which cause the loss of or the damage to the goods or damages of the warehouseman to be anticipated, the warehouseman shall without undue delay notify the person storing the goods, or where a warehouse receipt has been issued, the last legitimate holder of the receipt known to him, about the situation and ask for his instructions. If the warehouseman cannot obtain

ner Zeit Weisungen nicht erlangen, so hat er die angemessen erscheinenden Maßnahmen zu ergreifen. Er kann insbesondere das Gut gemäß § 373 verkaufen lassen; macht er von dieser Befugnis Gebrauch, so hat der Lagerhalter, wenn ein Lagerschein ausgestellt ist, die in § 373 Abs. 3 vorgesehene Androhung des Verkaufs sowie die in Absatz 5 derselben Vorschriften vorgesehenen Benachrichtigungen an den letzten ihm bekanntgewordenen legitimierten Besitzer des Lagerscheins zu richten.

instructions within a reasonable period of time, he shall take the measures which seem reasonable. He can especially have the goods sold according to § 373; if he makes use of this right, the warehouseman shall, if a warehouse receipt has been issued, direct the notice of the sale provided for in § 373 Subsection 3 as well as the notification provided for in Subsection 5 of the same provision to the last legitimate holder of the warehouse receipt known to him.

§ 472 Versicherung. Einlagerung bei einem Dritten

(1) Der Lagerhalter ist verpflichtet, das Gut auf Verlangen des Einlagerers zu versichern. Ist der Einlagerer ein Verbraucher, so hat ihn der Lagerhalter auf die Möglichkeit hinzuweisen, das Gut zu versichern.

(2) Der Lagerhalter ist nur berechtigt, das Gut bei einem Dritten einzulagern, wenn der Einlagerer ihm dies ausdrücklich gestattet hat.

§ 472 Insurance. Warehousing at a third Party

(1) The warehouseman is obligated to insure the goods upon request of the person storing the goods. Where the person storing the goods is a consumer, the warehouseman shall advise him about the possibility to insure the goods.

(2) The warehouseman is only entitled to warehouse the goods with a third party if the person storing the goods has expressly permitted him to do so.

§ 473 Dauer der Lagerung

(1) Der Einlagerer kann das Gut jederzeit herausverlangen. Ist der Lagervertrag auf unbestimmte Zeit geschlossen, so kann er den Vertrag jedoch nur unter Einhaltung einer Kündigungsfrist von einem Monat kündigen, es sei denn, es liegt ein wichtiger Grund vor, der zur Kündigung des Vertrags ohne Einhaltung der Kündigungsfrist berechtigt.

(2) Der Lagerhalter kann die Rücknahme des Gutes nach Ablauf der

§ 473 Duration of the warehousing

(1) The person storing the goods can demand delivery of the goods at any time. If the warehousing contract has been concluded for an indefinite period of time, he can terminate the contract only by observing a notice period of one month unless there is an important reason which would entitle to terminate the contract without observing the notice period.

(2) The warehouseman may demand that the goods be taken back upon ex-

vereinbarten Lagerzeit oder bei Einlagerung auf unbestimmte Zeit nach Kündigung des Vertrags unter Einhaltung einer Kündigungsfrist von einem Monat verlangen. Liegt ein wichtiger Grund vor, so kann der Lagerhalter auch vor Ablauf der Lagerzeit und ohne Einhaltung einer Kündigungsfrist die Rücknahme des Gutes verlangen.

(3) Ist ein Lagerschein ausgestellt, so sind die Kündigung und das Rücknahmeverlangen an den letzten dem Lagerhalter bekanntgewordenen legitimierten Besitzer des Lagerscheins zu richten.

§ 474 Aufwendungsersatz

Der Lagerhalter hat Anspruch auf Ersatz seiner für das Gut gemachten Aufwendungen, soweit er sie den Umständen nach für erforderlich halten durfte.

§ 475 Haftung für Verlust oder Beschädigung

Der Lagerhalter haftet für den Schaden, der durch Verlust oder Beschädigung des Gutes in der Zeit von der Übernahme zur Lagerung bis zur Auslieferung entsteht, es sei denn, daß der Schaden durch die Sorgfalt eines ordentlichen Kaufmanns nicht abgewendet werden konnte. Dies gilt auch dann, wenn der Lagerhalter gemäß § 472 Abs. 2 das Gut bei einem Dritten einlagert.

§ 475 a Verjährung

Auf die Verjährung von Ansprüchen aus einer Lagerung, die den Vorschrif-

piration of the storage period agreed upon, or in case of storage for an indefinite period of time, after the contract has been terminated by observing a notice period of one month. Where there is an important reason, the warehouseman can demand collection of the goods before the storage time has expired and without observing a notice period.

(3) If a warehouse receipt has been issued, the notice of termination and the demand to take back the goods are to be directed to the last legitimate holder of the warehouse receipt known to the warehouseman.

§ 474 Reimbursement of expenditures

The warehouseman is entitled to reimbursement of his expenditures made for the goods to the extent that he could deem them necessary according to the circumstances.

§ 475 Liability for loss or damage

The warehouseman is liable for the damage which arises from loss of or damage to the goods from the time they are accepted for warehousing until delivery unless the damage could not have been averted by the care of a prudent merchant. This also applies where the warehouseman warehouses the goods with a third party according to § 472 Subsection 2.

§ 475 a Statute of limitations

Section 439 applies analogously to the statute of limitations for claims aris-

Lagergeschäft	§§ 475a–c

ten dieses Abschnitts unterliegt, findet § 439 entsprechende Anwendung. Im Falle des gänzlichen Verlusts beginnt die Verjährung mit Ablauf des Tages, an dem der Lagerhalter dem Einlagerer oder, wenn ein Lagerschein ausgestellt ist, dem letzten ihm bekannt gewordenen legitimierten Besitzer des Lagerscheins den Verlust anzeigt.

§ 475 b Pfandrecht

(1) Der Lagerhalter hat wegen aller durch den Lagervertrag begründeten Forderungen sowie wegen unbestrittener Forderungen aus anderen mit dem Einlagerer abgeschlossenen Lager-, Fracht- und Speditionsverträgen ein Pfandrecht an dem Gut. Das Pfandrecht erstreckt sich auch auf die Forderung aus einer Versicherung sowie auf die Begleitpapiere.

(2) Ist ein Orderlagerschein durch Indossament übertragen worden, so besteht das Pfandrecht dem legitimierten Besitzer des Lagerscheins gegenüber nur wegen der Vergütungen und Aufwendungen, die aus dem Lagerschein ersichtlich sind oder ihm bei Erwerb des Lagerscheins bekannt oder infolge grober Fahrlässigkeit unbekannt waren.

(3) Das Pfandrecht besteht, solange der Lagerhalter das Gut in seinem Besitz hat, insbesondere solange er mittels Konnossements, Ladescheins oder Lagerscheins darüber verfügen kann.

§ 475 c Lagerschein

(1) Über die Verpflichtung zur Auslieferung des Gutes kann von dem Lagerhalter, nachdem er das Gut erhalten

ing from warehousing which is subject to the provisions of this Part. In case of total losses, the statute of limitations begins to run upon expiration of the day on which the warehouseman gives notice of loss to the person storing the goods or, where a warehouse receipt has been issued, the last legitimate holder of the warehouse receipt known to him.

§ 475 b Lien

(1) The warehouseman shall have a lien on the goods for all claims arising out of the warehousing contract as well as for undisputed claims arising out of other warehousing, freight and forwarding agent contracts concluded with the person storing the goods. The lien also extends to a claim out of an insurance contract and to the accompanying documents.

(2) Where a negotiable warehouse receipt has been transferred by endorsement, the lien exists towards the legitimate holder of the warehouse receipt only with respect to remuneration and expenditures which are obvious from the warehouse receipt or were known to him upon acquiring the warehouse receipt or were unknown as a result of gross negligence.

(3) The lien right exists as long as the warehouseman has the goods in his possession, especially as long as he can dispose of them by means of a bill of lading, an inland bill of lading or a warehouse receipt.

§ 475 c Warehouse receipt

(1) The warehouseman may issue a warehouse receipt pertaining to his obligation to deliver the goods after he

§§ 475c, d   Handelsgeschäfte

hat, ein Lagerschein ausgestellt werden, der die folgenden Angaben enthalten soll:

1. Ort und Tag der Ausstellung des Lagerscheins;
2. Name und Anschrift des Einlagerers;
3. Name und Anschrift des Lagerhalters;
4. Ort und Tag der Einlagerung;
5. die übliche Bezeichnung der Art des Gutes und die Art der Verpackung, bei gefährlichen Gütern ihre nach den Gefahrgutvorschriften vorgesehene, sonst ihre allgemein anerkannte Bezeichnung;
6. Anzahl, Zeichen und Nummern der Packstücke;
7. Rohgewicht oder die anders angegebene Menge des Gutes;
8. im Falle der Sammellagerung einen Vermerk hierüber.

(2) In den Lagerschein können weitere Angaben eingetragen werden, die der Lagerhalter für zweckmäßig hält.

(3) Der Lagerschein ist vom Lagerhalter zu unterzeichnen. Eine Nachbildung der eigenhändigen Unterschrift durch Druck oder Stempel genügt.

§ 475 d Wirkung des Lagerscheins

(1) Der Lagerschein ist für das Rechtsverhältnis zwischen dem Lagerhalter und dem legitimierten Besitzer des Lagerscheins maßgebend.

(2) Der Lagerschein begründet insbesondere die widerlegliche Vermutung, daß das Gut und seine Verpackung in bezug auf den äußerlichen Zustand sowie auf Anzahl, Zeichen und Num-

has received them; the warehouse receipt shall contain the following data:

1. place and day of issuance of the warehouse receipt;
2. name and address of the person storing the goods;
3. name and address of the warehouseman;
4. place and day of the warehousing;
5. the customary description of the type of goods and the type of packaging, in case of dangerous goods the description pursuant to the provisions relating to dangerous goods or otherwise the generally accepted description;
6. quantity, identifying marks and numbers of the packages;
7. gross weight or other designated quantity of the goods;
8. in case of mixed deposit storage a note thereto.

(2) Further data which the warehouseman considers to be useful can be entered in the warehouse receipt.

(3 The warehouse receipt shall be signed by the warehouseman. A facsimile of the signature by print or stamp is sufficient.

§ 475 d Effect of the warehouse receipt

(1) The warehouse receipt governs the legal relationship between the warehouseman and the legitimate holder of the warehouse receipt.

(2) The warehouse receipt especially establishes the rebuttable presumption that the goods and their packaging with respect to the external condition as well as the quantity, identify-

mern der Packstücke wie im Lagerschein beschrieben übernommen worden sind. Ist das Rohgewicht oder die anders angegebene Menge des Gutes oder der Inhalt vom Lagerhalter überprüft und das Ergebnis der Überprüfung in den Lagerschein eingetragen worden, so begründet dieser auch die widerlegliche Vermutung, daß Gewicht, Menge oder Inhalt mit den Angaben im Lagerschein übereinstimmt. Ist der Lagerschein einem gutgläubigen Dritten übertragen worden, so ist die Vermutung nach den Sätzen 1 und 2 unwiderleglich.

(3) Für das Rechtsverhältnis zwischen dem Lagerhalter und dem Einlagerer bleiben die Bestimmungen des Lagervertrages maßgebend.

§ 475 e Auslieferung gegen Rückgabe des Lagerscheins

(1) Ist ein Lagerschein ausgestellt, so ist der Lagerhalter zur Auslieferung des Gutes nur gegen Rückgabe des Lagerscheins, auf dem die Auslieferung bescheinigt ist, verpflichtet.

(2) Die Auslieferung eines Teils des Gutes erfolgt gegen Abschreibung auf dem Lagerschein. Der Abschreibungsvermerk ist vom Lagerhalter zu unterschreiben.

(3) Der Lagerhalter haftet dem rechtmäßigen Besitzer des Lagerscheins für den Schaden, der daraus entsteht, daß er das Gut ausgeliefert hat, ohne sich den Lagerschein zurückgeben zu lassen oder ohne einen Abschreibungsvermerk einzutragen.

ing marks and numbers of packages have been accepted as described in the warehouse receipt. If the gross weight or other designated quantity of the goods or the contents have been inspected by the warehouseman and the result of the inspection has been entered in the warehouse receipt, the warehouse receipt also establishes the rebuttable presumption that weight, quantity or contents are in conformity with the data in the warehouse receipt. Where the warehouse receipt has been transferred to a bona fide third party, the presumption pursuant to sentences 1 and 2 is irrebuttable.

(3) The provisions of the warehousing contract continue to govern the legal relationship between the warehouseman and the person storing the goods.

§ 475 e Delivery against return of the warehouse receipt

(1) Where a warehouse receipt has been issued, the warehouseman is obligated to deliver the goods only against return of the warehouse receipt on which the delivery has been acknowledged.

(2) The delivery of part of the goods is made against a corresponding entry on the warehouse receipt. The entry shall be signed by the warehouseman.

(3) The warehouseman is liable to the legitimate holder of the warehouse receipt for the damage which results from the fact that he has delivered the goods without having had the warehouse receipt returned to him or without having made an entry of partial delivery.

§ 475 f Legitimation durch Lagerschein

Zum Empfang des Gutes legitimiert ist derjenige, an den das Gut nach dem Lagerschein ausgeliefert werden soll oder auf den der Lagerschein, wenn er an Order lautet, durch Indossament übertragen ist. Der Lagerhalter ist nicht verpflichtet, die Echtheit der Indossamente zu prüfen.

§ 475 g Traditionsfunktion des Orderlagerscheins

Ist von dem Lagerhalter ein Lagerschein ausgestellt, der durch Indossament übertragen werden kann, so hat, wenn das Gut vom Lagerhalter übernommen ist, die Übergabe des Lagerscheins an denjenigen, den der Lagerschein zum Empfang des Gutes legitimiert, für den Erwerb von Rechten an dem Gut dieselben Wirkungen wie die Übergabe des Gutes.

§ 475 h Abweichende Vereinbarungen

Ist der Einlagerer ein Verbraucher, so kann nicht zu dessen Nachteil von den §§ 475 a und 475 e Abs. 3 abgewichen werden.

Fünftes Buch. Seehandel

§§ 476 bis 905 *(nicht abgedruckt)*

§ 475 f Proof of identity by means of the warehouse receipt

Anyone to whom the goods are to be delivered pursuant to the warehouse receipt or to whom the warehouse receipt, if it is negotiable, is transferred by endorsement is entitled to take delivery of the goods. The warehouseman is not obligated to check the authenticity of the endorsements.

§ 475 g Function of negotiable warehouse receipt

Where the warehouseman has issued a warehouse receipt which can be transferred by endorsement, the delivery of the warehouse receipt to someone whom the warehouse receipt authorizes to take delivery of the goods has, if the goods have been accepted by the warehouseman, the same effect as the delivery of the goods with respect to acquisition of rights in the goods.

§ 475 h Deviating agreements

Where the person storing the goods is a consumer, §§ 475 a and 475 e Subsection 3 cannot be deviated from to his detriment.

Book Five. Maritime Trade

§§ 476 to 905 *(not printed)*

Stichwortverzeichnis

Die Zahlen verweisen auf die Paragraphen.

Ablieferung an Empfänger 421
Abnahme
– Kauf 373
– Abschlußprüfer 316–324
Abschlußvertreter 55
Abschreibung 250, 253, 254, 279–282, 309
Abschriften vom Handelsregister 9
Abtretung einer Geldforderung 354a
Abweichende Vereinbarung 75d, 449, 451h, 452d, 466, 475h
Acht Tage als Zeit der Leistung 359
Angestellte 59, 83
– Handelsvertreter 84
– in Läden 56
Anhang 284
Anmeldung zur Eintragung ins Handelsregister
– Änderungen 13h, 31, 34, 107, 175
– Erteilung und Erlöschen der Prokura 53
– Firma 29, 157
– juristische Person 33 Abs. 2, 34
– Kommanditgesellschaft 162, 175
– Liquidatoren bei OHG 148
– offene Handelsgesellschaft 106–108, 143, 144 Abs. 2, 148, 157
– Nachweis der Rechtsnachfolge 12
– Zeichnung von Unterschriften 12
– Zweigniederlassungen 13, 13a, 13b, 13c, 13e, 13f, 13g
Annahmeverzug des Käufers 373, 374
Ansatzvorschriften für Jahresabschluß 252–256
Anschaffungs- und Herstellungskosten 255
Anteile anderer Gesellschafter 307
Antragspflicht 130a
Arbeitnehmer 83

Assoziierte Unternehmen 311, 312
Aufbewahrung
– beanstandeten Gutes 379, 391
– beschädigten Gutes 470, 471
– Proben 96
– Schriftstücke auf Bild- oder Datenträgern 8a
– kaufmännischer Unterlagen 257
– Unterschriften 12, 29, 35, 53, 108
Aufgebotsverfahren 365
Auflösung
– Bilanzrückstellungen 249
– OHG 131–144
Aufstellung
– Anteilsbesitz im Anhang 287
– Jahresabschluß 264
– Konzernabschluß, Konzernlagebericht 341i, 341j
Aufwands- und Ertragskonsolidierung 305
Aufwendungen
– Ersatz bei Handelsvertretern 87d, 88a
– Gesellschafter der OHG 110
– für die Ingangsetzung und Erweiterung des Geschäftsbetriebs 269
– Kommissionär 396 Abs. 2
– Lagerhalter 474
Ausführungsanzeige und Selbsteintritt des Kommissionärs 405
Ausgleichsanspruch des Handelsvertreters 89b
Auskunftsrecht des Pflichtprüfers bei Jahresabschluß 320
Ausscheiden eines Gesellschafters 139 Abs. 2, 160
Ausschließung eines Gesellschafters 140

Stichwortverzeichnis

Beförderungs- und
  Ablieferungshindernisse 419
Befreiende Konzernabschlüsse und
  Konzernlageberichte 291, 292
Befriedigung
– aus dem Gute 398
– aus Forderungen 399
– Kommissionär 396
– Pfandgläubiger 356
– Privatgläubiger eines
  Gesellschafters 135
– bei Zurückbehaltungsrecht 371,
  372
Befriedigungsrecht des Gläubigers 371
Begleitpapiere
– beim Frachtgeschäft 408, 413
– beim Speditionsgeschäft 455
– beim Lagergeschäft 468
Bekanntmachung der
  Handelsregistereintragungen 10,15
Beschlußfassung der OHG 119
Besichtigung des Lagerguts 471
Bestätigungsvermerk des
  Abschlußprüfers 322
Bestellung
– Abschlußprüfer 318
– Bevollmächtigter 54
– Liquidatoren 146
– Prokurist 48
Bestimmungskauf,
  handelsrechtlicher 375
Beteiligung an anderen Unternehmen
  271
Bewertung von
  Vermögensgegenständen 340e, 341b
Bewertungsvereinfachungsverfahren
  256
Bewertungsvorschriften 252–256,
  279–283, 308, 341b
Bezeichnung der Amtsblätter 11
Bezugsrechte 285 Nr. 9, 314 Abs. 1
  Nr. 6
Bilanz 266–274, 337
– Angabe der Haftungsverhältnisse
  251

– Anhang 284–288, 338
– Aufwands- und
  Ertragskonsolidierung 305
– Bewertungsgrundsätze 252–256
– Bewertungsvorschriften 252,
  279–283
– eingetragene Genossenschaft 337
– Gliederung 265, 266
– Inhalt 247
– bei Liquidation 154
– Rückstellungen 249
– Schuldenkonsolidierung 303
– Steuerabgrenzung 274, 306
– Stille Gesellschaft 233
– Umschreibung der Größenklassen
  267
Bilanzierungsverbote 248
Bilanzvermerke 268
Buchführung
– Inventurvereinfachungsverfahren
  241
– Pflicht zur 238
Bürgschaft, handelsrechtliche 350
Bußgeldvorschriften 334, 340n, 341n

Darlehen
– Rückgewähr bei KG 172a
– Rückgewähr bei OHG 129a
Dauer der Lagerung 473
DDR, ehemalige 62, 64, 73, 83,
  jeweils Fn. 1
Deckungsgeschäft 401
Delkredere 86b, 394
Delkredereprovision 86b, 394 Abs. 2

Eigenkapital 272
– Bilanz 266
– Wertansatz 283
Eigentumsfiktion bei
  Befriedigungsrecht 372
Eigentumserwerb 124, 366, 419
Einheitliche Bewertung 308
Einrede der Vorausklage 349
Einreden aus Handelsgeschäften 349
Einseitige Handelsgeschäfte 345

388

Stichwortverzeichnis

Einstweilige Aufbewahrung von Ware 379
Eintritt
- bestehende Handelsgesellschaft 24, 130
- Geschäft eines Einzelkaufmanns 28
- von Kommanditisten 173
- vor Eintragung 176 Abs. 2
Einwendungen des Gesellschafters gegen Verbindlichkeiten der Gesellschaft 129
Empfänger des Gutes 470
Empfänger, Rechte des 421
Entfernungen, vertragsmäßige 361
Entnahmen aus Gesellschaftskasse 122
Entschädigung für Gehilfen bei Wettbewerbsverbot 74
Entscheidung des Prozeßgerichts über Handelsregistereintragung 16
Entziehung
- Geschäftsführungsbefugnis 117
- Vertretungsmacht 127
Erben
- Fortführung der Gesellschaft 139
- Fortsetzung der Firma 21–25, 24 Abs. 2
- Liquidation 146, 148
- Recht zur Einsicht der Bücher 157 Abs. 3
Erhaltung des Gutes 471
Eröffnungsbilanz 242–256
Errichtung der Gesellschaft 105–108, 123, 161
EU-Richtlinien über befreiende Abschlüsse 291, 292

Fälligkeit der Provision 87a
- der Vergütung für den Spediteur 456
Fälligkeitszinsen 353
Firma
- Änderung 31
- Anmeldung zum Handelsregister 29

- Ausscheiden bzw. Eintritt eines Gesellschafters 24
- Begriff 17, 18
- Einzelkaufmann 19
- bei Erwerb des Handelsgeschäfts 22
- Fortführung 22, 24
- Fortführung bei Namensänderung 21
- juristische Person 33–36
- Kommanditgesellschaft 19 Abs. 2, 161, 173
- OHG 19, 24, 105–108, 124, 130
- Stille Gesellschaft 18
- Unterscheidbarkeit 30
- Unzulässiger Firmengebrauch 37
- Veräußerung 23
- Zusatz Zweigniederlassung 13
Fixhandelskauf 376
Forderungen
- aus Handelsgeschäften 353, 369–371
- aus Kommissionsgeschäften 392, 397, 399
- gesicherte durch Pfand 356
Formfreiheit bei Handelsgeschäften 350
Formkaufmann 6
Fortführung der Firma
- bei Änderungen im Gesellschafterbestand 24
- bei Erwerb des Handelsgeschäfts 22
- bei Namensänderung 21
Fortsetzung
- der OHG 134, 139, 144
- der KG 177
Frachtberechnung 420
Frachtbrief 408, 409, 451b
Frachtführer
- ausführender 437
- nachfolgender 442
Frachtgeschäft 407–452d
Frachtvertrag 407
Fristlose Kündigung des Handelsvertreters 89a
Fürsorgepflicht des Arbeitgebers 62

389

Gattungsschuld 360
Gattungsware 94, 96, 360
Gefährliches Gut 410, 451b
Gehalt des Handlungsgehilfen 59, 64
Gehaltszahlung 64
Geheimhaltungspflicht 333
Genehmigung
– bei Kommissionsgeschäft 386
– der Ware 377 Abs. 2
Genossenschaft 336–339
Gerichtsstand 440
Gesamtprokura 48, 53
Gesamtschuldner, Haftung 128, 356 Abs. 2
Gesamtvertretung der Gesellschaft 125 Abs. 2 u. 4
Geschäfts- und Betriebsgeheimnisse 90
Geschäftsbriefe 37a, 125a, 177a
Geschäftsbücher 157
Geschäftsführung
– Handlungsbevollmächtigter 54
– Kommanditgesellschaft 164
– OHG 110, 114–118, 148–152
– Prokurist 49
Gesellschaft auf Lebenszeit 134
Gesellschaftsvermögen 124 Abs. 2, 131 Abs. 3, 143–145, 149, 155, 158, 171 Abs. 3
Gesellschaftsvertrag
– Kommanditgesellschaft 163
– OHG 109, 114 Abs. 2, 115 Abs. 2, 119 Abs. 2, 125 Abs. 2, 3, 133 Abs. 2, 146
– Stille Gesellschaft 231
Gesetzlicher Zinssatz 352
Gesetzliches
– Pfandrecht 397, 404, 441–443, 464–466, 475b
– Wettbewerbsverbot 60
Gewinn und Verlust, Verteilung 121, 167, 168, 231
Gewinn- und Verlustrechnung 275–278, 284–288, 305, 340c
Gewinnauszahlung 169

Gewinnvortrag 264c, 266 Abs. 3, 268
Größenklassen 267
Größenabhängige Erleichterung 274a, 276, 288, 293, 326, 327
Gutgläubiger Erwerb 366, 367

Haftung
– Absender 451c
– eintretenden Gesellschafters 28
– des Erben 27
– des Erwerbers 25
– Frachtführer 414, 428–438, 451d–451h
– Geschäftsnachfolger 25–27
– Gesellschaft 110
– Gesellschafter 128–130, 159, 161
– Handelsmakler 98
– Handlungen vor Eintragung 176
– Kommanditist 171–173, 176
– Kommissionär 384–386, 390
– Lagerhalter 475
– Pflichtverletzung des Abschlußprüfers 323
– Spediteur 461–462
– Übernahme einer Firma 25–28
Haftungsverhältnisse, Angabe in der Bilanz 251, 268
Handelsbräuche 346
Handelsbücher 238–339
– Anhang 284–288
Handelsfirma 17–37
Handelsgeschäfte 343–372
Handelsgesellschaften als Kaufleute 6
Handelskauf 373–382
Handelsmakler 93–104
Handelsregister 2, 5, 8–16, 25 Abs. 2, 26 Abs. 2, 28 Abs. 3, 32, 53, 106–108, 143, 148, 157, 162, 175, 325, 329
– Abruf von Daten 9a
Handelsvertreter 65, 84–92c
Handlungsgehilfe 59–83
Handlungslehrling 59–83
Handlungsvollmacht 54–58
Hauptniederlassung im Ausland 13d

Stichwortverzeichnis

Herabsetzung der Einlage des
    Kommanditisten 174
Hinterlegung 373, 389

Indossament 363–365, 395
Inkassovollmacht 97
Insolvenzverfahren
– Eintragung in Handelsregister 32
– Inhaber 236
– Kommanditgesellschaft 171 Abs. 2,
    177a
– OHG 130a, 130b, 131 Abs. 1 Nr. 3,
    143–146
– Vermögen des Gesellschafters 236
Inventar, Erstellung 240, 241
Inventurvereinfachungsverfahren 241
Istkaufmann 1

Jahresabschluß 242–256, 340a–340d
– Gliederung 265
– Kapitalgesellschaft 264–288
– Offenlegung 325, 328, 340l
– Pflicht zur Aufstellung 264, 340i
– Stichtag 299
– Vollständigkeit 246
– Wahl des Abschlußprüfers 319
– Juristische Person 33–35
Jahresüberschuß/Jahresfehlbetrag
    264c, 266 Abs. 3, 268

Kannkaufmann 2, 3, 5
Kapitalanteile 264c
Kapitalgesellschaft
– Bewertungsvorschriften 279–283
– größenabhängige Erleichterung bei
    Offenlegung 326, 327
– Größenklassen 267
– Handelsbücher 264–335
– Jahresabschluß, Lagebericht
    264–288
– Konzernlagebericht 315
– Lagebericht 289
– Prüfung 316–324
– unrichtige Darstellung 331

Kapitalkonsolidierung 301, 302
Kaufleute 1–7
Kaufmann kraft Eintragung 5
Kaufmännische Orderpapiere 363
Kaufmännisches
    Zurückbehaltungsrecht 369
Kommanditgesellschaft 161–177a,
    264a, 264c
Kommissionär 383
Kommissionsgeschäft 383–405
Kommissionsgut, beschädigtes oder
    mangelhaftes 388
Kommittent 385
Kommittenten, Weisungen des 385
Komplementärgesellschaft 264c
    Abs. 3,4
Konossement 363 Abs. 2, 369, 397,
    410, 421
Konsolidierung, anteilsmäßige 310
Konsolidierungsgrundsätze 300
Konsolidierungskreis 294–296
Kontokorrent 355–357
Kontrollrecht
– Gesellschafter der OHG 118
– Kommanditisten 166
– Stille Gesellschafter 233
Konzern
– Anhang 296, 308, 313
– Aufwands- und
    Ertragskonsolidierung 305
– Bilanzerläuterung 313
– Gewinn- und Verlustrechnung 305,
    312, 313
Konzernabschluß 264b, 271, 290–314,
    325, 328, 340i, 340j, 341i
– befreiende Wirkung von EU/EU-
    Konzernabschlüssen 291, 292,
    292a
Konzernlagebericht 315, 340i, 340j
– befreiender 291, 292, 292a
Krämermakler 104
Kredit, Gewährung durch
    Kommissionär 393
Kreditinstitute 340–340o

Stichwortverzeichnis

Kündigung
- Frachtgeschäft 415
- Gesellschaft 131 Abs. 3, Nr. 3 u. 4, 132, 234
- Kontokorrent 355 Abs. 3
- Privatgläubiger 135
- Prüfungsauftrag 318
- Stille Gesellschaft 234
- Vertrag mit Handelsvertreter 89, 89a

Ladeschein 444–448
Lagebericht der Kapitalgesellschaft 264, 265, 289, 340a–340d
Lager-
- -geld 354
- -geschäft 467–475h
- -schein 475c–475h
- -vertrag 467
Land- und Forstwirtschaft, Betrieb 3
Laufende Rechnung 355–357
Legitimation zum Empfang des Gutes 446, 475f
Lieferfrist 423
Liquidation der Gesellschaft 145–158
Lohnanspruch des Maklers 99
Löschung einer Firma 3 Abs. 2, 31 Abs. 2

Mangel der Vertretungsmacht 91a
Maß, Gewicht, Währung 361
Meinungsverschiedenheiten zwischen Kapitalgesellschaft und Abschlußprüfer 324
Mindestarbeitsbedingungen, Festsetzung durch Rechtsverordnung 92a
Mußkaufmann 1
Mutterunternehmen 271, 290–314

Nachnahme 422
Nachträgliche Weisungen (Frachtgeschäft) 418
Nachweis der Rechtsnachfolge 12

Nichteinhaltung der Ladezeit 417
Notverkauf 379, 391

Öffentliches Recht 7
Offene Handelsgesellschaft 105–160, 264a, 264c
Offenlegung 325, 339, 340l, 341e
Offenlegung, Größenabhängige Erleichterungen 326, 327
Orderpapiere 363
Ordnungsgeld 335a, 335b, 341o, 341p
- wegen unbefugter Firmenführung 37
Ordnungswidrigkeiten 103, 334

Pensionsfonds 330 Abs. 5, 341m, 341n, 341o, 341p
Pensionsgeschäfte 340b
Persönliche Haftung der Gesellschafter 128, 161, 164
Pfändung
- Gesellschaftsanteil 135
- Saldo 357
Pfandrecht
- Frachtführer 441–443
- Kommissionär 366 Abs. 3, 368, 397, 404, 443
- Lagerhalter 475b
- Spediteur 464–466
Pfandverkauf 368
Pflichtangaben im Anhang 285, 314
Preisgrenzen beim Kommissionsgeschäft 386
Privates Rechnungslegungsgremium 342
Privatvermögen 264c Abs. 3
Prokura 48–53, 116 Abs. 3, 126
Provision 65, 74b Abs. 2, 87–87c, 354, 396, 403
Prüfung
- von Kapitalgesellschaften 316–324
- von Kreditinstituten 340k
- von Versicherungsunternehmen 341k

Prüfungspflicht des Registergerichts 329
Publizität des Handelsregisters 15

Rang mehrerer Pfandrechte 443
Rechnungsabgrenzungsposten in der Bilanz 250, 266
Rechnungslegungsbeirat 342a
Rechtliche Selbständigkeit der OHG 124
Rechtskraftwirkung bei Befriedigungsrecht des Gläubigers 372
Rechtsverordnungsermächtigung für befreiende Konzernabschlüsse 292
Registergericht 8–14, 329
Rücklagen 264c
Rückstellungen
– Bilanz 249, 266
– Pflichtangabe im Anhang 285
– noch nicht abgewickelte Versicherungsfälle 341g

Sammelladung 460
Sammellagerung 469
Schadensanzeige 438, 452b
Schadensort 452a
Schiffahrtsvertreter 92c
Schlußnote des Handelsmaklers 94, 95, 102
Schuldanerkenntnis, handelsrechtliches 350
Schuldenkonsolidierung 303
Schuldscheine, kaufmännische 344 Abs. 2
Schweigen des Kaufmanns 362
Seefrachtrecht, Anwendung von 450
Selbsteintritt
– Kommissionär 400–405
– Spediteur 458
Selbsthilfekauf 373, 389
Sicherheiten für Forderung 356
Sonderposten
– Allgemeine Bankrisiken 340g
– Rücklageanteil 273

Sorgfaltspflicht 86, 347, 384, 390
Spediteur, nachfolgender 465
Speditionsgeschäft 453–466
Speditionsvertrag 453
Sperrabrede unter Arbeitgebern 75f
Sprache bei Jahresabschluß 244
Steuer, in Gewinn- und Verlustrechnung 278
Steuerabgrenzung 274, 306
Steuerrechtliche Abschreibung 254, 281
Stille Gesellschaft 230–236
Straf- und Bußgeldvorschriften 130b, 331–335, 340m–340o, 341m–341o
Stundung des Kaufpreises 393

Tagebuch des Handelsmaklers 100, 101, 102
Taragewicht 380
Teilbeförderung 416
Tochterunternehmen 271, 290, 294, 295, 296
Tod
– Gesellschafter 131 Abs. 3 Nr. 1, 139, 143 Abs. 3, 148, 234
– Inhaber eines Handelsgeschäfts 52 Abs. 3
– Kommanditist 177
– Stiller Gesellschafter 234

Überschreitung der Lieferfrist 425, 426, 427, 431, 433
Überschuldung
– Eintragung in Handelsregister 32
– Kommanditgesellschaft 177a
– OHG 130a, 130b
Umlaufvermögen
– in Bilanz 266
– Wertansatz 253
Umzugsgut 451, 451a, 452c, 452d
Unterlassen von Angaben 286
Unternehmen
– assoziierte 311, 312
– verbundene 271

393

Unterschrift 12–14, 17, 101, 108, 153, 245, 321
Unterschriftszeichnung 29, 35, 53, 108
Untersuchungs- und Rügepflicht 377, 378, 391
Unterzeichnung des Jahresabschlusses 245

Verbote der Einbeziehung in Konzernabschluß 295
Verbundene Unternehmen 271
Verfügungsrecht über Frachtgut 418
Vergleichsverfahren 130a, 130b, 177a
Verjährung 26, 61, 88, 113, 139 Abs. 3, 159, 160, 323, 439, 452b, 463, 475a
Verladen + Entladen 412
Verletzung
– Berichtspflicht 332
– Geheimhaltungspflicht 333
– Wettbewerbsverbot 61, 113
Verlustvermutung 424
Verlustvortrag 264c, 266 Abs. 3, 268
Vermittlungsgehilfe 75g
Vermutung
– Handelsgeschäft 344
– Handelsregister 15
Verpackung, Kennzeichnung 411
Verordnungsermächtigung für Formblätter 330
Verrechnungsverbot im Jahresabschluß 246
Verschiedenartige Beförderungsmittel 452
Versender, Forderungen des 457
Versicherung (im Frachtgeschäft) 472
Versicherungs- und Bausparkassenvertreter 92
Versicherungsunternehmen 341–342
Versicherungstechnische Rückstellungen 341e–341h
Verteilung von Gesellschaftsvermögen 155
Vertragsstrafe 75c, 348

Vertretung
– Gesellschaft 75h, 125–127, 149, 170
– Handelsvertreter des 91, 91a
– juristische Person 33
Vertretungsmacht der Gesellschafter 106, 107
Verzinsungspflicht von Gesellschaftereinlage 111
Viehmängel 382
Vollkonsolidierung 300–307
Vorbehalt landesrechtlicher Vorschriften 263
Vorlagepflicht gegenüber Abschlußprüfer 320
Vorlegung von Handelsbüchern im Rechtsstreit 258–261
Vorschuß bei Kommissionsgeschäft 354 Abs. 2, 393, 397, 443 Abs. 2
Vorteilhafter Abschluß (Kommissionsgeschäft) 387

Währung bei Vertragserfüllung 361
Währungs-
– -einheit bei Jahresabschluß 244
– -umrechnung bei Anlagevermögen 340h
Wechselindossament 395
Wertansatz
– Anlagevermögen in der Bilanz 253
– Anteile an Tochterunternehmen 301
– Beteiligung und Behandlung des Unterschiedsbetrags 312
– Eigenkapital 283
– Vermögensgegenstände und Schulden 253
– Vorschriften 308–309
Wertaufholungsgebot 280
Wertpapier, Kauf 381
Wettbewerbsabrede 90a
Wettbewerbsverbot 60–75d, 61, 74, 74a–75d, 82a, 112, 113, 165
Widerruf
– Kommission 405
– Prokura 52, 116 Abs. 3, 126

Wirksamkeit der OHG im Verhältnis zu Dritten 123

Zahlung, Frachtberechnung 420
Zahlungspflicht des Empfängers 421
Zahlungsunfähigkeit
- Kommanditgesellschaft 177a
- OHG 130a, 130b
Zeichnung
- Handlungsbevollmächtigter 57
- Prokurist 51, 53
- Unterschriften 12
Zeit der Leistung 358, 361

Zeitliche Begrenzung der Haftung gegen Gesellschafter 159
Zeugnis 73
Zinsen 352–355, 357
Zurückbehaltungsrecht,
- Handelsvertreter 88a
- Kaufmann 369
Zwangsgeld 14, 335, 335b, 340o, 341o, 341p
Zwangsvollstreckung in Gesellschaftsvermögen 124
Zweigniederlassungen 13–13h, 15, 30, 50, 325a

Index

Numbered references are to sections and subsections.

Acceptance
- Goods in Warehousing Business 470
- Sale 373

Accompanying Documents
- in Carrier Business 408, 413
- in the Forwarding Business 455
- in the Warehousing Business 468

Accounting Board 342a

Accounting Panel 342
- in the Forwarding Business 455
- in the Warehousing Business 468

Accruals
- Balance Sheet 249, 266
- Insurance Cases not yet Settled 341g
- Mandatory Disclosures in the Notes 285

Accrued and Deferred Items in the Balance Sheet 250, 266

Acting Carrier 437

Actuarial Reserves 341e–341h

Administrative Violations 103, 334

Advance in Transactions on Commission Basis 354(2), 393, 397, 443(2)

Agent Authorised to Transact Business 55

Agreed Time for Performance; „Eight Days" 359

Agreement Prohibiting Competition 90a

Agriculture and Forestry, Enterprises 3

Amortisation 250, 253, 254, 279–282, 309

Annual Deficit 264c, 266(3), 268, 275

Annual Financial Statements 242–256, 340a–340d
- Choice of the Auditor 319
- Classification 265

- Closing Day 299
- Completeness 246
- Corporation 264–288
- Disclosure 325, 328, 340l
- Duty of Preparation 264, 340i
- Juridical Person 33–35
- Signing of 245

Annual Surplus 264c, 266(3), 268, 275

Appointment
- Auditor 318
- Holder of Commercial Power of Attorney 54
- Liquidators 146
- Prokura Holder 48

Apprentices 59ff.

Approval
- of Goods 377(2)
- of Transactions on a Commission Basis 386

Associated Enterprises 311, 312

Audit
- of Companies 316–324
- of Financial Institutions 340k
- of Insurance Companies 341k

Auditor 316–324

Authority
- of the Commercial Agent 91
- of the General Partner 114, 116, 126, 127
- of the Liquidator 151
- of the Limited Partner 170
- to represent 106, 107

Balance Sheet 266–274, 337
- Accruals 249
- Classification 265, 266
- Contents 247
- Contingencies and Commitments 251

Index

- Debt 303
- Definition of Class Sizes 267
- Expenses and Revenues 305
- General Principles of Valuation 252–256
- Notes 284–288, 338
- Registered Cooperative Associations 337
- Silent Partnership 233
- Tax Deferrals 274, 306
- Valuation Regulations 252, 279–283

Balance Sheet Notations 268
Bill of Exchange Indorsement 395
Bills of Lading 363(2), 369, 397, 410, 421, 444, 445–448
Bookkeeping
- Duty of 238
- Procedures for Simplifying the Keeping of Inventory 241

Branches of Corporations 13–13h, 15, 30, 50, 325a
Bulk Forwarding 460
Business Letters 37a, 125a, 177a
Business Operation by Voluntary Registration 2, 3, 5
Business Partnership 264a, 264c
Business Records 157
Buying and Selling Price Limitations in Transactions on a Commission Basis 386

Cancellation Proceedings by Public Advertisement 365
Capital Consolidation 301, 302
Capital Shares 264c
Carrier 414, 428–438, 451d–451h
Carrier Business 407–452d
Cash Due on Delivery 422
Cash Sale Coupled with a Contract for Subsequent Repurchase 340b
Certification of the Financial Statements by the Auditor 322
Civil Penalty Provisions 334, 340n, 341n

Claims
- Carrier Business 417–421
- Out of Commercial Transactions 353, 369-371
- Forwarding Business 456
- Secured by Pledge 356
- Transactions on a Commission Basis 392, 397, 399

Clerical Apprentices 59–83
Clerical Employee Capable of Soliciting for the Principal 75g
Clerical Employees 59–83
Close-out Agreements 75f
Coercive Fine 14, 335, 335b, 340o, 341o, 341p
- in Case of Improper Use of a Firm Name 37

Collection Authorisation 97
Commercial Agent 65, 84–92c
Commercial Broker 93–104
Commercial Companies and Partnerships-Merchant by Form of Organisation 6
Commercial Firm Name 17–37
Commercial Negotiable Instruments 363
Commercial Partnerships 264a, 264c
Commercial Power-of-Attorney 54–58
Commercial Practices 346
Commercial Records 238–339
- Notes 284–288
Commercial Records, Production
- In Litigation 258–261
Commercial Register 2, 5, 8–16, 25(2), 26(1), 28 III, 32, 53, 106–108, 143, 148, 157, 162, 175, 325, 329
Commercial Sale of Goods 373–382
Commercial Transactions 343–372
Commission 65, 74(2), 87–87c, 354, 396, 403
Commission Agent 383
Compensation Claim of the Agent 89b

Compensation for the Clerical
Employee because of Prohibition of
Competition 74 et seq.
Compensation Right of the
Commercial Broker 99
Consignee, Delivery to 421
Consignee's Rights and Obligation to
Pay 421
Consolidated Financial Statements
264b
Consolidated Group 294–296
– Capital Consolidation 301 et seq.
– Consolidation of Expenses and
Revenues 305
– Discussion of the Balance Sheet
313
– Financial Statements 271,
290–314, 325, 328, 340i, 340j, 341i
– Management Report 315
– Notes 296, 308, 313
– Profit and Loss Statement 305, 312,
313
– Proportionate 310
Consolidated Management Report
315, 340i, 340j
– Exemptive 291, 292, 292a
Consolidation of Expenses and
Revenues 305
Contingencies and Commitments,
Notation in the Balance Sheet 251,
268
Continuation of the Firm Name
– Change of Name 21
– Changes within the Partnership 24
– Firm Name in the Event of
Acquisition of the Business 22
Continuation of the General
Commercial Partnership 134, 139,
144
Contract Penalty 75c, 348
Contractual Prohibition of
Competition 74 et seq., 90a
Cooperative Association 336–339
Copies of the Commercial Register 9

Corporation
– Annual Financial Statements,
Management Report 264–288
– Audit 316–324
– Class Sizes 267
– Commercial Records 264–335
– Consolidated Management Report
315
– False Presentation 331
– Management Report 289
– Regulations as to Valuation
279–283
– Size-Related Relief for Disclosures
326, 327
Costs of Acquisition and Production
255
Court of the Commercial Register
8–14, 329
Covering Transactions 401
Credit given by Commission Agent
393
Credit Institutions 340–340o
Criminal Law and Civil Penalty
Provisions 130b, 331–335,
340m–340o, 341m–341o
Currency in the Annual Financial
Statements 244
Currency Conversion in the Capital
Assets 340h
Currency in Fulfilling Contract 361
Current Account 355–357
Current Assets
– in the Balance Sheet 266
– Valuation 253

Damaged or Defective Goods 388
Dangerous Goods 410, 451b
Death
– Business Owner 52(3)
– Limited Partner 177
– Partner 131(3), 139, 143(3), 148, 234
– Silent Partner 234
Debt Acknowledgement,
Commercial 350

Debt Consolidation 303
Default in Acceptance by the Buyer 373, 374
Defense out of Commercial Transactions 349
Defense to Execution on the Debtor 349
Defenses of the Partner against Obligations of the Partnership 129
Del credere 394
Del credere Commission 86b, 394(2)
Delivery 423
Deposit 373, 389
Depreciation under Tax Law 254, 281
Designation of Official Newspapers 11
Deviating Agreement 75d, 449, 451h, 452d, 466, 475h
Different Means of Transportation 452
Differences of Opinion between Corporation and Auditor 324
Disclosure 285 et seq., 314, 325, 339, 340l, 341l
Disclosures
– Mandatory in Notes 285, 314
– Omission 286
Dissolution
– Balance Sheet Accruals 249
– General Partnership 131–144
Distance agreed upon 361
Distribution of Partnership Assets 155
Documents accompanying Goods 413
Due Date of the Commission 87a
Due Date of Remuneration 456
Duty of Confidentiality 333
Duty of Care 86, 347, 384, 390
Duty to Examine and Object to Defects 377, 378, 391
Duty of Presentation to the Auditor 320
Duty to File a Petition 130a

EU-Guidelines on Exemptive Financial Statements 291, 292
Effectiveness of the General Partnership with Respect to Third Parties 123
Effect of Final Judgement Pertaining to the Right to Satisfaction of the Creditor 372
"Eight Days" as Time for Performance 359
Employees 59 et seq., 83
– Agent 84
– in Stores 56
– other 83
Employer's Duty to Provide for the Welfare of the Employees 62
Enabling Rule for Printed Forms 330
Enabling Rule for the Exemptive Consolidated Financial Statements 292
Enterprises
– Associated 311, 312
– Related 271
Equity Capital 272
– Balance Sheet 266
– Valuation 283
Establishment of the Partnership 105–108, 123, 161
Examination Duty of the Court of the Commercial Register 329
Exceeding the Term for Delivery 425, 426, 427, 431, 433
Exclusion of a Partner 140
Execution
– Account Balance 357
– Partner's Share 135
Execution on Partnership Assets 124
Exemptive Consolidated Financial Statements and Consolidated Management Reports 291, 292
Expenditures
– Commission Agent 396(2)
– Partner of the General Partnership 110

Index

- Reimbursement of Agent 87d, 88a
- Starting up and Expanding the Business 269
- Warehouseman 474

External Call for Commercial Register Data 9a

Fictive Ownership pertaining to the Right to Satisfaction 372

Filing for Registration with Commercial Register
- Branches 13, 13a, 13b, 13c, 13e, 13f, 13g
- Changes 13h, 31, 34, 107, 175
- Conferral and Termination of the Prokura 53
- Juridical Person 33(2), 34
- Firm Name 29, 157
- General Commercial Partnership 106–108, 143, 144(2), 148, 157
- Limited Partnership 162, 175
- Liquidators of the General Commercial Partnership 148
- Proof of Legal Succession 12
- Rider 13a
- Specimen Signatures 12

Financial Service Institutions 340–340 o

Firm Name
- Acquisition of the Business 22, 24
- Addendum to branch company name 13
- Change of Name 21
- Continuation in event of Name Change 21
- Definition 17,18
- Distinctiveness 30
- General Partnership 19, 24, 105–108, 124, 130
- Juridical Person 33–35
- Limited Partnership 19(2), 161, 173
- Registration in the Commercial Register 29
- Silent Partnership 18
- Sole Proprietor 17, 18, 19

- Termination 3(2), 31(2)
- Transfer 23
- Withdrawal or Joining of a Partner 24
- Improper use 37

Forced Sale 379, 391
Forwarding Agent, Subsequent 465
Forwarding Agreement 453
Forwarding Business 453 et seq.
Freedom from Requirements as to Form in Commercial Transactions 350
Freight Agreement 407
Freight Charges 420
Full Consolidation 300–307
G.D.R., former 62, 64, 73, 83, each in footnote 1
General Agency 48–53
General Commercial Partnership 105–160
General Partners 264c(3), (4)
Good faith acquisition 366, 367
Grace Period for Payment 393
Guaranty from the Point of View of Commercial Law 350

Handling the Shipment 454
Head Office or Domicile, Foreign 13d
Heirs
- Continuation of the Firm Name 22, 24(2)
- Continuation of the Partnership 139
- Liquidation 146, 148
- Right to Inspect the Books 157(3)

Hindrances to Shipment and Delivery 419

Inability to Meet Obligations
- General Partnership 130a, 130b
- Limited Partnership 177a

Identified Place Where Damage Occurred 452a
Indorsement 363–365, 395
Informationen Business Letters 37a

401

Insolvency
- Business Owner 236
- General Partnership 130a, 130b, 131(1), 143–146
- Limited Partnership 171(2), 177a
- Partner's Assets 236
- Registration in the Commercial Register 32
Insolvency Proceedings 130a, 130b, 177a
Inspection of Storage Goods 471
Inspection Right
- of the Commercial Register 9
- Limited Partners 166
- Partners of the General Partnership 118
- Silent Partners 233
Instructions of the principal 385
Insurance (in Freight Business) 472
Insurance and Building and Loan Association Agents 92
Insurance Companies 341–342
Interest 352–355, 357
Interest from the Date Due 353
Intermediate Forwarding Agent 408, 411
Inventory, Preparation 240, 241

Joining
- as Limited Partner before Registration 176 (2)
- Existing General Partnership 24, 130
- Limited Partners 173
- Sole Proprietorship 28
Joint and Several Debtor, Liability 128, 356(2)
Joint Prokura 48, 53
Joint Representation of the Partnership 125(2), (4)
Judicial Decision Registration in the Commercial Register 16
Juridical Person 33-36

Lack of Authority 91a
Language, Currency 244
Legal Personality of the General Partnership 124
Liability
- Auditor in case of Breach of Duty 323
- Business prior to Registration 176
- Carrier 414, 428–438, 451d–451h
- Commercial Broker 98
- Commission Agent 384–386, 390
- Continuation of the Firm Name 25–28
- Forwarding Agent 461–462
- Heirs on Continuation 27
- Joining Partner 28
- Limited Partner 171, 173, 176
- Partner 128–130, 159, 161
- Partnership 110
- Purchaser on Continuation 25–27
- Shipper 414, 451c–451h
- Warehouseman 475
Lien
- Commission Agent 366(3), 368, 397, 404, 443
- Forwarding Agent 464–466
- Freight Carrier 441–443
- Warehouseman 475b
Limited Partnership 161–177a, 264a, 264c
Liquidation of the Partnership 145–158
Livestock, Defects in 382
Loading, Unloading 412
Loans
- Repayment by General Partnership 129a
- Repayment by Limited Partnership 172a
Loss, Presumption of 424
Losses Carried Forward 264c, 266(3), 268

Index

Maintenance of Goods 471
Management of the Business
- General Partnership 110, 114–118, 148–152
- Holder of Commercial Power-of-Attorney 54
- Limited Partnership 164
- Prokura Holder 49

Management Report of the Corporation 264, 265, 289, 340a–340d
Maritime Shipping Law 450
Measure, Weight, Currency 361
Memorandum of Sale of the Commercial Broker 94, 95, 102
Merchandise 94, 96, 360
Merchant 1–7
Merchant by Form of Organisation 6
Merchant by Legal Definition 1
Merchant by Registration 2, 3, 5
Merchant by Voluntary Registration 5
Merchant's Right of Retention 369
Minimum Working Conditions, Establishment by Regulations 92a
Mixed Deposit Storage 469
More profitable Conclusion of Business 387

Negotiable Instruments 363
Non-competition Clause 60–75d, 61, 74, 74a-d, 82a, 112, 113, 165
Non-observance of Loading Time 417
Notes 284 et seq.
Notice of Performance and Substitution of the Commission Agent for the Third Party he would Otherwise Deal with on the Principal´s Behalf 405
Notice of Termination
- Agreement with the Commercial Agent 89, 89a
- Current Account 355(3)
- Examination Mandate 318
- Freight Agreement 415
- Partnership 131(3), 132, 234

- Personal Creditor of a Partner 135
- Silent Partnership 234

Notification of Damage 438, 452b

Obligation to Deliver Mechandise Specified only by Generic Characteristics 360
Obligation to Pay Interest on the Partnership Funds 111
Obligation to Recover Original Value 280
Offset Prohibition in the Annual Financial Statements 246
Opening Balance Sheet 242–256
Ownership Acquisition 124, 366

Packaging, Labelling 411
Parents 271, 290–314
Partial Shipment 416
Participation in other Enterprises 271
Partnership Agreement
- General Partnership 109, 114(2), 115(2), 119(2), 125(2), (3), 133(2), 146
- Limited Partnership 163
- Silent Partnership 231

Partnership Assets 124(2), 131(3), 143–145, 149, 155, 158, 171(2)
Partnership for a Term of Life 134
Passage of Resolutions by the General Commercial Partnership 119
Payment of Profits 169
Payment of Salary 64
Pension Funds 330(5), 341m, 341n, 341o, 341p
"Pension" Transactions 340b
Personal Liability of the Partners 128, 161, 164
Petty Broker 104
Place of Jurisdiction 440
Power to Represent
- Commercial Agent 91, 91a
- Juridical Person 33
- Partnership 75h, 125–127, 149, 170

403

Index

Preparation
- Annual Financial Statements 264
- Consolidated Financial Statements, Consolidated Management Report 341i, 341j
- Share Ownership in the Notes 287

Presumption
- Commercial Register 15
- Commercial Transaction 344

Principal 385
Principles of Consolidation 300
Priority among Multiple Liens 443
Private Assets 264c(3)
Procedures for Simplifying the Keeping of Inventory 241
Procedures of Simplifying Valuation 256
Profit and Loss Statement 275–278, 284–288, 305, 340c
Profits and Losses, Distribution 121, 167, 168, 231
Profits Carried Forward 264c, 266(3), 268
Prohibition of Competition 112, 165
Prohibition of Inclusion in the Consolidated Financial Statements 295
Prohibitions in Balancing Accounts 248
Prokura 48–53, 116(3), 126
Promissory Notes of a Merchant 344(2)
Proof of Identity to Deliver the Goods 446, 475f
Proof of Legal Succession 12
Publication in the Commercial Register 15
Publication of Registrations in Commercial Register 10, 15
Public Law 7

Reduction of Capital Contribution of the Limited Partner 174

Reference 73
Registered Cooperative 336
Registered Merchant 2
Related Enterprises 271
Relief depending up on Size 274a, 276, 288, 293, 326, 327
Repayment of Loans 129a, 172a
Reservation of State Law Regulations 263
Reserves 264c
Retention, Right of 88a, 369
Revocation
- Commission 405
- Prokura 52, 116(3), 126

Revolving Account 355–357
Right to Dispose of Goods 418
Right of Information by Auditor of Annual Financial Statements 320
Right of Retention
- Commercial Agent 88a
- Merchant 369

Right to Satisfaction of the Creditor 371

Salary of Clerical Employees 59, 63, 64
Sale of Pledged Items 368
Sale of Securities 381
Sale where the Buyer Specifies the Item 375
Sale to be Performed at a Fixed Point in Time 376
Satisfaction
- Out of Claims 399
- Commission Agent 396
- Out of Goods 398
- Out of Goods Retained 371, 372
- Lien Creditor 356
- Personal Creditor of a Partner 135

Security Interests to Outstanding Debt 356
Securities, Sale 381
Self-dealing
- Commission Agent 400–405
- Forwarding Agent 458

Self-help Sale 373, 389
Shipment of Goods
– Personal and Household Goods 451 et seq.
Shipper, Claims of 457
Shipping Agent 92c
Signature 12–14, 17, 101, 108, 153, 245, 321
– Holder of Commercial Power of Attorney 57
– Prokura Holder 51, 53
– Signatures for Submission to Registry Court 12
Silence of the Merchant 362
Silent Partnership 230–236
Size-related Relief for Disclosures 326, 327
Special Entries
– Capital Surplus 273
– General Bank Risks 340g
Specimen Signature 12, 29, 35, 53, 108
Statute of Limitations 26, 61(2), 88, 113(3), 139(3), 159, 160, 323(5), 452b, 463, 475a
Statute of Limitations for Claims against a Partner 159
Statutory
– Non-Competition Clause 60
– Interest Rate 352
– Lien 397, 404, 441, 464–466, 475b
Storage
– Commercial Records 257
– Damaged Goods 470, 471
– Documents by Photographic or Other Means 8a
– Refused Goods 379, 391
– Samples 96
– Signatures 12, 29, 35, 53, 108
Storage Charges 354
Subscription Rights 314(1) No. 6
Subsequent Carrier 442
Subsequent Instructions 418
Subsidiaries 271, 290, 294, 295, 296

Tare Weight 380
Tax Deferrals 274, 306
Taxes in the Profit and Loss Statement 278
Temporary Storage of Goods 379
Termination of a Firm Name 31(2)
Termination without Notice of the Commercial Agent 89a
Termination by Shipper 415
Time of Performance 358, 361
Trade and business secrets 90
Transaction Book of the Commercial Broker 100, 101, 102
Transactions on a Commission Basis 383–405
Transfer of a Monetary Claim 354a

Uniform Valuation 308
Unilateral Commercial Transactions 345
– Equity Capital 283
– Fixed Assets in the Balance Sheet 253
– Participation and Treatment of the Amount of the Difference 312
– Regulations 308 et seq.
– Share of the Subsidiary 301

Valuation
– Assets and Liabilities 253
Valuation of Assets 340e, 341b
Valuation Regulations 252–256, 279–283, 308, 341b
Violation
– Duty of Confidentiality 333
– Duty to Report 332
– Non-competition Clause 61, 113

Warehouse Receipt 475c–475h
Warehouse Receipt as Identification 475f
Warehousing 467 et seq.
Warehousing, Duration of 47
Waybill 408, 409, 451b

Index

Withdrawal
- Authority to Manage the Business 117
- of Funds 122
- Power to Represent 127

Withdrawal of a Partner 139(2), 160
Withdrawals from the Partnership Account 122